The Unwanted Child

The Unwanted Child

The Fate of Foundlings, Orphans, and Juvenile Criminals in Early Modern Germany

JOEL F. HARRINGTON

The University of Chicago Press
Chicago and London

The University of Chicago Press, Chicago 60637
The University of Chicago Press, Ltd., London
© 2009 by The University of Chicago
All rights reserved. Published 2009.
Paperback edition 2013
Printed in the United States of America

22 21 20 19 18 17 16 15 14 13   2 3 4 5 6

ISBN-13: 978-0-226-31727-4 (cloth)
ISBN-13: 978-0-226-10205-4 (paper)
ISBN-13: 978-0-226-31729-8 (ebook)
DOI: 10.7208/chicago/9780226317298.001.0001

Library of Congress Cataloging-in-Publication Data

Harrington, Joel F. (Joel Francis)
    The unwanted child : the fate of foundlings, orphans, and juvenile criminals
in early modern Germany / Joel F. Harrington
        p.   cm.
    Includes bibliographical references and index.
    ISBN-13: 978-0-226-31727-4 (cloth : alk. paper)
    ISBN-10: 0-226-31727-7 (cloth : alk. paper) 1. Orphans—Germany—
Nuremberg—History. 2. Unmarried mothers—Germany—Nuremberg—
History. 3. Infanticide—Germany—Nuremberg—History. 4. Street
children—Germany—Nuremberg—History. 5. Juvenile delinquents—
Germany—Nuremberg—History. 6. Germany—History—1517–1648.
7. Children—History. 8. Family—History. I. Title.
    HV1180.N9H37 2009
305.23086′9450943324—dc22
2009004285

For George and Charlotte, cherished beyond measure

CONTENTS

ILLUSTRATIONS

FIGURES

TABLES

NOTE ON USAGE

I have made the decision to leave the surnames of women in their feminine form, principally because this reflects how they were known at the time. The feminine form of early modern German surnames is typified by an occasional vowel shift in the penultimate syllable and the invariable -*in* ending. For example, Georg Widmann's wife would be known as Margaretha Widmänin or Widmenin, while Hans Krieger's wife becomes Magdalena Kriegerin or Kriegin, Jobst Fischer's daughter Catharina Fischerin, and so forth. All spelling of proper names reflects the most commonly used form in referring to an individual, often at variance with modern usage (e.g., Hanns, instead of Hans). I have similarly decided to employ the German word *Findel* for all references to Nuremberg's foundling home. This provides a more direct link to the era and also avoids referring to all of its occupants as foundlings, since the majority in residence were in fact orphans or foster children.

All translations are my own unless otherwise noted.

Currency rates fluctuated widely during the sixteenth and seventeenth centuries in Nuremberg as elsewhere, but for a convenient (if approximate) exchange standard, I will rely on the equivalent values ca. 1600: 1 Gulden (fl.) = 0.85 Thaler (Th.) = 4 "old" pounds (lb.) = 15 Batzen (Bz.) = 20 Schilling (sch.) = 60 Kreuzer (kr.) = 120 pence (d.) = 240 Heller (H.). For a common point of reference, all currencies other than Gulden will be accompanied by the equivalent value in Gulden (fl.), a coin used more in large-scale payments than in most day-to-day transactions.[1]

1. M. J. Elsas, *Umriss einer Geschichte der Preise und Löhne in Deutschland. Vom ausgehenden Mittelalter bis zum Beginn des Neunzehnten Jahrhunderts* (Leiden: A. W. Sijthoff, 1936); Gerald Strauss, *Nuremberg in the Sixteenth Century* (New York: John Wiley and Sons, 1966), 204.

ACKNOWLEDGMENTS

When I began this project, toward the end of the last century, I had little notion of just how long or interesting my journey would turn out to be. My conceptualization of the book, its thesis, and the overall format have all evolved considerably over the years. The friends who have assisted and accompanied me on the journey, however, have remained constant throughout, and it is a deeply gratifying pleasure to acknowledge their crucial support at every stage.

First, as always, is my wife, Beth Monin Harrington, who not only helped translate (or gently delete) my most impenetrable academic prose, but has patiently endured the countless manifestations of stress associated with the book, from the early days in the archives to the final challenges of the production process. As she knows well, I could not imagine a better life companion, or life at all without her.

Funding for two years of archival work in Germany as well as shorter trips was generously provided by the National Endowment for the Humanities, the German Academic Exchange Service (DAAD), the American Philosophical Society, the Herzog August Bibliothek Wolfenbüttel, and the Vanderbilt University Research Council. During my stays in Germany, I benefited greatly from the generosity and advice of a number of people, particularly Mason Barnett, Andrea Bendlage, Jill Bepler, Cornelia Blasberg, Martin Dinges, Heiko Droste, Dagmar Freist, Sigrun Haude, Uwe Hornauer, Robert Jütte, Craig Koslofky, Rotraud Ries, Thomas Schnalke, Gerd Schwerhoff, Heinrich Richard Schmidt, Otto Ulbricht, and Renate Wittern. My work at the Staatsarchiv Nürnberg was greatly enhanced by the experienced guidance of Dr. Peter Fleischmann (now director of the Staatsarchiv Augsburg). At the Stadtarchiv Nürnberg I similarly benefited from the expertise of Dr. Horst-Dieter Beyerstedt, Dr. Wiltrud Fischer-Pache, Dr. Paul Gebhardt,

Christof Neider, Herbert Schmitz, and Jürgen Zottman. Thanks also go to Dr. Christine Sauer of the Stadtbibliothek Nürnberg and Annemarie Müller of the Landeskirchliches Archiv Nürnberg as well as the graphics staff of the Germanisches Nationalmuseum.

In my work at Vanderbilt I have received indispensable support from several administrative mentors, and I would like to especially acknowledge Nick Zeppos, Richard McCarty, Tom Burish, Carolyn Dever, Jim Infante, and Liz Lunbeck. The *Findelkinder* database and resulting tables were largely compiled by my excellent research assistants—Maria Ebner, Andrea Eder, Alex Furches, and Kurt Johnson—with some timely assistance from Andrew Moe, Michael Filloon, Tom Filloon, and Hank Keeling. Brenda Hummel, Jane Anderson, Heidi Welch, Gulnara Namyssova, and Marilyn Pilley all helped in numerous ways throughout the project.

I have also shamelessly exploited the expertise and generosity of many friends and colleagues during the book's revision. Top honors go to those intrepid souls who read the entire manuscript in one of its incarnations and offered wise and very useful advice: Michael Bess, Joyce Chaplin, Phil Soergel, Tom Tentler, and Margo Todd. I am also very grateful for the insights of Tom Brady, Bill Caferro, Katie Crawford, Marshall Eakin, Jim Epstein, Paul Freedman, Mike Halverson, Robert Jütte, Jane Landers, Kate Lynch, Tom McGinn, Erik Midelfort, Dana Rabin, Matt Ramsey, Tom Robisheaux, Lyndal Roper, Alison Rowlands, Ulinka Rublack, Helmut Smith, Valentina Tikoff, Jeff Watt, Meike Werner, and Merry Wiesner-Hanks. Doug Mitchell at the University of Chicago Press has been a steady source of good-humored encouragement and wisdom through the publication process.

An earlier version of chapter 1 appeared as "An Unmarried Mother-to-be in Sixteenth-century Germany Weighs Her Options," in *Studies in Medieval and Renaissance History: Sexuality and Culture in Medieval and Renaissance Europe* 3rd ser., 2 (2005): 149–203, and parts of chapter 4 appeared in "Tortured Truths: The Self-expositions of a Career Juvenile Criminal in Early Modern Nuremberg," *German History* 23, no. 2 (2005): 143–71. I am grateful to both publications for permission to make use of revised versions of this material.

My parents, Jack and Marilyn Harrington, have provided me with a life-long foundation of unwavering love, confidence, and approval. My parents-in-law, siblings, nieces, and nephews likewise each contributed in his or her own way to my emotional well-being over the years so I would like to acknowledge each of them by name: Tom and Marilyn Monin; Sue, Tom, Nick, Michael, Maggie, Tim, Ben, and Peter Filloon; Jeff, Alyson, Noah, Bridget, and Cassie Harrington; Ann Monin; and Robert and Lea Ann Monin.

Finally, I owe a great personal debt to three scholar-mentors, each of whom offered invaluable encouragement and support at crucial times during my early career: Hans-Christoph Rublack, Bob Scribner, and Gerald Strauss. I am saddened that these great historians are no longer among us, and I hope that the final result of this project would justify the confidence they showed in me.

I dedicate this book to my children, George and Charlotte. The joy that they have brought into my life has unquestionably deepened my sympathy for the unfortunate children and parents I encountered in the archival sources. I hope that it has helped me to do right by these distant families and their stories.

Just before sunrise on August 7, 1599, Heinrich Herolt pounded impatiently on the front door of the Nuremberg foundling home, known as the Findel. In his arms was a bread basket containing a baby boy of about ten months old. When finally admitted, Herolt handed the basket to the head of the home, the Findel father, and told him how he had been out roaming with his companion Bastel Hoffman around 1:00 A.M. that morning and had stumbled upon the child in a meadow just outside one of the city's pesthouses. The Findel father recorded in his register that there was no note attached to the baby or the basket and since "nobody knows what it's called or who its parents are [so] until informed otherwise we've named it Lorenzlein." Later that same day, Herolt, a servant in suburban Gostenhof, came back and reported to the Findel father that the abandoned child's real name was Wölflein, its mother an unmarried bath maid named Margaretha from Unter Wöhrd (another Nuremberg suburb), and its father a married bath servant. Nuremberg's town councilors immediately ordered all of their officials to help track down, arrest, and imprison the absconded bath maid. Nine days later Margaretha Kriegin herself, whose last home turned out to be nearby Fürth, entered the Findel of her own volition. She named the baker-journeyman Hans Widman as the baby's father. He was not, she stressed, married. Kriegin also vehemently denied that she had abandoned her infant son—only left him instead in the care of her sister, bridle maker Margretha (sic) Widmenin, promising to be back for him in a few days and paying her sister the sizeable sum of 7 lbs. (almost 2 fl.) for her time, trouble, and expenses. When Margaretha returned, about a week later, she was told that her sister's husband, who couldn't stand to hear the baby crying anymore, had ordered it out of the house. Margaretha's sister had obeyed, handing the child off to a small boy to deposit elsewhere. Upon completion of her tale, Margaretha Kriegin had her son Wölflein restored to her. No criminal charges were filed against anyone involved.[1]

The story of the foundling Wölflein is at once familiar and alien to modern sensibilities. Abandoned children have populated folklore and literature since the time of antiquity, including among famous figures as Oedipus, Moses, Paris of Troy, Romulus and Remus, and Cyrus of Persia. European authors later produced such notable foundlings as Shakespeare's Perdita, Henry Fields's Tom Jones, Hugo's Fantine, Zola's Angelique Marie, and of course the Grimm Brothers' famously abandoned siblings, Hansel and Gretel. Child abandonment is so prominent in imaginative literature that the historian John Boswell once proposed that it might be a sentimental fiction or convenient plot device with little sociological reality. While Boswell instead concluded that child exposition (literally exposing to the elements) and abandonment were in fact common in the premodern world, his point about the potential of fiction shaping historical perception remains instructive.[2]

Of course foundlings as well as newborns or dead babies occasionally still turn up in dumpsters, public restrooms, or homeless shelters in modern developed countries. Yet on the whole, child abandonment as a common phenomenon seems to belong to an earlier, harsher, and frankly more primitive period in the history of the West. Economic and political development has clearly enhanced child welfare in many ways. The implicit contrast seems clear: Westerners today care more about children than their predecessors did (or more than many contemporaries in poorer parts of the world do). The callous treatment of young Wölflein by his own flesh and blood comes as no surprise to modern readers, nor does city councilors' lack of interest either in punishing his relatives or in assessing Margretha Kriegin's suitability as a mother. The assumption of governmental responsibility for child welfare itself appears to be a hallmark of the modern West, and one of relatively recent vintage at that.

Is this a fair and accurate assessment? Most people would admit that their understanding of the role of child abandonment in Western history—to the extent that they have reflected on it—is impressionistic, shaped more by half-remembered fairy tales than by critical study. Those dreamlike notions are also indirectly informed by two scholarly debates that have gradually penetrated the realm of informed general readers: the level of affection among premodern parents for their children and the role of the state in child welfare.

The first exchange is the older and probably the more familiar outside of academic circles. It can be dated quite precisely from the 1960 French pub-

lication of *Centuries of Childhood*, a wide-ranging treatise on European concepts of childhood during the past millennium. The most controversial assertion of its author, sociologist Philippe Ariès, was that these concepts were
not constant and that before the rise of sentimentalism in the seventeenth
and eighteenth centuries, parents did not "love" their children in the same
way that we understand that today.[3] During the 1960s and 1970s, many
scholars seized on this one aspect of Ariès's broader thesis, ever intensifying
the contrast between past parent-child relations and those of the modern
era. Lawrence Stone claimed that premodern parents were for the most part
"fairly remote" and mostly indifferent to high infant mortality, while Lloyd
de Mause proclaimed "the history of childhood is a nightmare from which
we have only recently begun to awake."[4] The subsequent scholarly reaction
against the so-called Black Legend of premodern childhood was equally ve-
hement. Beginning with the works of Linda A. Pollock and Steven Ozment
in 1983, a series of diverse historical studies of medieval and early modern childhood has effectively disproved the more extreme claims of Ariès's
followers, establishing multiple instances of parental affection and grief at
the loss of children long before the eighteenth century.[5] The current scholarly consensus strikes a balance, acknowledging that parent-child relations,
like all social relationships, vary within social contexts and that Ariès was
surely right to claim that there is no single, monolithic, unchanging, and
natural model of childhood. Virtually all contemporary historians, however,
would regard the last millennium of parent-child relations in the West as
substantially more continuous and similar than radically transformed at
some point in between.[6] Nevertheless, Ariès's assumption of an important
qualitative difference in premodern and modern attitudes toward children
continues to hold sway outside the halls of academe.

The other historiographical debate shaping our understanding of premodern child abandonment has to do with governmental interest in child
welfare. For most of recorded history, the abandonment of children was
considered an unfortunate but inevitable consequence of the human condition. By the sixteenth century, however, many European governments had
initiated a series of unprecedented bureaucratic and governmental attempts
to prevent, punish, and remedy such mistreatment. Until the 1960s, the
most common interpretation for this shift credited the Protestant Reformation, with its secularization and reorganization of poor relief, as well as its
leaders' emphasis on the social responsibility of every true believer. This
explanation necessarily ignored the achievements of Roman Catholic cities in the same areas, both before and after the Reformation, a fact futilely
pointed out by Catholic historians who challenged the prevailing Protestant

paradigm.[7] It was not until relatively recently that this orthodoxy began to crumble, chiefly from assaults by Natalie Zemon Davis and Brian Pullan, who undermined the assumptions of R. W. Tawney and W. K. Jordan that social reform was inspired principally by Protestantism. Whatever the influence of Luther and other evangelical reformers, Catholic civic leaders came to very similar conclusions as their evangelical and Reformed contemporaries about poverty and social order and instituted strikingly parallel reform agendas, largely as a result of shared humanist intellectual influences.[8] Other scholarly works have pushed the humanist inspiration back further in time and have shown that governmental concern about poor relief as well as child abandonment and infanticide can be seen as early as the fourteenth and fifteenth centuries, when all European cities witnessed a boon in new foundling homes and related legislation. Again, religious motives mixed with humanist aspirations in a revived classical model of civic harmony, particularly in Florence and other Italian city-states.[9]

Scholarly consensus over the chronology and ideological sources of new governmental intervention in child welfare does not mean that everyone views such attempts as socially progressive. Foundling homes already had a widespread reputation as disposal units for unwanted babies when the famous eighteenth-century demographer Robert Malthus made the acidic observation that "if a person wished to check population, and were not solicitous about the means, he could not propose a more effectual measure than the establishment of a large number of foundling hospitals."[10] Nineteenth-century writers such as Charles Dickens and Émile Zola portrayed orphanages and workhouses as wretched hellholes, thereby implicating the governmental authorities who created and maintained them. The antiauthoritarian atmosphere of the 1960s and 1970s gave impetus to scholarly criticism of virtually all governmental attempts to solve such problems as child abandonment and infanticide. The work of philosopher Michel Foucault in particular inspired many historians to accuse governmental reformers of harboring more cynical motives of social control and to despair of the very idea of progress through legal institutions. Richard Trexler and John Boswell both characterized the expanded state involvement seen in late medieval Italian city-states as "a tragic development" that, in the words of the latter scholar, transformed "the intricate, gentle complexities of the systems of [child] transfer developed in ancient and medieval Europe . . . into a simple technique of disposal—in a hauntingly literal sense."

All interpretations of the impact of new governmental intervention in child welfare—whether positive or negative—have ultimately reflected a referendum on "modernity" itself. Ariès and Foucault, who both despised the regulation and clinicalization of modern life, saw all governmental intervention in negative terms and Boswell barely concealed his contempt for the modernist project when he characterized the late medieval foundling hospital as "neatly organized, modern, discrete, and deadly" and "exquisitely calibrated to the times."[11] Historians who see the Renaissance and the Enlightenment as socially progressive, by contrast, have cast the overall effect on children and child rearing in a positive light. Failures to achieve the stated goals of governmental reformers may be alternately interpreted by proponents of intervention as genuinely disappointing to them or by opponents of such actions as irrelevant to government's true hegemonic agenda.[12] The contrast is even more evident in contrasting portrayals of the Middle Ages: either the cruel and backward "Dark Ages" that enlightened reformers attempt to overcome or conversely a sort of antimodern libertarian fantasyland, a *zone libre* in Foucault's terms, where spontaneous social mechanisms operated harmoniously until subverted by the ambitions of state hegemonists.[13] Both are anachronistic cartoons yet they remain powerful images for many, deeply influencing all discussions of child abandonment in the European past. Why is this?

One must start with the primary sources for this subject, particularly sparse for the medieval and early modern periods. Records of sentiment and emotions between parents and children, such as diaries and personal letters, are rare before the seventeenth century and even then are mostly limited to middle- and upper-class authors.[14] Ariès closely scrutinized paintings and sculptures of children during the Middle Ages but his evocative approach remains supplementary at best. Studies of medieval and early modern child abandonment and infanticide have mostly relied on legal sources, including public ordinances and forensic documents. Scholars have consequently been most successful at identifying large-scale patterns in legal prosecution as well as changes in law and legal procedures. The role of state institutions is especially pivotal in such discussions and too often serves as a proxy for more general changes in social attitudes and behavior.

The nature of historical evidence has consequently put blinders on our thinking about unwanted children of the past. "Child abandonment" and "infanticide" are legal characterizations of a number of different acts committed for a variety of reasons by many individuals. By viewing all of these diverse acts and their broader social context through the prism of the state—rather than the reverse—we almost certainly obscure the thinking, feelings, and thus the intent behind each of the acts themselves. This exclusive focus on the early modern state's perspective has begun to recede during the last decade or so, but studies from the perspective of abandoners and abandoned children remain rare.[15] The nature of evidence also distorts our understanding of large-scale historical change, implying that it is the product of some kind of social elite imposing some sort of change on passive or resistant parents. Earlier scholarly studies assumed a superstitious, tradition-bound, and generally backward "lower classes" resisting a progressive governmental innovation. In more recent works, a sensuous and uncomplicated people heroically but futilely resist cultural oppression by a social elite.[16] In either version, social change is assumed to be trickle-down, with the initiative almost always coming from above in a simplistic dualist power struggle. An author's verdict on "modernity" invariably reflects his or her assessment on the growth of the state, thereby bringing the tautological circle to a close, while revealing little about what child abandonment really meant in people's lives.

Take the story of baby Wölflein. The account in the Findel's register neatly unfolds like a three-act play: first there is the discovery of the foundling, later followed by the presentation of more evidence creating a hearsay portrait of a desperate unwed mother, with a dramatic conclusion where the accused mother herself appears and implicates her own sister and brother-in-law in the abandonment. Each of these individuals has a key role and a distinct perspective in the drama, as do the lesser characters of the baby's rambunctious discoverers Heinrich Herolt and Bastel Hoffman, the Findel father, the town councilors, and the unnamed boy who commits the actual act of abandonment. Yet of all of these perspectives, it is the one most commonly adopted by scholars—that of the town councilors—that turns out to matter the least in understanding this particular story. Any different action by any of the other characters for whatever reason could have significantly altered the course of events and possibly the outcome. Margaretha Kriegin, the unwed mother, might never have left Wölflein with her sister's family, or she might have left him with someone else, or might have actually abandoned him in a public spot herself. The Findel father might have turned Herolt and the baby away. The sister and brother-in-law might have refused to take Wölflein in the first place, or they might have kept him until his mother's return. Even the abandoning boy and Heinrich Herolt profoundly shaped the sequence of events, the former in his choice of an abandonment site, the latter by his decision to get involved at all. Town councilors, meanwhile, were completely ineffective in bringing any perpetrator to justice and in this case functioned more as a dismayed Greek chorus than as key protagonists. Admittedly their ultimate decision not to punish anybody made an impact, but even a guilty verdict against either sister would have almost certainly left the foundling reunited with its mother.

Does this imply that early modern state officials in fact played little or no role in child abandonment cases? That would be a hasty conclusion, based on one perhaps isolated incident. What this example does suggest is that historians' overemphasis on laws and governmental institutions has distorted our understanding of the diverse and complex human relationships involved in the phenomena we classify under the legal categories of child abandonment and infanticide. In other words, our narrow focus on the legal aspects of the problem of unwanted children tends to obscure whatever came before the crime in question. Any explanation of broad social change predicated on such a flawed foundation is self-serving at best and grossly misleading at worst.

How might we avoid the statist trap in discussing abandoned and other unwanted children?[17] Let's begin with the term "child abandonment" itself, which stresses something that parents or other caretakers do to children. There are many grounds for relying on this term, not least because it makes possible comparisons across time and space, particularly in quantitative terms. Yet because of this underlying premise, historians are from the start forced to frame their inquiries in terms of explaining this action—its motives, its forms, its repercussions—with little understanding of the action's broader context. Did the creation of foundling homes and orphanages spur parents to abandon more frequently? Was child abandonment sometimes a short-term strategy, with the parent(s) intending to reclaim the child in the near future, or was it a passive form of infanticide, with parents knowing full well the probable fate of the abandoned child? What role did governmental or religious institutions play in encouraging, mitigating, or restricting the practice of abandonment? How much of an impact did demographic factors such as famine and disease have on the rate of abandonment? Whatever the question, the boundaries remain the same, namely, a post hoc legally-defined category of actions that we call abandonment and that we proceed to explain in the same self-referential terms.

What would happen if we took the various acts that we call child abandonment and thought about them in a much broader context, such as what some historical anthropologists call the "circulation of children"? This term was first developed by U.S. anthropologists to describe the various forms of fosterage and adoption they encountered in their subject populations in eastern Oceania and North America and has since been employed in a variety of settings.[18] Depending on the cultural context, child exchanges and one-way fosterages can mean many different things, ranging from a profound familial alliance, to a kind of deposit on a debt, to a simple favor between friends—hence the usefulness of a broadly inclusive term such as child circulation.[19] The most immediate benefit of considering the parental act of abandonment as a form of child circulation is that both the act and subsequent state intervention are automatically decentered within scholarly studies. Instead we are forced to view both within the context of other key interactions, such as informal fosterage of children by relatives, friends, or strangers (whether voluntary or involuntary); the relative frequency of out-of-wedlock pregnancy and miscarriage as well the availability of options such as quick marriage, abortion, and infanticide; the nature and degree of independence among poor children on the street; other forms of child circulation such as apprenticeship and domestic service; and so forth.

This process in turn might also lead us to reconsider our very use of the terms "parent" and "child." If we think of a parent as an adult responsible for the care of a minor and do not restrict ourselves to the biological mother or father, we are forced to acknowledge that virtually every society, including that of early modern Europe, contains a variety of parent-child relationships, ranging from apprenticeship or domestic service positions to boarding school to foster households run by a relative or godparent to full legal adoption.[20] Each of these relationships represents a type of substitute parentage, widely differing in terms of affection and expectations, but all playing key parts in child circulation, where abandonment is far from the only option for a biological parent with an unwanted child.

The early modern significance of the term "child" has been much debated, as well, and is by no means uncomplicated.[21] For purposes of clarity and convenience we will refer to those under the age of twelve as children and those between twelve and twenty-one as youths (though twenty-five was the age of legal majority in Nuremberg, as elsewhere in Germany). But what should we call those children and youths like Wölflein Krieger, who appear to fall through the cracks of normal circulation? "Abandoned," as Catherine Painter-Brick has pointed out, has long been an especially loaded term, usually intended to arouse pity for the children involved, who are always presented as passive victims.[22] The term also does not capture the diversity of scenarios, since only a minority would fit the usual stereotypes of a child secretly left on a doorstep or in a public spot. Early modern records themselves use inconsistent and sometimes vague terminology in describing a particular case. In instances of babies left in the street or children found alone in their homes the Nuremberg city council tended to use the term *sitzen lassen* (literally "left sitting") or *entsetzt* (an archaic form of *ausgesetzt*: "put out" or "exposed"). Most of the time, however, the records used the more ambiguous word *verlassen* ("left behind") indiscriminately for children whose parents had clearly absconded, children whose parents happened to be away, and children whose parents had died (i.e., orphans). To this confusion we must add that at least some instances of children left with relatives or friends were informal service arrangements, common for boys and girls over the age of seven or eight. Sometimes money changed hands but other times it might merely be promised or implied. Should we consider all of these cases to be abandonments because they ended up before magistrates, or would it be more instructive to characterize them by the original intention? Can we ever be certain of what that original intention was?

The approach of this book will be to speak as broadly and generically as possible of "circulated" or "informally fostered" children. By this definition, most early modern children experienced some form of fostering, whether temporary care for a few days, as in the case of Margareta Kriegin's baby Wölflein, or for several months or even years. The motives of the biological or foster parents initiating the circulation will be notoriously hard to determine, so we will reserve the term "abandoned" for those parents who either left their children anonymously in a public place (anonymous abandonment) or those identified parents who apparently forced their unwanted children on friends, relatives, or strangers (known abandonment or forced foster). Those children whose incapacitated biological or foster parents petitioned to have them accepted into Nuremberg's Findel will be known as fostered children, as will all others circulated in a consensual manner. Only those children whose parents are both confirmed to be dead will be designated orphans.

All of these children whose circulation came to involve governmental intervention will be called "unwanted children." While this term is a distinct improvement over the misleading "abandoned children," it requires a few provisos. "Unwanted children" was not a common expression during the early modern era, though the German *Waisen*, usually translated as orphan, did often have this more expansive meaning.[23] In that respect, we have created still another artificial category and, on occasion, as in the discussion of beggar children still living with their parents, that artificiality might seem more pronounced. More problematically, the term is still heavily influenced by the criterion of state involvement, consisting primarily of those cases of child circulation that come before the Nuremberg Findel and city council. If we consistently situate these cases within the wider context of child circulation and informal fostering, however, we can nonetheless transcend this barrier and thereby resist statist distortions.

There is an additional advantage to this approach. Until now, historians' preoccupation with the state-defined offenses of abandonment and infanticide has occluded valuable evidence about the indispensable roles of various foster parents in all forms of early modern child circulation.[24] This information, to the extent that it may be recovered, might transform our very understanding of a variety of "horizontal" relationships, including those of consanguinity (parents, children, siblings, grandparents, and other relatives) and of affinity (neighbors, godparents, coworkers, etc.). Our quest to escape the bonds of top-down statist history thus impels us to seek as many of these different individual perspectives on child circulation as possible, drawing on the diverse experiences of unwed mothers, poor households, governmental officials, religious leaders, and of course the children themselves, including both life in a foundling home or other institutions and the alternative existence on the street. Our exploration of these multiple perspectives will recognize the role of emotion as well as rational choice in child circulation, and we will especially seek out those situations that best illustrate how individuals negotiate and interact with each other, such as through petitions from a parent, relative, godparent, or friend to a foundling home or alms administrator. In short, all of the activities and relationships that we have either ignored or put under the category of child abandonment would be atomized, to use the term of historians Michael Werner and Bénédicte Zimmerman, and we will be forced to look at them in new and revealing ways.[25]

Let's return to Wölflein's story as an example. To better understand the choices, intentions, and actions of his mother, Margaretha Kriegin, it would help to know her options. What were the conditions of her employment as a maid and the circumstances of her impregnation by a man who interestingly shares the same family name as her brother-in-law? What were the reasons she didn't marry, and to what extent could she rely on family and friends for support? What were the social implications of bearing an illegitimate child and the possible means of support for the same? Why did she decide against abortion, abandonment, and infanticide while other unwed mothers in her situation embraced these solutions to their problem? Obviously we cannot know all of the answers in each instance, but collectively these cases do allow us some sense of the range of experiences and choices available to these women. In the process, we can also get closer to Margaretha's own thinking, and we can also add another crucial perspective to the historical analysis of early modern child circulation.

Our analysis of the story can broaden still further. To this variable configuration we can add the perspectives of Margaretha's sister and brother-in-law. What was the state of their household finances, how many children were they supporting, what social networks of relatives and friends were at their disposal in issues of child care, and under which circumstances and for which motives did parents send away or leave behind their own children? Now we figure in the perspectives of Nuremberg's town councilors: how did they view the neglect, abuse, abandonment, and murder of children; which solutions did they formulate and why; what effect did poor relief and the growth of the Findel have on child circulation in general; what impact did intensified law enforcement efforts have on the rate of anonymous abandonment or infanticide; how did all of this vary over time? Finally, we can attempt to understand the experiences and perspective of the foundling himself. What would Wölflein's life had been like if he'd remained in the Findel's care; what were his chances of surviving to maturity, and what sort of future might he expect at that point? What would his life have been like if he had been definitively abandoned by his mother or simply neglected and left to fend for himself on the streets?

These are the types of questions that inform the first five chapters, each of which focuses on a different historical individual, with a different perspective on the question of the circulation of unwanted children: a desperate unmarried mother-to-be (chap. 1), a roaming mercenary who drifts in and out of his children's lives (chap. 2), a civic leader who orchestrates governmental responses to a variety of related problems (chap. 3), a homeless orphaned teenager who becomes a prolific thief (chap. 4), and a pair of orphaned twins who enter into governmental care at the age of nine (chap. 5). These are real individuals, not fictionalized composites, and they are not typical in all respects. (What person now or then is?) Apollonia Vöglin, the "unmarried mother" in the first chapter, is one woman confronted with many choices shared by other early modern women with unwanted pregnancies, but whose combined experiences and choices remain special, even unique, to her. The choices described in the course of each chapter's narrative should also not be viewed as a sequential checklist mentally consulted by every individual in a similar situation. As we will see, not everyone had the same options available or—just as importantly—perceived them to be available. Our overall goal in each of the five chapters is to come as close to each person's experience as possible (German, *Annäherung*), to have a more profound understanding of the spectrum of his or her choices, to situate those experiences and choices within a broader social context, and to identify any patterns shared with individuals in similar circumstances.

This close attention to the ideas and actions of people who do not normally fall within the scope of either intellectual or political history has a rich recent history of its own. For more than thirty years, scholars of "microhistory" and of "everyday history" have eschewed study of objectified ideas or social structures in favor of attempts to capture the subjective experience of unremarkable and sometimes untypical individuals.[26] Also known as historical anthropologists, they seek a qualitative understanding of life at the ground level, the "utmost concreteness" of a place and time, that effectively (some would say necessarily) complements the more generalized findings of social scientific and cultural historians alike.[27] This quest can be quite challenging for mostly illiterate subjects, particularly children, who left behind no "ego documents"—diaries, letters, autobiographies, or other deliberate accounts of their own perspectives and life experiences.[28] Instead we must continue to rely on official records—criminal interrogation protocols, conciliar decrees, Findel admission registers, etc.—seeking out isolated and often laconic references to individuals, and then carefully piecing together the "scattered fragments" of their lives.[29] Like archeologists unearthing the bones and pottery shards from a lost civilization, our method will sometimes involve "reading against the grain" of a source's purported function, as in the instance of reconstructing the daily life of a juvenile criminal based on interrogations about his burglaries. When successful, this technique can produce portraits as vivid as a traditional biography or autobiography, albeit with some frustrating gaps.[30]

This accomplishment is not the same thing as capturing the subjective experience of a historical individual, a much more daunting task whatever the sources at hand.[31] Historical anthropologists must also be ever vigilant of the seductive power of archival sources that put before us "misfortunes and mishaps without number, all bundled together in a handful of words . . . Inglorious lives put to rest in the few brief lines that brought them down." Are we attributing overmuch meaning to the sources available or are we being unduly cautious? "Rather than a reflection of the real," as Arlette Farge has mused, "might they not in fact be the oasis for satisfying our own thirst to see the poor and wretched spring to life?"[32] Trying to get at "feelings" without confusing emotion with sentimentality is particularly challenging, not least because "emotion . . . is a word which is almost taboo for anyone who professes to be a serious student of social matters."[33] Our probing of these intangibles, including the question of "motives" overall, must be suggestive rather than definitive, a sketch as opposed to a sharply defined photograph.

The very notion of capturing subjective experience from old texts, no matter how detailed, strikes some new historicists as a naïve, epistemologically flawed, and ultimately self-deceiving premise. Claiming that historians inevitably twist texts to fit the purposes of their arguments, these scholars conclude that experience itself "seems to be defined by its unavailability to language."[34] The chapters that follow, however, are predicated on what my colleague Helmut Smith has called a "middle way" on the question of textual interpretation and historical objectivity, namely, the premise that we may acknowledge the transformation of experiences by the text and other intermediaries, yet in most cases it is still possible to get some sense, albeit imperfect, of those original experiences.[35] No historical source can hope to provide more, and in that sense full understanding of another person's subjective experience will always elude us—just as it does today with the people we know most intimately. We will leave each of our historical individuals with some important unanswered questions, and that is just as it should be. In the words of Alf Lüdtke, one of the foremost proponents of everyday history, "ambivalences cannot be resolved; instead they have to be reckoned as fundamental to historical praxis and processes."[36] Put otherwise, there will always be a pastness to the past that remains fundamentally inaccessible to modern probing, regardless of the sources at hand.[37]

The other major controversy over the microhistorical method has existed from the beginning, namely, the "so what?" factor. Can a historical sketch of an individual or small community, however detailed, have any larger social significance? It is worth remembering that the origin of social history in the 1920s lay in this very impulse, the desire of its progenitors to liberate the craft of history writing from a narrow political or intellectual focus. Their pioneering work has broadened our gaze from famous and influential individuals to take in the rest of society, but always with an eye toward the "big picture" of social change. Whether the methodology in question relied more on quantitative evidence or theoretical abstraction, environmental influences or economic vectors, the question of large-scale social change has always remained paramount.

The rise of microhistory and other methods has not altered this fundamental orientation, despite some scholars' concerns about an epistemological crisis for social history's "totalizing ambitions."[38] As Charles Tilly has noted, "Social historians contend rather little about whether they ought to be linking big changes and small-scale experiences. They contend about how to establish the links."[39] The last thirty years have seen a plethora of imaginative and stimulating attempts to establish those links. Usually the microhistory provides the immediate narrative thread—based on a police investigation, a trial, a group migration, or a wartime incident—which over the course of the book is connected to a metahistorical narrative, such as racial or religious strife and intolerance.[40] Sometimes the events of an individual lifetime, revealed through diary entries or correspondence, are used to convey the broader social fabric and life rhythms of a community or people.[41] A microhistory might be presented as an example of a larger social trend or as counterevidence to prevailing historical wisdom or as simply an engaging story in its own right.[42] When presented skillfully, the connection between the micro- and macro- is seamless and the question of typicality becomes largely immaterial. When the link between the two perspectives breaks (or worse, is never established), the microhistory risks becoming an irrelevant diversion and the larger conclusions appear forced and unpersuasive.

This book will attempt to connect macro- and microperspectives in two complementary ways. First, within each of the first five chapters, I will employ the techniques of collective biography in contextualizing the experiences of the main figure within broader group patterns and common mentalities.[43] In addition to extensive criminal interrogations and decrees of the Nuremberg city council (*Ratsverläße*; see fig. 0.1), my chief source for this information will be a database compiled from the records of over 4,000 petitions for entrance to the Findel from 1557 to 1670, some 3,600 of them successful. The material and methods employed in putting this resource together are described in appendix 1. Viewed collectively, these records help provide a broader scope for the choices and actions of our six chosen protagonists. They inform but do not resolve the question of typicality. And though the size of the samples selected is often quite large, I will consign precise figures to the endnotes whenever possible, employing in text the less scientific but more sufficiently descriptive "most," "about half," "three out of five," etc.[44] In most instances, the collective biographies conform to current scholarly consensus on particular subjects; when they do not I will point out this distinction and its relative significance. The overriding goal is to convey a useful tension between individual experience and agency on the one hand and group patterns and social structures on the other. Again, the individuals who provide the narrative thread and focus for the first five chapters are by no means intended as prototypes but rather as personal examples within the range of experiences known to unmarried mothers, poor families, magistrates, and unwanted children. There will be no attempt to resolve perennial questions about the "free choices" of individuals, only to provide the parameters for choices available and the factors involved in individual decisions, what Annales school historian Fernand Braudel famously called "the limits of the possible."

Even so, one might ask, how could we possibly make sense of the multiplicity of perspectives that result within each chapter, not to mention the many temporal disjunctions among the six protagonists of our stories? Plurality of this kind is desirable to anthropologists but it poses some basic problems in comprehensibility for historians. How too do we talk about

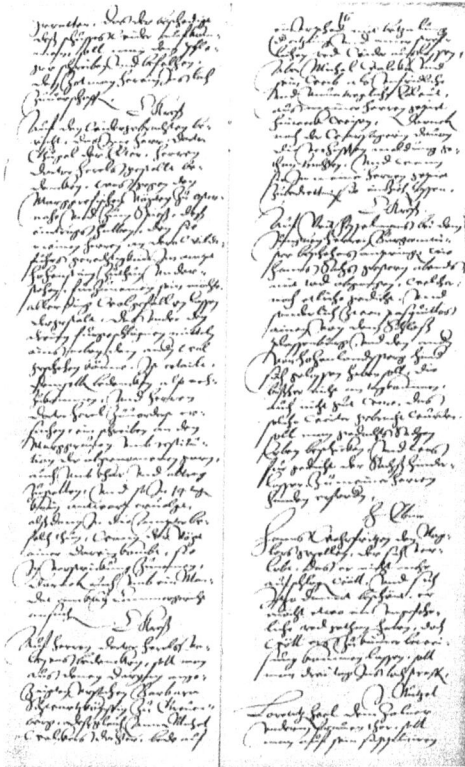

Fig. 0.1. Two pages from the transcripts of Nuremberg's inner council decrees, each paragraph dealing with an issue of varying magnitude in an average day (1594). Staatsarchiv Nürnberg.

long-term diachronic developments, changes over time, as they affected these individuals and groups within the confines of five relatively narrow narratives? In other words, how can we compare worldviews and experiences that are so disparate and do so in a way that speaks to the complexity of a society over the course of several generations? Can this be done, moreover, without imposing artificial categories or distorting terms such as "abandoned children"?

This book's second solution to these "big picture" challenges of microhistory draws on an approach developed by the modern Europeanists Michael Werner and Bénédicte Zimmermann, called *l'histoire croisée*. Related to, but not identical with, "connected history," "shared history," and "braided history," *l'histoire croisée* represents for Werner and Zimmerman an attempt to construct "a specific connection between observer positions, perspective, and object" without reliance on artificial—and in their view distortionary—categories of comparison.[45] This in effect describes the decision to suspend the use of terms and concepts generated by the category of "child abandonment" and instead to describe the interactions and networks that I see within the neutral context of child circulation. The resulting plurality of perspectives is not only tolerated but is in fact embraced by *l'histoire croisée* as a "foundational principle."[46] Although initially disconcerting, this decentering of the historian-observer in turn supplies its own constellation of points of reference, based on those points of interactions among individuals and groups. This way, it is the problems and questions that subsequently arise from such intersections—rather than preconceived and artificial categories—that in turn inform the historical agenda, a method sometimes called *Problemgeschichte*.[47]

The plurality of perspectives would seem to merely exacerbate the two historiographical problems just mentioned, namely, the difficulty in reconciling individual experiences with a social overview and the challenge of sustaining a scholarly argument in the midst of such multiple perspectives. To the contrary, it is the overlaying or crossing of these diverse perspectives that yields the type of big picture results promised by *l'histoire croisée*. To take the example of child abandonment or child circulation, it is only after we have re-created a constellation of involved individuals—as in the case of baby Wölflein—that we can thoroughly address such key macroquestions as the relative importance of different forms of early modern child circulation—in particular, anonymous abandonment—and the role of state involvement. This constellation of individuals and "networks of relationships"[48] is the subject of chapter 6. There we will identify recurring patterns among various people involved with unwanted children and analyze the significance of key social structures and concepts. We will also assess changes in these structures and patterns over time, before returning to the scholarly discourse about governmental involvement in child abandonment and infanticide, as well as the related issues of illegitimacy, poor relief, unruly youths, and household survival strategies.

Nuremberg

The setting for our stories is the southern central German city of Nuremberg (Nürnberg) from about 1555 to 1670.[49] During this era, the German empire, also known as the Holy Roman Empire of the German Nation, consisted of about twelve million people living in over 350 quasi-autonomous duchies, counties, margravates, landgravates, prince-bishoprics, baronies, monasteries, free knight estates, and city-states known as free or imperial cities—the latter over eighty in number in 1555, including Nuremberg. Most of the populace resided in the countryside, with fewer than one in five people living in towns of 2,000 inhabitants or greater, and only one in twenty-five in towns with more than 10,000 residents.[50] Nuremberg's populace of over 40,000 in 1600 thus made it atypical by sixteenth-century standards and one of the biggest cities in the empire, surpassed only by Augsburg, Strasbourg, and Cologne. It was also one of the most politically and economically powerful city-states of the era. Since attaining its great charter as a free city in 1219, the city had remained a staunchly loyal ally of the German emperors, including Charles IV, who in reward for Nuremberg's backing during a prolonged power struggle, proclaimed in his Golden Bull of 1356 that each new emperor thereafter was to hold his first diet in Nuremberg, an honor the city enjoyed until 1543. The city's maintenance of a castle (the *Kaiserburg*) as a royal residence, as well as the depository of the crown jewels (until 1796), reflected the prestige it enjoyed among subsequent emperors.

Possessing neither particularly rich farmland nor a navigable river, Nuremberg relied on its political and geographic advantages to develop into one of the leading economic centers of the empire by the sixteenth century. At the crossroads of northern routes to the Rhineland and southern roads to territories along the Danube, the city on the Pegnitz was famed for a variety of high-quality manufactured goods, including the local specialties of metal products (such as cannons, blades, and armor), precision instruments (compasses, clocks, musical instruments), as well as (even today) gingerbread and toys. Its banks and mercantile firms competed with the de Medicis of Florence and the Fuggers of Augsburg, establishing offices in Lisbon, Antwerp, Venice, Saragossa, Lyons, and practically every other major trade city in Europe. By 1500 Nuremberg had also become a center in the printing industry and quickly developed international fame for its maps and innovative "earth-apples," or globes, which incorporated information from the latest explorations of the New World. "What's good comes from Nuremberg" became a popular adage throughout the empire and abroad, thereby achieving a level of brand prestige that would be the envy of any modern marketing director or chamber of commerce.[51]

Like Florence, Nuremberg's economic and political golden age closely corresponded with an artistic flowering that brought the city still greater fame. By far the best-known local son was Albrecht Dürer (1471–1528), a drawer and painter of unrivalled skill in Germany who was even widely admired in Italy and France. The city was also home to sculptors Veit Stoss

(1447–1553) and Adam Kraft (ca. 1455–1508), poet Konrad Celtis (1459–1508), humanist Johann Pirckheimer (1440–1501) and his son Willibald (1470–1530), as well as Hans Sachs (1494–1576) the prolific dramatist, provocateur, and *Meistersinger* made still more famous by Richard Wagner.[52] It was with little exaggeration that Nuremberg's denizens during the city's golden age of 1500–55 proudly referred to their home as "the Florence of the North" and "the German Athens."

Despite Nuremberg's sixteenth-century artistic flourishing, its leaders remained conservative and "emphatically anti-intellectual."[53] Their continuing closeness to Emperor Charles V made the city an even more unlikely receptor of Luther's banned religious teachings. Nevertheless in 1525, partly due to the influence of evangelical preachers Lazarus Spengler (1479–1534) and Andreas Osiander (c. 1496–1552), the city council embraced Protestantism, banning the Catholic mass and other "papist" ceremonies and welcoming ministers of the new faith to the city. Five years later, Nuremberg's representatives signed the Augsburg Confession, the first formulaic statement of the Lutheran faith. When asked, however, in 1532 to join the new Protestant military alliance, the Schmalkaldic League, the city's longstanding imperial loyalties returned to the forefront. Instead, Nuremberg's leaders attempted—as they would almost a century later during the Thirty Years' War—to play a conciliatory role between the two religious factions. In both instances their efforts failed, but with the establishment of the Augsburg Religious Peace of 1555 Nuremberg and the rest of Germany were at least able to enjoy almost sixty-five years of relative religious peace—the first half of our stories' time frame.

During this period Nuremberg was at its zenith of wealth, power, and prestige. The French jurist Jean Bodin called it "the greatest, most famous, and best ordered of the imperial cities" and local son Johannes Cochlaeus dubbed it "the center of Europe as well as Germany."[54] Its surrounding rural territory was one of the largest of any city in the empire, stretching out in a thirty-five-mile radius of the city and encompassing the satellite imperial cities of Windsheim and Weissenburg as well as over five hundred villages and a dense forest known as the *Reichswald*. While still several miles off, a traveler would be able to glimpse the stunning city skyline that was so often the subject of artists and engravers (see fig. 0.2). First he would see the majestic *Kaiserburg*, a massive structure over 600 feet long and 200 feet tall, high on a hill overlooking a city of thousands of slate roofs and two especially prominent church spires—those of Saint Sebaldus and Saint Lorenz, the city's two main parishes. Approaching closer, our traveler would be able to make out within its total circumference of more than 17,000 feet a thick

Fig. 0. 2. Nuremberg as viewed from the southeast, with the Kaiserburg looming in the back and the city gallows drawn prominently just outside the city's walls (1533). Staatsarchiv Nürnberg.

sandstone wall about fifty feet high that completely encircled the city and castle. Along this intimidating fortification were eighty-three soaring towers, spaced approximately 150 feet apart, and before them was a moat 100 feet wide and about as deep. As we will see, the image of an island fortress is not far from the way Nuremberg's leaders imagined their home, and they would have been pleased at the sense of awe and admiration the city would inspire in our traveler. Arriving closer, the wayfarer would first have to pass by one small guardhouse before the city wall, then proceed across a narrow bridge through one of the city's eight gates, pass by another inspection point at the entrance to the gate and still another after he had passed through a tunnel in the wall to reach the inner city itself.

During our period of 1555–1670, the city of Nuremberg comprised over five hundred streets and alleys, mostly narrow and crooked, crammed with thousands of structures: stately public buildings, stunning patrician houses, modest artisan residences, and numerous storage barns and stables, as well as many makeshift shelters and stands. The streets, all paved, were often filled with rural folk and their livestock as well as countless horses, dogs, cats, pigs, and rats. Despite the great concentration of people and animals, Nuremberg's streets were reputed to be remarkably clean for the era, thanks to a well-developed water and sewage system in addition to a battery of waste disposal workers, who dumped waste outside the city walls and sometimes, illegally, into the Pegnitz River. Magistrates still frequently complained about unsightly accumulating garbage, but by early modern standards, the city was quite lovely and green, with a number of public parks, gardens, fountains, and decorated squares.

Politically, Nuremberg was governed by a city council, composed of local patricians and artisan representatives (discussed more in chap. 3). For administrative purposes, the council divided the city into eight districts (confusingly designated "quarters"), each with two district heads and numerous municipal guards, usually known as archers. Each district head also supervised several voluntary street captains, who kept track of arms, ammunitions, reserve supplies, horses, lanterns, ladders, and other communal property. This organizational structure was crucial in cases of fires and other local disasters as well as mobilizing for war, conducting surveys for the town council, and collecting taxes and alms. The city government employed teams of health inspectors and kept a close eye on craft production and prices, with all masters accountable to the city council rather than independent guilds, as was the custom in most cities of the day. Nuremberg also had a widespread and well-earned reputation as a law-and-order city, with an unusually active police network and practically the highest capital punishment rate in the empire.

Finally, the city and its magistrates were exceptionally generous in support of the social welfare of residents. The municipal alms bureau established in 1522 inherited an especially impressive array of diverse private and ecclesiastical foundations and institutions, at least 170 by one count, with some dating back as far as two centuries. These included several hospitals and hospices, a variety of poor-relief programs (including those targeted at poor parents with children and poor girls in need of dowries), and a number of private Latin and public German schools, some of the latter cost-free to all.[55] Most important for our story, the city also boasted the Findel, which played a pivotal role in caring for the unwanted children brought to the town council's attention.

When the Religious Peace of Augsburg in 1555 brought an official end to denominational strife and warfare within the German empire, the one major dark cloud on Nuremberg's horizon appeared to lift. The city was economically booming, politically powerful, legally sophisticated, religiously stable, artistically accomplished, and maintained a strong physical and bureaucratic infrastructure. Who could blame its residents for enjoying a genuine feeling of self-satisfaction and confidence as their beloved Nuremberg entered the second half of the sixteenth century, poised for greatness?

ONE

The Unmarried Mother

Until January 18, 1578, Apollonia Vöglin's life had been fairly typical of many rural young women of her day. Born in the Franconian village of Löhrberg, she had for the past three years lived and worked as a maid at the home of her sister and brother-in-law in nearby Immeldorf. The arrangement had been worked out by her father, Michl Vogler, after he learned that she secretly became engaged around the age of sixteen. Vogler had consented to pay for a formal wedding after Apollonia worked for two years, but the agreed upon date came and went with no wedding and after an additional year of pleading, her father remained as intractable as he had always been. Meanwhile, her fiancé, the journeyman Steffan Hassl, had purchased a cottage outside the town of Onolzpach and urged her to move in with him. But without a public wedding, Apollonia refused and Steffan was forced to sell the cottage and continue waiting. About the same time (that is, in March 1577), Apollonia attended a church wedding in Immeldorf as well as the riotous celebration that followed. There, according to her own later testimony, she met another journeyman named Cunz, better known as the Palm Cutter.[1] That evening Cunz accompanied Apollonia and her brother-in-law's male servants back to their house. When the other servants went out to their beds in the barn, Cunz stayed behind in the house, besieging Apollonia with declarations of love, promises of marriage, and plans about them running away together. Although they each knew the other was already engaged to another, she "allowed herself to be talked into it" and let him have his way with her. Over the next several weeks, they had sex at her brother-in-law's house about five times and then the affair fizzled. The following fall the Palm Cutter married his fiancée. Apollonia later claimed that besides Cunz, "no man had ever touched her." By Pentecost in early June of that year, she had begun to notice her abdomen getting bigger, so she

Fig. 1.1. A housemaid in Nuremberg (ca. 1650).
Germanisches Nationalmuseum Nürnberg.

started wrapping herself with a linen belt. Secret pregnancies were hardly unheard of, but the great majority of these were resolved by quick marriages, abortions, miscarriages, or even abandonments. Apollonia's misfortune by contrast had an especially tragic outcome. Early in the morning of Saturday, January 18, 1578, she gave birth in secret to a baby girl, which she later admitted strangling.[2] Seventeen days later she was arrested for the crime and thereupon began the fight to save herself from the executioner's axe.

Apollonia's sad tale is a variation on a familiar literary topos: an unmarried girl impregnated and jilted by a young cad, is forced by shame to hide her pregnancy, and finally, in desperation, murders her newborn child. In early modern Germany, a confluence of several demographic and social developments threatened to make infanticide a more common reality than at any time since antiquity. Most notably, an economic downturn from the mid-sixteenth century on exacerbated the late marriage tendency already common among Western Europeans. The extended period of premarital fertility that resulted multiplied the possibilities for single young women to be involved in voluntary and involuntary sexual encounters and thus the incidence of unwanted pregnancies. At the same time, both Protestant and Catholic secular authorities began much stricter punishment of sex outside of marriage, with particularly harsh consequences for unmarried mothers and their illegitimate children. The crime of infanticide was also vigorously prosecuted and punished as never before, particularly in some imperial cities such as Nuremberg. All of this undoubtedly made Apollonia's predicament worse and her crime presumably more commonplace. In fact, infanticide continued to be the rarest and most extreme option for a young woman in Apollonia's predicament. To explain this unexpected result requires an understanding of the circumstances behind her action as well as the various options she faced up until that fatal moment. Viewed in sequence, the choices available to women in her situation reveal much about early modern sexuality, domestic relations, marriage, and personal freedom as well as the centrality of informal child circulation within this framework. Viewed in combination with the various constraints Apollonia faced, such options also help to explain how such a desperate act might occur but how it was prevented in the great majority of cases.

Sex and the Single Maid

As was usually the case, Apollonia's unwanted pregnancy took place during the transitional period between childhood and full adulthood. For most girls, this began anywhere from ten to sixteen years old and ended at marriage, which could be as late as a woman's thirties. Like other early modern age transitions, the end of childhood was marked less by a biological development such as menarche—which appears to have started at fourteen at the earliest and more typically as late as sixteen or seventeen—than by a change in social situation.[3] The most readily visible marker was the girl's departure for domestic service in another household. Until the beginning of the modern era, perhaps 30–40 percent of all girls over fourteen worked as maids in other people's houses. About one-third of these had been employed since the age of ten, but most started later, like Apollonia Vöglin, who tells us that she was about sixteen when she moved to her brother-in-law's house to serve as a maid.[4] Most of those who did not enter into service remained in their parents' households until marriage, usually working in the house or nearby, sometimes begging for the family, and in a few cases knowingly sold by their parents into prostitution.[5] Before the eighteenth century, only a tiny minority of teenaged girls went away to convent or boarding schools and even those who attended small German schools or private "corner schools" received only brief and rudimentary training before the onset of full household chores, either at home or elsewhere as a maid.[6] After all, except for those girls in Catholic lands who became nuns, running one's own house-hold as a wife and mother was the universal vocation for women. In this respect, Apollonia's domestic service in particular had the double advantage of not only enabling her to develop her housekeeping skills but also—and more importantly—allowing her to build up a wedding dowry sufficient to marry. It also had the added benefit of relieving the financial strain on her family's household.

Significantly, the transitional period that encompassed domestic service coincided almost exactly with the time when girls reached their sexual maturity and first experienced some relative independence.[7] That transitional period, moreover, could be quite extended. Given the common northwestern European pattern of late marriage (on average, about twenty-five for women and twenty-eight for men), a young woman entering service at Apollonia's age might experience at least ten to fifteen years of fertility before marrying.[8] As today in industrialized societies, this life phase can be characterized as a distinctive and often unstable mixture of dependence and personal freedom. While working in their own homes or someone else's, young women such as Apollonia rarely had any kind of economic independence or security, yet unlike most married women (of whom the same might be said), teenagers and women in their twenties—particularly those living away from home—experienced for the first time a multiplicity of opportunities for voluntary or involuntary sexual relations. It is hardly surprising that these young women's lack of experience in dealing with men, combined with their new attractiveness to the same and a potentially long waiting period before marriage, resulted in a great number of illicit and unwanted pregnancies.

Yet were maids such as Apollonia truly more vulnerable to this undesired condition than their other unmarried counterparts? If not, why then were maids so prominent in legal records of fornication, abortion, abandonment, and infanticide?[9] Above all, domestic service entailed geographic and thus social displacement. Most young women, like Apollonia, served fairly near their homes but far enough away to require a new social network.[10] The site of their service might be determined in a variety of ways. In Nuremberg, the town council established official employment agencies for maids only.[11] Young maids could also turn to private individuals, who were not supposed to charge for their services. More often, girls and young women, especially from the countryside, flocked on their own to the job fairs held several times a year in town and country alike. Or, as was apparently more common with daughters than sons, the arrangement could be managed without any third party, with the girl often serving with acquaintances of her parents or, as in Apollonia's case, *en famille.*[12]

The role of a young maid in her initial placement was usually passive, with the position itself usually contracted between the employer and a girl's father or guardian; only older women made their own arrangements. Apollonia's placement and contract were all kept within the family and under the stern oversight of her capricious father. It is unlikely that she underwent the usual formal ceremony, consisting of a written contract, a handshake, and possibly a gift from the employer, such as a hairbrush or a "bond penny" (*dingpfennig* or *Mietpfennig*). Once "bonded" (*gedingt; verdingt*) in this way, a maid was not allowed to change masters before the specified time limit, two years in Apollonia's case; otherwise she forfeited the larger part of her salary and possibly faced a serious fine.[13] Apparently Michl Vogler promised to pay her the entire dowry at the end of the agreed upon time (though he did not live up to his end of the deal). Normally a maid was supposed to receive installments of her total salary, usually in semiannual or annual lump sums, as well as food, lodging, and presents (especially clothing) at Christmas and other times of the year. In return, she would reside at the employer's house (in Apollonia's case, that of her sister and brother-in-law), often sharing not only a room but a bed, until the contract ran out. Apollonia, as we know from her amorous encounters and secret childbirth, was fortunate enough to have her own room, but it is unclear whether she also received any spending money. Her duties were likely general and unspecified; only wealthy households could afford a full-time cook or nanny (the two highest paid female posts).[14] Ideally, by the end of this servitude she would have secured both her father's consent to marry and enough money to make a respectable dowry, enabling her to marry Steffan.

There were many ways Apollonia might have been derailed from this ideal path of respectability and become unintentionally pregnant. The inadequacy of domestics' pay in itself often made the ideal scenario unworkable. While overall demand for servants soared during the sixteenth and seventeenth centuries, only the minority of young women working in bourgeois or aristocratic homes appreciated any real financial benefits. Even then, the best-paid female servant always earned less than the worst-paid male servant of a household. On average, male servants and day laborers throughout Germany were paid two-and-a-half to five times as much as their female counterparts.[15] Under such conditions, the two essentials of attracting a mate—attractive clothing and a suitable dowry—remained long out of reach for many young maids. Consequently only one in four maids

were married by the age of twenty-five (compared to two-thirds of the remaining female population), and on average maids married ten years later
than other women.[16] In a few wealthy imperial cities such as Nuremberg,
this situation was mitigated by a dowry fund for poor girls, but unfortunately only a handful of awards of 20 fl. each were made annually (in a city
of over 40,000).[17] Maids from poorer backgrounds were naturally hit the
hardest by such conditions, but during the bad economic climate of the
sixteenth and seventeenth centuries many young maids from middle and
upper class families, such as Apollonia's, were forced to put off marriage or
marry beneath their social rank.[18]

Not surprisingly, many maids chose to leave their employers before
the end of their contractual period, sometimes after only a few months
or weeks. Employers found it particularly difficult to keep domestics during April through October, when the women could earn much more as
day laborers in the fields.[19] Given the demand for servants, such women
knew that there would then be no problem finding placement in the city
after the harvest. Secular authorities throughout Germany responded to this
perceived disorder with a flood of mandates and ordinances attempting to
freeze servants' wages and enforce maids' contracts. Meanwhile prospective employers continued to lure some women away from their positions
with promises of "more pay, tips, beer, money, or other devices," especially
clothing.[20] In some places the demand was so great that the requirement
of previous references was waived and maids could often have their pick of
employers. Some found markedly better conditions, most did not, but the
overall effect was the same: extensive job turnover and geographical instability among maids and servants in general, all during a prolonged period
of potential sexual activity and fertility.

The liberty of maids in Apollonia's situation should not be exaggerated.
Whichever job she chose and however often she changed, a maid's ability
to earn a sufficient dowry remained severely constrained. Frequent mobility
also made securing a marriage partner more difficult. In Apollonia's case,
her leaving would have jeopardized not only her engagement to Steffan but
also her father's willingness to pay any dowry. Like many maids, Apollonia
thus held up her end of the service contract, even if her employer (in her
case, her father and her brother-in-law) did not. Many did not run off to a
job fair once they started to get bored or dissatisfied with their position, and
a great number of maids apparently endured considerable abuse from their
employers. Fear of economic insecurity was probably the most common
reason for staying put, though this might be coupled with a sense of obligation to an employer, relative, or guardian or fear of reprisals.

Once in service, Apollonia would have been almost completely reliant on her master for food, lodging, and clothing. Maids were also vulnerable to accusations of theft (sometimes true) and other attacks on their reputation or person. A maid impregnated by her employer was in fact the most common adultery scenario among married men throughout the early modern era.[21] Often we encounter instances of a quid pro quo arrangement between an employer and his maid, with promises of money or even marriage in exchange for sexual favors, though marriage was at best a cruel delusion. Occasionally genuine love and affection surface in the records, whether or not marriage was promised or intended. On the other hand, an employer might apply various levels of coercion, from what would today be called sexual harassment to rape, considering it part of his privilege as the master. Close quarters undoubtedly intensified the temptation for such men, but a separate maid's room—such as Apollonia's—could not guarantee protection from unwanted advancements.[22] Household dynamics could produce a number of variations and combinations of all these themes.[23]

Some employers claimed that they were the victims, as maids blackmailed them with threats of crying rape. Certainly rape in general was drastically underreported, partly because of women's fear for their own reputations and physical safety, and partly because of the severity of the penalty it merited, namely, death. The government of Nuremberg stood out for its execution of six rapists between 1600 and 1692, though even this is an astonishingly paltry number of convictions for an entire century (which included long periods of military occupation).[24] Secular authorities generally favored male employers over female employees, in some cases forbade a woman from pressing charges of rape or seduction unless her reputation was spotless. According to a contemporary Neuchâtel legal formula: "A girl will be considered a virgin if she has good morals and a good reputation without any suspicion, and if she does not give in to the will of a young man unless he had first promised her faith of marriage in the presence of at least two honorable witnesses."[25] For some, an alleged rape that resulted in pregnancy in itself disproved the accusation since well into the eighteenth century it was commonly believed that orgasm (indicating the woman's willingness) was necessary for conception.[26]

A rape case involving a Nuremberg contemporary of Apollonia Vöglin illustrates the precarious status of a young woman's reputation at all times. In 1582 the two guardians of fifteen-year-old Apollonia Tortelein learned that the girl's master, Sebalt Kayser, had repeatedly forced himself upon her. They immediately petitioned the Nuremberg town council, which in turn summoned and questioned young Apollonia, asking her why she hadn't told either of her guardians about this earlier. Remarkably, her interrogator was even empowered to threaten her with torture if she refused to talk.[27] Upon his arrest the next day, Sebalt Kayser admitted taking the orphan in as a potmaker apprentice three years earlier, but maintained complete innocence as to all charges of rape. In his view, the accusation was part of a shakedown scheme by one of the guardians who demanded the exorbitant sum of 300 fl. for the girl's lost honor. According to Kayser, "He'd had her for about two years [and] she wasn't much good—had run away once or twice, and one time stayed for twenty weeks outside in the yard of her [married] sister—but each time she had returned and been rebonded."[28]

When this counter-accusation of personal instability failed to work, Kayser tried a different tack, admitting that one night while drunk he got into his wife's old bed in the children's room, not noticing until the morning that Apollonia was in the same bed with him. (His wife was away on a cure at the local spa—a common situation in such cases). The next morning he claimed to have awakened with no memory of what happened during the night but either way it couldn't have been rape since "the girl could have easily left when she saw that he'd laid down in the same bed."[29] Pressed further, Kayser admitted that it happened once more, but stood by the time-honored defenses that drunkenness on his part and silence on hers equaled a consensual act.[30] Bound and threatened with torture, he continued to deny more than two encounters, this time adding "after he did it with her the last time, he felt guilty about it and only half a year ago did he go [back] to communion with his wife, and he doesn't know how the evil adversary and drink had thus tempted him."[31] Only after Apollonia Tortelein was reexamined (again with threats if deemed necessary) did Kayser's already weak story begin to unravel fully. First he admitted that he had been awake the first time and that he whispered to her, "Apple, let me inside from behind," and she willingly let it happen and made no cry. He also conceded that she had been a virgin at the time. When his young charge was brought before him, he broke down completely and admitted his guilt.[32] His full confession and pleas for mercy did nothing to mitigate his sentence of decapitation, carried out four days later. What remains unclear is the effect all of this had on young Apollonia, who—after attempting to run away several times and then enduring not only the ordeal of repeated forced sex with Kayser but also a humiliating public investigation—was herself brought before the magistrates and berated for being less than forthcoming, and thereby branded a dishonored woman.[33]

Apollonia Vöglin never mentioned any sexual advances from her brother-in-law employer, but this immunity was hardly guaranteed by virtue of his kinship. Sexual coercion and dishonor also threatened those young women who remained at home or among relatives for their service. Incest, however, rarely escaped the "conspiracy of silence" within the household and thus—like rape—was seriously underreported. Also like rape and adultery, such abuse usually only came to light with an unexplained pregnancy or birth and thus usually after the usual early modern fertility age of sixteen–seventeen.[34] It is remotely possible that Apollonia had in fact been impregnated by her brother-in-law, which would have constituted incest, subject to execution at the stake (in which case her reticence in speaking out would have been quite understandable). Most incest cases involved girls in their mid- to late teens and their stepfathers. Occasionally a mother was also executed for complicity, such as Kunigunda Küflederin, who eventually confessed to learning within weeks of her second marriage that her new husband was molesting her daughter, but despite her anger and intention to make it stop, claimed that she was afraid to send her daughter out into the world as a beggar—a pathetic commentary on both the economic necessity of her marriage and the fragility of any girl's reputation.[35]

It is even more unlikely that Apollonia's impregnator was her own father, though it is not impossible. Reported instances of sex between siblings or a biological father and daughter were rare and as shocking to early modern sensibilities as to those of modern times. Valentin Goldner, executed for fathering seven children by his biological daughter, appears to have been truly an exceptional figure. There are only four instances of this type of incest in the criminal records of Nuremberg between 1550 and 1620.[36] Often these relationships also involved violence or the threat of it. In 1587, seventeen-year-old Gertraut Schmidtin told Nuremberg magistrates how four years earlier her brother had held her down and raped her at knifepoint. Rather than encountering sympathy from her interrogators, she was pressed to admit that their sexual encounters continued almost weekly, and that during the past year her biological father had also slept with her three times. Like most incest victims during the era, Getraut's claim that the two men had "treated [her] very poorly and beaten her badly" had little bearing on her case. The same was true of her description of attempts to escape through service positions, which were always thwarted by her father and brothers, who dragged her along with them to their constantly changing residences.[37] As in all rape cases, girls over fourteen were consistently assumed to be temptresses involved in consensual relations and then punished with their male relatives. Usually this meant a lesser punishment for them, such as public flogging or banishment, but in a few cases, such as that of Gertraut Schmidtin, the victim was actually executed alongside the perpetrator.[38]

A young woman who survived such ordeals emerged not only psychologically scarred but socially stigmatized, especially if her sexual contact had led to the birth of an illegitimate child. Here, as in other instances of illicit pregnancy, her options were decidedly limited. If no child resulted, she could flee to another position, as the young Apollonia Tortelein had repeatedly tried, but often this would require making the rape public—a dangerous option as already seen. Silence out of fear and shame no doubt often seemed the safer course, again, possible only without any visible pregnancy. If, on the other hand, the "stain" on the woman's honor became known, she would encounter great difficulty in securing a new position, let alone a respectable marriage.

Obviously not all unwanted pregnancies were the result of involuntary sexual intercourse. Apollonia enjoyed many opportunities to meet and become intimate by choice with members of the opposite sex. Early modern communities, particularly cities, teemed with young, unmarried people; by some estimates, perhaps two-thirds of the population was under the age of thirty, with about half of those young people between fifteen and thirty years old. Domestic servants constituted a particularly large proportion of this group, with three times as many maids as male servants in some areas.[39] The high presence and visibility of young and unmarried maids, particularly in large cities such as Nuremberg, were viewed with suspicion by many married contemporaries, male and female (see fig. 1.2). In popular literature, maids were often stereotyped as especially promiscuous, ostensibly accounting for their overrepresentation in fornication and illegitimate pregnancies. In his *Seven Devils* diatribe, Philemon Menagius warned of the many wiles of young maids, who were themselves "nothing but ashes and dirt," concerned only with new clothing and seducing men.[40] Certainly the new quasi-independence of many teenaged girls and young women played a role in this statistic, as did the typically long period most maids were forced to remain single.

The nature of young women's sexual encounters naturally varied widely but some common patterns are detectable, particularly in those instances where pregnancy resulted. The most typical scenario for premarital sex, and the one with the broadest popular approval among contemporaries, took place within the confines of a publicly announced—and therefore legitimate—engagement to be married.[41] In what most people viewed as the natural course of events, a young woman met a suitable beau (often through the matchmaking of female relatives) and if she felt sufficiently attracted or otherwise swayed, the two would secure the permission of their respective fathers and announce their intention to wed during a public ceremony,

Fig. 1.2. A broadsheet portraying various types of female servants conversing near Nuremberg's main market. The maid placement agent (A) gossips with the cook (C), who in her distraction allows a dog to eat some of her groceries. Both the nanny (B) and the farm maid (E) are also caught up in idle chatter, while the house-maid (D) is herself being chatted up by a young noble, with assistance from Cupid in the window at top left (1652). Germanisches Nationalmuseum Nürnberg.

usually at one of the families' homes. In traditional thinking, this secular event—which included certain vows, possibly a wedding contract, and a wedding toast—constituted the essential foundation of a marriage. By the sixteenth century, couples were still expected to "complete" their union with a church ceremony but the two events might be separated by several weeks, months, or as in the instance of Apollonia and Steffan, years. During this intermediate period, most members of the community considered the young man and woman exclusively committed to each other and effectively married. In some regions, the two were referred to as groom and bride or even husband and wife. There was consequently widespread toleration (except among zealous religious reformers) of sexual intimacy between engaged youths during this period before "coming to honor" with a formal wedding.[42] Throughout Germany, there was even a ritualized practice (variously known as *fensterlehen, nachtfreien,* and *gurgeln*) that consisted of a young man sneaking into a woman's bedroom (usually while her father was out) and then lying together in bed with their clothes on, having long discussions, some petting, and perhaps intercourse (see fig. 1.3).[43]

This relaxed attitude of most people toward premarital sex between fiancés was a matter of special concern to secular and religious officials. A 1582 Nuremberg ordinance forbade such a couple from taking full regalia during their formal weddings and ordered straw wreaths, as symbols of shame, for

Fig. 1.3. A young man beginning or concluding a clandestine overnight stay in his fiancée's bedroom (ca. 1650).

both the bride and the groom to wear. In addition to the downgraded wedding, each individual had to endure some type of punishment for fornication, usually an extended stay in one of the city's towers on a diet of bread
and water.[44] Most lay people apparently ignored such admonitions, but pastors in Franconia and elsewhere still attempted to apply a "chastity test"
for marrying couples. A 1655 account of the Nuremberger Georg Phillip
Hardörfer tells of a pastor earnestly inquiring of an engaged couple whether
"they have not had sinful relations with one another," to which both immediately respond "no." He then offers a toast to the health and salvation
of the couple and tells them that if they have told the truth the wine will
taste good, otherwise it will turn into gall and poison. And sure enough, as
soon as the guilty groom tastes bitter wine he admits the truth, condemning
his bride to wearing the shameful wreath of straw in the church ceremony.[45]
Certainly by the less tolerant seventeenth century, some of this moral rigor
had spread to the population at large, but traditional notions and the appar-

ent frequency of bridal pregnancies indicate that quick marriage remained a common and acceptable resolution of an out-of-wedlock pregnancy.

As an apparently unconsummated clandestine engagement, Apollonia's betrothal to Steffan did not exactly fulfill the communal expectations for courtship and marriage. The opposition of Apollonia's father posed a still greater obstacle. Even pregnancy within that context, however, was vastly preferable to the other common way that a young maid might become pregnant, through casual sex with a stranger such as the Palm Cutter. Yet such an encounter became much likelier once Apollonia entered domestic service, given that she would now spend a considerable amount of time on her own in the public sphere, going to wells or markets, delivering messages, and doing errands, even in the evening.[46] These activities allowed for many informal contacts with men, single or married, as did numerous social occasions such as feast days (especially May Day and Christmas) and weddings. Various single-sex youth groups, both formally and informally, conspired to find ways to meet eligible members of the opposite sex. Throughout Germany, girls organized dances and other events, while boys roamed in bands, visiting girls' homes or stopping in at the notorious spinning bees (Spinnstuben), held in private homes or inns, where they found spinning young women with whom they could eat, gossip, joke, sing (often lewd songs), and dance. According to historian Michael Mitterauer, "there were [numerous] social institutions which virtually forced adolescents into contact with the opposite sex."[47] Chaperones were usually expected among "reputable" girls, thus it was not surprising that when Apollonia Vöglin attended the wedding feast in Immeldorf, her brother-in-law's male servants accompanied her (see fig. 1.4). Obviously their concern was well placed (if not consistent); no sooner had the chaperones gone to bed than the young man she had just met proposed marriage to her and promised to take her away.

Who were these young men who wooed, impregnated, and then usually abandoned maids and other young single women? According to popular literature, soldiers were the most common cads in such situations, seducing vulnerable young women with declarations of love and promises of marriage and then absconding "once they'd had their way."[48] It was well known, moreover, that illegitimacy rates always rose during war years, with mercenaries roaming cities and the countryside alike (see fig. 1.5).[49] Yet at least one study has found that soldiers accounted for only 2.2 percent of the impregnators of single maids and that fellow servants, as in the case of Apollonia and the Palm Cutter, were by far the likelier culprits.[50] Most sig-

Fig. 1.4. Pieter Brueghel the Younger, *Peasant Dance*, ca. 1560. A wedding feast similar to this rural peasant festival was the site where Apollonia met the journeyman Cunz. The heady combination of dancing and alcohol often led to sexual trysts, as suggested by the embracing couple in the top left corner and the woman pulling a man indoors under the pennant. Kunsthistorisches Museum, Vienna.

nificantly, the great majority of "false suitors" were from the same age and class cohorts as the women they impregnated.

Like many early modern girls, Apollonia apparently had a quite limited knowledge of sex. Since her mother is never mentioned, it is likely that she had died, leaving any instruction on the facts of life to Apollonia's sister or female friends. Perhaps Apollonia knew how to acquire one of the many herbal potions or sprinkling powders (of varying efficacy) meant to inhibit conception. Certainly knowledge of *coitus interruptus*—sometimes referred to as "unloading before the barn"—was widespread during the sixteenth century, though many men refused to practice it. Many other contraceptive methods—including the use of sponges and tampons, douching, and condoms—were probably less known among women of Apollonia's background.[51] According to her testimony, the Palm Cutter visited and had intercourse with her about five times at her brother-in-law's house "in bed"; another time "he tried to get her to do it in a field but she refused to have anything to do with him [there]."[52] And while her chances of conception probably increased each time, frequent sex was and is by no means necessary to become pregnant: child murderer Agnes Lengin claimed that she only had intercourse once, while drunk.[53] Most likely, all of these encoun-

Fig. 1.5. Daniel Hopfer, *Soldier Embraces a Maiden*
(ca. 1535). Metropolitan Museum of Art.

ters involved no protective measures whatsoever, though perhaps afterward she ingested some contraceptive herbs.

Pregnant and Petrified

Then, as now, an unmarried woman who believed that she might be pregnant had to first make the crucial decision whether to reveal her suspected state to others or even to acknowledge it herself. Here the human potential for desperate hope or self-deception could be virtually unlimited. One of the most incredible aspects of secret pregnancies that ended in infanticide was the frequent claim by the accused—usually later in criminal interrogations—that the woman didn't know she was pregnant until the moment of birth. Convicted child murderer Agnes Lengin typically claimed "she really didn't know that she was carrying a child, since the same hardly moved within her and she wasn't being secretive when she said each time in her conversations with her mistress and other people that she wasn't carrying a child."[54] Was this a sincere conviction, a calculated lie, or some mixture of conscious and unconscious delusion? The question is complicated by the fact that plausible deniability was quite possible for early modern women, at least until the "quickening" at 4 ½ months. Various explanations other than pregnancy, for instance, might account for missed periods. "Interrupted flow" or "clogged up blood" was sometimes considered a seasonal malady, cured with the onset of spring. Certain foods or "wild dancing" were also viewed as triggers to this condition. Many of the symptoms—swelling belly, vomiting, loss of appetite, fatigue, moodiness, swollen breasts, and whitish urine with a hint of blue—were the same as those for dropsy. Intentionally or not, many women could easily have confused the two conditions, especially given their meager understanding of the entire biological process.[55] In some instances, the herbs used to unclog a woman might have acted as abortifacients, again, with or without intention. Whether a woman could go the full term of her pregnancy unaware of the movements within her growing belly is another question, though even here the possibilities for rationalized denial are not exhausted. Elisabeth Ernstin, for instance, claimed that she didn't know she'd been pregnant until she awoke one morning with a stillborn baby in her bed. The psychological nature of her denial and its relative truthfulness are of course impossible for us to ascertain.[56]

Apollonia Vöglin, on the other hand, tells us of her awareness early in the first trimester and her decision to bind her stomach with a girdle to conceal the pregnancy. Much clothing of the day could help a woman keep her pregnancy secret for a long time. The Nuremberg custom of women wearing "rain cloths" (*Regentücher*) was outlawed six times during the first forty years of the seventeenth century for this very reason (see fig. 1.6). One local wit even composed a couplet about this apparently common practice: "[A] raincloth can be used in many ways by [any] little fool / to conceal much from others in any event or rule."[57] According to the Carolina, the very influential imperial criminal codification of 1532, concealing a pregnancy in this matter was unlawful and tantamount to infanticide, but the deception was rarely if ever prosecuted as such within the empire.[58] Evidently Apollonia saw the risk of this course of action as minimal, or perhaps she convinced herself not to think about it. At the very least, this tactic would buy her some time.

Her plan, Apollonia says, was to marry Stefan and to remain quiet about the pregnancy until after the wedding.[59] Certainly she would not have stood out had this occurred. Bridal pregnancy was quite common in the early

Fig. 1.6. A Nuremberg maiden wearing a *Regentuch*
(1669). Germanisches Nationalmuseum Nürnberg.

modern era, with on average one out of three marriages followed by the
birth of a child in less than eight months.[60] Birth registers from Nuremberg's
two main parishes suggest that formal acknowledgement of this situation
(at least to a pastor) remained rare during the seventeenth century, even
after 1650, when such births averaged 2–4 percent of all baptisms.[61] There
is no way to ascertain how many of rushed marriages actually took place
among already engaged couples and how many unions were more hastily
arranged between relative strangers. Apollonia's hope to pass her impregnation by Cunz off as a more acceptable "early birth" following her long
engagement to Steffan was probably an infrequent solution but far from
unique among women in her predicament.

Why wasn't Apollonia able to take advantage of the relatively lenient
view of premarital relations by engaged couples? Most important were
her father's continuing objections to the match. Although she originally

thought his permission forthcoming, it never arrived. It is hard to make out the full nature of Michl Vogler's animus from Apollonia's testimony, though their secret courtship could not have endeared the young man to him. According to her, Steffan's father, Jobst Hassl of Schmallenbach, was a reputable man, yet the young journeyman was barred from the Vogler home.[62] Vogler's reaction to their marriage plans must have been anticipated by Apollonia and her fiancé Steffan, since they chose to exchange clandestine vows and keep quiet about them "for a long time" rather than engage in the usual semipublic contractual negotiations. Secret "corner marriages" (*Winkelehen*) were universally condemned by secular and religious leaders alike. Sixteenth-century Protestant and Catholic reformers as diverse as Thomas More, Desiderius Erasmus, Martin Luther, and Ulrich Zwingli all harshly condemned such private and secret marriages as diabolically inspired. The otherwise permissive Rabelais actually argued for the right of a father to kill the clandestine husband of his daughter.[63] In this instance, only a direct intervention by the deacon of Löhrberg softened Michl Vogler's adamant resistance to the union. Even then, the couple had to wait for full paternal approval, at least another five years, at which time Apollonia turned twenty-two and could marry of her own consent.[64]

The one loophole left to Apollonia and Steffan was the law recognizing a clandestine exchange of vows that at some subsequent point had been consummated as valid and binding, regardless of parental approval. In the face of her father's opposition, this legal tactic would seem to offer Apollonia a ready escape from her impending dishonor, yet she did not make use of it. Probably she simply was not aware of the law itself. A much more likely obstacle, and possibly the crucial one, was that she feared rejection by Steffan, who would know the child was not his, since according to her testimony, no man but her erstwhile lover the Palm Cutter "had ever touched her." To his credit, Steffan feared neither disinheritance nor public dishonor when he asked Apollonia to move in with him without her father's blessing or a public wedding. But that was before she became pregnant by another man. Risking the open ridicule of the label of cuckold was probably another matter. Perhaps she did tell him of her situation and he did reject her. A final and undoubtedly powerful reason for Apollonia's silence and rejection of a strictly legal solution was that by her own testimony she craved the communal and familial approval signified by the church ceremony and public feast that in most people's eyes "completed" the marriage. Put another way, she dreaded being discovered by an already recalcitrant father (who could legally disinherit her) and stigmatized as "a shameful whore" by her neighbors. A pregnancy that jeopardized both her reputation and Steffan's affections had to be hidden and ultimately dealt with in some way that preserved her honor and good name.

As time passed and no paternal approval or wedding with Steffan materialized, Apollonia's options for an honorable solution rapidly shrank. Obviously she could no longer pass off her child as Steffan's, at least to him. She still preserved the right to sue the Palm Cutter for marriage or at least support yet neither result was either fully practical or desirable. Most dauntingly, she faced a mighty struggle in attempting to enforce any of Cunz's casual promises of marriage, officially known as "frivolous vows." Like clandestine vows, frivolous marriage vows were universally condemned by all authorities of the day. In most people's eyes these promises were still worse, since the "suitor" apparently never had any real intention of marriage. Yet judging by the frequency of this pattern among convicted fornicators and child murderers—not to mention plaintiffs in marriage courts—such promises commonly, almost universally, preceded the initial sexual encounter.[65] Clearly Apollonia had her doubts about the sincerity of the Palm Cutter's proposal and she admitted that even though she knew "he was already half-engaged" (a fascinating obfuscation), she allowed his protestations of love and devotion to cloud her judgment. Similar vows from traveling journeymen or soldiers must have also been doubted by other women who eventually succumbed to "sweet words," yet a promise of marriage apparently provided the security they needed in case of pregnancy. One might even describe the encounter as a transaction (albeit one with unequal risk), whereby virginity is traded for marriage.[66] Marriage judges throughout Germany fumed about such vows exchanged "in heated and rash desire or with words of jesting or cursing" (such as eating a sausage "in the name of love") but remained powerless to prevent them.[67]

In the instance of the Palm Cutter, the greatest apparent impediment to establishing a binding marriage was his (as well as Apollonia's) preexisting engagement at the time of their first encounter, not to mention his subsequent marriage to someone else. Yet neither of these obstacles was insurmountable. In fact, this course of action (ironically) might have been Apollonia's best bet for a legitimate marriage and child. In Nuremberg the lawsuit would have come before its marriage court, established during the wake of the Reformation to handle cases previously referred to a diocesan court.[68] If Apollonia's father had chosen to pursue the matter (and here too was a problem from her point of view), her claim would be based on the still-honored canonical dictum that consummated marriage vows of any nature trumped previous, unconsummated vows.[69] If the Palm Cutter chose to contest both the vows and paternity, his strategy would probably focus on the wording of the vows or their very existence. Obviously corroborating witnesses could be helpful for either side but given the very nature of clandestine vows, these were often hard to come by. Such exchanges could take place in settings such as a crowded inn or an isolated forest, they could be formulated as simply as "Let us marry" or as vaguely as "I am yours," and consequently the disputes could drag on for months or even years. If Apollonia had been both literate and farsighted, she might be able to produce love letters or other written evidence; otherwise the case often came down to a contest of his word versus hers.[70]

Lawsuits concerning impregnation, with or without vows, were by contrast more straightforward. Given the fact that someone had impregnated the plaintiff, a defendant had to rely on proving either that he was elsewhere at the crucial time or that the plaintiff had "carnally mixed" with more than one man. One strategy related to this was to suggest that the woman had knowledge of contraception, thereby establishing a reputation for promiscuity. Another was that "he didn't go all the way with her, he only tried her"—a claim impervious to any forensic examination. Judges naturally viewed such defenses skeptically, placing more value on their own meticulous examination and interpretation of a single key piece of testimony or evidence, such as the actual words exchanged or symbolic items given (such as a ring or a coin).[71] Initially this highly subjective process of "he said, she said" had proven beneficial to female plaintiffs, who initiated at least two-thirds of marriage suits in both Protestant and Catholic courts, yielding an overall fifty-fifty chance of success. By the second half of the sixteenth century, however, when all women's reputations were increasingly suspect, the likelihood of winning had dropped to as low as one in ten in most places.[72] Visible pregnancy certainly helped—in seventeenth-century Schwäbisch Hall one-quarter of fornication cases ended in voluntary marriage and another one-quarter in court-forced marriage[73]—but this still meant that at least half of the "girls in trouble" involved could not find husbands and law courts were unlikely to assist them.

On the surface, Apollonia had little to lose in a marriage suit, apparently risking only personal embarrassment and court costs. If a woman was found to have falsely accused a man, he was entitled to claim injuries, while she would receive some sort of corporal punishment—as she would have anyway in the case of fornication. When Conrad Amshler's daughter claimed in 1645 that the servant Hans Georg Fuchs had impregnated her, the accused was immediately arrested and imprisoned. Upon discovering that Amshler had no more proof other than his daughter's word, however, the town council ordered Fuchs released and Amshler fined.[74] If, on the other hand, the marriage suit was successful, the man would be immediately escorted from the courtroom to the church, where he would be met by a deacon ready to say "I do" for him if necessary.[75] According to the 1564 Reformatio, the constitutional law of Nuremberg until the late nineteenth century, if the woman was pregnant the two had to marry each other whether they wanted to or not. More than one Nuremberg impregnator claimed that he preferred to sit in irons rather than marry, only to capitulate within a few days. The "shotgun" wedding (*Zwangstrauung*) was not a universal practice throughout the empire, however, at least not officially. The Elector of the Palatinate's 1563 marriage court ordinance stressed that the impregnator of a young maiden should be urged to marry her out of "Christian love and honor," but he was not to be compelled by any "worldly or physical force."[76] Yet the bias toward marriage was so strong in Nuremberg that two seventeenth-century decrees proclaimed that "even in the case of unclean wenches, the law nowhere forbids the forced marriage of a maiden."[77]

Why did Apollonia not take the Palm Cutter to court? True, he was by that time already married, but the consummated marriage vows she exchanged with him—if proven—would have annulled his current marriage. Quite probably she knew nothing of such legal matters and thought him unobtainable. In any event, as she made clear in her subsequent testimony, she wanted Steffan, not Cunz. This train of thought, combined with her dread of her father and of public scandal, also accounts for her unwillingness to pursue a less drastic kind of legal action, namely, a paternity suit for child support (*alimentatio*). If a man admitted paternity or had it forensically established and was already married or otherwise ineligible, he could at least be required to pay the costs of the birth and child support until the woman married or the child came of age (usually twelve). Usually a claim of this nature had to be filed within the first six months of pregnancy but in Nuremberg the suit could even be initiated after the child's birth—evidence of the strong magisterial interest in assigning paternal responsibility.[78] When Kunigunda Lessnerin set her illegitimate baby before the door of innkeeper Melchior Peldes, she immediately received the kind of attention she sought: a case before the marriage court, a dragnet for the absconded Hans Peldes (alleged father of her child), and imprisonment of Hans's father, Melchior, until he or his son made restitution.[79] Not surprisingly, Nuremberg's marriage and civic courts settled thousands of paternity suits during the course of the sixteenth and seventeenth centuries.[80]

Even this course of action carried risks though. Like frivolous marriage vows themselves, decrees of *alimentatio* were nearly impossible to enforce among traveling journeymen and soldiers—who generally could not be sued for child support in civic courts—as well as among other migrants.[81] Leinhard Feld succeeded in his marriage suit against Kilian Pfiz, whom he accused of deflowering and impregnating his daughter, but the culprit could not be found, forcing him to sue Kilian's father in civic court for damages.[82] Often it could be difficult to get even resident men to accept such a decree. A maid from the village of Schnabelveid was told by her accused impregnator that she was a "great slut" and that he would hunt her down after the birth; according to her, "he violently had his way with her and afterward forgot all about her child."[83] Apollonia might have risked the scandal of publicly acknowledging her pregnancy and still ended up without any financial support whatsoever, including from her outraged father.

Once exposed, an unwed mother-to-be faced intense pressure from family and government officials alike to name a father. Secular authorities at all levels had a practical as well as moral interest in achieving this result, since unmarried women and their children would inevitably turn up on their alms lists. In Nuremberg and elsewhere throughout early modern Europe, local officials always attempted to ascertain the name and location of the men who fathered illegitimate children so that the culprits could assume their financial and moral responsibility.[84] In instances of uncooperative mothers, Nuremberg's midwives were instructed to wait until the peak of the labor pain to demand the name of the baby's father.[85] In the harsher seventeenth century, the same unwed new mothers were sometimes ordered brought to the council in chains for interrogation and again questioned about their sexual partners, even if the child had died.[86]

Understandably, many young women in this situation yielded to combined familial and communal pressure and did indeed name a father. If a woman had had more than one sexual partner within the previous nine months, she might be genuinely confused yet rather than admit this and be thought of as a slut, she could simply name the man best suited to provide for her and her child. Others, occasionally with malice or greed aforethought, intentionally picked men they knew weren't even possibly the father yet who had deep pockets. An old German song mocks the practice:

> [U]nmarried I bring before you seven children.
> I did not give the right father for a single one,
> only whichever has the most,
> in front of his door I toss [the child],
> where the people go to and fro.[87]

Even among those pregnant maids who apparently named the true father, the information they provided remained spotty and made the authorities' task more difficult. Out of loyalty or genuine ignorance, a mother-to-be might identify the father in vague terms, such as "a cartman named Hans of whom by her testimony she can say no more" or "a baker's apprentice named Panle Schmauss" who lived "not far from Pforcheim in a hamlet that she can't name."[88]

Whatever her odds in court, a pregnant single woman such as Apollonia Vöglin risked her single greatest asset in acknowledging her condition: her reputation. Unless she was successful in her marriage lawsuit, her chances of finding a husband declined dramatically. Probably unemployed, saddled with an infant, and socially ostracized, a single mother might still succeed in attracting a mate if she had something to offer as a dowry. In the vast majority of cases, however, such women were disinherited (as Apollonia feared she would be) and because of their dishonorable status often remained ineligible for any public assistance in securing a dowry.[89] A woman who was brave and fortunate enough to secure some child support would lose this meager income if she married. A man who married an unwed mother also risked bringing shame and disrepute on himself, since, according to one seventeenth-century pamphleteer, the only men who would marry such "man-desperate" women could not be worth much themselves.[90]

Publicly acknowledging a "bastard" birth had many other costs as well—harsh social consequences that became even harsher over the course of the seventeenth century. First there was the religious stigma, whereby Apollonia would have been required to register her illegitimate baby and have it baptized, but would be prohibited from doing so in a church. Women who attempted to circumvent this rule and have their children baptized elsewhere or not at all were routinely arrested and forced to comply. In some places, the names of illegitimate children were entered upside down in the parish's baptismal records.[91] Nuremberg parish registers were even more explicit, specifying out-of-wedlock children (*spurii*), babies born too soon after a wedding (*Frühlingskinder*), and children born too late after a husband's death (*posthumi*). Overall, 3568 such children, two-thirds of them *spurii*, made it into the official record during the seventeenth century, giving the city of Nuremberg an official illegitimacy rate of 3 percent.[92] Still other parishes simply noted "soldier's whore" for the mother. In every instance, the mother's shameful status as well as that of her child—henceforth legally classified as a "whore's child" (*Hurenkind*)—was now part of the official records.[93]

This ordeal was typically accompanied by a series of criminal punishments and public humiliations for fornication. By the late sixteenth century, unmarried mothers in Nuremberg were regularly sent to prison in chains immediately after delivery, where they might stay for up to three weeks on bread and water.[94] Citizens might be spared the chains and women not yet delivered might be allowed to stay in the hospital until the birth, but ultimate punishment for both was the same as for most single mothers in Nuremberg, even if considered deranged: banishment for life with their offspring.[95] This treatment was admittedly milder than the death penalty officially prescribed for adultery and some other sexual offenses in Nuremberg, though this was rarely enforced, except in cases of incest. As in adultery (and most things for that matter), there was a double standard for men and women convicted of fornication, with married and sometimes single men punished only with a fine and/or public penance. Women in Apollonia's predicament, by contrast, regularly faced various forms of public humiliation, from being forced to wear distinctive clothing (such as red boots or a red hat), to public penance in the church, to being scourged in front of the town hall and chained to one of the stocks there for a brief period of public ridicule—before being banished with her child (see fig. 1.7).[96] Here too maids were overrepresented, in one sample accounting for only one-fourth of women convicted of fornication, but two-thirds of the women flogged and banished for the same offense. Apparently legal repercussions would have been somewhat lighter in a rural village such as Immeldorf, where labor was in demand, but the ecclesiastical sanctions and social ostracism of a small community more than compensated in severity.[97]

Finally, there were the economic costs of an illegitimate birth. If detected, an out-of-wedlock pregnancy usually spelled immediate dismissal for a maid. The effects of such a blow could be catastrophic. Apollonia might have found temporary employment as a wet nurse, ironically providing a much needed service for "moral" women and their legitimate offspring.[98] Day labor in the fields would have also been a possibility, although most of her pregnancy took place during the winter season. Once her child was born, though, she would have been virtually unemployable, particularly if the child's illegitimate status became known. Apollonia would have then belonged to a category of the dishonored that included prostitutes, "soldiers' whores," and other "loose" women, many of them victims of rape and incest. As always for single women, issues of reputation and economic solvency were so closely interwoven as to be indistinguishable from one another. Passing herself off in another town or village as a widow might have removed the stigma, but her earning and marriage prospects would have remained dim.

Fig. 1.7. Daniel Chodowiecki, *Flogging of Women*
(1782). An impassioned dramatization of young women
flogged for fornication. (ca. 1750) SLUB Dresden/
Deutsche Fotothek/Hans Loos.

Child support and poor-relief payments were also invariably meager—if
they came at all. Single mothers in Nuremberg received just enough to buy
two loaves of bread per week with nothing remaining for other food, drink,
clothing, or housing.[99] In eighteenth-century England and Sweden, poor
relief was equivalent to 6–26 percent of the salary of an unskilled laborer
and in some parts of Germany unmarried mothers were denied support altogether.[100] Of course none of this scenario takes into consideration the near
impossibility of finding any child care, unless such a dishonored woman

Fig. 1.8. Lucas Kilian, *A Soldier's Whore* (1609). Kunst-
bibliothek, Staatliche Museen zu Berlin; Art Resource NY.

was allowed to stay with relatives. Many women in this situation became
vagrants, living by begging, or entered into a criminal life of prostitution
and/or theft. Some committed suicide. One "very beautiful maiden" of Nuremberg who sought to marry the man who had impregnated her was so
distraught over her father's refusal of permission that she drowned herself
in the Pegnitz.[101]

Secret Pregnancy and Its Options

It should come as no surprise that the known illegitimacy rate plummeted
throughout Europe during the harsher moral climate of the late sixteenth
century onward. Reported illegitimate births in Nuremberg dropped from
perhaps 10 percent during first half of the sixteenth century to 1–2 percent

between 1600 and 1650.[102] Did this dramatic decrease in illegitimate births also mean a real increase in the number of secret pregnancies and related solutions, including quick marriages, abortions, abandonments, and infanticides? Obviously there is no way to measure this with any precision but the short answer is yes, perhaps significantly so. However much the actual number of illegitimate births declined during the late sixteenth and early seventeenth century, the number of secret pregnancies such as Apollonia's almost certainly increased. Despite the danger of criminal prosecution, pregnant single women who could not quickly marry had many good reasons to risk keeping their condition hidden. Most prominently, the chances that the pregnancy might naturally or artificially end in miscarriage were relatively high. Natural miscarriage ended perhaps as many as one in eight pregnancies and stillbirths made up another 2–4 percent of all births.[103]

Among women like Apollonia who kept their pregnancy secret, abortion was probably a frequent choice but again it is hard to be more specific based on the legal evidence. Certainly women in Apollonia's predicament risked little chance of prosecution for the offense before the eighteenth century.[104] Had Apollonia wished to abort, she probably stood a greater chance of being arrested in Nuremberg's jurisdiction than anywhere in the empire, yet even here detection and punishment remained rare. The great majority of those sixteen women tried in the city for attempted abortion between 1552 and 1792 were already condemned as child murderers and only two women during the entire 240-year period were actually convicted of a successful abortion.[105] To a large degree, this reluctance to prosecute stems from the limitations of early modern medical and other forensic evidence. Well into the nineteenth century, physicians were unable to distinguish between a naturally occurring and an induced abortion. In fact, all claims of pregnancy by condemned prisoners required multiple inconclusive examinations by midwives.[106] There was also much dispute among physicians and jurists about when a fetus became a person, with the "quickening" at about four and one-half months most generally accepted as the threshold.[107]

Just because abortion was difficult to detect doesn't mean it was common. Still, there are several grounds for suspecting that the "dark number" of actual abortions was indeed much higher than indicated by the tiny number of criminal prosecutions during the early modern era. First, there were the perceptions of contemporaries throughout Europe who considered the practice "epidemic" and far more common than the more often prosecuted crime of infanticide.[108] It is impossible to say how many of the high number of recognized miscarriages and stillbirths, together accounting for one in seven pregnancies, were spontaneous and how many were purposely induced. Still another final reason for supposing that abortion was drastically underreported in early modern Europe is the apparently widespread availability of abortifacients. For a long time, conventional historical wisdom held that almost all premodern abortifacients and potions were superstitious and ineffectual. Even those few that might have worked, moreover, were supposedly limited to the margins of society, that is, prostitutes and soldiers' whores. Recent studies, however, suggest quite a different picture, with functional purging remedies much more extensively known and available in early modern times than previously assumed.[109] One of these in particular, savin (*Segelbaum; Sadebaum*), was widely reputed to be a "shameful herb," popularly known as "child killer," "maids' tree," and "maidens' palm." It was by far the most frequently mentioned abortifacient in abortion and infanticide cases in Nuremberg. Other herbs—meadow rue, tansy, silk, and birthwood—required a certain degree of expertise to identify and obtain.[110] Many plants, such as sennet, grew wild in cemeteries, forests, and fields; others were carefully cultivated in private gardens. In all, over one hundred different means to induce abortion were known by the sixteenth century, in many instances as a result of Renaissance rediscovery of ancient practices.[111] Some of these methods were readily available to those able to read published Latin and German medical treatises, such as those found in Eucharius Rösslin (1470–1526), Otto Brunfels (1489–1534), and Hieronymus Bock (1498–1554). Each work listed about thirty abortifacients but warned that these should only be used to expel an already dead fetus, and then always under the supervision of a physician or midwife.[112]

Young women like Apollonia Vöglin might not have had direct access to any of these herbs, but they most likely knew of someone who did. If she had the money and the resolve, a pregnant single woman might "cure" her condition in a number of ways. A recent study of abortion in southwestern Germany during this era found that the majority of women consulted in such predicaments were described as "mothers" (often really "wise" or "cunning" women) or "healers," the term also frequently applied to the men approached—a broad category that included quacks, shepherds, root diggers, executioners, and cowherders. Only a little more than one in four women seeking an abortion consulted a professional physician or pharmacist.[113] This is understandable given that officially approved healers risked losing their licenses and thus usually refused to sell any potential abortifacients to an unmarried woman. After child murderer Anna Seyfridtin's confession, the council ordered the arrest of the pharmacist who sold her savin as well as the three women who told her about it in the first place.[114] Of course family members (especially mothers) or boyfriends might play an intermediary role but this too was somewhat hazardous (and apparently not an option in Apollonia's case). Steffan Reutter not only told his pregnant girlfriend how to abort but actually went and procured some savin for her, an intervention for which he was "out of mercy" flogged rather than banished.[115]

Other anecdotal evidence from Nuremberg follows the same general pattern, especially on the key role of oral traditions and older women in procuring the necessary herb. What Apollonia Vöglin's contemporaries knew as "women's secrets" (*Frauengeheimnisse; secreta mulierum*) has been described by modern historians as a "female sex culture," wherein popular knowledge about pregnancy and birth was conveyed almost exclusively from woman (or women) to woman.[116] Here again, Apollonia Vöglin was at a considerable disadvantage if her mother was indeed deceased and her sister considered untrustworthy. (Certainly she couldn't turn to her fiancé or her father on such matters.) In the 1606 case of Maria Ebnerin, both the girl's mother and a local cunning woman were convicted of helping her to obtain "highly prohibited means for procuring an abortion," namely, "safron oil and herbs," in exchange for "two ducats and a small polished white stone for a ring." Interestingly (and typically), the two older women were dismissed after stern lectures while the unmarried young mother and her illegitimate child were banished for life.[117] Another maid, Anna Schusterin, accused of drinking savin mixed in water, admitted that she had learned the potion from an itinerant female grocer but denied taking more than a sip "because it was such a bitter herb and miserable drink . . . and what little she tried she had to throw up."[118]

The bitter taste or other physical discomforts of an attempted abortion were minor considerations compared to the high risk of fatality to the mother. No doubt this was one of the reasons many pregnant maids relied on magical escapes from their predicaments. In addition to being painless, such solutions, like love magic, had the advantage of being secret—depending on the discretion of the magic worker. When Walburg Knechtlin got pregnant in the winter of 1608, she turned to her fellow maid Anna Maria Kreppin, who "tried to abort the fetus through magic learned from the [wisewoman] Agnes Klaiberin." Together, Kreppin and Klaiberin "not only aided and abetted but also wrapped the veil around the same [Walburg] with their own hands and said an incantation that the fetus should come from her."[119] Magical treatments such as eating the rind of a mandrake or binding a "blood stone" (*Blutstein*) to the thigh of the pregnant woman or wearing a girdle made of snakeskin were also described in medical treatises. In one case we hear of a man offering a pregnant woman an unspecified herb that if "she hangs over her naval, then nothing will come of the matter."[120] When neither herbal nor magical remedies worked, distressed pregnant women might try more direct (and dangerous) means, such as a large dose of alcohol or the rusty handle of a kitchen ladle. Anna Gräfin attempted to kill her fetus by "throwing herself [powerfully] over the bucket in which the cow's feed was made [so] that the child was thereby damaged and weakened but it [still] wasn't sticking out completely," leading her to force the fetus out and throw it on the floor, where it died.[121] A truly desperate woman, such as Kunigundt Dietmännin, might try all of the above—herbs, spells, slamming her stomach against a wall, carrying wood, laundering, and other chores— and thereby produce a premature, deformed, stillborn child, only to be discovered by authorities and banished for life after a thorough flogging.[122]

Employers' reactions to an illicit pregnancy could vary widely. When Margaretha Markhardtin's employers discovered her secret pregnancy, for example, she was fired immediately—the most typical course of events— but less on moral grounds than that they didn't want to have to support her and her child.[123] In other instances, women in the same condition were sheltered by relatives and employers—at great legal risk to themselves if discovered. It appears unlikely that Apollonia confided in her sister or brother-in-law and in fact she pointedly mentions denying the pregnancy to them. Dorothea Geyerin's employers had to take an oath that they knew nothing about her illicit pregnancy and even then were ultimately banished for not watching their maid "so that they might have intervened to [prevent] the infanticide."[124] Secret pregnancies could also pit members of the household against one another. In the case of accused child murderer Barbra Beerin, the family maid apparently unveiled a domestic conspiracy when she testified that the suspected Barbra and her mother "left the house last Monday night at 1:00 A.M. and didn't return until 6:00 A.M., [having] been at the tobacco maker Catharina Legatin's, and afterward talked very softly and secretly to one another"; later that day Barbra was inexplicably ill. Two weeks later the entire family was ordered arrested but all, including Barbra, were ultimately released on the lack of more than circumstantial evidence.[125] When Anna Emblin's lady employer noticed the maid's pregnancy she gave her a leave of absence but forced Anna to search for other lodging until she ended up with a woman "who puts up such people."[126]

This intriguing reference suggests an informal network of houses for unwed mothers in addition to immediate family members and out-of-town kin.[127] Known in England as "harbourers," those who ran such safehouses saw a young woman "in trouble" through the pregnancy and presumably helped with placement or public abandonment of the child.[128] Due to their shadowy nature, we know very little about such informal arrangements, including what must have been the common practice of giving an illegitimate child to a married relative or other willing foster parent to raise as his or her own. The maid Barbra Malerin denied an illicit pregnancy and even any fornication but after being threatened with torture she acknowledged not only her current condition but also a previous pregnancy, in both instances fathered by her employer Wolf Öttinger. After she got pregnant during her first year of work for him, "he put her on a cart to Hochstätt, giving her 6 fl., but instead of going there she went to a woman she knew in Bruck [who] met her and took her home." Like many other women in her situation, Barbra was thus able to avoid the stigma of illegitimacy by relocating among strangers and having the child baptized as the legitimate son of Öttinger. She still would have had the problem of support for the child but since it died after two weeks she was instead able to return to service at Öttinger's house, whereupon she again became pregnant, this time she was discovered and banished.[129]

Apollonia's options were more limited. Given her apparent inability to confide even in the sister with whom she lived, it is unlikely that she could have approached another relative for help, especially given her distance from home. Perhaps such a solution never occurred to her. Yet without such help, she had no place to go for her confinement and nobody to turn to with her illegitimate baby. Nor did the government or church offer any alternatives, at least until after the child was born. Despite several homes for reformed prostitutes (as Nuremberg maintained in its two former convents), formal institutions for unwed mothers were uncommon in Europe until the late eighteenth century.[130]

The one major complication in this respect was the involvement—if any—of a midwife—a more likely occurrence had Appolonia lived in a large, anonymous city instead of a tiny hamlet. Nuremberg's midwives were famed throughout the empire for their skill as well as their highly efficient organization and operation. They trained for four years (later five) under the four overseeing "honorable women," and each delivered from 55 to 300 babies during a year. They were among the very few individuals allowed to pass through the city's gates at night, and their expert testimony was key in all abortion and infanticide cases. Despite this privileged position, town councilors had a deep and perhaps not unfounded suspicion of some midwives' complicity in abortions and secret births and thus required these 25–50 women to report all illegitimate pregnancies and births or face severe punishment themselves.[131] In addition, "three or four unsuspicious women" were required at the burial of any dead illegitimate baby. Like laws against abortion and artificially induced labor, though, this ordinance proved extremely difficult to enforce. Some midwives did indeed become informers on their fellow women but at least a few remained complicit in an unknowable number of abortions and secret births.[132] Upon the interrogation of midwife Barbara Dallerin (aka "Barbie"), who was accused of helping Paulus Blümmet poison his wife, it was discovered that she was well known for supplying "poison or muck" to girls in trouble.[133]

Unmarried women like Apollonia who couldn't trust a midwife or anyone else gave birth alone. Just about any place could serve as a location for a secret birth. Naturally an out-of-town pregnancy and birth—at a relative's house or a safehouse for unwed mothers—was the safest, although even then the hint of scandal might arise. For those young women with fewer resources or foresight, though, the location might be improvised nearby. Already expelled from her employer's house, Anna Kißlingen was forced to give birth at a nearby shepherd's shack in suburban Gostenhof. Margaretha Marckhardtin gave birth in 1607 on "a big blanket in a field by the Pegnitz" (into which she immediately threw her unwanted baby). In 1604 Ursula Mauerin walked into Saint Sebaldus Church at night and gave birth under the pulpit, where she left the baby to be found at the next service.[134] Other places frequently mentioned in infanticide cases include barns, privies, alleyways, and in the woods.

The riskiest yet still common location was the maid's own bedroom (when she had one), sometimes when other members of the household were at home. In her interrogation Apollonia described the lonely scene of her labor and infanticide in almost biblical terms:

> . . . how she lay in her bed and had already fallen asleep when around midnight she felt the pain [of labor], and almost at the hour of Christ ['s birth], gave birth to the child in great pain. And [then] the afterbirth came from her and afterward she stood up and lit a pinewood torch from the oven [and] with the same burning torch went [back] to the bedroom to where the child lay and moved its arm and little leg while crying.[135]

Often the child did not survive birth under these circumstances and in some cases the mother died as well.

If the child lived, as in Apollonia's case, the new mother could follow one of three courses of action. Keeping the illegitimate child was not an option for Apollonia, as seen in her reasons for keeping the pregnancy secret in the first place. The second choice was to give the child away—either to place it with relatives, neighbors, friends—or to abandon it anonymously. Apollonia didn't have or didn't believe she had anyone she could turn to, but she might have simply done what many other young women did in her predicament and left the baby in front of the Findel or on a doorstep. Why did she not do so? For one thing, she was not at the time in a large, anonymous city, like Nuremberg, but rather in a small village where everyone knew her. The slightest possibility of being seen with a crying infant would have probably struck her as an unacceptable risk, particularly given her intense fear of exposure up to that point. Another factor would have been the lack of a common site of abandonment, such as the Findel or Heilig-Geist Hospital in Nuremberg, and accordingly the greater danger of detection in a village with few public spots. Both of these factors help account for the high percentage of convicted child murderers who came from the countryside.

In the city, by contrast, anonymous abandonment, particularly of newborns in front of the Findel, was a more common choice for unmarried mothers during the sixteenth and seventeenth centuries. There is no way to effectively measure the incidence of abortion and informal child circulation, but as figure 1.9 illustrates, at least anonymous abandonment and illegitimacy seem to have been inversely related during this period (though it should be noted that the number of such abandonments in Nuremberg remained much lower than the number of illegitimate births in question). We will see later that the infanticide rate has a more ambiguous relationship to the illegitimacy rate. In Nuremberg, 599 children were anonymously abandoned between 1557 and 1670, an average of 5.3 per year. While not all of these children came from unwed mothers, it is likely that the great majority of those under six months old did, accounting for about a third of total anonymous abandonments, or about 1.6 per year.[136] This is a strikingly low figure for a city of 40,000, particularly given that in Nuremberg, as in most German cities, the punishment for abandonment was no worse than for fornication itself—namely, flogging and lifelong banishment.[137] In 1692 this penalty was reduced to flogging, time in the stocks, and a two-year banishment. Only one abandoning woman was ever executed in Nuremberg and that was principally because she had had sex with a father and his son (considered incest).[138]

Apollonia would have thus risked no more in anonymous abandonment than she would have by publicly acknowledging the illicit birth. If she had the help of a friend or relative, the danger of detection would decrease significantly, though this choice would also put her accomplice at greater risk.[139] Informal circulation of this kind appears to have been more successful than not, and Apollonia could have even selected a childless household that she believed would welcome a child of their own. Instead she made a fateful and unalterable choice that put her own life in serious jeopardy.

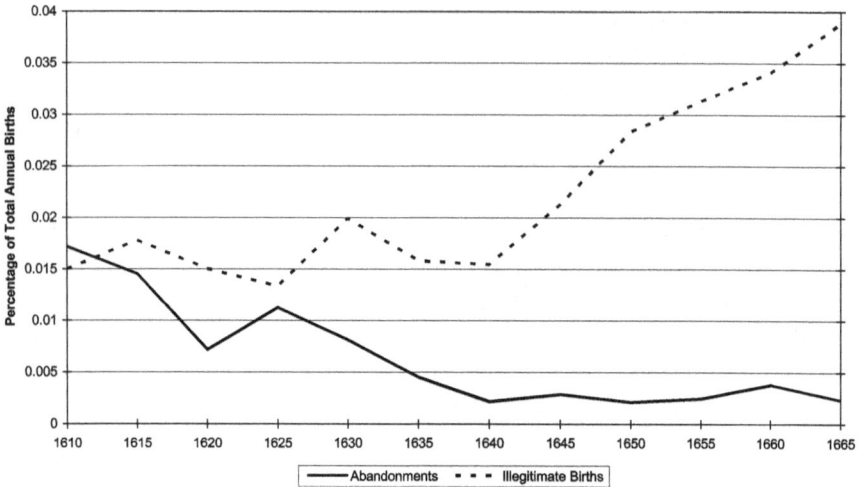

Fig. 1.9. Abandonment and illegitimate birth rate in Nuremberg, 1610–69 (five-year totals; total births n = 79,697). *Sources*: FKD; Rüger, *Die Kinderfürsorge*, appendix 1.

The Ultimate Act of Desperation and Despair

Perhaps anonymous abandonment never occurred to Apollonia in her frantic emotional state. Perhaps, out of desperation or by accident, she killed the baby before this option could be considered. In any event, her ultimate action was not unique: according to the statutes and mandates from the sixteenth century on, in fact, infanticide had become "almost common" in rural villages such as her own.[140] Certainly the offense was more frequently prosecuted than previously. In German states, the immediate legal trigger of more active prosecution and punishment of infanticide was the gradual promulgation of Emperor Charles V's comprehensive criminal code of 1532, the Carolina.[141] The new law's social impact in Nuremberg was dramatic, with the number of women prosecuted for infanticide almost quadrupling, from ten during the fifty years before 1549 (0.20 annually) to thirty-nine during the subsequent fifty years (0.72 annually) and twenty-four during the first quarter of the seventeenth century (0.89 annually). The number of executions during the same periods increased by an even greater factor, from about one every twelve years before the subsequent 1548 imperial ordinance to one every other year afterward (see appendix 2).

As with abortion, there are many reasons to suspect that the dark number of infanticides was still higher, though it hardly indicated a widespread phenomenon.[142] The magisterial perception—"that evils of this sort are more

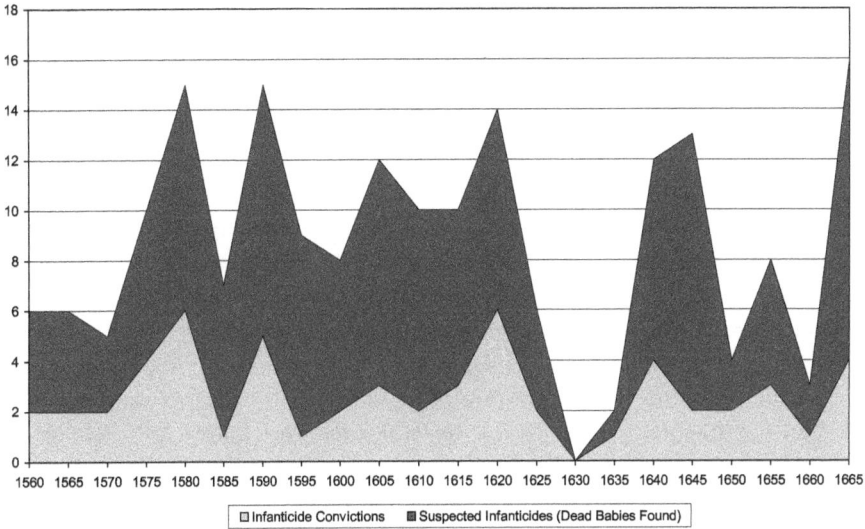

Fig. 1.10. Suspected infanticides and infanticide convictions in Nuremberg's territory, 1560–69 (five-year totals; n = 191). *Source*: appendix 2.

commonly encountered among peasants in the countryside"—was repeated enough elsewhere in Europe to suggest some basis in reality.[143] Nuremberg's rulers were also probably right to assume complicity of midwives in some cases of infanticide within the city itself. Some of the women convicted for infanticide admitted to having killed one or more children after previous births—another indicator of a greater dark number than even the number of newborn corpses would suggest.[144] Finally, the marked weakness of early modern law enforcement meant that in most instances only truly distraught or particularly inept perpetrators even stood a chance of being arrested. A relatively cool culprit would have had several opportunities to dispose of a corpse in secret and only bad luck (the occasional witness) or a guilty conscience (and self-incriminating statements) would give her away. Fewer than half of all known infanticides in Nuremberg between 1549 and 1675 even produced a suspect (see fig. 1.10).[145]

At the same time, magisterial concern about infanticide from the mid-sixteenth century on coincided with a more general anxiety about female sexuality and motherhood in general, similarly manifested in many contemporary witchcraft prosecutions.[146] In both instances, religious and legal reforms gave new impetus to old fears, not necessarily indicative of any correlating behavior (especially in the instance of alleged satanic pacts and cults). Official pronouncements on the frequency of infanticide should therefore be approached with some caution. Even if the actual infanticide rate were ten times the number of dead babies found, a very high estimate, it would still constitute less than 0.2 percent of all annual births in Nuremberg's territory. In that sense, it remained the rarest choice of women in Apollonia's predicament.[147]

In many ways, Apollonia Vöglin was typical of the early modern child murderer, particularly among neonatacides. She was young (approximately eighteen or nineteen), single, and female. Of the 116 individuals convicted of infanticide in Nuremberg between 1503 and 1743, only six were recorded as married or widowed women and one a man (see app. 2).[148] Other German cities and territories displayed the same pattern of single women, as well as the high preponderance of child murderers in their twenties — three out of four — with an average age of about twenty-four.[149] Also, though tried in Nuremberg, Appolonia came from a rural village, as did more than three-quarters of the same group of child murderers, rather than from the imperial city or its suburbs.[150] Illicit pregnancies were doubtless easier to conceal in the anonymity of a large city, thereby accounting for both the relatively greater social anxiety in village settings as well as the greater likelihood of suspicion and conviction. Finally, Apollonia became pregnant while serving as a maid, another extremely common characteristic.

It is important to note, however, that while most maids were far from financially secure or independent, they were not all from poor backgrounds. Apollonia herself came from a moderately propertied farming family, including a brother-in-law with three or more servants, and thus also had potential inheritance questions to consider in deciding what to do about her unwanted pregnancy.

One of the hardest facts to ascertain is the degree of premeditation involved in Apollonia's actions. In their interrogations, magistrates generally assumed that accused child murderers had long planned the evil deed, especially when the birth occurred in secret. Often the suspects' testimonies suggest a more spontaneous act, if not an accident or even natural death. Though pressed to admit such premeditation — "she [should admit that she] lied about the pregnancy for no other reason or grounds than that she intended all along to secretly give birth to her child and afterward kill it" — Apollonia continues to insist that the idea first popped into her head after the unexpected birth in the middle of the night. Again, the deep denial of the pregnancy itself figures prominently. Like many women in her situation, she ultimately attributes the thought to "the evil spirit," who tells her to "squeeze, squeeze" the silent child's throat until "its arms and little legs" stop moving.[151] Another young woman claimed that "a black cat jumped on her near a mountain and inspired her to do it."[152] Despite frequent references to the devil, though, accused child murderers were rarely accused of witchcraft, perhaps a reflection of maids' low visibility and relative lack of potential accusers.[153] In fact, it was the child-murdering maid's typical social isolation that helped create her quandary in the first place. Far from home, sexually involved with a man she probably knew very little about and who, in any event, had likely absconded, she literally had no one to turn to in her crisis.

Surprisingly, very few articulated what all contemporary jurists and reformers assumed was the most common motive, namely, shame and loss of personal reputation. Agnes Lengin feared more violent repercussions from her father and thus killed the child "because it would be a great burden and regret to her."[154] Both of these concerns were clearly shared by Apollonia Vöglin as well, as was fear of public punishment, though she does not use them as justifications. Perhaps the most common explanation was that the murder was an accident, neither planned nor intended by the perpetrator.[155] The common inarticulateness on the question of motive suggests an obvious confusion within the perpetrator herself, hence the frequent reliance on unexplained "bad thoughts" that must have come from "the evil enemy."

In the absence of fully reliable self-knowledge, the method of killing can also reveal much about the relative spontaneity of the deed. Obviously those women who admitted previously attempting to abort the child had to confess to some degree of premeditation. It was unusual, however, that someone displayed the foresight of Anna Dippoltin, who carried a piece of cloth around with her for weeks so as to immediately wrap up and bury the baby when it came.[156] Rarer still was the cold-blooded live burial of Hans Gumman's illegitimate six-month-old child (with his wife's assistance)—an atrocity that earned both of them the much more severe execution by the wheel.[157] Most accused child murderers acted only with what tools were available to them at the moment of birth. Suffocation, either by strangulation or by smothering, was by far the most common in the Nuremberg records, followed by pressing the forehead in, stabbing, and then sheer negligence.[158] One woman stuffed dirt in a newborn's mouth, another straw, others used pillows, and so on. Like Apollonia Vöglin, Veronica Köllerin gave birth in a bedroom at her sister-in-law's house. When the newborn cried a little, she held its mouth with two fingers and when she moved them away, the baby made two more little gestures and then was still.[159] Apollonia similarly admitted to pressing the baby's throat until it was dead. A more passive method was simply not to tie the umbilical cord and allow the child to bleed to death. The most common ancient practice, exposition to the elements, was a more ambiguous gesture in early modern times, since—depending on the intention of the mother—these cases might represent either failed abandonments (when the child was found too late) or failed infanticides (when the child was found too early). Margarethe Dörflerin claimed that she had given her baby to a woman gardener to hold while she went into a tavern to get some money changed and when she came out, the woman was gone and the child frozen to death.[160] General negligence of the newborn during its first days and weeks of life remained the most difficult to prove, yet it appears to have been widespread enough for one historian to characterize it as "an intentional or unconscious form of postnatal birth control."[161]

The treatment of the corpse also conveys some of the emotional turbulence that many women in Apollonia's situation experienced. Servants without their own bedrooms sometimes stowed the body under their bed or in a private chest until they could decide how to proceed—again suggesting a lack of premeditation that might prove fatal. The two most common means of disposal—at least among those caught—were throwing the child in some body of water (river, steam, well, or even fountain) and leaving the corpse among piles of human waste, either in a privy or on a street (see fig. 1.11). The advantages of each of these methods included that the child could be quickly dropped, thereby reducing the chance of being seen. The major risk was that the corpse was much more likely to turn up, prompting in turn some sort of investigation. In Nuremberg, for instance, about one newborn corpse a year surfaced somewhere along the Pegnitz (usually near a mill) or on the city's streets (see app. 2).[162] Secret burials, by contrast, were less common among the convicted and presumably more successful, with only the occasional witness or excavation by an animal (see fig. 1.12).[163] The significance of water and excrement go beyond sheer utility though. In Nuremberg, the Pegnitz, like rivers and streams everywhere, was the frequent destination of much of the city's garbage, and was filled with everything from wilted cabbage leaves to cattle carcasses.[164] Tossing an infant's body into either a privy or a river was effectively the same gesture of trash disposal, a pattern still seen in the modern use of dumpsters and public restrooms for the victims of infanticide.

Did this mean that murdering mothers formed no emotional attachments to their newborns? This is a difficult question to answer. After her late-night labor, Apollonia Vöglin took the child, wrapped it in an apron and stored it in a chest for two days until she had an opportunity to toss it unobserved into the nearby Petz River.[165] Do we interpret her behavior as a callous treatment of her own offspring's body, a denial of its humanity,

Fig. 1.11. A young maid tosses her illegitimate newborn under a waterwheel in Lucerne. Unknown to her, she is observed by a figure in the window behind her (1513). From the *Luzerner Chronik*. Luzerner Schilling.

Fig. 1.12. In April 1584, a large dog dug up the corpse of an infant who had been buried under a manure pile in Nuremberg. According to a 1605 chronicle, the dog ripped the body in half and went through the city's streets chewing on its portion (1605). Stadtarchiv Nürnberg.

or should we see instead look to cues in her description of its "little arms and legs moving" and otherwise gentle description of the newborn? Clearly the answer depends on the individual in question. Margaretha Markhardtin freely admitted that after her child's birth "she then took it and immediately threw it into the Pegnitz, before she had [even] seen whether it was a girl or a boy."[166] Apollonia, on the other hand, makes a point of noting that her child was a girl. To expect rational consistency in such a highly charged moment is probably a mistake. Otherwise, what do we make of Anna Emblin, who bore her child alone in the night and held it in her arms for at least a quarter of an hour before unceremoniously throwing it into the household privy?[167]

There is no indication in Apollonia Vöglin's interrogation records of how or why she was initially arrested in Immeldorf. She claimed to have confided in no one, yet in such situations the new mother's own physical appearance was often in itself the first indicator. Article 131 of the Carolina pointedly stated that a woman's sudden loss of girth and newly pale face were sufficient grounds for arrest on suspicion of child murder, even if no body had been found.[168] Both Apollonia's brother and sister-in-law had remarked on her apparent pregnancy, which she had nonetheless denied and they apparently declined to pursue.[169] Significantly, the same article of the Carolina added "or [possessing] a weak or bad reputation." Since almost anyone could make such an accusation, a single woman once more had to be especially careful that she maintained an honorable name. Only those informants deemed "bad or frivolous people" were doubted, "especially when they wanted to keep their names secret."[170] Otherwise, anyone could claim that a woman of reputed "loose character" or "whorish behavior" was hiding an illicit pregnancy.

Since such terms appear in other child murderers' interrogations but not in Apollonia's case, we might cautiously dismiss reputation as a factor. More likely, it was simply the discovery of a newborn's corpse that initiated an investigation by local authorities and resulted in her arrest. This type of dragnet was in principle easier in a village the size of Immeldorf than in a cosmopolitan center such as Nuremberg, where the number of potential suspects was many times higher and included many people passing through. In both the country and the city, magistrates relied on a network of local secular authorities and pastors to help identify culprits: "[W]hether [any] and which females were somewhat sick or [recently] travelled, or in any other way stood out as suspicious."[171] Midwives were also questioned about all recent births they had attended. When no names surfaced, the council turned to a carrot-and-stick approach, threatening anyone who withheld information with severe punishment and offering a reward (*Fanggulden*) for relevant information.[172] The dogged persistence of officials surprised some suspects. Susanne Reuthlin, later convicted for infanticide, naively claimed "she really hadn't counted on or known that my lords would pursue the matter so keenly and anxiously, otherwise she would have stayed in Bamberg."[173]

In Apollonia's case, we know only that she was arrested "with good cause." This decision would have been made by at least two of the city's jurists, possibly with both presiding mayors, and carried out by municipal guards or archers. Once arrested, Apollonia was detained in her home village until being transferred under darkness (to avoid spectators) to a cell in Nuremberg's "Hole"(*Loch*), where she languished for almost two weeks until her first interrogation.[174] Usually such women were put in the slightly brighter and better cells in the front of the dungeon; occasionally they were interned in the city hospital, where they were chained and guarded. The long waiting period that followed, sometimes lasting several weeks, could be especially torturous for women who had just given birth. Suicide was a special concern of the magistrates who repeatedly ordered jailers to keep close watch on their prisoners lest they do any harm to themselves. The town council appointed a special "watcher" for Appolonia immediately upon her entrance into the Hole.[175]

While incarcerated, Apollonia was visited by one of the prison's chaplains, who was charged with consoling her and offering reconciliation with God before it was too late. In his journal, the Nuremberg chaplain Johannes Hagendorn describes the misery of the accused child murderers he visited in some detail, usually involving a lot of weeping and in at least one case profound concern for the effects of the scandal on her family on the outside.[176] Hagendorn recorded with satisfaction that Anna Emblin "had otherwise conducted herself as a repentant sinner, heartily [acknowledging] her committed sins, and indeed wept such that, the first time I was with her, she required a second handkerchief, so that she might wipe away the tears that flowed so copiously down her cheeks."[177] Nurses were also brought in for ailing women such as Margreth Hainin who was "very weak and sick with pains in her side, also cannot keep any food down."[178] The city's magistrates remained always cognizant of the harsh effects of imprisonment, in one instance urging the municipal jurists to speed up the sentencing process so that the condemned "is not kept long in the squalor of incarceration."[179] This paternalistic concern for the well-being of imprisoned suspects strikes modern sensibilities as peculiar and contradictory, particularly when the woman is purposely given time to heal so that she can be effectively tortured or executed. The irony of the situation was not lost on some contemporaries. According to Hagendorn, the city's surgeon "remarked to him during the [condemned's] treatment that it troubled him that he spent so long healing what Meister Frantz [the executioner] would again ruin."[180]

During the first few days of incarceration, both Apollonia and the dead child would have been examined by midwives and occasionally a physician. The key question was whether or not she had recently given birth. Given the inconclusive nature of pelvic examinations at the time, this issue was usually resolved by midwives who checked Appolonia's breasts for milk. The suspect's overall mental and physical state were also assessed. Sometimes the midwives testified—unsuccessfully—on the defendant's side, arguing that a child was probably stillborn or that intentional excessive work could not have produced a stillborn child. Other times they confirmed that a suspected woman had indeed been pregnant and that a newborn showed signs of unnatural death.[181]

Meanwhile, the corpse of Apollonia's newborn would also be examined for signs of an unnatural death, especially if the magistrates were not satisfied with their initial examination of the mother. If this procedure did not turn up something obvious, like a crushed forehead or neck, a medical "commission"—consisting of one physician, two bathmaster-barbers, one midwife, and one nurse—was appointed to conduct an autopsy.[182] Until the development of the lung test at the end of seventeenth century (floating a cut-out lung in water to see if it held air), the examiners often had difficulty determining whether the child had ever been full term (*zeitig*).[183] Nonetheless, they always rendered a definitive finding for the magistrates, usually indicating foul play, for instance, "Upon the written statement of the sworn master of the barber and bath guild, how [the commission] examined the dead newborn baby found early last Sunday in the Vischbach and found that the forehead of the same had been pressed in."[184] Naturally, there were a few exceptions. In 1591, the grave digger at the new churchyard in suburban Wöhrd found the still-warm body of a newborn in the common grave, wrapped in a diaper and black cloth and apparently with the forehead pressed in. Subsequent examination by the city's surgeon, however, led the doctor to conclude that the head probably was not pressed in, that any wound probably occurred naturally during birth, and "the case should be left to the will of God."[185] Regardless of the cause of death, the infant was then buried in one of the city's cemeteries "at minimal costs."[186] Unlike Catholics, Lutherans usually did not deny church burial to unbaptized children. Thus the town council even ordered an infant's corpse dug up and reburied in hallowed ground when learning that a passerby had buried the body at the spot in the woods where he'd found it.[187]

Fig. 1.13. An eighteenth-century dramatization of the discovery of a murdered newborn under the mattress of a suspect young maid (ca. 1750). Bibliothèque nationale.

At the same time that Apollonia and her alleged victim were being examined, her bedroom and possessions were thoroughly searched for incriminating evidence. Together with the physical examinations, these searches constituted the first phase of the investigation, known as the "general inquisition." The premodern version of the smoking gun—the bloody knife—did turn up at times, as did stained bedsheets or clothing (see fig. 1.13). If so, the suspect was confronted with the suspicious items and asked to explain. More commonly, a case turned on careful deposition of various family members and neighbors, each of whom signed a sworn statement. Here too there were occasional bull's-eyes, such as the washwoman who claimed to see Veronica Köllerin burying a dead baby "in broad daylight," or another witness who merely saw Anna Seyfridtin near the grave of a newborn. Margaretha Markhardtin was even found moaning in a bloody tub by the local bailiff (*Hauptman*) but it wasn't until a newborn's corpse was found six days later that the case against her was made.[188] There is no mention of such incriminating evidence in Apollonia's case.

Given the severe limits of early modern forensic science, the type of evidence authorities relied on more than any other was the accused's own testimony. Ideally, the alleged murderer confessed immediately and without duress. This type of resolution appears to have been the exception rather than the rule. Instead, interrogators brought an ever greater degree of pressure on the accused, ranging from long confinement and hostile questioning to torture itself. One of the least violent (though still psychologically intense) methods of obtaining a confession was the so-called "bier test" (*Bahrprobe*), wherein the accused was forced to approach the newborn's corpse on its stretcher and touch it. If the body bled or gave any other sign of guilt, the killer's confession would supposedly be forthcoming. In a 1549 account, a suspected child murderer was confronted with the corpse of a newborn found in the household's common toilet. When "the master of the house said, 'Oh! You innocent baby, if one among us here is guilty [of your murder], then give us a sign,' then supposedly the left arm of the child immediately lifted up." Since this extrajudicial event appears nowhere in official records, it is hard to assess what role the cadaver's alleged dramatic testimony played in the subsequent conviction of the family maid, Margarethe Wagnerin. Nor is it clear how commonly the bier test was applied, especially since there are only two references in Nuremberg, both in the sixteenth century.[189]

It is clear that interrogators made use of every means of obtaining a confession possible. If Apollonia were found to have milk in her breasts, or other incriminating evidence surfaced, criminal authorities were empowered by the Carolina to instigate torture.[190] When the time for the "special inquisition" came, Apollonia was brought from her cell to the interrogation room, a windowless chamber also in the dungeon, located directly beneath a town council chamber with air ducts connecting the two rooms acoustically. There two members of the council posed questions, two secretaries wrote everything down, and the executioner, possibly with one or two helpers, restrained and upon instruction tortured the prisoner. After recording the subject's name, age, means of support, accused crime, and so forth, the interrogation itself got underway. Typically, Apollonia Voglin's opening statement acknowledges a secret pregnancy and unusual disposal of the body but maintains that the child was stillborn.[191] Her admission is essentially ignored by her interrogators who follow instead their own rough formula. By now it comes as no surprise that one of the first questions posed had to do with her reputation, particular in sexual matters: "Who is the child's father and where the same fornicated with her, also how often and which dates, this she should also testify."[192] Just as in marriage suits, a woman with multiple sexual partners immediately had less credibility with magistrates and was therefore more likely to be convicted.[193] Perhaps this bias helps account for Apollonia's repeated underscoring that her dalliance with the Palm Cutter had been her only sexual experience.

The second most common magisterial concern was the identification of any accomplices, before or after the fact. Apollonia testified more than once that no relative or friend knew about her secret pregnancy and birth or suggested infanticide to her.[194] Perhaps she did confide in her sister or even Steffan and received no comfort or help. Maybe Steffan urged her to abort or kill the child after its birth—not an uncommon reaction among some fathers-to-be in such situations.[195] On the other hand, a refusal on Apollonia's part to confide in others did not necessarily stem from genuine social isolation. Both Elisabeth Ernstin and Christina Zieckhin claimed that their fiancés would have come to marry them had they not waited until too late to write the men. Agnes Lengin similarly testified that her sister would have tried to help her but Lengin feared confiding in her "lest her father find out and beat [the sister] for it."[196] Interestingly, there is no record of any convicted child murderer ever implicating someone else as an accomplice; those very few individuals who were punished for complicity were apparently convicted on some other evidence or testimony. Is this evidence of courageous loyalty to supporters or of desperate isolation of those who actually got caught? Probably both, depending on the case, though there is of course no way to be sure. No person was ever convicted in Nuremberg of incitement to commit infanticide, and only two individuals were punished as full accomplices. [197]

This unwillingness of Apollonia and other accused women to provide the names of accomplices is impressive, particularly given the quite different trend among contemporary witchcraft trials, the other most serious criminal accusation against early modern women. Nor can witch hunters' frequent recourse to torture fully account for the difference, since at least one-third of infanticide interrogations (including Apollonia's) applied torture or the explicit threat of it.[198] Given the centrality of personal confessions in early modern criminal proceedings, the reliance on judicial torture is understandable (if still reprehensible to modern sensibilities). Early modern interrogators viewed this type of questioning as a last resort and even then required official approval of the town council each time a subject was to be tortured. The council in turn requested guidance from the city's jurists, who usually based their decisions on key passages from the Carolina on what sort of evidence was necessary to proceed to torture. The jurists also decided how long and to what degree a suspect should be tortured, generally agreeing on fifteen minutes at a time for a recently delivered or otherwise weak woman.[199]

The means of torture varied considerably. In Nuremberg, the first step was to bring the prisoner into the torture chamber with all of its assembled tools of pain on display, binding the subject into a chair and threatening to begin

Fig. 1.14. Various forms of late medieval and early
modern torture, including the strappado, at right.
From Ulrich Tengler's *Layenspiegel* (1509).

torture. This was usually enough in most infanticide cases, as in Apollonia
Vöglin's,[200] but for those individuals who still resisted the executioner and
his assistant would begin applying whatever method the council had approved: thumbscrews, "fire" (candles or torches applied to the subject's arm-
pits), "water" (a type of gagging and near drowning while seated), "the rack"
(the subject is strapped to a ladder and rolled back and forth on a spiked
drum), 'the wreath" (a metal and leather band is placed around the forehead
and tightened), or most commonly in Nuremberg, "the stone," or strappado
(the subject's hands are bound behind her back and slowly pulled upward
on a pulley with a stone weight; see fig. 1.14). When a confession ensued,
the prisoner was released and made to repeat the statement with at least two
witnesses and no further coercion (other than the specter of further torture).
If the suspect still denied the allegations, the interrogators sought permission

from the council to torture anew. Again, very few accused child murderers appear to have held out this long. Those who did quickly reached the point of exhaustion. Margaretha Schwammbergerin, who began as a cooperative subject was still tortured to the point where she pitifully responded to every question with " she doesn't know, even if she should die now."[201]

Was Apollonia's coerced confession genuine? Undoubtedly torture produced some false convictions for infanticide, but it is impossible to be more specific than that, particularly given the great emotional turmoil and confusion of accused women, whether or not they consciously killed their newborn. One Nuremberg jurist recognized this ambiguity and wrote that it was better "to let a hundred guilty [persons] go free, than to kill one innocent," yet this same judge went on to cast the deciding vote in convicting a young woman of child murder without a confession—the only case in Nuremberg's history where other evidence sufficed for conviction and execution.[202] If the question could be answered satisfactorily, it would turn less on acknowledging both the secret pregnancy and dead offspring—which almost all freely admitted after their arrest—than on establishing the suspect's active role and intentionality in causing the infant's death.[203] A secret birth in itself, in other words, was in practice treated as sufficient for arrest but not for conviction. This was one of the reasons that suspects were always asked about any previous children, a tactic that occasionally resulted in some fairly open-and-shut cases.[204] Several cases involved strong corroborating evidence, thereby weakening the dependence on a confession. Still, there would have always been certain instances where conscious intentionality or even guilt itself would have been difficult for the accused herself to ascertain, let alone distant observers from four centuries later. Clearly some accused women truly believed that their children were stillborn and only after the threat or application of torture confessed to murder. Apollonia Vöglin, for instance, claimed that she hadn't felt any movement in her womb for at least a week before the birth—a common phenomenon among late-term pregnancies, yet one that might have led her to genuinely believe that the fetus was already dead.[205]

After Apollonia's interrogation, her case was again referred to three or more of the city's jurists, who made their recommendations as to the appropriate punishment.[206] Usually the suspect had admitted her guilt by this point, and the legal experts' key determination was her understanding of the deed and its consequences. If, for instance, Apollonia had refused to acknowledge that her child was truly dead, the jurists might have sought the opinion of a physician as to her sanity.[207] A suspect who held to her statements of innocence after two or three torture sessions, such as Elisabeth Schusterin in 1611, was released for lack of evidence, though not without some form of punishment, ranging from an oath to flogging and banishment.[208] Here too the suspect's personal reputation and perceived intentions played the key roles. Ottilia Demerin, for instance was banished despite the absence of a confession, while Helena Schlauerspächin received merely a stern lecture and warning that if she again came before the council "one would undertake another serious action against her."[209] Overall, 64 of the 79 women accused of infanticide in Nuremberg from 1549 to 1675 were convicted, a rate of more than 80 percent.

Once convicted of infanticide, Apollonia faced an exceptionally high likelihood of execution, on average about three out of four convictions throughout the empire.[210] Again the influence of the Carolina and imperial police ordinance of 1548 is obvious. Only four child murderers were executed in Nuremberg before 1549; instead, banishment and other corporal punishment, such as branding, were the norm. From the mid-sixteenth century on, though, the prosecution of infanticide followed the same pattern of other crimes throughout the empire: more frequent prosecution and more severe punishments. Between 1549 and 1675, only six convicted child murderers were spared execution, all but one of those between 1592 and 1600 and none after 1621.[211]

There is no record of any plea for pardon on the part of Apollonia's relatives. This may have been in part because appeals of this sort, a common feature of late medieval justice, had become increasingly futile by this time. A massive appeals campaign for a young child murderer convicted in 1549, led by the imperial vice chancellor and other important personages, resulted in mitigation of her sentence in view of "youth and ignorance, as well as temptation by the evil Enemy." Just two years before Apollonia's case, convicted child murderer Margaretha Schüblin was pardoned upon the pleas of two Polish nobles.[212] Such exceptions were already unusual, however, and from that date on Nuremberg's magistrates intentionally made releases from execution for child murderers rarer still, "so that the people don't make light of it and give rise to more of the same evil business." It made no difference if the supplication came from an employer, family member, a community at large, a highly placed official, or even the "honorable women" who directed the midwives.[213] Mental competence apparently also played no role in sentencing, since the council still executed Anna Hupffauffin, "by nature a defective person, weak in the head," as well as Susanne Reuthlin, who "was very incomprehensible during the interrogation."[214]

Once Apollonia's guilt had been established through her own confession, the council moved swiftly to carry out a sentence of execution within if possible a few days. Her "trial," as such, consisted of her entering the council's chamber, whereupon the evidence against her as well as her own confession were read aloud to thirteen jurors. After her two interrogators certified her confession, the jury was immediately polled for a verdict and sentence pronouncement. The purpose of the entire ritual was to establish the accused's guilt and demonstrate the council's authority rather than to weigh the evidence in what was an already decided case. Immediately upon hearing the jury's decision, the main judge or representative of the town council would proceed to make a formulaic pronouncement of condemnation, typically ending "[that] amid the many, worsening, shocking, and appalling child murders, her well-earned punishment might serve as an example and abhorrence to keep others from similar misdeeds."[215] Apollonia was not permitted to make any statements on her own behalf; she merely watched and listened as her life was taken away from her. Once the judge finished speaking, she signed or made a mark on a copy of the verdict, and the procession to the execution site was underway.

Alone with No Options in Sight

Compared to the other details of her story, Apollonia's end is rather obscure. It is recorded that at sundown on Sunday, March 2, 1578, she was escorted outside the city's closing gates by four archers and for jurisdictional reasons transported twenty miles to Lichtenau, a journey that required four long days during which Apollonia was bound to contemplate her imminent violent end. Upon arrival in Lichtenau she was summarily drowned by Nuremberg's executioner, Frantz Schmidt (see fig. 1.15).[216] No gallows speech has survived, nor do we know whether any members of her family attended the execution and claimed her body or where that body was buried. This much of her story has been preserved, though, and thanks to it some sense of her plight has also survived. Most important, we see the usual effectiveness of dealing with unwanted children even before birth and how differently Apollonia's story might have ended had she felt able to turn to someone for support: a father who would (informally or in court) press her impregnator to marry her; a fiancé who would be willing to claim the child as his own in a somewhat downgraded wedding; a mother, sister, or female friend who would have helped her abort; relatives or friends who would have housed her during her confinement and taken or placed the baby.

Fig. 1.15. Drowning, shown here in an Anabaptist case, was the preferred form of execution for women during most of the sixteenth century in German lands. Two years after Apollonia's death, it was replaced in Nuremberg by beheading, considered more merciful (ca. 1592). München Kupferstichkabinet.

Infanticide, even more than anonymous abandonment, represented an extreme and relatively uncommon failure of informal child circulation, a rupture in the usual way that relatives, neighbors, and friends dealt with an illicit pregnancy or unwanted newborn child. Various demographic and legal factors, particularly more frequent and intense prosecution of fornication among single women, obviously worsened Apollonia's situation. It was nonetheless her perceived isolation—out of fear and inability to trust someone else—that eliminated all of the other options that the vast majority of pregnant single women pursued. Whether she had put her hope in a forthcoming wedding with Steffan or in a miscarriage, Apollonia very quickly embarked on a downward spiral of increasingly desperate choices. Given her desperately agitated frame of mind, it is not even certain whether her confessed murder was indeed a conscious choice or perhaps an accident of some sort. Even once the child was dead, she would have been much less likely to get caught if she had the assistance of one or more accomplice. The records, however, never mention any relatives or friends visiting during her imprisonment. A random omission or a significant one? We cannot know.

It is in fact an irony of the same sources that we know so much more about such cases of the least common resolution of an unwanted pregnancy than we do about the mass of pregnant single women who married, aborted, abandoned, or even kept their illegitimate children. Apollonia Vöglin was far from unique in her experience of an unwanted pregnancy and later an unwanted child but that truth provided her with no escape from her seemingly insoluble predicament.

TWO

The Absconding Father

On February 20, 1615, the bailiff of suburban Gostenhof reported to the Nuremberg city council that he had taken into custody three young girls "left sitting" by their father, soldier Christof "Stoffel" Baur of Nördlingen. As in similar cases—which seemed to be occurring with disturbing frequency—the bailiff immediately attempted to locate not only the absconded Baur but also any relatives or friends who might take in the children. Their mother, Magdalena, was recently deceased, but the bailiff was able to identify a grown son of Stoffel's, named Georg, who also lived in Gostenhof and worked as a potter. Following the council's instructions, the official interrogated Georg as to the whereabouts of his father, learning that the elder Baur had skipped town that very morning, leaving behind in his residence three young daughters, Margareth, Apollonia, and Annelein. Reluctantly, the council agreed to accept the girls into the Findel but only temporarily, ordering Georg Baur to notify them as soon as his father set foot back in town. Three weeks later, upon learning that Georg had exaggerated his own poverty, the council reversed its decision and ordered all three girls sent either to live with their brother in the poor suburb of Gostenhof or to be sent directly to their father, wherever he might be. Should Georg refuse to comply he would lose his citizenship and be expelled from the city. After nine days of deliberation, young Baur accepted the council's terms. Whether the girls then continued to live with their brother or were passed on to someone else was a matter of indifference to city leaders, who instead congratulated themselves at having relieved the Findel of still more dependents. Their role in the saga of three unwanted children was (at least for the time being) ended; the makeshift coping of the girls' relatives and friends might continue indefinitely.[1]

Like the unwed mother and the anonymous foundling, the absconding

Fig. 2.1. Pieter Quast, *A Begging Father and His Two Young Children* (ca. 1630). Bayerische Staatsbibliothek Munich.

father is a universally familiar figure. According to received wisdom, such ne'er-do-wells have been the cause of countless broken homes and many neglected or unwanted children. Their departures might be triggered by bad debts, a love interest, wanderlust, or some combination thereof. They might also be work-related. But how common were men such as Stoffel Baur in early modern Germany? Was he truly part of an epidemic of irresponsibility, as some contemporaries claimed, or has the scope of the problem been exaggerated? Just as important, what other options did he have in his predicament? This chapter explores the background of Stoffel and other absent fathers, looking at the frequency of their comings and goings, the reasons behind their departures, and the impact their decisions had on the wives and children they left behind. It describes the necessities of everyday life for such households, how these heads of households attempted to meet those necessities, and what happened when they failed. Most important, the relative roles of informal child circulation and of governmental intervention in sustaining the fatherless household will receive special attention, particularly in the context of paternal responsibility and affection.

Poor and Disreputable

What can be said with certainty about Stoffel Baur and the circumstances of his decision to leave his three young daughters behind? Most obviously, based on his place of residence and employment history, it is clear that he was poor, yet this characterization requires some clarification. "Poor," after all, is a highly relative term in any time and place and has qualitative aspects that elude historical records.[2] By modern Western standards, easily nine out of ten early modern Europeans would be considered as living below the poverty line. Even by early modern reckoning, likewise subjective, the magnitude of privation during the period is staggering. The tax records of sixteenth-century Augsburg, for instance, classified 44.5 percent of the city's residents as *miserabili* (completely propertyless) and another 48.0 percent with total possessions worth less than ten gulden (roughly six months' wages for an unskilled laborer).[3] In Stoffel Baur's Nuremberg, a city of similar size and wealth, this same proportion of the desperately needy translated to 17,000 destitute people, with perhaps just as many teetering on the edge of disaster (out of an overall population of 40,000). In early modern Europe as a whole, the Baurs and their fellow "have-nots" and "have-littles" together represented more than two-thirds of the population, or roughly forty-five million people in 1615.

These aggregate numbers fail to convey at least two important dimensions of poverty in Baur's day: first, that it had worsened considerably in scope over the course of the previous century; and second, that this economic decline hit poor families with children, such as the Baurs, especially hard. The population boom and European-wide inflation of the "long sixteenth century" (ca. 1480–1620) have been thoroughly documented and analyzed by historians, as has the subsequent "crisis of the seventeenth century.[4] Overall, Europe's population almost doubled during this 140-year period; the total for the German states of the Holy Roman Empire went from about nine million to sixteen million.[5] While this population increase might seem modest in comparison to modern demographic growth, its social impact was profound, particularly since the related rise in demands for products and services far outpaced the rate of increase for wages (see table 2.1). Between 1500 and 1625, the price of a pound of beef or pork, for instance, doubled and in some locations quadrupled. The average daily salary of an unskilled

Table 2.1. **Prices and Wages in Nuremberg, 1500–1600**

Prices/Wages	1500	1600	Total Increase (percent)
Price			
1 Pair of shoes	60 d	180 d.(used)	200
1 pair of pants	42 d.	150 d.	257
1 hen	38 d.	65 d.	71
1 shirt	17 d.	80 d. (used)	370
1 quart wine	6–8 d.	26–42 d.	225–600
1 quart beer	2–3 d.	7 d.	100–250
1 lb. beef or pork	4–5 d.	10–16 d	100–300
3 eggs	2 d.	6 d.	200
1 lb. bread	1 d.	3–4 d.	200–300
Wage			
Municipal jurist	300 fl. annually	500 fl. annually	66
Master construction worker[1]	18–30 d. daily (20–33 fl.)	77 d. (85 fl. annually)	158–325
Schoolmaster	30 fl.	60 fl.	100
Journeyman carpenter[1]	28 d. daily (31 fl.)	50 d. (55 fl.)	77.4
Male day laborer[1]	14–16 d. daily (15–16 fl.)	18–24 d. (20–26 fl.)	25–73
Female or child laborer[1]	4–6 d. daily (4–6 fl.)	12–14 d. (13–15 fl.)	117–275
Night watchman1	2 d. (2½–3 fl.)	3 d. (3–4 fl.)	0–60

[1] Annual salaries assume full employment (ca. 260 days) and thus represent the extreme high end of the salary range. More typically—due to famine, warfare, or other economic crises—this figure would have been at least 30–50% lower (e.g., a male laborer in 1600 would have taken home 10–16 fl. instead of 20–26 fl. annually). *Sources*: Strauss, *Nuremberg*, 204–5; Endres, "Zur wirtschaflichen," 21–25; Groebner, *Ökonomie ohne Haus*, 114–18; Elsas, *Umriss einer Geschichte*, 69, 726, 735; ASB 215: 248r, 296r.

laborer on the other hand increased by only 50 percent during the same 125 years. On the whole, the buying power of most workers decreased by about one-half over the course of the sixteenth century, meaning that Stoffel Baur and his contemporary heads of household, skilled or unskilled, had to work at least twice as long as their grandfathers for the same amount of food or rent money.[6] Given the high rate of unemployment and underemployment, the more typical result of inflated prices was greater impoverishment rather than longer hours, with an ever larger number of working-poor households falling deeper into debt and destitution. The seventeenth century, with its chronic warfare and multiple agrarian crises, saw a still greater exacerbation of this economic trend and a continued growth in the number of poor and destitute households.

Who were the unfortunate heads of these poor households and where did they come from? The largest single occupational group among the fathers of all children admitted to Nuremberg's Findel was that of unemployed artisans. Together masters and journeymen account for two-thirds of all fathers whose occupations were known. Young journeymen, typically under the age of thirty, were particularly conspicuous among petitioners, making up three-quarters of all artisans and about half of all occupations listed.[7] This is not particularly surprising, given that artisans typically comprised the largest part of most urban populations. By the lifetime of Stoffel Baur, Nuremberg alone claimed 227 different crafts, with some 3,400 masters, employing at least 5,500 workers.[8] Unfortunately, most of these crafts masters could afford to employ at most two journeymen and one apprentice each, another reflection of economic hard times. Those apprentices and journeymen lucky enough to find positions faced even more daunting odds against them eventually reaching master status. Consequently, almost every handiwork faced great unemployment at some point, even among masters, though some crafts were more regularly depressed than others, especially during the seventeenth century. Textile-related crafts in particular suffered everywhere during this period as did manufacturing jobs in general. Crafts such as cobbling and carpentry had long-established reputations as poor or at least irregular providers, while others—beer brewing, wine sales, baking, and merchantry in general—were commonly considered "rich crafts."[9] Potters like young Georg Baur appeared often in Findel petitions as did soldiers, belt makers, and wire drawers. Members of the so-called infamous (i.e., disreputable) occupations—including millers, barbers, butchers, executioners, grave diggers, night watchmen, and beggars—were surprisingly less common, and farmers only figured prominently as the parents of orphans (7 percent).[10]

It is likely that Stoffel Baur had trained in a craft in his native Nördlingen before becoming a professional mercenary; many young soldiers did.[11] Had he and Magdalena stayed in Nördlingen and attempted to make a go there they would have been part of the category of resident, working poor—sometimes known as the "shamefaced poor" or "house poor" (*Hausarme*).[12] The shamefaced poor, also called the "deserving poor" by secular and religious leaders, were those poor but reputedly upright artisans, shopkeepers, and wage earners who (through no fault of their own, went the argument) had dropped into near destitution, earning barely enough to feed their immediate families and rent a lodging. Some of these heads of household were permanently disabled and unemployable, forced to rely on alms and other supplemental forms of income. Beginning in the late fifteenth century, price inflation, job layoffs, and other calamities such as famine, war, or epidemics pushed an ever increasing number of previously able-bodied workers and self-sufficient household into their ranks. By Stoffel Baur's time, the shame-

Fig. 2.2. A vagrant family approaching a city.
From the *Liber Vagatorum* (1510).

faced poor constituted at least one-quarter of all urban populations (over 10,000 in Nuremberg); in the countryside the numbers were greater still.[13]

Once the Baurs left Nördlingen, their household joined another and older category of poor collectively known as vagrants.[14] During the sixteenth and seventeenth centuries, this term was increasingly applied to a variety of migrant workers, as well as the wandering peddlers, beggars, and entertainers of the Middle Ages. By some estimates, the number of such roving individuals and households tripled over the course of the long sixteenth century.[15] Adults and children like the Baurs faced seasonal employment in the countryside and often flooded cities during wintertime or periods of famine or war (see fig. 2.2). Depending on the season, the Nuremberg of Stoffel Baur would have hosted at least four to five thousand resident aliens of this kind, all struggling to survive by whatever means necessary. Most vagrants were unmarried "masterless" men between the ages of fifteen and thirty, but at least one-third were parents like Stoffel Baur with dependent children in tow.[16] Unlike the city's domiciled poor or established immigrants from nearby villages, new arrivals from more than twenty-five miles away (Nördlingen lies fifty miles from Nuremberg) usually had few if any personal ties in the communities they visited. Stoffel and his three daughters probably came to Nuremberg only after his adult son Georg had established himself as a potter and it is unlikely that he had any other contacts in the city.

This social marginalization that Stoffel experienced in Nuremberg was compounded by the disreputable nature of some of his identity as a soldier, a particularly odious profession, prominent among the infamous occupations. Professional soldiers were also especially numerous among the era's wandering people.[17] Their apparently small representation among the paternal occupations listed for Nuremberg's Findel children (only 2 percent) is somewhat deceptive, since in fact more than half the fathers labeled abandoners left home to fight as mercenaries; they simply continued to be identified in official documents by their craft.[18] During the early sixteenth century, soldiers were in high demand and thus relatively well paid, earning on average 4 fl. a month, about six times the salary of a domestic servant. Over the course of the next century, however, these soldiers' salaries too failed to keep pace with the rate of inflation and were especially hard hit by stagnation in exchange rates for silver, the usual currency of their wages. Higher positions with elevated salaries remained possible for Stoffel Baur and other enlisted men, but it was far more likely that they would have to supplement their monthly soldier salaries with wages earned as manual labors, often working for the army itself.[19]

When able-bodied, soldiers traveled in companies of several hundred fighting men, and they were usually accompanied by an equal or greater numbers of women and children trailing behind (see fig. 2.3).[20] The spouses and children who followed soldiers' camps had a precarious existence, perpetually haunted by the specter of the death or debilitation of the main breadwinner. Those women who toured with their men also regularly encountered the intense hostility that most civilians displayed toward mercenaries, considered by many to be the greatest curse of the age. To make matters worse, many "soldiers' whores" were not in fact officially married and their children thus bore the additional stigma of illegitimacy.[21] It is unclear whether Stoffel and Magdalena Baur were legally wed. We also can't say whether the rest of the household regularly traveled with him on campaigns or moved from town to town on their own. Either way their life was hard. If they moved around with his company, they would often have to endure great hardship and "the bitterest poverty"; yet if they stayed behind in Nördlingen, Dinkelsbühl, or other towns, they likely received very little if any income from Stoffel and were on their own economically.[22] His occasional return was unlikely to be an entirely jubilant event, since it meant

Fig. 2.3. Daniel Hopfer, *Landesknecht mit Frau*
(ca. 1600). Stadtmuseum Münster.

either increased consumption with little additional income or, worse yet, permanent unemployment due to a severe wound or other disability.

Even if Stoffel Baur returned to Nuremberg able-bodied, the job competition between a "foreign" soldier and one of Nuremberg's resident poor would be fierce. Civilian occupations were in principle forbidden to mercenaries, and the city's abundance of unskilled labor meant that any work Stoffel found would probably be temporary and his compensation at best half of what skilled workers got.[23] The Baur household's subsequent scramble to make ends meet by whatever means possible is known among historians as the makeshift economy.[24] Then, as now, it took many forms. In rural areas, this often entailed one or both parents, sometimes entire families, migrating for a few months or occasionally years, pursuing labor openings wherever they occurred, sending money home if possible. Usually agricultural work was seasonally specific and even then unreliable, with poor harvests and the ensuing economic depressions occurring on average every four years. Construction workers were relatively well paid, but this too tended to be short-term, summer employment (with occasional exceptions, such as Nuremberg's massive fortification project in 1503–4). Winter thus portended an especially desperate time for struggling households, with Stoffel and other poor fathers eagerly filling any openings in the city's "dishonorable" slaughterhouses and otherwise scrambling to provide for their families as a woodcutter, charcoal burner, or even as a poorly paid municipal gatekeeper or night watchman—all stopgap measures at best.[25]

Like many other young fathers, Stoffel Baur probably first decided to become a soldier during a difficult winter in Nördlingen, either taking his household with him or leaving them behind to fend for themselves.[26] If Magdalena and children accompanied him, she would have been expected to generate supplemental income from washing clothes, begging from town to town, plundering the dead of battlefields, and helping Stoffel loot cities. If left behind during campaigns, she might have supported her household through a combination of summer and fall fieldwork, spinning, some other type of cloth work, or by huckstering small quantities of food or other goods in streets, alleys, or door-to-door.[27] As the head of a migrant family, with irregular employment as a soldier, Stoffel too would have needed to be especially opportunistic and inventive in the struggle to stay afloat. Even while enlisted, a soldier necessarily relied on various odd jobs to make ends meet, including work as a woodchopper, manual laborer, rat catcher, rag picker, spindle maker, furniture repairman, knife grinder, or clog mender. Some "travelling folk" subsisted by providing some sort of entertainment: storytelling, singing, juggling, conjuring, fortune-telling, tightrope walking, and other acrobatic feats.[28] Finally, many migrants (all, in the popular imagination) were simultaneously engaged in some sort of illegal activity, from prostitution, smuggling, and dishonest gambling to confidence schemes (such as fraudulently disabled begging) to the more serious crimes of burglary, arson, extortion, and robbery.

Lest such flexibility and inventiveness among the poor be colored by the lighthearted adventures of later romanticizations, it should be underscored that this life frequently included lack of warm shelter or adequate food and the unrelenting anxiety of a literally hand-to-mouth existence. All workers (except soldiers) were paid daily, and even Nuremberg's well-remunerated construction workers had to fight for the right to be paid in the morning so that they could take their wages home to their wives at lunchtime.[29] Stoffel and his fellow mercenaries were often forced to go several months, occasionally more than a year, without pay—the trigger to infamous lootings at Rome in 1527 and Antwerp in 1571.[30]

The indigent life also came with a high degree of personal shame, a genuinely debilitating stigma often lost on many members of modern Western societies. An early modern father's inability to provide for his children could be crippling to both his self-esteem and psychological well-being—a frustration sometimes vented in the form of physical or emotional abuse of the rest of the household. The self-sacrificing *Hausvater* lionized by countless early modern tracts often provided a sorry contrast to the drunken, violent, and generally loutish heads of household who populate surviving court records.[31] In a world in which honor, even among the poor, was the most prized personal possession, "shamefaced poor" and "dishonorable poor" were not empty labels. Many of the shamefaced poor in particular considered manual labor almost as degrading as begging, an attitude reflected in the enduring tendency among unemployed artisans to continue identifying themselves by their craft rather than by the sack carrying, ditch digging, wood chopping, and other occasional labor by which they actually supported their households. Overall, only 3.4 percent of all fathers whose profession is known in Findel petitions were identified as manual laborers and only 0.6 percent as full-time beggars—again a reflection more of the era's definition of honor than of the social reality. Even these designations mostly came from a third person, rather than the father himself.[32] Not until the eighteenth century, when guild identity had sunk still lower and a new working-class consciousness had begun to emerge, do the fathers of poor children voluntarily call themselves manual laborers or daily wage earners.[33]

The Indigent Household

Like all poor parents, Stoffel Baur's day-to-day existence involved constant juggling of very limited resources. Obviously the degree of desperation he and other struggling parents experienced was affected by the number of children they had to feed. The size and structure of most poor households during this era were not necessarily what one might today assume. Stoffel Baur had at least four living children, born over a period of at least twenty years, with three still at home. Based on several lists of alms recipients and begging children detained in Nuremberg, this size was typical among poor households, which between 1529 and 1663 averaged 2.9 resident children each.[34] Poor families with six or more children do occasionally appear on alms lists for Nuremberg and elsewhere, but large families were much more common among propertied middle-class and wealthy households (which could afford to support them).[35] Well into the eighteenth century, the number of children in poor households remained consistently lower than the general European average of four to six children per household.[36]

The relatively small size of most poor households with children was less a function of widespread contraception and careful family planning than the consequence of an early modern demographic peculiarity. Natural birth control—by prolonged breast feeding, postnatal sexual abstinence, and extended separation of partners due to migration—clearly figured in the "reproductive strategies" of some poor households. It is difficult to say how commonly or deliberately such methods were applied. Certainly there was rarely any long-term family planning per se, evidenced by the fact that most births occurred during the most desperate months of winter, January through March.[37] The late marriage pattern of northwestern Europe, on the other hand, greatly aided in limiting the number of legitimate births, particularly compared to southern Europe, where much earlier marriage and thus higher fertility led to even more extensive poverty. A woman marrying between 30 and 35 (more common in German lands) usually had no more than three children, while one marrying much earlier, between the ages of 20 and 24 (more common in Italian regions), gave birth on average to seven children.[38] As seen in the last chapter, late marriages were especially common among maids and other lower-status individuals who put off the establishment of a new household until they had some financial security. For many poor people, however, that day would never come. Thus at some point they risked both marriage and procreation.

One aspect of early modern poor households that might be anticipated by twenty-first-century readers is the high proportion of them that were headed by women. Stoffel Baur's late wife Magdalena, who probably endured long periods as the sole head of household, was hardly unique. Women with absent husbands, widows, and never-married women made up at least a third of European populations during the sixteenth and seventeenth centuries—an astounding proportion compared to other historical and contemporary societies.[39] Unlike widowers, the great majority of whom remarried (usually within a year), widows found willing spouses much harder to come by, with most still unmarried ten years after their husbands' deaths.[40] Many deserted wives were no better off, unable to remarry without legal proof of their husbands' demise or a waiting period of up to ten years.[41] Female-headed households were particularly overrepresented among the ranks of the poor. One neighborhood survey of Nuremberg parents who regularly sent their children begging in 1663 yielded a list of thirty-one households, over three-quarters of them headed by women. The percentage among households receiving alms is similar—a fact that has changed little over the past five centuries. This too became more pronounced over the course of the sixteenth and seventeenth centuries in Nuremberg, where the balance shifted from an actual majority of male-headed households on the alms lists of the 1550s and 1560s to mostly female-headed households a century later.[42]

Poverty shaped every aspect of daily life for the Baurs, spawning a variety of coping and survival mechanisms. The most pressing concern of their household was food, which in large part consisted of some form of coarse dark bread, considered inedible by many middle-class and wealthy Nurembergers. All families except the very poorest observed a "morning soup" (around 10:00 A.M.) and an "evening bread" (around 6:00 P.M.). Meat was expensive and thus reserved for special occasions (if at all obtainable); instead, oatmeal porridge, boiled peas and lentils, or whatever vegetables were available constituted the main nourishment for most simple folk. Although highly taxed in Nuremberg, beer was much more affordable for the poor than wine and was thus popularly associated with the lower classes. Even this frugal diet, deficient in protein and several vitamins, was costly for the Baurs, accounting for two-thirds to three-quarters of their household's expenditures.[43] This budgetary proportion moreover could fluctuate wildly from year to year or even month to month, depending on the household income and the price of bread at any given time. During periods of extreme crisis, such as Nuremberg's famines and multiple epidemics during the early 1570s, bread prices could double over the course of a few months (especially during the winter) and quadruple within five years.[44] Not surprisingly, endemic hunger, and even starvation, were fixtures of life among the early modern poor, particularly in times of rapid inflation.

The other major expense of the Baur household was lodging. During the long sixteenth century home ownership fell precipitously, so that by Stoffel's time at least half of urban residents and virtually all poor people rented their living quarters.[45] Overcrowding in dark, cold, and cramped single-room dwellings was the norm among the poor; even in prosperous Nuremberg at least one-quarter of the population lived with five to six people within a few hundred square feet (see fig. 2.4). Since most families also lived in buildings with four or more households, privacy was virtually nonexistent, with every family quarrel instantly transformed into public knowledge and gossip.[46] Invariably poor families lived in the least desirable part of a building—an upper floor or cellar—and in the least desirable parts of town. Nuremberg had no public housing or tenements; instead its poor lived on the fringes of the city, in hovels near the city walls or in one of the surrounding suburbs, such as Gostenhof, residence of both Georg Baur and his father Stoffel, and also a frequent site for anonymous child abandonments during the sixteenth and seventeenth centuries.

Fig. 2.4. Andriaen van Ostade, *The Paterfamilias* (1648).
Rijksmuseum Amsterdam. The cramped apartment of
a poor married couple with two small children.

Lower rent in a suburban slum like Gostenhof came at a distinct cost, of course: polluted water, nonexistent public hygiene, and a high crime rate. Here was where the Baurs and other poor immigrants first landed, especially during plague and famine crises, and here too was the greatest concentration of inns and taverns, where many new residents found temporary or permanent lodging.[47] Nor was such dilapidated housing cheap: the rags-to-riches businessman Thomas Platter recorded as a student in 1520 paying 1.2 gulden a year for a tiny and shabby room in a house of ill repute; a century later the average annual rent was five times that (while most wages had only doubled).[48] For a day laborer earning at most only twelve gulden a year and with at least eight to nine of that sum going toward food, a rent of even five or six gulden a year often spelled crushing debt and eventually bankruptcy. Such housing was also precarious, subject to surprise rent increases from the landlord or immediate eviction for any cause. Not infrequently, we hear of homeless individuals and frequently entire families squatting in abandoned buildings and courtyards, or sleeping in outbuildings, in sheds, under market stalls, and in alleyways. Some migrant families lived in forests, collecting whatever food or firewood they could find.

With food and rent consuming all or most of the Baur household's income, there was little money left for other commodities, such as clothes or furniture, and certainly nothing to save. Those few items of clothing and linen that a poor family did possess were usually secondhand and on occasion had to be sold for food money or used as payment. As in middle-class households, the single most valuable asset was often a bedstead, though only one in two poor families actually owned more than a straw pallet or two for the floor (and even then the bed was generally shared by two or more people). Truly, "to be poor was to be virtually without worldly goods."[49] Of course, this sparseness came in handy during the frequent moves of the poor, particularly during surreptitious nighttime departures because of owed back rent, where virtually all of a household's goods could be packed into one wooden chest.

Making Ends Meet

The tremendous strain that only a few children placed on a struggling household cannot be overstated. As Olwen Hufton, the great historian of early modern poverty, has written, "for any poor family the mere existence of children spelt economic disaster."[50] All young children were a drain on a poor household's budget, at least until around age six or seven, when they could be put to work (often as beggars) or if lucky, placed as a servant or apprentice by the early teens. Of the three periods of greatest vulnerability in Benjamin Seebohm Rowntree's now-classic depiction of the poverty life cycle, two of these—early childhood and early marriage—coincided with the first years of a new household.[51]

How did Stoffel and Magdalena Baur cope under these circumstances? Some historians argue that the single most important development in the lives of early modern indigent families was the reorganization of poor relief throughout sixteenth-century Europe.[52] In Nuremberg, the most important public grants for poor families with children came from the Sailer Foundation (also known as the "Rich Alms") and the Keyper Foundation for shamefaced people (also known as the "Great Alms"). Founded in 1388, the Rich Alms initially provided forty "truly poor and resident (*Hausarme*) citizens" with 1/10 fl. worth of food every eight days for those with three or more children, every fourteen days for those with one or two. By the sixteenth century, the foundation's annual yield had risen enough to provide 150 households a week with either two five-pound loaves of bread and two pounds of meat or an equivalent cash stipend of twelve kreuzer (1/5 fl.).[53] The Great Alms of the Keyper Foundation, founded in 1481, was specifically intended to help the new poor among its citizens, especially "many pious, residential, and needy shamefaced poor who could not survive without personal aid and a helping hand." Eligible households with children received 60–90 d. weekly (about 1/5–1/3 fl.).[54]

To qualify for either program (but not both at the same time), parents and guardians needed to have a fixed address and at least six years of citizenship or approved resident alien status as well as a fixed address—qualifications that Stoffel Baur could not have satisfied, though his son Georg might have. If Georg were to seek such assistance to support his three young sisters, he would have applied in person to the director of the bureau during the posted office hours. If he could prove his need, he would then have received a special badge for identification and been limited to fifty quarters of aid, or twelve and a half years total, distributed weekly or biweekly in each of the city's quarters and Wöhrd as well as in his own poor suburb of Gostenhof. In addition to these stipends, both Georg and Stoffel could have benefited from one of the city council's many other public welfare programs, such as supplying greatly subsidized "emergency bread" during famines and other crises (in one instance the city government distributed more than 15,000 loaves of bread weekly at half price for several months).[55]

Yet despite such extensive and unprecedented governmental support, the numbers of unwanted children applying for admission to Nuremberg's Findel continued to rise over the course of the late sixteenth and early seventeenth centuries. How could this be so? Most fundamentally, poor relief in Nuremberg—despite its almost unique scope—still probably reached only 10 percent of the population as a whole and at its early seventeenth-century peak at most one in three of the neediest families in the city.[56] Alms were also generally limited to citizens and legal residents, thereby automatically excluding Stoffel Baur and thousands of other illegal aliens who regularly flowed through the city's gates. No doubt if deemed eligible, Georg and his wife would have welcomed the complimentary bread and meat, but these commodities hardly satisfied all of a household's needs, particularly lodging and other expenses. The annual cash equivalent, a little over ten gulden by 1600, had been quite generous by the standards of the early sixteenth century, but a hundred years of inflation had robbed this unchanged amount of its value, putting it well below the early modern poverty line, constituting at most one-half of a male day laborer's salary for a year.[57]

By the time Georg Baur and his wife took in his young sisters, the standard payment barely covered one-quarter of a childless individual's expenses; for a couple with three foster children and one of their own, the relief would have been even more inadequate. If a father were fortunate enough to have steady work, even in a low-paying job, the government relief might have made a crucial difference in his family's survival—but therein lay the catch. Georg Baur would have had to fraudulently claim unemployment (as he initially did) as well as that the three girls were his own, all the while successfully avoiding official detection. Otherwise he and the rest of his household would have been removed from the alms rolls and possibly expelled from the city. For the much greater number of poor households headed by genuinely unemployed women or disabled men, steady legitimate income was hard to come by and the free food distributed by the city might head off starvation, but no more.

Perhaps it was to be expected, then, that some alms recipients came to resent the very bureaucrats who thought they were helping them out. This antagonism is of course well known in modern social welfare contexts but apparently shocked sixteenth-century administrators of the new centralized poor relief. Repeatedly magistrates complained of ingratitude and a sense of entitlement among the recipients of municipal generosity. Many people, apparently, not only ignored the weekly sermon preceding alms distribution but were loud and disruptive as well. Others sent their children to pick up the food or stipend, despite frequent threats to end the family's relief altogether. Still others apparently made fraudulent claims about their poverty or the number of children in their household. And nearly everyone complained about being required to wear the shameful alms badges in public every day, with many simply ignoring the rule. Perseverance in any of these abuses, councilors warned, endangered not just recipients' alms but also their immortal souls.[58] Clearly such righteous indignation irritated many poor people, particularly when two alms inspectors began coming to their houses periodically, questioning neighbors and family members about the morality of their lives: whether they "[cultivate] public sins, such as immoral gambling . . .[or] live contentiously with their neighbors, with cursing, blaspheming, slandering, gossiping, and other improper matters as may be the case, [including] getting drunk senseless in taverns."[59] This price for small weekly or biweekly handouts was too high for many alms recipients, who continued to defy the bureau's ban on spending stipends on anything but food, on lending out or selling the alms badge, or especially on begging of any kind. Some recipients did indeed have their relief suspended as a result, but the frequency of official complaints conveys the fairly ineffectual enforcement of the bureau's empty threats.

Consequently, even the most fortunate minority of poor households that benefited from formalized poor relief was still forced to rely on various traditional and improvised stopgap measures to scrape by. Since even the combination of poor relief and cobbled-together work was generally insufficient to the needs of a poor household with children, almost all needy families—the Baurs among them—turned to the most common source of supplemental income in early modern Europe: begging. In addition to requiring little skill or exertion (though some might beg to differ on the former), panhandling could be three to five times as lucrative as unskilled day labor.[60] Equally important, anyone could beg and the usual obstacles to work, such as physical disabilities or small children, actually became assets. In Nuremberg, regulations since 1370 attempted to control who could legitimately beg, with strong preference given to local residents and especially the shamefaced poor, who were considered temporary or "part-time beggars" (*Nebenerwerbsbettler*) in times of crisis (especially during winter)—as opposed to full-time professional beggars.[61] In practice, many people of all backgrounds continued to beg without the council's permission even after the outlawing of all begging in 1522 and the centralization of all poor relief three years later. It is an understatement to note that criminal enforcement was sporadic and largely ineffective.

"Beggars," writes historian Otto Ulbricht, "moved within [early modern] society as fish in a river that carries plenty of water."[62] Begging children, alone or with their parents, were especially prominent throughout early modern Europe and probably accounted for one-third to one-half of all beggars on city streets.[63] Given the inadequacy of both official poor relief and occasional work for the parent(s), this outcome too seems inevitable. Begging children more often aroused—in a way adults often couldn't—the sympathy of passersby, thus enabling them to contribute to the household in a significant way, at times as the chief breadwinner. All boys and girls who regularly lived with family members were expected to contribute to the household income, sometimes by as early as seven or eight years old.[64] In the days before the Industrial Revolution's employment of children in factories and mines, begging "work" often made the difference in a family's survival, particularly during the high unemployment of the winter months.

Fig. 2.5. Rembrandt, *Beggars at the Doorstep*
(1648). Bibliothèque nationale.

Going door to door or crouched shivering on a street corner, the destitute mother with small children in rags constituted a pitiful but all-too-frequent sight in early modern cities (see fig. 2.5).

Begging parents with several malnourished children were common enough on the street to earn their own nickname of "shepherds" (*stäbuler*) in the street slang of early modern Germany.[65] If caught, begging families were supposedly expelled from the city, but in practice this punishment was only enforced against vagrants (and then irregularly).[66] It is very likely that Stoffel Baur sent his daughters out begging, perhaps regularly, though there is no explicit evidence of this.

The single most important resource for the Baurs' struggling household would have been help of various kinds from relatives or friends. Scholars have long referred to the availability of assistance of this nature as "social capital." An individual with a social network of several potential helpers is rich in social capital, even if he or she is struggling financially; a person with no human resources to draw on is poor in social capital. In this model, neighbors and other friends might be more valuable than kin, particularly for migrants whose relatives are far away.[67] Relationships of this type were usually reciprocal in nature, nourished by a series of small favors as much as by large financial ones. They tended to be strongest among people close in age and social station, but a vertical relationship with a landlord or employer could also be invaluable at points. The same combination of vertical and horizontal bonds was also found among relatives, with heads of households turning to parents and siblings alike when possible.[68] In early modern Germany, all of these supporters—kin and nonkin—were generally referred to as "friends" (*Freunde*) of the household. This typically imprecise description of the era is actually quite useful in terms of assessing social capital, focusing as it does on the pivotal issue of potential help, rather than secondary (and sometimes misleading) factors such as degrees of consanguinity and nature of affinity.[69]

"In a generally poor society," Robin Briggs has observed, "mutual aid was the norm, providing an elementary safety net for those in temporary difficulties."[70] This was even true in a large city such as Nuremberg, which scholars now recognize was not quite as anonymous and socially isolating as previously thought, but instead might be better viewed as a collection of multiple subcommunities such as Gostenhof, each containing several networks of collective support.[71] Given their greater day-to day familiarity with one another (as opposed to sporadic contact with often faraway relatives), it is not surprising that urban neighbors often borrowed money from one another, cosigned loans, gave each other job referrals, shared food or clothing, intervened in domestic disputes, and—most relevant to our enquiry— watched each others' children, an indispensable favor for many single parents. Informal aid of this sort was naturally easier to come by than loans, since most if not all of one's circle faced similar economic straits.

Would Stoffel Baur have built up any social capital during his brief residence in Nuremberg? As a recent arrival and a mercenary, it was unlikely. Whatever Stoffel's craft training, his chosen profession as a soldier robbed him of an essential craft identity while at the same time excluding him from the benefits from confraternities had he been Catholic or various other brotherhoods if he were Lutheran.[72] Those of his fighting comrades who were still alive and in the area were for the most part fellow foreigners with even less social capital in Nuremberg than he. Like most poor migrants, he was unable to meet the minimum property requirements for political enfranchisement and thus remained ineligible for a range of municipal benefits and protections.[73] Stoffel also had little to offer in the way of reciprocal services or loans. Here too, the death of Magdalena, who could have accumulated some social capital in this manner, figures prominently. With the sole exception of his son Georg, Stoffel apparently had no kin in the city to offer financial or other assistance. Help of different sorts from his new neighbors did possibly occur, but as historian Richard Grassby points out: "[L]iving in close proximity did not necessarily lead to frequent interaction [or] mutuality."[74]

Georg Baur, by contrast, had somehow achieved both master potter status and citizenship since his arrival in Nuremberg—a cherished status that the city council threatened to take away from him unless he agreed to care for his sisters. This was in itself a remarkable achievement given his background and even more uncommon as the seventeenth century progressed. He and his wife Barbara had likely also built up some social capital among their neighbors and his fellow potters and thus had something to spend as well as something to lose in exploiting those connections to support Stoffel and his three daughters. How much social capital they had already expended in this way by the time of Stoffel's latest departure is unknown. Perhaps they were already in social debt because of previous assistance to Stoffel in supporting his household. Whatever the reasoning behind George's actions, he and his wife eventually decided that enough was enough.

Direct financial assistance with debts would have been particularly elusive for someone with so little social capital as Stoffel Baur. Borrowing was also—as he undoubtedly knew—a short-term, temporary, and thus problematic solution. This was true of small loans from Georg or a friend as well as credit from a local grocer or tavernkeeper or advances from an employer against future wages—all common practices among soldiers, who only saw a small fraction of their monthly salary after deductions for provisions from the company store and for previous credit were taken out.[75] Every attempt to shift debts would merely postpone the inevitable crisis—robbing Hans to pay Franz. Yet as today, many low-income households did not have the luxury of planning for the future and continued to get ever deeper into debt with landlords and employers to the point where their work, if they had any, took on the form of indentured servitude.[76] That was often the moment that poor immigrants became poor emigrants and moved on to avoid prison for insurmountable debts. Soldiers were particularly bad flight risks and thus found it very difficult to obtain loans of any size. Had Stoffel been successful in borrowing any money from Georg or his "friends," he would have quickly expended whatever meager social capital he possessed, leaving him with still fewer and riskier options.

Perhaps, like many strapped parents, he resorted to a loan shark or pawnbroker, ignoring the exorbitant interest rates in favor of quick cash. This too was a desperate, dead end, and ultimately dangerous solution, yet for the poor of every era it at least solves that day's problems. Pawned objects—to the extent that they were available—rarely earned more than a tiny fraction of their actual value and were usually too expensive to redeem. A seasoned veteran, Stoffel also doubtlessly knew of the violent methods of collection favored by most moneylenders (who often employed ex-soldiers as their collectors). Since 1518, Nuremberg's city council had attempted to provide an affordable alternative for poor people through its own version of the Italian Monte della Pietà, a government-backed bank offering small loans at interest rates of 0–6 percent annually. Civic loan bureaus of this sort popped up in cities across Europe during the economic downturns of the sixteenth and seventeenth centuries, interacting with as many as half of all urban households in peak depression years.[77] Nuremberg's *Pfanleih-haus*—like private moneylenders (all of them Christians since Jews had been driven from the city in 1499)—required clothing, furniture, or other objects of equal value as deposits with each loan and quickly assembled a colorful miscellany of unredeemed objects. Concerned not to reward crime, the city's magistrates established strict regulation on which objects might be used as deposits, refusing to accept anything with the city's seal on it (which made it stolen public property), any liturgical items (stolen church property) or any ripped, wet, or bloody clothes (presumably the spoils of a personal assault). These and other restrictions tended to militate against ex-soldiers and their accumulated war booty.[78]

The city council's anxiety over the circulation of stolen property reflects another means of survival well known to a mercenary such as Stoffel Baur. In the early modern era as today, poverty and crime always existed in close proximity, with the latter regularly tempting those in need with quick and easy money. The boundary between legal and illegal means of support was rarely as clear to the poor as it was to upper-class magistrates and judges. In the words of Olwen Hufton, "[T]he poor had their own rules of conduct, their own standards—an alien set of values which, however hard the historian may try, are not easy to piece together."[79] With daily survival an unending struggle, Stoffel Baur and his neighbors expected trickery, petty crime, and intimidation from each other and often colluded in the illegal means used by friends and neighbors to scrape by. Stealing grass, vegetables, firewood, or even small livestock (usually chickens), was viewed as quite normal among the unpropertied, and not necessarily wrong from the perspective of hungry people living in the makeshift economy. Playing on the fears of wealthier members of their community met with even wider toleration. In a society where diseased beggars (possibly with concocted sores) implicitly threatened to touch and infect passersby unless a coin rang in their cup, begging and extortion were never entirely distinct from one another. Better-off town residents similarly bought a degree of safety (and quiet) and at least peace by "voluntarily" donating to beggars singing late at night outside their door. More aggressive panhandlers, often unemployed soldiers or journeymen, made even more explicit threats of violent assault, poisoning of a water supply, or most terrifyingly, arson.

There is no direct evidence of criminal acts by Stoffel Baur but the behavioral norms among migrant poor and especially soldiers make it likely.[80] Judging from legal as well as legislative evidence, Stoffel would have been far from unique among poor parents had he involved his young daughters in illegal activities. The crimes need not have been serious ones: stealing wood from a nearby forest or shoplifting food from a local grocer were apparently as ubiquitous as child begging.[81] Admittedly the entire household risked banishment, especially if they were non, but given the general ineptitude of early modern law enforcement, the odds against getting caught were quite favorable. Like begging and other parts of the makeshift economy, criminal activity usually provided supplemental income and was rarely the household's only or even chief means of support.

Stoffel Baur and his three young daughters were almost certainly not, however, among those families of full-time, professional criminals, each member with his or her specific assignment. One Nuremberg family specialized in stealing bedfeathers, with the father cutting a mattress open and taking some but not all of the stuffing, after which the mother and children sewed it shut to prevent discovery of the theft.[82] More infamous locally was the Elbach family counterfeiting ring, exposed in early 1607. For over five years, thimble maker Hans Elbach and his three adult sons forged various small coins, gradually moving up to the more valuable copper and silver currency. Tipped off about their impending arrest, the two surviving brothers (Hans senior and junior had since died) fled town, leaving behind their wives, children, and widowed sister-in-law. Their escape outraged Nuremberg's magistrates, who promptly imprisoned all three wives, interrogating them repeatedly about their complicity in the business as well as the whereabouts of the absconded husbands. After four months of imprisonment, an unusually long stay by early modern standards, all three women were finally to be released and banished with their children, but only after two of them had spent two days in the stocks (the third was pregnant and spared on that account). At the last minute, on account of their children, the women's public humiliation was reduced in duration to fifteen minutes. The court's mercy engendered neither gratitude nor greater maternal affection among the women, who immediately fled the city, leaving their five children behind, "sitting alone in their house." As had become routine in Nuremberg by this time, the council accepted the two youngest into the Findel and sent the other three to relatives, along with a stipend for each.[83]

A Burden Shared

Perhaps most important coping measure available to Stoffel Baur was informal fostering of one or more of his daughters. This ubiquitous form of child circulation spanned a variety of arrangements, ranging from temporary child care of a few hours during the day to fostering for periods of several weeks and occasionally years while a parent was out of town. The most popular form of long-term fostering was the custom of placing children aged seven to seventeen as servants or apprentices in other households for multiple years at a time. Employers of such youths frequently signed agreements where they promised "to raise" (*erziehen*) or "to provide for" (*pflegen*) children and youths as their own.[84] Arrangements of this sort eased the financial strain on a household considerably, although the cost of placement fees by the early seventeenth century had virtually eliminated the formal service option for poor families such as the Baurs. Even so, many different kinds of informal arrangements might have offered him at least some relief. In this sense, whether temporary or long-term, the circulation of children constituted a fundamental coping mechanism for struggling parents of all sorts, particularly those with small children.

The greatest testimony to the general success of informal fostering in various forms was its dampening effect on petitions for admission to the Findel. Of the several thousand children from Nuremberg's poor and struggling households with at least one parent still alive, at most one in three hundred ended up spending time in the Findel's care, mainly between 1570 and 1615.[85] Yet when it comes to identifying the precise nature and relative frequency of various private arrangements, the historical record is opaque, since it reveals only those cases of arranged or presumed care that failed, the ones that led an adult left with a child to petition the city council to admit his or her young charge. Even here generalization about care providers remains precarious. What does it mean, for instance, that grandparents, aunts and uncles, and older siblings appeared relatively infrequently (6.7 percent of the time) in foster and forced foster petitions for admission to the Findel?[86] It might signify that close relatives simply chose to keep the children left with them more often than nonkin. On the other hand, perhaps they were instead simply less entrusted with their children's children than might be expected. Both scenarios are possible for the early modern era (though evidence in favor of the latter explanation will be examined shortly). It is also generally impossible to track most unwanted children's multiple stops with various informal foster parents before coming to the Findel's attention. Some children had been through three or more homes before their petition for acceptance to the Findel. Except for formal service or apprenticeship contracts, fostering agreements were rarely written down, once again leaving only the self-interested accounts of petitioning foster parents.

The need for short-term child circulation or foster care in the seventeenth century was not significantly different from the modern era. Many married or widowed mothers, presumably Magdalena Baurin among them, worked for money, at home with some kind of spinning or other cloth work when possible but also outside the household when necessary. Like working widowers with children, these women could not always take young children to their place of employment and thus often required some sort of day care by a relative or neighbor (though children as young as five years old might be left on their own for long periods of time). Single mothers would also sometimes need babysitting when out shopping or doing other errands as well as during short trips to weddings or to visit out-of-town friends (as with Margaretha Kriegin, in the book's opening anecdote). Sometimes, for different reasons, these absences of a few days might stretch to one or two weeks. And then there was fieldwork and other seasonal employment, which might keep a father and mother out of town for several months. Long-term migrant work, most notably military campaigns, also led many mothers to leave their children behind while they toured with their husbands. Other times the mercenary father remained "abroad" on his own for years at a time, leaving his wife and children behind to fend for themselves—a situation the Baur children likely knew well. When serious illness or death struck the mother, the children were effectively orphaned, since the father was presumed dead or otherwise unreachable. Many soldiers never returned at all. Overall, fathers were dead or away in three-quarters of all Findel petitions.[87] Some of these fathers eventually returned to Nuremberg and picked up their children from the foster home where they had been living, genuinely surprised to learn that their offspring had been sent into the Findel during their absence.

To whom would Stoffel have been most likely to turn for long-term foster care? There was no universal and clear-cut hierarchy of preferred "secondary" or substitute parents. Nor did many people enjoy the full range of options. Poor parents could offer little monetary compensation and instead relied on whatever social capital they possessed—almost none in the case of Stoffel Baur. The most common resort for struggling parents would presumably be relatives, particularly their own parents, siblings, or older children. In the case of Stoffel Baur, this meant giving his girls to his grown son Georg and daughter-in-law Barbara, who already had a child of their own and who may have even shared the same quarters with Stoffel and the girls. Their scenario is the exact opposite of the more familiar situation in modern society, where it is often the child's grandparent who is left with the child when its parents leave.

In early modern Europe, neither choice was so straightforward or inevitable. Most modern preconceptions about premodern grandparents, in fact, are probably anachronistic, particularly regarding their privileged place in the affectionate multigenerational family. There is no evidence of a special sentiment toward grandparents in any of the art, literature, or so-called ego-documents of the early modern period.[88] Grandparents were instead shadowy figures, referred to largely in terms of lineage when mentioned at all. The era's common appellations of *Ahnherr* and *Ahnfrau* ("ancestor" and "ancestress") lack the domestic affection of the names of *Großvater* and *Großmutter* ("grandfather" and "grandmother") that gradually replaced them by the eighteenth century.[89] In petitions to the Findel, a widowed grandmother would usually be identified as caring for "her son's surviving child" or "her daughter's abandoned girl."[90] Sometimes the term "grandchild" (*Enkel* or *Enkelkind*) appears, but never "grandfather" or "grandmother," let alone "grandma" (*Oma*) or "grandpa" (*Opa*).

This too is a legacy of northwestern Europe's demographic peculiarity. Most people never even met their own grandparents. Because of the late-marriage pattern, six out of ten fathers and four out of ten mothers were dead by the time their children married.[91] Older grandchildren like Georg Baur might come to know one or two of their grandparents, probably on their mother's side (since women generally married younger). It would likely have been a brief acquaintance, however, since fewer than one in ten of early modern people made it to their late fifties, and only one in a hundred survived passed the age of sixty-five.[92] Did a grandparent care for Margareth, Appolonia, and Annalein (or Georg) Baur at some point in their early lives? The very fact that Stoffel had a grown son of at least thirty made it unlikely that any of his or his wife's parents was still alive. It was even more improbable that they would have been part of Stoffel's traveling household. Very

Fig. 2.6. Bartolomé Estaban Murillo, *Daily Toilet*
(ca. 1650). München Alte Pinakothek. An old woman,
presumably a grandmother, delouses a young boy.

few elderly people (usually women) lived with their children during the early modern era and then not until they were quite advanced in age and incapable of caring for themselves, let alone their grandchildren.[93] The majority of surviving grandparents, particularly in cities, lived alone, and most were also desperately poor—as attested in their frequent excuse in Findel petitions for giving up a grandchild "on account of poverty."[94]

That said, some grandparents did end up caring for their grandchildren for short or extended periods (see fig. 2.6). Perhaps as many as one in thirty households with children was headed by a grandparent.[95] On the whole, Nuremberg's magistrates considered this an acceptable situation. The very month of the Baur girls' entry into the Findel, when a grandmother with three grandchildren petitioned to have all three accepted into the Findel she was instead given a childcare stipend of 8–10 fl. per year. Similar requests "on account of poverty" were similarly denied, except for a few appeals from grandfathers.[96] Apparently grandmothers offered more assurance that fostered grandchildren would be properly cared for than grandfathers—still another manifestation of the gender double standard.

When Stoffel Baur and his three daughters moved to Nuremberg, they either lived with Georg and his family or near them in Gostenhof. Without their mother or other female relatives to care for Margareth, Apollonia, and Annalein, the responsibility likely fell to Georg's wife Barbara. It is hard to imagine a lifelong mercenary such as Stoffel Baur as willing or able to be involved in day-to-day child care and supervision. The more open question is how often and for how long he left the girls in his daughter-in-law's care. His most recent departure from the scene was likely only one in a series of comings and goings. Given that Georg and Barbara only had one child of their own, nine-year-old Katherina, Stoffel could have rationalized that such an arrangement gave Katherina some playmates and Barbara three ersatz daughters.[97] Georg, moreover, was apparently a successful master potter and property owner who presumably could provide better for the girls than their itinerant and often unemployed father. From Stoffel's perspective, this situation was the best he could hope for since the death of the girls' mother. Surely he was not the only widower-father who imposed himself in this way and his most recent disappearance would have likely been welcomed by Georg and Barbara were it not for the matter of providing for the three little girls he left behind.

Despite all of Georg's desperate scrambling during the nine days after the council's ultimatum, he failed to find anybody else to take the girls for an extended period. Apparently he did not have any other relatives nearby and his wife Barbara was also an immigrant (from Gunzenhausen), with no kin nearby. This was a common scenario among recent immigrants to Nuremberg and other big cities and helps account for the relative infrequency of relatives in Findel petitions, which again represented the minority of fostering arrangements that failed or were never possible.

The fact that none of the girls had been born in Nuremberg was unfortunate, because that meant that neither Stoffel nor Georg could turn to godparents, the most prominent nonparent represented in Findel petitions. Godparents were usually not even blood relations, but as the petitioners in roughly the same percentage of forced foster and voluntary foster cases as kin, they were regularly recognized as an important part of the broader definition of family.[98] Sometimes relatives were chosen for the honor, thus intensifying an existing kinship, but in Nuremberg the tendency was to extend kinship ties to nonrelatives. Canon law had even considered this so-called spiritual adoption of children the equivalent of blood ties in its definition of incest. Unlike kin, a godparent swore a sacred and specific oath at a child's baptism to provide for its spiritual and other needs. Children were in turn often named for their godparents and were sometimes thought to inherit traits from them (despite the widespread belief that such traits were normally passed on through the blood). Godparents were invited to every major event in the child's life and normally had a place of honor at the weddings of their godchildren. Judging from the many sumptuary ordinances limiting the value of gifts from godfathers and godmothers, these fictive parents frequently bestowed presents, sometimes expensive ones, upon their spiritual charges. Little surprise that many poor children fantasized about a fairy godparent who would magically lift them out of the dinginess of their everyday life.[99]

It is possible that in their plight Margareth, Appolonia, and Annelein Baur also dreamed of magical godparents, not least because they were unlikely to receive help even from their flesh-and-blood counterparts. One reason was the number of godparents involved. In other parts of Europe the usual number of godparents might be as many as six; in Nuremberg and surrounding Franconia, each child was traditionally limited to one.[100] This probably created a more intensive relationship in many instances but it also restricted the amount of social capital available to parents in time of need. Godparents from this part of Germany also tended to be gender-specific, meaning that each of the girls had a female benefactor, thus precluding a powerful male patron, such as the military officers often selected by rank-and-file soldiers.[101] Poor people often sought "vertical" godparenthood of this type, though some parents preferred to select peers for the honor, creating a "horizontal" spiritual affinity.[102] Whatever the social status of the Baur girls' godmothers, they lived at least forty miles away in their birthplace of Dinkelsbühl—today a short car drive from Nuremberg but in 1614 a journey of two to three days.

In the immigrant neighborhoods of Nuremberg's suburbs, neighbors and other friends thus acted as foster or secondary parents more often than the children's blood relatives.[103] Proximity and day-to-day contact regularly outweighed kinship for reasons of convenience as much as conviction. Based on patterns elsewhere in Europe, it is very likely that neighbors and other friends are greatly underestimated in our database's sample of petitioners to the Findel, since the relationship to the absent parent is usually only explicitly stated in the case of blood relatives and godparents.[104] More often the petitioner was simply listed by name. Some of these were neighbors, some coworkers, and others merely friends or acquaintances. Their care for another's children in some instances had been going on already for months or even years, and only financial necessity forced them to turn to the Findel for help. Possibly Stoffel Baur had already made use of such assistance; if so, it was no longer available to him (or perhaps deemed inferior to care by the girls' own brother).

Why did nonkin friends and acquaintances repeatedly take in others' children, sometimes for long periods of time, with no pay, in some cases raising them as their own offspring? Among relatives (including godparents), a sense of personal obligation emerges in many Findel petitions, though rarely stated explicitly and by no means universally. Among friends and acquaintances, child care assistance was sometimes offered in response to a past loan or other favor from the child's parent. Pity and simple charity naturally figured in to some degree, as did personal affection for the parent or child. More cynically, children of a certain age could be financial assets, particularly for their begging income, and thus readily welcomed (if not directly supervised) by relatives and friends. When thirteen-year-old Hans Frey was picked up for begging with his sick three-year-old brother, he informed officials that he had spent the last year moving between his mother's residence and the homes of his three siblings, finally ending up with his adult brother in nearby Schweinau, who daily sent the boys into the city to beg.[105]

The function of money in informal circulation of children varied. Given the nature of his self-interest, Georg Baur would have been disinclined to mention any payment Stoffel might have made before his departure, so this cannot be ruled out. Individual foster care for pay was common in early modern cities, whether the provider was a relative, friend, or mere acquaintance. As in the book's opening anecdote with Margaretha Kriegin and her married sister, the amount might be considered more of a compensation for time and expenses than a fee, especially among relatives and friends. The arrangement might involve daily supervision for certain hours or full-time care for several days or even weeks. Though common, the practice was completely unregulated in Nuremberg and led to many disputes and sometimes abandonments by foster mothers who had not been paid. Still, it is important to distinguish between the mom-and-pop fostering operations of individual Nurembergers (usually just mom), which involved a handful of children at most, and the large-scale baby farms and foster homes outside of the metropolises of London and Paris, where farming an infant out to a wet nurse was a virtual death sentence, especially for children under the age of one. As one church official in seventeenth-century London wrote, "He that loveth his dog would not put it in such a place to be brought up."[106]

Paid foster care in Nuremberg, by contrast, remained a popular and generally reliable option for those who could afford it and a modest moneymaker
for those who could not.

Running Away

Temporary child care is one thing. What could cause any parent, then or
now, to desert his own children so abruptly, coldly, and definitively as Stoffel Baur did? Some historical anthropologists have attempted to penetrate
the thinking of poor parents like Stoffel by framing such choices in terms
of "adaptive family strategy"—defined by a leading proponent as "a set of
interrelated family decisions and plans governing household membership,
marriage, and family limitation."[107] While useful in delineating the factors
involved in this form of child circulation, the notion of a family strategy
requires great sensitivity to the vast diversity of choices available, avoiding
the implication of any monolithic "poor family strategy of child abandonment."[108] It must also recognize that the volatile mixture of conscious and
unconscious factors, as well as emotions and other "nonrational" influences, is very difficult to assess in individual cases and that the range of
options available could in practice be quite constrained. For all of these
reason, the neutral language and conceptualizations of "child circulation"
and "informal fostering" remain preferable to the potentially misleading
"adaptive family strategy." Economic self-interest was merely one aspect of
an interwoven series of active and passive choices that lead a parent to leave
a child behind. Only with this important caveat in mind can the external
factors that might have shaped Stoffel Baur's actions be weighed.

The typical breaking point for desperate parents like Stoffel came amid
the multiple crises and overall vulnerability that perpetually haunted their
lives. Occasional hunger, unemployment, and other misfortunes were to
be anticipated, but some dire situations surpassed the coping abilities of
the most resilient fathers and mothers. The single most common structural
condition that preceded a child being left behind for a long period of time
was the absence of one parent, due to either death, serious illness, work-
related travels, or desertion. Sustaining the poor household was an intensely
collaborative balancing act, involving virtually every member of the family
(including small children as beggars). Losing just one member, particularly
the chief wage earner or "care provider," could be disastrous, sending the
entire family into a rapid, downward spiral of destitution. Even for those
families with extensive social capital, a crisis of this nature could stretch

their resources to an intolerable degree, to the point where sending a child away might be seen as the only way to insure its survival.

It was especially significant that Stoffel was a recent widower at the time of his departure. About one in three mothers seeking foster care for a child at the Findel was widowed, as was at least one in four abandoning fathers.[109] A generally high adult mortality rate meant that the death of a spouse before children were grown was unfortunately a common event among households at all social levels. Women had a lower life expectancy than men, mainly because of the one-in-twenty chance of dying during childbirth. The likeliest cause of Magdalena Baurin's premature death, though, was one of the epidemics that struck European cities with numbing regularity, on average every ten to fifteen years into the eighteenth century. Between 1505 and 1670, major epidemics hit Nuremberg fourteen times, each for a duration of one to three years, killing one-tenth to one-fourth of the population every time they struck. During the worst outbreaks as many as 10,000–15,000 people died within twelve months.[110] Poor suburbs, such as the Baurs' Gostenhof, with their dense housing and poor public hygiene, were naturally the hardest hit. During the plague of 1573–76, more than 6,500 people died in the small suburb of Wöhrd alone, versus about 5,400 for the entire city of Nuremberg proper.[111] Winter was the most vulnerable time for all poor people, but especially for migrant families living in poorly heated shelters or outside. Hardly a winter passed in Nuremberg and its environs without the discovery of some diseased and frozen beggar, with dead or alive children nearby, on a road, behind a barn, or in a field.[112]

The loss of his wife about a year earlier undoubtedly figured prominently in Stoffel Baur's decision to leave his girls behind in Gostenhof. The proximate cause of his departure, though, was more likely to have been an immediate financial crisis of some sort. Unlike illnesses, accidents, and death itself, all of which struck suddenly, the building of insurmountable debt was a household disaster that usually occurred gradually until reaching some definitive breaking point. True, a parent might suddenly be fired from his or her job, but most poor people expected unstable employment as a matter of course and, as already seen, could often temporarily rely on a social network of support to soften the blow. Parents who found themselves in such severe economic straits as to consider giving up their children had usually exhausted all supplementary sources of income and had borrowed as much as they could from friends or others, leaving them with few options, all of them drastic.

In Nuremberg, as elsewhere in Europe, bankruptcy protection did not yet exist and insolvent debtors could be imprisoned at the request of creditors or relatives until outstanding debts were paid off. By the time of Stoffel Baur this meant internment in one of the city's debtors' prisons—there was one for men and one for women—called stockades because of the barred ground-floor windows from which internees would accost passersby for help with their debts. Most debtors only spent a few days or a week in incarceration before being bailed out by friends or relatives, but some stayed on for several months. The number of prisoners in a given year likewise fluctuated greatly, from as few as three to as many as a hundred.[113] Until the opening of Nuremberg's workhouse in 1670, imprisoning whole families for debt was uncommon, though not unheard of. Instead, those debtors with children relied on spouses, relatives, or friends to care for their children until their release; there are only two official mentions of foster children entering the Findel on account of parental debt imprisonment.[114]

The psychological trauma of money troubles could be devastating. In the spring of 1574, one depressed young mother, upon her release from the debtors' prison, went directly to the executioner's platform and jumped in the Pegnitz, drowning herself. Sadly, she was not the only Nuremberg parent driven to this desperate act by financial woes.[115]

A more common response to insurmountable debts was simply running away, an option that was second nature to itinerant mercenaries such as Stoffel Baur. Skipping town in this situation was so common that the Nuremberg city council summoned any indebted citizens who were even suspected of such plans and made them swear not to leave the city without official permission. Various creditors, including landlords and employers, likewise always expected flight among poor households and thus similarly extracted solemn promises with ever larger deposits for advances.[116] Despite such precautions, many debtors still decided to resolve their financial troubles by fleeing from them, often leaving children behind, sometimes with relatives or friends, sometimes without any provision whatsoever. Crushing debt played a key role in at least one in six instances of child desertion, and perhaps many more (see fig. 2.8 below).[117]

There was often a blurred line between leaving the household for reasons of work (which Stoffel might have claimed) and for other, less admirable reasons, such as boredom or annoyance with family life, laziness, or an illicit sexual liaison. Even if prompted by physical or economic hardship, the decision to leave a child behind was more likely a complex series of choices, shaped by a conflux of emotions and personal demons as much as by economic necessity. Sometimes a father or a mother appeared to be just worn down and discouraged, merely seeking some time away from parental and familial responsibilities. Or, as in a great number of cases, the deserting parent might not even be thinking of the child(ren) and be instead driven by irreconcilable personal hostility toward a spouse. Known legally as "malicious desertion," this phenomenon was judged by many contemporaries, particularly Protestant reformers, as a scourge on the land. Two-thirds of single households in the era were headed by wives whose husbands had either died or unambiguously deserted them.[118] A sixteenth-century marriage ordinance from the Palatine-Electorate summarized the woes created:

> [S]ome men are so crazy and robbed of all human and fatherly sense that they take wives and stay with them for a while, seizing and enjoying all their worldly goods, even having children with them, before secretly deserting them or going off to war—out of sheer caprice and frivolity, without [the wives'] knowledge or approval, and often despite prohibition by the civil authority to whom they owe obedience and service. Thus the wives, with or without children, remain for many years without help or consolation, provided with nothing—against all that is just—pitifully left to ruin. Not only does this then lead to fornication among such wives, but sometimes even engagement and marriage, along with the great disputes, troubles, and terrible disturbances that necessarily follow.[119]

The loneliness of the spouse left behind and the potential for adultery and bigamy were of particular concern to legal authorities. Their worries were not misplaced, as numerous cases of this nature appeared before criminal and church courts.[120] During the sixteenth century, some Protestant jurisdictions, including Nuremberg, accordingly reduced the canonical waiting period for a missing spouse to be declared dead from seven to four years (Calvinist Geneva extended it to ten years).[121] Sexual appetites aside, this was a long time to wait before marrying a new provider. Not surprising, many individuals did not wait. Some remarried anyway and risked being charged with bigamy; others fled the city with a new lover, with or without children. Love and companionship could even trump financial assets, as in the case of carpenter Hans Schmid's widow, who left behind four children and 48 fl. of property to follow and marry a foreign journeyman.[122]

Did fathers like Stoffel play a disproportionately greater role in such household disruptions? Thirty years ago, Olwen Hufton claimed that virtually all broken homes among the early modern poor were caused by abandoning fathers. Many early modern contemporaries, particularly Protestant reformers, agreed. But in the Nuremberg sample, fathers were only somewhat more likely than mothers to be classified as abandoners (see fig. 2.7). Certainly large numbers of women were deserted by their husbands,

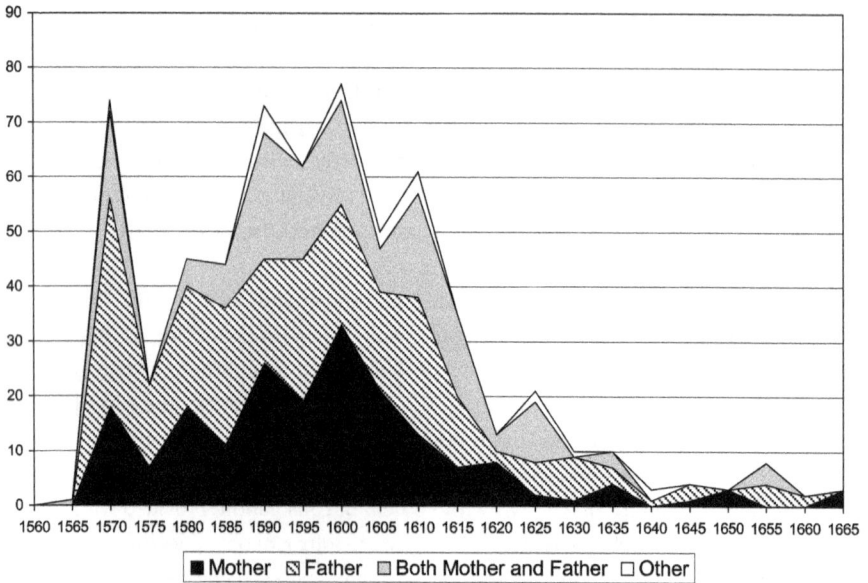

Fig. 2.7. Forced foster cases in Nuremberg, 1560–1669
(five-year totals; n = 621). *Source*: FKD.

but there were also many instances of women fleeing abusive husbands or otherwise dysfunctional households as well as absconding with new lovers, leaving dependent children behind.[123] Perhaps even more jarring is the unexpected scope of joint parental abandonments of children, a rarely described phenomenon that characterized as many as one in four cases where an abandoner was identified.[124] Considered as a whole, the many instances of deserting mothers make it clear that the presumed difference between men and women in this respect requires serious reevaluation.

The collective portrait of figure 2.8 reveals some other interesting patterns. For the majority of deserting fathers, going off to war (like Stoffel) appears to have been the most common destination. In other instances, a father left to become a soldier shortly after his wife's death, again leaving his children behind. A wife might also leave her children behind to join her mercenary-husband in a foreign location. It was be imprudent to infer motives from this information but at the very least the prominence of Stoffel Baur's chosen profession in this type of child circulation is obvious. Abandonment on account of debt also appears to have been a bit more of a male phenomenon or at least easier to identify as a motive in the case of men.[125] The motives and destinations of abandoning mothers, on the other hand, tended to be more complex and opaque, at least to official observers.

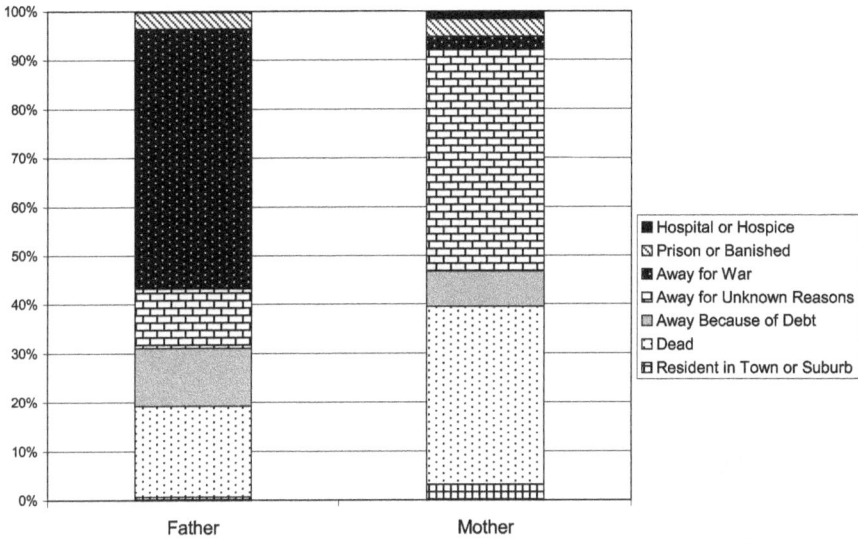

Fig. 2.8. Father and mother locations in forced foster
cases, 1557–1670 (*n* = 1085). *Source*: FKD.

In most cases, women seem to have left with men, either their husbands or
their illicit lovers, though these types of details are inconclusive. Perhaps the
most telling statistic is exemplified by Stoffel Baur: widowers were almost
two times more likely than widows to desert children widows.[126] Is this evidence of stronger maternal than paternal ties, of more options for men, or
of the relatively greater power of perseverance among women? Taking into
consideration how much easier it was for widowers to remarry compared to
widows, the indictment of male vulnerability appears even stronger.

Informal Circulation versus State Care

From a modern perspective, Stoffel Baur's decision to leave his three
daughters with their adult brother seems more understandable than young
George's decision to hand the girls over to the Findel. Most of Georg's early
modern contemporaries would apparently have shared this assessment,
with foster parents of all sorts preferring to keep young charges themselves
or to circulate them informally to another household. Again, the willingness and even desire of many people to raise someone else's unwanted
children should come as no surprise. After all, childlessness was often the
source of great despair in German fairy tales and folk stories. In real life,
excessive admiration of another's child could sometimes even lead to ac-

cusations of witchcraft, especially if the coveted child fell sick and died.[127] Fostering admittedly imposed a financial burden, but it also promised an affectionate companion, a potential worker and source of income, and the possibility of progeny. Many early modern married couples who were not childless by choice clearly found this arrangement appealing, as did some of the exceptionally high number of widows living alone with no living descendants.[128] Even if a single parent or married couple already had children in the household, a sense of obligation to deceased parents or of pity for "friendless" orphans and foundlings could overcome negative budgetary considerations.

One key reason that modern scholars have overlooked the frequency of informal child circulation is that fact that formal adoption, a common practice in ancient Greece and Rome, remained impossible in most parts of Europe, including Germany, until the twentieth century.[129] Some historians have argued for a medieval transformation of adoption into other practices—such as godparenthood, the oblation of children to monasteries and convents, and semi-informal *donato inter vivos* contracts—but this thesis does not hold up. Godparenthood did not involve the transfer of any parental (including property) rights, and neither religious oblation nor *donato inter vivos* contracts were widespread or the true equivalent of legal adoption.[130] Legal guardians (*Vormünder*), who were assigned by Nuremberg's Guardian Bureau, rarely welcomed children into their homes and for the most part remained tangentially involved in their upbringing.[131] There was simply no well-established equivalent of ancient or modern formal adoption during the medieval and early modern eras, hence no descriptive legal documents of long-term relationships. The very few times that Findel records referred to a nonbiological parent formally "adopting" a child out of the Findel (*an eines kindesstatt aufzuerziehen*) there was apparently little more than an oath involved, and it is unclear that this differed significantly from the myriad of other informal arrangements involving unwanted children.[132]

The number of unwanted children who came to the attention of governmental authorities, consequently, remained relatively small, making Stoffel Baur's case more the exception than the rule in child circulation. Combining forced foster cases such as his with the estimated number of anonymous abandonment cases that likely involved such parents yields an average of 8.8 unwanted children per year petitioning to the Nuremberg Findel for admittance from 1557 to 1670. If we add to this number those petitions from parents who appealed directly to the Findel for temporary fostering of one or more child, that number rises to 14.6 children per year with at least one living legitimate parent.[133] The great majority of these petitions came during the years 1565–1620, so the annual totals are actually higher for those fifty-five years and much lower for the subsequent fifty years. Nevertheless, the implication for a city of over 40,000 people is clear: informal and private fostering remained the norm for parents in need and governmental involvement in child circulation remained the exception.

A brief survey of the triggers to official intervention and official attitudes toward intervention helps explain why this was the case. The first scenario for magisterial involvement involved an existing foster arrangement between a parent and another adult that broke down. It is impossible to establish how often this situation occurred, since in most instances we have little information about the relationship of the abandoning parent to the petitioner.[134] The foster parent could potentially be anyone—a relative, friend, acquaintance, or stranger—and there were often reasons of self-interest preventing full disclosure. Usually, several weeks, months, or even years had passed before a foster parent approached the Nuremberg town council for assistance.[135] Since such agreements were virtually never written down, there was no way to determine what the original terms really were or which party truly violated them—a common problem with informal, oral contracts of all kinds. We have only Georg Baur's word, for instance, that no such understanding existed between his departing father and him. Obviously a long period without remuneration of any sort was the most common catalyst to action, but a petitioning foster parent might also be prompted by various changes in personal circumstances: the death or absence of a spouse, loss of a job, illness of the foster parent, or a number of causes of economic crisis for the household. The difficulties of caring for disabled children sometimes led a foster parent to petition for placement into the Findel as well as for financial compensation.[136] Disciplinary problems with a foster child were rarely specified but this too sometimes figured into an official request for help.

Again, it is likely that Georg and Barbara Baur had already cared for his three young sisters, since even the foster parents who surface in these petitions typically seemed willing to persevere a little bit longer if necessary. In 1572, the baker Michel Schmid had been caring for the small daughter of a poor farmer for six months when, upon the death of the farmer's wife, they took in his four remaining children—all of whom Schmid and his wife "kindly consented to raise," provided they received some financial assistance from the Findel.[137] Melchior Millenberger complained that he was already caring for "several of his friends'/relatives' children and he could not possibly handle the additional two children foisted on him; yet in the end he agreed to keep one and the Findel accepted the other.[138] Typically a successful petition of this nature came after a prolonged absence of the biological parent(s) and one or more previous requests for financial compensation.[139]

Foster parents who had hired out their services, by contrast, enjoyed little sympathy among magistrates when they claimed to have been cheated of money owed them for child care. Helena Homan's 1569 request for the Findel to take in the allegedly abandoned child of Hans Schmidlein was denied and she was told "that she had agreed to keep it and should she refuse she would be banished from the city for life."[140] When Anna Reshin complained that Margaretha Jenkin from Kulmbach made a fostering agreement with her and then disappeared completely, she was told that "she has herself to blame that she undertook the costs of the child and didn't secure payment for the same," to which the council helpfully added "she might inquire where this Margaretha went and send the child to her." Claims of poverty or other hardship did not usually soften the hearts of magistrates on this score, though in this instance the same child was accepted into the Findel five months later.[141] After hearing the petition of still another foster parent who claimed to have been cheated, in 1613 the council ordered its bailiffs to warn all foster parents "not only in Gostenhof but also at the Wöhrd market and also in gardens" not to take on foster children without assuring payment.[142]

Only when unhappy foster parents took extreme actions, such as public abandonment, did magistrates ignore their preference for informal circulation and modest financial assistance. Even then, when an anonymously abandoned baby or child was successfully traced back to a disgruntled foster parent, there were seldom any punitive consequences and the placement in the Findel often stood. After Hans Apfelbach and his wife moved to Prague, their child "was taken by its foster mother to the house of a third party, Margretha Suess, and left on the table." In this instance, rather than return the child to its abandoning foster mother, the council accepted the child into the Findel and ordered bailiffs to keep an eye out for Apfelbach if he returned.[143] In 1626 two small children left in a shopping basket at the market were similarly traced back to an abandoning foster mother and a year later a three-year-old child found on the doorstep of patrician Philip Harseldorffer was similarly connected to "a foster mother who couldn't get any more money." Shortly thereafter the latter child's mother returned to reclaim her child and after questioning was released, along with the foster mother, without punishment.[144] This didn't mean that the council passively encouraged this riskier type of child circulation. When Margretha Kreull's petition for the Findel to take her foster child was denied, she was told "she should take it up with those who vouched for the promised fostering money," to which the council—anticipating her reaction to the rebuff—added "not to abandon the child, since [they] will know how to find her."[145]

Fostering relatives appear to have been less likely to publicly abandon unwanted children in their care but occasionally—as in the instances of Margretha Widmenin (Introduction) and Georg Baur—they too chose this desperate form of child circulation.[146] In every instance, the Nuremberg council strove to place the child privately whenever possible, even if that meant returning it to an apparently irresponsible or at least unwilling adult. Whether Georg himself abandoned his three sisters in their house or merely denied his relationship to them when first contacted, he knew that the Findel would be compelled to accept the girls—at least until his ruse was discovered. Even impoverished grandparents might anonymously abandon a child, hopeful of a better home for their charge. In 1643 a three-year-old girl was found wandering the streets and immediately taken to the Findel, where she identified herself as Helena Sophia Kremerin from Regensburg. After initial inquiries, the council discovered that Helena Sophia's grandmother, Maria Petermänin, lived in Nuremberg and even though she was the likely abandoner, the child was returned "back to [Petermänin's] house" and the grandmother was granted a weekly stipend "so that she could raise [the girl] until she was old enough to be placed in service."[147] In a case of more naïve and optimistic honesty, a baby was found by a city gate in 1626 with note from its grandfather, Jörg Dressel, who humbly apologized that his son was away and that he was too poor to care for the child. The boy was promptly returned to him and he was instructed either to raise the child himself or to send it to his son.[148] Though relatively low-risk, this form of circulation appears to have generally been a last resort for relatives entrusted with a child.[149]

The second instance of governmental involvement occurred when a biological or foster parent formally petitioned the city council for temporary care of a child by the Findel. Requests of this kind accounted for about one in five of all petitions to the Findel.[150] In more than half such cases, the grounds were serious illness of one or both parents, usually requiring internment in the hospital or one of the city's pesthouses. The second most common reason given was general poverty, with varying specific circumstances. Ex officio fostering by the Findel, typically involving the children of banished or executed criminals, constituted the third and least common type of foster petition.[151] Roughly one-third of all foster petitions were initiated by parents themselves, one-third by governmental employees, and one-third by others (usually not specified as friends or relatives). Stoffel's failure to pursue this option was probably based on his status as a foreigner but his gender likely played a role as well. Again, the shameful concession of asking for help was too much for many fathers to handle. Mothers were much more likely than fathers to seek assistance of this type from the Findel, four times more so in cases where illness was not involved.[152] Hans Mayr had to make the humiliating request for help on behalf of his struggling brother-in-law Friederich Herdeger and his three children, only one of whom—after a thorough financial investigation of Herdeger's debts and assets—was ultimately admitted into the Findel.[153]

The most striking aspect of foster petitions to the Findel is the consistently ad hoc character they sustained throughout more than a century of practice, demonstrating that Nuremberg parents rarely intended them to be long-term child care solutions. Most frequently, particularly during epidemic years, the Findel accepted children for residence "until the parent(s) recovered." Other needs were also framed in temporary terms. In December 1572, Hans Apelshunder's two children were accepted into the Findel "until the weather changes" and indeed upon the arrival of spring, the two boys "were sent out of the home."[154] During an especially generous era, a widower-father could ask the Findel to take his two boys until he remarried; after winning approval, he returned three months later, freshly wedded, and reclaimed them.[155] Only nonparent petitioners tended to make their petitions more open-ended, promising to reclaim the child in two to three years, or more generally "when it is old enough to earn its own bread."[156] Just as significantly, the great majority of these foster petitioners kept their word, usually reclaiming their children within one year, or in the case of recuperated parents, three months. Only death of the parent or the child— also within a year—regularly stymied the planned reunions.[157]

Overall, 95 percent of all fostering petitions to the Findel were granted, ranging from virtually automatic approval in the case of ill or banished parents to 88.9 percent acceptance of petitions for other reasons, usually on account of poverty. That said, foster petitions clearly had a short-lived golden age in Nuremberg, from about 1565 to 1614, with the biggest surge during the famines and epidemics of the early 1570s (see fig. 2.10). In 1615, when the number of successful petitions began to decline precipitously, Cunrad Braun's petition to have his daughter's daughter accepted into the Findel met with the response that "the Findel is not intended for such children. He should thus take care that this child be raised without my lords' support," and that if he brought her back to the Findel, she would be banished from the city with her mother.[158] The following year, poor widow Christina Gshaf-

Fig. 2.9. Pieter Brueghel the Younger, *The Alchemist* (1558), detail. Berlin Kupfer-stichkabinett. Poor parents hand three small children over to a municipal hospital.

fin's petition was likewise turned down and she was instead granted an annual stipend of 10 fl. for her two young children.[159] In fact, although the acceptance rate for discretionary foster cases dipped somewhat after 1615, it was really the decline in the number of petitions submitted in this area that accounts for most of the drop. The degree to which this decline was influenced by a new conciliar policy is something to be discussed in the next chapter.[160]

The final and most common way that governmental authorities became directly involved in child circulation was through instances of forced foster-ing and public abandonment. Did Stoffel literally drop his three daughters on his son's doorstep or was there some sort of previous understanding between the two, which Georg no longer wished to acknowledge or honor? The extant sources cannot resolve this pivotal question but they can suggest how relatively more common this course of action was among biological and foster parents who involved the government in their travails. Whether out of low social capital, ignorance, pride, laziness, or malice, at least 1,000 children were allegedly foisted on people who in some way prompted gov-

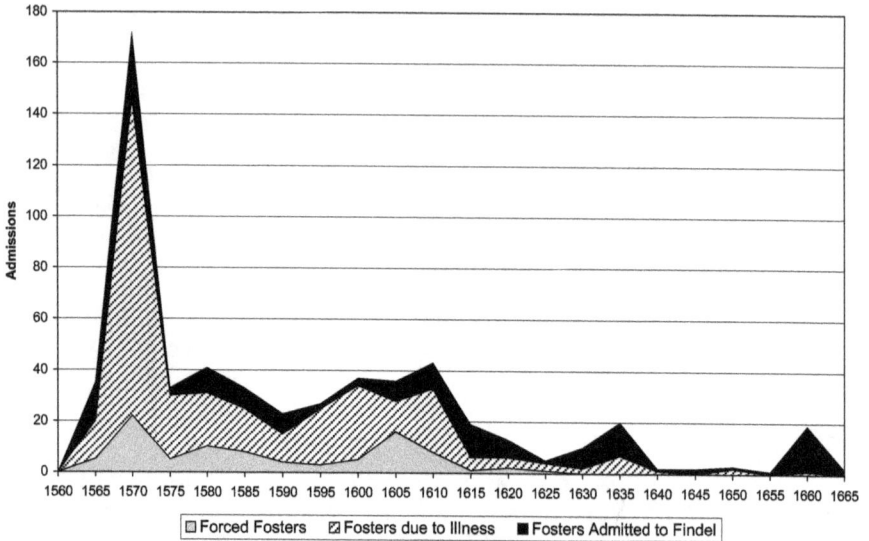

Fig. 2.10. Total foster admissions to the Nuremberg Findel, 1550–1669 (five-year totals; n = 576).

ernmental involvement between 1557 and 1670.[161] Most of these infants and small children ended up in Findel care, since neither parents nor relatives could be identified or located.

The majority of petitioners in such cases were apparently strangers to the departing parents. Only one in twelve admitted knowing the abandoner, though some might have lied to avoid getting stuck with the child.[162] Typically they claimed to have stumbled across a child in a public spot, such as a hospital or hospice, church, marketplace, tavern, or busy street corner.[163] Usually children found in this matter were handed over anonymously to an archer or other municipal employee, but in some instances alert functionaries insisted that discoverers accompany them and the children to the Findel, where their statements could be written down. Occasionally there was a delay of a few hours or even days before contacting authorities. In 1663 a tailor in nearby Glockenhof took in a newborn baby found on Christmas Eve night and cared for it a few days with his wife before asking local bailiff to get it into the Findel.[164] Often forced fostering resulted from hospitality offered to a stranger in need. On a December night in 1569 a "strange and sickly" woman came into suburban Thon with her two small girls and was put up by the local healer; the next morning she had died "and left nothing other than the two children, as she had been a poor shepherd's wife."[165]

Leaving a child at a private residence was the riskiest choice for a fleeing biological or foster parent, resulting in their identification nearly half the time.[166] The odds were better than 4:1 in Stoffel's favor that he would not be identified if he left the girls in a public building or on a street and 14:1 that he would not be caught leaving them in front of the Findel, yet only one in seven abandoners chose this much safer option.[167] One explanation for this tendency is a general unwillingness to expose a child to the many dangers of being left unattended in the street, especially during harsh weather. Indirect evidence suggests that many outside abandonments were made by unwilling foster parents rather than the biological parents (the one major exception being unwed mothers of newborns, where the Findel and other public buildings were preferred). In some instances, children were "left sitting" (*sizen lassen*) alone in their own homes, as were apparently the three Baur girls. According to scythe maker Heinrich Hirshlag, his journeyman Steffan Kraft moved out in the middle of the night, leaving all four children behind in his house.[168] More typically, relatives, friends, or acquaintances of various kinds were involved, though again the degree of coercion involved is difficult to ascertain from our perspective. An obliging neighbor who agreed to look after a friend's child for a few hours eventually learned that the mother had left town to join her soldier-husband, at which point the dismayed Good Samaritan contacted governmental authorities.[169]

Another reason for preferring a private residence to a safer public site to abandon children was the relative lack of negative consequences if identified. Even if he did not have some prior agreement with his son Georg about raising the girls (which Georg chose to disregard), he was well aware of how toothless early modern laws against child abandonment truly were. Article 132 of the Carolina prescribed corporal or capital punishment for abandonment, depending on the circumstances. In actual practice, such people were rarely apprehended or punished, even in exceptionally vigilant Nuremberg, where perpetrators like Stoffel were identified in more than half of all forced foster and anonymous abandonment cases.[170] As might be expected, there was moreover a gender double standard, where those few unmarried mothers caught in the act of abandonment were flogged and banished with their babies, while married men (and women) merely had their children returned to them, often with "stern words." In one unusually strict response, Hans Kreuselman's abandoning wife and her lover were both arrested and put in irons upon their return to Nuremberg, but even here her children were ultimately restored to the mother.[171] On this last point, Nuremberg's magistrates across the centuries were of one mind: if biological parents and children could ever be reunited, the council would gladly wash its hands of both, regardless of a parent's previous behavior.

Stoffel Baur likely knew that his actions could have no serious consequences for him should he ever return to Nuremberg, at the very worst suffering brief imprisonment and a lecture before being saddled again with his unwanted children (whom he could just as readily leave again). A few months after the Baur girls were abandoned in 1615, another small child was found alone in the same suburban slum of Gostenhof. Again, the council's very first instinct was to track down the abandoning father and restore his children to him. Unfortunately, the boy's identification of his father and hometown did little good, since "'Laughing Hans' [now] roams as a beggar" and thus remained outside of authorities' reach. Like the soldier Stoffel Baur, Hans was threatened in absentia with brief imprisonment upon return but even then his custody of the boy would never be in doubt.[172] One absconding father who was tracked down a few weeks after abandoning his daughter in 1618 had her returned to him and even "out of sympathy, [was] given a Findel stipend, with the warning not to abandon the child in the future or he will be seriously punished."[173] Another who had left his girls unattended for seven weeks also had his children promptly restored to him with no legal consequences whatsoever.[174]

There has been much historical speculation about the intentions of abandoning parents such as Stoffel Baur in respect to the Findel and other foundling homes. Many scholars of the early modern period have found evidence that poor parents routinely gave their children to state institutions temporarily, either as foundlings or foster children, fully intending to bring them back home once the household crisis had abated. "Do not take a fancy to this little girl," a note left with a foundling might say, indicating the parent's obvious intention to reclaim soon.[175] At first glance it seems as though some parents might have considered the Nuremberg Findel in just these terms. Among those forced foster or anonymously abandoned children whose nature of departure from the Findel is known, 16.5 percent of boys and 14.9 percent of girls were eventually picked up by their parents—twice the reclamation rate of contemporary homes in Florence and Lisbon.[176] These figures are deceptive, though, since the ultimate fate of two-thirds of nonorphans admitted to the Nuremberg Findel remains unknown, and the actual number of children confirmed to have been picked up over the course of 114 years—73 total or 1.6 per year—could hardly be characterized as a significant social trend.[177] Not until the "great century of child abandonment," from about 1750 to 1850, would this become a significant and discernible parental strategy anywhere in Europe, with retrieval rates of 25–30 percent in some Italian foundling homes.[178] In short, the overwhelming preference of all parties in early modern Nuremberg—biological parents, foster parents, and magistrates—remained informal child circulation and private placement.

Domestic Enemies

The most difficult assessment of all is the state of Stoffel Baur's affections and emotions when he left his three daughters sitting in their house. For some modern observers, such actions merely provide evidence of the coldhearted indifference of premodern parenthood.[179] With no direct statement from Stoffel or others like him, we must instead rely on the indirect evidence to the contrary, that is, the fact that the great majority of biological and foster parents took pains to place their children with other adults they thought capable of caring for them—relatives, friends, prosperous neighbors, or the Findel itself—and only a small minority made no provisions whatsoever. Even Stoffel, the archetypal absent father, probably thought that he was leaving his children in their older brother's capable care. Whether this action was indicative of parental love, by any standards, is unanswerable. At the very least, the Black Legend of premodern parent-child relationships requires much more unambiguous evidence to posit such a qualitative transformation over the intervening centuries.

There is, on the other hand, some indirect evidence that child circulation, particularly in the form of anonymous abandonment, was more common among stepparents. The disaffected and even evil stepparent has been a literary topos since at least Roman antiquity. Fairy tale stepparents, particularly stepmothers, certainly seemed eager to get rid of their dead spouses' children—by whatever means necessary. In the Grimms' "Hansel and Gretel," the stepmother (originally the biological mother) merely convinces her husband to commit passive infanticide, stranding their children in the center of a dense forest. In other stories stepparents murder children outright, sometimes in most grisly fashion.[180] Most people apparently considered such enmity a common occurrence. In a section of his "Marriage Mirror" devoted to childbeating, the sixteenth-century religious author Cyrakius Spangenberg makes the passing comment: "Each of us knows some strange types (*wunderliche Köpffe*)—found most often among stepfathers and stepmothers—who vent their bad tempers on helpless children or take out on them their vicious resentment of the care they are obliged to give them."[181] A contemporary Spanish proverb was even more succinct: *Madastra, el nombre la basta*—"Stepmother, the name says it all."[182]

Historians have too often taken this cultural stereotype of cruel stepparents to heart, but there does appear to be some historical basis for such beliefs. Before the nineteenth century, perhaps one-third of all children would lose at least one parent (more often the father) by the age of ten, resulting in a high number of single-parent households as well as a preponderance of stepparents.[183] Given the frequent disparity in ages between spouses as well as the general life expectancy and rapid remarriage (especially among widowers), some children might even end up being raised by two stepparents (e.g., the man who married their widowed mother and the woman he married after their birth mother died).[184] As in the modern West, where high divorce rates have made stepparents almost as common as in early modern Europe, there were inevitably antagonistic and even violent relationships that fit the stereotype.

It is also suggestive—and surprising, given the prominence of stepparents in everyday experience—that while godparents were consistently treated as kin, stepparents were hardly ever considered so. One stepmother's 1665 request typically referred to her late husband's offspring as "fatherless and motherless children, for whom not a single relative [*freund*] or godparent who could help them was available."[185] Some (perhaps even many) of the children considered orphans by the Findel actually had stepparents who were unwilling or unable to keep them. It is hard to be precise since stepparents were often able to stay in the background and let children's legal guardians do the actual petitioning. During the summer of 1613, for instance, the two guardians of Friedrich Herben's two orphans petitioned to get the children admitted to the Findel; only after three weeks of negotiation did the guardians acknowledge the existence of a stepfather who might be able to take one child (as he eventually did).[186] A few years later, the two guardians of Hans Ströbel's eight children tried to get his four youngest "orphans" into the Findel, and again the town council found out late about a stepparent who was forced to accept a stipend instead.[187] Some stepparents could be quite persistent: over the course of eight months in 1584 and 1585, the stepmother of Hanns Rucker's three children systematically placed each of her charges in the Findel.[188] On the other hand, the stepfather of Barbara Herbin's two sons had a last-minute change of mind and upon approval of his petition to the Findel decided to keep one of the children with him at home.[189]

Certainly there are also examples of abuse and abandonment by stepparents in Nuremberg's official records, though not to an inordinate degree.[190] The most infamous case of stepmother abandonment in early modern Nuremberg was undoubtedly in 1650, when a six-year-old boy wandering the city's streets was picked up by officials and taken to the Findel. Like Hansel and Gretel, young Georg Schäfer had been taken by his stepmother deep into a Bavarian forest and left there to fend for himself. Eventually he made his way out of the woods (there is no mention of bread crumbs or pebbles) and he was picked up by some cartmen on the road to Nuremberg, who in turn dropped him off at a city gate. For six months, magistrates endeavored in vain to track down and punish the stepmother, relaxing their efforts only when another female relative came forward and picked up the boy the following spring.[191]

Stepparents were also believed more likely to sell children, an ancient form of child circulation that apparently survived in some form into early modern times. During the Middle Ages, the practice was not only permitted but often perceived as indicative of parental concern for the children they were unable to support themselves. The thirteenth-century Schwabenspiegel, an influential legal code in southern Germany, specifically permitted the sale of children, adding only the restriction that the child should not be sold to someone who might kill or prostitute him; many local versions specified Jews and beggars.[192] Not until the 1532 Carolina was the practice prohibited altogether but even then the distinction between an outright sale and a negotiated "apprenticeship" was often blurred.[193] In 1665, for instance, Nuremberg's city councilors were scandalized to learn of the alleged sale of some children to a musketeer in a local tavern, but once the accused sellers produced some certified apprenticeship documents signed by the boys' parents they were released and merely warned to register all such future transactions with the municipal crafts bureau.[194] During the seventeenth century, similar forms of disguised impressments were not uncommon, though by no means limited to stepparents or other foster parents.

That other closely related topos of premodern folk tales that continues to haunt modern imaginations is the outright murder of children by stepparents or their own biological parents. Had he been apprehended and reproached as a bad father, Stoffel Baur could have retorted that at least he didn't kill any of his own offspring—undeniably the most extreme form of parental rejection. Here too the imaginary bent of many historical accounts of child killing casts some doubt on its actual frequency in premodern Europe. Fantastic stories of parents eating their own children in times of siege or pestilence—of dubious veracity in ancient and medieval chronicles— had virtually vanished by the late Middle Ages, but lurid accounts of the child feasts of witches and Jews continued to flourish well into the eighteenth century.[195] Infanticide was also a relatively common occurrence in early modern plays and other fictions. Is this possibly another instance of a popular literary topos distorting our perception of the historical reality?

Clearly some parents did intentionally kill some of their own children.

Neonatacide, as seen in chapter 1, was widely perceived to be a common practice, particularly in the countryside, and it almost certainly did take place at a greater incidence than successful prosecutions would suggest. Unlike single women, married women were not required to register their pregnancies or in any other way subjected to official surveillance and thus—with or without the support of their husbands—they could terminate unwanted pregnancies and infants with relative impunity. No one can know how many of the numerous baby and toddler deaths recorded as stillbirths and accidental bed smotherings were in fact intentional, any more than any governmental authority could detect or prosecute the more psychologically ambiguous crime of withholding or limiting nourishment from a baby.[196] Perhaps Lawrence Stone was right, that among some poor families with scant food resources, investment in weak or sickly infants might have been considered a luxurious indulgence and thus passive infanticide at an early age hardly viewed as a crime or sin. As in cases of infant abandonment, there could be a range of circumstances and parental self-justifications, ranging from mercifully ending an infant's suffering to economic need and self-preservation to mental instability or sheer malice. Like abortions and miscarriages, most smothering and deprivation cases would have appeared to early modern forensic medicine as natural occurrences (albeit occasionally suspicious ones). Neighbors might even formally question, as in the case of Elisabetha Greiffin, just what happened to her vanished children, but proving something other than the parent's plausible explanation was quite another matter.[197] Perhaps the most to be said on this subject is that passive and active infanticide were by no means limited to single mothers and illegitimate newborns and that both practices were not unheard of in the general population.

The only descriptive information of this phenomenon in early modern Europe (other than fairy tales) comes from those relatively few cases of parental murder that made it into the criminal justice system and the popular press. Nuremberg's infanticide convictions reflect the near invisibility of the active or passive murder of legitimate children, with only three confirmed cases of married women killing their own offspring during the entire period 1508–1806—a rarity typical throughout the empire.[198] In a fourth case, a farmer was arrested on suspicion of having murdered his stepchild and actually confessed to the crime during torture, at which point "God immediately provided a visible sign [of his guilt]" and the suspect fell dead, presumably of a heart attack.[199] In at least two of these instances, the crimes only came to light because of the relatively advanced age of the children (six years old and two years old) as well as the public nature of the murder (stabbing repeat-

Figure 2.11. The cover illustration of a broadsheet account of Jörg Kleck's 1561 strangling of his pregnant wife and two small children, followed by his own suicide (*right*). His corpse was subsequently dragged through the streets of Schaffhausen and later burned (*left*). Germanisches Nationalmuseum, Nürnberg.

edly at home and drowning amid a crowd of onlookers, respectively). This type of self-incrimination is also evident in the many domestic killings described by the sensationalist press in German lands.[200] For this very reason, neither literary nor legal sources can enlighten us much about the unknown number of parental child murderers who chose more subtle methods of killing. They can, however, reveal a great deal about the actual and imagined motives of murderous parents in general.

As today, such horrific acts often confounded ready explanation and divided those who learned of them as to the degree of moral responsibility and mental stability involved. Published accounts of child murders, predictably dwelling on the gory details, attempted to make the events both comprehensible and morally instructive. In this respect they bore striking resemblance to the later didactic fairy tales of the Brothers Grimm, speaking as much to popular perceptions and ascribed motives as to factual events and testimony. Men who murdered their children and wives, for instance, invariably were thought to have done so out of some combination of drunkenness, financial irresponsibility, and diabolical possession (see fig. 2.11). In 1599 a Silesian butcher and father of six supposedly spent all of the household's income on drink; when his virtuous wife reproached him he went on a rampage with a meat cleaver, slaughtering the entire family.[201] Obviously, the pamphlet's many dialogues were contrived and there were many other examples of poetic license, such as the 1607 account of a drunken father who supposedly murdered his pregnant wife, five children, and eighteen other people—all in one night.[202]

At least the murdering father's perceived failures as head of the household provided some credible explanation for the outburst of violence against his children and spouse. Male writers found the motives of murdering mothers, by contrast, decidedly more difficult to decipher, and thus proffered vague suggestions of melancholy as well as the all-purpose explanation of satanic influence. In a 1596 tale, a pregnant mother who poured pitch into her husband's mouth while he slept, wrung the neck of her youngest child, stabbed the second despite its cries and pleas, split the head of the four-year-old with an axe, then crushed her unborn child and hanged herself, was merely said to be "possessed by rage."[203] Interestingly, the tract's author also used the story as a moral lesson for pregnant women to beware of their own mood swings, which the devil would readily use against them. Sixteenth-century physicians and some laypeople were generally aware of the emotional fluctuations often brought on by pregnancy and birth, and medical experts had even identified postpartum depression (*puepera phrenitica*) as a real and dangerous phenomenon, urging similar caution.[204]

Neither medical nor moral circumstances, though, could fully account for the "unnaturalness" of such "heartless" acts of extreme violence against innocent children, and thus diabolical influence of some sort inevitably came into the picture. Typically the devil "took possession" (a consistently ambiguous phrase) only with the first killing. His presence might be presaged, however, in ungodly behavior of the future murderer or occasionally through actual appearances where he offered gambling fathers help with their debts, only to see them fall ever deeper under his influence. This common emphasis on the vulnerability of all men and women to the snares of the "evil enemy" distinguished German literature from contemporary English fare, which generally sought more psychologically sophisticated motives for child murder.[205] Accordingly, German pamphlets also dwelt more on the innocence of slaughtered children and their pitiful pleas for mercy. One account, reported by the Lutheran pastor Burckhard Waldis, tells of a mother who inexplicably hacks her four children to bits while her husband is at work. As she turns on her last child, he pathetically pleads:

> "O dearest Mother mine
> Spare me, I'll do whate'er thou'lt say:

I'll carry for thee from today
The Water the whole winter through,
O please don't kill me! Spare me, do!"
But no plea helped, it was in vain,
The devil did her will maintain.
She struck him with the self-same dread
As if it were a cabbage head.[206]

The key difference between German legal and literary evidence is the significance of the household's poverty in the murdering parent's decision. German literature, in contrast to elsewhere in Europe, was especially frank on the economic burden of children. In one account of a domestic killing spree, the fictitious dialogue has a child acknowledging such: "O Father, let me live! No longer needst thou food or drink / Or bread for school me give!"[207] Even in a child-murder case in which poverty played no role, the economic burden of children is clearly acknowledged. When sixteenth-century matron Anna Strölin was convicted of killing her young son, she made a point of saying that her life was quite comfortable and that there was no economic factor in her decision.[208] Still, Strölin's very mention of financial strain as a possible motive, as well as authorities' inability to detect purposeful child smothering and other more subtle murders, suggests that we are only viewing the tip of an iceberg of unknown dimensions.

A Father's Choices

The stereotype of the absconding house father, like many enduring stereotypes, continues to be popular because it is grounded on a few undeniable facts, namely, the relative frequency of disappearing fathers among poor families and the obvious destabilizing effects on the households left behind. That such extended paternal absences generally stimulated child circulation in some form is likewise indisputable. When situated within the broader context of early modern society, however, the actual circumstances and thinking of absconding fathers such as Stoffel Baur suggest a reality that is far more nuanced than might be expected.

First there is the common assumption about agency, that men of Stoffel's background had few options to begin with and were thus predisposed toward desertion. It is true that the fate of poor households was often determined by larger forces outside their members' control—epidemics, crippling accidents, chronic unemployment, wars, inflation, and so on. These and other demographic factors meant that there was a particularly high number of widows and widowers with children, as well as a large number of stepparents, thus potentially an equally high number of deserted or otherwise unwanted children. The evidence from Nuremberg has also demonstrated, however, that it is categorically erroneous to assume that poor fathers or mothers in such situations had few or no resources for coping with the financial or emotional hardship of small children. Odd jobs, begging, petty crime, and perhaps government assistance were all means employed by parents in straits similar to Stoffel's for keeping their households intact—not to mention nonfinancial help of diverse kinds from neighbors, relatives, and other friends. Many poor fathers were admittedly adamant about being self-reliant, but this attitude rarely precluded perhaps the most important coping mechanism of all, namely, child circulation.[209] Whether short-term or long-term, child care by nonbiological parents was an essential for struggling parents with children, be they roaming mercenaries, mothers working outside the home, or seriously ill or disabled parents. The foster parents might be friends or strangers and money may or may not have changed hands, but the phenomenon was clearly as widespread as any other coping mechanism of poor households, including child begging. A mercenary outsider like Stoffel Baur might have had much less social capital to draw on than other widowers with children, but he was by no means economically compelled to leave his children behind with no provision whatsoever.

The second popular but problematic assumption is that, in a city with a foundling home and sophisticated poor-relief system, a departing father or mother would be more likely to hand children over to a state institution. To the contrary, biological parents, foster parents, and governmental officials in Nuremberg all labored extensively to make the informal version of child circulation work, so that the Findel did not have to get involved unless absolutely necessary. Even Stoffel chose not to anonymously abandon his girls to the city's care, presumably to ensure that they would be cared for by their brother and his wife. Foster petitions to the Findel on behalf of ill parents—usually during citywide epidemics—were generally granted but were relatively few in number, mostly within a sixty-year period, and rarely resulted in a child staying in the Findel for more than one year. Only in cases of anonymous abandonment or if a foster parent (such as Georg Baur) claimed coercion did Nuremberg's city council willingly get involved and even then one or more of the children in question might very likely remain where they were or stay only briefly at the Findel—as was indeed the final result for the Baur girls. Or more precisely, this was the last destination recorded for Margareth, Apollonia, and Annalein, since it is likely that one or more was circulated elsewhere by their brother Georg. We cannot know whether their new home was a happy one for them, but their foster placement must be judged another success of the informal child circulation system, an amorphous process so efficacious that during the sixteenth and seventeenth centuries in Nuremberg, the Findel saw on yearly average fewer than fifteen unwanted children who had at least one living parent.

The greatest historian of the early modern poor has characterized people like the Baurs as being of "limited ambition . . . hop[ing] to make out, no more," and expecting very little help from anyone. "Poverty," Olwen Hufton also noted, "is acid: it corrodes and dissolves human relationships."[210] The story of Stoffel Baur, however, shows that deprivation did not always dissolve human bonds to the degree that Hufton assumed, and to the contrary poor parents with children regularly displayed the "bounce back qualities" that she so admired in the poor, drawing on more social resources than might have been presumed available.[211] Stoffel Baur faced a number of economic and cultural restraints that are completely alien to most members of a modern, affluent society, but his reliance on a relative to care for his young children is timeless. Whatever his immediate motivation in leaving them behind, he is in at least that respect not quite as alien a figure as he might first have appeared.

THREE

The Beleaguered Magistrate

At the beginning of 1635, perhaps the darkest hour in the Nuremberg Findel's history, city councilor and Findel administrator Albrecht Pömer assessed the institution's predicament. Since the outbreak of the Thirty Years' War in 1618, Nuremberg's leaders had attempted to steer a precarious path of official neutrality in the conflict. Given the city's widespread Protestant sympathies and the cost of "contributions" to both warring sides, that policy proved disastrously expensive and ultimately impossible to maintain. The turning point came in March 1632, when cheering crowds welcomed Swedish king Gustavus Adolphus through the city's gates. Fewer than three months later the imperial armies of Wallenstein, some 60,000 strong, set foot in Franconia. While Nuremberg troops hastened to shore up the city's walls and other defenses, as many as 25,000 refugees and their farm animals poured into the city from as far away as 100 miles, quickly overwhelming food supplies and available housing and filling the streets and alleys with massive human and animal waste. The ensuing "great stink" was a trivial consequence compared to the disease nourished by such conditions. Within a month, the first of three epidemics hit the city's population, ultimately resulting in over 10,000 corpses hauled outside the city's walls and thrown into mass graves or sometimes left unburied. A second wave of plague in 1634 left some 17,000 dead, including eleven city councilors, fourteen pastors, and eleven schoolteachers.[1]

Meanwhile a great many (perhaps a few thousand) orphaned or otherwise parentless children and youths roamed Nuremberg's streets. Between 1633 and 1637, the Findel admitted almost five hundred children, 294 just in the twelve months from June 1634 to May 1635, including four groups of 10–70 children each rounded up by the city's begging police.[2] Living conditions at the home accordingly deteriorated, as a building constructed to

Fig. 3.1. Albrecht Pömer at the age of fifty-seven
(1654). Stadtarchiv Nürnberg.

house at most 90 children was at times forced to accommodate more than
twice that number, with children literally sleeping on top of one another.
Merely feeding so many mouths was an enormous undertaking, but it paled
before the prospect of preventing contagion from wiping out most of the
Findel's young charges at one blow. Finding apprenticeships or maid positions for the Findel's older children appeared just as daunting, given the dire
economic situation of the city. Were Pömer and his staff up to such fearsome challenges? What would be the consequences for the city's unwanted
children if they were not?

The devastating war and plague years of 1632–39 constituted the worst
and most sustained economic, demographic, and political crisis in Nuremberg's nine-hundred-year history. Albrecht Pömer's challenge as Findel administrator was formidable, but it was extraordinary only in terms of the
number of children affected and the creative coping methods employed. In
Nuremberg, the magisterial tradition of patriarchal responsibility for such
pitiable castoffs of society dated back at least to the fourteenth century, and

by the sixteenth century it had taken on the form of a legal crusade. Fueled by a merger of traditional patrician sense of duty with Lutheran and humanist visions of the just civic order, ambitious reformers like Pömer attempted to eliminate child begging, provide for the education and placement of citizens' children, and effectively deter child abandonment and infanticide through rigorous law enforcement and sometimes harsh punishment. Goals of this magnitude were virtually unprecedented among European states and in many ways anticipated the aspirations and methods of much later nation-states. Their methods, meanwhile, remained fairly conservative, particularly in their strong preference for informal child circulation, with institutional care for unwanted children a last resort. The result was a mixed success. To grasp the significance of this typically early modern mixture of innovative social reforms and traditional bureaucratic methods, we must begin with the nature of all magisterial responsibility and action.

Patrician Paternalism

Albrecht Pömer's fierce dedication to Nuremberg had deep and ancient roots, though among his fellow patricians this was importantly a matter of degree. The Pömers were not among the fifty-seven patrician families listed as "council-eligible" (*Ratsfähig*) in the city's earliest documents from the thirteenth century, nor were they one of the twelve families declared eligible to serve on the Nuremberg council in 1318. In fact the Pömers were not listed as *Nobiles Norimbergenses* until relatively late, in 1395.[3] That still gave them seniority over the twenty-eight clans that joined the civic elect over the course of the next century. Most importantly they made the last official cut in 1521. That year, Nuremberg's city council issued its famous "dance ordinance," officially limiting the number of families who could partake in formal dances at the town hall and by implication be eligible to serve on the small council. By then, many of the "oldest dynasties" had died out or emigrated, and only twenty families remained. In addition to these, the dance ordinance further recognized seven "new" families (that is, admitted after 1385), including the Pömers, as well as fifteen houses "just admitted" (since 1440), making a grand total of forty-two council-eligible families. Nuremberg's dance ordinance was much more restrictive than Venice's closed oligarchy of two hundred families and it also came quite late (Venice's list dated from 1297). This endogamy of power, moreover, became even narrower over the course of the next century, with fifteen patrician families dying out by the time of Albrecht Pömer.[4] Not surprisingly, Nuremberg's inner council was widely known (and often envied) for its remarkable stability, continuity, and overall conservativeness in the face of much political and religious tumult.

The political privilege of so few families was based of course on their exceptional wealth.[5] Like many prominent local dynasties, the Pömer fortune dated back several centuries to mercantile and banking success, in their case with the Hanseatic League in Pomerania (whence the family name). At the beginning of the seventeenth century, only four hundred and sixteen households, 5 percent of Nuremberg's population, claimed property worth more than 5000 fl., or over four hundred times the annual wages of a manual laborer. Many of these households, including Albrecht Pömer's, had assets worth more than twice that amount.[6] The large living that usually went with such social status was often staggering. During the mid-sixteenth century, patrician Wilhelm Imhof spent almost 200 fl. annually on wine and beer alone and another 250 fl. on clothing for his family, together equivalent to the annual wages of thirty-five manual laborers.[7]

Preserving high social rank or possibly even climbing up a few rungs on the patrician ladder required extensive, virtually complete, endogamy. Just as their royal and aristocratic counterparts, Nuremberg's patricians were constantly searching for new and beneficial family alliances through marriage within a small circle of eligible mates. As the number of marital prospects continued to decline over the sixteenth and seventeenth centuries, many wealthy Nurembergers increasingly looked to their own relatives for possible spouses. Albrecht Pömer's parents, for instance, were second cousins, with his mother a member of both the Löffelholz and Welser families, two prominent (albeit fellow "new") patrician houses. His own wife Barbara was a Pfinzing, one of the very oldest families in Nuremberg, and her father served as a juror on the municipal court with Albrecht.[8] Kinship among fellow council members was not only common but—given Nuremberg's closed patrician circle—inevitable.

Political power within that circle rested in a series of ever smaller concentric rings (see fig. 3.2). The principal civic body, the "large council," was composed of about three hundred "selected" men, drawn from both the patricians and common citizens. As might be expected in a rigidly hierarchical society, this assembly was mainly a deliberative body, consulted only occasionally on serious measures such as war and tax increases. For the most part, selection to the large council bestowed more personal honor than actual influence on its members. The much more powerful "small" or "inner council," which governed the city's daily affairs, was made up of forty-two individuals: eight common craftsmen (each representing a respective craft) and thirty-four patricians.

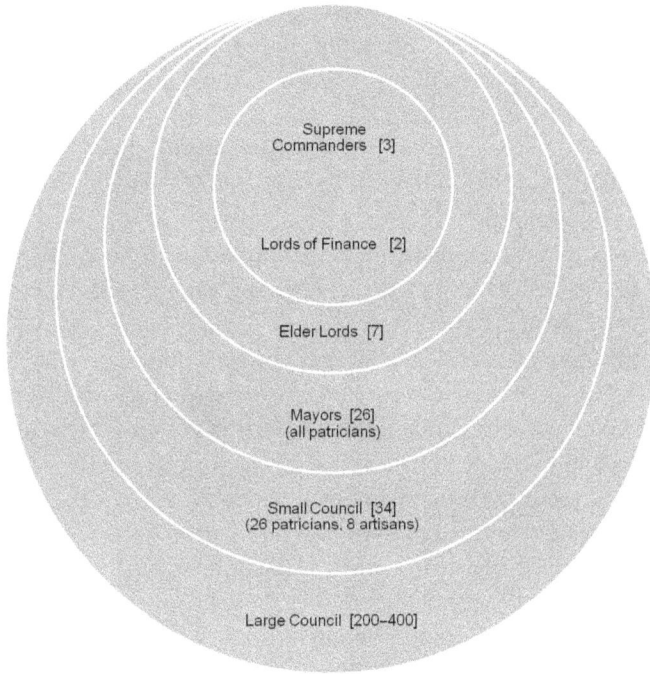

Fig. 3.2. Nuremberg's government (ca. 1600).

Within this group, thirteen "junior mayors" were annually selected from among the patricians and paired with thirteen "senior mayors" (also patricians); together each pair managed all council business during the four weeks of the year assigned to them.[9] During his twenty-eight days, the senior mayor would convene the inner council, put the questions, count the votes, and declare a council session over. He also sat with the seven Elders, also drawn from the forty-two patricians, when they met and he had the honor of receiving foreign dignitaries on the city's behalf. Traditionally, membership in the small council, though supposedly decided annually, was in effect a lifetime appointment, thereby reinforcing both the continuity and conservativeness of the council as a whole.[10]

The elite status of patricians as a group as well as the hierarchy within that group were both regularly reinforced by a series of civic rituals. Practically every public event, from religious festivals to Nuremberg's famed *Meistersinger* contests, provided the city's "first families" with an opportunity to assert their rank and privilege. Socializing among the patriciate meanwhile remained closed and restricted, whether dining in each other's homes or drinking in a private club, such as the *Herrentrinkenstube*, where patrician men gathered both to conduct business and to enjoy themselves.[11] As Thomas Brady has observed, the *Patriziat* of German imperial cities "was neither a class nor a caste, but it did have a social coherence."[12] The term itself was only just catching on in the Nuremberg of Albrecht Pömer; the more traditional way for social elites to refer to themselves was "honorable" (*ehrbare* or *honorabiliores*).

That emphasis on personal and familiar honor constituted the core of a patrician's self-identity as well as the chief motivation behind the prerogative to rule. Nuremberg's famed jurist Christopher Scheurl wrote with pride in 1516 that "the common folk have no power; it does not belong to their estate, since all power comes from God, and good government belongs only to those who have been endowed with special wisdom by the creator of all things and nature."[13] And Nuremberg's leaders would have likewise agreed with their Strasbourg counterparts that "He whom God has given riches also wants honor" and that service to one's *patria* was one of the surest ways to accumulate honor and glory.[14] Gatherings of the inner council of forty-two accordingly reflected patricians' close attention to hierarchy and honor. The body met in the appropriately ornate small council room in the heart of the magnificent town hall. The town hall itself was the very embodiment of civic dignity and authority, particularly after the fourteenth-century building was expanded at the beginning of the sixteenth century and later renovated in 1616–20 under the supervision of a famous Italian architect (see fig. 3.3). Within the small council chamber, each member of the inner council was assigned a seat based on the rank of his family, and the same prescribed hierarchy determined the order of speaking during a session (see fig. 3.4).[15]

Despite such apparent rigidity, the city council offered ambitious patricians such as Albrecht Pömer the possibility of still greater power and prominence among their peers. The rank of a public office might even outweigh the importance of a family's relative antiquity, providing considerable public prestige as well as greater financial compensation. At the top of the council hierarchy, the city's two finance lords accordingly had first place in all civic rituals and also earned the highest salaries, already 400 fl. by the beginning of the sixteenth century.[16] Next came the jurists, not patricians by birth but in recognition of their supreme learning paid 200 fl. per year and permitted to wear gold borders and lace on their garments and even to carry swords, like members of the nobility.[17] Each of the seven elders earned 100 fl. per year, and each council member was paid 50 pfennig per session attended (and fined 4 pfennig for each meeting missed). Of course these

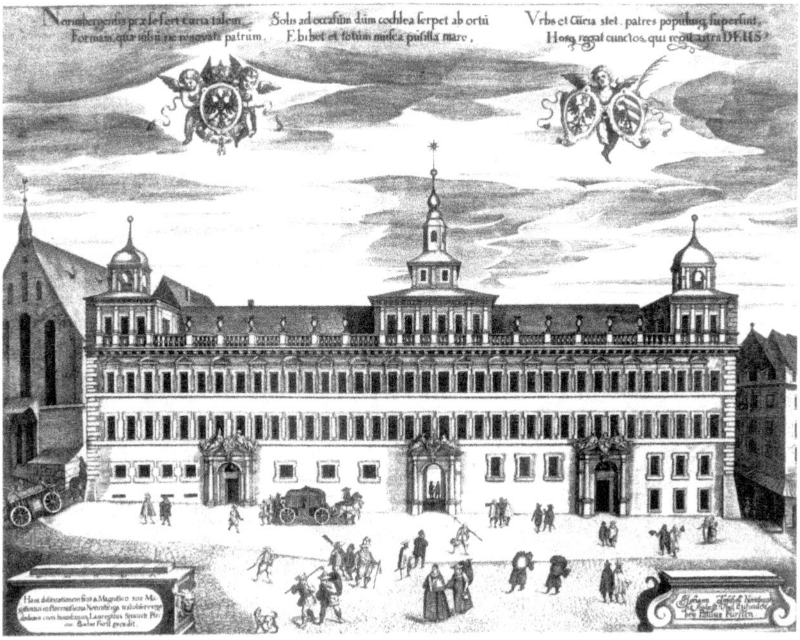

Fig. 3.3. Nuremberg's town hall, as seen from the west (ca. 1650). The main marketplace is just to the right (south) in this picture. Stadtarchiv Nürnberg.

salaries and fines were insignificant compared to the vast private fortunes involved. It was, rather, the greater honor associated with higher political rank that resulted in intense and sometimes bitter competition.

The considerable prestige bestowed by public office should not obscure the fact that such positions also usually imposed a significant burden in terms of time and personal expense. That genuine onus helps account for the pervasive sense of entitlement and self-righteousness Nuremberg's public leaders displayed, as well as their repeated invocations of hard work and self-discipline (see fig. 3.5). The inner council, for instance, met every day but Sunday and holidays, usually for sessions of at least three hours, often for the entire day. To this we must add at least as many hours in committee meetings and since every member of the inner council was also at some point in the year a mayor and in some instances a juror, still more hours of work. Most councilors also served on other public or private boards. In addition, all of these men paid high taxes and most contributed substantially to various charitable organizations. Yet on the whole they attempted some semblance of republican equality and moderation appropriate to a free imperial city, with large but moderately opulent houses and relatively small

Fig. 3.4. The meeting chamber of Nuremberg's inner council, with the seat of each patrician or artisan representative situated in a prescribed hierarchy (1677). Stadtarchiv Nürnberg.

Fig. 3.5. Nuremberg's magistrates carry the entire weight of the city on their shoulders, with the overhanging sword and scales symbolizing the key roles of force and justice in the execution of their duty (ca. 1600). Stadtbibliothek Nürnberg.

personal retinues. Most of Nuremberg's patricians continued to do their own annual wall and moat duty and otherwise mixed regularly with commoners in the city's markets and streets. They could be undeniably arrogant, hypocritical, and on occasion even brutal, but most of Nuremberg's political elite were also sober, diligent, and above all vigilant civic leaders.[18]

The emperor Ferdinand II (r. 1619–37) was said to have admiringly asked one Nuremberg councilor how he and his colleagues kept so populous a place in such good order. "With kind words and heavy penalties," came the typically laconic and somber response.[19] Early modern governance, particular in imperial cities, succeeded through the judicious combination of responsiveness to citizen concerns and consistent and expedient punishment of criminal transgressions, large and small. Had Nuremberg's magistrates been disproportionately concerned with either law enforcement or providing services, they would have been perceived as alternately tyrannical or pandering, in both instances effectively diminishing their authority and effectiveness. Hegemony over the citizenry, to the extent that it existed, depended as much on listening as on telling, on giving as well as taking.

The best illustration of this interdependence comes from our main source of documentation for the city, the council decrees (*Ratsverläße*). Throughout the sixteenth and seventeenth centuries, Nuremberg's councilors continued to hear or read petitions almost daily on a wide range of issues. From the modern bureaucratic perspective they were micromanagers, deciding not just questions about military fortifications and fiscal policy but also complaints about trash collection and street repairs, domestic disputes, religious practices, food preparation and prices, murder cases, grazing rights, and a thousand other topics both momentous and petty. Admittedly, the mayors on duty bore the brunt of the work on most petitions, but the other councilors remained involved in all binding decisions. The flow of proclamations, mandates, and ordinances that emanated from meetings of the small council thus represented not just the wishes of an isolated political elite but rather proposed solutions often shaped by the petitions themselves.

The interactive and often face-to-face nature of governance in Nuremberg should also dispel the common misperception of the inner council (or any early modern ruling body) as a distant, monolithic entity imposing its will on others. City-states such as Nuremberg are especially prone to such distortions, since all conciliar decisions were recorded and announced to the public as unanimous; dissenting arguments remained within the council chamber and are lost to history. Councilors' reasons for presenting a unified front to the public are easy to understand, as is the modern temptation to imagine their decisions in just these terms. The twenty-first-century observer must therefore make a deliberate effort to think of Pömer and his colleagues as individuals who—despite their common social background and frequent consensus—also had varying opinions on such issues as poverty and child welfare.[20]

The Making of a Civic Leader

Albrecht Pömer's life of public service was a model of patrician duty and honor. Upon his 1628 election to the small council at the age of thirty-one, he followed the traditional *cursus honorum* of a Nuremberg public leader. From 1628 to 1637, and later from 1643 until 1654, Pömer served as a juror on the city's criminal court (*Halsgericht*), helping to decide virtually every major case within that time period.[21] During all but six of the same twenty-six years, he also served as one of twenty-six monthly mayors, first as a junior and after 1639 as a senior member. His highest honor came in 1642, when he attained—at the age of forty-five—the rank of elder, an office second only to that of finance lord in prestige. After two years as an elder, Pömer returned to the ranks of the rotating mayors for another ten years. These duties alone would have consumed a considerable amount of time, but his sense of civic responsibility was expansive. During his public career, Pömer also served several terms as a guardianship and alms lord, a school superintendent, a delegate to the imperial court, and from March 1633 until his death in 1654 as administrator of the Findel. This last office had become a Pömer family tradition in 1573, when Albrecht's grandmother Anna, wife of the prominent Wolf Pömer IV, assumed the post. After her death in 1588, she was succeeded as Findel administrator by Wolf Pömer's second wife, Ursula (d. 1629), who upon her husband's death in 1603 was succeeded by Albrecht's father Jakob (1561–1607), followed in turn by Albrecht's first cousin once removed and his immediate predecessor, Hans Heinrich Pömer (1575–1633).[22]

By the time Albrecht Pömer joined Nuremberg's political elite in 1628, the city's days of economic and political preeminence within the empire were nearing an end. From the perspective of Pömer and his contemporaries, however, Nuremberg remained a supremely wealthy and influential urban republic. He and his magisterial colleagues fully appreciated the enormity of their responsibility, both for the roughly 100,000 souls within their regional jurisdiction and for the city's leadership in the major political and military struggles of the day.[23] Paternalistic concern for the city's poor and needy children was a particularly well-established tradition among civic leaders. As a child and young man Albrecht Pömer would have absorbed the ethos well from the many patrician leaders he encountered daily, including his own father Jakob, like his son an alms administrator, Findel administrator, and long-time member of the inner city council. This sense of noblesse oblige received vital reinforcement from the two most significant intellectual currents of the age, the Renaissance and the Reformation. For aspiring young Protestant politicians such as Albrecht, the principal site of convergence for these influences was the university. By the seventeenth century, virtually all members of Nuremberg's elite had a university education, many of them at prestigious foreign institutions. Albrecht began his study at the local academy (later university) of Altdorf, where his father was a member of the board of governors. From there he went on to the famed university at Heidelberg, following the conclusion of his studies with a leisurely six-year tour of the Netherlands, England, and France.[24] This kind of extended formative phase was unexceptional among patrician men and thus, like many of his colleagues, Albrecht was already married and in his thirties when he first assumed public office.

During his time at university and abroad, Pömer encountered numerous secular as well as religious justifications for paternalist governance and civic obligations toward the poor and neglected of a society. Most of the secular teachings about social order were the product of that complex phenomenon we now know as the Renaissance. And among those teachings, the most influential philosophical ideal for civic leaders such as Pömer was the notion of the *bonum publicum* (also *bonum commune; gemeiner nutz* in German), long translated into English as the "common weal" (whence commonwealth). The concept itself was an ancient one, revived during the fifteenth century by so-called civic humanist politicians, such as Florence's Coluccio Salutati and Leonardo Bruni. Nuremberg's 1478 legal codification, influential throughout Germany, was quite explicit on the magisterial duty "to the praise of God and the salutary and blessed increase of the common weal of this honorable city and the entire commune."[25]

By Pömer's university days, the numerous learned disputations on the common good were increasingly framed in terms of the body social and its health.[26] Definitions of a healthy body social naturally varied widely among theorists and rulers, but two recurrent themes would have resonated with young Pömer, particularly on the question of child welfare. The first was the close association between a city's public order and the reputation of its leaders. Like their Florentine and Venetian counterparts, Nuremberg's patricians viewed the quality of their own civic order, including social services, the same way they perceived their magnificent public buildings and monuments—as visible proof of the city's (and, by implication, its leaders') magnificence. The other significant theme was the importance, even necessity, of social planning and regulation. "Social engineering" would be a misleading (not to mention anachronistic) overstating of both magisterial goals and means during this period, but the humanists' optimistic confidence in the possibility of shaping the social order through legislation was undeniably strong.

The universities of Altdorf and Heidelberg were also Protestant institutions, dedicated to the evangelical shaping of society's future leaders. Since the earliest days of the Reformation, Lutheran pastors and theologians had regularly reminded secular rulers of their godly duties to help and protect the needy, while simultaneously disciplining and punishing the wicked. Luther himself wrote extensively about all Christians' responsibilities toward the poor, arguing that "there are no beggars among Christians." The 1523 ordinance he helped frame for the Saxon town of Leisnig provided an influential model for other poor-relief reforms throughout Germany.[27] Above all, Luther and other religious leaders wanted action from princes and magistrates, both in the support of the "deserving poor" and in the punishment of a variety of "public sins" (*öffentliche Sünden*). Professors at all Protestant universities shared these expectations and cherished their own roles in molding young evangelical leaders, who increasingly assumed the role of quasi-bishops within their own realms.[28]

These chief formative influences on Albrecht Pömer's view of governance—patrician duty, civic humanism, and Lutheran charity—were well-established components of Nuremberg's civic paternalism by the time he assumed office. The city had in fact become as famed for its aggressive social interventionist policies at home as it was for its extreme caution in diplomatic matters abroad. Concern for neglected, abandoned, and abused children came naturally to men who already viewed themselves as the city's fathers. Yet during his public service, Pömer would see the council's "true fatherly sympathy for poor and suffering children" tested as never before.[29] He and his colleagues would experience deep frustration in their concerted attempts to abolish child begging, provide for anonymously abandoned and other unwanted children, and effectively punish abusive and even murdering parents. Their responses to such failures, as well as to occasional successes, reveal a great deal about the consistently pivotal role of informal child circulation in their society as well as the self-limits it imposed on governmental attempts to aid that society's most vulnerable inhabitants.

The Conundrum of Child Begging

In every city that Albrecht Pömer visited during his youthful grand tour of Europe, he would have heard the same complaints about begging and rowdy children overrunning the streets. An English pamphlet of the 1640s remonstrated at length about children who "lie all day in the streets in playing, cursing, and swearing," while another contemporary wryly observed that in cities children "lous[ed] like swarms of locusts in every corner of the street."[30] The social reformer Juan Luis Vives bemoaned that in Spanish cities "the young children of the poor are villainously brought up, [mothers] and their sons lying outside of churches or running around begging."[31] Within the empire, Lucas Hackfurt reported in 1537 to the magistracy of Strasbourg that

the citizens complain that young boys and girls go up and down the streets
begging so that no one can eat in peace . . . Even if they should find a job,
they do not have the clothes they would need—and what citizen's wife (assuming they were given a servant's position) would let herself be followed by
such a ragamuffin . . . ? Nor is there any craftsman who would teach such a
lad for no pay.[32]

One could not walk more than a few feet in any early modern town, it was
said, without experiencing firsthand this universal blight of begging and
rowdy children and youths.

Virtually every educated person agreed that the pandemic of child and
youth begging posed multiple dangers to the body politic and thus required
some kind of official response. Not all secular authorities interpreted these
dangers in the same way, however, and the solutions proposed consequently
varied considerably. Nuremberg's leaders were especially precocious and active on the subject of child begging, issuing a prodigious number of related
mandates between 1478 and 1699.[33] For Pömer and other city councilors,
the issue represented an affront to their Christian sense of charity as well as
to their bourgeois work ethic and paternalist pretensions. In groping toward
a solution, the city's magistrates were able to draw on a long and venerated
tradition of poor relief in Nuremberg, dating back to the city's first alms
ordinance in 1370, well before any other city or principality in the Holy
Roman Empire.[34] Theoretically, that tradition made a clear and consistent
distinction between local citizen poor, who deserved assistance, and beggars
and their foreign counterparts, who did not. In actual practice those same
magistrates frequently transcended this citizen/foreigner boundary when it
came to children.

Pömer's sense of Christian duty to provide for the city's own "deserving poor," or "shamefaced poor," was reinforced by the patrician's embarrassment that such poor but honest people and their children were
"forced out of need to ask openly for alms and beg on the streets and in the
churches—which is no little affront and shame to our faith."[35] The initial
fifteenth-century impulse had been to license local beggars and to expel
their foreign competitors, but by 1522 the difficulties of enforcing begging
regulations led the council to the radical decision of prohibiting all begging, whether by locals or foreigners—a first in the empire.[36] At the same
time, the new alms ordinance secularized and centralized all poor relief
within the city proper, combining over 170 privately and publicly endowed
foundations into a "common chest," or almonry, administered by a municipal alms bureau (Stadtalmosenamt).[37] Thanks to several improvements

in fundraising, the budget of this office grew steadily over the course of the next century.[38] By the time Albrecht Pömer joined the city's alms lords in 1628, the bureau's annual expenditure often reached over 40,000 fl., a relatively massive amount of money, collected and distributed by a sizeable bureaucracy.

The centralization of poor relief in 1522 had been intended to eliminate the need for begging among any of the city's deserving—that is, local "shamefaced"—poor. A century later, however, it was obvious that this goal remained far from being realized. The cumulative effect of this failure was an increasing tendency among magistrates to characterize all defiers of the begging ban—citizen or foreigner—as "lazy beggars and sluts," effectively blurring the long-standing boundary between local and foreign poor.[39] The humanist concern about the social utility (*utilitatis publica*) of able-bodied beggars, which had shaped the city's earliest begging decrees, was now consistently overshadowed by complaints about molestation of the city's citizens and anxiety over public safety, culminating in near annual pronouncements about dangerous, able-bodied "sturdy" beggars, who sometimes physically assaulted local people in their quest for a handout.[40] Officially, foreign and local beggars continued to be classified and treated differently but in actuality more and more of Nuremberg's citizens and residents experienced the same contempt and occasionally banishment as outsiders. What was once an issue of economic misfortune was now increasingly viewed as a question of bad character.

Interestingly, the perception of adult beggars as immoral triggered a similar merging of conceptual categories among poor children, but with the opposite effect. Initially governmental intervention in child raising had been limited to children of the local poor, who were not only licensed to beg but also promised assistance in job placement once they were over eight years old (if healthy).[41] This startlingly innovative child welfare policy included financial aid in paying service fees and health costs and was reiterated throughout the sixteenth century right up until Pömer's time—but only for citizens' children.

Yet even after all child begging was prohibited in 1522, Nuremberg's magistrates consistently demonstrated a broader and more long-term interpretation of the problem than most private citizens, who were mostly concerned with the immediate annoyance factor. Councilors decried at length the widespread "shame, criminal acts, and frivolity" stemming from children "raised in begging and laziness."[42] According to an ordinance issued just two years before Pömer joined the alms bureau, negligent parents of this sort "raised their unwitting children from youth on by [their] shameful instruction to gamble, steal, whore, and [commit] other vices . . ."[43] Instead of learning trades and the importance of earning one's bread, these boys and girls roamed the city's street late at night, singing "shameless" and "worldly" songs, often in the company of "men and women who practiced all kinds of villainy and immorality on the streets," and thus growing up as socially useless beggars who "found it that much harder to take up a craft."[44] Often, physical, moral, and social well-being were intimately linked in legislation. One begging mandate typically compounded the immediate concern "that the poor young children, boys and girls, so freeze during the winter as to ruin their health," with the lasting consequence that the children "are so neglected and depraved that afterwards they never recover their health, but must remain sickly, weak, and infirm people for the rest of their lives."[45] (This recurrent concern about poorly clad children in severe winter weather also comes during the period known to historians as the Second Little Ice Age Event [1570–1635]).[46] The close association of beggars and other vagrants with disease generated an even more literal concern "that such persons could easily infect others," particularly children and youths.[47] Most distressing to the magistrates, the majority of these street singers apparently were sent out into this life by their own parents, often against their will.

Because Nuremberg's magistrates considered all children more vulnerable and less fully formed, they were willing to engage in a much higher level of social intervention, often transcending traditional insider/outsider boundaries in the implementation of their paternalistic mandate. The logical corollary to this *in loco parentis* activity was their signature identification of the problem with bad parenting. Fed up with the "howling, singing, and screaming of poor children in front of houses on the streets, day and night," the inner council in 1588 decreed that any child caught caroling or begging outright (other than a Latin student or a Findel child) was to be arrested and detained in the pesthouse until authorities could track down its parents. Parents would then be subjected to a stern lecture and warning; if a noncitizen or repeat offender, the child and his or her parents were to be banished (though this appears to have been irregularly enforced).[48]

By Pömer's time the magisterial obsession with bad parenting seemed to emerge in almost any context involving deviant children. The last chapter recounted official harangues of poor citizen parents who abused their alms, allowing their children to go hungry or sending them begging for food. Tirades about parents who let their children roam the streets "singing Latin and German songs and begging at all hours of the night on the streets and in front of houses" were often accompanied by complaints about "unruly youths" who threw stones and snowballs, fought among themselves on the street, and showed many other signs of wild and dangerous behavior.[49] In 1616, a violent street fight between two young boys that cost one of the combatants a finger prompted the sitting magistrates to reissue the begging ordinance condemning "the great noise and trouble" caused by poorly supervised children running in the city's street" and to admonish the boys' parents "to henceforth maintain better discipline over their children."[50]

This emphasis on paternal responsibility and proper upbringing had also been part of the very fabric of the Protestant Reformation. Nuremberg's own reformer, Andreas Osiander, frequently acknowledged that "God teaches everyone the very best and most valuable lessons through the mother and father."[51] His contemporary Otto Brunfels concurred that "[i]f one wants to reform the world and make it Christian, one must begin with children."[52] Conrad Sam expressed the apparently common evangelical sentiment that the growing numbers of mercenaries, murderers, and criminals were the direct result of bad upbringing. The magistrates of Augsburg came to the same conclusion about prostitution.[53] Each parent, particularly the father, thus assumed responsibility for not just their children but for the very health of the body politic.

The groundwork for secular intervention in child raising was likewise laid by the Reformation. Clerical reformers particularly resented the way many parents treated children as their own property (*eigenthumb*) rather than as God's temple (*heiligthumb*).[54] Children belonged first to God, Luther reminded parents, and thus by implication to His Church. Parental authority, he wrote, was natural and therefore fundamentally superior to the contrived and artificial authority of government, yet Luther did not oppose official intervention in cases when fathers and mothers were not carrying out their responsibilities. Luther thought basic literacy essential for any believing Christian and at one point wrote that if parents did not attend to the education of their children, then "children cease to belong to their parents and fall to the care of God and community." The reformer's religious colleagues in Strasbourg made a similarly revolutionary argument to the town council in 1547, that "children belong more to God and the community—we mean both the religious and political community—than to their parents."[55]

But what did this mean in the real world? One way to force poor citizen parents to live up to their divinely ordained responsibilities was to threaten to cut off their governmental aid. As chapter 2 revealed, however, this decision was difficult to enforce and in any event affected only the minority of parents who were sending their children begging. Banishment of entire families was likewise difficult to enforce. A more effective way to eradicate child begging would be to bypass "bad parents" altogether, with secular authorities themselves insuring that all children were inculcated with the proper Christian morals and work ethic, as well as providing job opportunities when possible. Here the humanist aspects of Pömer's training shine through, with a strikingly optimistic attitude about the malleability of children and the central role of education in promoting the health of the body politic. Thus in addition to the city's four Latin schools and six parochial German schools, the council maintained "poor" (i.e., free) grammar schools for boys and girls at both Saint Sebaldus and Saint Lorenz.[56] Nuremberg's city council also continued to pay placement fees, administer scholarships, and otherwise assist poor citizen children in finding an appropriate apprenticeship or domestic position. Orphaned and abandoned foreign children were regularly admitted to the city's Findel and even foreign youths were eligible for some financial assistance programs.[57]

Yet when Albrecht Pömer became a school superintendent in 1627, the dream of circumventing the "bad parents" of beggar children through education seemed as disappointingly distant from realization as it had been a century before. Church inspections over the previous seventy years continually showed a depressing state in Nuremberg's parochial education.[58] In the wake of one recent and particularly damning visitation of the city's parochial schools, the new superintendent promptly helped convince his colleagues on the inner council to issue a new directive on mandatory catechism classes. The next year the council issued a new instruction booklet for all schools and churches.[59] Pömer and his colleagues knew well that the greatest source of parental opposition was the economic hardship posed by a child in school, which cost them both instructional fees and lost household income from their children's begging. He also recognized that the poor schools at Saint Sebaldus and Saint Lorenz were grossly inadequate for the actual number of poor children in the streets. Thus in 1632, on the recommendation of Pömer and the other school superintendents, the council erected a new cost-free grammar school in the parish of Saint Jakob "for ill-raised youths." Two similar institutions followed soon after and by 1640 enrollment at the city's poor schools had almost tripled, from 175 pupils at the beginning of the century to more than 500 (of whom almost one-third were illegitimate).[60] Not until the Pietist reforms of the early eighteenth century would so many of Nuremberg's children be taught for free.

As refugee and other begging children continued to flood the city's streets during the ensuing crisis, more extreme measures were also proposed. In 1634, Pömer's senior colleague at the alms bureau recommended taking some "ill-raised" beggar children from poor parents and giving them to a worsted woodworker for training (as an alternative to constructing a work-house).[61] This radical suggestion was never implemented, but two years later Pömer and his fellow alms lords similarly proposed "that the city's poor wives and children be sent to designated houses to spin wool and yarn." One such *Spinnhaus* was established adjacent to the Findel with a small number of women and children but was dissolved once the city's immediate crisis passed.[62] "Discipline-houses" for unruly youths had been around since the late 1580s in England, where they were known as "bridewells." Their goal was ostensibly the same as that of Nuremberg's poor schools and all financial assistance programs: "so that youths may be accustomed to and brought up in labor and work." The methods of the discipline-houses, however, were considerably harsher, relying on not just occasional caning but also on food deprivation, extensive flogging, and—for unmanageable boys over fourteen—ear boring. Boys between five and fourteen were supposed to receive training and placement in a craft but there is no evidence that the latter ever took place.[63]

Nuremberg's magistrates had debated the establishment of a municipal discipline-house as early as 1588—seven years before the actual creation of the continent's first such institution in Amsterdam. They and their successors, however, consistently refused to join in the proliferation of the new institutions (now also for delinquent adults) until well after Pömer's death, in 1670.[64] Resistance to this austere alternative to voluntary poor schools likely stemmed from skepticism over the economic viability of a discipline-house rather than any squeamishness over physical brutality. Nuremberg had been, after all, a German pioneer in introducing the French punishment of chain -gangs for begging youths and young men about the same time they first debated establishing a discipline-house. Known as *Springbuben* or *Schellbuben* (for their foot irons and belled hats, respectively), these delinquents mainly performed street cleaning and repairs, as well as—most crucially during 1632–36—the cleanup of human and animal waste and other garbage.[65] The inmates of discipline-houses might have debated with *Springbuben* over who had the harder life, but in Nuremberg there remained one important distinction: the humiliating and generally distasteful punishment of the chain gang was reserved for foreigners. Citizen youths who repeatedly begged or committed vandalism might be briefly interned in the begging stockade but retained their immunity from the city's more severe "disciplining" of noncitizens—at least for the time being.

Despite all these magisterial efforts, supportive and punitive, child and youth begging in Nuremberg appears if anything to have grown rather than declined over the course of the seventeenth century. Shortly after Albrecht

Pömer's death in 1654, his successors and former colleagues launched a new "zero-tolerance" campaign against all street begging, arresting thousands of child, youth, and adult offenders between 1654 and 1668. In 1661 Pömer's brief experimental *Spinnhaus* was reinstituted in the same building next to the Findel. During the next seven years alone it admitted 1,645 women and children (in a city whose population had dropped to a mere 20,000). During the same period, the chain gang and begging stockade admitted at least 300 youths and adult males. Foreign children and youth beggars were now, like adults, regularly escorted to the city's gates and threatened with flogging or worse if they returned.[66] The impact of all this activity, however, was depressingly familiar. In his annual report of 1668, the chief alms lord complained that his bureau remained "swamped with children raised in and accustomed to beggary." His assessment—as well as his recommendation of a new study of "how many children had been picked up and how many times"—could have been written 150 years earlier, with only a slight difference in language and tone.[67]

Several crucial factors help account for the failed magisterial campaign against child begging in Nuremberg. Most obviously, the ambitious pedagogical reforms of the last century and a half had failed miserably, at least in terms of inculcating self-discipline and a work ethic among the city's children.[68] The agenda of the city's ecclesiastical session of 1657, for instance, was dominated by a series of accounts of the ineffectiveness and disorderliness of local poor schools:

> around Saint Jakob's courtyard, children create great disturbances with throwing, playing, or teasing, and accost the begging beadle with [thrown objects] and ridicule. Herr Volkart [added] that during catechism lessons in the Franciscan church [of the Findel], some journeymen played cards behind the altar and also spoke mockingly of the examiners. And then Herr Arnschwanger [recounted] that he was quite despised and mocked by the youths when he spoke to them.

After much deliberation, the body decided to ask the council for an additional beadle to patrol the area while school was in session (see fig. 3.6). This solution—like the following year's forceful declaration that parents were responsible for teaching their children the catechism—appears a small gesture toward what more and more seemed like an insoluble problem.[69] A few years later, the director of the city's German schools similarly complained " . . . that the local Teutonic Knights' courtyard is not only the site of schooling but also of the divvying up of bread and rolls as well as illu-

Fig. 3.6. Children taunting a city guard in Strasbourg
(ca. 1650). Munich Kupferstichkabinet.

minated pictures ripped [out of books] here, so that said schooling is completely impeded." This seems a minor annoyance compared to the master
of the city's small Reformed school's simultaneous report of an outing with
his pupils "where they displayed all sorts of cockiness [and] shot guns in
front of the pastor."[70]

Another source of magistrates' frustration was their continuing reliance
on inadequate and outdated approaches to criminal punishment. At its
peak population of 40,000, Nuremberg possessed only four "begging police," and even doubling that force in 1638 had little impact.[71] Alert children, who often took turns watching for the regular patrols, easily evaded
detection. New arrivals to the city ran a greater risk of being caught but
could still rely on small bribes of the begging beadles, who in Nuremberg
as elsewhere were better known for their brutality and corruption than for
efficiency. Popular hatred of these officials apparently often resulted in adult
collusion with child beggars on the street.[72] Not surprisingly, recidivism
among all beggars, particularly children and youths, was rampant, with the
beadles repeatedly chasing the same offenders, adults and children, out of
the city. When eighteen-year-old Martin Wildt was arrested by the begging
police in March 1661, he already had a record of three previous arrests for
the same offense. Although his late father had trained him in a craft, the
orphan complained that no master would hire him and thus he had no
alternative but to beg.[73] Most of the juvenile criminals to be encountered

in the next chapter had been banished as many as fifteen or twenty times before their ultimate arrests.

Another crucial factor was the city's fundamental inability to secure its own borders, despite a massive surrounding wall and deep moat. A 1668 memo from director of the alms bureau blamed the large number of begging children in Nuremberg on weak deterrence, especially at the city's gates, as well as numerous unwise marriages of couples without property, particularly involving Swedish soldiers during the Thirty Years' War.[74] Yet all attempts to prevent poor families with children from entering the city had proven self-defeating since the issue first surfaced in the late fifteenth century. Nuremberg's poorly paid guards, like their counterparts throughout Europe, relied on bribes from entering foreign beggars to get by. Given the porous boundaries of a supposedly inviolable walled city, banishment of beggars likewise proved nearly impossible to enforce, even when accompanied by flogging or other corporal punishments.

The universal ineffectiveness of local banishment led other seventeenth-century European states to experiment with the overseas version of child circulation known as "transportation."[75] Forced emigration of beggar children began in England with Elizabeth I but accelerated during the period 1618–22, when over three hundred youngsters, ages 9–16, were deported to the colony of Virginia. Though few survived to adulthood, the venture was repeated with 1,500 more children in 1627 and in 1653 with two ships carrying some four hundred poor Irish children, who were often enticed with small monetary rewards and promises of "good education and future maintenance."[76] From 1638 to 1671, cities and villages of the United Provinces sent over 8,000 poor children into various cloth trades in Leiden, a practice that grew exponentially during the Industrial Revolution of the nineteenth century. Both Louis XIV of France and Frederick the Great of Prussia considered mercantilist plans to use foundlings and orphans as soldiers in their rapidly expanding armies.[77] Most infamously of all, every ten to fifteen years between 1663 and 1750, poor children disappeared en masse from the streets of Paris. Only during the last episode were the abductions acknowledged to be the result of a genuine governmental conspiracy, the children having been shipped off to populate the crown's colonies in Quebec and Mississippi (where most of them perished before reaching adulthood).[78] Nuremberg, which possessed neither a fleet nor foreign colonies, apparently never participated in any such radical redeployments of unwanted beggar children.

A more formidable obstacle to official reforms was the steady resistance of poor parents to losing the income from child begging. As seen in the last chapter, often such money was the only thing that kept poor households—especially those headed by single mothers—from complete destitution. Not surprisingly, threats to drop entire families from the alms list or to expel them from the city apparently had little effect. Neither did promises of placement in a craft, a behavior that seemed to genuinely baffle Nuremberg's magistrates, who could not understand how parents could be so selfish as to sacrifice their children's futures in this manner. Occasionally councilors had the alms bureau and begging police draw up lists of parents known to send their children out begging so that the bad parents could be summoned before the council to explain their behavior.[79] In 1630 and 1631, Pömer and his fellow alms lords produced three such inventories of healthy children, apprehended while begging, who were eligible for placement in an apprenticeship or service position. Of the fifteen children in the first group, they ascertained, "[T]he majority (twelve) were intentionally sent out by their parents themselves, some of whom survived solely [on income] from the begging." Typically, a free service position was promised, but many parents refused outright. Benedict Fleyenzor, "a blind man in the Grassengasse with three boys who only roam in beggary and do no one good," nonetheless pleaded that he could not get by if his sons were placed with craftsmen. The next year, eight more parents of begging children were summoned to appear before Pömer at the alms bureau to explain themselves. All but one of them insisted on keeping their boys at home rather than sending them to poor schools or into apprenticeships, even if the council paid their placement fees. Only Hanns Dehnlein, a ring maker, actually requested that his fifteen-year-old son Niclas be placed with a master in the craft, a petition the alms lords immediately granted.[80]

In retrospect, the magisterial focus on parental character seems inevitable given the resilience of child begging. The apparent indifference of such parents when summoned to answer for their children's begging, however, continued to perplex already exasperated magistrates.[81] One particular incident not too long after Pömer's time vividly illustrates this dilemma. On October 16, 1668, the parents of three boys picked up for street begging were summoned before the inner council to account for their children's conduct. Anna Maria Salomonin, a nail maker's widow, explained that her son Bastl, age fourteen, was a "stupid, resentful boy who didn't get along well with anyone" and although she "tried with all her might to raise this foolish son well and keep him from begging and send him to the [poor] school at Saint Lorenz, she couldn't force the boy." No doubt, she added, much of the problem was that "she was rarely at home because of her job and thus couldn't give the boy sufficient attention." Shortly thereafter, on

November 24, the alms bureau raised her weekly allowance from 15 to 18 Kreuzer (about 1/3 fl.) "in consideration of her seven children."[82] The mother of the brothers Hans and Christoph Rössner, on the other hand, readily admitted that the boys (aged ten and eight) were routinely sent out by their father against their will to beg by a tavern ("which the Rössner youths also couldn't deny") and that she had often tried to persuade her husband, a roofer by training, to get a job and take better care of his children. She resisted sending them to the Saint Lorenz school, though, and assured the council that she would keep both sons from begging as well as she was able. To this effect, her weekly alms amount was increased by "a pair of Kreuzer" to twelve (about 1/5 fl.). The brothers Rössner also claimed to know nothing of certain house keys reported missing, and the case was dismissed.[83]

Two months later, the same three boys were back in official custody for the same offense of "almost nightly roaming around the city and molesting people with begging." Immediately, the municipal alms bureau notified the inner council of their parents' financial aid, including the recent increases. The same report also pessimistically noted a familiar pattern in such cases: "[A]lthough the apprehended children are warned with the greatest seriousness to stop begging, to which they promise, as soon as they are released, [they again] run around begging and molesting people." In this instance the boys made the mistake of begging once too often in front of the house of Councilor Andreas Baumgartner, who finally notified the city's archers and had them arrested.[84]

Appearing again before the inner council, Anna Maria Salomonin continued to lament the misery of her family's condition since the death of her husband two years before, including care for a mentally retarded ten-year-old son who just six months earlier had been accepted into the Findel (where he would remain until his death seventeen years later).[85] After her allowance was raised, she had tried to keep Bastl at home but on the day of his arrest "she was not at home but had taken care to lock the youth in without a shirt so as to keep him home [but] he got out and ran off to his begging." Once more she complained that he was "an especially clumsy and dirty boy, who didn't want to learn a craft or go to school on account of the rod." She in no way ever condoned his behavior, especially—she added pointedly—since when he did beg "it was a miracle if he even gave her a Groshen or half a Batzen" (small coins worth 1/16 and 1/30 fl., respectively).[86]

Christoph Rössner, summoned at the same time, claimed to be similarly mystified by his two sons' begging since he never approved of it and to the contrary had often beaten them on account of it. Like Bastl Salomon's mother, he also made the presumably salient point that the children never brought home much money anyway. On the day in question, he testified, the boys had asked his permission to go out to play. He consented, "with the express condition" that they return home by the proper time. When they didn't, he and his wife searched all over for them, only learning the next day that they had been picked up for begging. Now he respectfully asked the council to help him keep his sons from begging and to send them to school (which they allegedly refused to attend).[87]

Whatever the sitting magistrates made of the two parents' accounts, their options remained frustratingly limited. This time the inner council simply decreed that all three boys be given "a product" (that is, trained in a craft), and at the next report of any begging they and their families would be expelled from the city.[88] The same decree ominously included one new element in the by-then formulaic requests to the alms bureau for a satisfactory solution. In addition to stricter policing at the city's gates, preventing "such people" from entering in the first place, the council asked the bureau to investigate the costs involved in one other means of dealing with "lazy, shiftless riffraff," namely, a workhouse. This represented the first successful proposal for the Nuremberg discipline- and workhouse, ultimately opened two years later in September 1670.

The Salomon and Rössner cases provide revealing clues to the enduring social impasse behind this decision. In both instances, magistrates held to the traditional preference of aid rather than punishment for locals, threatening all three parents with banishment but in fact raising the weekly allowances of both families. Even when the boys were picked up a second time, they were presented with an offer of apprenticeship rather than an unpayable fine or presumably unenforceable ban from the city. The three boys, however, appear already submerged in an alternative urban street culture (to be explored in the next chapter). The deeper connections between their two families are never specified, but both had begun receiving public assistance on exactly the same day six years earlier, when Christoph Rössner had temporarily deserted his family and Anna Maria Salomonin's husband was still alive (but at home?).[89] Rössner, by his own wife's testimony, was well known as "a drunken and frivolous man" who routinely beat his children and refused to get a job. Anna Maria Salomonin, by her own account, worked to support her seven (later six) children, but even a yearly supplement of less than 16 fl. would have bought only about three loaves of rye bread a week—a grossly inadequate supplement, as was the Rössner's annual 10 fl.[90] Whether three young boys from such families begged on instruction or on their own initiative, everyone involved agreed on their current direction. The suspicious night wandering and accusation of stolen house keys in particular clearly pointed toward a profession learned not in the workshop but on the street.

Yet at this point the growing cultural divisions appear most striking. All three parents, by circumstances or personal failings, appeared to the council unable to raise their children "properly," no matter how much financial aid they received. The apparently criminal trajectory of the boys demanded immediate action, from the magisterial point of view, yet the parents seemed impotent or unwilling to prevent the inevitable. From the parents' perspective, governmental harassment of child beggars appeared one more obstacle in a world of hardships, yet one that they all skillfully negotiated and transformed into more money for their families. Thus while the magistrates lectured on parental responsibility and Christian duty, the parents readily admitted to their own inadequate guidance as well as to occasional panhandling by the children in order to establish the more important point that no professional, full-time begging was involved (which might lead to their own banishment). It is no exaggeration to see the two groups as speaking two different cultural languages, one concerned with law, morality, and decency, the other with scrounging, evasion, and sheer survival. Both sides had become trapped in a relationship of alternating dependency and adversity. Little surprise that within two years of its most recent mention in the Rössner and Salomon incident, the discipline- and workhouse that Albrecht Pömer and his fellow city fathers had resisted for so long opened its doors. Located directly adjacent to the Findel, its entrance bore a rhyming motto overhead:

> To the good of the bad has this workhouse been built,
> Who has never done much good or from working wilts,
> Herein finds work enough to be had,
> Where discipline rules and makes the best use out of bad.[91]

Negotiating Care for the City's Foundlings and Orphans

The opening of Nuremberg's discipline- and workhouse was still almost four decades away when Albrecht Pömer assumed the position of Findel administrator in April 1633. Pömer had just turned thirty-five and was married with three small sons. He brought to the position about six years of experience in various civic posts, most relevantly as a member of the inner council and as an alms lord, as well as a high degree of optimism about his own ability to achieve social order and peace, particularly on the question of the

Fig. 3.7. The forward interior courtyard of the Nuremberg Findel, facing Saint Lorenz (south) with the administrator's lodging on the left (top two floors) and the Franciscan church on the right. Pömer would have heard the sounds of children playing outside during those afternoons when he remained at home. The main Findel parlor, which served as a refectory and classroom, was on the ground floor of his residence (ca. 1725). Stadtbibliothek Nürnberg.

city's unwanted children. Even more important, he was a Pömer, long prepared to succeed his late cousin Hans Heidrich as Findel administrator, just as Hans Heidrich had followed Albrecht's father twenty-five years earlier. His first major challenge turned out to be a domestic one, namely, moving his family into the Findel itself. For several weeks, Hans Heidrich's widow, Sibylla, repeatedly petitioned the inner council to allow her and her seven children to remain living in the Findel for the duration of her lifetime. Not unsympathetic, the council "gently" refused her requests and even found her another residence, at least for temporary lodging, but Sibylla remained adamant in her desire to stay. After more than three months of delay, her husband's former colleagues on the inner council finally ordered her to vacate the premises by Saint Laurence Day (August 10) so that the rooms "could be cleaned and repaired as necessary for the new Findel administrator, Albrecht Pömer and his household."[92]

The institution Pömer and his family eventually moved into during September 1633 (see fig. 3.7) had evolved considerably in two significant ways since its late thirteenth-century origin with a large donation from a man named Fleinz.[93] First, the Nuremberg Findel was no longer exclusively or even mainly for foundlings. The original purpose of the hundreds of such institutions created between 1250 and 1450 had been to provide an alternative to those unmarried mothers who either killed their newborn bastards outright or left them exposed to the elements, where many eventually died.[94] Unwanted legitimate children were for the most part sent to private foster homes.[95] Beginning in the mid-sixteenth century, though, institutions specifically designed for legitimate orphans sprang up throughout Europe, particularly in Germany.[96] Many cities with foundling homes, such as Nuremberg, simply merged their legitimate and illegitimate populations into one institution.[97] The nature of admissions to Nuremberg's Findel, however, demonstrates how the apparent mixing of legitimate and illegitimate children in one institution can be misleading. Since fewer than one in five children admitted to the Nuremberg Findel was an infant foundling and virtually all of these died with private wet nurses before reaching the Findel's residential age minimum of seven, the Findel had become by Pömer's time a de facto orphanage and foster home.[98] Civic authorities explicitly recognized this new identity for the Findel as early as 1575, when an official report referred to the home's purpose as being "that fatherless and motherless and many other orphans left behind be therein raised to true fear of God, as well as to a virtuous and godly way of life, and be provided with necessary clothing, food, board, and other necessities."[99] Foundlings continued to be admitted to the Findel's care for centuries to come, but they would remain a small minority within the home itself.

The second major change since the Middle Ages was the size of the Nuremberg Findel. Until the beginning of the sixteenth century, the number of older abandoned children and orphans also remained low enough that the Findel itself could exist as a largely paper institution, with children housed around the city in the hospital, parish churches, cloisters, and ultimately a series of modified private residences, one each for the boys and the girls.[100] Between 1530 and 1594, however, the annual number of children in the Findel's care (one-third placed with wet nurses) rose steadily from 45 to over 200, making one central facility an increasingly appealing option. As early as 1525, Nuremberg's city council considered transforming the recently dissolved Franciscan (aka "Barefooted") cloister into a new Findel for the growing number of orphan boys, but nothing actually happened until thirty years later, when the girls' home was ravaged by a fire in May 1557.[101] Initially the girls were housed in the old Carthusian monastery, but within a few months the inadequate water supply and other difficulties resulted in the entire group relocating to the Franciscan cloister, vacant except for two elderly Franciscan monks who had been permitted to live out the rest of their days there.[102] Faced with an estimated cost of 2,000 fl. for a new Findel building, the council decided it was more economically feasible to leave the girls in the former monastery than to rebuild the burnt-out house. The Franciscan building complex, located directly across the Pegnitz from the city's hospital, was large enough to house the overcrowded boys' Findel as well. For reasons of propriety, though, their move was authorized only after a few councilors added the strict stipulation that the boys' and girls' homes remained separate—with their own entrances and facilities—and would not be merged into one "body" (corpus).[103] In July 1560 the boys' home was sold and a few months later the entire group joined the girls in the Franciscan cloister, where completely separate facilities for boys and girls were indeed maintained until 1623, shortly before Albrecht Pömer assumed his position as administrator.

Pömer's responsibility for the Findel's children began with the very question of their admission and continued over virtually all aspects of their daily care until they left the institution, through job placement, return to their parents, running away, or death. In Nuremberg, all unwanted children required a petition to the inner council in order to be accepted into the Findel. Usually this took the form of a brief written note, passed on by a council secretary to the session's two presiding mayors and then to the Findel administrator. Sometimes a petition was registered in council records as "verbally delivered" to one of the mayors and perhaps to the entire inner council.[104] Petitions generally identified the petitioner(s) and occasionally his or her relationship to the child(ren) in question. In most cases, the full nature of the petitioner's connection remains unknown. Among the remaining cases, though, some clear patterns emerge. For instance, in cases of anonymous abandonment (particularly of infants), the petitioner was most likely to be a city archer, the Findel father or mother (the resident heads, reporting to the Findel administrator), or another employee of the city. Sometimes more than one person petitioned and in a few cases entire neighborhoods made an appeal on a foundling's behalf.[105] In the cases of orphans or abandoned children whose parents were known, godparents and guardians made up the single largest identifiable group of supplicants. About a third of foster requests, a tiny group as a whole, came from parents themselves, usually the mother. Overall, almost three in four petitions on behalf of unwanted children came from outside the immediate family and kin (including godparents), or at least from individuals who were not identified as such. This pattern confirms the general success of informal child circulation and the common assumption of the era that it was mostly "friendless" orphans or other children without kin who ended up before the council.[106]

When Albrecht Pömer read or listened to a petition, whether in his capacity as Findel administrator or as mayor of the inner council, he sought the answer to one question: who could he get to take the child(ren) off the city's hands? In this quest he followed generations of Nuremberg's leaders before and after him, all of whom encouraged informal circulation and endeavored to minimize or to avoid governmental intervention as much as possible. To a certain degree, their reluctance was grounded in secular authorities' long-standing recognition of private parental authority over all matters of the household, the so-called realm of honor (*Bereich des Ehres*).[107] More fundamentally, Pömer considered himself a steward of the city's financial resources. Sometimes he could arrange for the care of the child with no cost whatsoever to municipal coffers; other times he was willing to authorize a modest stipend if necessary. The one central objective remained finding a private solution whenever possible. Otherwise, the Findel administrator and his surrogates enjoyed considerable latitude in their negotiations with petitioners.

Pömer's fundamental predisposition toward private care whenever possible also reflected the continuing prominence of informal fosterage and "blended families" during the sixteenth and seventeenth centuries. As already seen, many individuals—related by blood or not—were already caring for other peoples' children. Absent a truly compelling reason to change that, magistrates preferred to sustain the existing arrangement as long as possible, usually by means of an annual stipend. Most grandparents, for instance, who petitioned for their children's children to be admitted to the Findel, were instead sent away with cash stipends totaling 8 to 12 fl. a year to continue raising their charges.[108] There does not appear to have been any hierarchy of preferred foster parents among magistrates, other than a natural inclination toward "friends" (in the early modern sense), particularly blood relatives and godparents, who were most likely to feel obligated to care for an unwanted child.

Locating biological parents or legal guardians was the first priority. Every petition on behalf of an unwanted child triggered an official investigation to verify the stipulated facts and to identify and track down abandoning parents or any potential foster parents.[109] Within the city and its suburbs, this meant a general inquiry by neighborhood captains, with leads followed up by municipal archers and other minor officials already supposedly alert to "those [suspicious people] who creep into town and abandon children," particularly "all sorts of soldiers' women coming and going."[110] By Albrecht Pömer's time, there were regular patrols in the area surrounding the Findel all night long, so that often the time of abandonment could be specified within one-quarter of an hour.[111] When a pregnant "soldier's whore" was spotted abandoning her one-year-old child under an arch in the hospital courtyard, councilors ordered archers to identify and question neighborhood witnesses as well as to follow up in the nearby village of Schweinau, the woman's alleged home.[112] In the countryside, investigations of petitioning children were often initiated by the pastor of a village, who worked with the local bailiff or mayor. In every instance, location of a biological or willing foster parent remained the paramount objective.

In practice, however, there were three especially weak links in the chain of investigation. First, Pömer's inquiries were most often frustrated by the incompetence and ineffectiveness of lesser governmental personnel. Archers and begging police were consistently undermanned in patrols and stretched still thinner by frequent assignments to help in the interrogation, guarding, and sometimes execution of suspected criminals. Their meager salaries also compelled most to work at least one additional job or rely on bribes. Attempts to improve both the efficiency and reputations of their lawmen by quintupling annual salaries within a ten-year period and adding various benefits, including a type of pension, had negligible effects on either effectiveness or morale. Archers and sentries in Pömer's day were still widely perceived as low-class, dishonorable thugs, despised both for their brutality and corruption.[113] Often jurors suspected some complicity between child abandoners and guards, fomented out of sympathy or bribery, but there was little that could be done about it. In one case, the investigating jurors imprisoned an archer they believed had tipped off the parents in an abandonment case, but they were still unable to locate the culprits who had been identified by the abandoned children.[114] Instead, magistrates resorted to sporadic punishment of the city's guards for incompetence, such as the stern lecture given to the gatekeeper whose daughter saw a woman abandoning a two-year-old child but didn't tell him or chase after her, or the three-day prison sentence meted out to a different gatekeeper who let in a strange woman who later abandoned her child. Another even more negligent gatekeeper was berated for apparently sleeping through the nighttime break-in of a desperate mother into his watch house, only discovering her abandoned baby at daybreak.[115]

Accurate and accessible records, which might have somewhat mitigated police ineptitude and corruption, were also a challenge for Pömer. Following the investigation of an anonymously abandoned child in 1591, the council complained of statements being "completely erroneously and inconsistently recorded," particularly "the bad and unbearable custom since some time" of releasing witnesses before they had their statements read back to them to ensure accuracy.[116] Findel fathers were repeatedly admonished to keep their registers up to date "so that the parents might be sought" and were to notify the inner council if anyone inquired about a particular child.[117] Doorkeepers at Saint Sebaldus and Saint Lorenz churches were likewise ordered to make sure that all parents and sponsors at a baptism, "be they rich or poor," have their names recorded in the church's register so that parents or other responsible adults for unwanted children might be later tracked down if the name of the child could be determined.[118]

Even when anonymous abandonment notes provided incriminating information, the search for the parents was rarely successful. In one especially thorough investigation, a scrap of paper left with a three-year-old foundling, identifying the child as "Jörg Schmid" (roughly the equivalent of "John Smith"), led to a check of the marriage and baptismal records of all city and suburban parishes within the previous three or four years—without success.[119] When another note identified a newborn baby in a basket as Anna Margaretha and requested that she be raised as a Catholic, authorities immediately made inquiries among "Catholic females in and near this city," again in vain.[120] At least twice during the 1660s, councilors even instructed local officials to take the notes found with abandoned children and see if anyone recognized the handwriting, which in one case amazingly led to an unmarried mother's arrest.[121] If a child was old enough to speak and name its parent or guardian the chances of detection improved somewhat, though not as much as might be presumed.[122]

Pömer's greatest obstacle by far in tracking down anonymously abandoning parents, however, was the lack of public cooperation. Excluding the rare lucky strike of a police officer catching an offender in flagrante delicto, the initiative for all criminal investigations relied to an overwhelming degree on private complaint and eyewitness testimony. Yet assistance of this kind was notoriously hard to come by in child abandonment, so much so that magistrates had to require immediate reporting of any live child found under penalty of fine, flogging, and possibly banishment.[123] When a servant at the Golden Goose Inn turned in an infant foundling to a city guard he was immediately suspected of being the child's father and subjected to a rigorous interrogation (though a neighboring baker eventually acknowledged paternity).[124] Tavern keeper Steffan Weiss similarly had to anxiously endure two weeks of investigation before it was established that a married man from Landelberg and not he was the father of the six-week-old baby left on his doorstep, and that the unmarried mother (later identified and likewise unknown to him) had been told to leave the baby there by a passing beggar woman.[125] By Pömer's time, it had become standard to make such people swear to their innocence and complete ignorance of the child's background.[126] Of course, even if a petitioner could establish that he and a child were complete strangers, he still risked getting stuck with the child. One Good Samaritan scrap dealer who "out of sympathy" housed a five-year-old abandoned girl for a few days was turned away by the inner council with assurances of an annual stipend of 10 fl. a year to raise her.[127]

If Pömer was satisfied that a child's parents were either verifiably dead, incapacitated, or otherwise beyond his reach, as well as that "no friends were at hand who could take the child," he would then begin to negotiate with the petitioner to find acceptable terms for keeping the child where it was.[128] Usually this meant paying the petitioner an annual child care stipend, out of the budget of either the Findel or the alms bureau.[129] The amounts varied and sometimes fluctuated wildly, suggesting an inconsistency bordering on caprice. In one 1569 case, a grandfather was given 12 fl. a year to care for his three orphaned grandchildren; fifty years later a guardian was paid 32 fl. a year for care of only one charge. This was not simply a question of inflation. During Pömer's era, while prices remained high, the typical amount had sunk to a mere 8–12 fl. for one or two children, with some exceptional instances of higher grants.[130] A child care stipend might be combined with a service fee, such as the 32 fl. grant to a woman and her children in exchange for her treating the children of the Findel and hospital for eye diseases.[131] It also might be combined with other forms of assistance, as in the 1617 case of a destitute mother of eight being granted a Findel stipend for her youngest two, a weekly alms supplement for the next two youngest, and job placement for the oldest two.[132] Occasionally the council made block grants to groups of petitioners. It took not one, but two, villages to raise two children found abandoned in the woods near Weigenhofen and Huttenbach, with the inner council promising annual subsidies to both communities to be dispersed as each saw best.[133]

The degree of sympathy that a given petitioner might evince naturally influenced the size of the award, although most petitions were presented in a standardized written format rather than through impassioned personal appearances. Sometimes Pömer or a colleague expressed the council's gratitude for a kindness by simultaneously reimbursing a supplicant for past expenses incurred. Hans Eber was generously compensated for three years of care for his ten-year-old godson Hensle Anter, as was Steffan Müller for four years of keeping his mute, orphaned nephew. A petitioner who had no apparent blood ties to five-year-old Henssle Thanner was promptly recompensed for three months of costs since the boy's mother died.[134] The sitting mayors were no doubt pleasantly relieved that Leonhart Schimit, a knifesmith master who had already agreed to care for a fellow knifesmith master's son, requested only suitable clothing for the boy so that he could be placed in apprenticeship.[135] And when a farmer was reported to have "already taken in" a foundling on his own, the council recommended looking into the possibility of similar rural placements "so that the Findel is not burdened with the same." (Magistrates also did not trouble the willing foster father with a further inquiry about his expenses).[136]

Despite this magisterial inclination, direct requests for money rather than for admission to the Findel were surprisingly uncommon. When Saloman Zorn petitioned to have his one-and-a-half-year-old grandson accepted into the Findel, he added that he would find 20 kreuzer a week (about 18 fl. annually) an acceptable alternative and fortunately for him the inner council concurred.[137] A woman who was bold enough to request the sizeable sum of 40 fl. as reimbursement for the brief care of another woman and her child was viewed more suspiciously, particularly after testimony from the mother in question that "such demands were totally unreasonable, as I had to work like a maid as soon as I could walk and had certainly earned my keep." Magistrates accordingly denied the request and the grasping petitioner was sent away empty-handed, with a stern reprimand.[138]

If money alone did not satisfy the petitioner, then Pömer or another magistrate would offer to accept one or two siblings, usually the youngest, into the Findel if the petitioner would agree to provide for the remaining child(ren), often with governmental assistance.[139] In 1611, for instance, the two youngest orphans of Fritz Vogel were admitted to the Findel, with the understanding that the petitioning guardian would be granted "a modest child care supplement" to help support the remaining oldest brother "until he can earn his bread."[140] Here too Pömer and his fellow councilors instinctively reaffirmed the flexibility of family and household definitions in negotiations with petitioners. Keeping brothers and sisters together was rarely a priority. Splitting up multiple siblings became an especially common negotiating tactic after 1610, with the Findel administrator repeatedly asking petitioners to take on one or more siblings themselves in return for the admission of one or more children to the Findel.[141] On the other hand, in more than 90 percent of cases in which siblings were mentioned, at least two children from the same family were accepted into the Findel. Instances of three or more siblings admitted at the same time were not unheard of and overall at least one-third of all children admitted to the Findel entered with at least one sibling.[142]

When no relative or godparent could be found and petitioners consistently resisted taking on any children themselves, Pömer and his colleagues appeared willing to give unwanted children to just about anyone who would take them. This might take the form of an informal inquiry in the neighborhood where a foundling was discovered or even public proclamations of various sorts. In one instance, the inner council ordered the city's pastors "to query from the pulpit on the following Sunday whether there was anyone willing to take in [a two-year-old foundling]."[143] There is no record in Nuremberg of the notorious practice of French foundling homes "selling" children to professional beggars or others.[144] There was also, however, no background check whatsoever on adults who expressed a willingness to take in petitioning children, and there were no follow-up visits by governmental officials.

Even more jolting to modern sensibilities is the consistent willingness of Pömer and his fellow councilors to return publicly abandoned or even abused children to their the biological or foster parents who rejected them. In virtually every instance when abandoning parents could be identified and located, magistrates sent the children back to them, regardless of the parents' financial, physical, or mental capabilities. Hans Sturn, who "ran off and left his three children sitting" in June 1627, had all three children returned to him without question upon his reappearance almost a year later, as did the absconding Conrad Teuffel in 1598.[145] A newborn baby found exposed on Schütt Island in April 1666 was immediately baptized and accepted into the Findel, but upon its mother's emergence the next day, was restored to her and then banished with her. Another abandoning woman who was clearly deranged also had her baby returned to her, along with half a Gulder, before both were banished from Nuremberg's territory.[146] In 1611 we learn of a traumatized girl sent to the hospital by a woman nicknamed the "Tax Collector" (die Schosserin) who had promised the girl's father to care for her, "which, however, she has not until now done, but rather [knocked] the child about and beaten her lame." Despite this abusive behavior, the girl was returned to the foster mother, who was told "if she didn't fulfill her obligations, she would be banished from the city with the child."[147]

Nuremberg's magistrates could appear especially harsh when dealing with unwanted children from foreign jurisdictions. If the parents could be identified and located, they were summoned, admonished, and sometimes granted a small cash gift before being banished with their children. A child found by Hans Matthes Muller in 1615 was denied both admittance to the Findel and financial support, with the council instructing the Findel administrator to "tell him that foreign children cannot be accepted into the Findel."[148] Beginning about this time, councilors took the more aggressive measure of directly deporting such children on their own, as in the case of three children found abandoned in the Teutonic Knights' courtyard who were ordered loaded onto a cart, driven to their parents' village, "and the same abandoned [literally "set down"] there."[149] Two girls found in the streets of suburban Gostenhof who were determined to be from nearby Wasserzell were similarly ordered "taken back and abandoned there."[150] Once the father of a toddler named Georglein found on a Gostenhof street in May 1615 was identified, the child was immediately sent off to his grandparents' village of Hasloch.[151] Even Albrecht Pömer consented to removing four young orphans from the overcrowded begging stockade in 1634, giving each a piece of bread and then sending them back to their home villages in the Margravate of Ansbach.[152]

Shortly after the inner council began actively deporting unwanted foreign children, it began admitting some orphans on a fee basis for a set period, usually "until the child comes of age and can earn his own bread." Other European orphanages and foundling homes found this policy moderately profitable, but in Nuremberg the practice for the most part remained an ad hoc revenue generator during the worst times of the Thirty Years' War.[153] For prices ranging from 4 to 30 fl. annually (never advertised), the inner council agreed to accept a small number of orphans into the Findel, even during 1633–36, when the home itself was spilling over with residents.[154] Orphans who applied for admission during the 1630s were also routinely questioned on any family inheritance, particularly real estate, a practice first visible in 1614 and were in fact the only petitioners where property was mentioned at all.[155] In 1634, Pömer and his colleagues decreed that all property of any child admitted, without exception, had to go directly to the Findel, which would return the principal to the child upon release but in the meantime receive the earned interest. Guardians or relatives who failed to "effectuate" risked imprisonment.[156] During the first year of implementation this new requirement brought in 177 fl. in capital; in 1634–41 the total was over 700 fl.[157]

Since about 1615 onward, the council had also begun to investigate petitioners who claimed poverty as an excuse, such as last chapter's Georg Baur, who represented himself as incapable of caring for his three allegedly abandoned sisters. When Hans Mayr asked to have the three children of his brother-in-law, Friederich Herdeger, admitted on account of "great poverty," councilors demanded to know "in what manner the same came into poverty, what were his outstanding debts, how old the three children [were and] whether [they were] boys or girls, who [were] their friends and godparents, and whether they might not be cared for by the same." A week later they decided to accept Herdeger's youngest girl but left it to Hans Mayr to find other relatives to take in the remaining children.[158] The request of Elisabeth Miedlin, "a poor housemaid," that the Findel take in the orphans of her kinsman Caspar Deffinger was met by a similar direction "to inquire around the neighborhood and otherwise whether the supplicant's poverty was as great as she claimed," and also to seek out other relatives.[159]

Relying solely on official decrees risks overstating the importance of money in admission decisions and glossing over the many instances of counter evidence. Boarding payments by petitioning relatives or guardians were never frequent or substantive, and annual income from children's capital only exceeded 100 fl. three times during the crisis years of the 1630s. Accompanying property also did not guarantee admittance. Councilors continued to seek private foster parents for the four orphans of Thomas Ruchols, despite their collective inheritance of 500 fl., and the guardian of a mentally retarded boy with 180 fl. property was told that that there was no room for him in the Findel and that he would need to transfer to the Hospital as soon as possible.[160] Whether or not a beggar child claimed any inheritance (and many did during the 1630s) made no apparent difference in the decision to admit. The great majority of children admitted to the Findel at any time did not claim any property whatsoever and more than a few entered with significant debts. In 1638, the abandoned child of two banished thieves who left a 77 fl. debt behind them was still accepted, as was Matthes Christof Baur, whose recently deceased parents had left behind "great debts," which the Findel and alms bureau partially assumed.[161]

The same leniency in practice is true of the council's oft-repeated policy of not accepting foreign children, which often resembled less a strict rule than an exasperated parent's empty threat to really punish the next time. In 1616, after accepting noncitizen Friedrich Pellein's two orphans, the inner council decreed "to be mindful not to accept any foreign [children] except with considerable justification."[162] The proscription was especially difficult to enforce during periods of extreme need. In a group of seventy-one beggar children Pömer admitted to the Findel in March 1634, only five came from citizen families.[163] Even in January 1635, during the peak of overcrowding at the Findel, Pömer accepted the child of a noncitizen as long as his uncle paid off outstanding debts and gave the Findel the remainder of the child's inheritance.[164] One in ten petitioning fathers for whom citizenship was mentioned was a foreigner; the actual number was probably much higher.[165]

Day-to-day interactions with diverse petitioners also sometimes revealed a softer side of Pömer and his fellow magistrates not evident in official proclamations. Their profound desire to intervene only when absolutely necessary frequently collided with equally deep aversion to the sight of starving and suffering children in their streets.[166] Poverty itself was frequently the very grounds for acceptance of a petitioning child. A grandmother who professed great sorrow that she was too poor to raise any of three orphaned grandchildren clearly touched the hearts of the sitting mayors, who admitted all three children to the Findel.[167] Unwanted illegitimate children occasionally prompted similar sympathy and generosity. Successful early modern petitions were stories meant to persuade and appeal to the magnanimous inclinations of those in authority, so that cases with identical circumstances might yield quite different outcomes.[168] The changing cast of characters on both sides of the process also helps account for apparent arbitrariness in the decisive role of such factors as social connections.[169] Only in questions of religion did Pömer and other magistrates across the generations appear perfectly consistent. After ascertaining that the two orphaned daughters of Michael and Magdalena Weiss had "no blood relatives whatsoever," magistrates approached the girls' godmother, who declined due to her own six children. If the council handed the two over to a willing foster father, however, they "would be brought over to the Reformed [i.e., Calvinist] Religion." Both children were immediately admitted to the Findel. Another time, twelve-year-old Matthes Kramer was similarly accepted despite his advanced age, "so that [he] did not come into popery" with a foster parent.[170]

The council's apparent vulnerability to manipulation by shrewd petitioners was the necessary price of early modern hegemony, where compromise remained essential to effectiveness. Pömer and his colleagues knew well the possible consequences of a forced fosterage and thus attempted to reach an equitable agreement and avoid any hasty actions by a disgruntled petitioner. One of two women who claimed to have found a child abandoned in a field was given 10–12 fl. a year to care for the child (assumed by magistrates to be her own) and warned "she is not to harm or again abandon the child; otherwise they would know where to find her."[171] Preventing adverse reactions of this nature was the main reason that magistrates always preferred to find an acceptable common ground with a petitioner. After Hans Maisenbuch brought in a baby boy he had found deposited in his stable, the Findel administrator was ordered "to negotiate with the same to raise the child, giving him a yearly stipend from the alms bureau or should he not wish to keep it, to find another way to care for and raise the baby so that it doesn't [come to] ruin"; nine days later the child was accepted into the Findel.[172]

Contrary to the inner council's consistently expressed politics and tough rhetoric, the acceptance rate for Findel applicants was consequently quite

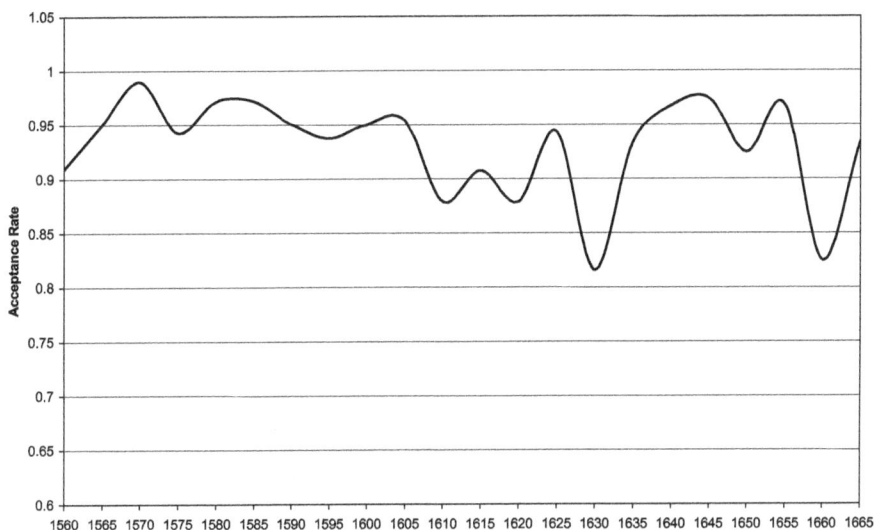

Fig. 3.8. Total Nuremberg Findel acceptance rate, 1560–1669
(five-year increments; n = 4018). *Source*: FKD.

high, ranging from 95 percent for foster children to 91 percent for orphans, and averaging 93 percent overall for the period 1557–1670 (see fig. 3.8). When petitioning children were turned away, it was rare that the Findel administrator had not identified an acceptable foster parent and provided some financial assistance for the child's upkeep. These precautions did not always insure that the child(ren) in question would not turn up at the Findel's doorstep later, but they did effectively remove virtually all parentless young children from the city's streets and in that sense satisfied Pömer's paramount duty toward Nuremberg's "poor orphans and foundlings."

The Findel Administrator amid Social Crisis

Were Albrecht Pömer's efforts to secure care for the city's unwanted children that came his way more successful than his campaign against child begging? Perhaps the best way to gauge the individual and social impact of his administration of the Findel is to examine it more closely during its years of greatest crisis. When Pömer took office as Findel administrator in the spring of 1633, the Findel housed about 75 children. During the next five years he would oversee the biggest sustained surge in the Findel's history, a total of 783 admissions from 1632 to 1638, with an average of 161 boys and girls in residence at any one time. He would also subsequently preside over the steepest decline in the institution's numbers, from 168 children in residence in May 1638 to only 49 residents just seven years later, in May 1645. That total would recover a bit during the remaining years of his tenure, but it would rarely go above 90 and usually remained around 75 for the next two hundred years.

But what do these fluctuations mean in terms of Pömer's effectiveness as a Findel administrator—failures, successes, or demographic forces beyond his control? In short, did he make a difference? The answer requires a slightly expanded definition of Albrecht Pömer's goals as Findel administrator. In addition to the care and eventual placement of the unwanted children that came before the council, Pömer had an overriding mandate to keep the Findel solvent. Admission of any unwanted child, no matter how great the need, always had to be weighed against the resources at his disposal. Like any administrator, he faced constraints of money and space. Pömer's success in this respect depended on making the most of what was available and finding additional resources when that proved inadequate. Since he did not maintain complete control over the numbers of children admitted to the Findel, these resources were regularly stretched, no more so than during 1633–38, his very first years on the job. His leadership during this crisis is a powerful illustration of Nuremberg's magistracy at its best, generating creative and sometimes desperate responses to the crushing demands imposed by marauding armies and devastating epidemics. His decisions also reflect the profound tension between the council's "citizens-only" policy for aiding such children and the reflexive pity and sympathy most magistrates experienced in the face of "friendless" infants and children. The immediate consequence of these conflicting agendas was severe overcrowding in the Findel, but also shelter and food for many homeless minors. The medium- and long-term consequences were a fiscal burden from which neither the city nor the Findel would ever fully recover.

In April 1633, the city and the Findel had already been in severe crisis for almost a year, ever since the arrival of Wallenstein's armies in Franconia the previous June. Almost immediately the inner council had experienced a dramatic surge in the number of petitions for admission to the Findel on behalf of foreign children. Since September 1632 the inner council had begun to accept numerous children, citizenship unspecified, who lay "poorly clothed [and] wretched" for several days in the street, fearing, in view of the unseasonably cold weather, that they would otherwise freeze to death.[173] The immediate result of such compassion was severe overcrowding at the Findel. During the eight months before Albrecht Pömer assumed office, his predecessor had admitted 129 children to the Findel, swelling the number of residents to over 150 at times, well beyond the home's normal capacity of 90. The new Findel administrator's frustrated appeals to the inner council for assistance encountered the same simplistic and unhelpful answer that his preoccupied colleagues had given his predecessor: send as many children as possible to relatives and place more of the older boys as apprentices "so that other needy poor children and orphans could be helped all the more."[174] Pömer proceeded to turn away almost half of all petitioning orphans during the rest of 1633—an unprecedented refusal rate for the Findel—but he was only able to place eight children in service or apprentice positions.[175]

At the same time, the new Findel administrator exhibited heartfelt sympathy for "the many orphans and children, both rural subjects of my lord and those citizens resident here [in the city], who upon the departure of their parents survive by begging and must lie overnight on the streets wretchedly rotting and freezing." (Once more, the colder winters of Europe's Second Little Ice Age played a key role). When the temperature began to drop in early November 1633, he ordered the municipal archers to pick up and take all such children at nightfall to the Findel, hospital, beggar stockade— anywhere they could "warm up . . . so that they might stay alive, and the following day to give each a piece of bread." The traditional distinction between local "poor orphans" and foreign "sturdy beggar rabble" still stood in principle, but at least for the duration of this one winter, the latter would "no longer be led out of the city and banished or left lying rotting day and night on the streets" but would instead be housed locally and permitted "to ask citizens for a small piece of bread."[176]

The subsequent influx of children into the Findel led Pömer again to complain to the inner council of dangerous overcrowding, with children literally "lying on top of one another." This time the war commissioners agreed to move out a number of chain-gang inmates (*Springbuben*) currently housed in the Findel's neighboring Franciscan church to make room for "the poor orphans."[177] On at least two more occasions during that desperate winter of 1633–34, large groups of seventy or more beggar children and other strays were crammed into both the Findel and begging stockade—any place "that could be kept warm," at least until spring.[178] When the "very sickly" five-year-old of a conscripted soldier was left behind in February 1634, Pömer ordered the usual check for relatives and promised aid from the Findel "so that [the child] not continue roaming around in beggary and its health further damaged."[179] In most institutions, such severe overcrowding and intense exposure to a variety of fatal diseases resulted in mortality of at least 60–70 percent of residents. But because Pömer immediately shipped all potentially contagious children to the hospital or another place of quarantine, the Findel lost only fifteen children during his first twelve months in office—one-fifth of the total fatalities during the preceding year.[180]

The inner council's "exceptional" decision regarding foreign beggar children turned out to be more than a one-time emergency stopgap. In the spring of 1634, the war bureau again reported high numbers of orphaned children on the city's streets, "having to ask and plead for nothing more than a piece of bread to stay alive, since they had no other means of getting by."[181] When asked once more to investigate the reports, Pömer and his committee replied that

> the orphans [on the street] are both foreign and local, and as to how to support the former, one might make inquiries about the same's [ruling jurisdiction] and investigate whether they might be sent to the designated [home town]; for those who cannot even name their home town, however, it would be an act of mercy to take the same into the Findel or another designated location . . . [and] to keep [them] there until they can be placed in either a service position or an apprenticeship.[182]

In the absence of a clear mandate from his colleagues, Pömer continued to oversee frequent sweeps of child street beggars that brought citizens and foreigners alike in the Findel.

The following fall and winter were the deadliest in the Findel's history and elicited new concerns. Responding to a surge in children whose biological or foster parents had died from the plague, Pömer asked the inner council in September 1634 what to do with the large number of sick children coming into the Findel. Again his fellow councilors told him what he already knew: send the contagious or "severely damaged" ones immediately to the hospital as before, those with fever or dysentery to the Lazareth Hospice, and those with plague to the pesthouse—all institutions already overcrowded.[183] Even with the transfers the Findel remained bursting with children. A few weeks later, in early October, the inner council suggested that Pömer "think of a special location that could contain children until it can be determined whether they are healthy and therefore able to be admitted into the Findel."

One month later, the council ordered the construction of a two-chamber annex to the Findel for just this purpose.[184] In the meantime Pömer continued to scour the city for any additional quarantine space, securing a small library and a fencing studio. Within a few weeks, though, the council's mood turned uglier, with the Findel's overcrowding blamed on foreign orphans and the city's deputies ordered " to quickly come up with a place where such parentless children might be transported and kept."[185] The decree had no apparent effect on the number of children who continued to flood the Findel. Once the weather began to turn warm again, in March 1635, councilors again urged the outright deportation of all healthy noncitizen children.[186] Instead, Pömer implemented a new policy that permitted only children under fourteen to be transferred into the Findel; the older remained in the hospital or other health facility until cured. By then about three hundred children, almost all orphans over six years old, had passed through the Findel's doors within the previous year. Half of them, 147 to be precise, had died before the fiscal year ended in May 1635.[187]

If not for a series of critical immediate responses and reform initiatives on the part of Pömer and his conciliar allies, the tragic outcome would probably have been even more disastrous. Already in mid-January of 1635, Pömer reported to the inner council that the Findel's grain supplies were almost depleted. In addition to securing two massive loans from the alms bureau totaling 4,500 fl., he began calling in past debts from millers, ranging from a few *Simmer* (approximately thirty-five liters) each to over 100 in one instance. Each time, debtors were given the choice of paying up or taking in "a number of poor children."[188] No Findel children changed residences. Over the next four months, Pömer also worked with his colleagues and local millers to develop a "voluntary" tax on all grain milled. Some millers vehemently resisted, but after the inner council threatened imprisonment of all dissenters the proposal carried and was endorsed by councilors on May 12, 1635. Though imperfectly enforced, this measure at least saw that the Findel had adequate grain supplies for the remaining three years of crisis.[189]

Pömer's efforts did not end there. Together with his fellow councilor Jakob Welser, he developed a complete relief package for the Findel's many needs.[190] Their working proposal focused primarily on creating additional revenue for the Findel and hospital through requiring "voluntary" contributions. What were in fact involuntary donations, or taxes, are never popular, but particularly so in times of great social turmoil. It took Pömer and Welser several months to convince their colleagues to endorse their plan and when the latter finally consented, in January 1636, the new decree was prefaced by a long and exculpatory justification that the council "had no greater wish than that the citizenry could be spared such burdens," but this was truly a time of desperate need and "the magistracy and its subjects formed a republic and could no longer live together unsociably (*unumgänglich*)," without sharing. Everyone affected by these charges, the two councilors stressed, could consider their contribution an act of true Christian charity.[191] The decree established new taxes on all precious metals in the city; a tax of one

Reichstaler (1.2 fl.) on several prominent occupations, including innkeepers, beer brewers, and craftsmen; a mandatory two-Reichstaler "contribution" at all wedding celebrations; and a progressive property tax on each new city officeholder upon the assumption of official duties.

The new taxes varied in success, producing an overall increased revenue of about 500 fl. in the first year.[192] They were in part a response to increased admission numbers, but also addressed the falling income from already existing Findel revenue sources that were particularly susceptible to various economic and demographic fluctuations. The Findel's wine tax, for instance, had dropped from a prewar income of over 1,000 fl. (over two-thirds of the Findel's income some years) to a mere 19 fl. during 1634.[193] The high mortality rate during the direst years of the 1630s, on the other hand, proved a boon for the custom of buying a "coffin pillow" (*Küssen* or *Lailach*) from the Findel, bringing in the massive amount of 1,609 fl in 1632–33 and 1,007 fl. in 34–35. Some preexisting taxes had withered to the point of insignificance, such as the 120-year-old practice of fining council members four schillings (1/5 fl.) for arriving late to a session, a tradition that only brought in 4 to 9 fl. annually during the 1630s.[194] Other income came from "the old custom" of fines for fornication being paid directly into its account (an appropriate source of income for a home originally dedicated to illegitimate foundlings). During the 1630s, the sexual peccadilloes of Nuremberg's populace provided the Findel with a reliable and steady income of 150–200 fl. per year.[195] Truly voluntary contributions were even more vulnerable to economic upheaval. By 1630, door-to-door collections were down dramatically and church collections for the Findel brought in next to nothing. Legacies to the Findel also dropped greatly during the same period.[196] Orphans' Christmas collections peaked at 275 fl. in 1631 and averaged over 100 fl. for the next sixty holiday seasons, while Easter egg collections garnered only 20–30 fl. annually during the 1630s.[197]

Albrecht Pömer's particular administrative genius in responding to the 1630s crisis lay in his utilization of the Findel children themselves in the support of their home. Instilling a work ethic had always been at the core of the institution's mission, but with the tumult of the 1630s that part of the mission received a new sense of urgency. After accepting two orphan sisters into the Findel back in February 1633, Pömer and his fellow alms lords expressed their dismay that "during this time the Findel children have absolutely no work to do," and they ordered the crafts bureau "to inquire among various craftsmen whether they have some work for these children, so that they can earn something and not just sit around useless."[198] Upon his installation as Findel administrator a few months later, Pömer targeted two aspects of Findel work in particular. First he addressed the perceived idleness of Findel children in combination with the institution's desperate need for cash. During Pömer's first two years as administrator, the Findel garnished only 34 fl. from sales of *Flinderlein* (small ornamental tin cutouts), but by 1635–36, that annual income had jumped more than sixfold to 217 fl., followed by a total of 344 fl. in profits in 1636–38, and averaged over 200 fl. during the subsequent decade.[199] In May 1636, he added the business of wool spinning to the children's work, yielding 54 fl. in first month alone, and a total of 420 fl. over the next six years. Since the principal aim remained economic survival, not exploited labor, the practice was discontinued once the immediate crisis had subsided.[200] Had he been more interested in profit, Pömer might have also considered expanding the Findel's milk and butter production, the source of over 100 fl. a year by 1635–36, but he did not and after 1640 that part of the Findel's businesses also declined until the next Findel administrator took over in 1654.[201]

Despite generating of this much-needed income, the Findel itself remained severely overcrowded, and the danger of insufficient quarantine facilities was acute. In September 1635, the inner council once again expressed anxiety about "the many wandering, poor, and underage children" in the city streets and the urgency of immediate action "on account of cold, [falling] nights."[202] The years 1635–36 were also difficult for the Findel, with the admission of an additional 116 children, all orphans, many of them ill. Even though roughly half of these new charges died, the Findel at times housed as many as 200 children—still more than twice its normal capacity.[203] This situation too could have been much worse. In that year Pömer successfully placed 79 older boys and girls in apprenticeships and service positions, thereby easing the overcrowding significantly. In all, 225 children were placed during Pömer's first decade in office—almost four times the total placed during the preceding ten years.

The seasonal ebb and flow of foreign children continued for the remainder of the crisis. In the spring of 1636, the council resumed its longstanding policy of banishing healthy foreign children and during the winter continued to accept them into the Findel. Incoming numbers actually declined significantly during the winter of 1636–37, so that by spring the total resident population was down to 137, the lowest in five years. But when new epidemics struck that fall, admission numbers again soared, to 120, this time with a slightly higher fatality rate and 168 children living in the home by the spring of 1638. By then, the worst of the city's demographic nightmare was over. During the next five years, annual admissions plummeted to under twenty and after that to below ten for the remainder of Pömer's tenure as Findel administrator. The home's population accordingly shrank to ninety-four by 1641 and then to under fifty by 1651. Admission numbers thereafter never exceeded twenty children a year nor the overall Findel population a total of ninety resident boys and girls—virtually the same statistics as a century earlier, before the Findel's major boom.

The cost of surviving seven catastrophic years cannot be overstated. By the time that Nuremberg's great economic and demographic crisis ended in 1639, the finances of both the Findel and the city were in shambles. Throughout the sixteenth century, the Findel budget had almost always run a surplus and despite a few difficult years, in 1632 it only owed the municipal coffers 1,368 fl. Beginning in July 1634, though, Pömer was forced to borrow more heavily from the alms bureau, including 4,300 fl. just within the last week of the year—the Findel's darkest hour. His fiscal innovations mitigated the situation somewhat but by the end of the 1630s, the Findel had borrowed over 14,000 fl. in multiple installments.[204] Virtually all of this particular debt was forgiven by the alms bureau and by 1653, Pömer had actually restored the Findel to the black, with a surplus of 1,203 fl. at the time of his death the following year. The institution would continue to struggle financially over the next two centuries, however, and was in particularly bad financial shape when the city was assimilated by Bavaria in 1806.[205]

The reasons for the Findel's money troubles are not particularly difficult to fathom. As a host of governments have since discovered, social services are costly. Most German states around 1600 spent on average 200 fl. per 1,000 inhabitants per year. Wealthy Nuremberg easily expended twice that amount, possibly three times as much, while Augsburg gave out still more.[206] Orphanages, foundling homes, and hospitals were particularly expensive, with high overhead and great vulnerability to inflation in food prices. Rising apprenticeship fees and staff salaries during the seventeenth century further exacerbated the situation. Because so many of the costs were fixed, limiting the number of admissions and other attempts to reduce costs had a minimal impact. Running a small home of fewer than twenty children in Regensburg on average cost one-half as much as operating an orphanage in Augsburg with ten times as many residents.[207] Put another way, while the number of admissions to the Nuremberg Findel fluctuated considerably over the course of the Thirty Years' War, the annual expenses of the home were almost exactly the same with 61 children in 1650 as they had been with 156 children in 1627.[208] Meanwhile, income to the Findel dropped precipitously, also due to the devastating effects of the war on the city's economy. By 1653, the municipal alms bureau reported drastically reduced revenue from its endowment and property taxes (down 75 percent and 50 percent, respectively, in just one year) "on account of impoverishment of the citizenry and declining real estate [values]."[209] Even more alarming was the decline of donations to the alms collection, particularly since the war's end in 1648.

The high expense of running social welfare programs such as the Findel, combined with the decline of private donations, hit traditionally generous and proud cities such as Nuremberg and Augsburg particularly hard. Unwilling to close down such institutions, Albrecht Pömer and other governmental officials were forced to rely on their own general coffers to supply an ever greater share of social welfare expenditures.[210] The expenditures remained high, with Nuremberg supporting at least 2,800 children annually in one form or another during the 1660s, even though the city's population had dropped to only 20,000, and its economy remained fragile.[211] Cost-cutting measures, including greater restriction of Findel admissions, could not make up the difference, and widely unpopular taxes on an impoverished and demoralized population had their own social costs. Overwhelmed with these and other crushing debts, Pömer and his fellow councilors brought the city back from the brink of bankruptcy in 1641 and were able to reduce the municipal debt from its wartime high of over 8 million fl. to just under 5 million fl. by the time of Pömer's death in 1654.[212] The Findel, like Nuremberg itself, survived the many blows of the war, but the price proved almost unbearable. Neither entity ever fully recovered its economic vitality and by the time that Nuremberg's independence ended in 1806, the municipal debt stood at over ten million fl.[213]

Yet as the crisis of the 1630 drew to an end, Albrecht Pömer could look back over the previous five years with some modest sense of accomplishment amid the citywide horror and misery. At a time when local bakers could not bake bread fast enough to feed the city's swelled population, the Findel administrator's collection on several past debts of millers and bakers and other finagling had insured that the institution always had an adequate supply of bread.[214] During the worst plague months, when three wagons in use around the clock could barely keep up with the mounting piles of cadavers from the hospital alone, Pömer's rigorous enforcement of quarantine in the Findel resulted in only about one-quarter of its children succumbing to the diseases ravaging the general population from 1633 to 1637—less than half the usual epidemic death rate in comparable institutions.[215] And in the midst of massive unemployment and the most severe economic crisis in the city's history, the Findel administrator had succeeded in placing eighty-nine boys and thirty girls in apprenticeships or service positions.[216] Pömer, who lost three of his own children during the same period, could not deny the universal suffering the crisis brought to Nuremberg nor the long-term damage to the city's economic and political stature. Perhaps, though, he found consolation that even in their darkest hour he and his fellow council members had honored their civic and Christian duty toward the unwanted children in their midst, saving many from certain death on the streets.[217]

A Life of Public Service in Vain?

Albrecht Pömer was nearly fifty-seven at the time of his death on March 10, 1654. During twenty-seven years of public life, he saw one of Europe's most admired cities, his beloved Nuremberg, successively blackmailed and humiliated by marauding armies, its population devastated by deadly epidemics, and its government slowly eviscerated by monstrous public debts. He also witnessed ever growing numbers of child and youth beggars on the city's streets, frustrating results in public education, a dramatic rise and equally dramatic fall in Findel admissions, as well as apparently undiminished instances of child abandonment and infanticide. Pömer had begun his governmental career as a privileged and highly educated member of Nuremberg's ruling class, confident that he could fulfill his paternal obligations toward the city's needy children while still respecting the moral, humanist, and fiscal imperatives of his various civic offices. There is no evidence that during his last days he considered his life's work a failure, and his continuous high level of governmental activity until that moment suggests the opposite conclusion. Surely he realized that he and his fellow civic leaders had critically underestimated the difficulty of achieving their ambitious child welfare agenda and that in some ways the situation was worse at the time of his death than thirty years previously. This at least was the conclusion of his conciliar successors, who, during the 1660s, initiated a zero-tolerance policy toward child begging, a greater restrictiveness in Findel admissions, and a new intensity in the prosecution of infanticide.

The view from Pömer's perspective is more ambivalent. He would undoubtedly (and rightly) take pride that his work as Findel administrator and in other public roles benefited many unwanted children and in some cases saved their lives and gave them a future. Pömer and his colleagues were proved especially effective and responsive in the face of widespread social crises, most notably the diverse disasters of the turbulent 1630s, where they were able to secure and distribute resources otherwise unavailable to Nuremberg's neediest children. He was clearly disappointed, on the other hand, by the apparent failure of many of his educational initiatives and by the intractability of numerous poor parents who continued to send their children begging and otherwise neglected to prepare them for life as pious and productive members of society. This impotence was hardly grounds for a crisis in confidence, though, especially for a university-educated student of Lutheran theology as well as human history. The City of Man belonged largely to the evil adversary, and self-destructive, sinful behavior was to be expected, even among members of the visible church. Again, Pömer's patrician and Christian duty lay not in perfecting such a world but in proclaiming God's will through his own assistance to the genuinely needy and his punishment of the wicked. The fact that fornication, infanticide, and other vices continued to thrive in Nuremberg despite the council's vigilance merely underscored the difficulty of magistrates' God-given responsibility and their faithfulness in nevertheless persevering in its execution.

Some aspects of Pömer's worldview strike the modern observer as alien and a few of his actions, such as returning children to abusive parents, seem incomprehensibly cruel. Here it helps to recall that he and his patrician colleagues were often as concerned about their own honor and escaping divine punishment of their beloved city as they were about reducing social inequality and individual suffering. Fiduciary responsibilities were also a prominent concern. For the most part, though, the reforms Pömer attempted, as well as their limited success, seem jarringly familiar—particularly regarding the importance of education and financial assistance to poor families and the practical futility of distinctions between citizen and noncitizen children.

Perhaps the most recognizable aspect of governmental involvement in questions of child welfare was the intrinsically moralistic nature of the entire endeavor. This characteristic was evident from the earliest paternalistic legislation of the fifteenth century and continued to grow more pronounced over the next two hundred years, as Nuremberg's magistrates felt ever more compelled to fill in for irresponsible parents. The simultaneously rising costs of governmental support for unwanted and neglected children only intensified their righteous anger and by the end of Pömer's career resulted in ever greater emphasis on discipline and punishment over education and nurturing, culminating in the establishment of Nuremberg's workhouse in 1670.[218] While the annual population of the Findel remained below sixty or seventy, the number of unruly adults and youths in the new discipline- and workhouse expanded steadily, peaking during the 1770s at over seven hundred adults and youth inmates. In an almost complete inversion of the Findel routine, young inmates of the workhouse spent almost the entire day in manufacturing work, with only the hour before bedtime reserved for schooling.[219] Pietist-inspired reformers countered with free poor schools in Nuremberg (1699) and elsewhere, but almost always with private, rather than public, financing.[220] It would be at least a century after Albrecht Pömer's death before governmental activists again became prominent, this time fired by Enlightenment notions of social reform and human perfectibility.

Sadly, Pömer's familial legacy did not fare much better than his political testament, the paterfamilias having outlived all but two of his ten children. None of the dead had reached adulthood and only one of his surviving daughters, Maria Helena, married and had children; Maria Magdalena died a spinster in 1726 at the age of eighty-seven. By then, five more of the city's forty-two patrician families had died out and the remainder continued to close ranks even more, jostling for social advantage in a thoroughly marginalized and inward-facing city. When Georg Karl Wilhelm Pömer, the last male member of the house, died without issue in 1814, the Pömer family line joined its extinct brethren and became one more vanished remnant of Nuremberg's once-glorious past.[221]

FOUR

The Street Orphan

Far beneath Nuremberg's ornate neoclassical town hall, in a damp, window-less chamber, a desperate Jörg Mayr knelt before his interrogators, plead-ing for mercy. He knew that the odds were heavily against him. Though only "sixteen or seventeen" years old, the youth more commonly known as "the Little Castle Seventh" (*der Schloss Sieptlein*, the diminutive of a type of sharecropper) had already been arrested and banished several times and was notorious throughout the Franconian countryside as the most prolific juvenile thief in memory. This time, the patience of the examining council-ors and jurors had obviously worn thin. During the six weeks since his arrest and incarceration in Nuremberg's dreaded Hole on April 14, 1604, he had been subjected to four extended interrogations, including repeated torture with the strappado. When his testimony concluded, Mayr had confessed to a life of crime since the age of six and to at least ninety-five thefts or bur-glaries within the past four years alone.[1] He had also provided—to the best of his ability—detailed descriptions of crimes, accomplices, items stolen, and even the amounts he received from his various fences. Now if only "my lords" could find it in their hearts to show mercy one more time, he swore that he would leave and never return to the territory of Nuremberg. He even volunteered to go directly off to Hungary, where the emperor needed young and willing mercenaries in his war against the Turks. "With all humility and for God's sake," Mayr begged his judges to give him one more chance to redeem the sins of one who as an "ignorant and stupid youth had been led into temptation by others." He asked only for the opportunity "to better himself and to become a completely new person."[2]

How did things reach this point for Jörg Mayr? Where did he come from and why was he on the street in the first place? What was that life like for him and other vagrant youths? Most important, how was a wandering

Fig. 4.1. *A Vagrant Beggar Boy* (1758).
Staatliche Museen zu Berlin, Kupferstichkabinett.

adolescent beggar transformed into a career criminal, "known throughout the land"?[3] In exploring this type of informal child circulation, we will see that some aspects of the Little Castle Seventh's background and experience were common to many youths, regardless of residence or criminal activity. Poverty, orphanhood, and the absence of any craft training were widespread structural realities of life that often produced aimlessly wandering teenagers such as Jörg.[4] Virtually all of these youths subsisted on begging, odd jobs, and the kindness of strangers. Many also occasionally filched food and small items of clothing. Only a small minority of poor children and youths, however, came to rely on stealing and other crimes for their principal livelihood and few of those, if any, achieved Jörg Mayr's precocious level of notoriety. Still, even this atypical individual can reveal much about the complex and varied experiences of those hundreds of thousands of unwanted children and youths who circulated on their own on the urban streets and rural roads of early modern Europe. This chapter will supplement Jörg's extensive testimony with qualitative evidence from fourteen other juvenile criminals interrogated at length in Nuremberg between 1582 and 1615, including one group of burglars (five boys and two girls), which for convenience we will call the Seven. Together, the experiences of Jörg and his contemporaries will illustrate how the few real options available to them greatly restricted but did not determine either their choices or the sad outcomes that often followed.

A Beggar Youth's Origins

By the age of sixteen, Jörg Mayr had already spent most of his life—perhaps as many as ten years—on the street. Today the term "street children" conjures up images of pathetic feral children who literally live on the street and spend their days begging and stealing as well as possibly using drugs and engaging in prostitution. Abandoned or orphaned at an early age, they roam aimlessly in packs through the concrete jungles of modern developing cities such as Bangkok, Calcutta, and São Paulo. Large cities in developed countries share this phenomenon to a certain degree, but the relative difference in scope tends to reinforce the self-serving Western notion that the modern phenomenon of street children, like unwanted children in general, is more of a "third world" problem. Given, moreover, the many demographic similarities between early modern Europe and modern poor countries, it is equally tempting to project this third-world street child stereotype backward and see it as an earlier developmental stage in the history of the now mature and affluent West.

The street children of these two worlds—Jörg's and today's developing countries—do indeed share many characteristics but their common reality is in a multitude of ways different than might be imagined. First there is the term itself. "Street children" has been in English usage since at least the nineteenth century, but only since 1979, the United Nations' "Year of the Child," has the term has gained widespread usage. Until the 1950s, the more common English names for such children were "waifs," "street Arabs," and "street urchins." In early modern Germany, the most common term was "beggar children" (*Bettelkinder* in German), followed by "masterless" (*herrenlose*) and "ill-raised" (*ungezogene*) children and youths.[5] These distinctions are important in correcting the most fundamental misperception about "street children" of the past or present (stemming largely from the neologism itself), namely, that the children have been abandoned to the street by one or both parents and are thus "homeless." In fact, the great majority of such boys and girls under the age of twelve in modern cities— perhaps nine in ten—have regular contact with at least one of their biological parents and often even continue to reside with them.[6] Most do not experience a definitive break with their families or regularly "sleep rough" on the streets, at least not until the age of sixteen or seventeen. Rather, these children typically spend their days and nights working, begging, stealing, fighting, and playing in the street, while drifting in and out of the lives and homes of their biological or foster parents—still another form of child circulation. They are independent in many respects but rarely to the absolute degree often presumed.

The same characterization was true of children and youths on the streets in Jörg's day. In our sample of Nuremberg juvenile thieves, at least eleven of fourteen kept in contact or resided with at least one living parent and one even stored all of his stolen loot at home with his mother.[7] Even Jörg Mayr, who liked to portray himself as a friendless and neglected orphan from an early age, did not strike out on his own until the age of eleven, and even then he occasionally relied on a network of relatives for shelter, including a brother Paulus, whom Jörg appears to have visited often up until a year before his latest arrest.[8] This in no way implies that domiciled children on the street enjoyed carefree or stable lives; their deprivation of food and affection often rivaled that of any literally homeless orphan (see fig. 4.2). Emotional and physical abuse easily qualified many of them as "unwanted children" in any but an economically exploitive sense. Their continuing relations with parents or other relatives, however, did set most of them apart in some important ways from the small minority of young children who were truly homeless and entirely on their own. Together all of these children and youths on the streets of early modern Europe—whether vagrant or domiciled—were known by their most common daily activity, that is, begging. Even though not all of them begged regularly and a few not at all, the term "beggar children" is thus preferable to the anachronistic "street children."

The great majority of beggar children on Nuremberg's streets under the age of ten almost certainly were not living on their own, at least not for any extended period of time. Clearly there were some genuinely lost souls like the fictional Simplicissimus, made homeless by war and wandering aimlessly until taken in at the age of seven by a sympathetic priest. In 1627, Nuremberg's Findel father admitted just such "a small peasant girl" who had been street begging and sleeping alone in a cloister stable for several days and who (like Simplicissimus) "could not even say where she was from or who her parents were."[9] A world perennially convulsed by war, contagion, and spiraling inflation routinely sent many orphaned or abandoned children to the street. During the city's crisis years of 1634–36 alone, the

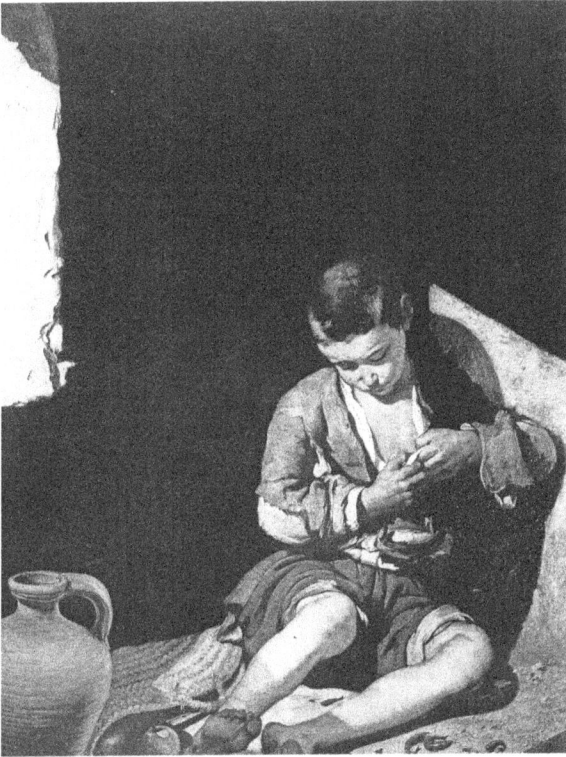

Fig. 4.2. Bartholomé Esteban Murrillo, *A Beggar Boy Picking Off Fleas* (ca. 1650). Louvre, Paris.

begging police picked up over 350 homeless beggar children and deposited them into the already overcrowded Findel. Many of these were so ill that they had to be immediately transferred to the hospital across the river.[10] More than half of the children were not yet twelve, the era's generally accepted age of independent self-support (see fig. 4.3 *on following page*).

Some were as young as four or five and overall the average age was ten and a half. Most of these smaller children, however, probably experienced only brief (though undoubtedly terrifying) periods with no fixed residence whatsoever. As already seen, the inner council followed a fairly consistent policy of picking up and immediately admitting into the Findel any beggar child under twelve who could not be claimed by a parent or placed privately elsewhere.[11] This was true of foreign children as well, a few of whom were actually deported, but most of whom were immediately accepted. Nuremberg's archers and begging police were particularly vigilant during cold

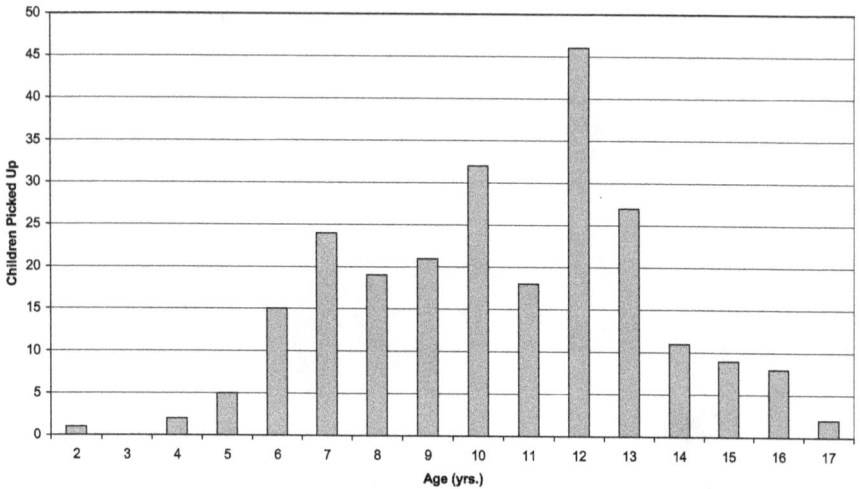

Fig. 4.3. Children picked up off Nuremberg's streets, 1634–36 (n = 240). *Source*: StadtAN 60A.

winter months. After her mother died in a street in suburban Gostenhof, twelve-year-old Barbara Mullerin wandered through Nuremberg with her one-and-a-half-year-old sister for less than two days during January 1567 before being picked up and admitted with her sister into the Findel's care.[12] It is more difficult to generalize about the number of homeless children in the countryside, though here too the situation was likely temporary in most cases.

Long-term homelessness among male teenagers such as Jörg Mayr, by contrast, was quite common throughout early modern Europe. By some estimates, one-third to one-half of all vagrants were boys under the age of eighteen.[13] Often magistrates lumped these "masterless youths" together with the slightly older cohort of "sturdy beggars." Also known as "roving country knockabouts," these vagrant youths annoyed and sometimes terrorized village and city residents with their aggressive panhandling, public drunkenness, threats, and general rowdiness.[14] They tended not to stay in one place for very long, walking two to three miles at a time and then staying for a few days to work, beg, or steal before moving on. Most remained within forty miles of their home village or city, often revisiting locations where they had been treated relatively well.[15] Based on the locations mentioned in his testimony, Jörg Mayr moved frequently during the previous four years but overwhelmingly within a twenty-five-mile radius of his hometown of Driessdorf (see fig. 4.4). The relatively few distant locations represented brief periods of his having to lie low for a while. A vagabond youth (particularly a thief)

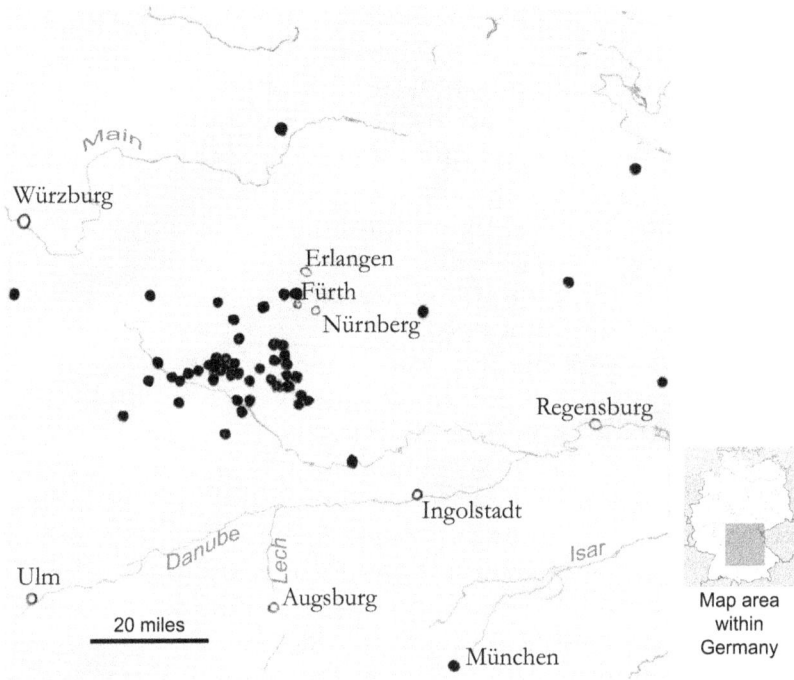

Fig. 4.4. Locations visited by Jörg Mayr, 1600–4. *Source*: ASB 215.

might acquire such a reputation as to be banned in some locations, but such prohibitions were very difficult to enforce, particularly in large cities such as Nuremberg. Several villages, for instance, had apparently banished Jörg for his thefts yet we only know of one location (Windsbach) where he was arrested and severely whipped for returning.[16] Notably, he apparently never entered the city of Nuremberg until his imprisonment and interrogation, a fact underscored by his frequent description as a *Landdieb*, or rural thief. Had he journeyed to the big city, he most likely would have resided in one of the poor suburbs of Wöhrd, Steinbühl, Schweinau, and Gostenhof, all popular destinations for vagrants of all ages.[17]

How many resident beggar children and vagrant beggar youths were actually on the streets of Nuremberg and other early modern cities? In this respect early modern societies in general shared another important demographic feature with modern developing countries. By most estimates, one-third to one-half of the entire population in Europe at this time was under the age of eighteen.[18] Based on vagrancy and residential poverty rates, this translated to a very large number of begging or idle children and teenagers on Nuremberg's streets during the day, at least a few thousand at any given time.[19] From dawn to dusk, every city and village would be filled with running and screaming children and youths (to the obvious annoyance of many adults, as we saw in the last chapter). Only a minority of all children under twelve would have been placed in a service position or a grammar school; the great majority would be at loose ends all day long. Boys and girls might assist with some household tasks, but among poor families most were left completely unsupervised in the city's streets—to play, to hawk some goods, perhaps to steal, and almost certainly to beg. Unemployed teenagers might get into even more mischief, especially if male.

For a variety of reasons, boys—under and over twelve, resident and vagrant, employed and unemployed—were more visible and audible on the streets than girls and much more disruptive. This was certainly true of the begging population. In a sample of nine groups of beggar children picked up in Nuremberg during 1634–37, boys outnumbered girls in all but two groups. Overall they comprised 58 percent of the total of 348 street children admitted during these four years—a pattern found elsewhere in early modern Europe as well.[20] Boys were also usually louder than girls. Adult residents of Nuremberg and other towns repeatedly complained about rowdy children and youths (especially boys) shouting and cursing on the streets all day long. Boys and young men also favored loud music and were especially prone to fistfights and brawls (often to impress each other, sometimes to impress girls). One of these youths' most annoying habits, according to town council decrees, was the common practice of *Jauchzen*, a kind of loud, high-spirited crowing, reminiscent of the squealing tires popular among modern teenage boys.[21] Another equally annoying practice—apparently motivated more by thrills than larceny—involved small groups of youths (boys and girls) begging house to house at night and then "creep[ing] into the house seeking a gift, especially wine."[22] Nuremberg's councilors repeatedly condemned this and other nocturnal disturbances of the peace, "when other people, healthy and sick, are taking their rest." For most townspeople this meant after 8:00 or 9:00 P.M., just when employed apprentices or journeymen would be getting off work and joining their jobless friends for drinking or other carousing.[23] The streets of Nuremberg were not lit at night, and youths who traveled without lanterns after the city's curfew risked being arrested by one of the city watchmen for burglary. The limited capabilities of a few two-man patrols, however, understandably emboldened many youths. Favorite hangouts during day or night included markets, church courtyards, outdoor plays and festivals, cockfights, horse races, weddings, funerals, and any sort of dance. Public parks, such as the Hallerwiesen or the Schütt Is-

Fig. 4.5. Nuremberg's Hallerwiesen, site of dignified Sunday strolls in
this portrayal, but more often filled with gambling and otherwise com-
peting young men (ca. 1700). Stadtbibliothek Nürnberg.

land, were particularly popular with Nuremberg's teenagers and youths, offering not only shady trees and fountains, but also space for ball playing,
bowling, wrestling, jumping, and crossbow shooting, all often including
gambling and thus frequently ending in noisy fights (see fig. 4.5).[24]

Teenaged boys like Jörg were also almost exclusively responsible for the
many acts of street vandalism and harassment that appear in official records. Whether throwing rocks or snowballs at passing coaches or playing
pranks, such as rolling a heavy stone in front of an unpopular sexton's door,
youths reveled in defying any authority they could.[25] Sometimes they could
be quite destructive, stealing or destroying lanterns, damaging conduits,
rolling timber or boulders onto highways. In July 1662, two leaders of a
pack of teenaged boys who congregated on Nuremberg's Schütt Island were
arrested for stealing large parts of the Saint Sebaldus fountain and then, in
good entrepreneurial spirit, pounding out and selling the iron. The group's
two leaders were banished to their hometown of Salzburg and five of their
followers were sentenced to chain-gang work for a few weeks.[26]

Why were Jörg and so many other unemployed youths on the street in the
first place? The single greatest structural reason had to do with the broaden-
ing gap between the early modern ideal of work and the economic realities
of the sixteenth and seventeenth centuries. According to the artisanal model
of labor that prevailed in Nuremberg and other cities, by the age of twelve
all boys would be placed as apprentices and all girls in domestic service,

Fig. 4.6. D. Teniers the Younger, *Urban Beggar Boys* (ca. 1650).

thereby simultaneously providing relief to their parents' household budget and the foundation of the youngster's economic life as an adult, either as a craftsman or as a housewife. In practice, the majority of early modern children between the ages of fifteen and nineteen were never able to secure even an initial position and were instead confronted with the choice of remaining at home, where they continued to be a drain on the family's resources, or striking out on their own ("to seek their fortune" is the way the fairy tales describe it).[27] Competitiveness for apprentice and journeyman positions had grown steadily since the late fifteenth century; by Jörg's era, up to half of all masters worked without any apprentices whatsoever; the remainder who did employ boys in this capacity could be quite selective based on the fee offered and whether other specified conditions were met.[28]

This basic structural failure of the early modern economy, obvious from today's perspective, generally eluded many people of the time. Nuremberg's magistrates, as seen in the last chapter, tended instead to locate the source for beggar children in the individual decisions of lazy, indifferent, selfish, or exploitative parents. By choosing to send their children begging instead of placing them in an apprenticeship or service position, such parents essentially condemned them to a life of inutility and likely crime. The reality was of course a bit more complex. A small minority of parents did in fact train their children to steal (what historian Norbert Schindler calls "a step with no turning back")[29] and others were truly negligent or abusive, but the great majority simply had few acceptable alternatives. Child begging in general brought in a steadier and relatively greater income than many part-time adult jobs. Single-parent households, usually headed by widowed or deserted mothers, were especially in need of money and not surprisingly predominated in lists of children arrested for begging or delinquency.[30] Jörg never mentioned his late father's profession, making it likely that he was a day laborer or vagrant but probably not a known criminal, since this type of damaging information would probably have made some appearance in either the magistrates' reports or in Mayr's own exculpatory testimony. It is known, however, that Jörg began begging at an early age, according to him at the instigation of his foster family.

In addition to parental poverty or exploitation, certain physical and mental disabilities prevented some children from pursuing an honorable trade or profession. Jörg was fortunate in this respect, since he not only had no such restrictions but appeared to be above average in intelligence and physical endurance. Nineteen-year-old Valentin Brunnmayr, on the other hand, attributed his own fall into years of thievery to a severe skin condition, possibly eczema or impetigo. No craft master would accept him because of the overwhelming stench, he told the prison chaplain, who later concurred in his journal entry that "he stinks so bad that nobody can stay near him for long." Brunnmayr also blamed his relatives, who refused to get him treatment for the disease, and threatened to shriek vengeance at them from the scaffold.[31] As with child supervision and job training, the causes of parental inaction in such cases cannot be generalized. Moreover, even if a concerned mother or father could afford consultation with a physician (an expensive proposition), early modern medicine offered few effective remedies for most disabilities and diseases. Here poor households were again trapped: Parents couldn't find employment for a disabled child and often the only way they could support the child at all was through sending him or her begging. Another juvenile thief and prostitute, Anna Geislerin, claimed that her epilepsy had prevented her from getting a domestic position and condemned her to life on the streets, a fate shared by her little brother Hans von Geiselwindt (aka Little Fatty) and his friend Hans Schober (aka Dusty), both of whom had "bad heads," presumably meaning some form of mental retardation.[32] When these suggestive references are considered alongside the large number of young people who were disabled due to an accident before or during service and the many disabled children who petitioned for entrance to the Findel, it is obvious how the ranks of the young unemployable must have been perpetually swollen.[33]

A bad reputation could be just as debilitating as any physical or mental infirmity, and here Jörg Mayr's alleged delinquency since the age of six undoubtedly made finding an apprenticeship difficult. His subsequent wandering in an age before photographs provided him some valuable anonymity but this would not have helped in any long-term placement, which required both money and character references—in other words, social capital. Juvenile offenders who remained within one locality faced much greater obstacles to obtaining honest work. When Nuremberg magistrates called the teenaged Maria Kürshnerin (aka Constable Mary) and Catharina Schwartzin (aka Farmer Kitty) "two crazy, frivolous sluts and thieves," they were acknowledging a public reputation as much as making a moral judgment.[34] No one would bring girls of this sort into their homes as maids (even though, or perhaps in part because, Maria was acknowledged by the city's executioner, Maister Frantz, to be "a handsome young creature.")[35] Similarly, in 1615, after a thieving young goldsmith apprentice was apprehended and severely flogged in public, no master in the city would have him.[36]

Even if any of these youths had been willing to emigrate, like Jörg, they would have been hindered by their own outsider status as well as by other disadvantages. As seen in chapter 1, unmarried mothers with children in tow, even when they traveled to a new village or town, found it virtually impossible to obtain a service position. The same was true when the marks of infamy were literally carved on a deviant's body, as was the case for young Catharina Schwartzin, whose ears were cut off after her penultimate conviction. A permanent disfiguration like this—not to mention Catherina's reputation in certain parts of Nuremberg as "a promiscuous wench"—effectively precluded any respectable and gainful employment for her no matter where she went. The same was true for young people who had one hand chopped off for stealing or, less drastically, one finger (known as the "oath finger") removed for perjury, as in the case of young Hennslein Creuzmayr (aka Bootsy).[37] Wherever such young people went, their own bodies advertised their infamy and thereby insured their unemployability.

The final and perhaps most frustrating barrier to the normal route of apprenticeship or service rarely appears in the firsthand testimonies of beggar children and youths, although it was a common obstacle throughout the entire early modern period. During the fifteenth and sixteenth centuries, the social stigma of illegitimate birth was in fact legally enshrined throughout most of the Holy Roman Empire, with masters who dared to hire bastards punished by steep fines and occasionally imprisonments. Once again, the leaders of Nuremberg appear relatively more enlightened, barring such youths from service only if they were the product of an incestuous union.[38] Of course this did not eliminate or prevent widespread job discrimination among masters, especially during the harder economic times of the sixteenth and seventeenth centuries. In Jörg's day Nuremberg was home to hundreds of illegitimate children of working age (7–17), the great majority of whom had no hope of obtaining training in a craft.[39] When Hans Neureter was picked up for begging with a group of boys in 1662, his father explained that he had already placed young Hans with a nail maker but that the latter had refused to keep him once he found out about the boy's illegitimacy.[40] Official legitimation was an option but one that was unaffordable and unknown to most poor illegitimate children or their parents. Was Jörg himself illegitimate? Possibly, though he made no explicit reference to this particular social disability.

Whatever the roles of illegitimacy and other social disadvantages in Jörg Mayr's story, it is important to acknowledge the key influence of more obscure psychological factors in the youthful entry into a more aggressive street life. A youth's own choices—whatever the motivation—could trump the best efforts of concerned parents, especially in the instance of juvenile delinquents. Sixteen-year-old Hennslein Creuzmayr, imprisoned the same year that young Jörg Mayr began his stealing, had attended school at Saint Sebald's since the age of four and had been apprenticed to a potter before he ran away because of severe beatings. His induction into street life began still later, after he had resumed studies at a different school in Nuremberg, where he met three of his future criminal associates (Little Sailor, Barber Jack, and Enderlein Vogel) and they began committing acts of vandalism and petty theft before graduating into more serious offenses. Like Mayr, Creuzmayr was said by magistrates "to have grown up in crime," despite the attempts by his mother and other relatives to provide him with an education and a trade.[41] The exasperated stepmother of sixteen-year-old Balthasar Reuth similarly complained that her husband's illegitimate child

had already been with a card maker and was able to help the same in his work of wire bending and shaving as well as a journeyman. The master was thus satisfied with him and would have kept him on . . . but [Balthasar] ran away in less than a quarter year and would do no good.

She and her husband both welcomed a chain-gang sentence, hoping that it would lead young Balthasar to straighten up.[42]

Initial parental success in securing job placement for their children thus might prove ultimately ineffectual or irrelevant. Four of five older youths hanged for multiple thefts in 1615, for instance, had already reached the level of journeyman in weaving, map making, and cobbling (two); at least three of them were also fully literate.[43] Overall, at least half of the male youths executed in Nuremberg between 1575 and 1615 had training in some type of craft. Some young thieves even used their training to get positions in houses they later robbed. Hensa Baur, the runaway son of a miller, actually relied on his early training to find numerous apprenticeships with millers throughout the countryside, working days, weeks, and sometimes months before stealing from them and fleeing.[44] Hennslein Creuzmayr, who was the son of a Nuremberg archer, worked for one miller for eight years, before stealing his master's life's savings from him.[45] It is doubtful that Jörg Mayr received any craft training whatsoever, though again he is never explicit on this matter.

Life on the Streets

Most independent young vagrants were runaways, either from home or work. Jörg Mayr testified that he was orphaned "at a young age" and ran away more than once from his foster home but he does not specify why, saying only that when he returned he was "led further astray by some of their company."[46] Possibly his final departure at age twelve stemmed from abuse of some sort, though boredom or a fight with his foster parents are equally likely motives. Many "masterless" apprentices or servants ran away from their positions because of beating, homesickness, a detected theft, to join a sweetheart, or simply "for no great reason." Youths in service were in general a highly mobile population, often changing masters yearly or even more frequently. Secular authorities were not sympathetic to fickle and selfish apprentices and maids who took off the moment "their service goes a bit sour, with no forethought or patience, also often against the will of parents or guardians."[47] Yet while many placed teenagers ran away more than once, the great majority apparently returned to their masters after a few days or weeks (unless they had stolen something upon their departure—a common occurrence).[48] Other youths on the street were the children of vagrants, forced to move from city to city with their parents. As magistrates suspected, most vagrant youths picked up for begging or theft in Nuremberg and its environs apparently came from elsewhere. In one sample of seventy-one beggar children and youths picked up off the streets in 1634, only one in fourteen, or 7 percent, came from Nuremberg or one of its suburbs. A similar proportion of "foreigners" prevailed among groups of convicted juvenile thieves.[49] Given all of these factors, it is not surprising that there was also great turnover in the population of young people on the street. Some died, others secured more reliable employment, but on the whole the single greatest cause of the constant change in population was probably migration, as young people left Nuremberg on their own or with family.[50]

While on the road, Jörg and his comrades stayed anywhere they could. Inns were preferable if one could pay, and a surprising number of youthful vagrants actually could (often through profits from thefts).[51] Mayr slept most frequently in the houses of hospitable strangers, as well as in barns, sheds, brick kilns, hospices, abandoned buildings, and when necessary, outside— under benches or bridges, in the doorways of public buildings, or in church courtyards, even in freezing or otherwise inhospitable conditions. Weather figured prominently in the lives of rural vagrants like Jörg, driving them from November through March toward towns, where the chance of public shelter and the begging prospects were best. As today, public gardens and parks were especially popular gathering places with young and old homeless people during the warm months of the year.[52] In the city of Nuremberg, citizens were repeatedly enjoined from housing vagrants and a few were occasionally caught and punished for the same. The people who housed the young vagrant-thief Anna Geislerin and those who sheltered Hans Windish escaped with only "stern talks" before the inner council, while the tavern keeper and his wife who had housed the Seven were arrested, imprisoned, and heavily fined.[53] In the city and especially in the countryside, by contrast, Jörg and his fellow travelers could pretty well count on coming across at least one hospitable stranger, usually asking no payment whatsoever.

Still, the scramble to get by was intense and relentless among vagrant youths. Large towns such as Nuremberg had great drawing power, promising excitement as well as better job opportunities. Jörg's reasons for avoiding Nuremberg remain unclear, unless perhaps he feared the competition, knowing that if he came to a big city he would find the marketplaces already jammed with local young people begging and seeking any kind of work. Like unskilled adults, unskilled children and youths faced a significantly different labor world from that of artisans, professionals, or farmers. For them, fluid makeshift employment was the norm, with individuals frequently changing jobs or holding more than one at the same time. Unskilled children under twelve were rarely used in construction or other heavy labor and instead relied on such low-paying occupations as hawking ballads or pamphlets; selling brooms, brushes, and other household items; ragpicking or other salvaging; rat catching; and chimney sweeping. Girls as young as eight might be put in charge of a market stand or hired out as babysitters or maids, although even these positions proved more difficult to find by the seventeenth century.[54] Many pick-up jobs were seasonally specific. Winter was an especially difficult time to make any money by working or by begging, which forced many youths to be creative and entrepreneurial in generating an income. When cold weather slowed down their regular business of stealing food and cutting purses around the wine market, young Hennslein Creuzmayr and his friends switched to stealing carp from nearby fishermen and reselling it in the town marketplace at a healthy profit.[55]

For those vagrant youths who like Jörg chose to remain in the countryside, on the other hand, just about any locality offered decent paying unskilled jobs in the field. Jörg spoke more than once of his occasional work at harvest time, a mainstay among vagrant men and women of all ages. Unfortunately such employment was seasonal and irregular, as was to some degree the option of joining traveling carnivals or acrobat shows (never mentioned by Jörg). Another work option for independent boys and young men, increasingly popular during the seventeenth century, was military service. When the imprisoned Jörg desperately offered to become a soldier in Hungary, he was making a credible proposition. Many teenaged boys and men, especially poor students or criminals on the lam, enlisted in armies as a last resort. If nothing else, the bonus they were paid upon enlisting served their immediate needs and they could always run off with the money and not return (see fig. 4.7).[56] In Jörg's time, enlistment was almost always by choice; a few decades later, during the Thirty Years' War, impressment of teenaged boys (dramatized in both *Simplicissimus* and Bertolt Brecht's *Mother Courage*) became more common, and was often used as an alternate sentence to jail or a workhouse. On average, one mercenary in eight was under the age of twenty and soldiers younger than fifteen were not unheard of.[57] This option apparently never appealed to Jörg until a moment of utter desperation in the torture chamber.

By far the most common source of income for both resident children and vagrant youths was begging, hence the most common label of "beggar children" and "beggar youths." Begging was usually more lucrative for children and teenagers than any other occupation except theft and thus was particularly common in large cities such as Nuremberg. By some estimates, one-third to one-half of all beggars were children under fifteen.[58] This could take a variety of forms, from door-to-door solicitations (day and night), to tableaus of several tattered children with their mother outside of

Nim hin das Werbegello, ob ðüglcich Jüng von Jaren
Das Hüren Lernstübald, flüchn müstu nicht Sparen.

Fig. 4.7. Christian Richter, *Juveniles Recruited
into the Army during the Thirty Years' War* (1643).
München Staatliche Graphische Sammlung.

a church, to street singing or other musical performances. Experienced child and youth beggars knew how to make the most of any physical disabilities or how to embroider tales of destitution and misery to maximize donations. Like their professional adult counterparts, they knew which bakeries and market stalls would give them old bread or produce. They knew to wait until a customer had made a purchase and then ask for a small portion of the change or to make the most of traditional religious moments of charity—a weekly church service, a wedding, or a funeral. Even the ancient custom of Christmas caroling for money was exploited by youths and some adults to make ends meet during the holiday season.[59] At several points in his confession, Jörg Mayr mentions begging alone as well as with others, and makes a specific reference to engaging in the Christmas tradition of street singing for money in the guise of the three Magi, an occasion upon which "he himself sang third [king]."[60] Many householders were so accustomed to begging children and families calling on them that they kept some stale bread or change by the front door for distribution.

The town's four (later six) begging police were no match for the masses of such children on the street and the children knew it, taking turns as lookouts and easily evading the authorities. Popular hatred of the begging police also often resulted in adult collusion with young offenders.[61] Even if a begging child or youth was nabbed, the consequences were not severe. On the first arrest, he or she was usually beaten with the rod carried by all law enforcers and then released with a warning. Older youths often complained of being forced to pay bribes in order to continue begging or just to avoid being beaten or taken into custody.[62] Upon second and third offenses, the begging youth was supposed to be transported to one of two locations for increasingly lengthy sentences. Until the late sixteenth century, the place of detention in Nuremberg was based on age: children under seven were taken to the Findel (and kept there if orphans or foundlings); those over seven were placed with adult beggars in the city's begging stockade.[63] In 1588, the council ordered the begging police and archers to instead bring local children of all ages to the renovated pesthouse, where they would be questioned about parental involvement in their begging before the same arrived to pick them up. The new location was intended to protect such youngsters from adult beggars and other deviants in the begging stockade—not to mention from the begging police themselves, who were at least twice convicted of raping beggar girls.[64] It also provided a venue for government officials to berate "irresponsible" parents who came to claim their offspring. Local orphans were placed either in the Findel or, if over twelve, in an apprenticeship or service position. All foreign beggar children, regardless of age, were supposed to be expelled from the city, though this was not regularly enforced, even among older youths such as Jörg. Humiliating scourging, such as Jörg received in the village of Windsbach, or brief imprisonment in the city's dungeon were usually limited to repeat offenders.[65]

Despite such measures, child and youth begging—as seen in the last chapter—remained ubiquitous. Based just on early seventeenth-century municipal expenditures on children in Nuremberg's pesthouse, hundreds of begging children and youths were annually picked up and detained.[66] There is no way to know how many of these were recidivists but the number is likely to be high. All of the juvenile criminals in our sample had been arrested and punished for begging multiple times before their latest arrest, many ten or fifteen times (though even that is a low estimate given the incomplete records of Nuremberg and the complete lack of any records in rural villages).[67] The institutionalization of chain gangs for young foreign beggars from the late sixteenth century onward apparently increased the number of arrests but did not significantly mitigate the growing problem itself. Nearly a century later, in a greatly depopulated Nuremberg, a new antibegging campaign resulted in over five hundred women and children being arrested and put to work in a revived *Spinnhaus*. During the same period, over two hundred men, at least half of them under the age of eighteen, served sentences of varying lengths in the begging stockade, working by day in chain gangs. This was undoubtedly a frightening prospect for some young males, but more hardened vagrants shrugged off the relatively mild sentences of a few weeks and upon release quickly returned to their old habits and haunts.[68]

The Path to Crime

Poverty was usually a precursor to crime, but it does not in itself account for Jörg's personal career trajectory. Not all beggar children became regular thieves; nor was the path to burglary, robbery, and other more serious crimes the same for all. The transition from begging in all of its most aggressive forms to stealing was also rarely clear-cut or self-conscious. After all, petty and opportunistic theft constituted a necessary part of life for many poor people and especially for vagrants like Jörg Mayr. Stealing to eat (*Mundraub*) was viewed as an especially excusable offense. In his first interrogation, Jörg confirmed the tangled relationship between beggary and petty theft, portraying himself as a hungry beggar who was also an occasional and even unwilling thief, rather than a habitual one. His first words after torture—"Says he did not always steal but also begged"—convey concisely how Jörg possibly conceived such petty thefts as an extension of begging. Bread, used clothing, and small amounts of cash were after all the same items he received from panhandling, the only difference being that in these few instances the donors were unaware of their own generosity (at least until it was too late).

Chronic hunger was part of the painful reality of life on the streets, and stolen food looms large in Jörg's and other juvenile burglars' accounts (as well as the tales of picaresque characters Simplicissimus and Lazarillo de Tormes).[69] In one instance, some members of the Seven actually stole a pet dove from a house and later cooked and ate it.[70] The group also regularly purloined cheese and bread and, in one instance, twenty-six *bratwürste*. Jörg readily admitted that to supplement the beggar's usual diet of rotted vegetables and stale crusts, he also occasionally stole cheese and bread, in addition to other household items. At the very instance of his last arrest, Jörg testified

Fig. 4.8. Bartolomé Esteban Murillo, *Beggar Youths Eating*
(ca. 1650). Melon and grapes—a veritable banquet for
most poor children, who struggled daily with insufficient
food (ca. 1650). München Alte Pinakothek.

that he had just begged a little bread from some women in Lichtenau and
had gone to the neighboring village of Zant to find more when he came
across a farmer's open house and walked inside "in broad daylight" looking
to take some bread. Instead he himself was grabbed and incarcerated—even
though he never got any bread, "much less swiped or stole anything else."
Hunger and desperation were also the initial justifications offered for his
crimes—"what he did steal was on account of poverty, when he couldn't
beg anything or come to Driessdorf (his hometown), since he was very frail,
thus he had to steal out of necessity."[71]

There were many compelling motives for moving beyond begging into regular theft. Stealing was much more lucrative, generally more reliable, and just plain easier in most instances than begging or occasional work. Theft was a constant temptation for all poor people, though usually in an opportunistic form, still supplemented by begging and odd jobs. The progression from odd jobs and begging to regular stealing, however, was never a purely rational choice based on economic self-interest.[72] As much as anything else, habitual stealing among early modern youths was the product of a type of acculturation, a natural progression from hanging with the "wrong crowd," with crimes gradually and almost imperceptibly escalating in gravity. With no school and irregular work, youths like Jörg Mayr had a lot of unsupervised time on their hands. Often this idleness led to "wild" and even criminal behavior among boys and girls alike. It was a further strike against accused burglar Hennslein Creuzmayr that he was widely reputed "to regularly eat, guzzle, and gamble with common sluts in the Sandpits."[73]

Jörg Mayr, who was alleged to have begun stealing at the age of six, blamed lack of parental guidance and the influence of bad company for his own descent into a life of crime: "His parents died when he was very young, so he had to go [live with] strangers, and after that moved around a lot, and did no more good, [and] though he did get away from it once and thought it behind him, when he went back to [the same people] for help, he was led even further astray."[74] It is difficult to know how much of this explanation is calculated for its effect on his judges or in which ways his foster family "led him astray." Despite Jörg's precocious thievery, at least some of his relatives maintained an open door toward him until he began to steal from them as well, including a theft of eight-and-one-half gulden hidden in the cradle of an infant cousin. Then, effectively banished from his home village, twelve-year-old Jörg began his five-year odyssey throughout rural Franconia.[75]

This was the age at which many youths began a quasi-independent life as apprentices or servants, but for Mayr the future looked bleak. Even if he had received some schooling or other training—which is doubtful—his forced vagrancy greatly diminished the likelihood of ever finding steady employment. Fortunately Jörg had no apparent physical or mental disabilities and thus was able to work in the fields during harvest.[76] Unfortunately, such day labor was seasonal and inadequate, forcing most vagrants such as Jörg and his traveling companions to survive the winter months mostly by begging, whether through song or dance or simple accosting of strangers. Even then there could be long periods without food or warm shelter. Thus Mayr's initial justification for his crimes—"what he had done was thus on account of hunger"—was probably not far off the mark—four years earlier.[77] In the intervening time, though, from roughly age thirteen onward, Jörg Mayr had gradually become a regular and even professional thief.

Whatever the motivation for Jörg's alleged childhood thefts, the street culture he entered as a teenager also made steady and honest employment improbable. Despite the meager possessions of its denizens, street life could often involve some expensive habits. Masterless youths, for instance, appeared particularly prone to card playing and gambling.[78] Legal authorities naturally knew of this inclination and often considered evidence of the same a sufficient motive for theft. The juvenile thief Hennslein Creuzmayr admitted habitually playing double-thalers (*Dölptäler*) on Nuremberg's bowling greens but vehemently denied that he gambled much or was a professional cheat, claiming to be "much too poor and unpresentable" for such a role.[79] More conspicuously, Jörg Mayr went through a large sum of stolen money in a relatively short period: by his own confession at least 200 fl. during the preceding four years alone, the equivalent of more than twenty years of wages for a domestic servant.[80] Though he never explicitly acknowledged gambling (and his interrogators never asked) his testimony did include frequent references to housing, food, and other unspecified debts to his sometime adult mentor Steffan the Grocer—another recurrent pattern among juvenile criminals and their older accomplices. Often Jörg's share of the loot from a burglary had to be handed over immediately to Steffan to pay such debts, thereby creating a cycle of debt and theft that he could only escape by going off on his own, which he eventually did.[81] The typicality of this situation was reflected in the popular German adage of the day, "A thief seldom steals himself rich."[82]

Another common incentive to theft was the preoccupation of many young people, on and off the streets, with new clothes and current fashions. Usually resident and vagrant beggar children were so shabbily dressed that members of the town council frequently worried about their health, particularly during winter. Many members of the Seven were "naked and bare" at their ultimate arrest and needed to be clothed by the prison staff.[83] Some, like the fictional Lazarillo de Tormes, were in their teens before they had their first pair of shoes. It was the high point of Lazarillo's tale when, after many years of careful saving, he had "enough to dress myself very decently in secondhand clothing," namely, "an old fustian jacket and worn coat with braided sleeves and a vent [and] a cloak that once had a fringe."[84] In denying that he was a professional gambler, Hennslein Creuzmayr argued plausibly that the other young men at the bowling green, all "finely attired or merchants' servants," were ashamed to be seen with him and repeatedly turned him away because of his shabby clothes. Little surprise then, that following

Fig. 4.9. Bartolomé Esteban Murillo, *Boys Playing Dice.*
Ragged clothing was always disreputable but less of a health
risk in Mediterranean climates than in German lands
during the winter (ca. 1650). München Alte Pinakothek.

one alleged major theft of 30 fl. at a Frankfurt fair, he is suddenly seen "in brand-new clothing from head to foot."[85] Hensa Baur reacted similarly to his first big score, immediately going to the market and buying a new hat, coat, pants, vest, and pair of gloves, as well as a pair of used shoes. After his arrest, the new clothing he was wearing was forwarded to his most recent victim as a partial compensation for the amount stolen.[86]

For those living primarily on the street with one set of worn and ragged clothes, more stylish vestments signified greater status and respect. Many youths on the street were in fact known by a distinctive piece of clothing that they always wore, such as Jörg's sinister associate "Green Cap" (whose birth name was unknown to him). Clothing also had an economic value as an easily liquidated asset, but most thieving teenagers were apparently more concerned about competitive personal appearance than property investment. Desirable clothing could even be a motive for theft, as certain sneakers or leather jackets are today. One of the first recorded break-ins by Catharina Schwartzin in fact occurred at a shoemaker's, when she and her accomplices made off with several pairs of new shoes and boots, at least one of which she kept.[87] Articles of clothing seem to have had particular importance among girls on the street. Catherina's friend Maria Kürshnerin recounted a fight among the prostitutes out in the New Forest, where another girl took the hairband off of her friend Elena's head and cut the latter's hair. Maria and Elena plotted to steal their enemy's dress as revenge, but unfortunately the other girl left town before they could act. Like gold jewelry today, furs were a particularly conspicuous sign of status. Maria was even still wearing some furs from a recent burglary during her interrogation while her friend Anna Steinfelderin similarly sported a stolen hair band. Finally, clothing could be given to friends, as Catherina did with several rings and as Maria did with a pair of boots, some hose, and an underskirt that was too long for her.[88]

What social form did the acculturation to street values and theft take? One of the most provocative but also potentially misleading aspects of street life is the frequent magisterial reference to these juveniles' *Diebgesellschaft*, which can be translated as "society of thieves" or more simply as "gang." Many criminals appeared to confirm this perception with their own vague references to a "cooked" or "funny" society.[89] Historians agree, however, that notions of a coherent "underworld counterculture" are extremely difficult to substantiate and probably tell us more about the anxieties of early modern secular authorities than the experience of criminals themselves. Several different models of street life existed, some supraregional and enduring, others highly localized and brief in appearance. "Gang" is also a problematic term for this period, similarly revealing—then as now—more about middle-class imagination and condescension than actual social organizations. This is especially true for the sixteenth and seventeenth centuries, when the larger groups of vagrants and thieves common in the eighteenth century were rare.[90] Groups of young thieves do appear in Nuremberg's criminal records for this period, but there are only two instances of groups that were both large and well organized. In 1575, thirteen boy pickpockets, "of whom none was over twelve years old," were all forced to watch the execution of their adult leader and then were flogged and banished from the city. Almost twenty years later, Steffan Kebweller was hanged for running a similar

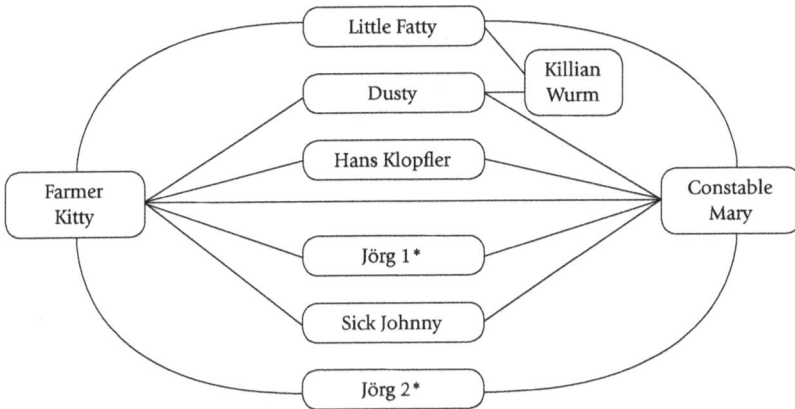

Fig. 4.10. Criminal accomplices among the Seven (1584).

group of young cutpurses whom he paid the extravagant weekly wages of one thaler (1.2 fl.) plus room and board for their labors.[91]

More often, the testimony of juvenile criminals reveals a fluid interaction of overlapping and shifting clusters of two to three people each. Each of the individual burglars of the Seven, for instance, knew and associated with the others but the crimes themselves were usually committed by subsets of the larger group. Intriguingly, the subsets themselves tended to organize around the two girls, Catharina Schwartzin and Maria Kürshnerin—at least until an older youth named Ule effectively took control of the group (see fig. 4.10). Only the circumstances of their recent cohabitation in a suburban inn and their joint execution might lead us to imagine them as a "gang" or distinctive group. These seven juveniles had no unified or exclusive criminal relationship and in fact regularly stole with other youths who were not arrested. Often the accomplices on break-ins were not all known to each other. Repeatedly, we hear of a job with "someone else named Margaret," or "a guy with a wide hat, called Cunz," or more simply "a student" or "two boys he didn't know," for example. When pressed by his interrogators for more names of his accomplices, Jörg Mayr appeared desperate to comply but was forced to acknowledge the extreme superficiality of most of his acquaintances, not even knowing whether many of them stole or not.[92]

At the same time, there were certain patterns of association among all early modern youth groups that resemble those of modern urban gangs. Drinking, for instance, was a key component of all male friendships in early modern Germany and had a particular significance in the coming of age among teenaged boys such as Jörg Mayr. It could establish the ephemeral bonds of drinking buddies or be a formal part of initiation into a local youth group, a military cohort, an occupational group, or even some form of blood brotherhood. Social groups based solely on the consumption of alcohol were also pervasive among German males in general, from the elite drinking clubs of patricians to the drinking fraternities of poor vagrants.[93] Taverns were usually the first stops of all migrants, including male youths, upon arrival in a village or town. There Jörg would be sure to find lodging, food, and drink if he could pay, and good criminal contacts if he could not.[94] Buying a round of drinks was a particularly effective way of making new friends, at least at a superficial level, and also provided some status to masterless new arrivals such as the teenaged Mayr.

German men were especially famous among their contemporaries for their drinking bouts and "duels" of wine and beer.[95] The competitive nature of male drinking led to much exaggeration and bragging about sexual feats—particularly those involving prostitutes such as Catharina Schwartzin and Maria Kürshnerin—played a role in all male youth groups. Jörg mentions that he drank occasionally and consorted with "loose females," so it is likely he also participated in such shows of virility. He was apparently never drunk or foolish enough to publicize his criminal exploits among relative strangers. Hennsle Baldauf (aka Sick Johnny), on the other hand, acknowledged bragging injudiciously of his burglaries while in the begging stockade, and Hennslein Creuzmayr similarly contributed to his own arrest by boasting to his drinking comrades about his recent big hauls at the Frankfurt fair and then throwing five Kreuzer coins at them, telling them to buy themselves some bread rolls.[96]

Neither Jörg nor any of Nuremberg's juvenile criminals ever mentioned any specific name for a group of youths or any ritualized induction to a "gang," but since including such incidentals would be counter to their interests during interrogation the existence of such associations cannot be ruled out. The same is true of criminal slang or cant, which was probably known to most of the young thieves but is likewise barely detectable in the official protocols.[97] At some point, many street youths involved in burglary and robbery did begin to identify themselves more generally as "bad boys" (*Ärgerbuben*), a turning point common to modern street children as well. By the time they became regular thieves, almost all juveniles had acquired colorful street names such as Frog Johnny, the Black Baker, Red Lenny, Ravenhound, Corky, Hook, Shifty, and of course, the Little Castle Seventh.[98] Despite the quaintness of such monikers to modern sensibilities, the anachronistic temptation to treat them as humorous—or even more condescendingly, as cute—must be resisted. In an age where the shame and embarrassment thresholds were much lower than today, nicknames often focused on an individual's appearance, such as "Pointy Head" or "Little Fatty," or on personal hygiene, such as "Dusty."[99] A nickname might also come as a play on someone's given name, such as the "Coal Girl" for Catharina Schwartzin ("Black").[100] These alternate identities permitted some degree of self-fashioning, but they also served an eminently practical purpose, namely, avoiding confusion in a society that over-relied on a few first names (four of five boys in the Seven were named Hans). Of course not everyone with a nickname ended up stealing but rarely did someone become a thief without a nickname.

Despite the absence of gangs per se, horizontal bonding of some sort remained essential to most youths living on the streets alone. Often this association was with peers; sometimes it included adults who formed a substitute family. Apparently, very few vagrant youths were quite as isolated as the young thief Hensa Baur, though even this development was relatively recent. Two years before his last arrest, Baur had been a known criminal associate of the executed robber Georg Müllner.[101] Escaping arrest, the itinerant miller's apprentice had wandered the countryside alone, working for at least twelve different millers during a span of eighteen months. His particular modus operandi was to lodge with an employer for several days or even a few months, waiting for the right opportunity to steal some money and then flee. Except for his last theft of 200 fl., his hauls were quite modest, ranging from a few pence to one gulden. On a few occasions Baur was caught by his masters, but since the amounts he stole were so small, he was simply dismissed and left to find his next victim.[102]

Not once during his entire testimony did sixteen-year-old Baur mention a friend or accomplice. Even his interrogators had difficulty imagining a truly solo thief at his age (especially given his criminal past) and thus repeatedly pressed him to name more accomplices, which he persistently refused to do, even during torture. Was this evidence of great loyalty to unnamed accomplices or of genuine distrust and social isolation, particularly after Müllner's hanging? There is no way to know for sure, though the latter characterization—given the paltry amounts stolen—seems much more likely. In addition to Baur's peripatetic lifestyle, some modern psychiatrists might account for his apparent friendlessness with the controversial "attachment" theory, an argument that children who do not develop attachment to a single mother figure by a certain age are likely to fail at future intimate attachments.[103]

Whatever the explanation for Baur's particular social isolation, the more striking observation is how anomalous his situation was among young vagrants in early modern Germany. The frequent lack of attachment to a central mother figure—as in the case of orphan Jörg Mayr—did not prevent many delinquent children and youths from developing what was obviously sincere affection for each other. Hennsle Schober of the Seven was visibly shaken when his friend Maria Schwartzin was brought "before his eyes" at the end of his interrogation. Kilian Wurmb began his interrogation defiantly but similarly broke down when immediately confronted with Schober and Hennsle von Geiselwundt, who "both expressly acknowledged that they knew him well, were part of the same society (*Gesellschaft*), and called him only Shifty."[104] When Hennslein Creuzmayr suddenly became violently ill, his friends put him up with an old woman in nearby Kleinhasslach and paid a barber to heal him.[105] Five young thieves sentenced to death in 1575 "wept greatly" as their criminal "master" was executed before them, "and often looked after their comrades and brothers." Before they were subsequently pardoned, they also asked for a deck of cards "so they could play to see which one of them would be hanged first."[106]

Perhaps the most moving example of friendship and affection among young thieves in Nuremberg occurred a few days before Christmas in 1615. After extensive investigations, five youths, aged between eighteen and twenty-one, were sentenced to be hanged for theft. The morning of the hanging, the five friends had been brought together for one last time in a small room of the municipal dungeon. Some prayed with the chaplains; most wept; all drank the executioner's wine. Finally, Meister Franz bound all five by hand and foot and led them first upstairs to the council chambers for the formal pronouncement of their sentence and then outside to the cart that would carry them the kilometer or so to the scaffold outside the city's walls. Immediately—one of the chaplains later recalled—the boys began to cry and scream at the top of their lungs, so loudly "that one couldn't hear his own words."[107] Though the clergymen and Meister Franz attempted to calm them, the baleful noise continued as the wagon slowly wended its way through the city. Suddenly, just as the procession reached the gate leaving the city, one of the condemned began to sing, "My Young Life Is at an End." Gradually the other four youths joined in and continued singing together until the cart reached the gallows. Each was then hanged in succession, after which the crowd of spectators was dispersed.

Even Jörg Mayr, who often operated solo, at age eleven took up with another youthful beggar-thief named Adam (who three years later hanged himself in his prison cell). After that Jörg joined the household of a thieving journeyman named Steffan the Grocer, his common-law wife, and their two small children. During his subsequent five years of wandering, young Jörg apparently spent more time with this surrogate family than with anybody else.[108] The Grocer, he explains, in fact had no grocery and was merely a wandering journeyman, living by begging and occasional work or theft. He describes the Grocer in colorful and affectionate detail as "a tall person with a red beard, wears black fustian knickerbockers [with] red London socks, a leather waistcoat with twill sleeves, and a black felt hat."[109] Steffan's "wife or cook," on the other hand, is only mentioned once by name (Margaret) and never described. The couple's two children are even more anonymous, not even distinguished by sex or age. Nonetheless, the image that Mayr conveys is that of an itinerant household, with an unemployed yet resourceful *Hausvater* scrounging to make ends meet.[110]

This image of his foster family was of course part of Jörg's defense strategy, but it clearly reflects his own need for companionship as well. As in poor biological families, everyone in the Grocer's household worked for the good of the whole, especially during burglaries. The previous fall, for instance, Jörg stood watch outside of a shepherd's house near Dinkelsbühl while Steffan went inside and stole a loaf of bread, some cheese, and two gulden, which he then proceeded to share with Jörg and the rest of the household. Two other times, Jörg accompanied Steffan's wife on break-ins while the Grocer stayed home and watched their two children. This time the haul was a bit more substantial—four gulden in coins, four men's shirts, a leather vest, a pair of pants, and some shoelaces. Again, the *Hausvater* distributed the spoils equally, giving Jörg an old shirt (which he tore up for rags) and the vest (which he sold for eight Bazen, or about half a gulden).[111] The four other thefts Mayr admitted to before stopping his testimony are similarly casual in method—crawling in an open window or walking through the door when the residents were at church—and likewise involved used clothing and small amounts of cash. Twice more during his subsequent testimony, Mayr underscores the domestic role of the Grocer, with references to his attending the birth bed of his wife and taking in a poor beggar girl (the "Mouse Girl") to care for the children. Of course, the beggar girl was later sent out stealing with Jörg Mayr, but the emphasis on makeshift provision for the household remains clear. At one point during this time, Mayr even experienced an extended period of domestic tranquility with Steffan's wife at the village of Osttaw, during which he continued to visit his brother in nearby Gnossaw.[112]

Such stability in personal relationships was rare among vagrant youths. Over the course of his mostly solitary travels, Jörg met up and "worked" with various acquaintances and friends, but except for this one time he apparently did not lodge for long periods with any of them. And whether or not he did experience some affection and loyalty for the Grocer's family or any of his other "fellows," it is worth remembering that all of these migrant people lived remarkably fluid lives with few long-term personal relationships. Of those friends Jörg mentions during the course of his testimony, at least five met violent ends, four through execution and one through suicide in jail. Of others, such as the Mouse Girl, he says merely that 'he doesn't know whether [they are] still alive or not.'[113] Throughout his testimony, Mayr also attempts to distance himself from those accomplices who are still around and instead chooses to give incriminating evidence about those already dead or apprehended.[114] Whether this is done primarily out of loyalty, some calculated purpose of self-interest, or is simply the truth is impossible to ascertain.

Friendship of any kind did not preclude young thieves fighting with one another over spoils as well as frequently stealing from one another. Maria Kürshnerin described breaking into the house of her friend Elena with two of their girlfriends and preparing to take off with several shirts from a trunk when Elena came in the door at 4:00 A.M. with a noble wearing a wolf fur. While the couple groped each other and made love on the landing, the girls tiptoed around them, only to be discovered by Elena as they ran down the steps and off into the night.[115] This is hardly surprising behavior among individuals for whom outsmarting the authorities and everybody else was the name of the game. Like his literary counterpart Lazarillo de Tormes, Jörg learned by hard experience the necessity of street smarts and the ability to scam and trick others himself. Like the cruel blind beggar to whom Lazarillo is apprenticed, Steffan the Grocer could promise Jörg, "I won't make you a rich man, but I can show you how to make a living."[116] Whether Jörg was ever forced to call his mentor "Dad" or eventually developed the same hatred for him as Lazarillo did for the blind beggar is unclear from his testimony. In fact Jörg's feelings for any of his friends and accomplices are difficult to infer. Most of his admitted friends often exploited or even cheated him at one time or another, yet there is no trace of any anger or resentment on his part in the transcripts.[117] Only a humiliating public scourging by the villagers of Windsbach appears to rile him during interrogation and perhaps prompted him to return later with his friends and threaten arson.

Whatever the nature of Jörg's intimate relationships, in other words, he apparently had low expectations and made few demands. Perhaps this attitude stemmed mostly from resignation, assuming that this was the way of a harsh and inconstant world.[118] Certainly Jörg had endured more than his share of insults, beatings, and betrayals during his short life on the road. Some of the incidents he mentions sound like excerpts from a picaresque tale of his literary counterparts. Once, he stole four gulden from a cartman who put him up, only to have most of it stolen from him the next night by a shepherdess with whom he shared a stable. Another time, he waited for a peasant and his wife to drive to a nearby town and then stole a woman's green skirt and one gulder, making a clean getaway until he was later spotted in town with the skirt by a barber, who informed the farmer, who in turn tracked Jörg down in the next town and forced him to give back both the skirt and the money.[119] On the other hand, Jörg was quite capable of treachery himself, regularly stealing from just about every cottager or farmer who put him up for a night or two, including his own relatives.[120] Occasionally his betrayals of hospitality and goodwill are jarring, such as watching the son of a widow he was staying with come home with wet clothes and stealing them right off the clothesline before sunrise. Or even more infamously, creeping into the bedchamber of a woman who had just given birth (and whose husband had taken him in from the cold) and stealing their life savings of over sixteen gulden from under the bed while she slept—all on Christmas Day![121] Overall, at least half of the ninety-five thefts to which he confesses involved violation of a benefactor's hospitality, including a former employer and another man who had put him up "for a long time."[122]

A Thief Known throughout the Land

The most important part of Jörg's street socialization was his escalation from occasional to regular stealing, whereby theft became his main, rather than supplemental, source of income. His progression in crime in fact corresponded to a pattern of increasing premeditation, even professionalization, that was common among beggar youths and thieves. The best analogy for this informal process is the advancement of any early modern apprentice to master status in a craft, with two crucial transitions for young criminals in training: first from spontaneous and occasional petty crimes to more frequent and better planned thefts (apprentice to journeyman), second from organized small-scale burglaries to more serious crimes of robbery, arson, and even murder (journeyman to master). Such a progression was neither constant nor irreversible. We must also be wary of succumbing to town councilors' underworld fantasies in their references to criminal Georg Mülner's "apprenticed youths," or to Hensa Baur "taking up the stealing trade."[123] Nevertheless, the crafts model of increasing gravity of crimes provides a useful framework for exploring the most dangerous form of street socialization.

At the bottom of the criminal hierarchy, the apprentice level, were the simple and nonviolent thefts favored by women and children under twelve:

picking pockets, shoplifting, cutting purses, cozening, pilfering, and rolling drunks. Like Jörg Mayr, Hennslein Creuzmayr began stealing at a young age. Together with his friends Enderlein Vogel, Little Sailor, and Barber Jack, he would take turns distracting one of the many street vendors at the marketplace while his companions made off with various items, from bread and cheese to belts, hats, crystal buttons, and twenty bars of soap. From shoplifting he and his friends moved on to assorted money-changing scams. After asking a traveling farmer or cartman to change a large coin, the boys would either switch in a coin of lesser value or more simply grab whatever they could from the purse and run off.[124] Creuzmayr bragged that usually he could pull it off without the victim noticing and that one time he had even gotten fifteen half-Bazen (about half a gulden) out of a cartman's purse and walked away, only to have the man later discover his loss and track Creuzmayr down to an inn in suburban Schweinau. Given the small amounts usually involved in such thefts, criminal authorities were apparently rarely contacted. Instead, justice might be meted out on the spot, such as the time when another cartman caught Creuzmayr's hand while snatching some coins and proceeded to pound the boy with his fists and then thoroughly whip him.[125]

Many young women and girls on the street who participated in thefts of various kinds also relied on another common source of cash: prostitution. Possibly Steffan the Grocer's common-law wife also made money this way during lean times for their travelling household. After most German cities closed down their civic brothels during the sixteenth century, prostitution simply went underground. Nuremberg, whose own house closed in 1562, was particularly famed for its high number of streetwalkers, who worked around markets and courtyards and just outside the city's walls in the New Forest by the Dutzen Pond.[126] Private houses, inns, and bathhouses might also serve as sites for paid encounters, some almost exclusively. It is difficult to estimate how many early modern prostitutes were minors like Farmer Kitty and her friend Constable Mary—perhaps as many as one in three.[127] A girl's initiation into the business usually fell along the lines of three themes: working to contribute to the household income, deception by a smooth-talking pimp or procuress, or the last resort of a lone vagabond. The role of parental pressure in the first case is ambiguous. Clearly some poor parents effectively sold their daughters against their will into the profession but in other instances the girls might have seen such work as their contribution to the household income.[128] The pay was usually not good, with a prostitute making at most 6 pfennig (the price of three eggs) for a quick trick and if lucky 4–8 Albus (1/6–1/3 fl.) for an entire night. Most prostitutes were thus forced to supplement their fees with begging, wage labor such as spinning or laundering, or—like the juvenile thieves Farmer Kitty and Constable Mary—with more dangerous illegal activities that paid at least four times as well.[129] During his travels, Jörg likely encountered many women who offered sex for pay and this is possibly how he contracted the syphilis that laid him up the winter before his final arrest.

Prostitution among young males was much less common in German cities, or at least much less visible. In Italian cities, arrests for sodomy between older men and younger males were common, averaging over 400 per year in Renaissance Florence alone. In the great majority of cases, boys under eighteen who had sex for money or other "gifts" were the passive parties in onetime encounters or the occasional long-term liaison.[130] There is no record in Nuremberg of any "houses of play" for boys with adult men, as in some other early modern cities.[131] Youths acting as procurers for girlfriends or other young women, on the other hand, turn up more often in official records. In 1584, executioner Meister Frantz recorded flogging a sixteen-year-old pimp named Hennsa Schmidt (aka Foxy and the Blade), who oversaw fourteen young prostitutes.[132]

The first transition of juvenile criminals, from apprentice to journeyman, typically began with burglary and other organized thefts. The members of The Seven, all but one aged between twelve and seventeen, illustrate the ways that youthful amateurs might be gradually acculturated to the ways of professional crime. By the time of their arrest in January, 1583, all had clearly advanced beyond sporadic panhandling and vandalism and had become fairly prolific and regular thieves. In his last statement, twelve-year-old Hennsle von Geiselwindt confessed to over thirty-eight burglaries in the previous two months alone; his friend, Hennsla Schober, admitted to thirty during the previous five weeks. Even discounting those break-ins that neither boy remembered or chose to mention, that works out to an average of five or six burglaries per week.[133] And while they and their accomplices did not disdain the occasional opportunity theft—a coat left unguarded on a wagon or a street vendor looking the wrong way—the majority of their heists were in fact planned, with advance information about the movements, trade, and sometimes possessions of the resident of a house or shop.[134] Sometimes they broke into more than one building in a night. Unlike petty theft, burglary was rarely a solo operation (Jörg Mayr being a notable exception) and it usually required two to seven people, thus a greater degree of organization and foresight. For this reason, burglars were outnumbered by common thieves at least 50–1.[135] Most significantly, by this point all of the juveniles involved had street identities and their jobs and pay indicated a clear (though not rigid) pecking order, with the youngest boys and the girls serving mainly as lookouts and also drawing the smallest shares of the loot.[136]

On the other hand, much about The Seven's recent exploits still smacked of thrill break-ins and adolescent impulsiveness. Their targets were just as often randomly selected and the background information itself sketchy or downright wrong. After breaking into one wood turner's shop with great difficulty, for instance, the group was chagrined to find absolutely nothing worth stealing. Another time, twelve-year-old Hennsle von Geiselwind (aka Little Fatty) struggled out of a burgled house with a heavy bag of loot, only to have to lug it back inside when none of his friends would agree to help carry it.[137] The juveniles' methods remained similarly crude: snatching drying clothes off of a line, finding a window or door left ajar, or at most using a table knife to pry open a stubborn lock. At first glance the spoils themselves also appear underwhelming: a pair of old shoes, two men's shirts, a pillow case, three undershirts, and so on—all divided in up to seven shares. Clothing and other everyday items, however, were often a household's most valuable property. They were very easy to liquidate and thus remained extremely popular with ordinary burglars well into the nineteenth century.[138] Occasionally small amounts of cash were discovered and divvied up. The youths did not deal with regular fences, but rather sold their items independently to a multitude of buyers—to a farmwife on the street, a servant at the market, a peddler, an innkeeper, a soldier, or in four instances to Jews, one "with many daughters and a big nose."[139] Perhaps most revealing of all, some of the items, especially among the boys, were destroyed, thrown away, or (among the girls) kept or given later as presents—again a refutation of pure economic motivation.[140] In sum, these were seven very active but hardly focused or particularly accomplished young thieves.

How and why did such amateurish thieves-in-training graduate to master status? Indisputably the key factor was their exposure to older, more experienced practitioners of their craft. In every one of our sample of juvenile theft cases, including Jörg's, at least one older person acted as an accomplice or mentor in some way.[141] Here the master-pupil analogy is most striking, though we should also recognize the often cynical self-interest at work behind the apparent care and support. Understandably, runaways and other juveniles living by their own means on the streets would welcome the generosity and "tips" of such worldly adults, who may not have actively recruited youths but at least exploited them. Jörg Mayr, we recall, recounted how Steffan the Grocer and his wife housed him and lent him money before they started sending him out on burglaries. This sort of patronage and apprenticeship was in fact common among juvenile beggars and criminals of both the early modern and modern eras. "Scabby George" and his wife similarly supplied food, drink, and even clothing to Hennslein Creuzmayr and other boys who brought them stolen goods.[142] In both instances, the boys were completely reliant on their mentors' fairness in compensation, especially considering the deductions made for various expenses and debts. Given the enormous difficulty and loneliness of a solitary life on the street, many vagrant children and youths quite naturally accepted almost any terms offered in exchange for a substitute family or mere companionship. Others maintained more flexible relations with their older comrades but were no less reliant on them for their livelihood.

This interaction between criminal masters and journeymen at the same time provided the young thieves' final acculturation into professional crime. During their last few months of activity, for instance, the Seven had increasingly been directed by a certain Ule, who was never captured. In addition to steering the group toward houses or shops with greater prospects of cash (as opposed to the usual old clothing), Ule brought a "special awl with which he can open locks everywhere."[143] Not surprisingly, the older Ule also took charge of divvying up the loot on such jobs, as did all of the older accomplices of the juveniles in our sources. So while the youths learned about the advantages of selective thefts, they also learned the harsh lessons of might makes right. After one job, seventeen-year-old Kilian Wurmb (aka Shifty) initially resisted the attempts of twenty-two-year-old Hans Windish (aka the Black Baker) to take some of his loot but was forced to relent when the older thief pulled out a weapon.[144] In another violent dispute over division of spoils, Bastlein Hofman chased Hennslein Creuzmayr through a field in suburban Gostenhof, shouting "You rogue, you thief, I'll carve you another leg," to which the fleeing Creuzmayr responded, "Be off you church robber (*Sackramendts dieb*), be off!" According to the testimony of Creuzmayr and other delinquent boys, confrontations of this nature appear to have been fairly common occurrences.[145]

Such stories reveal an especially ominous result of male juveniles' exposure to older and more experienced criminals, namely, the increased incentive to physical violence. One of the most striking aspects of the hundreds of juvenile crimes described in our sample is the almost complete lack of any violence or—in many cases—any contact whatsoever with the victims. The majority were burglaries, intentionally perpetrated when the residents were at the market, at church, working in the field, or at a wedding. Even Jörg, after he had gone solo, consistently displayed this *modus operandi*. Occasionally, young thieves mentioned sneaking in a room where someone else was asleep but on the whole personal contact was studiously avoided. Whether this was because of the younger youths' size, physical strength, or attitude is difficult to say but the same aversion to confrontation was true of women thieves in general.[146]

Meanwhile, more frequent drinking and gambling among the older boys made confrontations and violence ever more likely.[147] By the time of their final interrogations, a few of the older boys in our sample had begun roaming in what it is tempting to call gangs and occasionally engaging in what look like modern "rumbles." At least two of the boys of the Seven, Kilian Wurmb and Hans Klopfer (aka the Fat Farmboy), admitted during interrogation to consorting with older and more aggressive thieves and even being present at the violent robbery of two different groups of baker apprentices, although each insisted that he had only watched while their two older comrades beat the apprentices and took their money. They also boasted of having recently stolen two weapons from a farmer's wagon in the city, "in plain daylight."[148] Stolen or purchased guns appear in the testimony of Jörg and several older youths; even the nonviolent Hensa Baur who, after having completely re-outfitted himself, used some of the money from his big score to buy a flint-lock pistol.[149] A few of the Seven's boys were even present when a cartman's daughter was raped and killed, though each (predictably) claimed only to have held the girl after she attempted to flee, with the actual murder committed by two other boys.[150] Clearly these youths had moved beyond typical vagabond crimes against property and were now part of a criminal elite that included professional robbers and other violent offenders.

Hennslein Creuzmayr, by his own testimony, possessed a fierce disposition and frequently fought with friend and foe alike. Though always claiming victim status, he readily admitted to beating up several people, throwing knives at and trying to stab a certain shepherd, and even shooting at one of the city's guards (though he claimed it was with a toy pistol). Only the very serious accusation of threatening arson met with his fervent denial. Even after repeated torture—with the strappado, the "crown," and fire—he at most acknowledged "uttering a sacramental curse out of anger" at various individuals in Schweinau but never with any mention of arson.[151] Many of the older boys, including Creuzmayr, also forcefully resisted arrest, in the case of Claus Radler, seriously wounding one of the arresting archers and striking out at the others until he himself was eventually subdued by a near fatal blow to the head.[152]

The other sign of having attained master thief status was a dramatic increase in the amount stolen, also attributable to the influence of older companions. Whereas the great majority of earlier thefts in the Nuremberg sample involved used clothing and small amount of cash, some older teenagers were apparently moving on to bigger scores. As with more serious accusations of violence, Hensa Baur's interrogators waited until he had admitted to a plethora of small thefts before pressing him about his last and greatest heist, involving more money than all of the other thefts combined—200 gulden. Baur admitted only to taking two handfuls of money, not knowing how much he stole, and had only sixteen fl. on him when arrested (having already gone on a brief but extravagant shopping spree).[153] Hennslein Creuzmayr was similarly grilled about his suspected graduation to much larger takes at the Frankfurt fair of twenty and thirty gulden each (at least ten times as much as before), as well as the spectacular amount of 100 fl. at his final job.[154] When some members of The Seven went out with the older Hans Windish and Enderla Modtler (aka the Hook), they too became more ambitious and destructive, in one case taking not only the bed sheets from an inn but also all the pillows and two entire beds.[155] In every one of our sample cases, juveniles displayed the same progression toward better planned and more profitable crimes.

Jörg Mayr's apprenticeship in crime was no more formal but it did follow the same general life trajectory of other "professionals." In fact, once his randomly confessed ninety-five crimes are assembled in chronological order, the steady progression from accomplice to independent burglar and from occasional petty to more regular and more profitable burglary is quite striking. Like the Seven, his first efforts under the tutelage of Steffan the Grocer were small-time and unfocused, involving minimal planning and small profits. A few of his targets were chosen based on information about relatively large sums of cash kept at home but most householders were the victims of opportunity thefts, the result of open windows or unlocked doors while they were away. Initially Jörg entrusted Steffan to act as his fence for stolen clothing and bed linens but eventually he tired of relying on his mentor's fairness and decided to sell the stolen goods himself, apparently experiencing no difficulties at all finding ready buyers among peddlers, servants, farmwives, innkeepers, Jews, and others. Only large gold coins proved hard to get rid of, since it was assumed (usually correctly) that the only way they could have come into the possession of a young vagrant was through theft.[156]

By the time Jörg was fourteen or fifteen, he had begun the advanced journeyman phase of his career in theft, marked by his growing association with the older and more violent rural thief Georg König, better known as the Shepherd, and his menacing companion known only as Green Cap. While Jörg continued to "work" occasionally with the Grocer and others, he and his new accomplices planned more, stole far more often, and accordingly took ever bigger hauls. He also began to steal as much or more on his own, usually abusing the misguided hospitality of someone who put him up for the night. Mayr liked to portray himself to interrogating magistrates as a poor beggar occasionally snatching only food and clothing, with stolen cash an unintended byproduct of a burglary. By the time of his latest arrest, though, he knew that it had become entirely the other way around, with theft the main source of income and begging the supplemental. Now he unwittingly spoke of "casing a house," often through the intelligence of one of his rougher comrades, such as the Shepherd or Green Cap.[157] He went exclusively by his street name, drank regularly (sometimes in burgled houses), almost certainly gambled, and was sexually active.[158] This lifestyle is not surprising, given that Mayr now spent most of his time around adults. Many noncriminal teenage boys evinced such behavior, and the worldly Nuremberg magistrates did not even seem to notice this aspect of his maturation process during their interrogation. They did, however, note the premeditation and especially the violence in his recent exploits, including alleged extortion, arson, and assault. Whether or not Jörg was guilty of any of these charges, he couldn't deny that he spent long periods of time with young men who did commit such offenses, and thus was susceptible to guilt by association.

Fighting to Survive

The greater risk of violent death in his circle of friends and associates was just one of the threats to Jörg's long-term wellbeing. In a world where half of all children born alive never reached the age of fifteen, the mortality rates were undoubtedly higher among those minors who ate poorly and irregularly, endured long periods outside, with exposure to extreme temperatures, and had little or no access to medical care. Like all early modern children and youths, beggar children were highly susceptible to diseases such as smallpox and the plague.[159] Many of the beggar children admitted to the Findel, particularly during the 1630s, were already very sick and weakened, often requiring initial quarantine and treatment at the nearby hospital. Dead beggar boys and girls were regularly found on the sides of various country roads or curled up inside stables.[160] Most of Nuremberg's juvenile criminals mentioned long and debilitating illnesses at some point during their recent experience. Jörg Mayr recounts that shortly before his latest arrest "he was so sick and freezing that he had a cold fever for ten weeks, which left him so weak that he could hardly go from one village to another." Later in his testimony, he again mentions his recent illness and says that he mostly stayed inside "not only [violently] shaking three times a day but also with his entire body covered with the bad French things" (i.e., syphilitic sores).[161]

Still, Jörg Mayr's future was not foreordained by his life on the street or by his criminal activity. Early modern Germany had its own rags-to-riches stories, most famously that of the itinerant beggar boy Thomas Platter (c. 1499–1582) who became a very successful printer and teacher. Even the long-suffering Lazarillo de Tormes, after a series of colorful employers, eventually secures a position in the civil service as a town crier and is able to get married and settle down (albeit with a wife who regularly cuckolds him with their priest-landlord).[162] Marriage, children, and stable employment were admittedly unlikely prospects for someone in Jörg's situation, but they were not impossible. He had survived the most dangerous years of childhood, he had persevered and occasionally prospered amid great hardships, and he had successfully evaded serious punishment until this point. Why should one more arrest be any different?

Perhaps Jörg Mayr entertained such thoughts upon his most recent arrest in the tiny village of Zant on April 4, 1604. The seriousness of his current predicament was quickly evident, though, once he was transferred to Nuremberg's Hole and repeatedly tortured during a stay of almost nine weeks—an exceptionally long incarceration by early modern standards.[163] Jörg quickly recognized that his sole hope of escaping execution this time lay in convincing his interrogators that he had not yet become a "master" and therefore unreformable thief—a task to which he brought considerable ingenuity, mental toughness, and sheer physical endurance. Would he succeed?

The first major turning point in this fight for his life came early in his first Nuremberg interrogation on April 25, when after confessing to nine burglaries and suffering a session with the strappado, Jörg was confronted with "well-known" evidence of his long association with the notorious Georg König (aka the Shepherd). Faced with this irrefutable fact and the ever present reminders of further torture, Jörg acknowledged his relationship with the Shepherd, hanged in nearby Eschenbach almost a year earlier: "Since [König] himself already confessed that [Mayr] had stolen with him, he also wants to confess it and testify; he should just be allowed to reflect, so that he can tell one case after the other."[164]

His association with the infamous Shepherd put Mayr in a tight spot.

Fig. 4.11. Torture chamber of the Nuremberg "Hole," site
of repeated interrogations of Jorg Mayr. The pulley, stone, and
rack of the strappado are shown here; a room next to this one
displayed all of the different tools of torture available to the
executioner and was in itself often sufficient to elicit
confessions. Stadtarchiv Nürnberg.

Whatever Steffan the Grocer's faults, he was a nonviolent burglar and fence, a step or two below the violent robber König on the notoriety scale. Mayr therefore attempts, sensibly, to portray König and his violent companion Green Cap in a less threatening light. The initial thefts he mentions involving them sound as opportunistic and irregular as those of the Grocer's household, generally involving used clothes and small amounts of cash that happen to be lying around.[165] After reciting nine such petty burglaries, Jörg claims that he cannot remember any other crimes he committed with König. Threatened with further torture, he resumes his confession but shrewdly drops all references to the Shepherd, instead recounting eighteen more break-ins committed with Steffan's wife or on his own. The self-portrait Jörg paints is hardly flattering, frequently revealing treachery toward multiple strangers and even relatives who have taken him in at various points. Still, he must have been congratulating himself on shaking the more serious association with König and Green Cap when he stopped testifying after a total of thirty-seven crimes.

This time, though, the Little Castle Seventh's reputation has caught up with him, and he is asked why he had not mentioned his previous incarcerations in the villages of Ansbach and Windsbach and why he hadn't reformed after these punishments. Jörg brazenly attempts to turn this accusation around, exclaiming that no place had ever treated him as badly as Windsbach, where he was flogged while wearing a livestock feedbag and then expelled from the town. This outburst is a serious miscalculation on his part, as is more obviously the subsequent justification that "since then he hasn't stolen as much and what he did steal was on account of poverty, when he couldn't beg anything or come to Driessdorf (his hometown), since he was very frail, thus he had to steal out of necessity, but God help him just once more from that and he won't do anything else the rest of his life." This is too much for his two patrician interrogators, Christoff Behaim and Veit Georg Holtzschuher. "[Given] his multiple thefts he was not unjustly arrested but rather [on their account] has earned the gallows!"[166] More significantly, their angry retort is followed by the much more serious charge of recently threatening the villagers of Windsbach with arson when they refused to give him anything, as well as accosting them and running in and out of their houses with three accomplices, including the apparently not forgotten Green Cap.

Arson was a particularly terrifying crime in the premodern world.[167] A charge of even threatening such an action would escalate his case to a much higher level, and Jörg knew it. It would demolish his carefully constructed image of a beggar/casual thief and replace it with that of a violent, hardcore offender. Perhaps for the first time he suspected that these were the immediate grounds for his arrest back in Zant. More likely he knew that the favored method of Nuremberg's interrogators was to start with petty offenses and work up to more serious ones, in which case, the other shoe had finally dropped. Whatever Mayr's state of surprise or degree of guilt, he recognized that this accusation had to be fought at all costs. For an unspecified length of time, he endured another session of the strappado. Upon release he again swears, possibly weeping, "upon his poor soul's salvation that he didn't do anything except, at Green Cap's urging, go with him to these two villages, but stayed outside in the courtyards and can't [possibly] know whatever

Green Cap said to one or the other person or what he got from them."[168] He adds that he himself only received the tiny amount of five dreykreuzer (1/4 fl.) and three dreyhaller (1/9 fl.) from two of the accomplices and nothing from Green Cap. And then, to further blacken Green Cap as the dangerous instigator, Mayr states that he saw Green Cap pull out a pistol in one of the houses and threaten the other two boys who quickly climbed out of the window on a rope to join Mayr below.[169]

Unimpressed, the interrogators demand to know more of the crimes he committed with these associates, and when Mayr claims he has told all, he is confronted with a new accusation of actually burning down a stable with Green Cap and another friend known as the Fat Sieve. Again, Mayr knows that such a confession (whether true or not) could be his death warrant and his denial prompts a new torture session, the third within a few hours. When he has regained his senses, Mayr acknowledges that the bailiff of Lichtenau had already asked him about this incident shortly after his arrest four weeks earlier, and he swore then that he had nothing to do with it and doesn't even known any Sieve. Scrambling to avoid both the arson charge and more torture, Mayr volunteers that perhaps they mean the Black Boy, whom he saw only twice (and never during the day) and who went on to Rotenbach after Easter. Following this information with a new series of oaths, he again mentions his recent illness, and offers to provide names of those who can give him alibis during this period.

Sensing his vulnerability, the interrogators instead throw out still another serious accusation, that Mayr and Green Cap had recently robbed a peasant woman on the way to market in Schwabach, beating her and throwing her to the ground before taking her money. This too, the bailiff at Lichtenau had asked him, and Mayr pleads "for Jesus Christ's sake" that they believe his emphatic denial of any involvement or knowledge thereof whatsoever— "which God in his Kingdom" knows is true. Impressively, threats of further torture do not alter his position, and though he does provide the names of two more associates—Loud George and Shaky Dürrer—he does not give their current location and does not implicate them in any crimes, adding of the latter's group, "he doesn't even know if they steal or commit any other misdeeds."[170] In fact, when the daylong interrogation finally ends, an exhausted and brutalized Jörg Mayr must have felt some sense of accomplishment in fighting off the more sinister accusations against him. The cost was admittedly high, but he had resisted guilt by association with more visibly hardened criminals as well as any charges of the violence associated with such professionals. Thirty-eight confessed burglaries aside, the Little Castle Seventh had fared relatively well given the formidable odds against him.

Jörg might have further succeeded in shoring up his image as a fallen but redeemable petty thief had not new reports and information continued to flow into the Nuremberg chancellery. Three days after his initial marathon interrogation, the Little Castle Seventh was interviewed again, this time in front of his cell (rather than in the torture chamber). Apparently his account of a certain theft with Bird Johnny four years earlier claimed that only eight and one-half gulden had been stolen when in fact it was twice that sum, a sizeable amount. Mayr is quick to respond but not especially convincingly:

> Says on his soul's salvation he no longer knows exactly how much this stolen gold was since it happened so long ago but it might well have been seventeen gulden, he won't dispute it. He didn't use more of it than he already testified though: spent three kreuzer (1/20 fl.) for a roll and then, as he recollects, three Bazen (1/5 fl.) at Orberg for a pair of shoes and three kreuzer in Gunzenhausen for a white pearl hatband; the rest of the money was buried outside the village Aha, not far from Gunzenhausen. In the meantime, however, a tailor who had followed and observed him, dug up said money with the help of another and buried it in the bathhouse at Aha where it was [later] picked up by the aforementioned Bird Johnny in person, [who thus] as he reported got his money back.[171]

Even if this story were true, and his accomplice had made a fraudulent claim about the missing money, it seems unlikely that Jörg could remember the exact price of all his purchases four years later yet be so far off in his recollection of the amount stolen. Mayr's credibility, to the extent that he had any left, was crumbling, and he must have realized as much. The next discrepancy in his confession was even more damning. His version of a recent burglary in Niederdombach mentioned only ten gulden but according to the victim, two bags of coins totaling over forty-eight gulden—six times the annual salary of a domestic servant—were lifted. Again Mayr's explanation is often convoluted, surely testing his interrogators' patience:

> Says he just now rightly recalled and knows that there was a lot of money in two bags and that his comrade Green Cap was also present as they stole from the rooms and the trunk [and] divided said money among them and [Mayr] gave ten gulden of his share to the baker Enderlein at Riet to hold. Since he later learned that they had been banned by the peasants at Niederdombach, he never returned and thus the aforementioned baker Enderlein still has [Mayr's share] on hand. Of the remaining money, he and Green Cap

together gave the smith at Hirschlaw twenty-one gulden in a sack, including a deposit of three ducats for watching it. The next day, in the presence of his wife in a church, the aforementioned smith gave [Mayr] fifteen gulden back, saying that he could not keep the money since it might be dangerous. And when [Mayr] asked for the [six] gold pieces, which he did not find among the money, he was answered that the fifteen gulden should be enough for him. Another time [Mayr] tried to get him to [return] the rest which was withheld and—on his soul's salvation the pure truth, there's no more to be told—he again came up completely empty with said money.[172]

Though this still left six gulden unaccounted for, Jörg was undoubtedly relieved that no further questions or threats of torture followed that day. As his incarceration in the Hole wore on another three weeks, however, the desperateness of his situation must have become increasingly apparent.

When a new magistrate, Endres Imhoff, resumed interrogation May 21—almost seven weeks after Jörg's arrest in Zant and four weeks after his first Nuremberg interrogation—he was loaded with new information and fresh indignation: Mayr has stolen much more than he has admitted, from the age of six on; unless he now comes entirely clean the executioner will begin torture anew. Jörg sounds weary and defeated when he replies that he has done his best to remember everything up to this point and will try his best now. His attempts to avoid characterization as a professional thief have clearly failed and so instead of resisting further, he makes an about-face and he decides to throw himself at the mercy of the court, recounting his corrupted and misspent childhood.

This is the closest Jörg Mayr has ever come to expressing regret and even remorse during the course of all his interrogations. Whatever the degree of his sincerity, he undoubtedly believes that this is the type of contrition his moralistic judges like to hear from criminals and might just earn him one more chance. Hoping to build on this new persona, the abused and penitent orphan-thief, he then confesses in crisp fashion to fifty-seven more crimes. The duration of this session is not recorded but even at the breakneck pace of six cases per hour (one every ten minutes), it would have required more than nine hours. Now that Jörg has finally conceded the designation of lifelong criminal, he has no reason to stall or resist; torture is never even once threatened. To the contrary, his final strategic ploy depends on confessing more, rather than less, so as to appear both compliant and penitent.

This last self-representation—as Jörg probably suspected—was no more effective on Nuremberg's magistrates than had been his previous attempted characterizations of beggar and small-time thief. In fact, his third, lengthy statement merely sealed the case against him; while the first two interrogations had been followed by consultation with the municipal jurists, this final testimony went straight to the full Council, "since it didn't require much consultation [to decide] what he deserved."[173] When Jörg was interrogated a fourth and final time two weeks later, he clearly regretted his previous cooperation: "says with truth, he knows of nothing more to tell; what he has [already] confessed to is too much and he shouldn't have done it."[174] This last flash of defiance quickly gives way to utter desperation, and he admits to one more crime before literally throwing himself at the mercy of his judges.

Ultimately this last defense fails, too, but that should not distract us from the cleverness of Jörg's successive self-expositions and their likelihood of success under other circumstances. Like every street-smart criminal, he has a stockpile of defenses—most of which he has probably used before— suitable for every occasion. Among minors they range from the most basic excuse of poverty to various portrayals of inadequate or even criminal adult supervision. Knowing how highly magistrates value such oversight, he subtly adjusts this element in each successive self-representation, always preserving for himself the role of pawn or victim. Like his involuntary scaling of the ladder of notoriety in his statements, this aspect of Mayr's defense represents a dialogue with his interrogators. Together they successively create ever more sinister versions of the Little Castle Seventh, with the forced collaboration shattered only by the image of a violent career offender, which Jörg tenaciously resists. This too is a success on Jörg's part, requiring formidable endurance of torture and weeks of isolation in a dark dungeon cell.

Yet if he did everything right in his own defense, why in the end was he unsuccessful? The most basic answer is information. Because of Jörg's prolific activity within a relatively small area, Nuremberg's magistrates had no difficulty employing a network of local officials and informers to gather incriminating testimony against him. Immediately upon his transfer to Nuremberg's dungeon, city officials began an ongoing search for more information about his crimes, continually checking with various local authorities on the facts of Jörg's statements.[175] The sheer volume of those crimes that Mayr could recall in turn helped convince magistrates that the young criminal was both dangerous and unreformable: "[considering his] multiple and frequent thefts, burglaries, and break-ins far and wide throughout the land and in many localities, there is thus not the slightest hope of improvement to be found."[176]

Like the convicted child murderer Appolonia Vöglin, Jörg also had the misfortune of being prosecuted by one of the fiercest jurisdictions in the empire during its most active period. Most significantly for him, over two-thirds of those executed in Nuremberg during the peak years of 1560–1620 were thieves, previously a small minority of capital punishments in Nuremberg.[177] This new severity in punishing crimes against property helps account for the only period in early modern German history in which minors were executed for offenses other than murder or "crimes against God" (incest, sodomy, and witchcraft).[178] Burglary and common theft—as opposed to violent robbery—frequently involved juveniles, with fifteen- to seventeen-year-olds accounting for as many as one in three thieves in some areas.[179] Between 1560 and 1620, the city of Nuremberg executed at least fourteen thieves aged eighteen or younger. This appallingly extreme punishment for juvenile theft was nonetheless quite rare and appears in Nuremberg and other German lands only fleetingly within the same brief sixty-year window.[180] The same is true of the torture of young thieves such as Jörg Mayr (who endured the strappado four times during interrogations).[181] Still rarer was the execution of women under eighteen for theft. Catherina Schwartzin and Maria Kürshnerin of the Seven were the first women to be hanged in Nuremberg for theft, a shocking event that a chronicler noted "until this time was unheard of in [our city]."[182]

Even so, Jörg might have hope for a partial pardon and reduced sentence, long the normal course of events for convicted juvenile felons. As recently as 1575 and 1576 in Nuremberg, three different groups of condemned boy thieves aged seven to sixteen years were deemed "too young to hang" and had their sentences reduced to work in a chain gang before flogging and banishment.[183] The magistrates of contemporary Frankfurt condemned sixty-nine young thieves to death during a period of 130 years, yet all but nine had their sentences commuted to flogging and banishment.[184] Nuremberg's leaders, like those elsewhere in early modern Europe, were not blind to the mitigating factor of youth and indeed often invoked it in their ultimate decisions, even during this period of intensified executions. Less than half a year after Jörg Mayr's execution, another seventeen-year-old thief, Michel Brumbecker, had his death sentence commuted to two years on a chain gang. In Brumbecker's case, the appeals of his master "and the entire butcher craft" clearly played a decisive role, providing evidence of social capital that Jörg and his fellow vagrant youths crucially lacked.[185]

What led Nuremberg's magistrates to the exceptional decisions to execute Jörg Mayr and thirteen other minors "regardless of their youth?"[186] In each instance, the most decisive factor was probably sheer exasperation on the part of the magistracy. All of the condemned juveniles were repeat offenders, most with records of several arrests. Every member of the Seven, for instance, had supposedly spent at least ten detentions in the begging stockade or dungeon, usually followed by a public flogging.[187] Hennslein Creuzmayr had already been arrested seven times before his last detention, including one stretch in a chain gang (from which he escaped), as well as the usual flogging and banishment.[188] All of the older boys in the sample had served at least two or three terms in a chain gang, usually for sentences of a few weeks but in at least one case for an entire year. Most importantly, all of the condemned youths had previously received the penultimate punishment of permanent banishment, in some cases two or three times. Catherina Schwartzin, as already noted, had even had her ears cut off with her last banishment a few months before her execution. In every case, the final verdicts noted that "such warnings and mild treatment had been received with disdain," and the juveniles continued to return to Nuremberg and steal.[189] Why, a genuinely befuddled magistrate asked Catherina, after being "frequently arrested and imprisoned here for theft, escorted from my lords' territory by guards, even banished with flogging," why did she keep coming back? "She didn't know where she should go," came the reply," since no one would take her; otherwise she wouldn't have stayed here."[190] Having exhausted all other punitive means at their disposal, Nuremberg's magistrates finally yielded to the sentence normally reserved for adult or "master" thieves: death by hanging.

The 1594 case of Hennslein Creuzmayr provides an unusual glimpse of magisterial discussion and debate on this very question. Uncertain of the appropriateness and legitimacy of Creuzmayr's execution, town councilors requested the advice of their legal experts, just as they did with every death sentence for juveniles. Of the five opinions recorded, two actually opposed capital punishment, arguing that Creuzmayr was undeniably a bad thief and repeat perjurer but "despite being almost tortured to death . . . all the thefts that he has confessed to do not exceed five Hungarian ducats." Rather than execution, these jurists recommended chopping off his "bread" (i.e., oath) finger, followed by banishment.[191] Two other consultants strongly disagreed, arguing that one of Creuzmayr's recent thefts alone totaled thirty gulden (an unproven and unacknowledged allegation) and also that the large young offender was violent and dangerous, as evident in his resisting arrest that "severely injured" one of the officers. Citing this and other incidents (including threats of arson), they claimed that only execution would protect persons and property from Creuzmayr returning after banishment and causing further harm.[192] A fifth jurist found both arguments convincing—including that article 163 of the imperial criminal code, the Carolina, empowered the council to execute a minor under exceptional circumstances—and consequently presented magistrates with the choice to show mercy or not.[193] In Creuzmayr's case, the city's fathers ultimately decided that their "multiple mitigated punishments and warnings" had been consistently disregarded and that there was no hope of improvement; they hanged him next to young Hensa Baur five days later.[194]

Clearly all of the factors mentioned by the jurists weighed heavily in the Nuremberg council's condemnation of Jörg Mayr. Their practice of successively accusing Mayr of more and more notorious crimes during interrogation made clear the increasingly larger amounts Mayr stole and the allegations of violence in particular made Mayr in their eyes a serious threat to property and persons, despite his vigorous denial of the latter. Equally or more important to their decision was the explicit challenge to their authority: "The Little Castle Seventh is known throughout the land as a thief from whom nothing is safe."[195] Jörg's attitude at the outset of his interrogation, claiming complete innocence, constituted a brazen disregard for the council's authority and even an insult to their intelligence. Like their early modern counterparts everywhere, Nuremberg's patrician rulers craved and demanded submission from their subjects. It is unlikely that an immediate and unforced full confession would have gotten Jörg off this time, but his persistent resistance to their questions clearly outraged them. In fact anger permeates just about every question from the two examining councilmen, which is not the norm in other Nuremberg criminal interrogations. Even during Jörg's last interrogation, when he has already adopted a fully subservient position, he is excoriated for his numerous "freely undertaken" thefts and his "sinful" behavior, to which he has only "unwillingly" confessed.[196] Here, finally, was Jörg's most vulnerable spot. For while he could resist their portrayal of him as dangerous, he had no response to such reproaches for stubbornness, deceitfulness, ingratitude, and ultimately, unreformability. These were all essential parts of the one identity Jörg had sought to deny—the career criminal. In his judges' eyes, the friendless orphan, the misled teenager, and even the penitent sinner were no match for it.

Was this an accurate assessment? Certainly Jörg seemed unlikely to stop stealing were his captors to release him, but was he already irreversibly on the path to becoming the dangerous robber or arsonist that authorities feared? Here his astounding self-control under repeated torture makes it very difficult to see behind any of his assumed masks. His many years on the road had bred exceptional self-reliance and mental toughness, enabling him to survive in just about any circumstance, including his last and most desperate situation. Whereas most of us would confess to almost anything under such torture, Mayr endured four extensive bouts with the strappado, offering a resistance that was quite remarkable, albeit ultimately futile.[197] Like his interrogators, we are also aware of his intelligent manipulation of both facts and criminal stereotypes, a performance so skilled that only additional bits of information and his reputation itself could undermine it. His confession of ninety-five crimes committed over a four-year period—with only one detectable repetition and very precise information on stolen objects, sums paid by fences, and other details—testifies to either his outstanding memory or his great skills of invention, in both instances providing further proof of his intelligence. Jörg also does not lash out during his interrogations, either verbally or physically, as the mercurial Henslein Creuzmayr repeatedly did, the latter angrily arguing that "[the magistrates] were unfair to him and took away his life while comrades of his who stole just as much as he did came away with [their lives]."[198] Instead, Jörg makes his last-ditch offer to fight as a mercenary in Hungary (an idea that he likely got from a fellow prisoner, Hanns Wildt, whose confinement overlapped with his for three weeks, and who had been released under just such terms the week before).[199] Unfortunately, this appeal, as well as Jörg's final request "to better himself and to become a completely new person," fell on deaf ears.[200]

A Bad End

The story of Jörg May reveals the sporadic, intertwined nature of occasional work, begging, and sometime theft in the mostly monotonous lives of many beggar children and young vagrants. It shows the fallacy of any coherent "youth culture" or "criminal underworld," yet at the same time exhibits certain practices and attitudes common among society's marginalized, such as ubiquitous informal child circulation of various kinds—including at a child or youth's own initiation—as well as the gradual acculturation of some of these young people to stealing and violence at ever greater levels. Jörg's story of self-circulation as a runaway also confirms many relevant aspects of early modern life encountered in previous chapters, especially the indispensability of a family network (including biological or foster parents) and of training in a craft—the former resource rejected by Mayr and the latter probably never available to him. The subsequently strong momentum toward a life of crime from this point was something both he and his interrogators could agree upon, though both sides were also aware that the

Fig. 4.12. Hanging of the Seven, from a Nuremberg
chronicle (1605). Stadtarchiv Nürnberg.

process was not always irreversible and very few beggar children developed
into professional thieves of the caliber of the Little Castle Seventh.[201] Which
external and internal elements were most determinative in Jörg's case is of
course impossible to diagnose from our distant perspective.

The question before the Nuremberg magistracy appeared to be a much
simpler one: did Mayr's lifetime of theft and possibly more serious crimes
show any signs of possible reversal? On Monday, June 4, 1604, the final
version of his statement was put before the town council, which promptly
decreed that he was unreformable and that he should be hanged as soon
as possible. Normally, that would have meant the next day but the jurisdictional claims of the prisoner's native Lichtenau required more than a week

of correspondence on questions of prison expenses, hiring an executioner (since Lichtenau did not keep a standing one), and transfer of the prisoner. Finally, after nine days of waiting in his dim and dank cell, Jörg Mayr was released from the Nuremberg Hole and returned to the site of his initial incarceration in Lichtenau.[202] Three days later, on Saturday, June 16, he stood, bound by hand and foot, before the town's assembled residents while his sentence was first read aloud and then carried out. Like Apollonia Vöglin, executed in exactly the same spot twenty-six years earlier, he left behind no gallows speech or any record of his burial.

FIVE

The State Wards

By the spring of 1647, the pace of life at the Nuremberg Findel had slowed to a relative crawl. Just ten years earlier, during the crisis of the 1630s, the building had at times teemed with as many as 190 resident boys and girls, with a flurry of children and youths coming and going on an almost daily basis. Once the crisis abated, however, the annual influx dropped dramatically to the point where, during the ten months since May 1, 1646, a mere five children had been admitted to the Findel's care, bringing the total number in residence to twenty-nine boys and twenty-two girls. Only two of the residents had died during the same period, the fewest on record during the preceding 150 years, and only one boy had been placed as an apprentice, another unprecedented low. Overcrowding was hardly an issue, then, when on March 7, 1647, the inner council decided to admit an orphaned pair of nine-year-old twins named Eberhardt and Susanna Schier. The two children had lost their father, Stephan, before they reached their first birthday and their recently deceased mother, Sibylla, had never remarried during the intervening years.[1] We know nothing more about the life of the Schier twins before their entry into the Findel, and they probably knew equally as little about the life that awaited them within the same institution's walls. Would Susanna and Eberhardt find the daily routine and discipline therein stifling or would they flourish in an environment that guaranteed them sufficient food, shelter, health care, and even education? Would brother and sister become part of a closely knit surrogate family or would they leave the Findel at the first opportunity, even by running away? Most crucially, would both even survive to adolescence or would one or the other succumb to one of the many deadly diseases to cross the Findel's threshold?

The answers to each of these questions depended of course on a variety

Fig. 5.1. A boy and a girl from the Nuremberg Findel
(ca. 1650; 1915 reproduction). Stadtbibliothek Nürnberg.

of individual and sometimes unique factors. All Findel children shared the same unwanted status, at least in terms of the normal channels of child circulation, but each of their stories reflected a different subjective experience of life in the Findel (and one that is especially hard to capture given the absence of ego-documents—diaries, letters, recorded testimony—left behind). We can retrace the footsteps of Susanna and Eberhardt and reconstruct their daily routine and the range of social interactions available to them. Records of some 3,600 children who crossed the Findel's threshold between 1560 and 1670 can provide a statistical context for the twins' experiences and reveal patterns by age, gender, and the nature of admission.[2] Statistical data can also reveal which characteristics gave a child a higher *probability* of survival and post-Findel productivity, but they cannot predict whether individuals who fit into all the most favorable statistical categories would in fact live to see adulthood. To underscore the precariousness and uncertainty of the Schier twins' future, this chapter will therefore approach life in the Findel in the same open-ended manner as Eberhardt and Susanna experienced it, beginning with their moment of entrance into a new and mysterious world.

A Foundling's Passage

Neither town council protocols nor Findel registers mention where Eberhardt and Susanna were living at the time of their admission. We also don't know who escorted them to the Findel's door or the precise date of their crossing the institution's threshold. To even reach that point, however, they had already passed two important screenings. The first, examined in chapter 3, was the Findel administrator's determination that no private foster care could be found for the "friendless" twins. The second screening involved a preliminary sorting by age, a procedure common to orphanages and foundling homes everywhere in early modern Europe.[3] Because Susanna and Eberhardt had already attained the Findel's minimum residential age of seven, they were allowed to remain in the home itself until reclamation by a relative, death, or placement in a job.

Had the twins been younger than seven, their subsequent experience would have been quite different, as illustrated by the case of a young girl admitted to the Findel six months after their own arrival. When Findel father Conrad Heinrich Meyer answered the insistent pounding on the institution's front door just after dawn on October 9, 1647, he was greeted by the familiar sight of a guard holding a baby in an old basket, discovered just minutes earlier on that very spot. As usual, Meyer took in the baby and notified the Findel administrator, Albrecht Pömer, who promptly initiated inquiries as to the parents or other relatives of the foundling. After three days with no success, the inner council then approved the Findel father's petition to admit the child, now described as a girl of about eighteen months, named Anna Maria. Within a week, officials prepared to send Anna Maria off to a foster mother outside of the city's walls, where she would to be cared for until (if ever) she reached the age of seven, at which point she was to return to the Findel.[4]

This mundane account of an undoubtedly traumatic event in the life of any child, even a toddler, underscores the unexceptional nature of Anna Maria's experience. About three in four children admitted to Nuremberg's Findel during our period were under the age of seven, in most cases, under two years old.[5] This pattern was common throughout early modern Europe, as was the even more significant tendency that the great majority of these children were anonymously abandoned.[6] In each of these respects the foundling Anna Maria was commonplace, even typical among Findel children.

The intention to send a child of Anna Maria's age to a foster mother

Fig. 5.2. The front door of the Findel, site of many anonymous abandonments (ca. 1725). Stadtbibliothek Nürnberg.

was likewise the norm. These surrogate parents were appointed from a fluctuating list of twenty to forty women whom the Findel administrator had approved to act as foster parents to foundlings taken in by the Findel.[7] Early modern foundling officials throughout Europe frequently voiced the suspicion that some of their foster mothers might be the true mothers who had abandoned their infants, thereby obtaining a government subsidy to care for their own offspring.[8] It is possible that this occurred in Nuremberg as well. Was the maiden Clara Pfefferlin, who in 1662 sponsored and then raised a newborn foundling called Clara, in actuality the child's biological mother? If the Findel staff had any suspicions, they did not record them anywhere.[9]

Since the majority of foundlings were under the age of one, most of their foster mothers were first needed as wet nurses. Unlike larger foundling homes, Nuremberg's Findel maintained only one or two in-house wet nurses and thus nursing infants were dispatched to foster care as soon as possible. With rare exception that foster household would remain the foundling's home until it was old enough to reside in the Findel. Anna Maria was in fact one of these anomalies (found only in the mid- to late seventeenth century), remaining in residence at the Findel continuously since her admission.[10] No explanation for this decision was provided. Perhaps the personal affections of one of the staff prevailed or some mundane procedural snag kept her from being sent to a foster home.

Life with a foster family was in most cases probably not much different from life in the poor households many of the Findel children came from. The father of the household was frequently deceased, absent, or unemployed; the mother usually worked more than one job at a time. The foster family did at least offer a home of sorts for a Findel child, albeit under mean conditions. Foster mothers were not supposed to be nursing any other children at the same time, though this restriction was impossible to enforce. An unintended pregnancy could in itself endanger a Findel baby if the new child's birth led to a competition for nourishment.[11] In some instances, the mother's milk might run dry and an infant foundling would be fed pap, a pasty mixture of flour or bread with milk or water. The family's daily diet was typically meager and unbalanced so that the wet nurse herself was likely malnourished, thereby endangering her charge. As in all poor households, Findel children of all ages remained susceptible to disease and early death.

Naturally physical, verbal, and emotional abuse were all possible in such settings, but it was unusual that any cases came to the attention of the Findel administrator or the town council. The most common form of abuse, simple neglect, was probably practiced by many poor parents in general and it required some exceptional evidence to trigger an investigation and prosecution. As there was no official inspection of foster homes, this usually meant denunciation by a neighbor. In 1566, one such complaint brought foster parents Hans Maier and his wife before the inner council, where they were berated with questions: "How long they [had] been citizens why [had] they let [Hans Peck's leprous daughter] suffer thus?" Such cases surfaced quite rarely, and in general foster parents did not come under suspicion for neglect or physical abuse when there were clear signs of a communicable disease.[12] Young Hensslein Stöffel took matters into his own hands and ran away from his foster mother after two-and-a-half years, though this need not have been because of abuse. Another boy picked up off the streets by the guard at Thiergartner Gate in 1617 explicitly claimed to have run away from his foster family where he had been "very badly treated." Upon his immediate readmission to the Findel police authorities launched an investigation.[13] The most notorious case in Nuremberg came in 1634, when Findel administrator Albrecht Pömer ordered foster mother Anna Wernerin arrested and imprisoned for having beaten a boy in her care "so badly that a few hours later he died." Initial inquiries revealed that in fact "this Wernerin within a short period [had] had buried five such poor orphans." Despite repeated torture, though, Wernerin refused to confess to any murders, and the council regretfully released her with a large fine and banishment from the city until she paid up.[14] Even Wernerin's alleged murders pale in comparison to serial foster mother Eva Kellerin, who was arrested in nearby Würzburg for the deaths of seventy-seven of the eighty-one children entrusted to her in the course of fifteen years—a 95 percent fatality rate. No government official was indicted for negligent supervision, but Kellerin herself was ultimately executed.[15]

Foster parents and their charges might just as likely develop strong emotional bonds, particularly if the child survived several years. For children who had never known any other parents, leaving the foster home at the age of seven for the Findel could be a traumatic experience. Sometimes newly admitted Findel children ran back to their "milk families" after only a few days or weeks in residence.[16] On other occasions it was the foster parents who took the initiative, returning to the Findel after several months or even years to reclaim their former charges. After depositing her foster son in the Findel, Ursula Dennigerin was apparently struck with regret almost immediately, returning the next day and promising to raise the child as her own.[17] Nuremberg's officials naturally welcomed this relief of the public coffers, though there is no explicit evidence that they actively promoted intimacy within foster households with this objective in mind, as some of their French counterparts did.[18] Childless couples and particularly widows and widowers might have a number of reasons for wanting a foster child back, including the replacement of a recently deceased biological child. Perhaps some of these adoptive parents had selfish motives, though exploitation as a worker was probably not one of them, given the relative unproductiveness of such young children.[19] Genuine affection, rather, shines through in cases such as that of Steffan Diener, whose foster father Hans Ammen, an innkeeper from Gostenhof, reclaimed his former charge after almost two years and promised "to raise him and let him go to school for a year or two and then support him when he is ready to train [as an apprentice]." Nine years later, the Findel father noted, Ammen was true to his word, providing the 25 fl. apprentice fee when young Steffan began his apprenticeship as a blacksmith.[20]

Unlike virtually all foundlings under the age of seven, Anna Maria never left the Findel and thus never experienced life with a foster family. Wherever she resided, her chances of survival until adolescence were still dismally low by modern standards. Only one-half of all the children born in Europe before the nineteenth century would survive to the age of fifteen. Fortunately she had already weathered her first year of life, the most dangerous phase of

Table 5.1. Anonymous abandonment death rates in the Nuremberg Findel, 1570–1669 (twenty-year intervals; n = 202).

Interval	Within one month	Within one year	Within five years
1570–1589	62.5% (5/8)	75% (6/8)	100% (8/8)
1590–1609	42.9% (12/28)	75% (21/28)	92.9% (26/28)
1610–1629	32.4% (36/111)	67.6% (75/111)	96.4% (107/111)
1630–1649	45.7% (16/35)	97.1% (34/35)	100% (35/35)
1650–1669	40% (8/20)	85% (17/20)	95% (19/20)
Total	38.1% (77/202)	75.7% (153/202)	96.6% (195/202)

childhood that claimed from 15 to 50 percent of her cohort in the general population.[21] Living in a densely populated city put her at greater risk than life in the country but less so than if she had been living a bit further south in Bavaria and Austria, where infant mortality rates were twice as high as in northern regions. Her greatest jeopardy came from living in an institution, where on average children died at two to three times the general population rate. In Nuremberg, infants six months and younger predictably had the highest mortality rate: one-half died within the first month and only 13 percent were still alive after two years.[22] In foundling homes throughout Europe, a year with a fatality rate of 50–60 percent for foundlings under the age of one was reckoned as exceptionally fortunate; more typically the figure was closer to Nuremberg's overall foundling fatality rate of 96.6 percent within the first five years (see the sample in table 5.1).[23] The odds that eighteen-month-old foundling Anna Maria would survive her first year were three to one against—odds that she beat. The chances against her surviving for a total of five years, however, were much steeper, about thirty to one. And in fact on July 12, 1649, at the age of three, she succumbed to a deadly fever.[24]

Did Anna Maria's gender play a significant role in her fate? The evidence from Florence argues that it did, with an overall mortality rate of 72 percent for girls versus 65 percent for boys.[25] Thirty years ago, Richard Trexler argued that officials informally encouraged infanticide in general and female infanticide in particular by waiting longer to send girl babies to nurses or by negligent practices among nurses themselves.[26] In a more recent study of the same institution, Philip Gavitt countered that all infants were sent relatively quickly to nurses and suggested that perhaps overcrowding among girl babies (abandoned at a significantly higher rate than boys) provided a more plausible explanation than gendered passive infanticide.[27] Still more recent evidence posits that premodern girls on the whole were more susceptible to tuberculosis and some other fatal diseases than boys, though this does not resolve the issue of passive selection of conditions based on gender.[28] The pattern in Nuremberg's Findel is by no means straightforward: while overall girls comprised 55.7 percent of foundling deaths (and only 47.5 percent of admissions of this type), the death rate itself varied considerably based on age and the time period in question.[29] The significance of gender in foundling death rates, in other words, remains far from simple or unambiguous.

Would Anna Maria have been better off with a foster mother? If she had still been nursing (and in some places nursing at eighteen months was not unusual), the answer would be a qualified yes. On average, 80–90 percent of all infants and toddlers kept in foundling homes or hospitals during the early modern era died—a statistic that did not change significantly among such European institutions until the twentieth century.[30] Several scholarly studies have shown that survival rates improved dramatically, in some instances doubling, once a foundling got to a wet nurse, particularly one far from the city.[31] On the other hand, removal to one of Nuremberg's poor suburbs or nearby villages could not have assured Anna Maria of complete safety from the wide variety of infectious diseases that made premodern childhood such a dangerous passage.[32] She might still have been weakened by malnourishment and succumbed to the same fever that killed her at the Findel. Like all children under seven, her health would be repeatedly jeopardized by a variety of natural and man-made hazards wherever she lived in the early modern world. Clearly there was some correlation between the number of children living in foster care and the Findel's overall death rate, but this correlation might reflect more the young age (and therefore greater vulnerability) of the Findel children in foster care rather than any increased danger in that venue.

Daily Life at the Findel

As it turned out, both Susanna and Eberhardt Schier came to know the foundling Anna Maria, since she atypically remained at the Findel despite her young age. The twins were already resident for six months when she arrived, so they would have witnessed the flurry of activity set off by her arrival. They were also still there almost two years later, when she died, and almost certainly saw her in her deathbed and later attended her funeral service and burial. Close contact of this sort between the Findel's older orphans and young foundlings was very unusual, except for perhaps a brief encounter with a baby or toddler before it was sent off to a wet nurse.[33] Perhaps Susanna acted as an older sister to the young Anna Maria, watching out for her and playing with her. Certainly they saw each other repeatedly

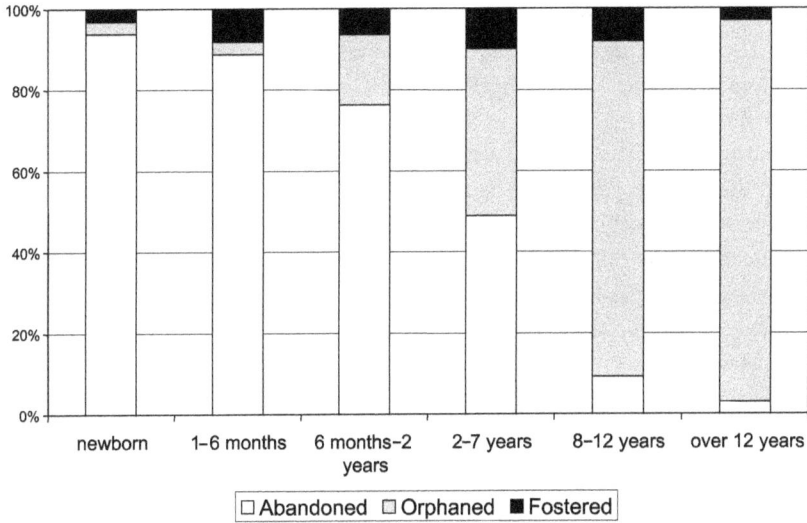

Fig. 5.3. Type distribution at Nuremberg Findel by age, 1557–1670 (*n* = 913). *Source*: FKD.

within the confines of their daily routine. As figure 5.3 shows quite starkly, the great majority of older children resident in the Findel were—like Susanna and Eberhardt—orphans, while the great majority of Findel children under seven living with foster families were—like Anna Maria—abandoned children. Some orphans were admitted under the age of seven and a small number under the age of two, but almost two in three applicants were of sufficient age to come directly to the Findel.[34] Just as significantly, very few of any children admitted at the age of two or less, typically foundlings, would live long enough to enter the Findel.[35] Only the third category of state wards, those children formally fostered to the Findel, maintained a relatively constant proportion across all age cohorts. This almost thorough segregation of illegitimate and legitimate children—based more on age than on the nature of admission or circumstances of birth—would have important repercussions for the Schiers' life experience at the Findel.

Entrance into the Findel marked a stark and often traumatic transition for all children. Orphans like Eberhardt and Susanna Schier were usually still reeling from the death of one or both parents and were possibly overwrought. Older children deserted by their parents were likely confused, sad, and perhaps angry. For those few children who had been with foster parents since a young age, that household was the only home and family they had ever known. The attitude of any child would obviously vary based on the quality of that previous life but inevitably each would have to make a great adjustment. Upon passing over the Findel's threshold, familiar faces and most other aspects of their old life abruptly disappeared. The many siblings who, like Eberhardt and Susanna, were admitted simultaneously could at least be near one or two people from that earlier time, though even that relationship would undergo a significant transformation, starting with their initial separation at the Findel's gate. From that point on, each would spend most of their time in the company of a single-sex cohort. There would be many opportunities for the brother and sister to see each other but they didn't yet know that and even if it had been explained to them, it is likely that their separation at the Findel gate remained a very emotional moment.

The experience was probably most analogous to entering a cloister or a boarding school, though even in those settings personal links with the past and other familiar points of reference did not vanish as thoroughly as they seemed to for Findel wards. Children were allowed to bring a few personal items with them, if they had any. Eberhardt and Susanna probably brought along some possessions, perhaps a favorite toy or book, some personal letters or mementoes—the list could not have been long. A rare surviving inventory of personal effects from 1597 notes that orphan Heinz Vogel brought with him "an old fur, a black fur cap, two pillows, a blue cap, a little farmer's stool, a black linen pinafore, a small towel, and some pictures wrapped up in an old towel."[36] Most children, even artisanal class orphans like the Schier twins, probably brought less.

The Findel that Eberhardt and Susanna first set foot in on March 7, 1647, had changed little physically since its days as a Franciscan cloister. There had been some important renovations and additions during the 1560s—including a new water wheel, mill, and bakery—and the usage of some rooms varied over time, but the overall layout remained unaltered.[37] That complex of buildings no longer exists, but fortunately during the 1720s, Markus Tuscher, a former Findel ward and later a celebrated artist, drew several sketches of his boyhood home that provide a convenient introduction (see fig. 5.4). The Findel was in most respects a self-sufficient community, much as the medieval Franciscan monastery had been. The property consisted of a completely enclosed complex of buildings, constructed around a front courtyard (A) and back courtyard (B), bordered by the Pegnitz in the north, the Findel garden in the east (C), the Findel church (far bottom left), still known as the Franciscan Church, in the southwest, and a multiuse building (after 1670 the discipline- and workhouse) in the west (off picture along left side). Only the southern wall, site of the Findel's sole entrance to the outside world, touched on open space, in this instance a public square. All the

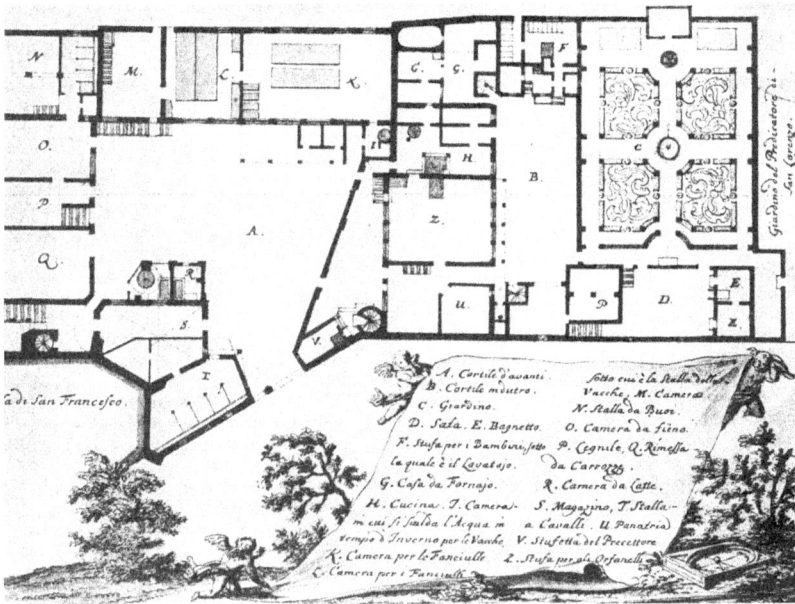

Fig. 5.4. Blueprint of the Nuremberg Findel (ca. 1722). Stadtarchiv Nürnberg.

buildings along the far western (left) side of the front courtyard were dedicated to livestock and food production, including a henhouse (P), horse stalls (T), a garage for wagons (Q), cow stalls (N), milking stalls (O), hay rooms (M), threshing floors and storage rooms (S), and a shack alternately used to house pigs and to warm water for the cows during winter (I). The ground floor of the building on the eastern side of the front courtyard and the western side of the back courtyard contained the boys' and girls' parlors (F), Findel kitchen (H), bakery (G), refectory (Z) and schoolmaster's study (V). The Findel administrator's family occupied most of the second and third floors, with small residences for the Findel parents and a few other live-in staff in the remaining space. Boys' and girls' dormitories were located on the shore of the Pegnitz (K and L) on the first and second floors, respectively. The southeastern corner of the cloister, separated from all living quarters, housed the multipurpose "firewood corner" (P), sick ward (D), and two baths (E).

The everyday routine that Susanna and Eberhardt encountered in their new homes bore striking resemblance to that of the Catholic monastery it succeeded. Nuremberg's Lutheran civil authorities recognized this uncomfortable affinity but nevertheless decided to maintain a Findel Rule well

Fig. 5.5. Boys' dormitory in the Nuremberg Findel (ca. 1725). Stadtbibliothek Nürnberg.

into the eighteenth century.[38] Like the monks whose cloister they inherited, Findel children divided their day—at least in theory—between prayer, meals, and study or work. At the beginning of their first full day, Eberhardt and Susanna would have been awakened at daybreak, 5:30 A.M. in the summer and 6:00 in the winter. Their separate dormitories each had their own heating ovens as well as large windows on the north and south walls of the rooms, allowing for much sunlight and good cross breezes when the weather was warm (see fig. 5.5). Immediately after dressing in their respective dormitories the children scurried downstairs to the refectory (see fig. 5.6), where they remained segregated by sex. There they briefly groomed themselves and when everyone was assembled began the usual morning prayers: an invocation and blessing by the Findel father, a psalm, the Lord's Prayer, and the Apostles' Creed. Sometimes boys and girls added their own prayers and special intentions. After singing a hymn, they then said the daily blessing for food—"All Eyes Await Thee, O Lord"—and recited another Lord's Prayer. Eberhardt and Susanna would then go to their respective parlors, also known as "milkrooms," where they were expected to eat in silence their meals of bread and cheese (younger children were given milk or strained soup).

Breakfast was followed by a prayer of thanks—"Lord, we have eaten, thanks be to the Lord"—as well as still another recitation of the Lord's Prayer and the Creed as well as a reading from the Luther bible. All but the youngest children would then spend at least four hours, two before lunch and two after, learning writing and possibly a craft. Lunch, the main meal, was served around noon and was preceded and followed by a similar ritual series of prayers, this time including a recitation of the Ten Commandments. After a few more hours of study and work, the boys and girls were then allowed to play outside in one of the Findel's two courtyards until late afternoon, when they gathered to sing "God wants to be merciful to us," followed by a supper of bread and soup or porridge. Bedtime followed shortly after that, with each child snuggling up next to one or possibly two bed companions before dropping off to sleep.[39]

What did Susanna and Eberhardt make of this highly regimented life? Did they feel nourished in body and spirit? Just as importantly, did the daily routine have the formative effect on their character that councilors hoped for, making them into pious, literate, and productive members of society? The most basic "civilizing" functions were toiletry and personal hygiene. According to a Findel ordinance, children were expected to maintain "clean bedding . . . [and keep themselves] daily brushed and combed."[40] The Findel maintained its own baths and both the children and their clothes (as well as the bed linen) were washed at least once a week—quite frequent by early modern standards.[41] The boys got their hair cut two to three times a year, the girls somewhat less often, usually before major holidays, when they were all also checked by the barber for skin lesions or dangerous scabs.[42] Their daily uniforms, while varying somewhat in fashion over the course of two centuries, were typically cut from common linen or cotton cloth. Girls wore simple dresses, accessorized with hose, gloves, and bonnets or caps (*Schlepplein*); by Susanna's time false pigtails or braids were also common. Older boys like Eberhardt wore plain shirts, vests of Augsburger cotton, and pants made of vellum or calfskin.[43] During special public occasions or door-to-door collections, Findel children dressed in their traditional uniforms, distinctive by their bright red color. Worn-out clothing was replaced at least annually and the twins would receive additional clothes, including new shoes or boots, upon departure for an apprenticeship or domestic position.[44]

An even greater difference that Eberhardt and Susanna would have noticed from their life until then was the relatively high level of health care they received. Salves, potions, powders, herbs, quicksilver, and other medicine regularly constituted a significant expenditure in the Findel's annual budget, as high as 100 fl. during the crisis year of 1637–38. This medical generosity did not escape the attention of the ever cost-conscious inner council, which repeatedly asked the Findel parents to keep medical expenses down—to no apparent effect.[45] The Findel also enlisted the services of a number of health care professionals, usually on a consultant basis. Bathmasters and barbers cared for a variety of "damaged" children—particularly those with leprosy, scrofula, syphilis, or other skin ailments—who were sometimes sent to the city's nearby spa for treatment.[46] Barbers also regularly checked Findel wards for worms, drew blood when deemed necessary, pulled teeth, cleaned and cauterized wounds, and set broken bones. Female eye specialists were occasionally engaged and nurses were hired as needed to care for sick children in two small "sick rooms."[47] By the beginning of the seventeenth century, Nuremberg's chief municipal physician received a small annual honorarium to treat Findel children and staff, and by 1638, a permanent nurse and barber had been added to the home's payroll.[48] Ever vigilant of the Findel children's welfare, Findel administrator Albrecht Pömer dismissed the first full-time barber a short time later, after hearing several complaints that he "treat[ed] the damaged children very badly and pretty much neglect[ed] them." Pömer then raised the salary offered and in 1640 hired the widely respected barber, Johann Daunestock, who was succeeded shortly thereafter by the barber-surgeon Dr. Gärtner, who first examined the newly admitted Schier twins in 1647.[49]

Susanna and Eberhardt would have quickly learned that proper nourishment was also a Findel priority, at least in principle. The menu at lunch and dinner naturally varied considerably, but by statute it was supposed to include bread and at least one vegetable (no portions mentioned), as well as meat on Saturdays, Sundays, and holidays for the children. (The Findel father and mother and some staff members were served meat everyday.)[50] The eligible "vegetables"—barley porridge, lettuce, turnips, pease porridge, cabbage or sauerkraut, and mashed bread in milk—were each assigned a day of the work week, though again the actual offering would depend on the season and the cook's preferences. Potatoes, a staple of later orphanage meals, were not available in Franconia until the early eighteenth century. The nutritional value of this diet would not have met modern standards, particularly since the Findel (like most early modern institutions) greatly relied on bread, noodles, porridges and other food heavy in carbohydrates and fats to fill the children up. Deficiencies in certain vitamins naturally also led to the pediatric problems most associated with them, namely, scurvy from a lack of vitamin C, rickets from insufficient vitamin D, and particularly blindness and various eye ailments from inadequate vitamin A. The imbalanced diet of the Findel could also stunt children's growth or emaciate them, thus making them more susceptible to dysentery or the various contagious diseases around them. This vulnerability was of course exacerbated by the children's practice of eating directly out of common dishes, with their

Fig. 5.6. The Findel's main parlor, which served as a refectory
and a classroom (ca. 1725). Stadtbibliothek Nürnberg.

spoons, well into the eighteenth century. Despite these shortcomings, most
of the foundlings ate as well as or better than their counterparts in private
artisan-level households, particularly in view of the relative frequency of
meat in their diet, a key source of protein.[51]

On the surface, then, Eberhardt and Susanna would have quickly become accustomed to relatively high standards of personal hygiene and propriety, received comparatively high-quality medical attention, and always
had enough to eat. So much for the body, what about the mind and soul of
the Findel child? Education offers one measure and here too the Findel was
quite progressive for its time. Since 1530, all of its boys and most of its girls
had been trained in basic German reading and writing as well as elementary
mathematics.[52] Few children had such skills upon entry into the Findel and
those who did—such as ten-year-old Joachum Reutmayr, who had been
taught by his scribe father—would have stood out as precocious.[53] Perhaps
Eberhardt or Susanna had some rudimentary training of this sort or had
even briefly attended a school before they came to the Findel. In their new
home, all of their learning would be separated by sex as well as by age, with
at least two groups of pupils in each of the two homes' parlors (see fig. 5.6).
Before 1644 both boys' and girls' instruction took place under the tutelage
of part-time student-teachers, the home's clerk, or the Findel father himself;
by the time of Eberhardt and Susanna, Master Johann Sauer, the chaplain

from Saint Lorenz, had assumed that role, assisted by Master Peter Hoffman from 1647 on. On Sundays, all children attended catechism lessons before the service at the adjoining Franciscan church (or, during winter, in each home's parlor).[54] Particularly adept pupils were aided by an endowment that provided for the annual "instruction, clothing, stipend, and other needs" of four girls as well as four boys to attend the German schools of Saint Lorenz or Saint Sebaldus. The most gifted boys were tutored by the Findel scribe in his small office and eventually sent to one of the city's Latin schools—in every instance with tuition and books paid for by the Findel.[55]

The effectiveness of this instruction or the actual skill level achieved by most of the children is not easily gauged. The majority of those boys and girls who survived to adolescence were sent into craft apprenticeships or domestic servitude, so literacy was perhaps advantageous but by no means essential to a successful career. Adding and subtracting, multiplying and dividing, were much more practical skills in that respect. Fundamental literacy was indispensable, however, to regular reading of the bible and to the inculcation of Lutheran doctrine. In this sense, both the objective and the method of the Findel's reading lessons resembled those of all German Protestant grammar schools following the Reformation, with the bible and Dr. Luther's small or large catechism for children providing the substance of most daily lessons. Perhaps the constant repetition of certain prayers as well as the catechism's questions and answers did eventually make an impression on even the most stubborn young minds in the Findel. Perhaps some children were even able to move beyond rote memorization to actual comprehension of Lutheran doctrine. If so, the Findel would have been more successful than most schools throughout the empire. It is surely worth noting, however, that amid the multiple cases where a Findel child's later adult experiences are recorded, there is not a single reference to a boy joining the ministry.[56]

Another character-shaping goal of the Findel Rule—again similar to its monastic counterpart—was the inculcation of self-discipline through daily labor. Laziness, willfulness, and disobedience were all obstacles to the children's ultimate success in "finding a living" (*eine Nahrung finden*).[57] Like all early modern children, Findel residents were expected to contribute to the operation and income of their household. Some of the daily labor consisted of routine tasks such as carrying water, working in the Findel garden, helping with the groceries and food preparation, or feeding the Findel's livestock, which at the time of the Schier twins consisted of five or six cows, a few pigs, and some two dozen hens. Before the sixteenth century, the children had also grazed and milked the cows, but by the seventeenth century these tasks were performed by the Findel's own full-time shepherd and milkmaids. Some tasks tended to be gender-specific: laundry, cleaning, and mending for girls; loading and moving heavy supplies for boys.

In addition to their lessons and assigned chores, Eberhardt and Susanna were also required to devote a few hours of most days to rudimentary craftwork. Like all of the girls, Susanna was trained in spinning and sewing by the Findel mother or one of her maids; by the late seventeenth century the Findel employed a full-time seamstress for this purpose.[58] These domestic skills were intended to help her secure a husband and subsequently contribute to the household income, rather than to make a significant contribution to the Findel's revenue. Only once, during the crisis years of the 1630s, did the girls' work approach large-scale production; after that there is no subsequent mention of income from spinning until 1774. Other craft activities for boys and girls—including belt making, hatchet bending, button sewing, and comb making—provided modest income for the Findel but were also mainly intended to teach the work ethic and a few practical skills more than to generate significant revenue.[59]

The most financially successful of the Findel's products were the thin brass or silver ornamental figures known as *Flinderlein*. Findel boys and girls cut and stitched the shiny little metal sheets together and then handed them over to craftsmen who turned them into finished gold leaf products. The children's handiwork was so popular that, at one point, a complaining metalworker successfully lobbied the inner council to limit the Findel's production of *Flinderlein*.[60] All of this made the institution the Schier twins entered a far cry from the protoindustrial orphanages and foundling homes elsewhere in Europe. With its consistent emphasis on literacy and religion over vocational training, the Findel's daily routine more closely resembled the medieval monastery's training of young oblates than the eighteenth-century workhouse's forced and underpaid labor by juvenile internees.[61]

The apparent rigidity of this routine obscures the fact that on most days Susanna and Eberhardt had at least a few hours of free time, with ample opportunities for friendship and enmity, fun and mischief, pleasure and pain. This was also the only regular occasion where the brother and sister would have been able to engage in genuine conversations with one another. Work, study, and sleep were all strictly segregated by sex, as were meals, with male staff members and older boys eating at the neighboring Krauss Foundation's house, and all younger children and female staff members taking their meals at the Findel.[62] In theory, even this playtime was supervised

Fig. 5.7. Tuscher, drawings of children playing in the Findel's courtyards, detail (ca. 1725). Stadtbibliothek Nürnberg.

though it is hard to believe that most boys and girls weren't able to sub-
vert surveillance at various times.[63] Play in the courtyards was also the one
time when children were permitted to be loud—a precious outlet from the
rest of their day, when they were expected to be silent or speak only when
spoken to (see fig. 5.7). Even within their highly regulated daily routine,
the Schier twins, like all children, would be exposed to teasing, gossiping,
singing popular songs, shirking work, or cleaning indifferently. By contrast,
those few privileged children permitted to work in the Findel's garden, away
from such activity, were permitted the other indulgence rare to the daily
routine—time alone.

In addition to informal games and play, Susanna and Eberhardt could
look forward to numerous festivities and other special occasions throughout
the year. The Lutheran calendar preserved a surprising number of traditional
feast days, albeit without any of the "papist" trappings. Christmas reigned

supreme as the special day on which, in addition to a relatively sumptuous dinner, all Findel children would enjoy gifts of candy, Nuremberg's signature gingerbread, forks, knives, toys, clothes, and possibly other gifts from private donors. Each boy and girl also received an article of clothing and a pastry on five occasions throughout the year: Easter (March or April), Saint George's Day (April 23), Pentecost (May or June), Saint John the Baptist's Day (June 24), and Saint Michael's Day (September 29). On each of these and other major feast days, older children were also given a draught of beer, and everybody enjoyed a special meal with lamb or veal.[64] There is no evidence of birthday or nameday celebrations in the Findel (generally a later development in society at large), though by the second half of the seventeenth century the birthdates or baptismal dates of all orphan and foster children were at least carefully recorded by the Findel scribe.[65]

Local philanthropists established other special events for Findel children, such as the annual spring picnic with games and dancing in the Wöhrd meadow, just outside the city's eastern wall. The most famously endowed celebration was a gift of Elisabeth Kraussin, who came to Nuremberg as a ten-year-old peasant girl in 1569 and died seventy years later the very wealthy widow of a prominent local businessman.[66] With funding from a small portion of her massive endowment of over 127,000 fl., every Saint John's day (or Midsummer; June 24) the Findel's children and staff (including all foster mothers if they wished) marched in a slowly winding procession from the Findel to the Krauss Foundation's house nearby, singing religious songs (see fig. 5.8). Upon arrival, boys and girls continued to sing songs and then recited a memorial prayer to the memory of Elisabeth Kraussin, with formal acknowledgment of any of her descendents who might be present. Each child then received a meal of soup, meat, and roasted vegetables as well as a quarter liter of wine and three-quarters liter of beer. The entire daylong ritual, later including a trip to Kraussin's grave in the Saint Rochus Cemetery, survived well into the nineteenth century.

On some occasions, work and play overlapped. As wards of the state, Findel children often sang at public ceremonies, such as the dedication of a bridge or the reception for a visiting delegation from Moscow.[67] Their oldest and best-known public activity was the custom of singing door to door or in the marketplace for bread or money, particularly during the Christmas season.[68] Originally, Findel children identified themselves by special badges cut out of old red cloth, but by the time of Susanna and Eberhardt the children's entire uniforms were an easily recognizable bright red. They roamed the city in four groups, each containing one lead singer, one alms collector

Fig. 5.8. The winding annual procession of children and staff from the Findel (*lower right*), to the Krauss Foundation (*top left*), for a banquet and other festivities (ca. 1600). Stadtbibliothek Nürnberg.

and seven additional singers, making thirty-six children total.[69] Two of the groups were exclusively boys and two exclusively girls, with each sex having a "rich" and a "poor" group (based on the affluence of their assigned neighborhood). Sometimes the carolers circulated during the weeks before Christmas, but normally they made their rounds between 6:00 and 8:00 P.M. during the twelve days following Christmas. It is not known how the children were selected for this privilege or which songs they sang (they were supposed to be evangelical hymns). But apparently these unchaperoned outings could be quite exciting for the children—too much so, according to one seventeenth-century preacher, who complained of wild and "unspiritual" behavior.[70] Undoubtedly the beer listed among the expenses as well as the novelty of being out after dark each played a part in the merriment.[71] Still, not until the eighteenth century were singing orphans accompanied by adults or their stops announced to residents in advance.[72]

Findel children also left the home to collect money door-to-door at other times during the year. One pre-Reformation custom, the Maundy Thursday collection and resale of "indulgence eggs" (*Antlasseier*), continued to be a source of good revenue long after Nuremberg embraced Protestantism (and rejected both Purgatory and indulgences) and long beyond the time of Susanna and Eberhardt (see fig. 5.9).[73] The medieval traditions of foundlings

Fig. 5.9. Findel children collecting eggs on Easter
(ca. 1700). Stadtbibliothek Nürnberg.

and orphans collecting money after church services and soliciting free bread, fruits, and vegetables from market vendors likewise remained Findel staples throughout the eighteenth century. After Christmas caroling, the single most significant source of both revenue for the Findel and outings for its children was funeral singing.[74] For modest fees, boys and girls would hold candles as they processed in corteges and would then sing at the graveyard. The Findel also rented out special pillows for the casket of the deceased. As in Christmas caroling, the Findel's attempted monopoly on a practice formerly open to students and other poor children met with resistance from various quarters. Pastors frequently complained that parish children were suffering from their exclusion from such ceremonies, and one local gravedigger who tried to prevent "the poor foundlings" from collecting their alms for singing at a funeral was ordered to abide by "ancient custom" and return to them their money.[75] More than sixty years later, another gravedigger's widow attempted to confiscate and sell some of the Findel's coffin pillows, but she too was reprimanded and ordered to return the pillows to the Findel children immediately so that they could continue to rent them out.[76]

A World unto Itself

Upon their admission into the Findel, Eberhardt and Susanna Schier joined a distinct community, a minisociety, with its own rules, tensions, and traditions. Modern historians often debate whether that community was more like a family or an impersonal institution.[77] This dichotomy is misleading, since characteristics of both models were present and by no means mutually exclusive. Like many medieval and early modern institutions (including monasteries and convents), the Nuremberg Findel was consciously modeled on the household, with a benevolent but strict father figure at its head. It also contained elements we might associate with modern state institutions, such as regimentation and an emphasis on individual utility and productivity. Like all human communities, the Findel knew various levels of personal affection, enmity, and indifference among its members and was also defined by various implicit or explicit hierarchies within that community. These social hierarchies and the quality of relationships that were possible within such constraints are particularly useful indicators of subjective experience in a setting that was at once familial and institutional.

In overtly appropriating the structure and language of the household, Findel authorities surpassed even their monastic and convent inspirations, since the Findel possessed not only a father and a mother but actual children as well. Appointed by the Findel administrator, who also resided at the home with his wife and children, the Findel father and Findel mother represented the most important adult influences on these children's lives. Until 1623, the boys' and girls' homes each maintained its own set of fictive parents, even though the two homes had shared the same roof since 1560. After that, except for the crisis years of 1635–45, one married couple presided over all the boys and girls. Some of these substitute parents stayed at the Findel for many years, others more briefly.[78] Findel parents Conrad Heinrich and Catherina Meyer had only been at the Findel for a year when Schier twins arrived in 1647 and they remained at the Findel just four more years, when they were replaced by Georg and Margaretha Heinlein.[79] Heinlein, himself a former Findel child, was appointed by Albrecht Pömer and served as Findel father for a total of fifteen years before succumbing to a deadly fever in 1665.

Most Findel parents came from humble backgrounds, though at least the father was required to be literate. Husband and wife were together paid the modest salary of 24 fl. per year and were supposed to be individuals of good personal character, for like biological parents, their charge was moral as well as financial, ultimately aimed at producing "useful and pious" individuals.[80] Thus, in addition to overseeing the household's day-to-day budget and tasks, the Findel parents led their children in daily prayers and were expected to provide occasional religious instruction outside of the weekly catechism with a local chaplain. Normally the Findel father personally picked up all newly admitted children who were not yet resident in the Findel and he accompanied them months or years later when they were placed in a job outside the home. Like any other early modern *Hausvater*, his authority over the children was near absolute, subject only to the Findel administrator and in turn the city council itself. (The Findel father's authority over Findel property was in fact more carefully prescribed than his moral imperative over the children, as the inner council strictly forbade him or his wife to sell any Findel property or to house any guests without explicit permission from the administrator).[81]

Eberhardt and Susanna would also have had near daily contact with a residential staff of adults that included a cook, a nanny, and a milkmaid, as well as one or two bakers, one or two shepherds, two male servants, the Findel scribe, a nurse, and the Findel dungmaster, who regularly hauled away the Findel's waste (and who earned the biggest salary of anyone, including the Findel parents).[82] Even when the size of the staff shrank after the 1630s, the ratio of adults in staff to children remained high relative to the low admissions of the 1640s.[83] These adults obviously exercised great influence over the Findel's children but were not necessarily as carefully screened for upright character as the Findel father and mother. The Schier twins would likely have spent more one-on-one time with one of these staff members than with the Findel father or mother. Perhaps Susanna helped in the kitchen and Eberhardt frequently worked with the baker or a shepherd. Maybe he was one of the boys assigned to help the dungmaster with his malodorous duties of keeping the Findel and surrounding grounds clear from refuse (especially trash dumped by peasants) and once or twice a week hauling waste to a dump outside the city walls.[84] Christmas singing and other organized outings put children in brief contact with adults outside the Findel, but that was the usual extent of their connections with the wider world. Findel children apparently did not receive any relatives or other adult visitors, as did children in some Italian and French homes, perhaps because adults in Nuremberg feared having the children returned to them.

The emotional and psychological impact that staff members had on the children within this mostly closed society must have been profound, at least in the short term. Unfortunately the personal relationships that developed between these adults and the Schiers or other children are mostly hidden from us. For better or worse, these adults likely provided the only

role models most of the children knew. Some Findel staff members probably attempted to teach minor skills to the wards or otherwise took a special
liking to one boy or girl. Others no doubt verbally, physically, or perhaps
even sexually abused them. Above all, these adults taught Findel children
by example about the hierarchies and rules of interactions within the larger
society outside their walls, particularly the gender roles expected of them.
Of course, not all of the adults at the Findel set the sort of example that
town councilors would have hoped for. On more than one occasion, male
servants were reproached or imprisoned for physical assault. More scandal-
ously, in 1619 two of the Findel's unmarried maids were found to be pregnant by the home's baker.[85]

Did Findel parents and their staff form emotional attachments to their
charges? Death entries in the Findel register, such as "this Mayerin died
on 4 March 1623" or more laconically "this child died," evoke the sort
of institutional indifference to the deaths of foundlings and orphans that
many modern people assume prevailed in the Findel. It is important to
distinguish, though, between infant and other young foundlings—most of
whom were sent almost immediately to a wet nurse, where they eventually
died—and those older children who actually resided in the Findel. Most
register entries for the latter consistently call the child by name in the death
entry, usually by a diminutive, such as "this Hanslein died of a bad fever," or
"Annalein Schmidtin died on Saint Ursula's Day, 1588." By the time that Susanna and Eberhardt entered the Findel, it had become standard to include
more personal details in the entries for children who died while resident in
the Findel, such as cause and description of death and time of burial.[86] Thus
we hear that Hans Caspar Lanng "was very swollen and suffered greatly"
and that Michael Saloman "departed blessedly after 6 A.M. in the night of
December 17, 1685, of frailty and a breast ulcer."[87]

If the Findel father and mother or any of the staff showed affection toward Eberhardt and Susanna it is likely that it was reciprocated. But how
did the twins feel about their peers in the Findel? Did they think of them
as brothers and sisters, the logical corollary to Findel father and mother?
Perhaps, though there is absolutely no explicit mention of the terms "Findel brother" and "Findel sister" in any official documents. Each child likely
acquired both friends and enemies during their years of residence in the Findel. In addition to personal predilections and individual encounters, these
relationships were shaped by those hierarchies that the children had absorbed from both their small community and the larger society. First there
was the gender double standard, evident to all the children in their daily
treatment in the home as well as in placement. Age and size also determined

the daily pecking order, as they do today in most school or other institutional settings. Finally, there was the rigid social order of the day, whereby bastards and all foundlings were at the bottom, the offspring of beggars and other dishonorable people next, and so on, up the social hierarchy.

As orphans of a respectable artisan and his wife, Susanna and Eberhardt were from the start far better off than those few foundlings who had survived to age seven and were surrounded by constant reminders of their shameful birth and rejection by their parents or other relatives. The Schiers were admittedly lower on the totem pole than the two resident daughters of Findel administrator Albrecht Pömer—Maria Helena (fifteen when the twins arrived) and Maria Magdalena (eight)—though the two patrician girls probably still interacted frequently with the Findel's orphans and foundlings. It is ironic that parental social status meant so much among parentless children, but it is also quite understandable considering the amount of stigma that they all experienced because of their residence in the Findel. Additional shame of any degree allowed some "poor orphans" an opportunity to lord it over the even less fortunate. Life in the Findel could not have been easy for Hennslein Ziegler and Michael Piggel, both the sons of publicly executed murderers, nor for the four children of a family counterfeiting ring, most of whom remained at large.[88] How much did peers torment the child of a former monk and later mercenary, or the son of a mad student, not to mention the offspring of various more infamous social deviants?[89]

Perhaps the most difficult question to answer is whether Eberhardt and Susanna were on balance happy during their residence at the Findel. The greatest historian of the Nuremberg Findel, Ernst Mummenhoff, writing in 1915, thought it "a truly sad, monotonous, and depressing life,"[90] but surely this is a modern projection on an existence that had both ups and downs. On the positive side, the twins were part of an easily identifiable community of children similar to themselves in many ways, cared for by adults who professed concern about their physical, mental, and spiritual well-being. The daily routine and other traditions of Findel life could offer comforting structure and stability, especially for younger children who had previously experienced much familial turbulence. They had clean clothes, warm shelter, and enough to eat. They were taught to perform basic arithmetic as well as to read and write—still uncommon skills among children in the world outside Findel walls. If either Eberhardt or Susanna displayed an aptitude for learning they could receive extra tutoring at the Findel or one of the city's Latin schools. Most importantly, Susanna and Eberhardt were able to remain in close contact with one another and their experience in this respect was not unusual. Half of the children admitted to the Findel entered—like the Schier twins—with at least one sibling.[91] Their own time in the Findel in fact overlapped with six pairs of brothers and sisters.

On the negative side, some of the older children doubtlessly found the same Findel routine and emphasis on silence stifling. Susanna and Eberhardt were probably teased at some point or possibly even assaulted by fellow Findel children or staff members. Again, their situation in that respect was not that different from that of children at a modern boarding school, with the significant exception of the ubiquity of corporal punishment in premodern times. By the time Susanna and Eberhardt were adolescents, they may have longed for dances or other opportunities to become intimate with members of the opposite sex. This type of encounter, no matter how chaste, was emphatically discouraged by the Findel father and mother. All outside activities, including Christmas caroling, also remained segregated by sex. Most Findel children had not yet experienced puberty by the time they left the Findel so perhaps sexual frustration was not as great as we might imagine. The only known case of pregnancy among Findel girls came to light in January 1624, when Barbara Wächterlein, a mentally retarded albino, was discovered to be pregnant by one of two visiting workers.[92] Still, the reassuring comfort of the Findel's regimented daily life had likely been transformed into a source of oppression for many young teenagers, who were also daily reminded of their great debt to the charity of others. There are no recorded suicides or suicide attempts but the latter were not likely to show up in official records.

Boredom, laziness, raging hormones, and other common teenage experiences often collided with the Findel's central goal of producing virtuous, God-fearing, and law-abiding citizens. In the daily contest of wills between the adult staff and noncompliant children, discipline was more than a watchword. Most infringements were minor: forgetting or botching a task, lying, playing with or ruining food, talking during prayers, breaking a window, and so forth. Such offenses and their punishments leave no historical record, nor do most cases of drunkenness, fighting, or general rowdiness. Even petty theft appears in institutional records only when a foundling runs away from the Findel after stealing or if civic authorities became involved. Such was the case for Hans Christoff Korner, who absconded after stealing 10 Batzen (2/3 fl.) from a blind fellow ward in 1583 as well as for four boys who ran away in 1600 "on account of thievery" from a visiting official asleep in his room.[93]

Like any other paterfamilias of the day, the Findel father had a wide range of punishments at his disposal, from simple scolding to beating to expulsion from the house. Public humiliation of various kinds could be an

Fig. 5.10. The Findel garden, a quiet oasis amid the institution's
busy daily routine (ca. 1725). Stadtbibliothek Nürnberg.

especially potent form of discipline, particularly in such a closed society.[94] Disobedient boys or girls might be forced to wear visible signs of shame (such as a humiliating hat), to stay inside during playtime, or to miss certain meals, particularly on holidays. Bed wetters were tormented by other children and staff alike.[95] Corporal punishment was common, and while there is no evidence of excessive cruelty, traumatic events of this nature were unlikely to be recorded or known outside the Findel's walls.[96] The Findel father and mother also might effect positive reinforcement with small rewards to children who excelled in certain activities, such as sewing, gardening (see fig. 5.10), catechism lessons, reading, or writing. Clemency has always been a prerogative of any sovereign authority, and Findel parents exercised this power with varying frequency. Generosity of this sort could backfire, as with the Findel father's initial leniency toward a delinquent boy who subsequently attempted to burn down the boys' home in 1559 (resulting in a stern reprimand for the Findel father by the inner council for his permissiveness).[97]

City councilors often showed their readiness to assist in the exercise of paternal discipline. In 1601 they immediately complied with Findel father Hans Rudreff's request to put Findel boy Veit Geitmüller in the city dungeon, following the discovery of his sexual relations with an already absconded female grocer.[98] In 1635, the Findel teacher ordered accused thief Lorenz Lenzer to be brought before inner council, which gave him a stern lecture and ordered him "to find a product" (i.e., learn a craft).[99] Another Findel girl was imprisoned for "various thefts" in 1640, as was Georg Vischer, who briefly overlapped with the Schier twins at the Findel.[100] The precise nature of young Elisabeth Visherin's 1625 offense(s) is unclear, but the situation must have been serious to merit a brief sentence on the city chain gang—something virtually unheard-of for girls or women.[101] By 1667, eleven-year-old Maria Magdalena Castarinsin's temper and "impetuousness" were enough to get her permanently expelled from the girls' home.[102]

Sometimes the discipline, pressure to conform, or other motivations led children to flee the Findel. On average, there was one runaway every three years between 1557 and 1670 (though in fact thirteen children ran away during 1600–12 and none at all for long stretches of time, such as 1569–84 or 1616–32).[103] Most of these flights also took place during the late sixteenth and early seventeenth centuries, before the Findel had shrunk to the modest size it maintained during the twins' time and absconding had become relatively rare. There was only one runaway during Eberhardt Schier's six years of residence in the boys' home, fellow teenager Georg Bishoff, who skipped out the year before Eberhardt himself left for an apprenticeship.[104] Some children, as already noted, ran away to escape imminent punishment for a crime or misdeed. Others became homesick for blood relatives or for foster families. The orphan Wolffla Schmidt left the Findel "at the urging of his sister" and went straight to a position she had arranged with a potter.[105] The severe overcrowding of 1635–37 prompted several older children to take their chances on the street, especially when the weather was warm.[106]

Usually the Findel father and mother didn't know (or didn't wish to acknowledge) the motivation in such cases and merely noted that a ward "ran away without any cause whatsoever."[107] In most instances, an absconding child left after several years in residence at the Findel, and usually did so alone. Only one in eight runaways was a girl, further substantiating the preponderance of boys on the street.[108] That existence, as we have seen, was hardly the carefree life some of these runaways might have imagined. In a few instances the tragic results of leaving the Findel in this way are known: A runaway Findel boy was found drowned in the Vishbach in 1558 and runaway Anna Bernreüterin was known to have "died in suffering" on the street.[109] Children who wished to return were almost always accepted back by the Findel parents. Catharina Kremerin, for instance, was taken back in 1568 but "sternly told" that if she didn't behave she would be expelled.[110] Orphan Peter Loner in 1597 ran away from the Findel an unprecedented

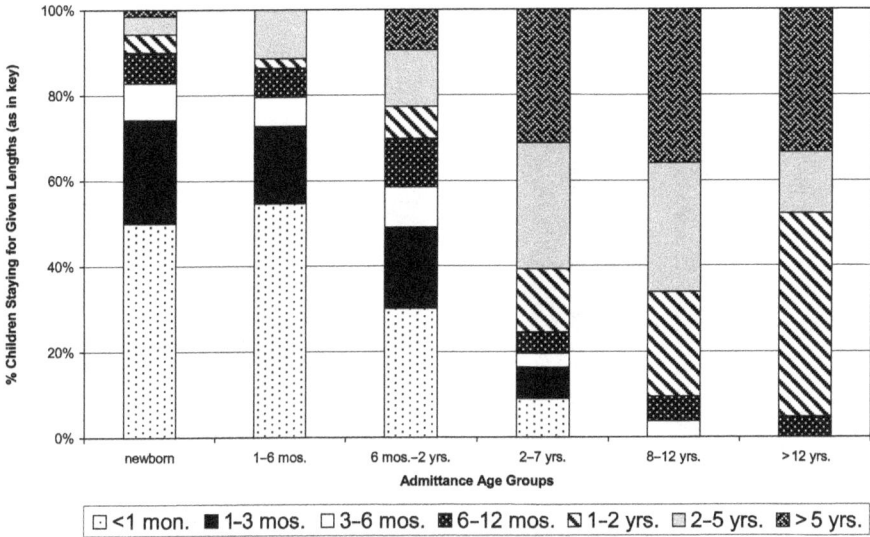

Fig. 5.11. Length of time spent in the Findel's care by age at
admittance, 1557–1670 (n = 363). Source: FKD.

four times within sixteen days, though "the fourth time the Findel administrator personally accompanied him into the pesthouse, where he was later
picked up by one of his relatives."[111]

One of the great constants during the twins' residence at the Findel would
have been the steady turnover of children. On average, only four in ten children admitted to the Findel's care stayed longer than one year, and only
half of those were still around after five years.[112] As figure 5.11 illustrates,
however, these numbers are skewed by the differing experiences of the two
main groups within the Findel population. Children under two years old,
who tended to be foundlings sent to wetnurses, usually died after a short
period of time, with only a small number still in foster care after five years.
Children seven or older at time of admission, who were mostly orphans,
had a much higher life expectancy. Thus almost all of them, by contrast,
spent at least a year in residence at the Findel, with more than one in three
staying for more than five years, as did Eberhardt and Susanna Schier.[113]
Boys tended to stay a little longer in the Findel's care than girls, though this
sample too might be skewed; in the twins' case, Susanna remained in the
Findel fifteen months longer than Eberhardt.[114]

The most likely cause of departure from the Findel was death. The rampant epidemics of the day—in particular, cholera, typhus, smallpox, and
tuberculosis—had a disproportionately fatal effect on children. Overall,

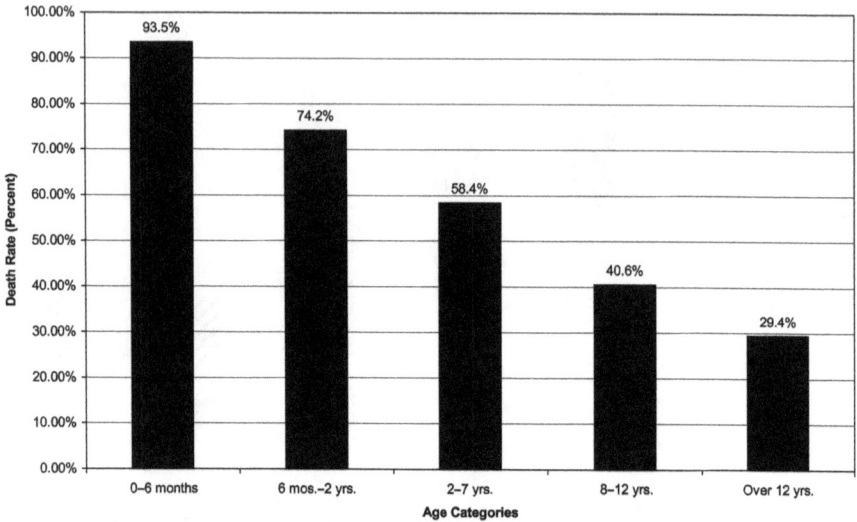

Fig. 5.12. Death rate by age of admission to the Nuremberg
Findel (all types), 1557–1670 ($n = 555$). *Source*: FKD.

about six of every ten children admitted, including those placed with foster parents, died while in the Findel's care. This death rate is much lower
than that of most foundling homes of the era but higher than that of most
orphanages, a difference that results from the Nuremberg Findel relatively
unusual practice of combining younger foundlings with older fostered children and orphans in its records. When Findel deaths are broken down into
these three main categories, abandoned children (most of whom were under two years old) had the highest mortality rate, about two in three, and
formally fostered children (who usually only stayed for brief periods) had
the lowest death rate, about one in three, while orphans (usually over seven
years old) had about a fifty-fifty chance of survival at the Findel.[115] As figure
5.12 illustrates, the odds of dying, regardless of admission type, declined
steadily with every passing year.

In terms of both age and admission type, then, Susanna and Eberhardt
had highly favorable odds of surviving their Findel experience. Yet even
among older children like them who were resident at the Findel, the overall
mortality rate is still greater than one in three—shockingly high by modern
standards.[116] The chances of death for Susanna were still greater than for
her brother. Between 1557 and 1670, 40.8 percent of all girls admitted to
the Findel died in custody, while only 33.2 percent of all boys did. Girls
are markedly overrepresented among deaths of children under the age of

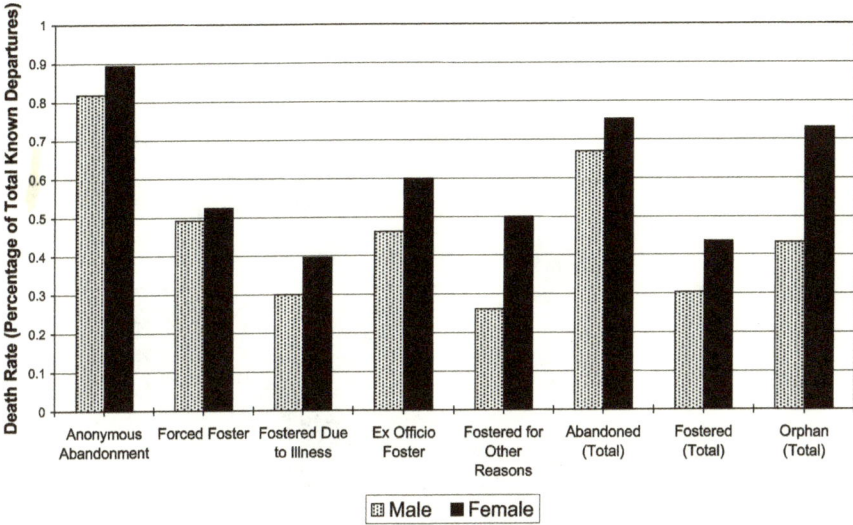

Fig. 5.13. Male versus female death rates in the Nuremberg Findel by type and subtype, 1557–1670 (*n* = 2014). *Source*: FKD.

two, but they also lead boys in every type and subtype in our sample (see fig. 5.13).

Death was a constant presence among Findel children, varying only in the scope of its destruction at different times. The worst years were undoubtedly those of the 1630s crisis, when the annual number of children dying averaged over sixty children a year, with 147 dead during 1634–35 alone.[117] During massive and recurring epidemics of this nature, each new calendar year brought only a mild respite of at most six months before a new onslaught of deaths in the late summer and early fall. Four in ten of Nuremberg's foundlings, including young Anna Maria, died during the peak months of August through October, while only one in ten passed away during May and June.[118] This phenomenon was virtually ubiquitous in premodern Europe, had been linked in folklore since antiquity to the appearance of the Dog Star in late summer, giving rise to the term "dog days of summer." Nonepidemic years followed the same seasonal cycle of sickness and death, albeit at a reduced rate of about ten to twenty deaths annually in the years before 1632 and about five a year after 1640. Most of these deaths occurred at foster households, but the Findel was by no means spared.

Even in a society accustomed to half of all children dying before they reached the age of fifteen, the high concentration of children in the Fin-

Fig. 5.14. Burial of a child in Nuremberg (ca. 1700). Stadtbibliothek Nürnberg.

del meant that Eberhardt and Susanna were directly exposed to suffering and death with much greater frequency than they would have been in a private home. During fewer than eight years in the Findel, they experienced at least sixteen deaths firsthand, including the demise of the three-year-old foundling Anna Maria. Seen in comparison to death rates over the four-hundred-year history of the Findel, mortality numbers during the Schier twins' time there were uniquely low. Still, it would have been impossible for them to escape the sadness and unspoken terror that each child's death brought to the Findel community. Whether either of them actually saw a severely fevered or convulsing peer confined to a sickroom or merely heard about it in prurient detail on the playground, the effect would have been profound. Each death must have reinforced the *memento mori* tenor of their daily religious lessons: who would be next—a friend, a sibling, oneself? The orphans' regular participation in funeral corteges and burials only further accentuated the omnipresence of death in their young lives.

The toll of such incessant sickness and death on the Schiers' psyche was a constant fear of contagious diseases that enveloped them. The slightest suspicion that a child might be a leper or carrier of another disease led to the burning of that child's clothes and immediate quarantine in one of the

Fig. 5.15. The Findel as viewed from the Heilig-Geist Spital, on the
other side of the Pegnitz. Both the boys' and girls' dormitories looked out
directly over the river (ca. 1725). Stadtbibliothek Nürnberg.

Findel's small sick rooms or elsewhere. The incoming boy or girl was then
carefully examined by a physician and, if deemed contagious, either denied
admission or sent to a pesthouse or "French" house (for syphilis) where the
quarantine could last up to six months.[119] Beginning in the 1590s, abandoned beggar children, sickly or not, were increasingly sent first to one of
the pesthouses or to the begging stockade for a probationary period.[120] The
so-called children's house in suburban Wöhrd served the same quarantine
function from the epidemic of 1562 until around 1600. When it reopened
in 1607, it too began to serve as a routine screening site of all beggar children as well as a long-term quarantine facility.[121] In 1627, the Wöhrd house
was joined by a new quarantine house at Saint Rochus—site of the Findel
children's cemetery—but by 1634 both it and the Wöhrd children's house
had disappeared from Findel records.[122]

The constant exchange of sick or cured boys and girls between the Findel
and the hospital directly across the river (see fig. 5.15) undoubtedly also
made an impression on Susanna and Eberhardt. Sometimes noncontagious
sick children from the hospital were transferred to the Findel for conva-
lescence, including a twelve-year-old girl with chin injuries in 1605, three
older children with fistulas the next year, and a girl with severe rheumatism
in 1636. Other new arrivals were merely the orphans of recently deceased

hospital patients and had no kin willing or able to take them.[123] Continuous exposure to death from contagion made Findel children understandably wary of any newcomers, particularly those from the hospital or a pesthouse. Their anxiety was hardly eased by well-intentioned city councilors who sometimes ordered that medically approved children continue to be kept apart from other residents for an indefinite period.[124]

Epilepsy had a particularly terrifying effect on the Findel's children, both because of the spectacle of a seizure as well as the unrelenting fear of contagion. To their credit, magistrates were skeptical when informed in 1619 that young Hans Jörg Bauman, afflicted with "the falling disease," had supposedly infected two other boys in the Findel. In response to their official inquiry "whether this sickness can be passed on from one to another as a disease and whether this boy might be helped," physicians scoffed and told them that the other children in the Findel were simply frightened by Bauman's seizures. The danger of mass hysteria outweighed expert opinion, though, and the inner council ordered the Findel administrator to arrange for transfer somewhere else, possibly to the children's house at Wöhrd, at the city's expense.[125] Almost fifty years later, the same scenario repeated itself with Magdalena Heusserin's daughter, who was "afflicted with the great sickness, has repeatedly fallen down, and [is] thus the source of a great fright among the Findel children, who fear that she might infect others." Despite a dismissive response from the city's surgeon, the girl was swiftly returned to her mother and promised an annual stipend from the alms bureau.[126]

A similar reaction to children with other disabilities might be expected but apparently several blind, deaf, dumb, or lame wards caused no such stir, at least none considered worthy of recording.[127] Findel records explicitly mention more than a hundred disabled children admitted between 1560 and 1670, sometimes simply described as "particularly infirm," "very damaged," "quite wretched," or simply "sickly."[128] Based on the general pattern among early modern orphanages and foundling homes, there were undoubtedly many more.[129] To this number we must add Michael Kraus, an albino who "can't use his five senses," teenager Georg Regenandt, who "on account of his [mental retardation] remains a two-year-old," as well as a four-year-old boy found in front of Tiergärtner Gate "who can neither talk nor stand."[130] Disabled children were as common during the early modern era as today, but Eberhardt and Susanna's exposure to disabled peers—like their exposure to death itself—was more concentrated and thus more intense than when they lived at home with their mother. Whether this frequent contact made them more or less compassionate toward such individuals we cannot say. There were probably diverse reactions among the children,

ranging from pity to curiosity to disgust, when the Findel made a rare exception to its normal age limitation of fourteen and admitted twenty-year-old
Friedrich Heinsel, who had no hands or feet and "was also a small person
like a dwarf." And surely the arrival of hermaphrodite Wolflein Kranniger
caused a sensation, albeit a short-lived one, as he was reclaimed after only
two weeks by his recuperated mother.[131]

Children with mental problems received much the same treatment as
those with other disabilities. The merely "slow-witted" could continue to
call the Findel home well into adulthood. Only a few severely retarded or
mentally ill youths who frightened residents or appeared dangerous were
sent away almost immediately, either to the hospital's special ward for mentally disturbed children, back to relatives, or to one of the city towers for an
indefinite period.[132] Here too the fears of resident children probably outweighed any real danger posed. In 1639 maid Anna Schäferin petitioned
the council to care for her depressed young niece in the Findel "until she re-
cuperates and can be placed somewhere." The council reluctantly complied
until receiving a report from the chaplain at Saint Egidien that the girl suffered "more [from] a melancholy than anything," whereupon, like the adult
mentally ill, she was transferred to one of the city's towers for an indefinite
period.[133] In 1663, young Maria Magdalena Widmänin was similarly judged
"crazy in the head" but was nevertheless permitted to live in the Findel until
she had been examined by a physician and a member of the clergy. A week
later, councilors listened to a report on her behavior and heard how "at first
she conducted herself well in prayer and work but after a while, because she
had no sleep at all, became very crazy again and thereby demonstrated that
she posed a danger to the Findel orphans should she remain." Even then,
the council decreed that she "should not be left alone but rather transferred
to the women's tower and there observed, first by a physician and any other
specialists on account of [her lack of] sleep . . . that she might be restored
to health."[134]

Amid the frequent comings and goings of children at the Findel, one
kind of departure held special hope for Eberhardt and Susanna. One in
four of all children admitted were eventually reclaimed by an adult. In most
instances that adult was a parent, meaning that more than half of all formally fostered children, admitted on a temporary basis, were eventually
reclaimed, while only one in eight orphans left the Findel in this manner.[135]
Reclamation by a parent or relative also became much less common in Nuremberg by the 1640s, though it never disappeared altogether. During the
Schiers' residence at the Findel, five boys and three girls were reclaimed
by relatives. This average of about one per year (actually four in 1650) is

miniscule compared to the numbers of reclaimed children at contemporary French and Italian foundling homes but it might have sufficed to suggest to Eberhardt and Susanna the possibility that they too might leave the Findel in this manner.

The passing of time diminished but did not necessarily extinguish this hope. Susanna witnessed Helena Sabina Donusin and Anna Wolfin each reclaimed by a godmother after seven and fourteen years, respectively, and Elena Rogenfuss's aunt waited ten years before picking her up at the Findel. Girls were in fact reclaimed at a slightly higher rate than boys, again refuting facile assumptions about a gender double standard. Among the boys, Ludwig Weidner was reclaimed by his father in 1650, ten years after Ludwig's entry into the Findel, and Hans Wagner was similarly reclaimed by his mother after more than nine years had passed.[136] Reclaim after long periods of time, however, was far from the norm. Most children who left the Findel in this manner were picked up sooner rather than later: one-fifth within a month of admission, one-half within three months, and three-quarters within a year. Parents and godparents were especially likely to pick up children within a year. If a child had not been claimed by then, the odds were high that he or she would never be picked up, with fewer than one in fifteen reclaimed children being picked up after more than five years.[137] Not having such statistics at their disposal, the reunions the twins witnessed firsthand possibly haunted their dreams. They could not hope for deliverance by *parentes ex machina*, but the sudden appearance of a benevolent godparent, magical or otherwise, might have remained at least a hope, however remote.

The Path to Self-sufficiency

If no relative or friend had come to claim Eberhardt or Susanna within a year or two, it became more likely that they would leave the Findel to begin an apprenticeship or service position, the normal path to attaining respectable self-sufficiency. In the general population, boys usually started work outside the home earlier than girls, sometimes as young as seven or eight. The typical range for boys as well as girls was between twelve and eighteen, with an average age of fourteen. Both Eberhardt and Susanna were slightly older than this when they were placed in service, at ages fifteen and a half and sixteen and a half, respectively.[138] In Eberhardt's case, Findel father Georg Heinlein played the pivotal role in finding the appropriate apprenticeship for his young charge. For Susanna, it was "the maid bringer" who would attempt to find her a reputable and otherwise suitable employer.[139] Given the Findel's relatively small size by 1653, the two adults should have been able to screen potential employers much more carefully than their counterparts in London and Paris, who were confronted with placing between 500 and 1,500 foundlings annually.[140] In securing Eberhardt a position in Nuremberg, Heinlein was to work closely with the Findel administrator—in this instance Albrecht Pömer—as well as the director of the alms bureau.[141] When Eberhardt went to register for his apprenticeship, he carried a brief letter of recommendation not unlike one that a previous Findel administrator, Wolf Pömer, had written for another ward:

> Bearer is Hans Ritscher, admitted to the Findel with his brother Leonhard Ritscher by the Honorable Council on the 27th of July in the long past year of 1583, after his father, carpenter Wendel Rütsch, went off to war and his mother died here. Upon his request, I hereby [send] this certificate via my usual envoy.[142] Actum Nuremberg, Wednesday the 27th April A[nn]o [15]97.
>
> [P.S.] So far as I know he has until this time conducted himself honorably and well.

All contracts except those with goldsmiths were prepared and notarized by the city's crafts bureau. In Nuremberg, apprenticeship and service agreements normally took effect on one of four traditional dates: Candlemas (February 2), Saint Walpurgis's Day (April 4); Saint Lawrence's Day (August 8), or All Saints' Day (November 1). Eberhardt was apprenticed on May 3, 1653, and Susanna on Saint Lawrence's Day the following year. Upon their departure from the Findel, each was given a complete set of new clothes and a new pair of shoes.[143]

In the case of orphans or foster children, family members might identify a suitable master. Sometimes a brother, uncle, or godfather would take on a Findel charge to train in a craft. After seventeen years, Hans Jacob Halle was removed from the Findel by his uncle who taught him sail making, the same as his father.[144] Eberhardt was apprenticed in his father's craft of spectaclemaker, possibly to a former colleague or friend of his late father. It is not clear what role if any, his own preferences (*Lust und Liebe*) played in the initial selection of this craft. Occasionally Findel records mention a boy who "wants to learn compass making" or "wants to be a tailor," and in any case (as we will see), unhappily placed boys and girls were always accepted back into the Findel and found new masters.[145] Virtually all crafts make appearances in the Findel's placement records, most commonly book-binding, sieve making, goldsmithing, turning, card making, and metalwork of various kinds.[146]

Until the late Middle Ages, most apprenticeships lasted under two years; by the sixteenth century they often ranged up to seven years before leveling out at an average of four years by Eberhardt's time.[147] Eberhardt's contract has not survived but for reasons that we will learn later, the term cannot have been more than five years. Usually the length of service depended on the age of the child in question, that is, a boy of ten or eleven might contract for six years while an older teen, such as the nearly sixteen-year-old Eberhardt, would agree to one to three years of "learning time." Hanns Kopp, for instance, was apprenticed for six years "because he is young," while Hans Durr, who was at least twenty-three years old at the time of his placement, had only one year of training before he became a salaried employee.[148] It was also a common practice that the master would promise to engage the youth for "an appropriate weekly wage" after his apprenticeship had concluded. In 1595, Hennslein Seywoldt's contract specified no salary the first four years, but if he remained two additional years, he would receive two Bazen a week (about 7 fl. per year) the fifth year and 10 Kreuzer a week (about 8.5 fl. per year) the sixth year.[149]

A key factor in finding the appropriate match was a properly negotiated apprenticeship fee (*Lehrgeld*), the money paid to a master for taking on an apprentice. These charges varied widely, by Eberhardt's time averaging about 25 fl.—not an insignificant amount (perhaps analogous to a year of tuition at an expensive private U.S. university today). In some German cities the fee was waived for orphans or a few years were added to the length of the contract.[150] The city council of Nuremberg went still further, not only subsidizing placement fees for poor citizen children but also coming up with various financial incentives for masters to take on apprentices from the Findel. Even during the turbulent 1630s, the city government continued to pay fees for needy citizen and Findel children.[151] Of course the Findel administrator was always charged with first attempting to obtain funding from a child's relative or from an inheritance a child had brought into the Findel. If necessary, the official would arrange for installment payments, more to maintain some influence over the master than because of inadequate funds.[152]

Eberhardt and Susanna were fortunate that they were not foundlings, since virtually everyone would have assumed that they were bastards and most employers would have declined to take them. Many early modern governments even codified this discrimination, threatening masters who hired illegitimate apprentices with heavy fines.[153] Nuremberg had no such official prohibition, but the council nevertheless often had great difficulty in getting craftsmen to take on illegitimate apprentices from its Findel and poor citizens lists. The successful placement of illegitimate Findel youth Alexander Mener in 1589 was apparently an exception to the rule, worthy of notation.

Beginning in the 1630s and continuing throughout the rest of the century, Nuremberg mandates explicitly required masters to take all Findel children, legitimate or not.[154] But custom and prejudice died hard. A 1648 complaint of discrimination from the Findel youth and would-be cress shirtmaker Endres Kreuzer prompted the council to ask Findel administrator Albrecht Pömer if it was true that "those Findel children of whom nothing certain is known, whether they were legitimately or illegitimately born, are not accepted into the crafts, or how this is handled." Pömer's response was not recorded, but the evidence suggests that implementation of the council's official policy remained problematic.[155] Conrad Lang, who entered the Findel's care in 1664 as a three-year-old of unknown origins, was forced to keep working as a servant at the Findel until the age of twenty-seven, when he was finally successfully placed with a grocer.[156] The illegitimacy issue continued to plague the directors of German orphanages and foundling homes into the eighteenth century, with many civic leaders arguing—partly based on the realities of apprenticeship placement—that German orphanages should only admit legitimate children. A 1731 imperial ordinance attempted to resolve the question and ordered all craftsmen to accept illegitimate apprentices. In Nuremberg as elsewhere, though, the town council continued to have to negotiate with masters, placing fewer than one illegitimate foundling every three years into the 1770s.[157]

Eberhardt and Susanna were also lucky that their father had been a citizen of Nuremberg. Before contracting a foreign apprentice, all of the city's masters were legally required to inquire at the city's schools, alms bureau, and Findel for an available "citizen's son." When craftsmen complained in 1631 that they couldn't get any citizen apprentices and therefore were forced to accept foreign youths, the inner council reiterated that local boys were always to get first preference and ordered the Findel administrator to bear this in mind.[158] This admonition was apparently followed during the tumultuous years of 1633–37, but even then the great majority of boys and girls placed were noncitizens—a reflection more of the city's generosity than any deprivileging of citizen children.[159]

By the time that Eberhardt came of age, there was little economic incentive for a master to accept an apprentice.[160] Craft guilds had become increasingly exclusive since the fifteenth century, in most cities requiring a strong family connection and some capital to secure even a short-term apprenticeship. Nevertheless, in Nuremberg almost one in five children admitted to the Findel eventually left for an apprenticeship or service position.[161] As a boy, Eberhardt had a much greater chance of finding a position than Susanna. During the nine years that the twins lived at the Findel, the home placed nineteen boys and only eight girls. This was a typical proportion among German orphanages and actually a better rate of placement for girls than Nuremberg's overall average among orphans, where boys were placed at almost three times the rate of girls.[162] Possibly this gender disparity emanated from some sort of bias among Findel officials, though the explanation more likely lay with the preferences of prospective employers in a buyer's market. Nuremberg's city council and crafts bureau were also able to exert more direct influence over craftsmen than private employers of maids. Almost two-thirds of the placement gap between boys and girls occurred between 1635 and 1640, suggesting that it was even more difficult to place girls than boys during periods of extreme economic distress.[163]

Finding a position did not insure that Eberhardt or Susanna would keep it. As seen in the previous chapter, the streets of early modern Europe were filled with runaway servants and apprentices (known in England as "ronnegates").[164] Most of these took flight after the probationary period of two to eight weeks had passed.[165] According to the official policy of the Nuremberg crafts bureau, any apprentice could withdraw from a contract during this trial period on grounds of bad or inadequate food, poor sleeping arrangements, "too much" corporal punishment, overwork "which is not customary to the craft," or too many household chores. On the other hand, a master could dismiss an apprentice for laziness, dishonesty (e.g., theft), "improper words or deeds," or excessive absences without permission (especially at night).[166] Municipal authorities generally responded quickly to any reports of negligence or abuse on the part of masters. In 1570, the inner council ordered Hans Chilling and his wife arrested for beating the young Findel girl in their service; their punishment is unknown but the girl was returned to the Findel.[167]

Neither Susanna nor Eberhardt ran away from their positions, but many of their fellow wards did, particularly during the troubled years of 1634–37.[168] One common motive for absconding was the imminent discovery of theft from a master. Findel youth Jochum Weiersmuller spent four years as an apprentice and two as a journeyman at a local spoonmaker's before he stole money from his master and ran away; shortly thereafter he was apprehended, imprisoned, and banished from the city.[169] Enderla Pilman came back to the Findel after a few months from his potter apprenticeship claiming he had "learned nothing."[170] Beginning in the time of Eberhardt Schier, a growing number of apprenticed youths left their apprenticeships early to become soldiers or go off to sea.[171] The reason a Findel child ran away from his or her position varied considerably: it might be abuse, homesickness, or simply a desire for independence. Of Catharina Mollebreünin, one of few girls known to run away from a maid position, the Findel register simply notes that she "has run off without cause."[172] Placement success rates could vary considerably from year to year, based on the individuals involved, the economic situation, and countless other factors, including the death of a youth before completion of his or her service term. On average probably fewer than one in six placements ended badly.[173]

Many Findel children and youths who fled service or apprenticeship ran away to places unknown and were never heard from again. A surprising number, almost half, came back to the Findel, where they were without exception taken back and typically placed again within a year or two.[174] Shortly before Eberhardt himself was apprenticed, he witnessed nineteen-year-old Nicholas Beuerlein come back to the Findel from his goldsmith apprenticeship after only a few months and later be placed with a dyer. Hanns Kummpass was similarly received after running ran away from his initial placement with a knifemaker and ten months later reapprenticed to a carpenter.[175] Occasionally the Findel father was successful in getting a returning ward to reconsider and, after a brief respite, give his or her master another chance.[176] By contrast, a few youths returned to the Findel and never again ventured beyond its walls. Mertha Schwarz and Valentin Kostner left their apprenticeships because of unspecified illness and bad eyesight, respectively; neither ever left the Findel again. Clara Leissnerin, known to Susanna Schierin, also quit her maid position in 1640 because of ill health and when she died seventeen years later was still a resident in the Findel.[177] Barbara Huberin, Anna Wickin, Elisabeth Engelmayerin, and Christof Brabi each came to the Findel as young children and remained until their deaths more than thirty years later.[178] The longevity record was apparently held by Maria Magdalena Lieserin, who after forty-five years at the Findel had attained revered status there when "on March 27, 1699, at 5:45 A.M., [her] soul departed" and a stately funeral ensued.[179] Some of these wards were probably in some way disabled, as in the case of mentally retarded Michael Salomon, who died at the age of twenty-seven, after spending most of his life at the Findel. At least three wards in their twenties or thirties were resident at the same time as Eberhardt and Susanna, a common phenomenon into the eighteenth century.

Success and Failure in the Wider World

The connection between the Schiers and their adopted home was not severed immediately upon their placement. Even if they stayed in their positions, the twins could have turned to their former home for help in job disputes, money for appropriate work clothes, or even a dowry.[180] After five years with a jewelrymaker, alumnus Hensa Plannckh could find no work so the Findel secured his placement with an armorer. Michael Hübner similarly returned to the Findel at the age of thirty-one and was employed there for at least a few years until he found work elsewhere.[181] In one infamous case, the orphan Hans Gsell, admitted to the Augsburg orphanage in 1618, abandoned his highly promising studies for a life on the street, only to be retrieved and placed by the orphanage father shortly thereafter. After stealing 50 fl. and absconding from his new employer, Gsell was punished and returned again to the orphanage, only to run away once more, this time to Nuremberg, where goldsmiths in suburban Wöhrd communicated that he was passing himself off as the son of an Augsburg smith. Another theft of about 54 fl. forced Gsell to flee once more, yet it did not impede him from writing his flabbergasted orphanage parents from Ulm, brazenly requesting that they certify him as a farrier. Finally, he had found the limits of the orphanage's generosity and was definitively disowned by its administrators.[182]

The strongest indication of the affection or at least responsibility the Findel's adults felt toward their charges is the consistent effort they made to keep track of children and youths after they left the home. In the instance of runaways, genuine concern for the welfare of the youths surfaces more often than anger or despair. After Hensa Remp ran away from the Findel on November 22, 1598, the Findel staff took pains to follow his whereabouts as long as possible and appeared surprised that he did not stay in touch once on the outside: "He went and begged to [a neighboring] baker woman, who gave him some bread [but] he didn't take it because he wanted a bread roll (*Semmel*); since then we have not been able to learn a thing more [about] him from reliable sources."[183] There is a note of disappointment and at least surprise in the entry recording that after Mattheus Hoffensummer ran away from his apprenticeship, "nothing more has been heard from him."[184] Even though Wolff Barthel "impetuously and with no grounds whatsoever ran away from the Findel," the Findel parents continued to correspond with him and make inquiries on his behalf, "because he is infirm."[185] Hieronymus Giesswein informed the home that he had left his buttermaker master to go to Regensburg but in the case of Hans Rost, the Findel staff knew only that after he had left his first position with a wire bender for another position with a gunsmith "[he] did no good [and] ran away from there."[186] Maria Magdalena Castorinsin, expelled from the Findel in 1667 because of her temper, likewise remained in touch with staff members until her premature death at the age of twenty-five.[187]

By the time of the Schier twins, it had become standard practice for the Findel's register to record subsequent successes and failures in the lives of its alumni, though never in a thorough manner. Of over four hundred boys placed from 1557 to 1670, the home's register only identifies eight alumni, including Eberhardt Schier, as achieving master status in their respective crafts, mostly during the 1660s and 1670s.[188] This outcome may in fact reflect improved record keeping (as well as fewer alumni to track) rather than an improved success rate. Findel alumni Georg Heinlein and Peter Hoffmann both went on to work at the Findel, as Findel father and Findel teacher, respectively.[189] It is also necessary to bear in mind the great difficulty of social mobility even among youths outside the Findel with far more blood connections and other social capital. The town council made attempts to compensate for this inequity, including the granting of citizenship to the most promising Findel boys, but by the time of Eberhardt and Susanna—themselves already citizens—this practice seems to have been discontinued.[190] All Findel children knew the rags-to-riches stories of local notables such as Barthomäus Viatis and Elisabeth Kraussin, both of whom came to Nuremberg as impoverished orphans and went on to become fantastically wealthy.[191] Most also knew, however, that their own chances of even modest success in the larger society were far from assured.

The measure of success for Findel girls was a respectable marriage, often made possible by the dowry money accumulated during domestic service. Susanna was not one of the fortunate few who brought property into the Findel that she might use for a dowry and thus had to rely on whatever she could save of her post-Findel earnings.[192] The Nuremberg council provided some additional incentives for potential suitors, such as granting citizenship to any man who married a "Findel daughter."[193] It is possible that this perk occasionally produced the desired outcome, though there is no explicit mention of it in any Findel records.[194] There is also no evidence of a marriage between two Findel children, a phenomenon that occasionally appeared in the records of the London Foundling Hospital and is vividly portrayed in the Pellegrino fresco of the Santa Maria della Scala Orphanage in Siena.[195] Once again, though, references to wards' lives after service positions were rare before the mid-seventeenth century, so we should reserve judgment on this possibility.[196]

Many of the boys placed in apprenticeships would not find employment as journeymen once their terms finished, let alone aspire to mastership, and a good number of the girls working as maids would work well beyond their specified terms, watching their prospects for marriage steadily decline as time passed.[197] One indicator of the difficulty in finding a craft position is the growing number of Findel boys who joined the military upon completion of their apprenticeships, at least six during the 1660s alone, including one by impressment and another "against the express will of his godfather."[198] Many teenaged boys likely considered this choice as a quicker path to manhood and independence and would have concurred with orphan Bernhard Abraham Reinhard, who became a soldier in rebellion against "the harsh regime of the aforementioned orphanage in which they treat him not only like a boy . . . but like a dog, not even permitted to smoke a pipe of tobacco."[199] Wolf Wahlman, known to both Eberhardt and Susanna, was described twelve years after his release as a vagabond singer/beggar and his wife Sabina "a useless wench" was often seen begging in the streets with her children.[200] Former Findel daughter Barbara Kornlein (aka "Little Corn-flower," because of her discovery in a cornfield) was allegedly imprisoned sixteen times for her begging and petty theft.[201] Initial successes did not necessarily translate into long-term accomplishment. Jochum Weyer served for six years as an apprentice then journeyman spoonmaker, but upon the discovery of multiple stolen items and a large amount of cash in his chest, he was imprisoned, banned from his craft, and banished from the city.[202] More heartbreakingly, Findel alumnus Peter Herdegen succeeded in rising to become a master ringmaker, but when he died prematurely of a fever at the age of thirty-two, his three orphans were left with no option but to apply for admission to the Findel.[203]

Is it possible to generalize about the average Findel child's long-term prospects? Consider six pairs of siblings who coresided with Eberhardt and Susanna Schier at the Findel, four boy-girl pairs and two pairs of girls. Christoph and Anna Schell, admitted to the Findel the year after the twins, both survived until adolescence and both were, like the Schiers, successfully placed, Christoph with relatives who would teach him goldsmithing and Anna as a maid to a local family. Christoff Wilhelm and Gerdtraut Sauber were also successfully placed about the same time as Susanna and Eberhardt Schier.[204] Both pairs of sisters, however, died in the Findel's care.[205] The two remaining pairs of brothers and sisters were reclaimed in one instance by the father after only five months and in the other instance after seven years by a godmother.[206] Thus, of fourteen children (including Susanna and Eberhardt), six were placed in service positions, four were reclaimed, and four died within the Findel.

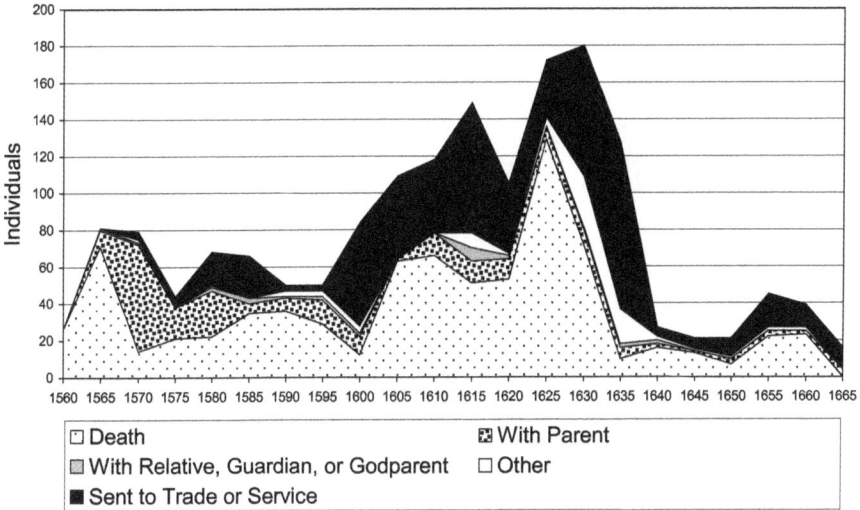

Fig. 5.16. Nature of departure from the Nuremberg Findel by admission date, 1560–1669 (five-year totals; *n* = 1677). *Source*: FKD.

The more typical nature of departure from the Findel throughout the period of our study was somewhat different; with more than two-thirds of all children admitted to the Findel's care (mostly underage foundlings with wetnurses) dying before adolescence, about one in five picked up by an adult, about one in five placed in an apprenticeship or maid position, and at most one in one hundred running away or released on their own recognizance (see fig. 5.16).[207] Certain outcomes were more likely in certain case types, namely, death among abandoned children (mostly under the age of two), reclaim among fostered children, and placement among older orphans (as in the Schiers' cohort).[208]

The role of gender in the nature of departure from the Findel remains ambiguous (see fig. 5.17). On the one hand, there were no significant distinctions between fostered or abandoned boys and girls in this respect. The great majority of all abandoned children died before release, and the great majority of all fostered children were eventually picked up by parents or others. Among male and female orphans, however, there were two striking divergences. The first is the greater frequency of death among girls than boys, particularly among orphans, where girls apparently died at an almost 30 percent higher rate.[209] The second is the much greater placement of boy orphans compared to girl orphans, a disparity we have already discussed. The fact that both high female death rates and low job placement were exacerbated during the crisis of the 1630s suggests that the inability of Findel

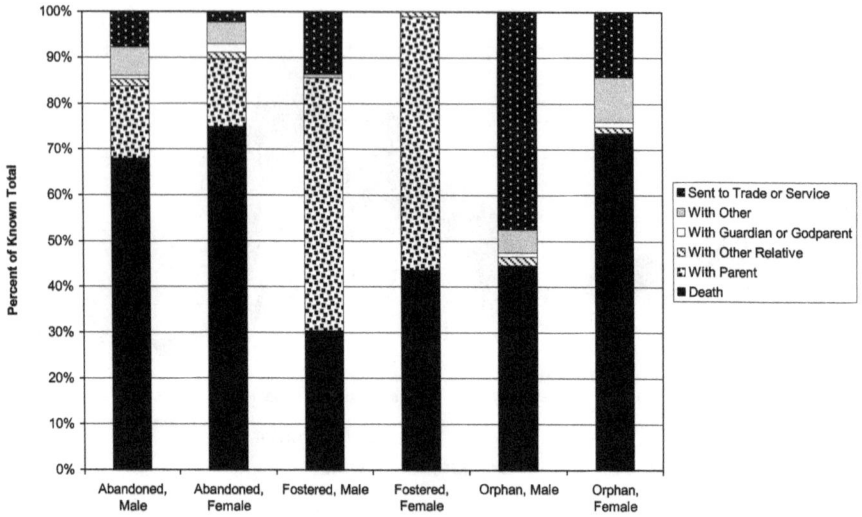

Fig. 5.17. Male versus female nature of departure from the Nuremberg
Findel by type, 1557–1670 (*n* = 1259). *Source*: FKD.

officials to place girls in domestic positions meant that such children spent
more time in the Findel and were thus more likely to die, but this is not an
entirely satisfactory answer.[210] In any event, for a variety of reasons, hard
economic times clearly hit the Findel's girls more severely than its boys.

A Happy Ending?

What of Susanna and Eberhardt Schier? After Eberhardt left the Findel in
May 1653, he worked for only five years as an apprentice and journeyman
before being accepted as a master into the spectaclemakers' craft guild.
At about the same time, when he was not quite twenty-one years old, he
married Magdalena Schwartzin, a twenty-four-year-old widow with two
small girls, Maria Magdalena (age three) and Anna Catherina (twenty-four
months). Attaining both master status and marrying at such a precocious
age was a tremendous achievement for any man of the era, much more
so for a former Findel child. The source of this joint success is shrouded
in mystery. We know only that Magdalena's first husband, Hans Schwartz,
had also been a spectaclemaker and that Eberhardt not only likely knew
the couple earlier but had probably attended their wedding with all of his
craft brothers in September 1654. Perhaps Eberhardt had even been placed
as an apprentice with Schwartz upon his release from the Findel a year

earlier; the Findel records are silent on this. It is also enticing but futile to speculate about when the attraction between the young apprentice and his fellow craftsman's wife began or about the relative roles played by genuine affection and professional ambition. The most salient public fact at the time was that Magdalena waited a respectable seventeen months after Schwartz's death in May 1657 before marrying Eberhardt on October 12, 1658.[211]

Susanna Schierin was placed as a maid on Saint Laurence Day in 1654, more than a year after the commencement of Eberhardt's apprenticeship and three months before her seventeenth birthday. We do not have any information about her employer either, and the historical record remains mute until more than twelve years later, shortly after she turned twenty-nine, when Susanna married the widower and journeyman carpenter Hans Schörbel. How Susanna met Schörbel is not clear; he and his late wife might even have been the young woman's employers, perhaps from the beginning. Susanna's marriage to Schörbel came a full eight years after her twin brother's union, and her new husband was not yet a master, although he did own some property. Compared to other young women of her social status, particularly alumnae of the Findel, she had nonetheless married very well. At the time of her wedding, she inherited two stepchildren, nine-year-old Johannes and three-year-old Georgius. (A pair of twins, like Eberhardt and Susanna a boy and a girl, had been born to Schörbel and his first wife in October 1663 but had died a month later.) Fourteen months after marrying Susanna gave birth to her own son, Nicolaus, followed in 1672 by Jacob, and in 1675—when she was thirty-eight—by another Nicolaus. There is no record of the first Nicolaus dying during this period, though we are informed that Susanna's stepson Johannes passed away at the age of seventeen.[212]

After that, Eberhardt and Susanna Schier and their new families vanish from historical view. At least initially each household remained in the Nuremberg area for several years, albeit in different suburbs. Did the twins remain in contact after leaving their Findel home? It would be touching if one of Susanna's children were named after her brother or at least if he had stood as godfather but it did not happen that way. There is no trace whatsoever of children born to Eberhardt and Magdalena. By choice or by necessity, release from the Findel marked the beginning of still another new life for each of the twins, akin to the way that their entrance into that same institution seven years earlier had punctuated life with their mother. The absence of death or burial references suggests that one or both new households moved away, but there are also other, more mundane, explanations for such lapses in the official record.

That both Eberhardt and Susanna reached this point was a resounding success story. As older orphans they entered the Findel with the greatest probability of survival and placement of any admission type, but that fate was still far from assured. Had they started out as baby or toddler found-lings, such as the young Anna Maria, the odds against them would have been fearsome. Of the approximately six hundred children admitted to the Findel as anonymous foundlings between 1557 and 1670, only one, Anna Regina Mayin, is known to have survived the passage from infancy to ado-lescence.[213] Susanna Schier was especially fortunate in that girls were even less likely to attain the Findel triple crown of survival to adulthood, success-ful placement, and establishment of her own household. Did their Findel experiences help the twins reach their respective goals? The basic literacy and mathematical skills they learned probably made them more attractive to potential employers, as did their personal cleanliness and manners. And despite the danger of contagion in such close quarters, the health care that they received at the Findel undoubtedly surpassed the attention they would have otherwise received, thereby making their survival to an able-bodied adolescence more likely. The psychological impact of their Findel life is much harder to assess, given how little we know about their personal ex-periences of affection, disdain, or indifference there. Some Findel children clearly considered that community their home and its residents their substi-tute family. Perhaps Eberhardt and Susanna were among them. In any event, their subsequent stations in life were as much as the great majority of their contemporaries could have asked for, let alone two "friendless" orphans taken in and raised by strangers. For that outcome alone they must have felt at least some gratitude.

SIX

From Micro- to Macro-:
Individuals and the Big Picture

We have now viewed the circulation of unwanted children from the distinct—and in some ways unique—perspectives of six historical individuals: an unmarried pregnant maid, an itinerant widowed mercenary, a patrician magistrate, a teenaged street orphan, and a brother and sister pair of orphaned twins. We consequently have a much better sense of the circumstances and the choices of some adults with unwanted children, as well as the experiences and destinies of a few such children themselves. Our understanding of and our empathy for all of these fellow human beings has hopefully expanded considerably—a worthwhile achievement in itself. But might this handful of life stories offer something of broader significance and relevance to the big picture of their times and our own? How in other words, might our historical camera zoom out from such close-ups to capture the wide panorama of society at large?

The situating of these stories of illegitimacy, abandonment, and infanticide within the broader context of child circulation provides the very means to address the question of long-term continuities and changes in a number of important areas. Putting these five microhistories of unwanted children—and the thousands other from our database—side by side with a multitude of foster parenting situations helps us understand the interconnectedness of such experiences among early modern households. Just as significantly, thinking in terms of child circulation provides us with a more flexible vocabulary and more inclusive frame of reference within which we may compare many phenomena previously treated as unrelated and in the process identify significant affinities and patterns. At the same time this approach's focus on the many perspectives involved restores governmental involvement—the preoccupation of early modern sources and modern theorists alike—to its proportionate role in most people's lives. This final chapter assesses the general lessons drawn from these stories, first by using them to develop a new framework for analysis of such diverse historical experiences and second by probing them as valuable source material for postulating some general patterns and cross-cultural comparisons about the overall social significance of child circulation and informal fostering.

The Ubiquity and Diversity of Child Circulation

As the preceding chapters make clear, everyday life was rife with reasons for the circulation of children outside their biological parents' home. By far the most frequent cause of long-term circulation was the serious illness or death of one or both parents, a much more common occurrence for that era's children than for those in the developed countries of the twenty-first century. Absence of a parent for reasons of work, such as soldiering or other migrant labor, also frequently triggered the circulation of a child, as did other sources of financial stress on a household. The most highly formalized and respectable form of child circulation was the placement of young teenagers into apprenticeships or service positions, though the fees usually involved put this option increasingly out of the reach of most struggling early modern families. Many poor households circulated their children as street beggars and some of the latter circulated further by running away from home. On the other hand, anonymous abandonment—contrary to popular assumptions—represented a less common and less reputable way of dealing with a burdensome child, occurring on average only five times per year in early modern Nuremberg. Infanticide was apparently even rarer and more disparaged, with only one or two corpses discovered annually in Nuremberg, each followed by a vigorous governmental effort to track down and prosecute those responsible.

Far from representing an anomaly or a system failure, informal child circulation in various forms was in fact one of the core mechanisms that held together early modern communities and thus society as a whole. It also remains largely invisible to surviving historical sources, emerging more in its marginal and less common forms.[1] The great majority of unmarried pregnant young women, for instance—unlike Apollonia Vöglin—resolved their predicament by marriage, abortion, or by successfully circulating their infants to the households of relatives, friends, or strangers. Married and widowed parents such as Stoffel Baur, who were itinerant or for other reasons unavailable, likewise regularly left their own children with relatives or other adults, most often for brief periods but sometimes for months or years. Foster parents also sometimes relied on the children circulated to them for income or free or cheap labor, and some children seemed to have been passed serially from one household to the next. Only in a minority of instances, most notably in cases of apprenticeships and some domestic servant positions, were formal agreements the norm. Usually arrangements were oral, possibly involving money, and the people involved might just as often be friends, neighbors, or coworkers as blood relatives. In several instances, foster parents were strangers, given or promised money to care for a child for an agreed upon length of time. Contrary to the assumptions we might make about a generally impoverished society, willing foster parents appear to have been everywhere (including during times of economic hardship). Even itinerant teenagers such as Jörg Mayr consequently experienced little difficulty in finding hospitable strangers or more exploitive sponsors, such as the thieving Stefan the Grocer. Only because foster care in all these guises was rarely formalized into legal adoption have so many modern historians profoundly underestimated its persistence in medieval and early modern societies.

The prominence of fostering in various forms also reaffirms a defining characteristic of the early modern household, namely, its flexibility. As countless scholarly studies during the last thirty years have demonstrated, there was no such thing as "the traditional" European household. The many instances of child circulation that we have viewed, successful or not, demonstrate that a highly elastic model of the household is most appropriate in our attempt to better understand the reality of life in early modern Europe. For a household of the era, changeability was the key to survival, so much so that it is better to think of the early modern family itself as a process rather than a rigid structure.[2] The coming and goings of a parent or child were not exceptional, nor was everyone in residence a blood relative. Blended households were the norm, particularly given the high number of late marriages, widows and widowers, remarriages, stepparents, and orphans—not to mention the comings and goings of relatives, servants, boarders, and other individuals. Foster children, biologically related or not, fit right into these permeable minisocieties, even if only for a brief time. Illegitimate children admittedly faced greater obstacles in finding foster parents but not to the degree that we might expect, especially when a child's true identity could be concealed by a relative or other willing surrogate.

Our collection of individual stories, moreover, demonstrates that limiting child circulation to fundamental categories such as "abandonment" or "institutional fostering" distorts the inherent multiformity of the phenomenon itself. Many cases that secular authorities classified as "abandonment" actually involved individuals who not only knew each other but frequently came to an informal agreement about care of a child. The level of coercion involved is usually indecipherable from a modern perspective, not least because the participants themselves generally had mixed and fluctuating intentions. Stoffel Baur, for instance, might have considered his sudden departure without his three daughters as mostly consensual on the part of his adult son, possibly involving some vague assurance of future compensation. Georg's immediate involvement of governmental officials might have stemmed from an honest misunderstanding, a cynical abuse of his father's trust, anger at still one more imposition, or other more psychologically complex motives. Even among apparently unambiguous fostering agreements, there could be countless permutations of diverse elements in the deal itself: duration (a day, several months, indefinitely), the foster parent involved (a relative, a friend, a stranger), the terms (cash payment, a reciprocal favor, no compensation whatsoever), and so on. Diversity likewise characterized child circulation involving a governmental figure or an institution, with official involvement perhaps consisting of a financial incentive to prevent or effect child circulation, a promise of temporary or permanent Findel care for a child, or the expulsion from the city of an unwanted child with its parent.

At this point the historiographical usefulness of such a sprawling categorization of action begins to look dubious. The highly contingent dynamics involved in each instance of child circulation seem by their very nature to preclude any meaningful generalization whatsoever. This diversity regarding an unwanted child is complicated still further by each individual's available social capital, perceptions of the choices available, as well as by highly variable notions of parental responsibility—not to mention the equally inconstant emotional responses among third parties to the plight of unwanted children and their biological or foster parents. Unwanted children and youths themselves, moreover, were not always (or merely) victims and some played a very active part in their own circulation outside their household as well as their own subsequent self-destruction.

This apparent quandary is not merely a restatement of the epistemological problem of the ultimate unknowability of others, historical or contemporary. Nor does it imply a simplistic call for radical subjectivism based on the impossibility of historical objectivism. It merely reflects the fundamental interconnectedness of all human action and "motives," particularly within an analytical realm as broad as child circulation as well as the hazards of imposing rigid boundaries to make sense of them. No incident of child circulation, even the seemingly solitary choice of anonymous abandonment, was unaffected by that individual's social relations. Not only family members and friends but a number of individuals from the underground child circulation economy often played a part, including those who sold contraceptives, harbored pregnant unwed girls, performed abortions, fostered infants or older children, or other related services. These persons defy categorization by intent or expected outcome, as do the more familiar figures of the (not always benevolent) godparent and the (not always malevolent) stepparent. On the other hand, placing such a vast array of human activity under the umbrella of child circulation appears to have merely exacerbated the cacophony. The relative closeness to these individuals' experience enabled by the microhistorical approach not only obscures the big picture but appears to make it unintelligible and virtually unobtainable.[3]

In the practice of *l'histoire croisée*, this moment is akin to Saint John of the Cross's dark night of the soul, the moment of utter desolation and confusion before the emergence of clarity and connectedness. Having "atomized" previous categories such as child abandonment, we must now gather together all of the diverse and seemingly discrete experiences described in these microhistories and lay them atop one another, looking for points of intersection and areas of overlap. The specter of radical nominalism can only be overcome by this equally radical form of construction from the ground up. We will start by looking for significant commonalities among all the individuals we have thus far encountered (not just the six main characters), then expand our scope to include entire communities and finally conclude with some hypotheses for cross-cultural comparison.

Intersections and Commonalities among Individuals

One of the most pronounced themes in all of our stories is the centrality and indispensability of female networks in the success of informal child circulation.[4] Mothers, sisters, aunts, grandmothers, and female friends, as well as midwives and wise women, all played pivotal roles in a variety of scenarios. In the case of Apollonia Vöglin, it was the absence of her mother or any other female ally (apparently including her sister) that limited her matchmaking potential, denied her crucial information about contraception and abortion, cost her an advocate in getting Apollonia's father to sue for marriage, prevented her from placing the baby with a relative or friend, and eliminated a potentially vital accomplice in a secret birth, anonymous abandonment, or even infanticide. Like virtually all women in her situation, Apollonia herself played a much more central role in determining the fate of her unwanted child than its alleged father (who might not have known of the pregnancy until she was arrested for infanticide).

Female networks also appear to have helped widowed, deserted, or otherwise single mothers with burdensome children to cope better than most of their male counterparts. In the indigent Baur household, it was the children's mother who had kept the family together, particularly in the wake of Stoffel Baur's many comings and goings. Denied sufficient income of her own, Magdalena Baurin instead accumulated social capital through numerous services to neighbors and other friends. Like most de facto single mothers, she was then in turn able to rely on female friends and acquaintances to look after her children for periods of a few days or possibly longer. No more than a year after she is permanently out of the picture, however, Stoffel leaves his three daughters behind—a pattern common among widowers with children and other single men (though much less so among women in similar circumstances). Given his own meager social capital and his distance from most female relatives, he is able to turn for help not to a network of women but only to a single woman, his daughter-in-law, who refuses to accept responsibility this time but nonetheless ends up with the three girls as a result of the inner council's decision.

Albrecht Pömer and his fellow magistrates were of two minds on the value of female networks. On the one hand, they recognized the importance of mutual assistance among single mothers forced to work outside the home or otherwise scrape by. They also knew that not all women could rely on informal child care by a relative or friend and thus they agreed to provide weekly stipends for poor citizen households and free poor schools for their children. On the other hand, magisterial sympathy for pregnant young women like Apollonia Vöglin was less expansive, particularly in instances that resulted in infanticide. Here Pömer and his fellow male council members turned suspiciously on that same informal female network of midwives, common healers, and "harbourers," who they believed actively contributed to an allegedly high incidence of abortion, abandonment, and infanticide, by providing forbidden abortifacients and other aid and by willfully concealing the identities of abandoners and child murderers.

In the instances of orphans such as Jörg Mayr and the Schier twins, male relatives and friends tended to play the most important legal role but it was the presence or absence of women able to care for these and other circulated children that usually determined whether or not legal guardians became involved in the first place. Most orphans and half-orphans came from homes where the most recent death was the mother. Widows, in other words, tended to hold onto their children more consistently than widowers, who often left children with paid or informal foster parents. Had only Jörg's father died while his son was still young, it is likely that Jörg's mother would have continued to care for him, with the help of a female network, as did Sybille Schier for Erhard and Susanna. Whether his mother could have prevented Jörg from entering a life of crime is harder to say—many juvenile offenders in fact came from female-headed households—though certainly his chances of resisting would have improved somewhat.

The great activity of women in making child circulation work was not unrelated to the fact that they bore much more of the burden when it did not work. Personal reputation was an early modern woman's most precious possession and also the most fragile, whether she was single, married, or widowed. In cases of fornication and adultery (usually revealed by an illicit pregnancy), the consequences were almost always worse for the woman, who was not only socially stigmatized and often flogged and banished, but was also expected to support the illegitimate child—even though jobs for single mothers were notoriously hard to come by. This all took place in an economic climate of ever declining wages for working women and the prolonged period of marital insecurity that resulted for most poor maids, struggling to save enough money for a respectable dowry. Widowed or deserted mothers likewise had it hard, unable to earn sufficient income themselves or get by on weekly alms (if they were even eligible) and often forced to rely on the income that their children brought in from begging or even less reputable work.

The centrality of female networks in caring for unwanted children was also based on the cultural situation of pregnancy, childbirth, and child rearing within a separate women's realm, a parallel world, mysterious to men, which the latter usually invaded only in moments of criminal suspicion or other exigencies. Segregation by gender was a common aspect of early modern life, with the unrestricted mingling of the two sexes in street life the major exception to the rule. Often this social bifurcation resulted in a gender double standard that was also evident in most aspects of the lives of unwanted children. Life in the Findel was consistently harder for girls, who were also less likely to survive to adulthood than their male counterparts and were placed in service much less often—Susanna Schier being a notable exception to the rule. Magistrates and many people apparently had lower expectations of fathers than mothers, merely admonishing irresponsible fathers but banishing "bad mothers"—almost always with their deserted or abused children once more in tow. Grandmothers' petitions to the Findel were likewise turned down more frequently than those of grandfathers, who were thought less able to raise children and thereby released from their obligation. Only in cases of anonymous abandonment, where we might assume a prejudice against baby girls, does the gender double standard in fact vanish, with boys abandoned at exactly the same rate as girls.

The disproportionately significant role that women, particularly relatives, played in solving the problem of unwanted children through informal circulation was complemented by the disproportionately significant role that men, particularly soldiers, played in creating the problem in the first place. Soldiers like Stoffel Baur appear almost everywhere in stories of unwanted children, little surprise since the number of mercenaries in Europe increased tenfold during the early modern era, while the general population merely doubled.[5] The implications for premarital and other unwanted pregnancies, by force or suasion, are obvious. Many young unmarried women, particularly maids who did not marry until their late twenties or thirties, yielded—willingly or under force—to young soldiers, men who were often long gone by the birth of a child and in any event remained untouchable by most civil courts. The economic vicissitudes of the era also meant that many mercenary fathers were forced to leave their children with their mothers or foster parents, where they often had to fend for themselves for extended periods of time. Many youthful beggars and delinquents came from such households, denied apprenticeships or basic schooling because of the absence and dishonorable status of the chief breadwinner.

Like most people, Albrecht Pömer and his fellow magistrates frequently deplored the great number of unruly and dangerous mercenaries roaming Nuremberg's territory, particularly during the Thirty Years' War, who—among their other disruptions—often left behind unwanted babies and older children. The city fathers were also well aware that many beggar youths and boys joined the army out of financial desperation and that if they returned at all it was as maimed or otherwise incapacitated breadwinners, highly vulnerable to the temptations of drink, crime, and desertion of the household. Some of Jörg Mayr's older road companions were former soldiers and they undoubtedly played a key role in introducing the teenager to the weapons and greater violence that proved his ultimate downfall. His last desperate plea for mercy in fact included an offer to go abroad as a mercenary. Even some Findel alumni who received training in a craft were prompted by the lack of employment opportunities and perhaps by the lust for adventure to join passing military regiments. Eberhardt Schier's dazzling success in attaining master status by the age of twenty-one should not obscure the fact that more of his fellow Findel alumni ended up as soldiers than as craft masters.

Other commonalities in early modern child circulation are evident in the type of breakdowns that triggered governmental intervention in the process. The most common cause was that a biological or foster parent in need had simply outstretched his or her support network, due either to that individual's depleted social capital or a general social crisis, such as an epidemic. This was the case with Stoffel Baur, an unemployed newcomer to the city whose relatives, with the exception of his probably already overburdened son, were either far away or dead. The two other most frequent sources of breakdown in informal child circulation were more subjective in origin. As in the instance of Apollonia Vöglin and other pregnant young women with unclear marriage prospects, the perception of social isolation, whatever the actual circumstances, could impair an individual from seeking help in the first place and thus lead to tragic consequences for mothers and their children. This scenario is found in any time and place, not just early modern Germany. A final impediment to normal child circulation focused on problems with the child itself that made it difficult to find a willing foster parent. Usually this meant a physical or mental disability, requiring extra care and expense, but sometimes the issue was more behavioral in nature. Given their own self-interest, petitioners to the Findel tended to minimize such problems with a child in their official requests and instead stressed their own inadequate resources. Again, this barrier to fostering or adoption is not unknown today.

All of these reasons for the success or failure of informal child circulation make clear the continuing centrality of individual agency, contingency, and personal dispositions in early modern Germany. Then as now, each case of an unwanted child involves a tangle of individual perceptions, emotions, and rationalizations, often impervious to objective analysis by observers (particularly those living four centuries later). Most of the biological and foster parents we have encountered had relatively few real choices and in many instances perceived still fewer. Outsiders, whether early modern magistrates or modern scholars, have not always taken sufficient care to find the balance between this subjectivity and its social context. The paternalistic and legislative perspective of Nuremberg's town councilors often led them to moralize first and punish second, generally minimizing the role of poverty and other structural conditions in parents' decisions. Modern historians, more sympathetic to the desperate circumstances of such individuals, often go to the opposite extreme and exaggerate to an almost predeterminative degree the influence of sociological factors, whether in assessing the responsibility of a murdering mother, the culpability of indifferent or exploitative parents, or the criminal trajectory of a homeless young thief. Striking the right balance on this question is never easy and—given the information available—in most instances ultimately impossible. However, by using the approach of *l'histoire croisée* and identifying points of intersection and areas of overlap among these five microhistories, we can eschew the distorting lens of paternalistic magistrates and reductionist scholars alike and perceive the richly detailed panorama of human experiences and responses that shaped the actual circulation of unwanted children.

Patterns and Commonalities at the Communal Level

Communities, like households, had a considerable stake in the successful circulation of unwanted children and responded in different ways to collective challenges. Here too the parameters for action, Braudel's "limits of the possible," displayed considerable continuity throughout the early modern period. The most obvious and influential social structures were the fixed demographic realities of the premodern world, namely, high infant mortality and overall low life expectancy. Combined with the northwestern European late marriage pattern, these constraints resulted in a great number of orphans and half-orphans as well as fewer available foster parents than today (especially grandparents, who were likely deceased). The typically long delay until marriage also meant that premarital conception was more likely, though this did not necessarily translate into a high illegitimacy rate, especially given the prominence of quick marriages, abortions, and informal fostering of unwanted children.[6]

Even more than individual households, communities tended to experience these structural factors in waves, producing in turn a cyclical pattern of child circulation. During relatively prosperous times, for instance, work was plentiful, bread and housing were affordable, and mortality rates were steady. In bad times, various combinations of deadly epidemics, marauding armies, and spiraling prices made life much harder for poor families with children, intensifying the pressure on the informal and formal circulation of children. An overview of all Findel petitions between 1560 and 1669 (fig. 6.1) reveals a clear pattern indicative of these influences. The overall number of admissions spikes in all categories dramatically upward from 1560 to 1574, then it peaks four more times—1585–89, 1600–4, 1610–14, and significantly, 1630–39—before plummeting during the 1640s to a level that it would maintain for the next 250 years. Not surprisingly, each of those spikes represents a period of epidemic, famine, and in the last instance, warfare. Obviously when more parents died or were hospitalized, more children became orphans or half-orphans, more were circulated informally to whoever can take them, and more were anonymously abandoned and sent to the Findel. During the crisis of 1570–74, the number of all three type

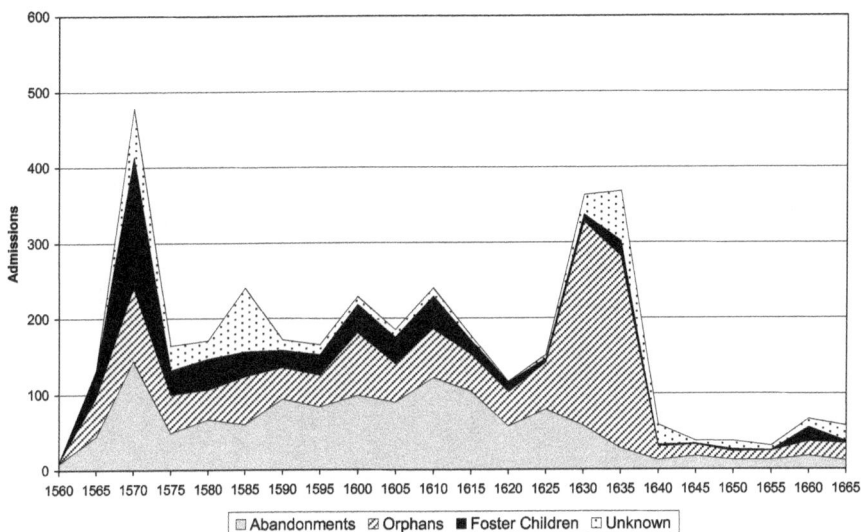

Fig. 6.1. Total admissions to the Nuremberg Findel by type,
1560–1619 (five-year totals; *n* = 3452). *Source*: FKD.

admissions—orphans, foundlings, and foster children—increased. Many
children also entered the Findel during the much more numerous nonepidemic years but it is noteworthy that the plague outbreak of 1613–14
possibly took the life of Magdalena Baurin (wife of Stoffel) and one of the
many epidemics during the 1630s likely killed Stephan Schier, father to
Susanna and Eberhardt. Whether informal child circulation increased accordingly during such difficult periods is unverifiable but likely.

Usually times of famine and disease were also economically difficult,
so the problems of supporting a household with children were likewise
exacerbated, again triggering various forms of child circulation. Some historians believe that the number of unwanted children, or more specifically
foundlings, correlates directly to times of economic distress.[7] A comparison of grain prices and Findel admissions in Nuremberg (see fig. 6.2) suggests that there does indeed appear to be a close relationship between this
price index and the number of all types of unwanted children sent to the
Findel—at least until 1615, when Findel admissions continued to decline,
while grain prices escalated and remained high until the 1640s (as a direct
result of the Thirty Years' War), at which point Findel admissions dropped
much more steeply than grain prices and remained low (for other reasons
to be discussed). Given what little we know of our subjects' motivations, it
is hard to move beyond this general correlation. Stoffel Baur's decision to

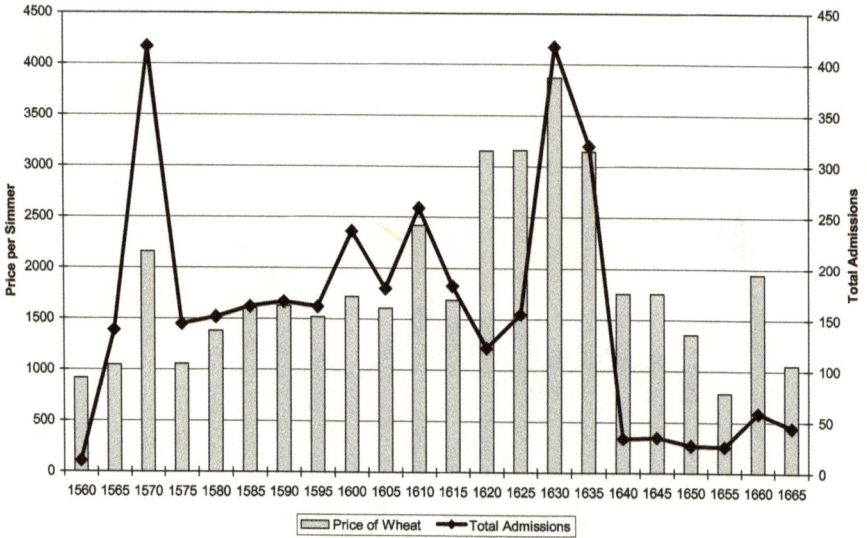

Fig. 6.2. Rye prices and total Findel admissions, 1560–1669 (five-year totals; $n = 3452$). *Sources:* FKD; Bauerfeind, *Materielle Grundstrukturen*, table A12.

leave town alone, for instance, was likely influenced by his lack of suitable employment opportunities (by his own assessment) as well as the precarious economic climate of Nuremberg in 1614, but such an act might just as likely have occurred in a generally prosperous year—neither scenario reveals much about an individual's particular decision, only that circulation in some form was more likely.

Sometimes detecting a communal cycle requires a more expansive chronological framework. If, for instance, we look at the patterns of anonymous abandonments between 1520 and 1700 (see fig. 6.3), what emerges is not a progressive increase in numbers but rather cycles of approximately twenty-five to forty years each, roughly one to two generations. These cycles are not demographically based, at least between 1520 and 1640, when the city's population grew steadily. There is also evidence of a new cycle underway at the end of the seventeenth century, during a period of zero population growth. The cycles also do not correspond to any economic developments in Nuremberg. Their somewhat complementary relationship to the incidence of known infanticides, on the other hand, suggests that what we might instead be viewing are cycles of law enforcement, in this instance related to the prosecution of fornication and illegitimacy, which intensified considerably between 1585 and 1630 and eased notably during the rest of the seventeenth century.[8] In other words, both incidences of anonymous

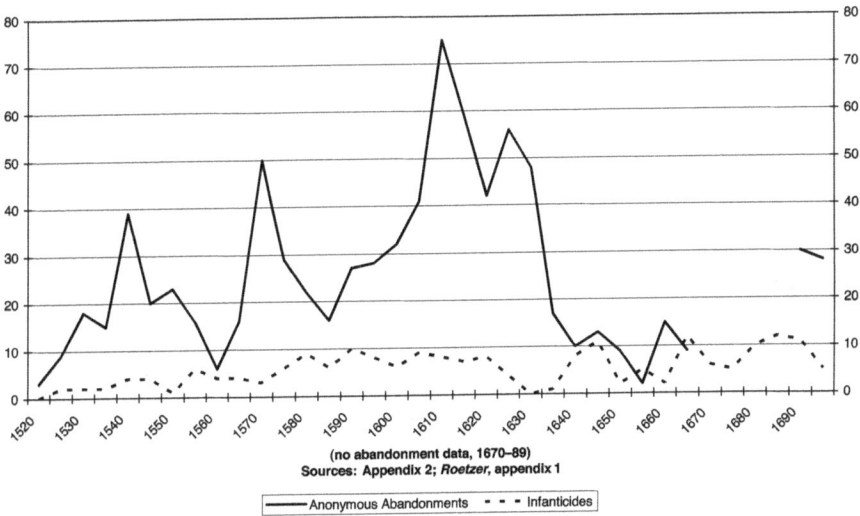

Fig. 6.3. Anonymous abandonments and known infanticides in Nuremberg, 1520–1699 (five-year totals; *n* anonymous abandonments = 622; *n* infanticides = 58).

abandonment and infanticide might have been more affected by law enforcement than by economic or demographic factors.

A comparison of anonymous abandonment, infanticide, and illegitimacy on a per capita basis (see fig. 6.4) further clarifies the relationship among the three phenomena. As we saw in chapter 1, abandonment and illegitimacy rates are at times inversely related—a logical correlation. In 1610, both anonymous abandonment and illegitimacy rates were about 1.5 percent; by 1665, the former had declined to about 0.3 percent of all births, while the illegitimacy rate had risen to almost 4 percent. Known infanticides, meanwhile, appear to be completely independent phenomena, at least in terms of collective trends and overall frequency, thereby precluding any significant generalization.

Collective cycles of child circulation thus for the most part appear to conform to common sense: in times of collective stress—economic crises, wars, epidemics—biological and foster parents were more likely to circulate their charges. Female networks of support weakened and the entropic effect of deceased or absent parents increased. Such periods placed enormous pressure on the usual options for formal and informal fostering but not necessarily to the breaking point. These demographic forces, moreover, did not have the same effect in every instance and could be mitigated or exacerbated themselves by religious, cultural, and legal factors—the basis for still greater generalization and comparisons, to which we now turn.

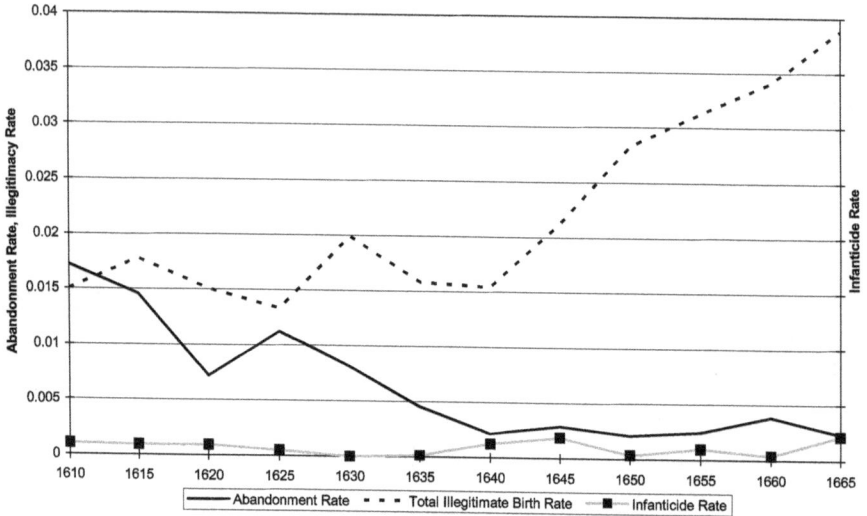

Fig. 6.4. Abandonment rate, total illegitimate birth rate, and infanticide rate in Nuremberg, 1610–69 (five-year totals; *n* total births = 79,697). *Sources*: FKD; Rüger, *Die Kinderfürsorge*, tab. 1, app. 2.

Cross-cultural Comparisons

How do the individual and communal commonalities in Nuremberg's experience of child circulation compare to those elsewhere in early modern Europe? This is an important question and by no means an uncomplicated one. We must be especially cautious in generalizing simple causal relationships and linear developments in child circulation. Illegitimacy rates, for instance—presumably inversely related to anonymous abandonment and other newborn circulation rates—fluctuated greatly over time and space, influenced by a number of factors such as household size, inheritance patterns, nature of local economy, migration patterns, local marriage market, and so on. Social attitudes toward illegitimacy likewise varied considerably throughout early modern Europe and generational shifts in these did not necessarily have a straightforward and immediate effect on the practice of anonymous abandonment. In general, regions or "cultures" where premarital sex and bastardy were highly stigmatized—such as Spain and France— did tend to experience high anonymous abandonment, while societies that were more tolerant of these occurrences, such as the Basque country, had very low infant abandonment.[9] Nuremberg's evidence from the seventeenth century similarly appears to support a direct inverse relationship of the two phenomena, albeit within a very narrow range.[10] But when the illegitimacy rate in many French and Italian cities shot up to as many as one in three

births during the eighteenth and nineteenth centuries, anonymous abandonment rates not only failed to decline but simultaneously soared to unprecedented heights.[11] Meanwhile, in many other regions—most notably
the British Isles, Scandinavia, northern Germany, and the Balkans—both
illegitimacy rates and child abandonments remained very low during the
sixteenth and seventeenth centuries and only modestly elevated during the
eighteenth and nineteenth centuries.[12]

Nor can such differences in anonymous abandonment rates be simply
ascribed to different attitudes among the religious denominations, another
"cultural" factor. Scholars have long noted, for instance, that early modern foundling homes were more common in Catholic than in Protestant
regions.[13] The reason for this distinction is far from clear, however. The
continuing prominence of private and informal child circulation in Nuremberg and the city's low child abandonment numbers cannot be characterized as a Protestant phenomenon, especially considering that foundling
numbers were also low during the two centuries before the Reformation.
More obviously, as the story of Apollonia Vöglin makes abundantly clear,
early modern Protestants could be just as punitive toward unwed mothers
as their post-Tridentine Catholic counterparts, which logically should have
spurred much more child abandonment than it did. Germany and the rest
of northwestern Europe, characterized by a distinctive late marriage pattern,
should likewise have seen more illicit pregnancies and higher circulation of
newborns than areas typified by early marriage and extended households,
but there is no evidence that this is true—in fact, the contrary.[14] Meanwhile,
many German Catholic areas, such as Bavaria, continued to have low abandonment rates well into the nineteenth centuries.[15] If there is one external
factor that appears to have significantly influenced the number of anonymous abandonments more than any other it is the presence (or in Nuremberg's case, the absence) of a *ruota*, or turning wheel, at a foundling home's
entrance for the deposit of unwanted babies. Even this pattern, however,
raises the question of why the *ruota* was so popular in Mediterranean countries and so rare in German and Scandinavian regions—a mystery at the
core of early modern child circulation.[16]

Perhaps the most vexing question in any cross-cultural comparative analysis concerns the role of governmental bodies such as the Nuremberg city
council in early modern child circulation. Virtually all learned discussions
of this topic, focusing primarily on foundling homes and other institutions,
proceed from three historical axioms about unwanted children. First, all
assume a primary catalyst role for the state and its leaders in a transformation of child circulation practices. Usually the motives of governmental

reformers emanate from some new ideological inspiration, whether the humanist movement of the fourteenth and fifteenth centuries in Italy, the Protestant Reformation in sixteenth-century Germany, the social agenda of seventeenth-century Pietism, or the Enlightenment project for human improvement during the eighteenth century.[17] Second, whatever the immediate trigger, the scholarly assumption has been that an expansion of governmental involvement in this area is unidirectional and irreversible, at least until the rate of abandonment in European cities reached a crisis point around the mid-nineteenth century.[18] The image is that of a runaway freight train: admissions to Florence's Innocenti Children's Hospital expanding from under 200 foundlings per year before 1475 to almost three times that number within sixty years and several thousand by the eighteenth century; the foundling homes of Paris growing from 300 annual admissions in the 1640s to over 1,400 in the 1720s and more than 7,000 annually during the 1770s; and all European foundling homes rapidly expanding from 1750 on to the point where in metropolises such as Prague and Vienna every other infant born was anonymously abandoned.[19] Third, these scholars argue, that because early modern state involvement always triggered more abandonments, the inevitable social impact was profoundly negative, resulting in many more suffering and dying children. David Ransel describes modern Russian interventions as causing "unintended consequences on a massive scale," and David Kertzer similarly considers the expansion of nineteenth-century Italian foundling homes "a tale of human tragedy on a vast scale, the result of good intentions gone wrong, of historical change running out of control."[20] Other scholars have been less generous about the motives for state intervention, positing official complicity in what amounted to passive infanticide among the lower classes.[21] Well intentioned or not, all agree that governmental attempts to remedy the problems of anonymous abandonment and infanticide clearly had an overwhelmingly negative impact and in most instances made matters much worse.

How well does the evidence from Nuremberg support this paradigm? The first axiom, regarding ideological inspiration, applies only indirectly. The Findel's origins in the late fourteenth century put it at least a century ahead of the earliest traces of the Renaissance in Germany, and its institutional reconfiguration in 1560 had much more to do with logistical considerations than with specific Lutheran inspirations. Obviously both humanist and Protestant teachings influenced the general outlook of the city's magistrates but this affinity cannot be directly correlated to changes in the Findel's operation, at least chronologically speaking. As with the founding of the city's workhouse over a century later, Nuremberg's supremely cautious city

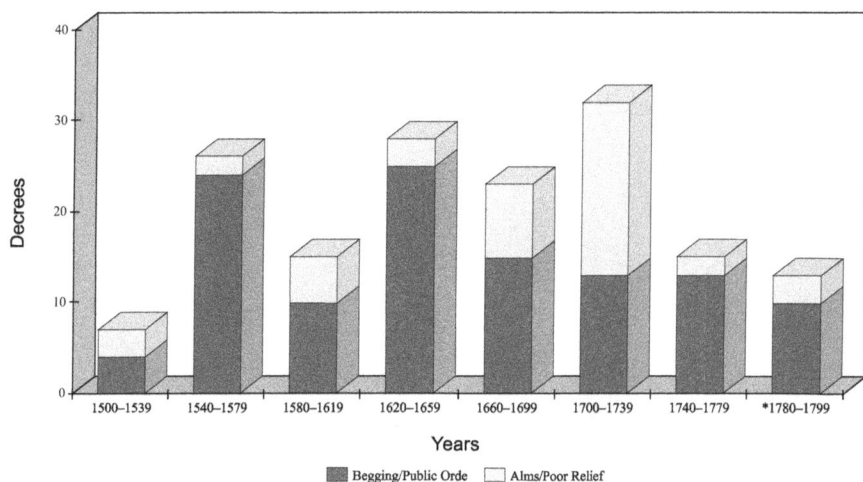

Fig. 6.5. Poverty related legislation in Nuremberg, 1500–1799. *Source*: StaatsAN 63IA.

councilors could never be accused of susceptibility to intellectual or religious trends and showed much more inclination to adapt existing institutions to fit the resources and needs at hand than to create new ones.[22]

Rather than imagine one crucial and irreversible turning point in governmental intervention on behalf of unwanted children, triggered by an intellectual movement such as the Renaissance or the Enlightenment, we might better view official attitudes toward child circulation in cyclical—perhaps generational—terms. As the evidence of anonymous abandonments in Nuremberg suggests (see above, fig. 6.3), city councilors and other leaders as a group tended to respond to various social disorders in alternately supportive and punitive manners. The specter of anonymously abandoned babies, for instance, might be interpreted as a social welfare question, requiring governmental resources for the care of such children, or as a disciplinary matter, mandating stricter surveillance of unmarried women and harsh legal consequences for fornication, illegitimate births, and infanticide. Since all governments involve multiple individuals and perspectives, we should never assume a monolithic response at any given moment. Clearly, though, Nuremberg's patricians were affected by their respective *Zeitgeist* as much as their fellow citizens. Focusing just on the related issue of legislative responses to begging in the city, for instance, figure 6.5 shows a general generational fluctuation between more supportive and more reactionary tendencies. This is not a conclusive trend but certainly a suggestive one.

The second historiographical axiom—that creating governmental insti-

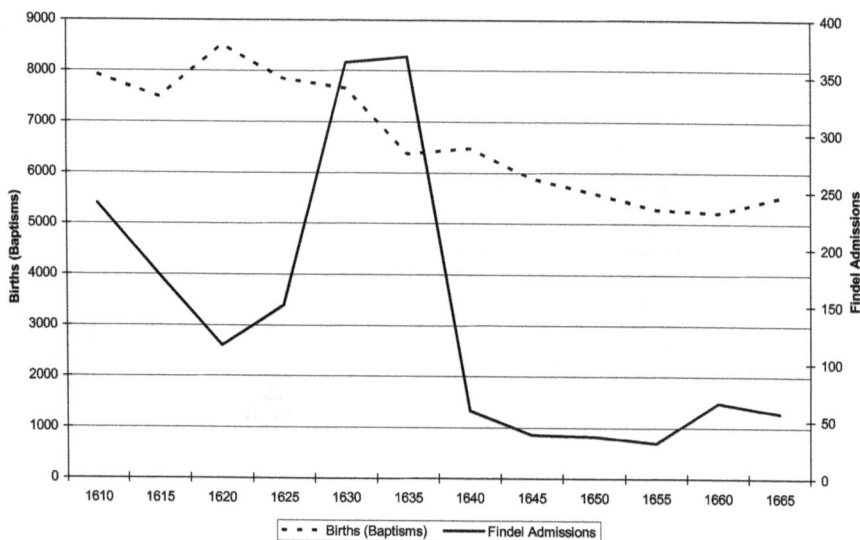

Fig. 6.6. Births (baptisms) and total admissions to the Nuremberg Findel,
1610–69 (five-year totals; *n* births = 79,697; *n* admissions = 3452).
Sources: FKD; Rüger, *Die Kinderfürsorge*, tab. 1.

tutions for unwanted children always triggered irresistible growth in public
abandonments and other institutional circulation—shows more initial signs
of promise. The great rise in Findel admissions during the 1560s and 1570s
was clearly the direct result of two magisterial decisions: the centralization
of the boys' and girls' Findels in the old Franciscan cloister in 1560 and
the council's general response to the number of orphans and other needy
children produced by a deadly series of famines and epidemics during the
period 1570–74. This initial growth spurt was in fact typical of most premodern foundling homes and orphanages, as was an initial drop after the
crisis passed, followed by a gradual expansion in admission numbers over
the course of the next decades. Here, though, we once again come to the
burst of Findel activity during the 1630s, followed by a momentous drop
in admissions, which remains at pre-1560 levels for the next two centuries.
This is not supposed to happen, according to the second axiom, at least not
before the late nineteenth century. How do we account for this?

At first glance the explanation seems to be a simple case of supply and
demand. As figure 6.6 illustrates, the seventeenth-century drop in admissions to the Nuremberg Findel clearly correlates to the city's declining birthrate, both starting at least two decades before the decimation of the city's
populace during the epidemics of the 1630s. Between 1610 and 1669, the

annual number of baptisms within Nuremberg declined from over 1,600 to under 1,100. During the same period, the number of admissions to the Findel declined from about fifty new children per year to about ten, with of course the major exception of 1630–39. The decline in admissions affected all age and type cohorts equally and profoundly transformed the Findel itself. Born during this period of declining birthrates, for instance, Susanna and Eberhardt Schier thus enjoyed a much better adult: child ratio at the Findel and significantly better job placement opportunities than any of their counterparts in nearly a century (not to mention beds of their own).[23]

A decline in demand for the Findel's services is not in itself the whole answer, however. Births between 1610 and 1669 declined 31.4 percent, for example, while Findel admissions dropped 80 percent. Put differently, Findel admissions went from a peak of 3.1 percent of the number of annual baptisms within the city to 0.9 percent over the course of sixty years.[24] While a rising and declining population can help explain the general rise and decline of the Findel's numbers, we need to consider at least one other key structural influence in order to account for the rapidity of the growth and shrinkage alike, namely, the financial imperative of reduced operations.

The soaring costs of Nuremberg's various social welfare programs were already of concern to the city's leaders by the beginning of the seventeenth century. Around 1610, simultaneous with the falling birthrate, the inner council began a new hard-line approach to admissions, marked by more magisterial references to the "overburdening" of the Findel, more property checks, more negotiations, and greater attempts to track down abandoning parents.[25] This fiscally motivated decline in the acceptance rate was modest, but it did have some visible results, which are obscured by the huge influx of children during the 1630s, most of whom were older orphans. Abandonments, for instance, show a sharp decline over the first half of the seventeenth century, from a peak of almost twenty-seven per year in 1610–15 to an average of about three per year in 1640–49, a level that would remain virtually unchanged for the next 150 years. Most of this initial drop is driven by a decrease in the number of known abandonments (aka forced foster cases; see fig. 6.7). In other words, before 1610 abandoners made fewer attempts to conceal their identity, perhaps confident that the Findel would nevertheless take in their children, with no legal consequences for the parents, but once the council's new attitude became known, more parents (not many) began to abandon their children anonymously. Most significantly, the overall number of abandonment cases coming before the council continued to decline steadily (with one brief surge) over the course of the Thirty Years' War. At the same time the inner council doubled its normal rejection rate

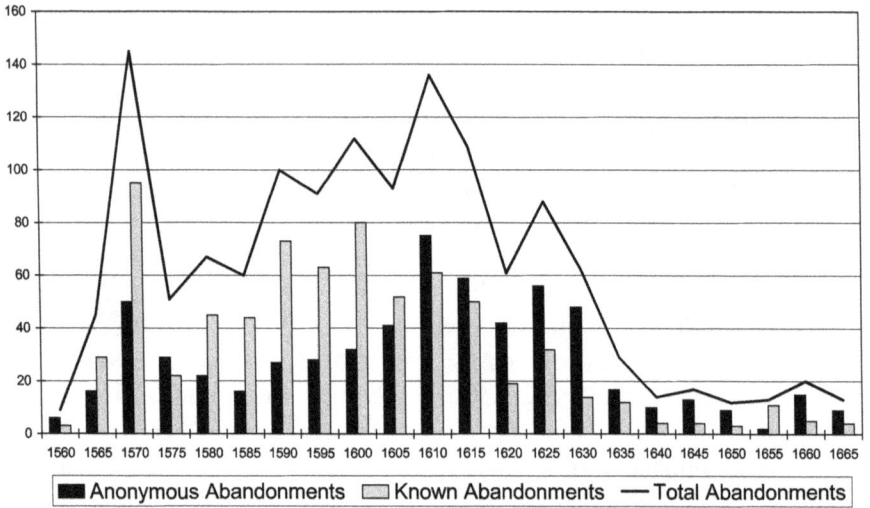

Fig. 6.7. Total abandonments in Nuremberg, 1560–1669, with breakdown of known and anonymous abandonments (five-year totals; *n* = 1347). *Source*: FKD.

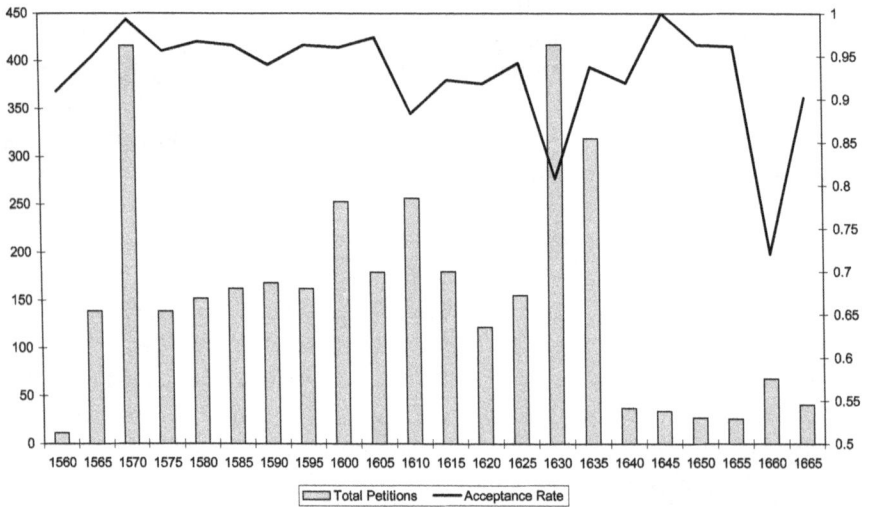

Fig. 6.8. Total petitions and acceptance rate over time for the Nuremberg Findel, 1560–1669 (*n* = 4018). *Source*: FKD.

of 7 percent for known abandonments and quadrupled the percentage of rejections in the instance of foster petitions, the case type with the greatest degree of magisterial discretion.[26]

It is unlikely, however, that this policy shift alone could have produced such a dramatic decline in overall applications and admissions, particularly given the council's repeated tendency to return to its traditionally high acceptance rate of 93 percent (see fig. 6.8).[27] Even during the crisis of the 1630s, when the overall number of petitions skyrocketed, only the year 1633 saw a significantly low acceptance rate (55 percent); the following six years averaged 89 percent acceptance and even 1634, when the Findel received an unprecedented 233 petitions for admission, also saw a success rate of 86 percent.[28] Not until the crisis subsided in 1639 did the number of children admitted drop steeply, though not because of a change in the official acceptance rate, which hovered around 95 percent for the rest of Albrecht Pömer's tenure as Findel administrator, taking another brief downturn during the 1660s.

Even Nuremberg magistrates' own best efforts at resisting bureaucratic momentum and mission creep were thus in themselves insufficient. Instead, Albrecht Pömer and his fellow magistrates frequently found themselves enmeshed in problems that they had sought to relegate to the private sphere and their attempts to extricate themselves proved mostly futile, confined mostly to tinkering with law enforcement and other means of implementation. It required the combined pressure of a financial crisis and a demographic decline—something the Findel's French and Italian counterparts would not experience until two centuries later—to significantly reduce the number of admissions. The modification of axiom two should therefore be that while resisting institutional expansion in early modern foundling homes was difficult it was by no means impossible, given the proper stimuli.[29]

The third axiom of early modern governmental involvement in child circulation, that it invariably made matters worse, is perhaps the most pervasive belief among scholars and the most resistant to modification. Just as we have underestimated the persistence of informal child circulation, though, we have tended to overestimate the universal influence of premodern bureaucracies and institutions on phenomena such as child abandonment and infanticide. Nor was government involvement always linear in nature (i.e., ever expanding) or universally harmful in effect. The results of institutional participation in child circulation in fact varied considerably over time and space—hardly surprising given the diversity of individuals and situations involved. Once more, many of our misconceptions stem from the very concepts and terms we use in phrasing our questions. There was no such thing as "the early modern state," and given the range of social structures, political and religious agendas, and effectiveness in enforcement, any essentialist generalization risks serious distortions. Instead of anthropomorphizing "the state"—in similar terms as "the Church" (or that modern favorite, "the market")—we need to think of the state as a negotiated process, a multivalent and dynamic construction of various individuals and groups, as opposed to a bludgeon used by one group to get something from another (which was admittedly one possible application, but not the most common one).

Magistrates such as Albrecht Pömer obviously had a greater voice in this social conversation but not to the extent we often imagine, nor did they truly speak with one voice, despite their pretensions to the contrary. Like their fellow citizens, most individual magistrates were evidently moved by the sight of real poor and starving children on their streets and often acted contrary to their own official policy toward foreigners. In a few instances, most notably in the prosecution of infanticide, outraged legal authorities initiated action and prefigured popular indignation over the offense by several decades. Here we might justifiably speak of state initiative as determinative. More often, though, the inner council and other governmental apparatuses were profoundly reactive, drawn into a variety of specific situations as a last resort by petitioners who sought financial assistance or foster homes for children, punishment of a suspected fornicator, or arbitration in a dispute over responsibility for a child. For fiscal and ideological reasons, Nuremberg's councilors consistently tried to find private homes and private solutions and to that end preferred negotiated settlements to autocratic decrees, knowing that the latter would more often than not backfire. Despite their authoritarian stance and adherence to a rigid social hierarchy, Albrecht Pömer and his colleagues were much closer to today's city councilors and aldermen, immersed in the more mundane aspects of the community's life, than to the majority of less accountable modern civil servants at the national and international level.

It is easy to be misled about the extent of early modern governmental involvement with unwanted children. After all, Nuremberg's rulers intervened to a virtually unparalleled extent in a variety of social contexts and encouraged citizens to come to them with all sorts of disputes and other problems, hoping to thereby secure civic order and bolster their own hegemony over the populace. They also made frequent decrees and pronouncements on a variety of topics, often repeatedly within the space of a few years. Some of their legislation did indeed have an immediate impact. In addressing the blight of child begging, for instance, they not only fumed about bad parents but also provided alms and other assistance for poor local families as well as free education and job placement for their equivalent of at-risk youths in the city's poor schools. Even publicly abandoned and otherwise circulated foreign children were regularly accepted into the Findel and given other material support. In law enforcement, councilors greatly increased the number and extent of inquisitorial investigations of dead infants and strictly punished fornication, illegitimate pregnancies, and to a much lesser degree, child abandonment itself. They were especially effective during short-term crises, most notably the 1630s, when the usual social networks broke down and only a careful marshalling of collective resources mitigated the combined effects of epidemics, food shortages, inflation, and overcrowding.[30]

In the big picture, however, the effect of governmental intervention in Nuremberg remained decisively limited. The thousands of Findel petitions examined from our period show an overwhelming official preference for private placement in questions of unwanted children and great reluctance to interfere with anything remotely identified as "parental discipline." This mostly passive attitude about various forms of what we would consider child abuse led them to return just about every abandoned or beaten child to its parents. Consequently the Nuremberg Findel functioned as a safety net for a small minority of the city's circulated children, and even then authorities made repeated and sometimes successful attempts to find private foster care for the unwanted child petitioners. Such restraint seems paradoxical for a council that inserted itself into such a variety of social issues yet Albrecht Pömer or one of his associates could say the very same thing about our modern national and international governments, which likewise tend to prefer legislation and pronouncements to costly or otherwise difficult actions.

If we consider this question from the perspective of our stories' protagonists, the limited practical impact of expanded governmental involvement is obvious. For Apollonia Vöglin the greatest single effect of magisterial action was the increased surveillance of virtually all women for fornication and illicit pregnancies, especially following the discovery of abandoned or murdered infants. Yet investigative methods remained primitive, vulnerable to manipulation, and for the most part ineffective in preventing any of these desperate actions. The most notable achievement of this atmosphere of heightened paranoia was in compounding the misery of an unmarried pregnant woman or mother through corporal punishment and banishment.

Intensified prosecution of infanticide also made her desperate situation more dangerous. Had Apollonia lived fifty years earlier (or two centuries later), she almost certainly would not have been executed and her offense might not even have been detected. Meanwhile, governmental threats to cut off alms to parents with begging children had no impact whatsoever on foreigners such as Stoffel Baur, nor did the frequently reiterated ultimatum of banishment, which was also extended to abandoning parents (who were in most instances already far away). The juvenile thieves we encountered also repeatedly defied their numerous banishments and ignored floggings and corporal punishments as severe as the cutting off of ears. Their executions admittedly put a stop to their own criminal careers but this solution was viewed even then as extreme and impractical and was therefore rare.

On the other hand, some poor parents and their children were unquestionably helped by poor relief and other governmental assistance. Eberhardt and Susanna Schier clearly benefited from their residence at the Findel, which provided not only housing, food, health care, and education for several years but also facilitated key job placement that led to their subsequent marriages and new households. This did not ensure financial success and personal happiness, but what human institution can? Nuremberg's relatively efficient and aggressive legal system also probably gave Apollonia Vöglin a much better chance of tracking down her baby's father and making him marry or pay than medieval women enjoyed, but neither result was guaranteed and both came at the cost of a demolished personal reputation. And undoubtedly various forms of financial assistance from the city government allowed some poor households to survive, if not exactly thrive, in treacherous times.[31]

Conclusions

Is Nuremberg a typical example of early modern child circulation? This is *une question mal posée*, since no city or territory can serve as a satisfactory microcosm for all German lands, let alone Europe as a whole. A more useful query would seek to establish which parts of the Nuremberg experience we have witnessed appear to resonate on a universal or regional level and which aspects appear unusual or even unique. Certainly all of the triggers to child circulation described, as well as the importance of female networks and social capital, were common throughout early modern Europe. So too was the diversity of forms of child circulation, though this has rarely been explicitly recognized as such among historians. The relative frequency of particular forms, on the other hand, appears to be a regional phenomenon, with Nuremberg's anonymous abandonment rate even low by German standards. By 1850, when the foundling homes of the metropolitan Milan and Florence were taking in thousands of foundlings per year and Europe overall saw more than 100,000 babies abandoned annually to governmental institutions, Nuremberg's Findel averaged a mere fifteen new children (all orphans) annually, and had admitted no foundlings whatsoever since 1831.[32] Was private and informal circulation simply much more prominent in northwestern regions, and if so, why? John Boswell intriguingly noted that in northern Europe it was the unwanted child's "found" status that was stressed in the common name (foundling; *enfant trouvé*, *Findelkind*), while in southern lands it was the rejection that was underscored (*gettatello*; *expósito*; *exposto*).[33] Can such widespread distinctions be traced back to ancient Roman and Germanic times or to other large-scale cultural divisions? The basis for such apparently deep regional tendencies has yet to be satisfactorily explained and remains a fertile topic for future research.

Ironically, Nuremberg is most instructive in the area where it is most unusual, namely, the high level of governmental involvement in certain societal contexts relevant to child circulation, most notably its generous social welfare support and its zealous prosecution of fornication and infanticide. Few European cities could match the extent of either activity. Yet even here, in one of the most interventionist jurisdictions in early modern Europe, the impact of such governmental action remained minimal. The example of Nuremberg likewise demonstrates how diverse and inconsistent governmental officials in the same city could be in their approaches and how much they were subject to the same emotional reactions and practical compromises as their fellow residents.[34] Finally, the Nuremberg evidence demonstrates the abiding resilience of medieval notions of hospitality and personal charity among countless foster parents—undiminished by the Reformation's reconceptualization of good works and the rise of the Findel and other charitable institutions. The "kindness of strangers," Boswell's evocative translation of the long-lauded *aliena misericordia*, did not become the social relic he so lamented but continued to thrive into the modern period.[35]

These are valuable lessons but not conclusive in any all-encompassing manner. The search for a unified theory of early modern child circulation, in other words, remains inherently futile, prone to the same teleological distortions as any other self-serving narrative of child abandonment in the West. What the language of child circulation instead provides is a useful conceptual framework for broader analysis, a way to compare apples and oranges. What our tales of unwanted children offer is a greater appreciation of the diverse faces of human coping and of human compassion in the midst of great suffering and want, much of it brought on by human fear, intolerance, and selfishness. If these two perspectives on the unwanted children of Europe's past have truly broadened and deepened our understanding of the crying baby on the doorstep, then perhaps those wails will no longer sound quite so distant.

The Findelkinder Database

The statistical foundation of this study is a database composed of 4,018 cases of unwanted children in the city of Nuremberg from 1557 to 1670. The timeframe for the study represents a substantial historical period starting just before the joining of the boys' and girls' homes in 1560 and ending with the burning down of the adjacent discipline- and workhouse in late 1670. The database was compiled by combining and cross-indexing selected cases from almost daily petitions to the city council and the body's subsequent decrees (*Ratsverläße*) from 1 January 1557 to 31 December 1670 with the admission records of the Findel from 23 February 1557 to 28 November 1670. The first set of records comprises 1,506 manuscript volumes of ca. 80–150 pages each and required locating and transcribing assorted cases amid a myriad of petitions and issues, guided mostly by each volume's original index. While surprisingly thorough for the era, these indexes can be idiosyncratic at times and thus do not ensure that every petition relevant to unwanted children was transcribed. The Findel's admission records, on the other hand, appear to have been more standardized and are thus more reliable in terms of comprehensiveness of children taken into the Findel's custody. They do not, however, give any indication of how many children were refused entrance or why. Also during periods of crisis, particularly during the period 1632–36, the flood of incoming children resulted in some omissions or other errors. Finally, the admission registers often leave out important details about the children, parents, or circumstances of admission.

For all of these reasons, the cross-indexing of both sets of records has yielded a much fuller view of many cases than either set alone could provide. Predictably, the two sets do not match up perfectly: Of the total 4,018 cases, only 1,716 are recorded in both the *Ratsverläße* and the admission registers. 70 of the 660 cases (10.6 percent) recorded only in the *Ratsverläße* represent unsuccessful petitions for admission to the Findel; the remainder are successful petitions that for various reasons (again, usually mass admissions) do not appear in the Findel admission registers. The 1,642 cases that appear only in the registers, on the other hand, reflect both the occasional unreliability of *Ratsverläße* indexes as well as several instances where children might have been admitted without a formal petition.

After complete transcription and cross-indexing of both sets of records, the available information was entered into a database using Microsoft Access. For this purpose I devised a form containing multiple choices for each of the following bits of information: name, age, and gender of child; date(s) of petition and/or admission; case type (explained below); petitioner and relationship to child (if known); property of child; whether admitted; siblings; name, origin, marital status, citizenship, occupation, and status/location of father; name, origin, marital status, citizenship, occupation, and status/location of mother; length of time spent in the Findel's care; and nature of departure from the Findel's custody. Cases were divided into eight subtypes: anonymous abandonment, abandonment by a known person (aka forced foster), temporary foster care for reasons of illness, foster care at the government's initiation (e.g., because of an executed or imprisoned parent), foster care for other reasons (e.g., poverty), orphanhood, combination (a rare exception), and unknown. Clearly any categorization maintains a somewhat artificial rigidity, but I found these distinctions useful in conveying an accurate picture of the circumstances surrounding each unwanted child that came to the city council's attention. Statistical queries of the completed database were then converted into Microsoft Excel for purposes of analysis.

APPENDIX TWO

Known Infanticides in Nuremberg, 1384–1806

Such a list has been attempted twice before for Nuremberg, by Gustav Bode (1914) and by Karl Roetzer (1957). Whereas Bode (used uncritically by some contemporary historians) is so unreliable as to appear quasi-fictitious, I have found Roetzer about 85 percent accurate before 1640 and 100 percent thereafter. Still, as the inconsistency in criminal record keeping makes clear, even this list cannot be considered a definitive list, only the best one possible given the sources available (see especially the lacuna during the war and plague years of 1628–39). S indicates suspected but not convicted; F, flogged; B, banished; and E, executed.

Date	Name of Accused	Source
Before 1549: 23 dead babies reported; 15 infanticide suspects; 12 convictions (10 since 1508), 4 executed (3 since 1527)		
27 March 1384	Else Stadelmännin	ASB 204: 24v
1408	Kunigunde R. (S)	ASB 205: 54r
1443	Undetermined	RB 1b: 84v
5 May 1492	*eine fraw*	A-Laden, 33c: 92v–93r
11 Aug. 1497	Agnes Pörtlin (B)	A-Laden, 33c: 110r
5 Oct. 1498	Agnes Nehingerin (S)	A-Laden, 33c: 118r
25 Nov. 1508	Els Merklin (F)	RV 497: 8v, 14r; RV 498: 6r, 9r
8 March 1510	Anna Malerin (F)	A-Laden, 33b: 37v–38r
26 July 1513	Elisabeth Näglin (E)	HS 440: 167

NOTES: The date given is the day of execution for those condemned; for all others the first mention of suspicion. *Sources:* A-Laden: Staatsarchiv Nürnberg, 15a, Ratskanzlei, Differentialakten. ASB: Staatsarchiv Nürnberg, 52b, Amt und Standbücher. F1 Nr: Stadtarchiv Nürnberg. FS: *Maister Franntz Schmidts Nachrichter in Nürmberg all sein Richten,* ed. Albrecht Keller (1913; reprint: Neustadt a. d. Aisch: Ph. C. W. Schmidt, 1979). GNM: Germanisches Nationalmuseum. HS: Staatsarchiv Nürnberg, 52a, Handschriften. MNG: Johann Christian Siebenkees, ed., *Materialien zur Nürnbergischen Geschichte,* 4 vols. (Nuremberg: V. G. Schneiderische Kunst- und Buchhandlung, 1792–95). RB: Staatsarchiv Nürnberg, 51, Ratschlagbücher. RV: Staatsarchiv Nürnberg, 60a, Ratsverläße.

Date	Name of Accused	Source
7 March 1515	Kunigunda Cuntzin (F)	A-Laden, 33c: 201r
11 Oct. 1515	Barbara Ott Karlin (B)	A-Laden, 33c: 204v
12 May 1518	Margaretha Behaimin (B)	RV 623: 4r, 8r, 12r, 14r
28 Feb. 1525	Gerhaws Störchin (B)	HS 440: 565; HS 447: 699; RV 713: 22r; RV 714: 4v, 5r, 7r, 8v, 10r, 11r, 15v
3 Dec. 1527	Margaretha Schefferin (E)	HS 440: 272; ASB 226a: 28r
20 Feb. 1534	Undetermined	RV 833: 2r
26 March 1534	Catharina Lierin (E)	RB 8: 84ff.; HS 440: 276; ASB 221: 109r; ASB 226a: 29v; GNM HS: 19r
8 March 1536	Undetermined	RV 860:8r
14 Feb. 1536	Undetermined	RV 870: 17r
18 Sept. 1540	Undetermined	RV 921: 3r
5 Feb. 1541	Undetermined	RV 926: 5r
12 Dec. 1542	Margaretha Dhomanin (E)	RV 943: 27r, 31v, 32v, 33r, 34r, 36r, 38r: RV 950: 1v, 2v, 3v, 7r, 20r, 24r, 29r, 31r
29 April 1543	Undetermined	RV 956: 9v
22 April 1544	Undetermined	RV 969:15r

1549–1675: 152 dead babies reported; 79 infanticide suspects; 64 convictions; 57 executed

Date	Name of Accused	Source
2 May 1549	Dorothea Nicklin (F)	RB 24: 266r; RV 1034: 8r, 24v; 1035: 2r, 8r; 1036: 2r, 7r, 11r, 15v, 18r
14 May 1549	Undetermined	RV 1036: 36v
26 Sept. 1549	Margaretha Wagnerin (E)	HS 440: 177–78, 282; ASB 221: 135v; ASB 226a: 32v; RV 1040: 39v, 42r; 1041: 12v, 18v, 21r, 23r
28 Sept. 1549	Margaretha Hessin (E)	RV 1041: 24v, 38v; RV 1042: 6r, 15r, 16r, 27r, 29r; RV 1043: 3v, 8r, 10r, 12r
30 Oct. 1554	Susanna Anna Schimidtin (E)	HS 440: 285; 226a:33v; RV 1108: 39r; RV 1109: 1v, 3r, 9r, 25r, 28v
17 Sept. 1555	Undetermined	RB 29: 9r; RV 1121: 17r
25 March 1557	Undetermined	RV 1141: 17v
1 June 1557	Barbara Schwenderin (E)	HS 440: 286; ASB 221:157r; 226a: 34v; RV 1141: 33v, 34r, 35v; RV 1142: 28v, 31v; RV 1143: 8r, 9v, 18r–v; GNM HS: 23v
1 Oct. 1557	Undetermined	RV 1147: 36v
13 Oct. 1557	Undetermined	RV 1148: 9v
31 Jan. 1558	Undetermined	RV 1152: 6r, 7v, 11v
23 July 1560	Margarethe Hänin (E)	ASB 222: 6r; ASB 226a: 36v; RV 1183: 36r; RV 1185: 10r, 13r, 14r, 17v, 20r, 22r, 43r
17 Sept. 1560	Barbara Seegerin (E)	HS 440: 222; ASB 222: 6v; ASB 226a: 36v; RV 1185: 43r; RV 1186: 4r; RV 1187: 8r, 10r, 11r, 15v, 19v, 21v–22r; GNM HS: 25v
1 June 1564	Undetermined	RV 1237: 1r
26 June 1564	Undetermined	RV 1237: 31r, 34r
3 July 1568	Getrude Hoffmännin (E)	RV 1290: 10v; 1291: 5r, 7r, 10r, 22r
6 July 1569	*ein frembd. weib*	RV 1304: 29v
16 Aug. 1569	Gertraudt Peurin (S)	RV 1306: 18r, 26v, 29r; RV 1307: 3r
6 Dec. 1569	Helena Nusserin (E)	RV 1309: 2v, 4r, 12v, 13v, 20r, 21v 35v; 1310: 2r, 11v, 16v; GNM HS: 29v
29 May 1571	Margaretha Steinlin (aka Fuchsin) (E)	HS 440: 306; ASB 222: 47r; ASB 226a: 42r; GNM HS: 30v

Date	Name of Accused	Source
11 Nov. 1572	Elisabeth Geuderin (E)	RB 42: 280r–284v; HS 440: 309; ASB 226a: 43v
5 Nov. 1574	Undetermined	RV 1376: 14v
24 July 1576	Hans and Kunigunda Gumman (E)[1]	RB 42: 17r–19r, 48v–49r; HS 440: 314–15; ASB 226a: 45v–46r; F1 110: 34v–35r; GNM HS: 34r
28 Sept. 1576	Undetermined	RV 1400: 27v, 33r, 35r
27 Nov. 1576	Margaretha Schublin (F)	RB 42: 80r–81v; RV 1401:50r, 1402: 24r. 1403: 20r, 29r, 33r; GNM HS: 34r
6 March 1578	Apollonia Vöglin (E)	ASB 209: 21r–23r; RV 1419:22r, 1420:31v–32r; FS 6; MNG, 1: 696
23 June 1579	Margaretha Wallenhelderin (E)	ASB 209: 115v–166v; FS 8; MNG, 1: 693
1579	Anna Fiechtin (S)	RB/43: 63v–64v
26 Jan. 1580	Agnes Lengin; Elsbeth Ernstin; Margaretha Dörflerin (E)	HS 440: 325–36; HS 447: 1025–26; ASB 209:167r–172v; ASB 220: 91r–v; ASB 222: 91r–v; ASB 226a: 50v–51r; RV 1444: 43v, 55v, 59v, RV 1445:7v, 9r, RV 24v, 30v, 31v, 34v, 39r–v, 43v 43v; F1 Nr 109: 32; GNM HS: 36v–37r; FS 8–9
29 Feb. 1580	Kunigunde Dietmänin (S)(F)	RB 43: 62v–63v; FS 82
3 Dec. 1580	Anna Strölin (E)[2]	RB 51: 106r–109r; HS 440: 328; HS 447: 1033; ASB 209: 235r–236v; ASB 222: 99r–v; GNM HS: 37v; FS 10
14 Aug. 1582	Christina Zickhin (E)	RB 43:154v–156r; HS 440: 334; ASB 210: 43v–45r; ASB 222: 110r–v; ASB 226a: 52v; RV 1478: 74v–75r, 1479: 19r, 22v, 56v–57r, 61v; GNM HS 3857: 39r; FS 13
25 June 1583	Undetermined	RV 1491:46r
5 Nov. 1583	Undetermined	RV 1496: 31r, 32r
17 Nov. 1584	Anna Freyin (E)[3]	RB 43: 250r–253v; HS 440: 339; ASB 210: 146v–148r; ASB 222: 128r; FS 16
28 Aug. 1585	Undetermined	RV 1520: 39r–v; ASB 222:128r
21 June 1586	Undetermined	HS 447: 1092
15 Dec. 1586	Undetermined	HS 447: 1113; RV 1538: 2r
19 April 1587	Undetermined	HS 48: 538
18 Jan. 1588	Margaretha Hörnlein (E)	HS 440: 354; ASB 210: 303v–307v; ASB 226a: 57v; GNM HS: 43v; FS 24
25 June 1588	Undetermined	RV 1557: 41r
5 May 1590	Kunigunde Schedlin (E)	HS 447: 1142; ASB 211: 98r–100r; FS 28
7 July 1590	Margaretha Schwambergerin (E)	HS 447: 1144; RB 43: 19–20; ASB 211: 108v–110v; FS 28
20 Jan. 1591	Undetermined	RV 1590: 44v, 51r
2 April 1591	Elisabeth Rentzin (B)	RV 1593: 1r, 26r; F1 Nr 14: III: 1453
6 July 1592	Dorothea Hoffmännin (F)	HS 447: 1155; FS 99
6 Oct. 1593	Undetermined	RV 1625: 8r
11 Nov. 1593	Anna Arnoldin (F)	RB 45: 437r–438v; FS, 101
25 Feb. 1594	Appolonia Haasin (S)	RB 45: 331–335
6 June 1594	Undetermined	RV 1594: 16r
6 Sept. 1594	Undetermined	HS 447: 1180; RV 1637: 24r

[1] The victim was six weeks old.
[2] The victim was six years old.
[3] The victim was two years old.

Date	Name of Accused	Source
11 March 1595	Undetermined	RV 1644:9r
14 Aug. 1595	Undetermined	RV 1650:1r
15 March 1597	Veronika Kölerin (E)	RB 45: 198v–199v; HS 475: 140; ASB 213: 80v–81r; ASB 226a: 64v–65r; RV 1670: 37v, 39v, 40v, 44v, 46v, 53r; GNM HS 3857: 49v–50r; FS 44; StAN F1/109: 70
1 April 1597	Ottilia Demerin (S)	RB 45: 102–105; RV 1668: 36v, 41v, 1670: 25v, 37r, 41v, 46v, 50r
9 May 1598	Undetermined	RV 1684: 38r, 44r
11 July 1598	Undetermined	RV 1687: 4v
10 Sept. 1599	Undetermined	RV 1702: 23v
10 Dec. 1599	Margarethe Seelin (S)	RV 1705: 22r, 25v
26 Jan. 1600	Margaretha Teutschin (F)	FS 108
13 April 1600	Ursula Märvin (S)	ASB 226a: 68v
20 May 1600	Anna Kisslingen (F)	HS 440: 533; RB 44: 252ff.; FS 108
5 Feb. 1601	Undetermined	RV 1721: 15r
5 Sept. 1601	Undetermined	RV 1729: 9v
12 April 1602	Undetermined	HS 447: 1282; F1 Nr 47: 810r
28 April 1605	Undetermined	HS 50: 335v; HS 475: 22v; F1 Nr 14: 1598; F1 Nr 47: 835r
17 May 1606	Dorothea Meulin (E)	HS 50: 502; ASB 199:78v; ASB 216: 168v–176v; F1 Nr 14: 1612; FS, 65
18 May 1606	Undetermined	HS 447: 1330; HS 475: 18v;F1 Nr 47: 841v
26 June 1606	Susanna Reuthlin (E)	RB 46: 190ff.; HS 440: 417; HS 447: 1339; HS 475: 40v; ASB 216: 177r–191r; ASB 199: 89v; ASB 226: 40v–41r; 226a: 74r; F1 Nr 14: 1610; F1 Nr 47: 841v–842r; GNM HS: 62r–62v, FS 65
16 March 1607	Undetermined	F1 Nr 47: 844v
9 June 1607	Undetermined	HS 447: 1336; HS 475: 43r; F1 Nr 14: 1618
4 Aug. 1607	Margaretha Marckhardtin (E)	HS 440: 418; HS 447: 1339; 216: 226v–230v ASB 226: 31–32; 226a: 74r; F1 Nr 47: 848r; GNM HS: 64r–v; FS 66
8 Aug. 1609	Barbara Malerin (S)	ASB 200: 46v–47r
2 Oct. 1609	Elisabeth Greiffin (S)	ASB 200: 66r
4 Aug. 1610	Magdalena Fischerin (E)	HS 440: 420–421; HS 475: 32r; ASB 216: 289v–295v ASB 226: 40v–41r; ASB 226a: 75v; FS 69
8 Sept. 1610	Undetermined	HS 447: 1366
9 March 1611	Undetermined	HS 52: 294
3 April 1611	Elisabeth Schusterin (S)	HS 52: 273; ASB 200: 228r–v
6 July 1611	Magdalena Schottin (S)	HS 52: 337) ASB 200:441v–442r
8 Feb. 1614	Anna Emblin (E)	ASB 223: 184v–185r; ASB 226: 61r; ASB 226a: 79r; F1 Nr 14: 1764; F1 Nr. 47: 934r; GNM HS: 88v–89r; FS 74
4 March 1614	Undetermined	RV 1893: 62v
2 Oct. 1614	Undetermined	RV 1902: 41v
7 March 1615	Margaretha Lindnerin (E)	HS 475: 75v; AB 218; AB 226: 68v–69r; ASB 226a: 81r; F1 Nr 14: 1778; F1 Nr 47: 939v; GNM HS: 97r–v; FS 77

Date	Name of Accused	Source
28 Aug. 1616	Undetermined	HS 447: 1482; RV 1927:13v
13 Jun 1618	Undetermined	RV 36v–37r
13 Aug. 1618	Barbara Dallerin (E)	HS 475: 83v; ASB 218; ASB 226: 81r–82v; ASB 226a: 83r–v; F1 Nr 111: 9r–10r; GNM HS: 115r–116v
30 Jan. 1619	Elisabeth Pöppin (S)	RV 1959: 52r, 63r
4 Feb. 1619	Anna Dieppoltin (E)	HS 475: 83/lv; ASB 219: 9v–18r; ASB 226: 84r–v; ASB 226a: 84r; RV 1958: 38r, 52r, 55r; F1 Nr 14: 1810; GNM HS:120v–121r
22 Dec. 1619	Undetermined	HS 447: 1560
12 Nov. 1620	Undetermined	HS 447: 1580
7 Jan. 1621	Undetermined	HS 447: 1581
8 Feb. 1621	*ein magd* (B)	HS 474: 270
17 April 1621	Elisabeth Bräunin (E)	HS 447: 1587
16 Jan. 1622	Ursula Fuchsin (E)	ASB 219: 161r–165r; MNG, 1: 691ff.
14 March 1622	Margaretha Friedlin (E)	HS 447: 1704–1705
27 March 1623	Anna Maria Hupffauffin (E)	HS 447:1709; ASB 219: 260r–266v; ASB 226: 101v–102r; ASB 226a: 86v; F1 Nr 14: 1856; F1 Nr 111: 15v; GNM HS: 129v
9 Dec. 1624	Kunigunde Stammin (E)	HS 163: 154r; HS 475: 84r; ASB 219: 389r–393v; ASB 226: 101v–102r; ASB 226a: 167; F1 Nr 111: 16r; GNM HS: 130r
25 Feb. 1625	Margaretha Ferchin (E)	ASB 219: 394r–396v; RV 2040: 45v; MNG, 1: 696
4 Feb. 1626	Undetermined	RV 2052:36r–v
22 Nov. 1626	Barbara Kellin (E)	HS 474: 293; ASB 220:136v–139r; ASB 226a: 87v; F1 Nr 14: 1884; F1 Nr 47: 950v; F1 Nr 111: 17r
29 Nov. 1627	Undetermined	RV 2076: 75r–v
28 June 1639	Ursula Böhmin (E)	MNG, 1: 696
16 March 1641	Margaretha Voglin (E)	HS 475: 180v; ASB 226: 120r–122r; ASB 226a: 91v–92v; RV 2249: 16r–v, 24v, 45r; RV 2250: 6r, 9r, 13r–v, 15r–v; F1 Nr 47: 974v–975r; F1 Nr 111: 23r–24r; GNM HS: 131r–v
7 April 1641	Undetermined	RV 2250: 78r
20 April 1641	Undetermined	RV 2250: 119v
16 Oct. 1641	Magdalena Gemlin (E)	ASB 226: 122r; F1 Nr 111: 24r–25r; MNG, 1: 691
8 March 1642	Barbara Wernauerin (E)	HS 475: 186r; ASB 226: 123v–125r; ASB 226a: 92r–v; StAN F1 Nr 111: 25r–v; GNM HS: 131v
21 April 1642	Anna Teuflin (E)	HS 475: 186r; ASB 226: 125r– 126v ASB 226a: 92v; F1 Nr 111: 26r–v; GNM HS: 131v
18 Sept. 1643	Undetermined	RV 2282: 94r–v
14 Dec. 1644	Undetermined	RV 2299: 34r, 43r, 47r, 2307: 14r, 2308: 5v, 12v, 15r, 36r, 43v
29 March 1645	Undetermined	RV 2303: 5r
2 June 1645	Undetermined	RV 2305: 80v
18 June 1645	Undetermined	RV 2306: 51v, 57v
22 Dec. 1645	Undetermined	RV 2313: 19v–20r

Date	Name of Accused	Source
29 June 1646	Undetermined	RV 2320: 12v–13r
19 Oct. 1646	Undetermined	RV 2324: 11v
8 Jan. 1647	Kunigunde Riederin (E)	HS 475: 206v; ASB 226: 130r–131r; F1 Nr 111:28v–29r
28 Feb. 1648	Undetermined	RV 2342: 14v–15r, 37r
31 May 1649	Undetermined	RV 2359: 39r
13 Nov. 1649	Catharina Mayrin (E)	ASB 226: 136r–137r; ASB 226a: 94v; F1 Nr 111: 31v–32r; GNM HS: 132r
23 Nov. 1649	Undetermined	RV 2365: 73v
23 April 1650	Dorothea Geyrin (E)	ASB 226: 139v–140v; ASB 226a: 95r; RV 2370: 24v–25r, 49r–v, 2371:9v, 24r, 33r, 102v; GNM HS: 132r
9 June 1653	Anna Gräfin (E)	HS 475: 249v; ASB 226: 141r–142v; ASB 226a: 95v; F1 Nr 47: 1076v
17 April 1655	Undetermined	RV 2438: 16v
29 May 1655	Ursula Poppin (E)	HS 475: 259r; ASB 226: 145r–146v; ASB 226a: 96r–v; F1 Nr 47: 1055r; GNM HS: 132v
14 April 1657	Undetermined	RV 2464: 59r
16 Jun 1657	Anna Lenningerin (E)	HS 475: 267r; ASB 226: 150r–151r; ASB 226a: 97r; GNM HS: 132v
9 May 1658	Katharina Haasin (E)	ASB 226: 148v–149v; F1 Nr 47: 1095v; MNG, 1: 691
9 Oct. 1661	Undetermined	RV 2524: 15r–v
22 Oct. 1663	Anna Seyfriedin (E)	HS 475: 293v; ASB 226: 165v–167v; ASB 226a: 100r–v; RV 2550: 29r, 31r–v, 46r, 56v–57r, 85r, 2551: 20r–v, 23r–v, 28v, 30r, 32r–v, 33r, 38r–v, 43v–44r; F1 Nr 47: 1125v–1126r; GNM HS: 133r
31 Aug. 1665	Margarethe Götzin (E)	HS 475: 305r–v; ASB 226: 176v–178v; ASB 226a: 103v
11 May 1666	Undetermined	HS 475: 308v; F1 Nr 47: 1140v; F1 Nr 57
30 July 1667	Undetermined	HS 475: 374r; F1 Nr 47: 1147v; F1 Nr 57
2 Aug. 1667	Barbara Beerin (S)	RV 2602: 3v–4v, 10v–11r, 41v–42r, 45r, 52v, 56v–57r; RV 2603: 7r–v, 25v
31 March 1668	Undetermined	HS 475: 378v; RV 2611: 22r, 24r; F1 Nr 47: 1158v; F1 Nr 57
29 Oct. 1668	Undetermined	F1 Nr 47: 1156v; F1 Nr 57
8 Dec. 1668	Margarethe Irnsingerin (E)	HS 475: 321r; ASB 226: 182v–184r; ASB226a: 104v; F1 Nr 47: 1157r; GNM HS: 134r
26 Jan. 1669	Margarethe Wölfflin (E)	HS 475: 323r; ASB 226: 184r–185v; ASB 226a: 105r–v; F1 Nr 47: 115r–v; NM HS: 134r
10 Sept. 1669	Undetermined	HS 475: 325r; RV 2630: 32v; F1 Nr 47: 1161r; F1 Nr 57
14 Oct. 1669	Barbara Kresslin (E)[4]	HS 475: 325v; ASB 226: 187r–189r; ASB 226a: 105v–106r; RV 2631: 42r, RV 2362: 7v, 26v
15 Oct. 1669	Undetermined	HS 475: 325v; F1 Nr 57; F1 Nr 111: 57

[4] The victims were five and three years old.

Date	Name of Accused	Source
6 Nov. 1669	Agnes Dechmännin (S)	RV 2632: 7v, 26v
16 April 1670	Undetermined	RV 2638: 35r–v; F1 Nr 47: 1165v; F1 Nr 57
11 July 1670	Undetermined	HS 475: 331v; F1 Nr 57
9 Aug. 1671	Undetermined	RV 2655: 69r
9 Jan. 1674	Undetermined	HS 475: 352r; F1 Nr 47: 1101v; F1 Nr 57
12 March 1674	Undetermined	HS 475: 352v; RV 2690:9r, 38v; F1 Nr 47: 1102r; F1 Nr 57
6 April 1674	Undetermined	RV 2691: 28r
23 Feb. 1675	Margaretha Hofmännin (E)	HS 475: 356v; ASB 226: 203r–204r; ASB 226a: 108r–v; F1 Nr 47: 1106r; GNM HS: 135r
12 March 1675	Undetermined	HS 475: 357r; F1 Nr 47: 1106r; F1 Nr 57

1676–1806:[5] 130 dead babies reported; 66 infanticide suspects; 52 convictions; 41 executed

TOTAL

305 dead babies reported (273 since 1549)
160 infanticide suspects (145 since 1549)
128 convictions (116 since 1549)
102 executions (98 since 1549)

[5] After Karl Roetzer, "Die Delikte der Abtreibung, Kindstötung sowie Kindaussetzung und ihre Bestrafung in der Reichsstadt Nürnberg" (Ph.D. diss., Friedrich-Alexander Universität Erlangen, 1957).

ABBREVIATIONS

ASB	*Amt- und Standbücher* (Bayerisches Staatsarchiv Nürnberg, Bestand 52b)
FB1	Findelbuch 1 (Stadtarchiv Nürnberg D 10/3/4)
FB 2	Findelbuch 2 (Stadtarchiv Nürnberg D 10/3/6)
FKD	Findelkinder Database (see app. 1)
GNM	Germanisches Nationalmuseum (Nürnberg)
LKAN	Landeskirchliches Archiv Nürnberg
MVGN	*Mitteilungen des Vereins für die Geschichte der Stadt Nürnberg*
RV	*Ratsverlaß* (Bayerisches Staatsarchiv Nürnberg, Bestand 60a)
StaatsAN	Bayerisches Staatsarchiv Nürnberg
StadtAN	Stadtarchiv Nürnberg
WA	*D. Martin Luthers Werke: Kritische Gesamtausgabe* (Weimar: Herman Böhlau, 1883–; reprint, 1964–68)

INTRODUCTION

1. FB 1: 173 (7 and 16 August 1599); also RV 1701: 12v (7 August 1599). The Findel register gives the baby's age as "about one year old," and the RV says "three-quarters of a year old"; I have used an average of the two figures.

2. John Boswell, *The Kindness of Strangers: The Abandonment of Children in Western Europe from Late Antiquity to the Renaissance* (New York: Pantheon, 1988), 6–7.

3. A self-described "Sunday historian," Ariès based his argument on whatever scarce historical sources he could find for the premodern period, chiefly brief and scattered textual references, material artifacts such as clothing and toys, and artistic representations of children. His objective, he readily admitted, was not so much a reconstruction of the experience of children (and in particular their relationship with their parents) as a philosophical exploration of how and when adults became so "obsessed with the physical, moral and sexual problems of childhood." Philippe Ariès, *Centuries of Childhood: A Social History of Family Life*, trans. Robert Baldwick (New York: Knopf, 1962), esp. 395ff.

4. Lawrence Stone, *The Family, Sex and Marriage in England, 1500–1800* (London: Harper & Row, 1977), 105–7; Lloyd de Mause, ed., *The History of Childhood* (New York: Psychohistory Press, 1974), 3. See also Edward Shorter, *The Making of the Modern Family* (New York: Basic Books, 1975); and Elizabeth Badinter, *Mother Love: Myth and Reality; Motherhood in Modern History* (New York: Macmillan, 1981). Explanations for the relatively recent rise in sentimentalized views of children varied, though most focused on reasons variously connected to social transformations wrought by capitalism, such as the rise of the middle class and the separation of the home and workplace, which in turn triggered the subsequent "cocooning" role of the nuclear family and greater idealization of children and childhood.

5. Linda A. Pollock, *Forgotten Children: Parent-Child Relations from 1500 to 1900* (Cambridge: Cambridge University Press, 1983); Steven Ozment, *When Fathers Ruled* (Cambridge: Harvard University Press, 1983). Ozment later credited the spread of the Ariès thesis to "many scholars and pundits" employing "quasi-scientific" methods and ahistorical thinking, with the worst culprits being Michael Mitterauer, Reinhold Siedler, Edward Shorter, Jean-Louis Flandrin, and Lawrence Stone. He also held many gender studies works of the 1980s and 1990s responsible for perpetuating this flawed model. See Ozment, *Ancestors: The Loving Family in Old Europe* (Cambridge:

Harvard University Press, 2001), 5ff. Other influential attacks on the Ariès thesis were Ralph A. Houlbrooke, *The English Family, 1450–1700* (London and New York: Longman, 1984); Valerie Fildes, "Maternal Feelings Reassessed," in *Women as Mothers in Pre-Industrial England: Essays in Memory of Dorothy McLaren*, ed. Valerie Fildes (London: Routledge, 1990); Shulamith Shahar, *Childhood in the Middle Ages*, trans. Chaya Galai (London: Routledge, 1990); Hugh Cunningham, *The Children of the Poor: Representations of Childhood since the Seventeenth Century* (Oxford: Blackwell, 1991); Ilana Krausman Ben-Amos, *Adolescence and Youth in Early Modern England* (New Haven: Yale University Press, 1994); and Louis Haas, *The Renaissance Man and His Children: Childbirth and Early Childhood in Florence, 1300–1600* (New York: St. Martin's Press, 1998).

6. Hugh Cunningham (*Children and Childhood in Western Society Since 1500* [London: Longman, 1995], 187 ff.) actually argues that the most transformative period for Western concepts and experiences of childhood has been the twentieth century.

7. Cf. Léon Lallemand, *Histoire des enfants abandonnés et délaissés: Études sur la protection de l'enfance aux diverses époques de la civilisation* (Paris: A. Picard, 1885).

8. Natalie Zemon Davis, "Poor Relief, Humanism, and Heresy," in *Society and Culture in Early Modern France* (Stanford: Stanford University Press, 1975); Brian Pullan, *Rich and Poor in Renaissance Venice* (Cambridge: Harvard University Press, 1971); R. W. Tawney, *Religion and the Rise of Capitalism: A Historical Study* (1926; New York: Harcourt Brace, 1952); W. K. Jordan, *Philanthropy in England, 1480–1660: A Study of the Changing Pattern of English Social Aspiration* (New York: Russell Sage Foundation, 1959).

9. See, especially, Philip Gavitt, *Charity and Children in Renaissance Florence: The Ospedale degli Innocenti, 1410–1536* (Ann Arbor: University of Michigan Press, 1990).

10. Thomas Robert Malthus, *An Essay on the Principle of Population*, 7th ed. (London, 1872; reprint, New York: A. M. Kelley, 1971), 151.

11. Boswell, *Kindness of Strangers*, 426. David Ransel has characterized the "transparent and political purpose" of Boswell's work as to convince readers "that the conventional family models based upon blood or marital relations are recent impositions and not the typical family arrangements known to history." "Child Abandonment in European History: A Symposium," *Journal of Family History* 17, no. 1 (1992): 19.

12. Thomas Safley perceives some modern cultural patterns among historians' characterizations of the motives of early modern governmental leaders in dealing with social welfare, ranging from an Anglo-American group who stress good intentions overwhelmed by the sheer magnitude of the problem, to French historians who characterize relief efforts as futile and often cynical gestures toward an insurmountable problem, to scholars of "Central European studies" who stress continuity and tradition in governmental responses from the medieval to modern eras. The "Anglo-American" group consists of Cissie Fairchilds, Allan Forrest, Olwen Hufton, Colin Jones, Linda Martz, Katherine Norberg, and K. D. M. Snell. The sole French scholar cited by Safley is Jean-Pierre Gutton. Under the "Central European studies" rubric, he includes Mack Walker, Max Bisle, Thomas Fischer, Robert Jütte, Werner Moritz, Christoph Sachße, and Florian Tennstedt, as well as Philip Gavitt, a scholar of Florence, and Brian Pullan, an expert on Venice. Safley, *Charity and Economy in the Orphanages of Early Modern Augsburg* (Atlantic Highlands: Humanities Press, 1997), 9.

13. For a stimulating discussion of these historiographical tendencies, see Paul Freedman and Gabrielle Spiegel, "Medievalisms Old and New: The Rediscovery of Alterity in North American Medieval Studies, *American Historical Review* 103 (1998): 677–704.

14. This has been a consistent criticism, for instance, of Lawrence Stone's *Family, Sex, and Marriage.* Steven Ozment's *Three Behaim Boys Growing Up in Early Modern Germany: A Chronicle of Their Lives* (New Haven: Yale University Press, 1990), like his *Magdalena and Balthasar: An Intimate Portrait of Life in Sixteenth-century Europe* (New York: Simon and Schuster, 1986), provides a fascinating insider's view of youths in a prosperous mercantile family but cannot speak to many experiences of those much more numerous children and youths from the lower ranks of society. For a thoughtful reflection on the difficulties of getting at the perspectives of the poor, see Tim Hitchcock, Peter King, and Pamela Sharpe, eds., *Chronicling Poverty: The Voices and Strategies of the English Poor, 1640–1840* (London: St. Martin's Press, 1997), 1–8.

15. See Robert Jütte, *Poverty and Deviance in Early Modern Europe* (Cambridge: Cambridge University Press, 1994), 1 ff., on both historiographical tendencies. The most important development in changing perspectives has been the growth of scholarship on "family strategies," described by Tamara K. Hareven, "The Impact of Family History and the Life Course on Social History," in *Family History Revisited: Comparative Perspectives*, ed. Richard Wall, Tamara K. Hareven, and Josef Ehmer, with the assistance of Markus Cerman (Newark: University of Delaware Press, 2001), 25–28.

16. See, for example, Beate Schuster, "Der Widerspenstigen Zähmung? Anmerkungen zu Norbert Schindlers Buch *Widerspenstige Leute. Studien zur Volkskultur in der frühen Neuzeit*," *Historische Anthropologie* 1 (1993): 294–305, followed by a rejoinder from Schindler, 306ff.; also Martin Dinges, "Ehrenhändel als 'Kommunikative Gattungen': Kultureller Wandel und Volkskulturbegriff," *Archiv für Kulturgeschichte* 75 (1993): 359–93.

17. On problems with a statist perspective, see especially Heinrich Richard Schmidt, "Sozialdisziplinierung? Ein Pläyoder für das Ende des Etatismus in der Konfessionalisierungsforschung," *Historische Zeitschrift* 265 (1997): 639–82.

18. See especially Esther Goody, *Parenthood and Social Reproduction: Fostering and Occupational Roles in West Africa* (Cambridge: Cambridge University Press, 1982); C. Fonseca, "Orphanages, Foundlings, and Foster Mothers: The System of Child Circulation in a Brazilian Squatter Settlement," *Anthropological Quarterly* 59 (1986): 15–27; Suzanne Lallemand, *La circulation des enfants en société traditionelle. Prêt, don, échange* (Paris: Éditions L'Harmattan, 1993); Isabel dos Guimarães Sá, "Circulation of Children in Eighteenth-century Portugal," in *Abandoned Children*, ed. Catherine Painter-Brick and Malcolm T. Smith (Cambridge: Cambridge University Press, 2000), 27–40; Ann Blum, "Public Welfare and Child Circulation in Mexico City, 1877–1925," *Journal of Family History* 23, no. 3 (July 1998): 240–71; and Nara Milanich, "The Casa de Huerfanos and Child Circulation in Late nineteenth-century Chile," *Journal of Social History* 38, no. 2 (Winter 2004): 311–40.

19. "En tout cas, lorsqu'elle y apparaît, la prise en compte de la circulation enfantine et ses modalités (fréquence, unilatéralité ou réciprocité, sexe, âge, etc.) confère un éclairage plus précis à l'entité familiale considéréré, et au mécanisme de recrutement de ses membres." Lallemand, *La circulation des enfants*, 39. The term "child circulation" plays a key role in Boswell's *Kindness of Strangers*, particularly as he approvingly contrasts the informal model of most of the Middle Ages with the insidious influence of new foundling homes from the thirteenth century on. His usage of the term "child circulation," though, remains limited to anonymous child abandonment, what he calls "the social redistribution of surplus children," and does not include informal and temporary fostering among friends and relatives or service positions among teenagers.

20. In addition to fosterages based on nurturance, training, sponsorship, and jural identity, Esther Goody mentions the new category of genitor/genitix (donator of sperm or an egg in artificial insemination or proxy pregnancy). "Sharing and Transferring Components of Parenthood: The West African Case," in *Adoption et fosterage*, ed. Mireille Corbier (Paris: DeBoccard, 1999), 369–88. On "delegated motherhood," see C. Bledsoe, "'No Success Without Struggle': Social Mobility and Hardship for Sierra Leone Children," *Man* 25 (1990): 70–88; and S. Blaffer Hrdy, "Fitness Tradeoffs in the History and Evolution of Delegated Mothering with Special Reference to Wet-nursing, Abandonment, and Infanticide," *Ethnology and Sociobiology* 13 (1992): 409–42. Legal adoption was actually rare in Europe during the medieval and early modern eras.

21. The best survey on this sprawling literature is Hugh Cunningham, *Children and Childhood in Western Society since 1500* (London: Longman, 1995). See also the learned terminological exposition in Boswell, *Kindness of Strangers*, 26–39.

22. Catherine Painter-Brick, "Nobody's Children: A Reconsideration of Child Abandonment," in *Abandoned Children*, ed. Painter-Brick, 1–11.

23. In the sixteenth and seventeenth centuries, the term *Waise* was often used interchangeably with *Frembdling* to describe a minor with no foster parent. The term *Waisenhaus* was current during the sixteenth century, but there was no feminine form of the word *Waise* until the eighteenth century, when *Waisenmädchen* appeared. *Grimms Deutsches Wörterbuch* (Leipzig: S. Hirzel, 1922), 27: 1043–57; also Heide Kallert, "Waisenhaus und Arbeitserziehung im 17. und 18. Jahrhundert" (Ph.D. diss., Johann Wolfgang Goethe University Frankfurt am Main, 1964), 11.

24. This is even true of two admirable recent works on abandoned children and orphans: Thomas Max Safley, *Children of the Laboring Poor: Expectation and Experience among the Orphans of Early Modern Augsburg* (Leiden: Brill, 2005) and Nicholas Terpstra, *Abandoned Children of the Italian Renaissance: Orphan Care in Florence and Bologna* (Baltimore: Johns Hopkins University Press, 2005). Both repeatedly acknowledge the roles of parental agency and informal networks of support, but the emphasis of both studies is overwhelmingly on institutional care as opposed to the broader context of child circulation.

25. *De la comparaison à l'histoire croisée*, ed. Michael Werner and Bénédicte Zimmermann, special ed. of *Le genre humain* (April 2004): 7.

26. The pioneering microhistorian Carlo Ginzburg addresses the question of typicality in his celebrated *The Cheese and the Worms: The Cosmos of a Sixteenth-century Miller*, trans. John and Anne Tedeschi (Baltimore: Johns Hopkins University Press, 1980), xx ff., as well as in his coauthored article with Carlo Poni, "Was is Mikrogeschichte?" *Geschichtswerkstatt* 6 (1985): 48–52, and "Mikro-Historie. Zwei oder drei Dinge, die ich von ihr weiß," in the "new" social history journal, *Historische Anthropologie* 1, no. 2 (1993): 169–92. On the methods of *Alltagsgeschichte* in Germany, see *The History of Everyday Life: Reconstructing Historical Experiences and Ways of Life*, ed. Alf Lüdtke (Princeton: Princeton University Press, 1995); and Martin Dinges, "'Historische Anthropologie' und 'Gesellschaftsgeschichte': Mit dem Lebensstilkonzept zu einer 'Alltagsgeschichte' der Frühen Neuzeit?" *Zeitschrift für historische Forschung* 24 (1997): 179–214. For examples of *Alltagsgeschichte* in early modern Germany, see Richard van Dülmen, *Kultur und Alltag in der frühen Neuzeit. 16. Bis 18. Jahrhundert*, 3 vols. (Munich: C. H. Beck, 1990–94); Arthur E. Imhof, *Lost Worlds: How Our European Ancestors Coped with Everyday Life and Why Life Is So Hard Today*, trans. Thomas Robisheaux (Charlottesville: University of Virginia Press, 1996); and Albert Schnyder-Burghartz,

Alltag und Lebensformen auf der Basler Landschaft um 1700—vorindustrielle ländliche Kultur und Gesellschaft aus mikrohistorischer Perspektive: Bretzwill und das obere Waldenburger Amt von 1690 bis 1750 (Basel: Verlag des Kantons Basel-Landschaft, 1992). For two very different examples of microhistory in the same field, see David Sabean, *Power in the Blood: Village Discourse in Early Modern Germany* (Cambridge: Cambridge University Press, 1984); and Michael Kunze, *Highroad to the Stake: A Tale of Witchcraft*, trans. William E. Yuill (Chicago: University of Chicago Press, 1987).

27. Walter Benjamin's phrase is appropriated by Norbert Schindler in describing his own attempts to capture "lived experience." Norbert Schindler, *Rebellion, Community and Custom in Early Modern Germany*, trans. Pamela E. Selwyn (Cambridge: Cambridge University Press, 2003), 16–18. See Geoff Eley, foreword, in *History of Everyday Life*, vii–xi, on the extraordinarily slow acceptance of microhistory among established German academics. See also Schindler, *Rebellion, Community and Custom*, 1–18, on resistance to historical anthropology among German historians.

28. On the development of the field since its founding by the Dutch historians Jacob Presser and Rudolf Dekker in the late 1960s, see *Ego-Dokumente. Annäherung an den Menschen in der Geschichte*, ed. Winfried Schulze (Berlin: Akademie Verlag, 1996), especially the editor's "Preliminary remarks for the conference 'Ego-Documents' [held in 1992 in Bad Homburg]," 12 ff. See also Jan Peters, "Wegweiser zum Innenleben? Möglichkeiten und Grenzen der Untersuchung populärer Selbstzeugnisse der frühen Neuzeit," *Historische Anthropologie* 2, no. 1 (1993): 235–49; and *Das dargestellte Ich. Studien zu Selbstzeugnissen des späteren Mittelalters und der frühen Neuzeit*, ed. Klaus Arnold, Sabine Schmolinsky, and Urs Martin Zahnd (Bochum: Winkler, 1999).

29. Schindler, *Rebellion, Community and Custom*, 15. Arlette Farge similarly aims to "perceive outlines of some shattered figures." *Fragile Lives: Violence, Power and Solidarity in Eighteenth-century Paris* (Cambridge: Harvard University Press, 1993), 5.

30. French historians have the longest history of successful use of "juridico-literary" material for this purpose, dating from Pierre Chaunu, "Inquisition et vie quotidienne dans l'Amérique espagnole au XVIIe siècle," *Annales ESC* 11 (1956): 228–36. Natalie Davis describes her own method of reading against the grain as "attending closely to the means and settings for producing the stories and to the interests held by both the narrator and audience in the storytelling event." Natalie Zemon Davis, *Fiction in the Archives* (Stanford: Stanford University Press, 1987), 4. Winfried Schulze makes the case for including such material in an expanded understanding of ego documents in *Ego-Dokumente*, 20ff., and Wolfgang Behringer weighs the advantages and difficulties of using such sources as ego-documents in the same volume, "Gegenreformation als Generationskonflikt oder: Verhörprotokolle und andere administrative Quellen zur Mentalitätsgeschichte," 275–93. For a useful summary of the field, see Richard van Dülmen, *Historische Anthropologie: Entwicklung, Probleme, Aufgaben* (Cologne: Böhlau, 2000).

31. In this respect, I echo Lyndal Roper's call for "an approach to early modern subjectivities which will recognise the collective elements of culture without trivializing individual subjectivity." Roper, *Oedipus and the Devil: Witchcraft, Sexuality, and Religion in Early Modern Europe* (London: Routledge, 1994), 26.

32. The first quotation is from Michel Foucault, "La vie des hommes infâmes," *Cahiers du chemin* 29 (January 1977): 12, as translated in Farge, *Fragile Lives*, 1.

33. Farge, *Fragile Lives*, 3. Farge adds that "emotion is not fusion between oneself and the archives or the annihilation of all capacity to think in concrete terms, but rather the development of a reciprocity with the object, by which access is given to meaning"

(4). See also *Subjektive Welten. Wahrnehmung und Identität in der Neuzeit*, ed. Martin Rheinheimer (Neumünster: Wachholtz, 1998).

34. Stephen Greenblatt and Catherine Gallagher, *Practicing New Historicism* (Chicago: University of Chicago Press, 2000), 63. According to Greenblatt and Gallagher (49ff.), "most mainstream historians" are fated to interpret all past sources and evidence within the context of their respective grand historical narrative, thereby distancing the modern observer still more from the actual voice and "experience" of his or her subject(s). This characterization of "mainstream historians" strikes me as curiously dated, however, particularly on the inability of modern scholars to imagine "a multiplicity of pasts" or historians' resistance to anecdotes that puncture grand narratives, treating them only as "rhetorical embellishments, illustrations, or moments of relief from analytic generalization." My method could of course be interpreted by a new historicist as another instance of a historian attempting to exercise a "stabilizing and silencing function in analyses that [seek] to declare the limits of the sayable and thinkable" (16).

35. Helmut Walser Smith, "Geschichte zwischen den Fronten. Meisterwerke der neuesten Geschichtsschreibung," *Geschichte und Gesellschaft* 22 (1996): 592–608. The history of early modern "experience" was the subject of a relatively recent German conference and resulted in the published collection, *"Erfahrung" als Kategorie der Frühneuzeitgeschichte*, ed. Paul Münch, Historische Zeitschrift Beiheft (Neue Folge), 31 (Munich: Oldenbourg, 2001). See especially the editor's introduction, 11–27, on the epistemological and methodological challenges of the subject.

36. Introduction, *History of Everyday Life*, 9.

37. I am indebted to Tom Brady for underscoring this important point to me.

38. The central issue here is not merely the difficulty in reconciling differences in scale and subjects but also the coherent theoretical underpinnings of past social history as opposed to the dispersed and unconnected experiences described in microhistories. In a recent forum on the subject, Geoff Eley declares the old social history project dead and calls for a basic pluralism of approaches and questions, while William Sewell, Gabielle Spiegel, and Manu Goswami suggest other coherent theoretical frameworks or approaches, including "semiotic practices" and "built environments." "AHR Forum: Geoff Eley's 'A Crooked Line,'" *American Historical Review* 115, no. 2 (April 2008): 393–437.

39. Charles Tilly, "Family History, Social History, and Social Change," *Journal of Family History* 12, nos. 1–3 (1987): 322. See also van Dülmen, *Historische Anthropologie*, 95–101; Winfried Schulze, "Mikrohistorie versus Makrohistorie? Anmerkungen zu einem aktuellen Thema," *Historische Methode*, ed. Christian Meier and Jöen Rüsen (Munich: Deutscher Taschenbuch Verlag, 1988), 319–44; and Jacques Revel, ed., *Jeux d'échelles: La micro-analyse à l'experience* (Paris, 1994).

40. See the outstanding examples of Kevin Boyle, *Arc of Justice: A Saga of Race, Civil Rights, and Murder in the Jazz Age* (New York: Henry Holt, 2004); Helmut Walser Smith, *The Butcher's Tale: Murder and Anti-Semitism in a German Town* (New York: W. W. Norton, 2002); Mack Walker, *The Salzburg Transaction: Expulsion and Redemption in Eighteenth-century Germany* (Ithaca: Cornell University Press, 1992); and John Demos, *The Unredeemed Captive: A Family Story from Early America* (New York: Knopf, 1994).

41. See, for instance, Laurel Thatcher Ulrich's innovative and compelling *A Midwife's Tale: The Life of Martha Ballard, based on Her Diary, 1785–1812* (New York: Random House, 1990).

42. Ozment's *Madgalena and Balthasar* and *Three Behaim Boys* offer counterexamples to the Ariès and Stone theses, while his engaging *Bürgermeister's Daughter: Scandal in a Sixteenth-Century German Town* (New York: St. Martin's Press, 1996), is less concerned with links to larger academic debates.

43. For two excellent examples of the prosopographical, or collective history, methodology in early modern Germany, see Thomas A. Brady, Jr., *Ruling Class and Regime at Strasbourg, 1520–55* (Leiden: Brill, 1978); and Peter Wallace, *Communities and Conflict in Early Modern Germany, 1557–1730* (Atlantic Highlands: Humanities Press, 1995).

44. Boswell makes a similar stylistic decision for *The Kindness of Strangers* (45–46), though the lack of available statistical evidence for the medieval period is also crucial in his choice.

45. "eine spezifische Verbindung von Beobachterpositionen, Blickwinkel und Objekt." Michael Werner and Bénédicte Zimmerman, "Vergleich, Transfer, Verflechtung. Der Ansatz der *Histoire croisée* und die Herausforderung des Transnationalen," *Geschichte und Gesellschaft* 28 (2002): 609. See also *Le travail et la nation. Histoire croisée de la France et de l'Allemagne*, ed. Bénédicte Zimmermann, Claude Didry, and Peter Wagner (Paris: Éditions de la MSH, 1999); Michael Werner and Bénédicte Zimmerman, "Penser l'histoire croisée: Entre empirie et réflexivité," *Annales Histoire, Sciences sociales* 58, no. 1 (Jan.–Feb. 2003): 7–36; Michael Werner and Bénédicte Zimmermann, *De la comparaison à l'histoire croisée* (Paris: Seuil, 2004). The immediate concern of Werner and Zimmerman is overcoming the difficulties inherent in most transnational or international comparisons, particularly in their own comparative work in modern German and French social history. They also readily acknowledge the influence of postcolonial debates and their own desire to reconcile the post-1989 forces of globalization with "le caractère irreducible du local." Werner and Zimmerman, "Penser l'histoire croisée," 7. On connected history, see *The Making of the Modern World: Connected Histories, Divergent Paths, 1500 to the Present*, ed. Robert W. Strayer (New York: St. Martin's Press, 1989); and Serge Gruzinski, "Les mondes mêlés de la monarchie catholique et autres 'connected histories,'" *Annales Histoire, Sciences Sociales* 56, no. 1 (2001): 85–117. For an example of shared history, see the example of Ann Laura Stoler and Frederic Cooper, "Between Metropole and Colony: Rethinking a Research Agenda," in *Tensions of Empire: Colonial Cultures in a Bourgeois World*, ed. Ann Laura Stoler and Frederic Cooper (Berkeley: University of California Press, 1997), 1–56. On braided history, see Natalie Zemon Davis, *Trickster Travels: A Sixteenth-century Muslim between Worlds* (New York: Hill & Wang, 2006).

46. Werner and Zimmerman, "Vergleich, Transfer, Verflechtung," 619–20.

47. Werner and Zimmerman, "Penser l'histoire croisée," 10. Cf. O. G. Oexle, *Geschichtswissenschaft im Zeichen des Historismus. Studien zu Problemgeschichten der Moderne* (Göttingen, Vandehoeck & Ruprecht, 1996).

48. Katherine A. Lynch, *Individuals, Families, and Communities in Europe, 1200–1800: The Urban Foundations of Western Society* (Cambridge: Cambridge University Press, 2003), 15.

49. The single best overview of daily life in early modern Nuremberg remains Strauss, *Nuremberg*. I have also found the following surveys particularly helpful: Emil Reicke, *Geschichte der Reichsstadt Nürnberg* (Nuremberg: Joh. Phil. Rawschen, 1896; reprint, Neustadt an der Aisch: Ph. C. W. Schmidt, 1983); Werner Schultheiß, *Kleine Geschichte Nürnbergs*, 3rd ed. (Nuremberg: Lorenz Spindler Verlag, 1997); *Nürnberg. Eine europäische Stadt in Mittelalter und Neuzeit*, ed. Helmut Neuhaus (Nuremberg:

Selbstverlag des Vereins für Geschichte der Stadt Nürnberg, 2000); and the indispensable reference work, *Stadtlexikon Nürnberg*, ed. Michael Diefenbacher and Rudolf Endres (Nuremberg: W. Tümmels Verlag, 2000).

50. Lynch, *Individuals, Families, and Communities*, 28–30.

51. "Was gut sein sollte, wurde aus Nürnberg verschrieben." Reicke, *Geschichte der Reichsstadt Nürnberg*, 998.

52. For an overview of Nuremberg and the arts during the sixteenth century, see Strauss, *Nuremberg*, 231–83.

53. Ibid., 234.

54. Ibid., 12; *Brevis Germaniae descriptio*, 74; cited in Klaus Leder, *Kirche und Jugend in Nürnberg und seinem Landgebiet: 1400–1800* (Neustadt an der Aisch: Degener, 1973). 1. My brief description of Nuremberg's appearance is greatly indebted to Gerald Strauss's much more lyrical and evocative description in *Nuremberg*, 9–35.

55. Reicke, *Geschichte der Reichsstadt Nürnberg*, 620–21, 724–25; Willi Rüger, *Mittelalterliches Almosenwesen. Die Almosenordnungen der Reichsstadt Nürnberg*, Nürnberger Beiträge zu den Wirtschafts- und Sozialwissenschaften, 31 (Nuremberg: Krische, 1932), 26–29; Rudolf Endres, "Armenstiftungen und Armenschulen in Nürnberg in der Frühneuzeit," *Jahrbuch für fränkische Landesforschung* 53 (1992): 1ff.

CHAPTER ONE

1. Possibly a reference to "maiden's palm" (*Jungfernpalm*), a well-known abortifacient, suggesting that Cunz already had a reputation as a cad.

2. ASB 209: 21r–23r (12 February 1578); RV 1419: 22r, RV 1420: 31v–32r (4 and 27 February 1578).

3. Heide Wunder, *He Is the Sun, She Is the Moon: Women in Early Modern Germany*, trans. Thomas Dunlap (Cambridge: Harvard University Press, 1998), 24–25; John Gillis, *Youth and History: Tradition and Change in European Age Relations, 1770–Present*, expanded student ed. (Orlando: Academic Press, 1981), 7.

4. In her early seventeenth-century sample, Renate Dürr found that 30 percent of maids had started work by age ten and 70 percent by the age of sixteen. *Mägde in der Stadt. Das Beispiel Schwäbisch Hall in der Frühen Neuzeit* (Frankfurt: Campus, 1995), 147–48, 160. Domestic service cut across all social strata: 30 percent of the maids in Schwäbisch Hall, for instance, came from upper-class families (153–54). Earlier estimates of 75 percent of all youths in service (Alan MacFarlane, *The Family Life of Ralph Josselin, a Seventeenth-century Clergyman: An Essay in Historical Anthropology* [Cambridge: Cambridge University Press, 1970], 209) and even 50 percent (Michael Mitterauer, "Gesinddienst und Jugendphase im europäischen Vergleich," *Geschichte und Gesellschaft* 11 [(1985]: 185–87) are now generally discredited as too high for most of early modern Europe.

5. See chapter 4 and Nuremberg ordinances forbidding the selling of a daughter to the city's brothel or trading of them by its keeper. Merry E. Wiesner, *Working Women in Renaissance Germany* (New Brunswick: Rutgers University Press, 1986), 94; also Lyndal Roper, *The Holy Household: Women and Morals in Reformation Augsburg* (Oxford: Clarendon Press, 1989).

6. A small minority of girls were trained in spinning and sewing in their own houses by *Lehrfrauen* (female instructors). Some others attended German schools, which were common in many cities, including Speyer, Bern, Regensburg, Mainz, Zurich, and Nuremberg. Small "corner schools" (*Winkelschulen*) were also a common urban phenomenon of the early modern era: Braunschweig, for instance, had 39 by

1673, with a combined enrollment of about 600. Gillis, *Youth and History*, 217; Christopher R. Friedrichs, "Deutsche Schulen nach der Reformation: Einige Belege aus Braunschweig," *Braunschweigisches Jahrbuch* 63 (1982): 127–35; Olwen Hufton, *The Prospect Before Her: A History of Women in Western Europe: Volume 1, 1500–1800* (London: HarperCollins, 1995), 213ff.

7. See Judith M. Bennett and Amy M. Froide, "A Singular Past," in *Singlewomen in the European Past, 1250–1800*, ed. Judith M. Bennett and Amy M. Froide (Philadelphia: University of Pennsylvania Press, 1999), 1–37.

8. Marriage ages represent a composite of thirty-eight early modern family reconstitution studies, cited in Antoinette Fauve-Chamoux, "Marriage, Widowhood, and Divorce," in *The History of the European Family*, ed. David I. Kertzer and Marzio Barbagli (New Haven: Yale University Press, 2001), 1: 245–47. On the original and revised "European" models of late marriage, see John Hajnal, "European Marriage Patterns in Perspective," in *Population in History: Essays in Historical Demography*, ed. D. V. Glass and D. E. C. Eversley (Chicago: Aldine, 1965); as well as the later "Two Kinds of Preindustrial Household Formation System," *Population and Development Review* 8, no. 3 (1982): 449–94; also Jan de Vries, "Population," in *Handbook of European History, 1400–1600: Late Middle Ages, Renaissance and Reformation*, ed. Thomas Brady et al. (Leiden: Brill, 1994), 28, table 3; Rainer Beck, "Illegitimität und voreheliche Sexualität auf dem Land. Unterfinning, 1671–1770," in *Die Kultur der einfachen Leute*, ed. Richard van Dülmen (Munich: C. H. Beck, 1983), 118; and Maryanne Kowaleski, "Singlewomen in Medieval and Modern Europe: The Demographic Perspective," in *Singlewomen*, ed. Bennett and Froide, 38–81.

9. See Dürr, *Mägde in der Stadt*, 99ff., on the common representation of maids as loose women, and 229ff. on their apparent overrepresentation in such cases. This pattern continued well into the nineteenth century. Two-thirds of unwed mothers in eighteenth-century Paris and Moscow were maids. Louise A. Tilly et al., "Child Abandonment in European History: A Symposium," *Journal of Family History* 17, no. 1 (1992): 9.

10. Dürr's study found that although most maids left their hometown, 80 percent remained within a twenty-five-kilometer radius of the city. A few cities such as Basel were known to attract maids from as much as eighty miles, away but this was not the norm. Dürr, *Mägde in der Stadt*, 186–87; Wunder, *He Is the Sun*, 133.

11. By the sixteenth century, these agencies (first mentioned in 1421) were restricted to eight in number and were usually no more than small stands in the marketplace or private residences with special signs hanging outside. After a minimal background check, the applicant was placed in an "appropriate" position and the agency was paid a commission. In 1579 women agents were forbidden to place male servants and were supposed to refuse servants who could not give just cause for their departure from their most recent employment. Agents were also supposed to show no favoritism in placement, excluding only those employers who had a history of abuse. Merry E. Wiesner, "Paternalism in Practice: The Control of Servants and Prostitutes in Early Modern German Cities," in *The Process of Change in Early Modern Europe: Essays in Honor of Miriam Usher Chrisman*, ed. Phillip N. Bebbs and Sherrin Marshall (Athens: Ohio University Press, 1988), 180–81; Wiesner, *Working Women*, 84ff.

12. Michael Mitterauer, *A History of Youth*, trans. R. Graeme Dunphy (Oxford: Blackwell, 1992), 103.

13. Walter Hartinger, "Bayerisches Dienstbotenleben auf dem Land vom 16. bis zum 18. Jahrhundert," *Zeitschrift zur Bayerischen Landesgeschichte* 38 (1975): 604. Sometimes

a deposit, known, for example, as a *Weinkauff* in Schwäbisch Hall, was required to make a contract binding. Dürr, *Mägde in der Stadt*, 215.

14. On servant wages, see R. Engelsing, "Einkommen der Dienstboten in Deutschland zwischen dem 16. und 20. Jahrhundert," *Jahrbuch des Instituts für Deutsche Geschichte der Universität Tel Aviv*, 2 (1973): 21–23; also Dürr, *Mägde in der Stadt*, 149ff.; and Merry Wiesner, "Gender and the World of Work," in *Germany: A New Social and Economic History: Volume 1, 1450–1630*, ed. Bob Scribner (London: Arnold, 1996), 209ff.

15. In the early sixteenth century, female workers earned on average one-third that of male day laborers. Still, there had been some increase over the very low salaries at the beginning of the fifteenth century. Valentin Groebner, *Ökonomie ohne Haus. Zum Wirtschaften armer Leute in Nürnberg am Ende des 15. Jahrhunderts* (Göttingen: Vandenhoeck & Ruprecht, 1993), 150, 152–56; Engelsing, "Einkommen der Dienstboten"; Wiesner, *Working Women*, 92; and see also Ulinka Rublack, *The Crimes of Women in Early Modern Germany* (Oxford: Oxford University Press, 1999), 102, on the 1579 Württemberg *Taxordnung*.

16. Dürr's study of seventeenth-century Schwäbisch Hall found that 70 percent of maids served more than eleven years and almost 20 percent over twenty years, while only 6.6 percent completed their service in five years or less. As a result many poor young women were forced to work until their late twenties, thus greatly increasing the likelihood of premarital sex and the possibility of an unwanted pregnancy. Only one-half of maids were married by age twenty-nine and over one-tenth were older than forty at their first marriage. Dürr, *Mägde in der Stadt*, 162, 174–75. For instance, in seventeenth-century Hofmark Messenheusen, daughters of wealthy peasants married on average at age 25.6, while those of cottagers at age 28.5. Wunder, *He Is the Sun*, 29.

17. The Guldener Trunk in Nuremberg, established in 1427 with an endowment of 12,000 fl. from Otilia and Hilpolt Kress. StadtAN D1/2, 52v. Memmingen and Munich had similar funds.

18. Dürr, *Mägde in der Stadt*, 164.

19. Among women, post-hole digging and manure hauling paid the most, with the less arduous work of hoeing and sickling beneath that, and weeding and gleaning paying the least. Wiesner, *Working Women*, 92–93

20. A typical Nuremberg ordinance of 1521 threatens three years' banishment for a maid who left her job within the first six months and a ten gulden fine for anybody who attempted to coax a maid away from her master. One move per year was supposed to be the maximum. Wiesner, *Working Women*, 86–88, also 181–83 on similar restrictions in Strasbourg and Munich. See also Hartinger ("Bayerisches Dienstbotenleben," 619) on continuances into the eighteenth century; and see Engelsing ("Einkommen der Dienstboten," 14–16) on attempts to limit the amount of Christmas and other presents. By the end of the sixteenth century, these "voluntary" gifts outweighed the salary itself in value and often determined whether a maid would come and if she would stay.

21. In Germany, maids constituted the most commonly cited category of partner of married men in adultery cases, at least 50 percent in the bishopric of Speyer during the sixteenth century and 35.5 percent in seventeenth-century Schwäbisch Hall. Joel F. Harrington, *Reordering Marriage and Society in Reformation Germany* (Cambridge and New York: Cambridge University Press, 1995), 227–28, 241ff.; Dürr, *Mägde in der Stadt*, 259–63. In England, maids accounted for perhaps 70 percent of all legiti-

macy cases before the Salisbury Episcopal and London courts during the sixteenth and seventeenth centuries. Paul Griffiths, *Youth and Authority: Formative Experiences in England, 1560–1640* (Oxford: Clarendon Press, 1996), 173–274; Ingram, *Church Courts, Sex, and Marriage,* 264. See also Sara Maza, *Servants and Masters in Eighteenth Century France: The Uses of Loyalty* (Princeton: Princeton University Press, 1983), chap. 4; and Markus Meumann, *Findelkinder, Waisenhäuser, Kindsmord und unversorgte Kinder in der Frühen Neuzeit* (Munich: Oldenburg, 1995), 123–24. On accusations of theft, see Rublack, *Crimes of Women,* 100–2, and Martin Ingram, *Church Courts, Sex, and Marriage in England, 1570–1640* (Cambridge: Cambridge University Press, 1987), 266–67.

22. Griffiths (*Youth and Authority,* 271–72) notes that 83 percent of 230 pregnant female servants before the London Bridewell (1559–78) testified that sex took place in the master's household.

23. In one 1601 melodrama, the pregnant cook Margaretha Mauerin accused her former employer Steffan Scheuffelein of impregnating her. After questioning the two of them, Scheuffelein's mother and young sister, as well as "the ill-behaved, loathsome maid" Helena Kröpffin (who had had sex with both Steffan and his brother Paulus), the magistrates discovered that Mauerin's illegitimate child in fact belonged to Steffan's brother Paulus—even though Steffan had acknowledged the child as his own and compensated the mother accordingly. As if this weren't confusing enough, bewildered magistrates ordered Steffan interrogated on his action, especially why he claimed the child and allegedly conspired to have its mother killed. RV 1725: 2v–3r, 4v–5r, 8r–v, 14r, 19r (14, 15, 16, 19, and 22 May 1601).

24. Four of these included violent robbery. Richard van Dülmen, *Theatre of Horror: Crime and Punishment in Early Modern Germany* (Cambridge: Polity Press, 1990), appendix: table 5. Frankfurt am Main (van Dülmen, table 4) only convicted three men of rape during the same period; all were flogged and banished. Death for rape is defined in article 119 of the imperial law code, the Carolina, discussed in Richard Martin Allen, "Crime and Punishment in Sixteenth-Century Reutlingen" (Ph.D. diss., University of Virginia, 1980), 258, 277, n. 79. For the literary treatment of rape in Germany and England, see Joy D. Wiltenburg, *Disorderly Women and Female Power in the Street Literature of Early Modern England and Germany* (Charlottesville: University of Virginia Press, 1992), 223ff.

25. Jeffrey Watt, *The Making of Modern Marriage: Matrimonial Control and the Rise of Sentiment in Neuchâtel, 1550–1800* (Ithaca: Cornell University Press, 1992), 90–91. Cf. a similar 1585 ordinance of Württemberg in Rublack, *Crimes of Women,* 137. German and Swiss magistrates contrasted with their English counterparts, who sided with complaining servants in two-thirds of such cases. Giffiths, *Youth and Authority,* 321.

26. Merry E. Wiesner-Hanks, *Christianity and Sexuality in the Early Modern World: Regulating Desire, Reforming Practice* (London and New York: Routledge, 2000), 81.

27. RV 1475: 1r–2r (29 March 1582); ASB 210: 29r–32v.

28. "als er etwan bey zwein Jarn bei sich gehabt, kein gut thun wollen, sey ein mal od. zway davon gelauffen, auch eins mals bei zwainzig wochen draussen In ein gartten bey Irer verheyrat. Schwester . . . geplieben, aber stetigs wider eingedingt worden." ASB 210: 29v–30r.

29. "hette das Maidlein wol khonnen davon gehe, do es gesehen, das er sich in dasselb peth gelegt hette." ASB 210: 30r.

30. Cf. Ulinka Rublack "Viehisch, frech vnd onverschämpt. Inzest in Südwestdeutschland, ca. 1530–1700," in *Von Huren und Rabenmüttern. Weibliche Kriminalität in der*

Frühen Neuzeit, ed. Otto Ulbricht (Cologne, Weimar, and Vienna: Böhlau, 1995), 180, idem, *The Crimes of Women,* 239ff. The same defense had been used in Nuremberg by Hans Muller three years earlier, followed by an assertion of consent on the part of the fourteen-year-old shepherd girl. After extensive torture he made a full confession and was executed on 3 July 1579. ASB 209: 63r–70r.

31. "nach dem er das letzer mal mit Ir zuthun ghabt, sey er hernach in sein gewissen gangen, unnd erst vor eim halben Jar mit sein weib zu Gottes Tish gangen, und wisse nit wie Ine der böse feindt unnd der Trunck also verfuhrt gehabt." ASB 210: 31r–v. He also claimed that a certain Dutch smith had led him astray in Wöhrd, but had since moved away.

32. "Appel lass mich hinein zu die rucken, das hab sie gutwillig geshehen lassen und kain shrey gethan." ASB 210: 32r–v.

33. RV 1475: 15r–v (6 April 1582).

34. Rublack, "Inzest," 181, 192, idem, *Crimes of Women,* 235.

35. Executed with her husband Philip Lohner on 5 March 1611. GNM Hs 3857: 73v–74v; also StadtAN F1–111, 4r.

36. ASB 226a: 62 (30 December 1558). Valentin Goldner was executed on 20 December 1568 for incest with his daughter; Christoph Thurm was also beheaded for the same crime on 13 July 1569, as was Gertraud Hoffmännin for incest with her father, followed by infanticide in 1568. Seventeen-year-old Gertraut Schmidtin, member of a criminal family, was executed on 20 July 1587 for incest with her father and brother. Twenty-seven year-old Elisabeth Mechtlin, after her conviction on 28 February 1611 for "great harlotry" was revealed by her eight-year-old son to have slept with her two brothers. RV 1543: 47r, 51r, 53r; RV 1544: 7v, 10v, 16r, 22r–v, 27r–v, 39v; RV 1555: 2r; ASB 210: 248v–251r; GNM Hs 3857: 72v; StadtAN F1–111: 3v–4r; StadtAN F1–2/VII: 428–429; StadtAN 226a: 69. Meumann finds similar patterns in eighteenth-century Celle (*Findelkinder,* 88–90).

Incest cases involving biological mothers and sons were even rarer. Of the 130 incest cases examined by Rublack for 1533–1700, only one involved a mother and a son ("Inzest" 180, n. 45). Nuremberg had no such cases, and the seven incest cases found in Frankfurt during roughly the same period all involved stepfathers and stepdaughters. Maria Boes, "Public Appearance and Criminal Judicial Practice in Early Modern Germany," *Social Science History* 20, no. 2 (1996): 269.

37. "gar lech gehalten, und ubel geshlagen." Gertraut also claimed that she had been bonded several times but her father and brothers constantly made enemies and had to move. ASB 210: 248v–251v (12 July 1587).

38. RV 1555: 2r, 11v (13 and 19 July 1587); also ASB 210: 248v. Cf. the more typical case of Philip Lohner, who was executed (along with his wife, who had failed to intervene in the goings-on) for sex with his stepdaughter Catherina. "In view of her sweet words and age," the victim received only banishment. GNM Hs 3857: 73v–74r. See also Rublack, "Inzest," 180, 184–87.

39. About half of the overall female population was under the age of twenty, while maids as a group made up anywhere from one-fifth to one-third of the general population, and one-third to two-thirds of women between the ages of twenty and twenty-four. Wiesner, *Working Women,* 91; Wunder, *He Is the Sun,* 17, 129; Schubert, *Arme Leute,* 104; Mitterauer, "Gesindedienst," 185ff.

40. Philemon Menagius, *Die Sieben Teuffel / welche fast in der gantzen Welt die heutige Dienst-Mägde beherrschen und verführen . . .* (Frankfurt, 1693), 66–67. See also Dürr, *Mägde in der Stadt,* 99.

41. For more on engagement and wedding rituals in early modern Germany, see Lyndal Roper, "Going to Church and Street: Weddings in Reformation Augsburg," *Past and Present* 106 (1985): 62–101; and Harrington, *Reordering Marriage*, 169–214.

42. In some areas of Austria and southern Germany, especially poorer ones, concubinage was even viewed as a preliminary stage of marriage, and in early modern Sweden, the children of engaged couples were even entered as legitimate in church registers. Michael Mitterauer, *Ledige Mütter: Zur Geschichte unehelicher Geburten in Europa* (Munich: C. H. Beck, 1983), 14–16. Griffiths (*Youth and Authority*, 263–65) has found the same popular tolerance in early modern England.

43. Susanna Burghartz, *Zeiten der Reinheiten, Orte der Unzucht. Ehe und Sexualität in Basel während der Frühen Neuzeit* (Paderborn: Schöningh, 1999), 237ff. Rainer Beck argues that there were, however, relatively few children born out of wedlock, because *Fensterlehnen* consisted mostly of wooing and petting rather than intercourse ("Illegitimität und voreheliche Sexualität," 142). Griffiths (*Youth and Authority*, 259–61) concurs with these findings for England, where the practice was known as "night visiting" or "nights of watching" in the south and "sitting up" in the north.

44. Moser, "Jungfernkranz und Strohkranz," in *Das Recht der kleinen Leute. Festschrift für Karl-Sigismund Kramer zum 60. Geburtstag*, ed. Konrad Köstlin and Kai Detlev Sievers (Berlin: Schmidt 1976), 143, 147, 148, 153–54; see also Alfons Felber, "Unzucht und Kindsmord in der Rechtsprechung der freien Reichsstadt Nördlingen vom 15. bis 19. Jahrhundert" (J.D. thesis, Universität Bonn, 1961), 55. On the legal origins of this custom in Franconia, see Karl-S. Kramer, *Grundriss einer rechtlichen Volkskunde* (Göttingen: Schwartz, 1974).

45. Moser, "Jungfernkranz und Strohkranz," 154.

46. Wunder, *He Is the Sun*, 83.

47. Mitterauer, *Youth*, 163; see also 155–70 on rural and urban youth groups. On *Spinnstuben*, see Hans Medick, "Village Spinning Bees: Sexual Culture and Free Time among Rural Youth in Early Modern Germany," in *Interest and Emotion: Essays on the Study of Family and Kinship*, ed. Hans Medick and David W. Sabean (Cambridge: Cambridge University Press, 1984), 317–39; also Harrington, *Reordering Marriage*, 212–14, 222–24. Griffiths (*Youth and Authority*, 121) makes the important point that while "youth culture" was pervasive, it was far from cohesive.

48. Matthias Rog, "Wol auff mit mir, du schoenes weyb! Anmerkungen zur Konstruktion von Männlichkeit im Soldatenbild des 16. Jahrhunderts," in *Landsknechte, Soldatenfrauen und Nationalkrieger: Militär, Krieg, und Geschlechterordnung im historischen Wandel*, ed. Karen Hagemann and Ralf Pröve (Frankfurt: Campus, 1998), 51–73, esp. 56ff

49. Mitterauer, *Ledige Mütter*, 19; also William W. Hagan, *Ordinary Prussians: Brandenburg Junkers and Villagers, 1500–1800* (Cambridge: Cambridge University Press, 2002), 466ff.

50. Based on a sample of 88 court cases of pregnant maids suing for marriage, Dürr found that 42 percent were fellow servants, 24 percent journeymen, masters, or masters' sons, and only 2.2 percent soldiers. *Mägde in der Stadt*, 256. Of course, highly mobile soldiers might have been harder to bring to court, thus skewing their apparent frequency in such cases, but many servants were also itinerant. Peter Zschunke (*Konfession und Alltag in Oppenheim* [Wiesbaden: F. Steiner, 1984], esp. 149–51) also found that the majority of unmarried fathers were soldiers, travelling journeymen, and students, though he does not provide a breakdown.

51. Sponges and tampons as contraceptives date back at least to Chaucer. Though well

known in the sixteenth century, condoms were mainly used to prevent infection until the eighteenth century. See Robert Jütte, *Lust ohne Last: Geschichte der Empfängnisverhütung von der Antike bis zur Gegenwart* (Munich: C. H. Beck, 2003), esp. 11–24 and 102–20; Angus McLaren, *A History of Contraception from Antiquity to the Present Day* (Oxford: Basil Blackwell, 1990); Patricia Crawford, "Sexual Knowledge in England, 1500–1750," in, *Blood, Bodies and Families in Early Modern England* (London: Pearson, 2004), 148–58; and Burghartz, *Zeiten der Reinheit*, 245–50.

52. "Und ob er Ir gleich Ir Ins Veldt auch nachgangen, so hab sie doch im Veldt mit Ime nichts zuthun gehabt." ASB 209: 22v.

53. "hab sich in ainem trunckh, nicht mehr als ein mahl." ASB 209: 170r (26 January 1580).

54. "sie hab nicht aigentlich gewusst, dz sie ein kind trage, dann sich dasselbig gar wenig bey Ir geregt, und sey nicht hain, dz sie uf besprachen Irer frawen, und anderer Personen, jedesmals gesagt, sie trueg kein kindt," ASB 209: 170r (28 December 1580). Anna Seyfridtin violently denied her pregnancy to her mother and even during the late interrogation maintained that she had not known she was pregnant (StaatsAN 226a: 193 [1663]). Cf. frequent denials of child murderers also found in Alison Rowlands, "In Great Secrecy: The Crime of Infanticide in Rothenburg ob der Tauber, 1501–1618," *German History* 15, no. 2 (1997): 181–82. For modern examples of this phenomenon, see Lita Linzer Schwartz and Natalie Isser, *Endangered Children: Neonaticide, Infanticide, Filicide* (Boca Raton: CRC Press, 2000), 45–60.

55. Rublack, *Crimes of Women*, 174ff., idem, "Public Body," 58–60.

56. ASB 209: 168v–169r (19 January 1580). Laura Gowing ("Secret Births and Infanticide in Seventeenth-century England," *Past and Present* 156 [1997], 107–8), considers the word "denial" to be "too simplistic" in such instances.

57. "ein regentuch kann viel bey einem Närrchen / Auf manche Art und Weis in allem Fall verbergen." Karl Roetzer, "Die Delikte der Abtreibung, Kindstötung sowie Kindesaussetzung und ihre Bestrafung in der Reichsstadt Nürnberg" (Ph.D. diss., Friedrich-Alexander Universität Erlangen, 1957), 87.

58. *Hals- oder Peinliche Gerichtsordnung Kaiser Carls V*, 8th ed., ed. Johann Christoph Koch (Goldbach: Keip, 1966), article 122.

59. ASB 209: 22v.

60. Wiesner-Hanks, *Christianity and Sexuality*, 81. Peter Laslett estimates that at least one-quarter of early modern English brides were pregnant (*Family Life and Illicit Love in Earlier Generations* [Cambridge: Cambridge University Press, 1977], 21ff.), and Schubert one-third of couples in eighteenth-century Würzburg (Schubert, *Arme Leute*, 126). David Cressy (*Birth, Marriage and Death: Ritual, Religion, and the Life-Cycle in Tudor and Stuart England* [Oxford: Oxford University Press, 1997], 277–78) estimates that only half of all brides in England were still virgins on their wedding day, and Gwyneth Nair (*Highley: The Development of a Community, 1550–1880* [Oxford: Basil Blackwell, 1988], 120) has a figure of 22 percent of marriages in seventeenth-century Highly were followed by a birth within eight months. Beck, "Illegitimität," 122; see also Paul E. Hair, "Bridal Pregnancy in Rural England in Earlier Centuries, *Population Studies* 20, no. 2 (1966): 233–43, and "Bridal Pregnancy in Earlier Rural England Further Examined," *Population Studies* 24, no. 1 (1970): 59–70.

61. Only 24 *Frühlingskinder* are officially recorded during 1600–49; from 1650 to 1699 (0.48 annually), though, the parishes of Saint Sebald and Saint Lorenz baptized a total of 930 *Frühlingskinder*, an average of 18.6 per year—an increase of 3,875 percent! Willi Rüger, *Die Kinderfürsorge im Almosenwesen des XVII Jahrhunderts*, Nürnberger

Beiträge zu den Wirtschafts- und Sozialwissenschaften, 47–48 (Nuremberg: Krische, 1934), 126–29, table 1.

62. ASB 209: 22r.

63. Joel F. Harrington, "*Hausvater* and *Landesvater:* Paternalism and Marriage Reform in Sixteenth-Century Germany," *Central European History* 25, no. 1 (1992): 55ff. As a result of sixteenth-century legal reforms among both Protestants and Catholics, such vows were no longer binding in themselves and could in fact be punished with fines, banishment, or excommunication.

64. The age of twenty-five for men comes from Roman law; Bertha Kipfmueller, *Die Frau im Rechte der Freien Reichsstadt Nürnberg. Eine rechtsgeschichtliche Darlegung auf Grund der verneuerten Reformation von 1564* (Dillingen an der Donau, 1929), 4 ff., 14. The lowest anywhere during the early modern period was 18 for boys and 16 for girls. The one outstanding exception were the canonical ages of consent of 14 and 12, respectively.

65. See, for instance, child murderers Elisabeth Ernstin, executed 26 January 1580, Christina Zieckhin, executed 14 August 1582, and Anna Emblin, executed 8 February 1614. ASB 209: 168r; 21: 44r; GNM Hs 3857: 88v; also Beck, "Illegitimität, 133ff.; and Burghartz, *Zeiten der Reinheit,* 155ff.

66. "mit süßen Worten." Burghartz, *Zeiten der Reinheit,* 238. The transaction characterization is from Beck, "Illegitimität," 135ff. See also the frequency of this scenario in English ballads, described in Margaret Spufford, *Small Books and Pleasant Histories: Popular Fiction and Its Readership in Seventeenth-century England* (Cambridge: Cambridge University Press, 1981), 158ff.

67. From the 1563 Ehegerichtsordnung of the Rhineland Palatinate, in Emil Sehling, ed., *Die Evangelischen Kirchenordnungen des XVI. Jahrhunderts, vol. XIV (Kurpfalz),* ed. J. F. G. Goeters (Tübingen: Mohr, 1969), 30. See also Watt, *Making of Modern Marriage,* 65–70, on the sausage and other informal vows.

68. Other cities and territories, Protestant and Catholic, continued with some sort of ecclesiastical court of broader jurisdiction. See Harrington, *Reordering Marriage,* 101–66, on medieval and early modern marriage jurisdiction. The Nuremberg marriage court, established in 1526, met twice weekly. Roetzer, "Die Delikte der Abtreibung," 65.

69. Harrington, *Reordering Marriage,* 55ff., 92–93.

70. For a fascinating instance of this scenario, see Steven Ozment, *The Bürgermeister's Daughter: Scandal in a Sixteenth-Century German Town* (New York: St. Martin's Press, 1996).

71. "er habe die that nit recht mit ihr vollbracht, er habe sie nur probiert." Burghartz, *Zeiten der Reinheit,* 243, 245, 273. For examples of pregnancy by a married man, see Barbara Wernauerin (8 March 1642, ASB 226a: 177) and Margareth Dörflerin, who gave birth to five illegitimate children by a married man, four of whom died of natural causes (4 January 1580; ASB 209: 173r). Surprisingly, the great majority of marriage suits did not involve pregnancy. Samples from Basel's marriage court, for instance, show pregnancy rates of 18.9 percent (1536–40), 12.2 percent (1585–90), 15.4 percent (1645–49), and 15.1 percent (1685–89) among female plaintiffs in marriage suits. Burghartz, *Zeiten der Reinheit,* 163.

72. In Basel, for instance, Safley found that 82 percent of the marriage suits before the marriage court from 1550 to 1592 were initiated by women. Burghartz found comparable rates for the same court in her samples of 1536–40 (59 percent), 1585–89 (78 percent), 1645–49 (85 percent), and 1685–89 (71 percent). The success rate for women plaintiffs from the years 1536–40 was 41 percent (versus 45 percent for

men). By the seventeenth century, women's rates of success were 11 percent (1645–49) and 14 percent (1685–90).Thomas M. Safley, *Let No Man Put Asunder: The Control of Marriage in the German Southwest; A Comparative Study, 1550–1600* (Kirksville: Sixteenth-Century Journal Press, 1984), 173; Burghartz, *Zeiten der Reinheit*, 129–30.

73. Burghartz's four samples from the sixteenth and seventeenth centuries show similar overall success rates for marriage suits in Basel at 22.8 percent, 21 percent, 40 percent, and 23 percent. Burghartz, *Zeiten der Reinheit*, 114; Dürr, *Mägde in der Stadt*, 234–35.

74. Amshler unsuccessfully mentioned that the two young people had been seen on strolls together and that his daughter had confessed her sin to her pastor. RV 2301: 56v, 72v–73r, 81r; RV 2302: 34v, 87r–v (15, 20, 25 February and 3 March 1645). In another case, farmhand Hans Schmidt admitted that "he pursued his maid until he brought her to his will," but denied that he had exchanged marriage vows with her. Based on the jurists' recommendation, "this marriage thief" was flogged, put in the stocks, and then banished. The petitioning maid was spared on account of her "innocent fruit of her womb" but was also sternly warned that if she ever became involved in a similar situation that she would be severely punished. StaatsAN 51/42: 17r (1576).

75. The "Ja-Wort." Roetzer, "Die Delikte der Abtreibung," 65–67.

76. Harrington, *Reordering Marriage*, 202.

77. "unsauberen Dirnen." Kipfmüller, *Die Frau im Recht*, 16; and decrees of 11 November 1613 and 11 January 1643. Rüger (*Die Kinderfürsorge*, 69) claims that pressure to marry was greatest before the early seventeenth century.

78. Nuremberg was exceptional in the respect that marriage to any eligible man could legitimize a woman's illegitimate child(ren). According to the *Reformatio* of 1564, "Wann ein ledige mannsperson mit ainem ledigen wibspild kinder erzeugt het und nachmaln dieselbig weibsperson eelicht, so werden die kinder, so davor ledig geborn, durch solche ee für rechte eeliche kinder gehalten und mit den andern in der ee erzeugten kinder zu erben zugelassen." Tit. XXXIV, Ges. 5, cited in Rüger, *Die Kinderfürsorge*, 70–71. In 1619, for instance, Nuremberg's magistrates order Vieter Herwort to pay child support for his illegitimate child by Leonora Sellmennin "bis einen andern vatter stelle." RV 1959: 12r (23 November 1619). In Basel, a woman with multiple sexual partners would have her support divided among them, but only if she filed within the first six months of pregnancy. Burghartz, *Zeiten der Reinheit*, 102; see also 78–79, 271–73.

79. RV 2554: 44r–v; RV 2555: 8r–v (16 and 29 January 1664). See the similar example of RV 1778: 57v–58r (26 March 1606). In a more modest example of magisterial generosity, a Nuremberg woman who had gone to Regensburg to have her illegitimate child and then returned to abandon it in Nuremberg was banished with "a full quarter year's stipend" so that she didn't abandon the baby again. RV 2585, 36r (27 April 1666).

80. See StadtAN B14/II.

81. Rublack, *Crimes of Women*, 183ff.

82. Feld also said that Killian Pfizsher promised his daughter marriage and thus sued the father, Wezel Pfizsher for defloration, impregnation, birthbed costs, and alimetation. RV 1748: 2r, 28v–29r (10 and 19 February 1603).

83. "grosse kötzer . . . habe er sie sich so hefftig zu gemuth gefurt, und sich hernach an ihrem kind vergessen." ASB 211: 101v (21 April 1590).

84. See StaatsAN 51, 68: 568 (1611) on tracking down fathers of illegitimate children born in the Spital; also StaatsAN 51, 31: 197 (1561). See also Ingram, *Church Courts, Marriage, and Sex*, 282, on concern in English villages about the sheltering of poor unwed mothers and the perceived burden it imposed on the community.
85. Wunder, *He Is the Sun*, 125, 190; and see examples of three young mothers in RV 1683: 38v (22 March 1598).
86. RV 2372: 56r (27 April 1650); RV 2391: 24v (22 October 1651); and see instances where the child did not survive but the mother was still vigorously interrogated: RV 1509: 9v (13 October 1584); and RV 1536: 31v (8 November 1586).
87. "Ich truog euch ledic siben kint. / keinz ich den rechten vater gab, / nur welcher het die moisten hab, / dem warf ichs morgens für die thür, / da die liut gingen hin und für." Jacob und Wilhelm Grimm, *Deutsches Wörterbuch* (Leipzig, 1854), 459, 632, quoted in Roetzer, "Die Delikte der Abtreibung," 41. Olwen Hufton, *The Poor of Eighteenth-Century France, 1750–89* (Oxford: Clarendon Press, 1974), 324, describes a similar practice in eighteenth-century France of unwed mothers naming more than one father for support.
88. "ein fuhrknecht namens Hans von dem sie weiters ihren furgeben nach nichts wissen zu zeigen." Margaretha Marckhardtin, executed on 4 August 1607; GNM Hs 3857: 64r. "nit weit von Vorchaim in ein dörffle, das sie nicht nennen khone." Christina Zieckhin, executed 14 August 1582; ASB, 210: 44r. For typical instructions to track down an accused father, see RV 1896: 10v (29 April 1614).
89. Unmarried mothers were ineligible for Nuremberg's *Jungfernalmosen* (also known as the *Aussteuerhilfskasse*), in operation since 1427. Rüger, *Mittelalterliches Almosenwesen*, 28.
90. Menagius, *Die Sieben Teuffel*, cited in Dürr, *Mägde in der Stadt*, 252. Menagius also predicted that such marriages would not last.
91. *Taufordnungen* of 1625, 1627, 1647, 1652, 1662, 1705, see Siebenkees, *Materialien*, 229–33. For examples of arrested single mothers, see RV 1896: 10v (29 April 1614), RV 1936: 33r (3 May 1617), RV 1963: 16r (5 May 1619), RV 2018: 63v (1 July 1623); Rublack, *Crimes of Women*, 154.
92. Specifically, 3,568 of 119,168 total births listed in the birth registers of Saint Lorenz and Saint Sebaldus parishes, or 3.0 percent. 2290, or 64.2 percent, of those were *spurii*. Rüger, *Die Kinderfürsorge*, 126–29, table 1.
93. Peter Burschel, *Söldner im Nordwestdeutschland des 16. und 17. Jahrhunderts. Sozialgeschichtliche Studien* (Göttingen: Vandenhoeck & Ruprecht, 1994), 243. In Nuremberg, *spurii* could still serve in some trades but were banned from the *Ehrenämter* of doctors, lawyers, or magistrates. Rüger, *Die Kinderfürsorge*, 63–64.
94. See the example of Barbara Meiglerin, put in irons and summoned before the town council (RV 1963: 16r; 5 May 1619) and Anna Lochnerin, who received the same punishment as well as church penance and banishment (RV 2018: 63v; 1 July 1623). Both were impregnated by soldiers. A 1623 decree of the town council specified three weeks in the tower on bread and water for unmarried fornicators, four to six weeks for adulterers. Recidivists received sentences twice as long (Rüger, *Die Kinderfürsorge*, 69–70). In parts of Württemberg, pregnant brides were not even to be allowed public weddings and were instead to be punished with a tower sentence. The Reformed states of Zweibrücken and Geneva maintained the most severe punishments of both imprisonment and public penance. Both Nördlingen and Schwäbisch Hall were relatively easier on fornicating women, who in most cases spent less than one week in

prison. Felber, "Unzucht und Kindsmord," 55–56; Dürr, *Mägde in der Stadt,* 233; also Harrington, *Reordering Marriage,* 239–40, and see 228ff. on church penance for sexual crimes.

95. See, for example, RV 1916: 16r (2 November 1615). This practice was still common fifty years later (RV 2546: 50r–v; 3 June 1663) even though Hermann Knapp (*Das alte Nürnberger Kriminalrecht* [Berlin: J. Guttentag, 1896], 1: 110, 390) claims that it was only for foreign women. In a few instances, couples apparently received only a stern lecture: RV 1896: 10v (29 April 1614), RV 1933: 67r (3 March 1617), RV 1936: 33r (3 May 1617). The widow Elena Weisin provides an example of a citizen spared chains but still banished (RV 2033: 27r; 30 July 1624). The expenses for a single woman staying in the hospital until birth were charged to the alleged father. Mummenhoff, "Die öffentliche Gesundheits- und Krankenpflege," 61.

96. August Jegel, "Altnürnberger Hochzeitsbrauch und Eherecht, besonders bis zum Ausgang des 16. Jahrhunderts," *MVGN* 44 (1953): 265–69. See also Harrington, *Reordering Marriage,* 254ff. Dürr (*Mägde in der Stadt,* 241) found fornicating women almost three times more likely to be banished. During this time there were four stocks on the south wall of the town hall. Schultheiss, *Rechtspflege,* 198. See Dürr, *Mägde in der Stadt,* 238ff. on red boots and other honor punishments; also Hans Conrad Ellrichshausen, *Die uneheliche Mütterschaft im altösterreichischen Polizeirecht des 16. bis 18. Jahrhunderts* (Berlin: Duncker & Humblot, 1988).

97. Dürr, *Mägde in der Stadt,* 242, 246. Ironically this milder enforcement included the famously disciplinarian governments of Scotland and Prussia (Wiesner, *Christianity and Sexuality,* 82). Mitterauer (*Ledige Mütter,* 74) claims that German cities were generally more tolerant than rural areas in this respect, though this clearly only applies to a later period. Rublack (*Crimes of Women,* 137) found that measures against illegitimate births were harsher in areas with partible inheritance.

98. See especially Gordon DesBrisay, "Wet Nurses and Unwed Mothers in Seventeenth-century Aberdeen," in *Women in Scotland, c. 1100–c.1750,* ed. Elizabeth Ewan and Maureen Meikle (East Linton: Tuckwell Press, 1999), 210–21. Both Wunder (*He Is the Sun,* 140–41) and Meumann (*Findelkinder,* 156ff.) note the hypocrisy in this transaction.

99. See below, chapter 2. Alimentation was no more sufficient. In parts of sixteenth-century Bern, the standard *alimentatio* was 3 lb. For the birth bed and 5 schilling (1/4 fl.) a week thereafter. This weekly amount was never raised, though the birth bed payment was increased to 10 lb. In the 1640s and later consolidated into a one-time payment of 20–50lb in the 1680s. Burghartz, *Zeiten der Reinheit,* 271.

100. Rublack, *Crimes of Women,* 90.

101. StaatsAN Hs 440: 99 (22 July 1572). See similar examples on 98 (2 February 1571) and 113 (24 April 1602).

102. Rüger, *Die Kinderfürsorge,* table 1; de Vries ("Population," 34) estimates an illegitimacy rate of 4–10 percent of all European births between 1400 and 1600.

103. Miscarriage rates are based on averages from seventeenth-century Lancashire (2.9–9.6 percent) and from Nuremberg infant death statistics, where twenty-nine (13.4 percent) of the 217 children buried at Nuremberg's Saint Johanis and Rochus Cemetery in 1667 were designated "abgänglein." Houlbrooke, *English Family,* 128; Roetzer, "Die Delikte der Abtreibung," 88. Stillbirth figures are based on statistics from the eighteenth-century Prince-Bishopric of Bayreuth (4 percent) and Rothenburg ob der Tauber (2.4 percent), nineteenth-century Maine (1.8 percent) and New Hampshire (3 percent). Griffiths, *Youth and Authority,* 246; Schubert, *Arme Leute,* 184; Ulrich, *Midwife's Tale,* 171.

104. Larissa Leibrock-Plehn ("Frühe Neuzeit. Hebammen, Kräutermedizin und weltliche Justiz," in *Geschichte der Abtreibung. Von der Antike bis zur Gegenwart*, ed. Robert Jütte [Munich: C. H. Beck, 1993], 85) reports none in Frankfurt am Main during 1500–1700, one in Freiburg during the same period, and one in Cologne between 1568 and 1583. See also Maria Boes, "Public Appearance and Criminal Judicial Practices in Early Modern Germany," *Social Science History* 20, no. 2 (1996): 269 on Frankfurt. Rublack ("Public Body," 63ff.) finds sixty-two cases of attempted abortion in the southwestern German cities of Memmingen, Schwäbisch Hall, Essligen, Bad Mergentheim, Ludwigsburg, Freiburg im Breisgau, and Constance from 1515 to 1690, most in the course of testimony from infanticide cases.
105. 30 October 1663, StaatsAN 226a: 193 (13 August 1613); GNM Hs 3857: 115r. In addition to the fourteen women listed in Roetzer, "Die Delikte der Abtreibung," appendix 1, I have identified two more: Barbara Dallerin (GNM Hs 3857: 115r) and Katherina Büttnerin (RV 2052: 45r, 83r; RV 2053: 22v, 46v). Rublack (*Crimes of Women*, 164) estimates that one-quarter of the infanticide cases she examined included previous attempted abortions. For examples of abortions coming to light because of crimes other than infanticide, see RV 2944: 13r, 38r, 43v, 57r, 72v; also ASB 199: 139v–140r.
106. Examples in Nuremberg include a 1582 case of a condemned woman examined four times (Roetzer, "Die Delikte der Abtreibung,", 72); the 1604 case of a thief examined eight times with her execution postponed thirty-two weeks (RV 1470: 40r, 43r; 1471: 18r, 22v; RV 1472: 35v; RV 1473: 34r, 40r, 41v, 48r); and the 1667 case of accused abortionist Barbara Beerin, who after repeated inconclusive examinations by the midwives and city physicians was eventually released (RV 2602: 10v–11r, 41v–42r; 5 and 14 August 1667). Even the doctor who examined the famous eighteenth-century child murderer Susanna Brandt couldn't be sure whether she'd ever been pregnant (Richard van Dülmen, *Frauen vor Gericht. Kindsmord in der Frühen Neuzeit* [Frankfurt am Main, 1991], 20). I have found only one instance in Nuremberg where a surgeon concluded that a woman had actually attempted abortion and had her arrested (RV 2052: 45r; 7 February 1626).
107. Some jurists also argued for fifty or ninety days. Article 135 of the Carolina spoke of *Umbeseelung* at five months. Roetzer, "Die Delikte der Abtreibung," 152; Leibrock-Plehn, "Frühe Neuzeit," 70; Knapp, *Kriminalrecht*, 184.
108. Felber, *Unzucht und Kindsmord*, 94; Ulbricht, *Kindsmord und Aufklärung in Deutschland* (Munich: Oldenburg, 1990), 184.
109. See especially Jütte, *Lust ohne Last*, 111ff.
110. *Kindermord, Mägdebaum, Jungfernpalm*. All three of these herbs were forbidden by the Nuremberg council in 1592 because of their use as abortifacients (Roetzer, "Die Delikte der Abtreibung," 90). In her study of southwestern Germany, Ulinka Rublack found twenty-three different abortifacients mentioned in legal records, including laurel and penny royal (nine times each), hazelroot (seven times), and savin (five times). Rublack, "Public Body," 76, n. 27, 61–62, 66. Other common abortifacients included hemlock, vervein, woodbine, camphor, cannabi, dill, female fern, and honeysuckle. On the question of early modern knowledge and usage, see John M. Riddle, *Contraception and Abortion from the Ancient World to the Renaissance* (Cambridge: Harvard University Press, 1992), viiff.; Leibrock-Plehn, "Frühe Neuzeit," 81; Burhartz, *Zeiten der Reinheit*, 245–50; and McLaren, *History of Contraception*.
111. Riddle, *Contraception*, 144–57; Roetzer, "Die Delikte der Abtreibung," 90.
112. Leibrock-Plehn, "Frühe Neuzeit," 76–79.

113. The statistics come from Rublack, "Public Body," 63 and 77, n. 36. Exact numbers are nine female healers, nine male healers, nine physicians, seven "mothers," four pharmacists, three unspecified men, two unspecified women, two widows, two barbers, one mistress, and one midwife. I have seen no evidence in early modern Germany of the abortion rings found in contemporary England (Peter Hoffer and N. E. H. Hull, *Murdering Mothers: Infanticide in England and New England, 1558–1803* [New York: New York University Press, 1981],156) or in nineteenth-century Germany (Regina Schulte, *The Village in Court: Arson, Infanticide and Poaching in the Court Records of Upper Bavaria, 1848–1910*, trans. Barrie Selman [Cambridge: Cambridge University Press, 1994], 87–118), but it is likely that such informal associations of women later known as *Engelmacherinnen* ("angel makers") existed in some form.

114. RV 2551: 28v (17 October 1663).

115. Albrecht Keller, ed., *Maister Franntzn Schmidts Nachrichters inn Nürmberg all sein Richten* (1913; reprint, Neustadt an der Aisch: Ph. C. W. Schmidt, 1979), 106; Roetzer, "Die Delikte der Abtreibung," 90.

116. The earliest textual reference to *secreta mulierum* comes in a thirteenth-century manuscript falsely attributed to Albertus Magnus. On the importance of female networks in this area, see especially Crawford, *Blood, Bodies and Families*, esp. 62–72; also Gowing, "Secret Births," 92ff., and Sara H. Mendelson and Patricia Crawford, *Women in Early Modern England, 1550–1720* (Oxford: Clarendon Press, 1998). On the particular importance of the mother-daughter relationship in passing on this information, see Hufton, *Prospect Before Her*, 210–16.

117. "hoch verbottenen mitteln, abortum zu procirn . . . saffron öhl undt kreutter . . . zwei Dukaten und ein klein spizig weiss steinlein, zum ringlein." The mother was a well-known vagrant who associated with loose company, accused of "regularly held parties [with] frivolous gaming, dancing, and other boisterousness," thereby "corrupting her daughter," who had just given birth to an illegitimate child. Most notoriously, she had allowed her daughter to say at the house of Margaretha Linckin, who was reputed to put up many "maidens, maids, and young journeymen . . . which were paired off and corrupted by her." Linkin countered "with great swearing and protestation that she [neither] coupled, corrupted, or led astray the smallest [minor] or adult, nor provided instructions, encouragement, or shelter to such highly punishable and dishonorable gatherings; her whole lifelong [she] had never thought or suggested much less effected [such], nor talked about the same or carried it out; nor did she recall a single word about the Ebnerin pregnancy, nor did she sell or provided the same with a penny's [worth] of herbs the day before." She also claimed to be pregnant herself, a shrewd move given the mitigating force of this condition with magistrates. ASB, 199: 65v–67v (8 April 1606). In a similar case two years later, a fellow maid played the intermediary part and was banished with the unwed mother; the wise woman was released with a fine. ASB 199: 37r–v (30 September 1608).

118. "weil es so ein herb bitter und ärmlich getranck gewesen, nicht trincken können, auch das wenig so sie versucht wieder geben mussen." Despite her continuing denials, Anna Schusterin was banished for life. ASB 199: 139v–140r (1606). Cf. 1668 case of Elisabeth Maurer of Schordorf who swallowed a potion from her mother that made her vomit and feel "as if her heart were being pushed away." Rublack, "Public Body," 63.

119. "die Frucht durch verbottene von der [wise woman] Agnes Klaiberin angelehrte zauberei, abzutreiben . . . nicht allein Rhath und thatt gegeben sonder auch derselben [Walburg] den shlayer mit eigner hand übergebunden und einen seegen darzu ge-

sprochen, das die frucht von ihr kommen soll." ASB 199: 379r–v (30 September 1608).

120. "wenn sie dieselbig auf den nabel pendt, so wurde nichts aus der sachen." 17 February 1578, cited in Roetzer, "Die Delikte der Abtreibung," 92. The same power was sometimes ascribed to eaglestones, haemites, agate, and bezoars. Leibrock-Plehn, "Frühe Neuzeit," 80.

121. "und sich uff und über den kübel darinnen dem viehs essen angemacht worden gelegt, damit das kind ein schaden bekommen mögt, dadurch zar dasselbst geschwächt, aber gar nicht abgestanden." ASB 226a: 184 (26 May 1653).

122. "holz tragen, washen und anderer arbeith." StaatsAN 51, 43: 62v–63v (1580). Cf. the similar case of Katharina Buchnerin, whose dead child was judged by the municipal surgeon to be the product of an abortion. Buchnerin eventually confessed to drinking savin for four weeks. RV 2052: 45r, 87r; RV 2053: 22v, 46v (7 and 20 February, 1 and 8 March 1626).

123. GNM Hs 3857, 64r (4 August 1607). Dürr (*Mägde in der Stadt*, 247) could not find a single case in which an unwed pregnant maid was not dismissed from her position.

124. "damit d. kindtsmords halten vermitteln bleiben können." RV 2370: 49r–v; RV 2371: 9v, 24r (8, 18, 20 April 1650).

125. "an verwiesen Montag nachts umb 1 Uhr auss dem haus gangen und erst umb 6 Uhr wieder heimkommen, bey Catharina Legatin, Tabacmacherin gewesen sein, und nachmals gar leiss und heimlich miteinander geredt haben sollen." RV 2602: 10v–11r, 52v; 2603: 25v (5 and 17 August, 5 September 1667).

126. Emblin was ultimately executed for infanticide on 8 February 1614; GNM Hs 3857: 88v.

127. Rublack (*Crimes of Women*, 88–89) found many examples of parents and other relatives hiding and caring for young pregnant women and their offspring.

128. Griffiths, *Youth and Authority*, 285.

129. "hatt er sie uff ein karrn nach hochstätt geschickt und Ir 6 fl. eingefast, sie sey aber dahin nit sonder zu Bruck eine Ir vohie bekandte fraue . . . angetroffen mit der sie haim gefahren." ASB 200: 46v–47r (8 August 1609).

130. Sherrill Cohen, *Women's Asylums: From Refuges for Ex-prostitutes to Shelters for Battered Women* (New York: Oxford University Press, 1992), 3–4, 18, 159.

131. The Nuremberg 1522 ordinance was similar in this respect to those of Regensburg (1452), Munich (1488), Freiburg im Breisgau (1494), Strasbourg (1500), Frankfurt (1509), Württemberg (1549) and Memmingen (1578). Wiesner, *Working Women*, 60; also Wunder, *He Is the Sun*, 99–104, Roetzer, "Die Delikte der Abtreibung," 75, Friedrich Baruch, "Das Hebammenwesen im Reichsstädtischen Nürnberg" (Ph.D. diss., Universität Erlangen, 1955), 7–8, 11, 36–38.

132. In this respect, I would dissent slightly from Rublack's generalization that "[f]ar from helping them, female midwives had themselves become chief agents in the control of women who practised 'deviant' sexuality and motherhood, while the notion that knowledge about contraception and abortion was exchanged within a 'separate female sexual culture' implies a homogeneity of attitudes and a solidarity among women that is hard to verify and ignores potential conflicting feelings about fertility and motherhood." Rublack, "Public Body," 58. Cf. Rowlands, "'In Great Secrecy,'" 188, on the "crucial, yet potentially ambivalent" role that midwives could play in infanticide cases.

133. "die Berbel . . . Gift oder Muck." Dallerin was also convicted of bigamy and executed. GNM Hs 3857: 115r–116r (13 August 1618).

134. Kißlingen: StaatsAN 51, 44: 252 (1600); Marckhardtin: GNM Hs 3857: 64r (executed 4 August 1607); Mauerin: RV 1759: 33r (18 February 1604). Cf. similar case to Mauerin's in Saint Lorenz: RV 1803: 27r (19 May 1607).

135. "wie sie sich an Ir beth shlaff gelegt. Unnd albereit eingeshlaffen gewesen, do wer Ir nach Mitternacht zum kind wehe worden. Unnd als sie vasst zum stund Krissten, und Ir wehe gewesen het sie das kind geborn. Und wer die nachgeburt mit dem kind von Ir gangen darnach were sie vom kind ufgestanden, und het ein shlaissen Im Ofen anzundt, were mit derselben brinnenden shlaissen Ir kammer gangen, do het das kind gelegt und arm unnd bunlein geregt aber mit geshryhen." ASB 209: 23r (7 February 1578). Meumann (*Findelkinder*, 132) found the woman's bedroom to be the most common birth choice for unwed mothers. See also Gowing, "Secret Births," 98–108, on secret labors.

136. FKD: 182 infants (30.4 percent) of 599 anonymously abandoned children.

137. Article 132 of the Carolina qualified its pronouncement on abandonment as "depending on the circumstances." Knapp, *Kriminalrecht,* 1: 189. Cf. the imprisonment and banishment in 1645 of a "wench" who tried to abandon her six-week-old baby. RV 2302: 84r (26 May 1645). Another abandoning mother was apprehended and imprisoned but before she could be banished with her child it died. StadtAN D10/3–4: 98.

138. Magdalena Fischer, executed on 6 November 1610. Keller, *Maister Franntzn Schmidts,* 69.

139. In 1622 both an abandoning mother and her own mother were apprehended and imprisoned for their attempt to get rid of an illegitimate baby; afterward the grandmother and mother, "once she is strong enough," were both banished, while the infant remained behind in the care of the Findel. RV 2010: 40v, 61r; RV 2011: 18r (20 and 26 November, 11 December 1622).

140. "fast gemein." See Van Dülmen, *Frauen vor Gericht,* 58–75, for various statistics on the frequency of infanticide cases in the sixteenth and seventeenth centuries. Otto Ulbricht (*Kindsmord und Aufklärung,* 6) disputes the presumed high incidence of early modern infanticide in Germany.

141. The relevant articles in the Carolina were 131, 135, and 136. Article 133 also prescribed capital punishment for accomplices to abortion. The 1548 imperial criminal ordinance's prohibition of infanticide was followed by an influential French ordinance in 1556 and later by prohibitions in England (1624), Sweden (1627), Württemberg (1658), Denmark (1683), Scotland (1690), and Bavaria (1751). Cunningham, *Children and Childhood,* 117.

142. Estimates of actual infanticide rates naturally range considerably, given the amount of speculation involved. Keith Wrightson ("Infanticide in Early Seventeenth-Century England," *Local Population Studies* 15 [Autumn 1975]: 19) argues that the actual rate was probably at least 2.5 times that of convictions, while Gerd Schwerhoff (*Köln im Kreuzverhör: Kriminalität, Herrschaft und Gesellschaft in einer frühneuzeitlichen Stadt* [Bonn: Bouvier, 1991], 71–72) argues that infanticide was very difficult to conceal and thus the number of killings was probably not much more than the number of infant corpses found. I can see no basis on which to suggest a concrete number or percentage of all illicit pregnancies.

143. "Unnd dergleichen ubels merers teils under dem paurs volck ufm Lannd begangen werde." RV 1420: 18r (22 February 1578).

144. Cf. Dorothea Maulin (ASB 199: 78v;17 May 1606); Elisabetha Greiffin (ASB 200: 66r; 2 October 1609); Barbara Käsin (StaatsAN 226a: 204–5; 14 October 1669).

145. During 1549–1675, there were 152 dead newborns discovered, 79 women charged as suspects, 64 of those convicted, and 57 of those convicted executed. See appendix 2.

146. Here I see strong affinity between the simultaneous rise of witchcraft and infanticide prosecutions in German lands during the sixteenth century and concur with the conclusion of Lyndal Roper about the centrality of anxiety over motherhood. See her *Witch Craze*, esp. 247ff.; also *Oedipus and the Devil*, 199–225.

147. Based on an estimated population of 100,000 for the entire Nuremberg territory and an average of 2,000 infants baptized yearly within the city of Nuremberg during the late sixteenth and early seventeenth centuries. Wiesner, *Working Women*, 55.

148. Barbara Weiherin (RV 1185: 43r; 3 August 1560), Anna Gummanin (StaatsAN 51, 42: 48v; 24 July 1576), and Anna Teuffelin (F1–111: 26r–v; 21 April 1642). Hans Gumman was also executed with his wife and there is mention of one widow, Margreth Dörflerin (ASB 209: 167r; 26 January 1580). See also RV 2271: 18v; RV 2376: 110; 2380: 21r; StadtAN Imhof'sche Chronik III. Hoffer and Hull, *Murdering Mothers*, 54–55, 97, table 4.1, found a particular preponderance of unmarried women in the killing of newborns (neonaticide), 95 percent in the instance of colonial Massachusetts and an adjusted frequency of 85.6 percent among 139 cases in Essex, Hertford, Middlesex, and Sussex during the period 1558–1623.

149. Van Dülmen, *Frauen vor Gericht*, 82; based on eighteenth-century samples from Danzig, Prussia, and Schleswig-Holstein. Meumann found a similar pattern in Saxony, with 74 percent under the age of thirty and the average age twenty-five (*Findelkinder*, 120, table 3). Most unwed mothers gave birth at the same age as married mothers (Wunder, *He Is the Sun*, 26).

150. Based on background information collected on 49 of the 64 child murderers listed in appendix 2 between 1549 and 1675. The same pattern is evident in eighteenth-century Saxony (70 percent from rural areas), Paris (80 percent), and Moscow (90 percent). Meumann, *Findelkinder*, 118; Tilly et al., "Child Abandonment in European History," 9. Rowlands ("In Great Secrecy," 195) also found that most of the women tried in Rothenburg ob der Tauber for infanticide were "foreigners."

151. "Sie hab die Shwengerung aus keiner andern ursac od fursatz geleugnet, dann das sie Ir unnd allmahl dess willen gewesens, Ir kind heimblich voerborgener weiss zugeberen, und es hernacher umbzubringen." ASB 209: 22v–23r. This motif is common in infanticide confessions; cf. RV 1445: 31v (23 January 1580); ASB 209: 167r–172v; StaatsAN 51/43: 62v–63r (30 December 1579); ASB 209: 169r (19 January 1580); GNM Hs 3857: 88v (8 February 1614). Cf. the 1693 testimony of Katherine Conrie in Scotland that "she had cutted her child's throat and the divile hade given her a kniff to do it with." Deborah A. Symonds, *Weep Not for Me: Women, Ballads and Infanticide in Early Modern Scotland* (University Park: Pennsylvania State University Press, 1997), 163.

152. "ein schwartze katz sei an ihr gein Perg gesprungen und ir eingeben, sie soll solches thun." ASB 211: 108v (12 June 1590).

153. Van Dülmen, *Frauen vor Gericht*, 87, also notes that maids as a whole are very underrepresented in witchcraft trial records, for the same reason.

154. ASB 210: 44v (14 August 1582). "weils Ir ein gross laidt und bererrung sey," ASB 209: 171r (26 January 1580). Rublack (*Crimes of Women*, 183ff.) found more explicit statements of concern about scandal and shame.

155. See, for example, Elisabeth Ernstin (ASB 209: 169r; 19 January 1580); also Clemens Zimmerman, "'Behörigs Orthen angezeigt.' Kindsmörderinnen in der ländlichen

Gesellschaft Württembergs, 1581–1792," *Medizin, Gesellschaft und Geschichte* 10 (1993): 71.

156. GNM Hs 3857: 120v (4 February 1619).

157. StaatsAN 51, 42: 49r (24 July 1576).

158. See, for example, Dorothea Maulin on 17 May 1606 (ASB 199: 78v), and Barbara Schwenderin on 25 May 1557 (RV 1143: 8r, 9v, 18r–v). Here Nuremberg differs from Clemens Zimmerman's study of Württemberg where stabbing was the most common method ("Behörigs Orthen angezeigt," 74). For the variation of infanticide methods, see Roetzer, "Die Delikte der Abtreibung," 93–97.

159. 15 March 1597; GNM Hs 3857: 50r. See also Roetzer, "Die Delikte der Abtreibung," 94; Zimmerman "Behörigs Orthen angezeigt," 75.

160. Dörflerin's tale failed to convince Nuremberg's magistrates, who had her executed as a child murderer. ASB 222: 110r–v, 209: 167r (executed 26 January 1580). It was unusual that the perpetrator was caught, let alone executed, in the case of a fatal abandonment. See also the case of 4 February 1626, where a dead baby was found "unharmed in all limbs and undoubtedly must have suffered from the extreme of this cold weather." (RV 2052: 36r–v). Other examples of failed abandonments include RV 1520: 39r–v (28 August 1585) and RV 2447: 2r (27 December 1655).

161. Burghartz, *Zeiten der Reinheiten*, 269.

162. Based on the recorded 282 dead infants found between 1549 and 1803.

163. Gertraud Hoffmännin's dead baby that she buried in a field was dug up by some dogs and found by a shepherdess (*Gras Magd*), StadtAN F1-2/VII: 428–429 (1568). Margarethe Dörflerin (ASB 209: 167r; 30 December 1579;), Veronica Kölerin (StaatsAN 51, 45: 199v; 15 March 1597), and Dorothea Meulin (ASB 199: 78v; 17 May 1606) were all observed burying their children. Other secret burial sites included cemeteries (RV 2282: 94r–v [18 September 1643]; RV 2313: 19v–20r [22 December 1645]), fields (RV 1625: 8r [6 October 1593]; RV 1951: 36v–37r [13 June 1618]), and the woods (RV 1594: 16r [1554]).

164. Strauss, *Nuremberg*, 192. The Vischbach, a tiny tributary of the Pegnitz, was an especially popular location with garbage disposers and child murderers alike.

165. ASB 209: 23r (1578). See similar modus operandi of Barbara Schwenderin (ASB 226a: 62 [1 July 1557]), Elisabeth Ernstin (RV 1445: 30v [18 January 1580]), and Susanna Reuthlin (GNM Hs 3857: 62v [26 June 1606]). Anna Schmidin (ASB 226a: 60 [30 October 1554]), Christina Zieckhin (ASB 210: 44v [14 August 1582]), and Anna Dippoltin (GNM Hs 3857: 120v [4 February 1619]) also delayed disposal for a few days but buried their dead children rather than throwing them in the Pegnitz.

166. "da hat sie dann daselbe also bald genommen, ehe sie gesehen, ob es ein Mägdlein oder büblein gewesen und in die Pegniz geworffen." GNM Hs 3857: 64r (4 August 1607).

167. "[Anna Emblin] hat das kind in der nacht allein gebohren, ein viertel stundt in armb gehalten und dann in das Privat geworffen." ASB 223: 184v–185r (8 February 1614).

168. Sections 35 and 36 of article 131 of the Carolina (see Wilhelm Wächtershäuser, *Das Verbrechen des Kindesmordes im Zeitalter der Aufklärung. Eine rechtsgeschichtliche Untersuchung der dogmatischen, prozessualen und rechtssoziologischen Aspekte* [Berlin, 1973], 61 ff.; Roetzer, "Die Delikte der Abtreibung," 78–79; and cf. Meumann, *Findelkinder*, 102, where at least one-third of the infanticide cases from a sample of fifty were instigated by suspicious pregnancies.

169. ASB 209: 22r.

170. "immassen schlechten oder liederlichen leuten nicht sogleich zu glauben, zumahlen wo sie ihren Namen wollen verschwiegen wissen." Roetzer, "Die Delikte der Abtreibung," 121.

171. "ob und was für weibspersonen etwas krankh oder verreist seyn, oder sonsten sich wieder gewohnheit, einerhalten, oder auch in einige weg sich verdächtig bezeigen." RV 2638: 35r–v (18 April 1670).

172. As early as 1536, councilors began offering a reward (*Fanggulden*) of ten gulden—ten to twenty times the normal premium paid—for information leading to the arrest of the killer of a baby found in the Pegnitz. RV 870: 17v (14 December 1536). A later reward for the murderer of an infant found buried near the customhouse was 2 fl. RV 1168: 24v (14 June 1559). By the beginning of the seventeenth century, magistrates had also begun using wanted posters (*Steckbriefe*) and raised the amount of frequently offered rewards to as high as 50 fl. in some instances—all to no apparent effect. The same reward was offered seventy-five years later. RV 2690: 99r (19 September 1674). Once, the council even offered a reward of 100 fl. (RV 2342: 14v–15r; 28 February 1648). For the most part, though, reward offers ranged from six to twelve gulden each. See RV 870: 17r (14 December 1636); RV 1080: 31r (9 July 1551); RV 1400: 27r, 33r, 35r (30 August, 1 and 2 September 1576), RV 1538: 2r (3 February 1587); RV 1874: 34r (14 September 1612); RV 1886: 78r–v (25 August 1613); RV 1895, 10r (11 April 1614); RV 1927: 13v (28 August 1616); RV 1933: 75r (13 March 1617); RV 1942: 46v (22 October 1617); RV 2299: 34v (17 December 1644); RV 2342: 14r and 37r (26 February, 3 March 1648); RV 2638: 35r–v (18 April 1670).

173. "sie habe es so weit nicht aussgerechnet, noch gewusst, das meine Herren den sachen so genawe und embsig nachforschen lassen, sonnsten wollt sie wol zu Bamberg geblieben sein." ASB 216: 177r–191r (26 June 1606). Another suspected child murderer who attempted to flee Nuremberg's jurisdiction didn't realize that Haroldsburg was still within the city's scope. Margaretha Friedlin (executed 14 March 1623), cited in Roetzer, "Die Delikte der Abtreibung," 129.

174. Both her transportation from and back to Lichtenau occurred at night. RV 1419: 22r, 26r (4 February 1578); RV 1420: 31v–32r (2 March 1578).

175. "Ir ein Wechter zuordnen." RV 1419: 28r (8 February 1578). See similar concerns about Barbara Schwenderin (RV 1141: 34r [8 April 1557]), Margreth Hainin (RV 1183: 36r [6 June 1560]), Elisabeth Ernstin [RV 1445: 30v; 29 December 1580]), Agnes Lengin (RV 1445: 15v–16r [10 December 1579]), and Margaretha Voglin (RV 2249: 16r–v [17 February 1641]). The cells were collectively known as the *Lochhüter-stublein.* Roetzer, "Die Delikte der Abtreibung," 130–31. According to Gerald Strauss (*Nuremberg,* 227), there were many suicides in the cells of the *Loch,* despite the religious beliefs of the times.

176. According to Hagedorn, Anna Dippoltin was very concerned about her parents and three siblings, including two small boys at home and a sister in service. GNM Hs 3857: 120v (4 February 1619).

177. "hat sich sonsten als eine bussfertige Sünderin erzeuget, ihre begangenen sünden herzlich, und zwar also beweinet dass man ihr, als ich das erstmahl bey ihr gewesen, das andere tüchlein reichen müssen, damit sie die zähren, so ihr mildiglich über die backen herab geflossen, abgewishet." GNM Hs 3857: 89r (8 February 1614).

178. "ganntz schwach und kranckh und sich in der seiten klagt, auch kein speis bei Ir behalten khan." RV 1185: 13v (17 July 1560).

179. "nicht lang in squalore carceris aufgehalten werde." RV 2551: 23r–v (10 October 1663).

180. "soll haben verlauten lassen sie währender Cur, er trage leider Sorge, das er eine lange Zeit gut gemacht habe, das würde Meister Franz wiederumb verderben." GNM 3857: 88v–89r (8 February 1614). The interrogators of both Helena Nusslerin (RV 1309: 16v [12 November 1569]) and of Barbara Schwenderin (RV 1142: 31v; 1143: 8r [8 May 1557]) were ordered to wait eight days before further torture. Similarly, Margarethe Voglin was allowed two weeks to grow stronger before her execution was carried out (RV 2249: 24v [19 February 1641]).
181. For midwife testimony on behalf of the defendant, see the cases of Kunigundt Diemännin (StaatsAN 51, 43: 62v–63r [1579]) and Christina Zieckhin (StaatsAN 51, 43: 154v [1 April 1582]). Their support of the accused Barbara Beerin was unusual in that it resulted in her release (RV 2602: 10v–11r, 41v–42r [14 August 1667]). For example of midwife testimony on behalf of the prosecution, see the case against Veronica Kölerin (RV 1670: 39v [9 March 1597]).
182. Articles 147 and 149 of the Carolina called for the examination of all suspicious cadavers. The Untersuchungskommission might also be composed of the hospital physician, two other physicians, one of the "ehrbare Frauen" who directed the midwives, and one midwife. The autopsy itself was normally conducted in the Freisskammer of GostenhofGostenhof or the Spital. Roetzer, "Die Delikte der Abtreibung," 116–20, 131.
183. The Wasserprobe was introduced in 1696. Felber, Unzucht und Kindsmord, 35.
184. "uff der geschwornen Maister der barbirer und baderhandwercks, verlesene Ansag, wie sie das am jungst vergagnenen Sontag an frue in dem Vischbach todt gefundenen neugebornen kindtlein besichtiget und befunden, das demselben die hirnschalen eingedrückt worden." RV 1557: 41r.
185. "das sie doch zweifelich ob Ime das hirn eingedrukt worden . . . soll man den fall Gott befohlen sein lassen," 20 and 22 January 1591; RV 1590: 49v, 51r.
186. "mit den geringsten Unkosten." During the sixteenth century this tended to be in the common grave at Saint Johannes, chosen to save space rather than because of any dishonor associated with the deceased. By the seventeenth century, the New Churchyard in Wöhrd was the usual destination, though other cemeteries, such as Saint Lienhard's, were also used. See, for example RV 1625: 8r (6 November 1593), RV 1644: 9r (11 March 1595); and Roetzer, "Die Delikte der Abtreibung," 121.
187. RV 1594: 16r (12 May 1591).
188. "bey hellem Lichten tag," StaatsAN 51, 45: 199v; GNM Hs 3857: 50r (1597), 64r (4 August 1607); RV 2250: 29r, RV 2251: 56v–57r (17 September and 6 October 1663). For other examples of obvious Wahrzeichen, see GNM Hs 3857: 88v (8 February 1614) and 120v (4 February 1619).
189. "da sagte der Meister im haus O! du unschuldiges Kindlein, ist einer unter unss allhie schuldig an dir so gibe ein Zeichnen, das sol alsbald das kind das linke kinder armlein empor gezogen haben." ASB 226a: 32v. The executioner Frantz Schmidt reports seeing a red spot on a child appear under similar circumstances on 6 July 1592 with Dorothea Hofmännin (Keller, Maister Franntz Schmidts, 99; StaatsAN 52a: 447, 1155). Rublack finds references to the Bahrprobe in some seventeenth-century criminal records (Crimes of Women, 58).
190. Article 36 of the Carolina. These grounds for torture of a suspected child murderer were later adopted in France (1556), Sweden (1627), Württemberg (1658), Denmark (1683), Scotland (1690), and Bavaria (1751). David Ransel, "Orphans and Foundlings," in Encyclopedia of European Social History from 1350 to 2000, ed. Peter Stearns (New York: Scribner, 2001), 4: 497.
191. ASB 209: 21v. See also Elisabeth Ernstin (RV 1444: 55v [28 December 1579]), Agnes

Lengin (ASB 209: 169v–170r [26 January 1580]), and Ottilia Demerin (RV 1668: 36v, 41v [1 April 1597]).

192. "Wer des kindvatter sei unnd wo derselbig die unzuch mit ir getriben, auch wie off und zu was zeiten es geshehen, das soll sie anzeigen."ASB 209: 21v. See Roper, *Holy Household*, 115ff., on a similar magisterial obsession with the sex lives of prostitutes and other criminal women brought before them. Here my findings differ from those of van Dülmen, who claims that "during the interrogations the judges paid surprisingly little attention to the partners or fathers of the children" (*Frauen vor Gericht*, 83).

193. Cf. case of Barbara Krellin, ASB 226a: 168 (25 October 1626).

194. "one Irer freund und herrshafft vorwissen . . . on ainichs menshen beisein . . . hab sie niemand geraitzt, dagelernt . . . hab auch niemand wissen darumb tragen." ASB 209: 21r, 22v.

195. Cf. examples cited by Meumann (*Findelkinder*, 127) such as the advice one young woman received from her boyfriend: "if she had a child she should throw it into the water."

196. "dann sie besorgt, es möchte Ir vatter fahren, und sie also handtschlagen." ASB 209: 171r (26 January 1580). Ernstin: ASB 209: 169v (20 January 1580); Zieckhin: ASB 210: 45r (14 August 1582).

197. Geyerin's father was also punished for conspiring to hide her pregnancy. RV 2370: 49r–v; RV 2371: 9v, 24r (8, 18, 20 April 1650). Anna Seyfridtin's parents were arrested but eventually released on the same charges (RV 2550: 31r–v, RV 2551: 56v–57r [19 September and 6 October 1663]) and Veronica Köllerin's sister and brother-in-law were banished as "losen leute" (RV 1670: 40v [10 March 1597]).

198. See, for example, Barbara Weiherin (RV 1187: 8r, 10r [17 September 1560]), Margrethe Dörflerin (ASB 209: 172v [4 January 1580]), Elisabeth Ernstin (ASB 209: 169v [20 January 1580]), Christina Zieckhin (RV 1479: 56v–57r [1 August 1582]), and Anna Seyfridtin (RV 2551: 20r–v [14 October 1663]; also Zimmerman, "Behörigs Orthen angezeigt," 73. Van Dülmen, however, insists that torture was rarely applied to suspected child murderers, only threatened (*Frauen vor Gericht*, 39). Given the gaps in criminal documentation, it is impossible to compute a precise figure, though Meumann's sample of fifty infanticide cases correlates with the Nuremberg figure of one-third (*Findelkinder*, 105).

199. Rublack (*Crimes of Women*, 54) cites a 1677 recommendation of the Tübingen law faculty on a time limit for torture. See also Strauss, *Nuremberg*, 225–27, on methods of torture employed in Nuremberg; also Roetzer, "Die Delikte der Abtreibung," 46, and 78–80 on paragraph 36 of article 131 on sufficient grounds for torture in infanticide cases.

200. Her interrogators were instructed by the council "speak somewhat harshly to her" and "seriously bind and threaten [her]." RV 1419: 26v (6 February 1578).

201. ASB 211: 110v (7 July 1590).

202. The abhorrence of a wrongful execution is a common supposition in Roman law. Cf. StaatsAN 51, 8: 84ff. (26 March 1534).

203. Margaretha Dörflerin was an exception, claiming "she knows of nothing that she did except to give birth to a child and have it baptized." ASB 209: 171r (4 January 1580).

204. Dorothea Meulin admitted killing another illegitimate baby two years earlier, ASB 199: 78v (17 May 1606). Barbara Käsin confessed to killing two of her previous three illegitimate babies. ASB 226a: 204–5 (14 October 1669).

205. ASB 209: 22v.

206. For explicit references to legal consultation, see RV 1185: 43r (3 August 1560), RV 1444: 58v (29 December 1579), RV 1445: 34v (15 January 1580), RV 1670: 40v, StaatsAN 51, 45: 199r–v (10 March 1597), RV 2249: 24v (19 February 1641), and RV 2551: 20r–v, 23r–v (14 October 1663).

207. See H. C. Erik Midelfort, *A History of Madness in Sixteenth-century Germany* (Stanford: Stanford University Press, 1999), 183–94, on infanticide and the insanity defense in sixteenth- and seventeenth-century Germany.

208. ASB 200: 228r (3 April 1611). Schusterin persisted in denying both a secret pregnancy and infanticide during repeated torture sessions and eventually only admitted that the child was hers and had been born dead. She was fined and banished for life.

209. "werde man einen anderen ernst gegen ihr fürnehmen." Ottilia Demerin (StaatsAN 51, 45: 102–5 [1 April 1597]); Helena Schlauerspächin (ASB 200: 44v–45v [9 February 1611]). The Carolina of 1532 required secular authorities to release a suspect after denial of charges during three separate torture sessions. See Roetzer, "Die Delikte der Abtreibung," 152, on the use of the *sträfliche Rede* and *Denkzettel* in infanticide cases with insufficient evidence.

210. Nuremberg (1549–1675) executed 58 of 64 convicted (90.6 percent) and 58 of 79 accused (73.4 percent). Frankfurt am Oder (1562–1696) executed 18 of 26 accused (69.2 percent). Rothenburg ob der Tauber (1501–1618) executed 8 of 11 accused (72.7 percent). Geneva (1592–1712) executed 25 of 31 accused (80.6 percent). Württemberg (1581–1792) executed 65 of 75 accused (86.7 percent). The Electorate of Saxony and Hildesheim (1600–1809) executed two-thirds to three-fourths of all accused. Augsburg (1620–1786) executed all of its 17 accused child murderers (100 percent). Van Dülmen, *Frauen vor Gericht* (63, table 6); Rowlands, "In Great Secrecy," 179; William Monter, "Women in Calvinist Geneva," *Signs* 6, no. 2 (1980): 189–209; Meumann, *Findelkinder*, 110; Zimmerman, "Berhörigs Orthen angezeigt," 78ff., and see appendix 2.

211. Elisabeth Rentzin (2 April 1591), Dorothea Hoffmännin (6 July 1592), Anna Arnoldin (11 November 1593), Margaretha Teutschin (26 January 1600), Anna Kisslingen (20 May 1600), "ein magd" (8 February 1621). See appendix 2.

212. "Jugendt und unverstandt, auch dess pösen feinds verfürung." StaatsAN 51, 41: 107. See also Theodor Hampe, *Die Nürnberger Malefizbücher als Quellen der reichsstädtischen Sittengeschichte vom 14. bis zum 18. Jahrhundert* (Bamberg: C. C. Buchner, 1927), 82–83, and appendix 2.

213. "damit das volk nit leichtfertiger gemacht und zu der gleichen bössen händeln mehr ursach gegeben werde." RV 1185: 22r (23 July 1560). Other examples of popular but unsuccessful appeals include the cases of Barbara Schwenderin (RV 1143: 18r–v [1 June 1557]) and Agnes Lengin, whose father was the court gardener to the Count of the Rhineland-Palatinate in Heidelberg (ASB 209: 169v [26 January 1580]). See also Knapp, *Kriminalrecht*, 1: 184 ff., on pre-1542 leniency; and Van Dülmen, *Frauen vor Gericht*, 46, on the decline of clemency during the sixteenth and seventeenth centuries.

214. "von Natur ein Spröte Persohn, im haupt blöt" (27 March 1623; cited in Roetzer, "Die Delikte der Abtreibung," 157). "sehr unbeständig in der frage gewesen," GNM Hs 3857, 62v (26 June 1606). Cf. successful examples of these defenses in Rublack, *Crimes of Women*, 60ff. Several modern studies have found diagnosable disorders in as many as 80 percent of neonatacide cases, including 35 percent classified as mentally retarderd. Schwartz and Isser, *Endangered Children*, 40–41.

215. "ihr selbst zur wohlverdienten Straff andern bey so viel und oftmahlig einreissenden erschröklichen und entsetzlichen Kindsmorden zum abscheu und Exempel sich vor dergleichen Übelthaten zu hüten," ASB 224: 124v (April 1674), See also Strauss, *Nuremberg*, 229; and Richard J. Evans, *Rituals of Retribution: Capital Punishment in Germany, 1600–1987* (Oxford: Oxford University Press, 1996), 65.
216. RV 1420: 35r (2 March 1578); Keller, *Maister Franntzn Schmidts*, 6.

CHAPTER TWO

1. RV 1906: 50v–51v, RV 1907: 34r–v (20 and 21 February, 16 March 1615); FB 1: 288.
2. The subject of early modern poverty has accumulated a massive bibliography on such issues as governmental poor relief and vagrants in literature, as well as the prosecution of begging and other crimes. The best introductory survey of this sprawling literature is Robert Jütte, *Poverty and Deviance in Early Modern Europe* (Cambridge University Press: Cambridge, 1994). See also the magisterial Hufton, *Poor of Eighteenth-Century France*, 1 ff., on the historiographical problems of tracking and understanding the largely invisible poor of this period. Several studies of the 1980s attempted to convey the experience of early modern poverty and begging in Germany but lacked access to firsthand perspectives. See, for instance, Ernst Schubert, *Arme Leute, Bettler und Gauner im Franken des 18. Jahrhunderts* (Neustadt an der Aisch: Degener, 1983); Carsten Küther, *Menschen auf der Straße. Vagierende Unterschichten in Bayern, Franken und Schwaben in der zweiten Hälfte des 18. Jahrhunderts* (Göttingen: Vandenhoeck & Ruprecht, 1983); Arnold Lassotta and Franz Irsigler, *Bettler und Gaukler, Dirnen und Henker. Randgruppen und Außenseiter in Köln 1300–1600* (Cologne: Greven, 1984); and Adalbert Nagel, *Armut im Barock. Die Bettler und Vaganten Oberschwabens* (Weingarten: Drumlin, 1986). Even the recent work of Gerhard Ammerer (*Heimat Straße: Vaganten im Österreich des Ancien Régime* [Munich: Oldenbourg, 2003]), while a fascinating prosopography, has only occasional firsthand testimony. More satisfying in this respect are Norbert Schindler, "The Origins of Heartlessness: The Culture and Way of Life of Beggars in Late Seventeenth-century Salzburg," in *Rebellion, Community and Custom in Early Modern Germany* (Cambridge: Cambridge University Press, 2002); and Otto Ulbricht, "The World of a Beggar around 1775," *Central European History* 27 (1994): 153–84.
3. Even tax records can be inconsistent and therefore misleading, since the city of Cologne only recorded 4 percent of its sixteenth-century population as propertyless, clearly an underestimate, while contemporary Verona recorded 77 percent of its population as indigent. In England, Gregory King estimated that 47 percent of the kingdom's 5.5 million subjects in 1688 were poor cottagers, wage earners on the edge, or vagrants. Bronislaw Geremek, *Poverty: A History*, trans. Agnieska Kolokowska (Cambridge: Blackwell, 1994), 119. Rudolf Endres, "Zur wirtschaftlichen und sozialen Lage in Franken vor dem Dreißigjährigen Krieg," *Jahrbuch für fränkische Landesforschung* 28 (1968): 17; and Jütte, *Poverty and Deviance*, 2, 195–96.
4. See the summary in Jan DeVries, "Population," in *Handbook of European History, 1400–1600: Late Middle Ages, Renaissance, and Reformation*, ed. Thomas A. Brady, Jr., and James D. Tracy (Leiden and New York: E. J. Brill, 1994–95), 1: 13–36.
5. David Kertzer, introduction, *Family Life in Early Modern Times, 1500–1789*, ed. David Kertzer (New Haven: Yale University Press, 2001), ix; Christian Pfister, "The Population of Late Medieval and Early Modern Germany," in *Germany: A New Social and Economic History*, vol. 1 (1450–1630), ed. Bob Scribner (London: Arnold, 1996), 39–41.

6. Neither prices nor salaries increased uniformly throughout Europe. In sixteenth-century Hamburg, for instance the average wages of men increased only 150 percent and those of women a mere 40 percent, while the price of grain went up 380 percent (Geremek, *Poverty*, 90). Endres estimates that in Nuremberg and its environs the price for a *Simmer* of grain tripled during this period, from fifteen to forty-five days of unskilled labor in 1500 to twenty-eight to eighty days in 1600 (Endres, "Zur wirtschaftlichen und sozialen Lage," 23). Meanwhile in neighboring Würzburg, salaries increased 200 percent from 1505 to 1622 (Elssas, *Umriss einer Geschichte*, 69). Abel, long the standard interpretation for Germany, estimated that on average, prices tripled during the long sixteenth century and wages doubled; more recent data refine these increases to 255 percent and 157 percent, respectively. See also Werner Rösener, "The Agrarian Economy, 1300–1600," in Scribner, ed., *Germany*, 72.

7. FKD: 1606 of 2424 (66.2 percent) total occupations were artisans; 1186 of those (73 percent) artisans were journeymen, who as a group composed 48.9 percent of all occupations listed. Anita Obermeier, "Findel- und Waisenkinder: Zur Geschichte des Sozialfürsorge in der Reichsstadt Augsburg," *Zeitschrift des historischen Vereins für Schwaben* 83 (1990): 129, finds a similar pattern among the parents of orphans and foundlings in Augsburg, as does Ammerer (*Heimat Straße*, 67) in his sample of 1,884 eighteenth-century vagrants.

8. Artisans constituted up to one-half of early modern urban populations. Christopher R. Friedrichs, *The Early Modern City, 1450–1750* (London and New York: Longman, 1995), 147–48; Endres, "zur wirtschaftlichen und sozialen Lage," 19–20; Ekkehard Wiest, *Die Entwicklung des Nürnberger Gewerbes zwischen 1648 und 1806* (Stuttgart: G. Fischer,1968), 167.

9. Ellis L. Knox, "The Lower Orders in Early Modern Augsburg," in *Process of Change*, ed. Bebb and Marshall, 167.

10. FKD: 77 of 1106 cases in which the father's occupation was known. Of 27 households with children in one sweep of street children, six listed soldier for father's occupation, followed by belt maker and wire drawer (four each). Stadtalmosenamt report of 8 April 1663 (StadtAN D1/564). The top five crafts among the city's alms recipients for 1700–42 were belt maker, wire drawer, wheelsmith, ring maker, and weaver. Wiest, *Die Entwicklung des Nürnberger Gewerbes*, 200–1.

11. In a 1696 sample of five recruiting rolls from the tiny principality of Schleswig-Holstein-Gottorf, the proportion of men who claimed training in a craft were 32.3 percent, 19.1 percent, 39.4 percent, 26.9 percent, and 55.4 percent. Baker, tailor, and cobbler were the top trades. Burschel, *Söldner im Nordwestdeutschland*, 58.

12. On the *verschämte* poor and their special status, see Geremek, *Poverty*, 39ff. On differentiations among the poor in this period, see also Bernd-Ulrich Hergemöller, ed., *Randgruppen der spätmittelalterlichen Gesellschaft* (Warendorf: Fahlbusch, 1990); Bernd Roeck, *Eine Stadt in Krieg und Frieden: Studien zur Geschichte der Reichsstadt Augsburg zwischen Kalenderstreit und Parität* (Göttingen: Vandenhoeck & Ruprecht, 1989), chap. 7; and the excellent study by Valentin Groebner, *Ökonomie ohne Haus: Zum Wirtschaften armer Leute in Nürnberg am Ende des 15. Jahrhunderts* (Göttingen: Vandenhoeck & Ruprecht, 1993).

13. Ingomar Bog, "Über Arme und Armenfürsorge in Oberdeutschland und in der Eidgenossenschaft im 15. und 16. Jahrhundert," *Jahrbuch für fränkische Landesforschung* 34–35 (1974–75): 1800.

14. See Ammerer, *Heimat Straße*, 30 ff.

15. In England, for instance, while the population of London tripled between 1550 and 1650, the number of arrests for vagrancy went up twelve times. A. L. Beier, *Masterless Men: The Vagrancy Problem in England, 1560–1640* (London and New York: Methuen, 1985), 40. Intensified enforcement cannot account for all of the increase.

16. Based on an estimate of 4,800 illegal aliens in Nuremberg in 1622 and an overall population figure of 15 percent for the sixteenth and seventeenth centuries, in Rudolf Endres, "Zur Einwohnerzahl und Bevölkerungsstruktur Nürnbergs im 15./16. Jahrhundert," *MVGN* 57 (1970): 261. Katherine A. Lynch (*Individuals, Families, and Communities*, 38) estimates that migrants constituted 3–8 percent of most German urban populations. See Friedrichs, *Early Modern City*, 217ff., on early modern urban problems associated with immigration; also Schubert, *Fahrendes Volk im Mittelalter* (Bielefeld: Verlag für Regionalgeschichte, 1996); and Beier, *Masterless Men*, 51–52, for England.

17. The seminal article on soldiers as vagrants is Bob Scribner, "Mobility: Voluntary or Enforced? Vagrants in Württemberg in the Sixteenth Century," in *Migration in der Feudalgesellschaft*, ed. Gerhard Jaritz and Albert Müller (Frankfurt: Campus, 1988), 65–88.

18. FKD. Only 60 of 2,424 were identified as soldiers in instances in which the occupation of the father was specified. There were no fathers listed as soldiers in foster petitions and 4.1 percent among orphans. Meumann (*Findelkinder*, 331–38) found soldiers particularly overrepresented in questions of abandoned children and child welfare a century later.

19. Daily laborers in military construction earned two to five Groschen a day during the seventeenth century. Burschel, *Söldner im Nordwestdeutschland*, 166–67, 173, 180, 199, 206–17.

20. When the imperial army left Buxtehude in February 1632, it comprised 501 soldiers, 355 women, and 367 children; in Lippstadt (November 1645), an army contained 220 officers, 1614 cavalry and infantry, 800 women and 900 children; another army in Münster (1662) had 55 officers, 1417 under-officers and troops, 689 women, and 1272 children; finally a Hannoverian army in Einbeck (1677) contained over 700 soldiers, 355 women, and 430 children. Burschel, *Söldner im Nordwestdeutschland*, 241–42.

21. See Burschel, *Söldner im Nordwestdeutschland*, 27–53, on the rich literary tradition of despising soldiers, and 244–46, on the legal restrictions regarding soldiers and marriage. In one eighteenth-century sample of vagrants, 40.4 percent of couples lived in common-law marriages (Ammerer, *Heimat Straße*, 265). See also Gerhard Fritz, *Eine Rotte von allerhand räuberischem Gesindt* (Ostfildern: J. Thorbecke, 2004), 279–91 and 319–23, which argues for a high degree of stability among such illicit unions.

22. Burschel cites contemporary sources describing how military families lived in "bitterster Armut" and rarely had sufficient income for the entire household. *Söldner im Nordwestdeutschland*, 216, 244.

23. Groebner, *Ökonomie ohne Haus*, 118ff.

24. As early as the sixteenth century, the word "makeshift" had the dual meanings of "one who is making shifts" and "a shifty person or rogue" (*OED*, 9: 167). During the late twentieth century, many historians, particularly Olwen Hufton, used the term to describe an entire way of life or an economy. According to Hufton, the nature of a makeshift economy was very closely linked to local migrational patterns, which were in turn influenced by geography, sex, local traditions, time available, and what one

344 / Notes to Pages 81–82

left behind (i.e., a small parcel of land or the possibility of a big inheritance). Hufton, *Poor of Eighteenth-Century France*, 70–73. See also Ammerer, *Heimat Straße*, 379–457, on the economic life of vagrants.

25. On the seasonal nature of vagrant work, see Ammerer, *Heimat Straße*, 387; also Groebner, *Ökonomie ohne Haus*, 123–28.

26. Cf. 1654 comments of Raimond of Montecuoli that military service often presented a welcome opportunity among rural people "to play hooky during the work off-season." Burschel, *Söldner im Nordwestdeutschland*, 81.

27. See especially the example of the soldier's wife who helped her husband carry bed linens, wine, clothes, and silver belts from a burning Magdeburg. Jan Peters, ed., *Ein Söldnerleben im Dreißigjährigen Krieg. Eine Quelle zur Sozialgeschichte* (Berlin: Akademie Verlag, 1993), 226–27; also Lynch, *Individuals, Families, and Communities*, 47. In German lands, peddlers were variously known as *Hausierer, Ausrufer, Hockerer, Kiepenkerle, Gäukler,* and *Krämer.*

28. Laurence Fontaine, *History of Pedlars in Europe*, trans. Vicki Whittaker (Cambridge: Polity Press, 1996), esp. 1–4; Werner Danckert, *Unehrliche Leute: Die verfemten Berufe* (Bern: Franke, 1963), 213–20; Beier, *Masterless Men*, 87; and see Groebner, *Ökonomie ohne Haus*, 145–47, on noncitizen workers in Nuremberg.

29. Friederichs, *Early Modern City*, 215–16.

30. According to Burschel, "the complete and punctual payment of the salary was more the exception than the rule." (*Söldner im Nordwestdeutschland*, 192–94).

31. See Harrington, *Reordering Marriage*, 39–49, 73–78; also Fritz, *Eine Rotte*, 326–29; and Susan D. Amussen, *An Ordered Society: Gender and Class in Early Modern England* (New York: Blackwell, 1988), 96–98 and 123–28.

32. FKD: 14 of 2,424 (0.57 percent) cases in which the father's occupation was known were identified as beggars, 83 (3.4 percent) as manual labors.

33. FKD: 77 of 2,275 known father occupations as daily laborers and 113 of 2,275 as beggars. In 79.5 percent of laborer listings (61 of 77), the father was dead or absent. The top four occupations listed for fathers of fifty apprehended beggar children in 1769 Würzburg were sack carriers, wheel barrowers, tobacco workers, and day workers. Schubert, *Arme Leute*, 111.

34. Based on *Reichenalmosen* lists of 301 households in 1529 and 760 households during 1557–64, as well as one 1663 list of twenty-seven Nuremberg households that sent minors begging. The number of children in households ranged from one to eight, with an average of 3.5 children per household for 1529, 2.7 for 1557–64, and 3.44 in 1663. StaatsAN *Reichenalmosen; Stadtalmosenamt* report of 8 April 1663 (StadtAN D1/564).

35. A recent study of the Saxon village of Belm during the same period has found not only a comparable average of 3.61 among poor families, but also that only 17.6 percent of poor households actually had three or more children resident at the same time. Large families were much more typical of propertied middle-class and wealthy households, where 72.9 percent of households had three or more children, yielding an average of 6.64 each. Jürgen Schlumbohm, *Lebensläufe, Familien, Höfe. Die Bauern und Heuerleute des Osnabrückischen Kirchspiels Belm in proto-industrieller Zeit, 1650–1860* (Göttingen: Vandenhoeck & Ruprecht, 1994), 201, 297.

36. Introduction *Family Life*, ed. Ketzer, x; in the same volume, Pier Paoloa Viazzo, "Mortality, Fertility, and Family," 169. In 1530, for instance, about half of all couples in the bishopric of Speyer had three or more children. Pfister, "Population of Late Medieval and Early Modern Germany," in Scribner, *Germany*, 39. A large family was

only cited as one out of ten times as the main cause of poverty in eighteenth-century Würzburg and Cologne. Jütte, *Poverty and Deviance*, 41.

37. Pfister, "Population of Late Medieval and Early Modern Germany," in Scribner, *Germany*, 50.

38. Schlumbohm, *Lebensläufe, Familien, Höfe*, 116, 134, 149. Pier Paolo Viazzo, "Family Structures and the Early Phase in the Individual Life Cycle: A Southern European Perspective," in *Poor Women and Children in the European Past*, ed. John Henderson and Richard Wall (London: Routledge, 1994), 31–50. On the "European" (later "northwestern European) late marriage pattern, see John Hajnal, "European Marriage Patterns in Perspective," in *Population in History: Essays in Historical Demography*, ed. D. V. Glass and D. E. C. Eversley (Chicago: Aldine, 1965), idem, "Two Kinds of Preindustrial Household Formation System," *Population and Development Review* 8, no. 3 (1982): 449–94; also the discussion in Lynch, *Individuals, Families and Communities*, 44ff.

39. Rublack, *Crimes of Women*, 139, 152–53; Wiesner, *Working Women*, 4–5.

40. In Oppenheim, 76 percent of widowers remarried within one year while only 44 percent of widows remarried within ten years (Zchunke, *Konfession und Alltag in Oppenheim*, 189–93). In Belm, 45.1 percent of all widowers married within one year, while only 31.1 percent of widows remarried within ten years (Schlumbohm, *Lebensläufe, Familien, Höfe*, 176). On average, widows tended to wait two-and-a-half times as long as widowers to remarry, if at all. Antoinette Fauve-Chamoux, "Marriage, Widowhood, and Divorce," in Kertzer, *Family Life in Early Modern Times*, 221, 244.

41. During the sixteenth century, many Protestant legal codes permitted divorce and remarriage for malicious abandonment, but the legal process involved was rigorous and often expensive. Waiting periods ranged from one year (Basel) to seven years (canon law) to ten years (Geneva). Harrington, *Reordering Marriage*, 88–89, 260–62, 267.

42. In 1529, 134 (53 percent) of *Reichenalmosen* households were headed by men; 1557 and 1564 that proportion had risen to 68.4 percent, *Stadtalmosenamt* report of 8 April 1663 (StadtAN D1/564). A 1769 survey of beggar children in Würzburg found that half (16 or 32) came from female-headed households. Schubert, *Arme Leute*, 111. See similar figures among early modern households receiving alms elsewhere in Thomas A. Brady, Jr., "The Social and Economic Role of Institutions," in Scribner, *Germany*, 279; and see Jütte, *Poverty and Deviance*, 41 (table 3). In 2000, the World Bank estimated that girls and women made up 70 percent of the world's poor. Laurence Fontaine and Jürgen Schlumbohm, eds., *Household Strategies for Survival 1600–2000: Fission, Faction and Cooperation; International Review of Social History Supplement* 45 (2000): 13.

43. White bread cost at least twice as much as less palatable dark bread in Nuremberg, leading Groebner (*Ökonomie ohne Haus*, 84) to observe that "with bread, as with other food items, there is a clear and fairly drastic social differentiation." The inedibility comment is based on a 1545 observation of Nuremberger Sebastian Frank, cited in Jütte, *Poverty and Deviance*, 72–73. See also Ulf Dirlmeier and Gerhard Fouquet, "Diet and Consumption," in Scribner, *Germany*, 89ff.; Groebner, *Ökonomie ohne Haus*, 99–100. Henderson and Wall, introduction, *Poor Women and Children*. By the time of the French Revolution, Parisian wage earners were spending 88 percent of their wages on bread alone (Hufton, *Poor of Eighteenth-Century France*, 46).

44. Groebner, *Ökonomie ohne Haus*, 71–72, 75. Groebner considers such wild fluctuations as typical of the bazaar economy at work, where prices are geared toward immediate

profit rather than lasting consumer relations (112). Endres, "Zur wirtschaftlichen und sozialen Lage," 29–32.

45. Sample rent figures are 57 percent in 1522 Rostock, 23–65 percent in 1554–56 Leipzig, 62 percent in 1589 Cologne (one parish sample), and 63 percent in 1563 Vienna. In every instance, figures for the fifteenth century had been lower. By the eighteenth century, nine out of ten wage earners in Paris rented. Robert Jütte, "Daily Life in Late Medieval and Early Modern Germany," in Scribner, *Germany*, 329ff.; Daniel Roche, *The People of Paris: An Essay in Popular Culture in the Eighteenth Century* (Berkeley: University of California Press, 1987), 105.

46. In early seventeenth-century Augsburg, 70 percent of families lived in such multi-dwelling buildings. Friedrichs, *Early Modern City*, 39. See also Raffaella Sarti, "Material Conditions of Family Life," in Ketzer, *Family Life in Early Modern Times*, 3–23; Brady, "Social and Economic Role of Institutions," 279.

47. Jütte, *Poverty and Deviance*, 59ff., 166; Geremek, *Poverty*, 69–70; Beier, *Masterless Men*, 78–82, on vagrants and alehouses, often associated with theft and stolen goods.

48. Jütte, *Poverty and Deviance*, 65.

49. Hufton, *Poor of Eighteenth-Century France*, 52. A sample of Gloucestershire and East Kent during the period 1650–1700 found that 80–90 percent owned a bed of some sort, though only 50 percent owned a single chair. Sarti, "Material Conditions of Family Life," 6–9. See Groebner, *Ökonomie ohne Haus*, on the use of material and clothing for payment (152–57), on clothing of the poor in general (235–43), on small tin and silver objects (243–46), and on beds (246–52); also Ammerer, *Heimat Straße*, 313–17.

50. Hufton, *Poor of Eighteenth-Century France*, 329.

51. Benjamin Seebohm Rowntree, *Poverty: A Study of Town Life*, 4th ed. (London and New York: MacMillan, 1902). See also Ammerer, *Heimat Straße*, 123–58; and introduction to Henderson and Wall, *Poor Women and Children*, 4–5. Only old age in the days before pensions rivaled the tremendous strain that young children placed on a family's economic resources.

52. See, for instance, Carter Lindberg, *Beyond Charity: Reformation Initiatives for the Poor* (Minneapolis: Fortress Press, 1993). This shift is discussed in greater detail in chapter 3.

53. Recipients also received quarterly payments of one pound of lard and one *Nietzen* of salt. Rüger, *Mittelalterliches Almosenwesen*, 18–21.

54. "viele frommen, hausarme, bedürftige [verschämte Arme] ohne persönliche Hilfe und Handreichung nicht zu leben vermögen." *Ordnung des grossen almosen hausarmer leut* (1562), StaatsAN 63Ia: Vol C: 45v–46r.

55. The example is from the famine and plague of 1570–75. During the famines of 1482 and 1501, the council subsidized 7,000 and 5,000 weekly loaves of *Notbrot*, respectively. Groebner, *Ökonomie ohne Haus*, 114; Endres, "Zur wirtschaftlichen und sozialen Lage," 27, 32–33.

56. Despite the sizeable alms expenditure of nearby Würzburg (2354 fl. in 1600), Schubert estimates that relief reached at most 4 percent of the general population (*Arme Leute*, 209). The Nuremberg figures are based on an estimate of 4,666–6,666 poor children in the city under the age of sixteen (one-third of the population of 40,000 in 1615 was under sixteen and 35–50 percent of those in struggling families); figuring an average of 3.0 children per household yields 1,555–2,222 poor households, of whom 616 (27.7–39.6 percent) were receiving some form of government assistance at its peak in 1610. StadtAN D1/128.

57. This was actually much higher than contemporary England, where relief declined from 20 percent of a day laborer's wages in 1600 to 12–13 percent in 1700. Another study estimated relief at 27 percent of a worker's wages in 1707, while by the beginning of the next century in Netherlands and Flanders, stipends were valued at only 6–20 percent of a worker's wages. Henderson and Wall, introduction, *Poor Women and Children*, 18–19.

58. *Ordnungen des Reichenalmosen*, 1579 and 1609; StadtAN A6, D1/3. Cf. decrees about alms recipients who were ashamed to wear badges: RV 16 December 1631 and RV 8 January 1633; Stadtalmosenamt Bericht. See also a request (RV 25 and 28 February 1633) for exemption from the requirement from widow Margaretha Bauerin, turned down by the council. StadtAN D1/126.

59. "die ofenlicher Sünden pflegen, als mit unkeüsch spillen . . . od. unfriedlich mit Iren nachbarn leben, mit scheldenn, Gotlesterlichenn fluchen, nachreden, shlaben, und andern unzimblicher sachen, wie das kummen mag, auch vol und truncken wehrn, do Ire unnüzlich verzehrn in wirtsheüsern." *Ordnung des Reichenalmosen* (1579, 1609) StadtAN D1/3: 8r–v.

60. Ulbricht, "World of a Beggar," 164–65; Jütte, *Poverty and Deviance*, 139; Beier, *Masterless Men*, 27. The same might be said of begging in a modern U.S. city, where a full-time minimum wage earner would receive about $40 per day after taxes (based on a 2008 minimum wage of $6.55).

61. For the text of the 1370 ordinance, see Rüger, *Mittelalterliches Almosenwesen*, 68–70. Ordinances of 1478 and 1518 both permitted shamefaced poor to beg house to house as long as they took their official badge and lantern (to avoid accusations of burglary). See also Christoph Sachße and Florian Tennstedt, *Geschichte der Armenfürsorge in Deutschland, Volume 1: Vom Spätmittelalter bis zum 1. Weltkrieg*, 2nd rev. ed. (Stuttgart: Kohlhammer, 1998), 28ff.

62. Ulbricht, "World of a Beggar," 171.

63. Jütte, *Poverty and Deviance*, 39. The report of the Comité de Mendicité in the 1770s estimated that 1,886,935 children were unable to be supported by their parents and were thus forced to beg. A 1724 annual report for Aix-en-Provence similarly shows that 42 percent of all registered beggars were under twenty years of age. Hufton, *Poor of Eighteenth-Century France*, 108, 111.

64. This is also common among modern street children. See Rachel Baker and Catherine Painter-Brick, "Comparative Perspective on Children's 'Careers' and Abandonment in Nepal," 165.

65. See Jütte, *Poverty and Deviance*, 182–85 on *Rotwelsch*, a mixture of the Latin of wandering medieval monks, Yiddish, Romany (Gypsy), and various German dialects.

66. See the example of begging day laborer Georg Schmid, his wife, and their two sons: RV 2376: 110r–v (27 September 1650).

67. Pierre Bourdieu was the most influential theorist of social capital. See his *Outline of a Theory of Practice* (Cambridge: Cambridge University Press, 1977), 32ff., on the distinction between "official" and "practical" kin. Based on a study of self-help and reciprocity among the poor of seventeenth-century Bordeaux, Martin Dinges concludes that "working relations are as effective as personal relations in coping with poverty, and that neighbourhood relations may have the same useful effects as family relations during a period of distress." Martin Dinges, "Self-Help and Reciprocity in Parish Assistance: Bordeaux in the Sixteenth and Seventeenth Centuries," in *The Locus of Care: Families, Institutions, and the Provision of Welfare since Antiquity*, ed. Peregrine Horden and Richard Smith (London and New York: Routledge, 1998), 113–14. For

a summary of the application and interpretation of "social capital" by early modern historians during the past thirty years, see Sheilagh Ogilvie, "How Does Social Capital Affect Women? Guilds and Communities in Early Modern Germany," *American Historical Review* 109, no. 2 (April 2004): 325–28.

68. Jeremy Boulton, "'It Is Necessity That Makes Me Do This': Some 'Survival Strategies' of Pauper Households in London's West End during the Early Eighteenth Century," in Fontaine and Schlumbohm, *Household Strategies,* 61–62.

69. Jakob and Wilhelm Grimm, *Deutsches Wörterbuch,* new ed. (Leipzig: Hirtel, 1964ff.), 4.1: 161–64, s.v. *"Freund,"* definition 2. In most parts of sixteenth- and seventeenth-century Europe, "friend" had the ambiguous sense of "one joined to another in mutual benevolence and intimacy" as well as "a kinsman or near relative" (exclusively the latter in most Scandinavian languages), *OED,* 6: 192–93. On the ambiguous nature of "friend" during this era, see Naomi Tadmor, *Family and Friends in Eighteenth-Century England: Household, Kinship, and Patronage* (Cambridge: Cambridge University Press, 2001), esp. 167–70 and 272–79. Tadmor defines early modern "friendship" "as a moral and reciprocal relationship," regardless of blood relationship. Richard Grassby advocates a similar understanding of the term in his *Kinship and Capitalism: Marriage, Family, and Business in the English-Speaking World, 1580–1740* (Cambridge: Cambridge University Press, 2001), 241–49.

70. Robin Briggs, *Witches and Neighbours: The Social and Cultural Context of European Witchcraft* (New York: Viking, 1996), 139.

71. In London's Saint Saviour parish from 1655 to 1665, 83.1 percent of residents married within parish, and 13.9 percent in neighboring parishes or elsewhere in London. Within the same sample, more than three-quarters of all wills had at least one neighbor as an executor and two-thirds of all lawsuits relied on the supporting testimony of a neighbor. Jeremy Boulton, *Neighbourhood and Society: A London Suburb in the Seventeenth Century* (Cambridge: Cambridge University Press, 1987), 206–7, 227ff., 235–36, 240. See also Ammerer, *Heimat Straße,* 379–457, on the *Ökonomie des Notbehelfs;* Boulton, *Neighbourhood and Society,* 230ff., on the problems of defining "community" in an urban context; and David Garrioch, *Neighborhood and Community in Paris, 1740–1790* (Cambridge: Cambridge University Press, 1986), 257ff, on social networks in Paris.

72. Geremek, *Poverty,* 65–66, 68.

73. By one estimate, almost 80 percent of the early modern urban poor could not afford citizenship. Lynch, *Individuals, Families, and Communities,* 38.

74. Grassby, *Kinship and Capitalism,* 244.

75. Burschel, *Söldner im Nordwestdeutschland,* 188.

76. A 1443 Nuremberg statute forbade employers to make loans to employees but apparently the law was generally disregarded. Groebner, *Ökonomie ohne Haus,* 199–200. In 1700 Paris, debts comprised two-thirds of wage earners' estates at their deaths; by the end of the century the proportion had risen to 83 percent. Rent was by far the chief source of debt. Roche, *People of Paris,* 83.

77. Strauss, *Nuremberg,* 198–99. At its peak in 1764, Barcelona's Mont de Pietat aided over 10,000 households, or one-third to one-half of the city's population. Such a level of activity was short-lived, however, and the number of loans plummeted within the next ten years. Montserrat Carboneller, "Using Microcredit and Restructuring Households: Two Complementary Survival Strategies in Late Eighteenth-Century Barcelona," in Fontaine and Schlumbohm, *Household Strategies,* 72ff.

78. Grain and other food commodities were also unacceptable as were the scrounged or

stolen glass and metal that were often sold for great profit on the black market. The city's official purchasing agents had the authority to buy outright any used goods, but items of this quality could usually fetch more and faster cash on the street, where there was never any trouble finding a willing buyer. Groebner, *Ökonomie ohne Haus*, 179–83, 207ff., 217–23; Wiesner, *Working Women*, 137–47.

79. Hufton, *Poor of Eighteenth-Century France*, 355.

80. See especially Burschel, *Söldner im Nordwestdeutschland*, 291–303, on ex-soldiers and crime.

81. In eighteenth-century France, perhaps as many as one million people, a large portion of them children, were involved in the smuggling of salt and tobacco. Hufton, *Poor of Eighteenth-Century France*, 284–91.

82. Schubert, *Arme Leute*, 257. See also Farge, *Fragile Lives*, 153–54, on family crime units.

83. ASB 199: 228r–229r; RV 1800: 48v–49r, 59r; RV 1801: 2r–v; RV 1804: 77r, 1805: 3r, 56v–57r, 60v, 62r; RV 1808: 37r (14, 18, 27 March; 30 June; 20–22 July; 9 October 1607).

84. Other German terms include *ernähren* and *unterhalten*. The legal status of children taken in by relatives was not always clearly defined. In *familles-souche méridionales*, celibate aunts or uncles often adopted their brothers' nephews as heirs, but the legal nature of "affiliation" is ambiguous, as is whether the *ahidada* niece the same as one who is legally *adoptada*. In Brie, a family council of up to twenty relatives (depending on the amount of money involved) took responsibility for orphans, but like the "food lease" (*bail à nourriture*), which involved a notary, this was probably "nothing else than a peculiar form of fosterage, functioning within the kinship network under very close family control." Anita Guerreau-Jalabert, "Nutrius / oblatus: Parenté et circulations d'enfants au Moyen Âge," in *Adoption et fosterage*, ed. in Mireille Corbier (Paris: De Boccard, 1999), 271–73, 280; Kristin Elizabeth Gager, *Blood Ties and Fictive Ties: Adoption and Family Life in Early Modern France* (Princeton: Princeton University Press, 1996), 76, 127–31; Antoinette Fauve-Chamoux, "Introduction: Adoption, Affiliation, in Family Recomposition; Inventing Family Continuity," *History of the Family* 3, no. 4 (1998): 387; David E. Vassberg, "Orphans and Adoption in Early Modern Castilian Villages," *History of the Family* 3, no. 4 (1998): 44; and Antoinette Fauve-Chamoux, "Beyond Adoption: Orphans and Family Strategies in Pre-Industrial France," *History of the Family* 1, no. 1 (1996): 9.

85. Between 1557 and 1670, the population of Nuremberg fluctuated between 25,000 and 45,000. Using an average of 35,000 inhabitants and the formula for poor children described above in n. 56, there were approximately 3,733–5,333 children under the age of sixteen in poor Nuremberg households. Annual admission to the Findel for the same years averaged roughly 14.6 legitimate children with at least one living parent (FKD: estimated 1,562 over the course of 114 years), or 0.27–0.39 percent of all poor children in the city. Since at least some of the Findel admittees came from outside the city, this is a high estimate.

86. FKD: petitioners were identified as neighbors in 7 of 263 forced foster petitions (2.7 percent) in which relationship to parents was specified, 7.6 percent (20) as relatives, 6.5 percent (17) as godparents or legal guardians. Among 243 voluntary foster petitions of the same nature, 14 (5.7 percent) came from relatives and 9 (3.7 percent) from godparents or guardians. Cf. eighteenth-century English parishes, in which about one-half of petitions for aid come from either grandparent, parent, or sibling. Boulton, "It Is Necessity," 63.

87. FKD: 2057 of 2721 petitions (75.6 percent) in which location of the father was indicated. While not necessarily typical, the experience of one Swedish company sent off

to fight in Germany and Poland during the Thirty Years' War is emblematic: of the 230 men and boys who left Sweden in late 1632, only five eventually returned, and each of those disabled. Burschel, *Söldner im Nordwestdeutschland*, 55, 248, 258–71.

88. Erhard Chvojka, *Geschichte der Großelternrollen vom 16. bis zum 20 Jahrhundert* (Vienna: Böhlau Verlag, 2003), 52–64, 72–96, also 349–50 on the eighteenth-century bourgeois notion of the affectionate grandparent.

89. In the north of Germany, the terms *Eldervader* and *Eldermoder* were more common until the eighteenth century. The same pattern is found in France, with *aïeul* and *aïeule* gradually replaced by *grand-père* and *grand-mère*, and in England, where the older terms of *ealdfader* and *ealdmother* yielded to grandfather and grandmother, along the same timeline as in Germany. Chvojka, *Großelternrollen*, 97–98, 104–6. See also John Demos, *Turning Points: Historical and Sociological Essays on the Family* (Chicago: University of Chicago Press, 1978) on the alleged "invention" of grandparenthood in seventeenth-century New England.

90. "das Barbara Hannsen Schedners kreushlapers Wittib Irer sohns hinderlassen kind." RV 1338: 27r–v (14 January 1572).

91. In eighteenth-century Haute-Maine, Anne Fillon found that at the average age of first marriage for men (27.5), only 38 percent still had a father alive and 62 percent a mother alive; among women at first marriage (25), 40 percent still had a living father and 62 percent a living mother. Anne Fillon, "À la Recherche des Aïeuls du Maine," *Annales de Démographie Historique* 82 (1991): 33–50.

92. Chvojka, *Großelternrollen*, 27, 47.

93. In 1569 Salzburg, only 2.4 percent of craftsmen households had a grandparent in residence; Zurich in 1637 had 8 percent of people over 60 in a household headed by another; in later Belm (1772), the figure for poor households was 8 percent (vs. 23 percent of prosperous farmers). Schulmbohm, *Lebensläufe, Familien, Höfe*, 264; Chvojka, *Großelternrollen*, 34–43, 51–52.

94. "armut halben." RV 1338: 27r–v (14 January 1572).

95. In England, 1650–1749, the figure was 3 percent, including both orphaned and semiorphaned children. *Family Forms in Historic Europe*, ed. Richard Wall (Cambridge: Cambridge University Press, 1983), 500.

96. RV 1905: 31r (17 January 1615). See a similar response to Dorothea Behaimin's petition for admission of her two grandchildren. RV 1272: 18v (11 February 1567). RV 1916: 55v–56r (18 November 1615); RV 2097: 28v (12 June 1629).

97. Georg Baur married Barbara Kargin on 13 August 1604 in Saint Sebaldus Church and their daughter Katherina was baptized on 24 October 1606. LKAN L-52 Proclamationen, 1602–10, 124; S23 Trauungen, 1587–1616, 106r.

98. FKD: Godparents were the petitioners in 31 of 486 such cases (6.4 percent) where petitioner's relationship to the child was specified, as compared to relatives other than the parents cited in 29 (6.0 percent) of such cases. See, for instance, the 1666 request "ob kein Taufdot oder ander befreundte, so zu dessen alimentation etwas beytragen möchten" (RV 2591: 54r–v; 24 October 1666), or the petition from a stepmother regarding her late husband's "vatter = und Mütterlose Waisen . . . und das einiger freund oder Taufdot, der etwas an ihnen thun könt, nicht vorhanden" (RV 2568: 33v–34r [30 January 1665]; also RV 2581: 59r–v [24 January 1666]).

99. Perrault alone used fairy godmothers in the stories of Cinderella, Peau-d'Ane, and Little Annette. See Agnès Fine, *Parrains, Marrains. La parenté spirituelle en Europe* (Paris: Fayard, 1994), 45, 51, 69ff., 92.

100. In Sweden, where six godparents was the norm, the number might reach as high as eighteen, based on a study of the baptismal records of Helsingburg, 1688–1709. Solveig Fagerlund, "Women and Men as Godparents in an Early Modern Swedish Town," History of the Family 5, no. 3 (2000): 348; Reicke, Geschichte der Reichsstadt Nürnberg, 659–60. The Council of Trent set the limit for Catholics at three godparents per child, with two of the three the same sex as the child. Fine, Parrains, Marrains, 24.

101. In one sample of early modern Sweden, 56 percent of all godparents were female, while in Nantes (1560–1660) only 10 percent female. Fagerlund also found that there were far more unmarried women as godparents than unmarried men in Sweden. Fagerlund, "Women and Men as Godparents," 348–49, 355–56. See also Jan Peters, Ein Söldnerleben, 239–40; and the classic study by Benjamin D. Paul, "Ritual Kinship, with Special Reference to Godparenthood in Middle America" (Ph.D. diss.: University of Chicago, 1942), on "intensive" (intensifying relations between kin) and "extensive" (including nonkin) godparenthood.

102. Zschunke's sample from Oppenheim (1568–1798) shows more of a patron-client pattern in lower classes, with almost two-thirds of godparents identified as officeholders. Konfession und Alltag in Oppenheim, 160, table 18.

103. Garrioch, Neighborhood and community in Paris, 94; Boulton, Neighbourhood and Society, 239; Gager, Blood Ties and Fictive Ties, 25.

104. R. B. Outhwaite, "Petitions to the London Foundling Hospital, 1768–1772," Eighteenth Century Studies 32, no. 4 (1999): 497–510, finds much evidence of help from employers, neighbors, and kin. Hans Humel and Niclaus Dörnhafer were both identified as neighbors of Balthasar Neuman when they requested admission for his epileptic son, as was Sebastian Hübner, who offered to continue caring for Endres Hartman's oldest son Jorg for an annual stipend of 15 fl. from the city council. RV1956: 29r–v (20 November 1618); RV 2072: 39v–40r (1 August 1627).

105. Stadtalmosenamt Actum of 22 October 1662; StadtAN D1/560.

106. Cited in Beatrice Gottlieb, The Family in the Western World from the Black Death to the Industrial Age (New York: Oxford University Press, 1993), 146.

107. Tamara K. Hareven, "The Impact of Family History and the Life Course as Social History," in Family History Revisited: Comparative Perspectives, ed. Richard Wall and Tamara K. Hareven (Newark: University of Delaware Press, 2001), 25–28. Hareven admits that this approach risks obscuring the roles of individuals.

108. See especially Fontaine and Schlumbohm, Household Strategies, 5–7; also Michael Anderson's much earlier description of the "rational actor" model of kin behavior in "critical life situations," in Family Structure in Nineteenth-Century Lancashire (Cambridge: Cambridge University Press, 1971), 136–61.

109. FKD: 52 of 173 (30.1 percent) of female foster petitions and 52 of 209 (24.9 percent) of male known abandonment cases in which marital status was indicated.

110. The major epidemics in sixteenth- and seventeenth-century Nuremberg came in 1505, 1507, 1520–22, 1532–34 (5,600 dead), 1543–44, 1561–63 (officially 9,186 dead of plague), 1570 (ca. 1,600 children dead of smallpox), 1572, December 1573–August 1576 (12,000 dead), 1582, 1585 (over 5,000 dead), 1599, 1600, 1602, 1609, 1620, 1632–33 (over 15,000 dead), 1634 (18–20,000 dead). StadtAN F1–2/VII: 682; Ernst Mummenhoff, "Die öffentliche Gesundheits- und Krankenpflege im alten Nürnberg. Das Spital zum heilige Geist," in Festschrift zur Eröffnung des Neuen Krankenhauses der Stadt Nürnberg (Nuremberg, 1898; Reprint: Neustadt/Aisch: Schmitt, 1986) 107–9;

StadtAN F1–2/VII: 374; StaatsAN 52a,476: 83r. See also Friederichs, *Early Modern City*, 281–83, on the effects of epidemics on urban life.

111. ASB 253: 4v, 39r.

112. During the worst epidemics, the city's archers also reported finding live children in the street next to mothers who literally dropped dead, including a two-year-old in 1632 and a newborn in 1669, both of whom were immediately admitted to the Findel. RV 2141: 89v–90r (13 November 1632); RV *2628*: 84r–v (3 August 1669). See also Schubert, *Arme Leute*, 202–3; and Burschel, *Söldner im Nordwestdeutschland*, 242, on frequent accounts of finding "ein unbekanntes Soldatenweib" or "eine alte Reitersfrau" dead on the side of the road.

113. Schultheiss, *Rechtspflege*, 202, on the men's and women's stockades (*Männereisen* and *Weibereisen*). Before 1498 debtors were put in the dungeon of the town hall (Groebner, *Ökonomie ohne Haus*, 225–230). Since 1483, those imprisoned in the debtor's tower (*Schuldturm*) were recorded in a special *Inhaftionsbuch* (e.g., ASB 201). The average from 1484–1510 was twenty-two internees per year. Groebner, *Ökonomie ohne Haus*, 228.

114. A 1574 chronicle of the great plague of 1573–76 mentions four children housed in the men's begging stockade. ASB, 253: 3r. The two references to parents sent to debtors' prison are RV 1410: 6v–7r (13 May 1577); RV 1467: 50v (6 September 1581). During the 1630s and again in the 1660s, the city maintained a *Spinnhaus* for delinquent women, some of whom brought their children with them.

115. StaatsAN HS 440: 100 (4 April 1574). See 100–8 for similar cases of fathers and mothers committing suicide because of debts. See also below, pp. 122–23, on household debt as a contributing factor in domestic homicides.

116. Groebner, *Ökonomie ohne Haus*, 190–91, 223–26.

117. FKD: 65 (12.2 percent) of fathers and 39 (7.3 percent) of mothers in a known sample of 532. This includes some cases of dual desertion but does not consider the large share of mothers and fathers—45.3 percent and 12.6 percent respectively—for whom the reason for desertion is unclear.

118. Of children living with only one parent, 64.5 percent were with the mother. Based on a sample of nineteen English communities from 1599 to 1811 in Laslett, *Family Life*, 166.

119. 1563 *Eheordnung* in *Die Evangelischen Kirchenordnungen des XVI. Jahrhunderts*, vol. XIV (*Kurpfalz*), gen. ed. Emil Sehling, vol. ed. J. F. G. Goeters (Tübingen: Mohr, 1969), 286. Cf. the more indulgent description of deserting wives in the same ordinance (326).

120. On informal divorces and malicious abandonment, see Harrington, *Reordering Marriage*, 261–262 Burghartz, *Zeiten der Reinheit*, 215–17; and Safley, *Let No Man Put Asunder*, 152–57.

121. Harrington, *Reordering Marriage and Society*, 88–89.

122. RV 1338: 19v (10 January 1572).

123. See Bernard Capp, *When Gossips Meet: Women, Family, and Neighbourhood in Early Modern England* (Oxford: Oxford University Press, 2003), 118–19, for the departing mother's perspective.

124. FKD: In a sample of 674 cases where an abandoner was identified, fathers were the sole abandoners in 256 cases (38.0 percent), women solely in 235 cases (34.9 percent), and both parents in 156 cases (23.1 percent), or overall 95.6 percent of such cases. Hufton's claim is found in *Poor of Eighteenth-Century France*, 115.

125. FKD: In cases where a key reason was mentioned for desertion: 65 of 532 men (12.2 percent) versus. 39 of 732 women (7.3 percent).

126. FKD: 36.3 percent (193 of 532 cases) of abandoning men were widowers, while 19.4 percent (103 of 532 cases) of abandoning women were widows.

127. Briggs, *Witches and Neighbors* 239; Roper, *Witch Craze*, 41–43, 61–63, 135.

128. One in five married couples were childless. E. A. Wrigley and Philip Abrams, *Towns in Societies: Essays in Economic History and Historical Sociology* (Cambridge and New York: Cambridge University Press, 1978), 150–51; Richard M. Smith, *Land, Kinship, and Life-cycle* (Cambridge and New York: Cambridge University Press, 1984), 40–46. Gager (*Blood Ties and Fictive Ties*, 95) found that widows were especially active in pseudo-adoption cases.

129. The Napoleonic Code of 1804 provided for limited adoption, but full legal adoption was not available in France until 1923, Finland 1925, Germany 1928. In the U.K., legal adoption required an act of parliament until the late nineteenth century. *Handwörterbuch zur deutschen Rechtsgeschichte*, ed. A. Erler and R. Kaufmann (Berlin: E. Schmidt, 1964–67), s.v. "Adoption," 1: 56–57; Mireille Corbier, "Introduction: Adoptés et nouris," in *Adoption et fosterage*, 3; Gager, *Blood Ties and Fictive Ties*, esp. 37–70.

130. Jack Goody, *The Development of the Family and Marriage in Europe* (Cambridge: Cambridge University Press, 1983), 39–45, 71–75; Boswell, *Kindness of Strangers, passim.* Some historians consider the *donato inter vivos* contract—found in the areas most influenced by Roman law, such as France, Spain, and Portugal (but rarely Italy)—to be the semiformal equivalents of adoption (not unlike today's civil unions and marriage). This practice, however, appears to have remained relatively uncommon. Gager, for instance, has found only forty-five surviving cases on record from la Couche and the Hôtel-Dieu in Paris, 1540–1677, an average of one every three years (Gager, *Blood Ties and Fictive Ties*, 10, 72). On the question of monastic oblation, Anita Guerreau-Jalabert argues that contrary to the assertions of John Boswell's *Kindness of Strangers*, the practice did involve the complete transfer of parental rights to the abbot, but it was more the equivalent of educational fosterage than of either legal adoption or exposition. She adds that it was certainly not common and that oblation was rarely free and mainly aristocratic. Guerreau-Jalabert, "Nutrius / oblatus," 271–73.

131. The relationship between a child and its legal guardian, was not one shaped by personal affection or even familiarity. Legal guardians were rarely related by blood and not necessarily even friends of the family. Unlike godparents, the number of guardians per child in Nuremberg was not fixed: there might be as many as three guardians for one child and in another case one guardian for four children. Tutors were always male, and enjoyed full paternal power up to age twelve for girls, fourteen for boys, and custodial authority over the child's property until age twenty-five (as defined by Roman law, most customary law during the Middle Ages, and Tit. 39 Ges. 7, §2 of the 1564 Reformatio); cf. also Tit. 21, Ges 2 §2; Rüger, *Die Kinderfürsorge*, 3, 73–74. A guardian, however, was forbidden from selling a ward's property without the permission of the inner council.

132. Only once was a legal commitment explicitly mentioned in Nuremberg's records, when Kunigunda Reuterin's former foster mother reclaimed her at the Findel in 1642 and "dieselbe an kindtsstatt zu ziehen bey gericht versprachen." FB 2: 91 (16 September 1642). The other six references all occurred within a narrow chronological window between 1595 and 1616: FB 1: 149 (17 November 1595), 150 (20 December

1595; 6 June 1601), 176 (9 February 1600), 188 (23 May 1601), 205 (18 February 1603); FB 2: 5.

133. FKD: Based on 727 cases of known abandonment and 623 cases of anonymous abandonment, where 154, or 20 percent of the latter figure, are assumed because of their age of two or older to be legitimate (that percentage based on a sample of 367 cases where the age was indicated). Even if some of these were in fact orphans circulated by adults other than their parents, that number is balanced out by the number of those anonymously abandoned children under two who are probably legitimate. My estimate of 1035 total abandoned legitimate children is admittedly conservative, though at most that figure could not go more than 150 higher, based on the known incidence of abandoning unwed mothers. I have also increased that combined figure by an extrapolated number of cases where type was not indicated, based on the percentage of anonymous abandonment (20 percent, thus one-fifth of that) and known abandonment (39 percent), yielding an additional 22 and 102 children respectively, or a total of 1007 cases over the course of 114 years, or 8.8 children per year. The known foster case number of 576 is similarly extrapolated by its percentage of the total petitions to add 88 cases from those of unknown type, for a total of 664 or 5.8 per year. The total for all legitimate children with at least one parent known to be alive thus totals an average of 14.6.

134. FKD: In 538 of 750 known abandonment cases, the location is not specified. We know that some of the 148 cases where the location is known to be a private house involved a situation of this sort, but there is no way to know how many of the unknown sort represented a failed agreement. The same is true of all anonymous abandonment cases.

135. There were, of course, exceptions, such as the 1558 case where a widow left her child with a foster family and then immediately skipped town, counter to the agreement, resulting in the child being taken into Findel and the mother ordered arrested upon return. RV 1159: 17v (18 August 1558).

136. Cf. the 1628 case of a "three- or four-year-old [boy] who could neither talk nor stand." RV 2083: 54r (27 May 1628).

137. "die er in der fewrung nicht ernehmen koennen ohne dz Allmussen und vermelt . . . haben gutwillig angenohmen zuerziehen." FB 1, 35 (27 February and 26 August 1572).

138. "das ihnen d. Schiemesher kinder wollen auffgedrungen werd. das er doch vorn viel seiner freundt kinder ernehren muss, auch albereit bey den Schirmaishen geshlecht gleich vermosen getraget, sein gegentheil aber Georg Göpner und ander gerne solche nit gestehen." RV 2147: 126v–127r (18 May 1633).

139. Nuremberg's magistrates were skeptical when knife maker journeyman Jacob Kurz refused to take back his own child from his godfather, claiming "he was afflicted with horrible French sores (i.e., syphilis) and he did not want to harm his child by having it near him," but they nevertheless provided the foster father with a stipend and asked him to be patient just a little longer. Two months later, when Kurz's godfather and his wife passed the child on to a neighbor, the council agreed to accept the child into the Findel until Kurz checked out of the "French" pesthouse. StaatsAN 199: 145v (18 October 1606); RV 1796: 16r, 27v (13 and 18 November 1606).

140. "hab sies angenummen dasselb zubehalten do sies waigert Ir die stadt Ir lebenlang verpieten und solchs shwern lassen." RV 1302: 6r (16 April 1569). Heinrich Fleisher's similar 1576 petition that the Findel admit the two children he was fostering for Conrad Baur was likewise denied and the petitioner was told either to send the

children after the father or keep them himself or see if he can find other accommodations for them. RV 1400: 20r (25 August 1576).

141. "und Ihr sagen sie hab selbs zuzumessen, dass sie solch kind in die Cost augenummen, und sich dess Costgelts halben nitt versichern lass., sie mög demnach erkundigen wo dise Margretha hinkammen und Ihr das kind nachshicken." RV 1985: 61r–v; RV 1991: 57v (19 January and 15 June 1621). In another rare exception, a foster mother was told in 1581 that "von wegen Irs grossen leibs, und Ire Zwaier ziehkinder halben, noch langer zu Gostenhof pleiben zu lassen alleinen, und sitzen, Iren Man nach zu ziehen, da sie dann gemelte Ir ziehkinder hinder Ir lasssen wurde." RV 1466: 24r (29 July 1581).

142. RV 1885: 21r (8 July 1613); RV 1886: 26 (7 August 1613).

143. "der mitt seiem weib von hinnen nach prag gezogen, von seiner Ziehmutter zu haus [of Margretha Suess] getrogen und auff den Tish gesetzt worden." RV 1797: 47v (20 December 1606).

144. RV 2062: 118r (22 November 1626). "vermuttlich von einer Ziehemutter hingesezt worden sey, dern man kein ziehgeldt mehr geben wollen." RV 2073: 41r, 50v, 62v (27, 29 August, 1 September 1627). The final entry concluded "soll man sich ruhen lass. und das händelein aussleygen."

145. "und Ihr sagen, sie soll sich an die jenigen halten, die Ihr wegen dess versprachenen ziehgelts vertröstung gethan . . . das kind nitt hinsezen, man werde sie sonsten wol darumb zu finden wissen." RV 1897: 46r (RV 14 June 1614).

146. FKD: Friends and relatives constituted only 4 percent of all known abandoners (27 of 674 such cases where an abandoner was identified).

147. "aus dem allmosen eine wochentliche steuer zu ertheilen, damit dieselb. sie erziehen könne, biss sie zu dienst konne." RV 2278: 65r (24 May 1643). Cf. a similar case where a grandmother caught abandoning a baby was held for a three days until the baby's mother could be located. RV 2021: 65r (23 September 1623).

148. RV 2053: 54r–v (1 March 1626). For a similar case of anonymous abandonment by a grandfather, see RV 1794: 23r (20 September 1606).

149. Shortly after anonymously abandoning her two-year-old nephew in the marketplace, Madelena Scheilin had second thoughts and picked up young Georg at the Findel, telling officials that her sister had run off and left the child with her. FB 2: 21 (10 January 1623). By contrast, two children found abandoned on Schütt in 1610 turned out to be offspring of a recently deceased soldier / beggar and were left there by their older brother, who since disappeared and never returned. RV 1840: 30v, 35r (8 and 10 March 1610).

150. FKD: 576 of 3199 (18 percent) of all petitions to the Findel in which type was indicated.

151. FKD: Foster on account of illness made up 332 (57.6 percent) of all 576 foster cases, on account of poverty or other hardships 180 of 576 (31.3 percent) and *ex officio* fostering 93 of 576 (16.1 percent). Jeorg and Katharina Prew were accepted into the Findel in May of 1581 on account of their father's banishment and their mother's hospital internment yet almost two years later were picked up by both parents (FB 1 90; 30 May 1581, 17 April 1583). Sometimes an absent but nonabandoning parent would redeem children left in the Findel, such as the wife of thief Niclas Praun and their children Cuntz and Ottilia. Both children were picked up within two months of their father's abandonment on 27 October 1581 (FB 1: 91). After Hans Pair was hanged as a thief, no relatives could be found to take his three small children, so they were admitted to the Findel (FB 1: 23; 26 May 1571).

152. FKD: Overall, mothers were the petitioners in 46 of 223 cases (20.6 percent) in which the petitioner was named and fathers in 18 cases (8.1 percent). In petitions not involving illness, the proportions shot up to 30 percent (30 of 100) and 8 percent (8 of 100).

153. RV 2534: 42r–v, 65r (10 and 17 July 1662).

154. "bis zur wetter wirdt aus dem heim shieben." RV 1339: 29v (12 December 1572).

155. FB 1: 174 (admitted 8 November 1599; picked up 19 February 1600). Thirty years later, a poor widow with eight children whose husband was killed by Tilly's troops succeeded in placing two of her offspring in the Findel. RV 2134: 9r (15 March 1632).

156. "bis sie Ihr Brod selbs erwerben mögen." RV 1545: 58v–59r (9 August 1587). See FB 1: 277 (19 December 1612), 281 (27 August 1612), 281 (14 August 1613); FB 2: 9 (25 November 1617), 41 (29 February 1630), 45 (5 October 1630).

157. FKD: Recovered parents picked up their children in 55.7 percent (131 of 235) where the nature of departure was indicated. 35.3 percent (83) of children died in Findel custody and 7.6 percent (18) were placed in an apprenticeship or service position. In cases where the length of the child's stay in the Findel was indicated, 63.9 percent (46 of 72) of these parents reclaimed the child within three months, 88.9 percent (64) within one year.

158. "die Findel sey nitt fur solche kinder gestifftet, Er soll dannach bedacht sein, wie diss kind ohne Meiner herrn beshwerung erzogen werde, dann wann man es In die Findel ausse einnemen, werd man die Mutter zur Statt hinaus shaffen." RV 1916: 55v–56r (18 November 1615).

159. RV 1928: 37r (2 October 1616).

160. FKD: 106 of 116 miscellaneous foster petitions (91.3 percent) were granted from 1565–1619 and 54 of 64 (84.4 percent) from 1620 to 1670.

161. See below, chapter 3, pp. 155–65.

162. FKD: 47 of 581 (8.1 percent) cases of forced fosters where petitioners were named. 295 were identified as city employees.

163. FKD: 59.5 percent of cases (446 of 750) where site of abandonment was specified.

164. RV 2553: 62v–63r (28 and 29 December 1663).

165. "und nichts dann die zwein kinder verlassen, wie sie dann eins armen hirten weib sol gewest sein." Both children were accepted into the Findel. RV 1310: 42r (15 December 1569).

166. FKD: Parents were identified in 64 of 148 cases (43.2 percent) when a private residence was identified as the site of abandonment. One-third of the abandonments in Meumann's sample of 69 occurred at inns or private homes where parents were staying. *Findelkinder,* 148.

167. FKD: 117 of 750 (15.6 percent) of all forced foster and anonymous abandonment cases where the location was specified. Parents were identified in 71 of 296 cases (24 percent) where a public building or street was the abandonment site, 8 of 117 (6.8 percent) where the site was in front of the Findel.

168. RV 1271: 27v–28r, 1272: 4r (17 and 27 January 1567).

169. RV 2018: 84r.

170. FKD: 727 of 1350 (53.9 percent) of all forced foster and anonymous abandonment cases. During the eighteenth century, most German states commuted this sentence to a life sentence in the local workhouse. Roetzer, "Die Delikte der Abtreibung," 84; Meumann, *Findelkinder,* 164.

171. RV 1945: 47v (19 January 1618).

172. "der lachner Hans in Bettel umziehe." RV 1910: 4r, 11r–v, 44v (11, 15, 29 May 1615). Roetzer, "Die Delikte der Abtreibung" (126) describes a similar case where the city's archers returned a child to its disappointed father in Fürth but were unable to punish him while he remained outside of Nuremberg's jurisdiction.

173. "ime aus mitleiden das (in der Findel angelaufene) Kostgeld schenken, mit warnung, das künftten das kind nit hinzusetzen, man wird ihn sonst mit ernst strafen." RV 1953: 8v, 16v (31 August 1618).

174. RV 1655: 4r (3 January 1596); FB 1: 150.

175. Gavitt, *Charity and Children*, 195. Many notes also promised forthcoming child support payments.

176. The reclamation rates during the sixteenth and seventeenth centuries were 6 percent in Florence and 8.8 percent in Lisbon. Gavitt, "'Perche non avea chi la ghovernasse,'" in Henderson and Wall, *Poor Women and Children*, 68; Sá, "Circulation of Children," in Painter-Brick, *Nobody's Children*, 34.

177. FKD: 41 of 249 (16.5 percent) abandoned boys whose nature of departure from the Findel was known; 32 of 215 (14.9 percent) girls. The actual number of children known to have been reclaimed in cases where the parent was also known is even smaller, though the percentage of the sample is higher: 56 of 189 (29.6 percent) cases from 1557 to 1670.

178. 3.4 percent of children were reclaimed from the Milan Foundling Home in 1673–93, 30.1 percent in 1842. Only 2.1 percent of children were reclaimed from Florence's Innocenti in 1700–2, 24.1 percent in 1841. Volker Hunnecke, *Die Findelkinder von Mailand. Kindesaussetzung und aussetzende Eltern vom 17. bis zum 19. Jahrhundert* (Stuttgart: Klett-Cotta, 1987), 127; Viazzo, "Family structures," in Henderson and Wall, *Poor Women and Children*, 40.

179. The motives of married couples who abandoned small children to others have particularly baffled some modern historians. Cf. Beatrice Gottlieb: "Since it is not likely they were all crazy, we must believe either that many of them, [like unmarried mothers] were desperate or else that they didn't care." *The Family in the Western World*, 139.

180. These include "Old Mother Frist," "Cinderella," "Riddle," "The Almond Tree," "Old Mother Frist," "Cinderella," "The Tree Bride," "The Poor Boy in the Grave," "Three Snake Leaves," and of course, "Hansel and Gretel." *The Complete Grimm's Fairy Tales*, ed. Padraic Colum (New York: Pantheon, 1972). On the ancient roots of this topos, see Suzanne Dixon, "The Circulation of Children in Roman Society," in Corbier, *Adoption et fosterage*, 224.

181. *Ehespiegel /Das ist / Alles was von dem heyligen Ehestande / nutzliches / noetiges / und troestliches mag gesagt warden / In LXX Brautpredigen / zusammen verfasset* (Strasbourg: Theodor Rilel, 1570), 48r–v.

182. Vassberg, "Orphans and Adoption," 442.

183. The average early modern marriage lasted twenty-one years and 10 percent of children under nine (13 percent age 10–14) lived with a stepparent. Schlumbohm, *Lebensläufe, Familien, Höfe*, 170–72, 301.

184. Only 0.4 percent lived with two stepparents in Laslett's sample of nineteen early modern English villages. *Family Life*, 166.

185. "vatter- und Mütterlose Waisen und das einiger freund oder Taufdot, der etwas an ihnen thun könt, nicht vorhanden." RV 2568: 33v–34r (30 January 1665). Laslett (*Family Life*, 169) concurs that most stepparents felt little or no obligation to stepchildren after their natural parents had died.

186. RV 1884: 48r, 1885: 6v, 17v, 29r, 40r (21 June; 3, 7, 12 15 July 1613).
187. RV 1936: 33v (3 May 1617). Cf. the similar case of RV 2209: 28v (25 January 1638).
188. FB 1: 107 (21 November 1584; 22 March 1585; 9 July 1585). Cf. the appeal of one stepmother "doch vorhin ein alt verlebt weib zu versorgen" (presumably her mother or mother-in-law) who requested that the Findel take her three stepchildren. RV 2568: 33v–34r (30 January 1665). The Findel accepted the two youngest but told her to keep the oldest child, for which she was given a small stipend.
189. FB 1: 280 (15 July 1613).
190. Knapp (*Kriminalrecht*, 188) describes the 1610 censor of one abusive stepmother. For instances of abandonment by a stepparent, see the case of two-year-old Hans Caspar Waldmann in RV 2271: 18v (3 November 1642). See also RV 2376: 110r (4 October 1650); RV 2380: 21r (11 January 1651). On emotional strangers, Ernst Benz, "Population Change and the Economy," in Ogilvie, *Social and Economic History of Germany*, 43.
191. RV 2376: 88v–89r, 110v–11r (23 and 27 September 1650); RV 2380: 21r (30 December 1650); RV 2383: 22r (26 March 1651); FB 2: 105.
192. "Und ist das ain man sin kind verkoft durch ehalf not das tuot er wol mit recht. Er sol es aber nit verkoffen das man es toet oder in das huorhuss." Quoted in Boswell, *Kindness of Strangers*, 326.
193. Article 118. "Kinderraub," in *HRG* II: 733–35. The practice did not receive its first full treatment until the Prussian Allgemeine Landrecht of 1794.
194. RV 2570, 10r–v, 11r, 21r (25 and 29 March 1665). See also Franz Schmitt's account of a murderer reputed to have sold children to Jews. Keller, *Maister Franntzn Schmidts*, 55.
195. Cf. Yahweh's threat of punitive starvation in Lev 26: 29: "You shall eat the flesh of your sons, and the flesh of your daughters you shall eat." Also Deut 28: 63–56, and 2 Kings 6: 28–29. "Betteln," in *Handwörterbuch des deutschen Aberglaubens*, ed. Hanns Bächtold-Stäubli (Berlin and Leipzig: W. de Gruyter & Co., 1927–42), 1: 1195. See also Roper, *Witch Craze*, 69–81 and 97–98, on early modern anxiety about cannibalism, children, and witches.
196. The common sharing of a bed with an infant, among biological and foster parents alike, frequently resulted in overlaying, or accidental suffocation. Some of the incidents labeled this way probably included cases of sudden infant death syndrome (SIDS). If the early modern rate for this phenomenon were comparable to that of a modern developing nation, the result would be an occurrence two to three times greater the current incidence in the U.S. Based on a modern U.S. rate of 2.3–3 per 1000; a modern developing country would be about 6.56. Gavitt, *Charity and Children*, 237.
197. ASB 200: 66r (2 October 1609). See also ASB 226a: 204–205 (14 October 1669).
198. Anna Schmidtin, executed 30 October 1554 (ASB 226a: 60); Barbara Segerin / Weiherin, executed 17 September 1560 (ASB 226a: 66); and Anna Strölin, executed 3 December 1580 (ASB 209: 235r–236v). There are also four other cases of married women and one of a married man killing their illegitimate offspring (see appendix 2). The two cases described above are Strölin and Anna Freyin, executed 17 November 1584 (ASB 210: 146v–148r). Other German jurisdictions followed the same pattern with only three married women out of fifty-four cases in Württemberg (1568–1785), two out of thirty-seven in Prussia (1774–1801), three out of seventy-six in Frankfurt (1562–1696) and just three examples of parents killing older

children in Saxony (1691–1810.) Van Dülmen, *Frauen vor Gericht,* 19, 77; Meumann, *Findelkinder,* 159.

199. "solt GOTT alsbalden ein sichtbarlich zeichen an ihm thun, und ist darauf zuhörzlich gestorben." StadtAN F1-2/VII (1586).

200. See especially Wiltenburg, *Disorderly Women,* which looks at more than twenty published accounts of domestic murders in sixteenth- and seventeenth-century Germany.

210. *Zwo Warhafftige Newe Zeitung / Die erst / Von einem Mörder / der sein Ehelich Weib / unnd Sechs Kinder ermördet hat / geschehen inn der berümpten Statt Prüsseln / in der Schlessien* . . . (1599), cited in Wiltenburg, *Disorderly Women,* 224. Cited also in Wiltenburg is a similar 1616 case of a man found by his wife at an alehouse after a two-day drinking binge, who proceeds to kill her and the rest of the family: *Ein warhafftiger / grundtlicher Bericht und newe Zeitung: Was sich mit einem vollen Weinschlauch und seinem ehelichen Weib / die gross schwanger gewesen* . . . (Erfurt, 1616). According to Ann Tlusty (*Bacchus and Civil Order: The Culture of Drink in Early Modern Germany* [Charlottesville: University of Virginia Press, 2001], 115ff.), the woman reproaching the drunken and irresponsible husband at the tavern was a frequent theme in contemporary literature.

202. *Warhafftige* . . . *Zeitung. Von etlichen Jesuwittern* . . . *Die ander Zeitung. So sich zu Hall im Ihnthal mit einem Burger* . . . (1607), in Wiltenburg, *Disorderly Women.*

203. *Zween Erschreckliche geschicht / Gesangs weise. Die Erste / von einem Wirt im Allergaw / Bastian Schönmundt genandt / Die Ander / Eine erschreckliche und Warhafftige Newe Zeitung / . . . zu Langenberck* . . . (1596), cited in Wiltenburg, *Disorderly Women,* 227.

204. See, for example, the advice of Pieter van Foreest, "the Dutch Hippocrates," in Midelfort, *Madness,* 168–69.

205. See *Warhafftige Zeitung / So niemals erhört / . . . zu Quedelburg in Sachsen mit einem Becken / mit Namen Heinrich Rosenzweig / welcher durch dess Teuffels List und Rath sein Weib und 6. Kinder jämmerlicher weise umbgebracht* . . . (Erfurt, 1621) and *Zuo warhafftige trawrige newe Zeitungen* . . . *Die erste / Von einem Undervogt zu Bergen* . . . (Freiburg, 1623), both described in Wiltenburg, *Disorderly Women,* 225–26, 260. English publications also tended to focus more on the couple's relationship than their parental duties and worries.

206. "Er sprach hertz liebste mutter mein/ Verschon mein doch vnd lass dir sagen/ Ich wil dir all das wasser tragen/ Das dir den winter thut von nöten / Verschon mein doch wölst mich nit tödten. Da halff keyn bitt es war vmb sunst / Ihrn willen schafft des Teuffels kunst / Sie schlug vff jn gleich nach der schwer / Als obs eyn frisches krautheupt wer." from Burckhard Waldis, *Eyne warhafftige und gantz erschreckliche historien / Wie eyn weib jre vier kinder tyranniglichen ermordet / und sich selbst auch umbbracht hat / Geschehen zu Weidenhausen bei Eschweh in Hessen* . . . (Marburg, 1551), translated in Wiltenburg, *Disorderly Women,* 227–28.

207. Wiltenburg, *Disorderly Women,* 226.

208. As a counterexample, cf. Hufton's citing of the eighteenth-century case of a woman near Sélestat who kills her child before parting with any of four chickens. *Poor of Eighteenth-Century France,* 54.

209. Olwen Hufton writes that "those who look closely at the eighteenth-century poor cannot but be struck by their aggressive independence and their desire to be left alone to live out their lives without intrusion from higher authority, police, government official, ecclesiastics." *Poor of Eighteenth-Century France,* 355. Martin Dinges also emphasizes the importance of autonomy and independence to the poor, more in the

form of self-help than reliance on others, the latter termed by him a "sozialromanti-scher Bilderbogen," literally a socio-romantic broadsheet. "Aushandeln von Armut," 9–10.

210. *Poor of Eighteenth-Century France*, 114, 355. She concludes that "their very survival was a triumph of human ingenuity" (367).

211. Ammerer (*Heimat Straße*, 492–94) also emphasizes the value of social networks among the poor, even vagrants, and rejects the image of "a sub-culture of passive victims."

CHAPTER THREE

1. For a detailed account of Nuremberg during the crisis years of the 1630s, see Ernst Mummenhoff, *Alt-Nürnberg in Krieg und Kriegsnot (Aus d. schlimmsten Tagen des 30jäh-rigen Krieges)* (Nuremberg: Selbstverlag des Stadtmagistrats, 1917).

2. StadtAN 60a. There were also large transfers on 28 November 1633, 12 and 28 November 1633, 23 March 1634, and 23 March 1636. StadtAN D1/561; RV 2185: 73v–74r. From 1633 to 1637 the Findel admitted 456 new children, 294 between 1 June 1634 to 31 May 1635 alone.

3. Christoph Hans Imhof, *Berühmte Nürnberger aus neun Jahrhunderten* (Nuremberg: A. Hofmann, 1984), 389–90. A sixteenth-century *Sammlung von kurzen Nachrichten über Nürnberger Familien* (StaatsAN 52a: 257, 104v) dates the Pömer entry into *Ratsfähigkeit* at 1420. On the political elites of German imperial cities, see Thomas A. Brady, *The Politics of Reformation Germany: Jacob Sturm (1489–1553) of Strassbourg* (Highlands: Humanities Press, 1997), and idem, *Ruling Class, Regime and Reform in Strassbourg, 1520–55* (Leiden: Brill, 1978). See also Barbara B. Diefendorf, *Paris City Councillors in the Sixteenth Century: The Politics of Patrimony* (Princeton: Princeton University Press, 1983).

4. In 1536, an exception was made and the Schlüsselfelder family was added to the list of forty-two. Later, in 1729, six families were added to the list, and another three in 1788, shortly before the end of the city's independence. Imhof, *Berühmte Nürnberger*, 387.

5. Here I diverge slightly from Wolfgang Reinhard, who argues that "[w]ith a certain simplification we might claim that earlier European ruling classes did not rule because they were rich, but were rich because they ruled," "Introduction: Power Elites, State Servants, Ruling Classes, and the Growth of State Power," in *Power Elites and State Building*, ed. Wolfgang Reinhard (New York: Oxford University Press, 1996), 14–15. See also, in the same volume, Neithard Bulst, "Rulers, Representative Institutions, and Their Members as Power Elites: Rivals or Partners," 41–58.

6. Endres, "Zur wirtschaftlichen und sozialen Lage," 18.

7. Strauss, *Nuremberg*, 204.

8. Johann Gottfried Biedermann, *Geschlechtsregister des Hochadelichen Patriciats zu Nürnberg* (Nuremberg, 1750), 578.

9. See Strauss, *Nuremberg*, 58–64 for a more detailed description of the council's composition and offices.

10. Strauss, *Nuremberg*, 60. Strasbourg had a senate of thirty-two members and a smaller council of thirteen. Friedrichs, *Early Modern City*, 45.

11. Schultheiss, *Rechtspflege*, 196–98.

12. Brady, *Ruling Class*, 93. See also Kathryn A. Edwards, *Families and Frontiers: Re-creating Communities and Boundaries in the Early Modern Burgundies* (Boston and Leiden: Brill, 2002), 267ff., on the importance of civic privilege.

13. Hans-Christoph Rublack, "Political and Social Norms in Urban Communities in the Holy Roman Empire," in *Religion, Politics, and Social Protest: Three Studies on Early Modern Germany*, ed. Kaspar von Greyerz (London: German Historical Institute, 1984), 44.

14. Brady, *Ruling Class*, 122.

15. For a good representation of a council session during an earlier period, see *Beschlüße des Rats der Stadt Köln, 1320–1550*, ed. Manfried Huiskes and Manfred Groten (Düsseldorf: Droste, 1990).

16. Strauss, *Nuremberg*, 62.

17. Strauss, *Nuremberg*, 215. Robert von Friedeburg and Wolfgang Mager, "Learned Men and Merchants: The Growth of the Bürgertum," in Ogilvie, *Germany*, 169–77.

18. Roetzer, "Die Delikte der Abtreibung," xvi; Strauss, *Nuremberg*, 25–26, 83. Thomas Brady writes that "soft words [were] as much a Nuremberg specialty as Lebkuchen, the famous honey-cakes." *Turning Swiss* (Cambridge and New York: Cambridge University Press, 1985), 213.

19. Strauss, *Nuremberg*, 69.

20. As Margaret DeLacy has eloquently argued about later prison reform in England, we must not assume "that a united elite was acting with a clearly defined motive, the maintenance of domination," and we should instead recognize "both the multiplicity of intentions and the fact that many actual changes had not been intended at all." *Prison Reform in Lancashire, 1700–1850: A Study in Local Administration* (Palo Alto: Stanford University Press, 1986), 227. See also Christopher Friedrichs, *Urban Politics in Early Modern Europe* (London and New York: Routledge, 2000), 7–8, on the pluralist interpretation of conciliar power; as well as Rudolf Schlögl, "Vergesellschaftlichung unter Anwesenden. Zur kommunikativen Form des Politischen in der vormodernen Stadt," in *Interaktion und Herrschaft. Die Politik der frühneuzeitlichen Stadt*, ed. Rudolf Schlögl (Constance: UVK Verlagsgesellschaft, 2004), 9–60; and Urs Hafner, "Gravamina im Rathaus. Zur sozialen Übergabe kollektiver Beschwerden in süddeutschen Reichsstädten des 17. und 18. Jahrhunderts," in *Formen der politischen Kommunikation in Europa vom 15. bis 18. Jahrhundert. Bitten, Beschwerden, Briefe* (Bologna and Berlin: Duncker & Humblot, 2001), 289–307.

21. ASB 12. Pömer served as a Bürgermeister in 1628–29, 1634–36, and 1639–54.

22. *Geschlechtbuch*, 352r–353v; Ernst Mummenhoff, "Das Findel- und Waisenhaus zu Nürnberg, orts-, kultur-, und wirtschaftsgeschichtlich," *MVGN* 21 (1915): 57–336, and 22 (1918): 1–146, here, pt. 2, 112–13.

23. Gerald Strauss has best characterized their common ideal of governance as civic paternalism wherein the ruling patriciate perceived their society as less a mere aggregate of competitive producing and consuming groups, than as "an extended family, engaged in a common civic pursuit and held together by mutual political duties and social responsibilities." *Nuremberg*, 145. On the importance of paternalistic imagery among German rulers of the sixteenth and seventeenth centuries, see Harrington, *Reordering Marriage*, 39–47.

24. Biedermann, *Geschlechtsregister*, 578. In this sense, Nuremberg had changed significantly from the "emphatically unintellectual society" of the sixteenth century. Strauss, *Nuremberg*, 234, 240.

25. Rublack, "Political and Social Norms," 26, n. 8.

26. Today we would probably call their subject "social welfare," but the phrase itself was not coined until the nineteenth century by John Ruskin. Paul Slack, *From Reformation to Improvement: Public Welfare in Early Modern England; The Ford Lectures Delivered in the University of Oxford, 1995–96* (Oxford: Clarendon Press, 1999), 1ff.

27. Responding chiefly to Ernst Troeltsch and Reinhold Niebuhr on the "quietist" and "defeatist" attitude of Luther on social issues, Carter Lindberg argues that Catholic poor laws such as those of Ypres were adaptations of "Lutheran social innovations" (*Beyond Charity*, 146, 161ff). Geremek, *Poverty*, 136ff.

28. Sachsse, *Geschichte der Armenfürsorge*, 34–35. On Nuremberg, see Günther Vogler, "Erwartung—Enttäuschung—Befriedigungen. Reformatorischer Umbruch in der Reichsstadt Nürnberg," in *Die frühe Reformation in Deutschland als Umbruch*, ed. Stephen E. Buckwalter, and Bernd Moeller (Gütersloh: Gütersloher Verlagshaus, 1998), 381–406.

29. das ein Rhat mit den armen und nothleidenden kinder / ein Vätterliches getrewes mitleiden hab." Ordinance of 17 November 1556. Similar language is found in discussions of child begging in the earlier ordinance of 24 March 1553; StaatsAN Ia, Bd. B: 105.

30. Cunningham, *Children and Childhood*, 100.

31. Pamphlet by Samuel Harttib, cited in Slack, *From Reformation to Improvement*, 79; Cunningham, *Children and Childhood*, 100; Vives, *De subventione pauperum* (1526), quoted in Cunningham, 114. See also Natalie Z. Davis, *Society and Culture in Early Modern France* (Stanford: Stanford University Press, 1975), 24, on similar complaints in France.

32. Cited in Jütte, *Poverty and Deviance*, 39.

33. Alms ordinances of 1478, 1519, 1522; mandates of 30 December 1537, 8 May 1552, 17 November 1556, 19 March 1562, 24 July 1566, 3 December 1566, 2 July 1567, 25 October 1571, 16 August 1615, 25 April 1616, 26 August 1619, 8 September 1619, 29 September 1620, 25 June 1633, 21 June 1634, 17 March 1636 (renewed 9 June 1637; 8 June 1653), 22 June 1666, 31 December 1668, 18 December 1669, 11 December 1670, 27 October 1683, 11 May 1699, and 11 November 1699. StaatsAN 63 Ia. Legislation on this subject continued to appear through the eighteenth and into the nineteenth centuries.

34. Frankfurt am Main's ordinance dates only from 1488 and Augsburg from 1491. Jütte, *Poverty and Deviance*, 161. For the text of the 1370 ordinance, see Rüger, *Mittelalterliches Almosenwesen*, 68–70. The town council had begun to assume authority in this area since the beginning of the fourteenth century (7).

35. "Eins Rats der Stat Nürmberg ordnung des grossen allmusen haussarmer leut" (ca. 1562); StaatsAN 63IA, vol. C: 35v. The ordinance echoes the poor-reform sentiment made popular by Martin Luther that "there should be no beggars among Christians." "An den christlichen Adel deutscher Nation" (1520) and "Ordenung eyns gemeynen kastens" (1523), in WA, 6: 381–469, 12: 11–30.

36. The alms ordinance of 1522 (see Rüger, *Mittelalterliches Almosenwesen*, 144ff) was an influential model for similar reforms throughout Europe.

37. The prohibition of begging had already been considered twenty-five years earlier at the imperial diet in Lindau. Luther also proposed it in his *Sermon vom Wucher* (1519) and *Nobility of the German Nation* (1521). During its first three years, the new municipal alms bureau (*Stadtalmosenamt*) distributed 13,000 fl. before expanding into a regional alms bureau (*Landalmosenamt*) with even more funds in 1525. This model of rationalization and centralization represented an innovative and much emulated alternative to the more traditional practice of parochially administered alms. Rüger, *Mittelalterliches Almosenwesen*, 36; Reicke, *Geschichte der Reichsstadt Nürnberg*, 823. On the *Heimatprinzip* of poor relief, see Meumann, *Findelkinder*, 77ff.; also Jütte, *Poverty and Deviance*, 100–42.

38. Chief among these was the 1626 Acht-Viertel plan, which divided the city into eight parts, each corresponding to a different craft, with two paid collectors for each, collecting every Friday (each paid 1 fl. a week). In this way 9,323 fl. were saved at the end of fiscal year but the alms bureau spent over 26,000 fl. the next year, leaving only 1,839 fl. remaining. Almosspfleger Gutachten (22 April 1668); StadtAN D1/564. For the text of the 1626 ordinance, see Rüger, *Mittelalterliches Almosenwesen*, 51–53.

39. "faulkeit von starken streuner and schupfel." RV of 20 December 1549; StadtAN D1/563. Friday begging was permitted for anyone until 1564. Rüger, *Mittelalterliches Almosenwesen*, 46.

40. The 1478 alms ordinance, for instance, opined that "the poor should not sit lazily about on any workday but rather spin or do some work of which they are capable." Rüger, *Mittelalterliches Almosenwesen*, 33. Cf. other Protestant begging ordinances, Kallert, "Waisenhaus und Arbeiterziehung," 4–6, 50–80.

41. The offer to pay apprenticeship fees and doctor's costs was limited to one child per family. Reicke, *Geschichte der Reichsstadt Nürnberg*, 71. See also alms ordinance of 1478; 22 June 1518; 1 September 1522; 24 July 1588. Rüger, *Mittelalterliches Almosenwesen*, 30–36, 70–76, 76–90.

42. "auch bey den kindern, so die im pettel und müssiggeen aufgezogen, vil schand, sträfflicher handlungen und leichfertigkeyt erwachsen ist." *Almosenordnung* of 1 September 1522, ibid., 78, 82–83.

43. "ja wol auch die unwissende Kinder von jugend auf darzu erzogen, schendlichen underricht und dardurch zum spielen, stehlen, hurerey und andern lastern, so gemeinlich aus dem entstiehen der arbeit zu folgen pflen von ihren selbst eygenen eltern verwiesen und also zugleich umb Leib und Seel gebracht werden." *Almosenordnung* of 1626; ibid., 95. Similar language is found in mandates from 27 November 1556, 19 March 1562, 24 July 1566, 3 December 1566, 25 October 1571, 16 August 1615; Almosen Bericht from 22 April 1668. StaatsAN 63Ia. See also ibid., 45, 50.

44. "darunter sich mehrmals begibt, das von Manns und Weibs Personen, allerley Püberey unnd unzucht auff den Gassen geübet unnd getrieben . . . und sich desto beshwerlicher zu der handtarbeit begibt." 1522 ordinance in Rüger, *Mittelalterliches Almosenwesen*, 147. "Ungewöhnliche Zeiten" apparently meant more than two hours after sundown, the city's traditional curfew (mandate of 17 November 1556; StaatsAN 631a/B 143; Reicke, *Geschichte der Reichsstadt Nürnberg*, 567–71, 625). Cf. similar complaints about bad parents in the begging mandates of 15 October 1567, 10 March 1569, and 9 June 1651, as well as the police ordinances of 29 September 1571 and 12 May 1572. StaatsAN 63 Ia, Bd. C: 158, 203; Bd. D: 52, 76; StadtAN D1/564.

45. "die armen Jungen kinder von knaben unnd Maidlein, zu WintersZeiten dermassen erfrieren, das es Inen an Irem gesind shedlich, und dermassen verwarlost und verderbt werden, das sie hernach zu Iren gesundt nimmer mehr kommen, sondern also gebrechliche, shweche und arbeitselige leuth bleiben nussen." Mandate of 3 December 1566; StadtAN D1/543. Cf. a 1557 begging ordinance similarly excoriating parents who "allowed their children to suffer in cold, frost, hunger, and wetness in the streets, forcing them to work outside as public beggars." StaatsAN 63 Ia, Bd. B: 45v.

46. See especially the pioneering work of Christian Pfister, best summarized in "Weeping in the Snow: The Second Period of Little Ice Age-type Crises, 1570 to 1630," in *Kulturelle Konsequenzen der "Kleinen Eiszeit*," ed. Wolfgang Behringer, Hartmut Lehmann, and Christian Pfister (Göttingen: Vandenhoeck & Ruprecht, 2005), 31–85.

47. "daß dergleichen Personen leichtlich andere davon inficirt warden könten." Stadtal-mosenamt report of 20 October 1649; StadtAN D1/563.

48. Cf. RV of 23 and 24 July, and 22 November 1588, collected in StadtAN D1/544, as well as the pronouncement of an ordinance of 15 May 1588 (RV 1556: 16v–17r) and the full text of the ordinance itself in Rüger, *Mittelalterliches Almosenwesen*, 90–93.

49. Mandate of 3 December 1566; StadtAN D1/543. Cf. RV 1922: 75r (25 April 1616). Stadtalmosenamt report of 20 October 1649; StadtAN D1/563. "muthwillige Jugent . . . hochmuth wid.shlagen und waffen, so wol under wehrenden Gottesdienst, als sonsten treiben." RV 2137: 17r (2 July 1634); also RV 2353: 6r–v (14 December 1648). See also Irsigler and Lassotta, *Bettler und Gaukler*, 62–67, on child and youth begging.

50. "und allenthalben in diser Statt, die gassen uebl.kinder lauffen, die grosses geshrey und Muttwillen treiben . . . und Ihr kind forthin in besserer zucht zuhalten." RV 1922: 27r, 47v, 60v, 75r (10, 16, 19, 25 April 1616).

51. "so leret uns Gott am allersten die allerbesten und köstlichsten lere durch vater und muter." Emil Sehling, *Die Evangelischen Kirchenordnungen des XVI. Jahrhunderts*, vol. 11.1 (Tübingen, 1969), 218.

52. *On Disciplining and Instructing Children* (Latin ed., 1519, 1530; German ed., 1525), quoted and translated in Ozment, *When Fathers Ruled*, 136.

53. Sam, *Davids Eebruch* (Ulm, 1534), F3b, cited in Ozment, *When Fathers Ruled*, 133; Lyndal Roper, "Discipline and Respectability: Prostitution and the Reformation in Augsburg," *History Workshop* 19 (1985): 3–28.

54. Leonhard Culmun, *Jungen gesellen /Jungkfrauuwen und Witwen /so Ehelich wöllen werden* (Augsburg, 1568), E4a, quoted in Ozment, *When Fathers Ruled*, 134.

55. "Eine Predigt, dass man Kinder zur Schulen halten sole" (1530), in *WA*, 30.2: 509ff., 532, 586–87. By 1525, Luther had already accepted the superiority of schools to home for nurturing and education, though he still maintained that the governance of the state—unlike that of parents—remained more like a cat-and-mouse relationship. "Tischreden," no. 386 (352), *WA*, vol. 41, and see Strauss, *Luther's House*, 36, 120ff.

56. The Latin schools were founded at Saint Lorenz (1325), Heilig-Geist Spital (1333), Saint Sebald (1337), and Saint Egidien (1526). The poor schools were established at Saint Sebaldus in 1454 and Saint Lorenz in 1478. Johannes Müllner, *Die An-nalen der Reichsstadt Nürnberg von 1623*, ed. Gerhard Hirschmann, Teil 2: 1351–1469 (Nuremberg: Selbstverlag des Stadtrats, 1984), 506. Leder, *Kirche und Jugend*, 18–20, and see 25ff. on the pedagogical reforms inspired by Luther and Melanchthon; also Siebenkees, *Materialien*, 1: 269–288 and 333–338; and Strauss, *Nuremberg*, 234ff., on Lutheran schools in general.

57. The Konrad Gross Foundation, for instance, dated back to 1331 and supported twelve *scolares pauperes*. Sothmann, *Das Armen-, Arbeits-, Zucht- und Werkhaus in Nürnberg*, 28. The inner council also continued to administer various scholarships for poor students, as well as other assistance programs, such as the All Saints' Day custom of the city fathers bestowing a pair of shoes, a shirt, and a wool cloak upon 150–200 poor apprentices and domestic maids, whose masters might not employ them otherwise. Based on the assumption of a four-year contract, the young people received clothing their first and third years of service, if the craft were eligible. Rüger, *Die Kinderfürsorge*, 48–49; Rüger, *Mittelalterliches Almosenwesen*, 87ff.; and see StadtAN D1/430 for mag-isterial attempts to place poor children between 1621 and 1676.

58. *Nürnberg, Eine Stadt*, 282–83.

59. Rüger, *Die Kinderfürsorge*, 22; *Nürnberg, Eine Stadt*, 282–83; Leder, *Kirche und Jugend*, 158–67.

60. "für die übel gezogene jugent." RV 26 April 1632; StadtAN D1/ 563. The other poor schools were in Wöhrd and in the city on Rössler Street. Rüger, *Die Kinderfürsorge*, 116.

61. Bericht des Almosenpfleger Sig. Held on 26 April 1634; Rüger, *Die Kinderfürsorge*, 50.

62. "dass die armen weiber und kinder, so hiesiger stadt zugethan, mit garn und wollen spinner in denen darzu bestimbten haüsern." *Almosenordnung* of 17 March 1636, StadtAN D10. Cf. founding mission of Christ's Hospital in London: "to take oute of the streates all the fatherless children, and other poor men's children, that were not able to keep them." Cited in Jütte, *Poverty and Deviance*, 39.

63. See Catherine Lis and Hugo Soly, *Disordered Lives: Eighteenth-century Families and Their Unruly Relatives* (Cambridge: Polity Press, 1996), 49–50, on uncontrollable children in discipline-houses; also Griffiths, *Youth and Authority*, 203ff., 368; and Beier, *Masterless Men*, 10.

64. On the origin of Nuremberg's discipline- and workhouse, see Joel F. Harrington, "Escape from the Great Confinement: The Genealogy of a German Workhouse," *Journal of Modern History* 71 (1999): 308–45. Following the opening of discipline-houses in Amsterdam in 1595–96 and Leiden in 1598, the institution spread to the German cities of Bremen in 1608–13, Lübeck in 1613, Hamburg in 1622, and Danzig in 1629.

65. Already common in sixteenth-century Paris and Rouen, the revived medieval practice of the *atelier public*, or *opus publicum* apparently spread to German cities via Strasbourg, though the precise dating is unclear. When Strasbourg, one of the apparent pioneers of *opus publicum*, mentioned the punishment in 1595, "wie in vielen andern grosen stätten," it is possible the magistrates were referring mainly to French cities. The first explicit mention of *Springbuben* in Nuremberg appears in the diary of executioner Frantz Schmidt in 1593 (Keller, *Maister Franntzn Schmidts*, 33), but other evidence suggests that the punishment was already in use since at least the 1580s and by the time of a war bureau recommendation in 1614 it is clearly a well-established practice. Harrington, "Escape from the Great Confinement," 330–32.

   On the etymology of *Schellenwerk*, which first appeared in Bern ca. 1614, see Georg Fumasoli, *Ursprünge und Anfänge der Schellenwerke. Ein Beitrag zur Frühgeschichte des Zuchthauswesens* (Zurich: Schultheiss Polygraphischer Verlag, 1981), 51–62. On the origin of *Springbuben*, see Grimm, *Deutsches Wörterbuch*, vol. 10, sect. 2, pt. 1: 105 (no. 5).

66. See especially the decrees of 23 June 1660 and 8 March 1661; also StadtAN D1/252. Many arrest and release records of *Springbuben* during the 1660s have been collected in StadtAN D1/560, but the list is certainly not complete.

67. "theils durch Ihn überhäuffe kinder, welche von Jugend auff zum bettlen gewehnet und aufferzogen warden, mit furschreib: und ansezung eines geraisen quanti, wievil sie den lag, oder die wochen über, Ihren Eltern heimbringen müssen, welches die Eltern nochmals liederlicher weiss durch die gurgel jagen, und die kinder einen als den andern weeg dorben und noth leiden lassen." Stadtalmosenamt Bericht of 22 April 1668; StadtAN D1/563. This was reissued on 11 December 1670, 13 November 1671, 29 November 1674, and in a slightly modified form on 27 February 1682, 7 January 1683, and 24 September 1674.

68. See especially Strauss, *Luther's House of Learning*, passim.

69. "dass um Kirchhof St. Jacob herum die Kinder mit Werfen, Spielen und Spötteln grossen Unfug treiben und dem Streifer überlegen wären, auch ihn werfen und schänden täten. Herr Volkart aber, dass unter während Kinderlehre bei den Parfüssern etliche Handwerksgesellen bei sich eine Karten gehabt und hinter dem Altar gespielt, auch spöttlich von den Examinatores geredet hätten. Und dann Herr Arnschwanger, dass er von der Jugend sehr gehönet und gespöttelt wurde, wenn er ihnen zureden täte . . . Worüber absonderlich Herr Leibnitz, Herr Volkart, u. Herr Arnschwanger geklaget, u. zwar Herr Leibnitz," *Konventsitzung* of 20 November 1657; GNM Merke 1 HS 164.2°. Cf. Leder, *Kirche und Jugend*, 204ff., on similar complaints of the body on 25 November 1659, 24 November 1660, 24 November 1665, and 23 November 1666.

70. "dass in den Teutschordens hof alhie nicht allein Schul gehalten: sondern auch durch austheilung brod und knuffestücklein, auch illuminiter bilder die Jugendt heirein geraizt, so gar hiesigen schulhaltern abgespant würde . . . da sie allerhand hochmuth getriben, und unter dem fahrn mit schlüsselbüchsen geschossen." RV 2562: 20r (10 August 1664).

71. *Bettelstreifer Ordnung* of 4 September 1638; StadtAN D1/99.

72. See *Pettelrichter Ordnung* of 29 November 1566 on daily rounds and commissions of 5–10 d, later 8d, per beggar apprehended. StadtAN D1/2. Adult protection of young beggars from the *Bettelrichter* and *Almosendiener* was frequently cited in the city's begging ordinances. Rüger, *Mittelalterliches Almosenwesen*, 45.

73. Bettelstreifer Actum of 21 March 1661; StadtAN D1/560.

74. Almosspfleger Bericht (22 April 1668); StadtAN D1/564.

75. Transportation to foreign colonies was more popular in England during the eighteenth century and France during the nineteenth century. In both instances, however, the punishments were always for more serious crimes than begging or vagrancy. See André Zysberg, "Galley and Hard Labor Convicts in France (1550–1850). From the Galleys to Hard Labor Camps: Essay on a Long Lasting Penal Institution," in *The Emergence of Carceral Institutions: Prisons, Galleys and Lunatic Assylums, 1550–1900*, ed. Pieter Spierenburg (Rotterdam: Erasmus Universiteit, 1984), esp. 78–85; also Spierenburg, *Prison Experience*, 266–68.

76. Hundreds of others were also settled in Bermuda and the Barbados or simply sent "to sea." Beier, *Masterless Men*, 163; Geremek, *Poverty*, 218.

77. Frederick the Great was prepared to send a thousand children, ages 10–12, to the Hirschberg merchants to improve yarn production. After the French Revolution, manufacturers urged to bid for the "children of the nation" and one linen manufacturer in Bourges asked for five hundred girls. Cunningham, *Children and Childhood*, 129; Fauve-Chamoux, "Beyond Adoption," 9; McClure, *Coram's Children*, 15; Endres, "Armenproblemen," 1014.

78. In the years 1663, 1675, 1701, 1720, 1749–50; the last episode triggered the most public resistance. Farge, *Fragile Lives*, 55–62.

79. One such list of parents known to send their children begging was compiled on 8 April 1663 (StadtAN D1/564). Alms bureau reports of 11 and 22 April 1668 and a subsequent mandate of 3 April 1670 also addressed the issue of children raised in laziness and begging. StadtAN DI/564; StaatsAN 63IA.

80. "dargegen aber der mahrer theil [twelve] von den Eltern selbst mutwillig auff: aund zum theil nur uf das betteln gehaltten worden, als haben die Ruegherrn befohlen solches obehengedachten herrn Allmosspflegern anzudeuten, und iren herrlb herinzustellen, ob sie die Eltern erfordern, darüber zu rett halten, und zu gebüer vermahnen lassen wollen . . . ein blinder mann in d. Grassengassen, der hatt 3 Puben,

welche nur in Pettel umziehen, und niemand gutthun." Memorial an die wolver-
ordente herrn Almospflegers, betreffendt die burger kinder, die zu hanndwercken
tüchtig, dern Eltern das Almosen haben" (4 May 1630); "Bericht aus dem Rugsampt,
die in Allmosen Ufgezeichnet Jungen, so hanndwerck zulassen begern betr." (late
1630); and "Leerjungen, so ire Allmosen zufinden, und hanndtwerck lernen wollen"
(10 May and 12 Juny 1631); StadtAN DI/ 430, nos. 3 and 4. In 1633 the alms bureau
compiled another list of thirty-one families who send children begging; Bericht des
Almosenpfleger 8 April 1633; StadtAN D1/560.

81. RV 19 February 1651, RV 1 March 1656, RV 17 April 1668; StadtAN D1/563 and 564.
Cf. earlier versions of the same complaints in a mandate of 29 September 1571, police ordinance of 12 May 1572; *Reichenalmosen Ordnung* of 1579, begging ordinances
of 20 August 1588 and 16 August 1615 (StaatsAN 631A, Bde B, D, and E); StadtAN
D1/3.

82. "dess es ein tummer unbaulig knab ist, mit dem nirgen fortzukamm, seyn wirdt . . .
nach allen ihren vermögen dieser sohn und erziehen von den betteln und in eine
schuel etwas nach St. Lorentzen gehen lass. woll., sie sey aber das Knaben nich mäch-
tig, zumaln die wegen ihrer nahrung wenig zu hauss sey und also end. den knaben
nicht genug achtung geben könne." RV 16 October 1668 (StadtAN D1/563). "in
ansehung ihren 7 kinder." Stadtalmosenamt Actum of 14 December 1688 (StadtAN
D1/560).

83. "auch die Rößnerin Jungen nich verneien können." RV 16 October 1668 (StadtAN
D1/563).

84. "fast alle Nacht in der Statt herumb vagirn und da leuth mit betel molestirn." "Aussag
des herrn Andr. G. Baumgartner" (14 December 1688) StadtAN D1/563.

85. Michael Salomon was admitted to the Findel on 29 June 1668 and died on 17 December 1685. FB 2: 127.

86. "alss aber am vershienen Sonntag nicht zu hauss gewesen seye der jung ohne hembt
welches ir ihne mit fleiss eingespirten damit er desto eher zu hauss bleiben möchte,
davon: und seinen betteln nachgelauffen. Er seye gar ein ungeschickhter und unsau-
ber knab, der nicht wohl zu einen handwerkh druge, auch in den schuelen, wegen
des gestrukhs, nicht gelitten werde . . . habe ihr gar wunder selten etwan 1 grosh oder
½ batz gegeben." Stadtalmosenamt Actum (15 December 1668); StadtAN D1/563.
   The topos of taking away a youth's clothes to keep him at home appears as early
as the fourth century, in Eusebius's tale of the youthful Origen's would-be martyrdom
in *Ecclesiastical History, Book VI–X*, trans. J. E. L. Oulton (Cambridge: Harvard University Press, 1932), 2: 343. Heather Shore (*Artful Dodgers: Youth and Crime in Early
Nineteenth-century London* [Bury St. Edmunds: Royal Historical Society, 1999], 46) has
found the same topos in the testimony of a nineteenth-century juvenile delinquent.

87. "jedoch mit dem ausdrucklich beding." StadtAN D1/563.

88. RV: 18 December 1668; StadtAN D1/563.

89. Rössner's deserted wife was granted a weekly 20 kreuzer 12 shillings on the same
day Anna Maria Salomonin received her first 15 kreuzer (6 December 1662) but
payments for the former were stopped when Christoph Rössner returned sometime
afterward. On 10 October 1668 the Rössners were restored to the rolls but at a lower
10 kreuzer 12 shillings rate, while Anna Maria Salomonin's stipend was raised by 3
kreuzer 12 shillings to 18 kreuzer. Stadtalmosenamt Acta 14 and 15 December 1688;
StadtAN D1/563.

90. "als einen vertrunckenen liderlich mann." RV 14 December 1688; StadtAN D1/563.
Although prices across Germany had by this time fallen to about a third of their level

during the 1620s, 16 fl. a year would have only bought about three loaves of rye bread (ca. 3400 grams) per week (calculated at 2.4 Albus, or about 0.10 fl. each; price based on figures in Dietrich Ebeling and Franz Irsigler, *Getreideumsatz, Getreide- und Brotpreise in Köln, 1368–1797* [Cologne: Bölau-Verlag, 1976], ix, xv; and Thomas Robisheaux, *Rural Society and the Search for Order in Early Modern Germany* [Cambridge: Cambridge University Press, 1989], 150).

91. "dem Bösen ist zu gut, diss Arbeits haus gebaut, Wer nit viel guts gethan, od. den vor Arbeit graut, der find hie werkzeug gnug, hierinnen wohnt die Zucht, der bösen bester Nutz wird hie damit gesucht." StadtAN F1/57; 11 March 1671.

92. Refused "mit Glimpf . . . nach Notdurft repariert und gesäubert und Herr Albrecht Pömers Herrlichkeit als jetziger Findelpfleger bis nächst kommende Laurenzi ohnfehlbar einziehen könne und ferner nich daran gehindert werde." RV 2146: 137v (16 April 1633); RV 2150: 4r–v (26 July 1633). Pömer's oversight of the Findel was shared with two fellow council members, Leonhard Grundherr and Lucas Welser, until he finally moved into the Findel in August. RV 2147: 84v (9 May 1633).

93. See Mummenhoff, "Das Findel- und Waisenhaus," 1: 100–10, on the early history of the Nuremberg Findel.

94. The oldest institution specifically for foundlings was that of the archbishop of Milan, founded in 787. The practice was slow to catch on, with only four more foundling homes, all but one in Italy, created by the end of the millennium. A few more institutions followed in the eleventh and twelfth centuries, including a home in Laibach (1041) and nine homes founded by the Brothers of the Holy Spirit throughout Germany (by 1198). German foundling homes included Memmingen (by 1200), Einbeck (by 1274), Saint Gallen (1228), Strasbourg (by 1300), Cologne (by 1341), Ulm (by 1355) and Eßlingen (by 1400). The oldest foundling homes in Spain date a bit later, such as that of Toledo, founded in 1483. Most Spanish foundling homes originated in the sixteenth century, including ones in Seville, Madrid, Valladolid, Salamanca, Córdoba, and Santiago de Compostela. Mummenhoff, "Das Findel- und Waisenhaus," 1: 71–74; Vassberg, "Orphans and Adoption," 448; Linda Martz, *Poverty and Welfare in Habsburg Spain: The Example of Toledo* (New York: Cambridge University Press, 1983), 224–25.

95. A few medieval hospitals—Freiburg, Constance, Munich, Landshut, and Mainz— maintained separate child clinics (*Kinderstuben*), where illegitimate foundlings and a few legitimate orphans were mixed, but for the most part civic and ecclesiastical authorities attempted to keep the two populations apart, with foundling homes catering exclusively to those babies assumed to be bastards. Mummenhoff, "Das Findel- und Waisenhaus," pt. 1, 71–74. The Parisian orphanage that opened at Place de Grève in 1363, by contrast, accepted only legitimate boys and girls; anonymously abandoned babies were taken to the foundling hospital of La Couche, next to the Cathedral of Notre Dame in order to preserve the reputation of the orphanage (and thereby the employment prospects of its children upon their release). Paris also had the Hôtel-Dieu (next to Notre Dame) for orphans, and the Trinité, founded in the twelfth century, for foundlings. Gager, *Blood Ties and Fictive Ties*, 106–10.

96. Only three German cities (Basel, Bamberg, and Breslau) maintained homes specifically for orphans before 1500; by the end of the seventeenth century, virtually every German town with a population greater than 10,000 operated at least one orphanage. Orphanages founded between the mid-sixteenth and mid-eighteenth centuries included Lübeck (1546), Leipzig (1556), Augsburg (1572; 1737 Catholic), Würzburg (1579; 1659), Speyer (1583), Münster (1592), Prague (1602), Bremen

(1602 and 1684, both Reformed; 1692 Lutheran), Hamburg (1604), Donauwörth and Zurich (1637), Hannover (1643), Frankfurt am Main (1650), Regensburg (1666; 1731 Catholic), Altenburg (1671), Bremen (1684), Dresden (1687), Goslar (1693), Celle (1696), Darmstadt (1697), Halle (1698), Berlin (1702), Wolfenbüttel (1704), Pforzheim (1718), Stuttgart (1710), Wiesbaden (1725), Göttingen (1746), Helmstedt (1752), and Hildesheim (1754). Mummenhoff, "Das Findel- und Waisenhaus," 1: 70, 75–85; Meumann, *Findelkinder*, 259.

97. In some locations, such as Breslau, orphanages were prohibited from admitting illegitimate children without a special privilege from the emperor. Zurich contemporaries also prohibited their municipal orphanage from accepting illegitimate children. Separate foundling homes also continued to be established throughout the seventeenth and eighteenth centuries, most famously Saint Vincent de Paul's Hôpital des Enfants Trouvés in Paris in 1638, and the London Foundling Hospital in 1739. Mummenhoff, "Das Findel- und Waisenhaus," 1: 75, 85; Cunningham, *Children and Childhood*, 125; Meumann, *Findelkinder*, 181; and Ruth McClure, *Coram's Children: The London Foundling Hospital in the Eighteenth Century* (New Haven: Yale University Press, 1981), *passim*.

98. FKD: Anonymous abandonments constituted 599 of 1,262 (47.5 percent) of all abandonment cases; 599 of 3,199 (18.8 percent) admission cases where type was known. This function became even more pronounced during the crisis years of 1633–38, when orphans went from comprising roughly a third of all admissions to accounting for almost nine in ten children accepted into the Findel (372 of the 425 whose type could be identified; of 576 total).

99. "das darinnen vatter- und mutterlose, auch sonst von menniglichen verlassene waisen aufgenommen, zu wahrer gottesfurcht, auch züchtigem gottseligem leben und wandel aufgezogen und mit notwendiger kleidung, kost, liegerstatt und anderer notdurft zur gebühr und versorget würden." Quoted in Rüger, *Die Kinderfürsorge*, 80.

100. Mummenhoff, "Das Findel- und Waisenhaus," 1: 100–1. During the Middle Ages, Augsburg, Dresden, and Leipzig regularly sent foundlings out to foster parents. The Couche of Paris tried very hard to get abandoned children raised in foster homes; on holidays, some infants were placed in cradles in churches to be picked up and taken home. Ibid., 76–79; Gager, *Blood Ties and Fictive Ties*, 117.

101. At that point the girls were living in a house able to accommodate about fifty children as well as a staff of six or seven, located at the corner of Maxplatz and Weissgerbergstrasse. The boys' home was located on Breitengasse with back buildings going on to the Brunnengasse. The girls' home had suffered a less destructive fire in 1537. Mummenhoff, "Das Findel- und Waisenhaus," 1: 103–7, 110.

102. StadtAN F1–2/VII, Bd. VI: 244. Mummenhoff, "Das Findel- und Waisenhaus," 1: 111–3.

103. The resulting blueprint for renovations also attempted to accommodate Brother Peter Pfingstetter, by then the sole remaining Franciscan, whose only complaint about "the good children" was that they didn't visit him as much as they did when the girls first moved in. RV 1181: 2r–v, RV 1182: 6r (28 March and 18 April 1560); Gutachten from 2 April 1560, cited in Mummenhoff, "Das Findel- und Waisenhaus," 1: 117.

104. For more details on the early modern petition process, see Jörg Walter, *Rat und Bürgerhauptleute in Braunschweig, 1576–1604* (Braunschweig: Waisenhaus, 1971).

105. FB 1: 278 (19 March 1613).

106. FKD. Of 1,842 non-orphan cases in which petitioners were identified, parents were

mentioned only 6.3 percent of the time (116) and other relatives 5.5 percent of the time (101). Of course some relatives probably did not identify themselves as such to avoid having the children returned to them.

107. See H. Heidrich, "Grenzübergänge: Das Haus und die Volkskultur in der frühen Neuzeit," in *Kultur der einfachen Leute*, ed. van Dülmen and Heidrich, 17–41.

108. See, for example, RV 1298: 16r (15 January 1569); RV 1776: 48v (15 April 1605); RV 1905: 31r (17 January 1615); RV 2153: 60v–61r (25 October 1633).

109. Zimmerman, "Behörige Orthen angezeigt," 70; Meumann, *Findelkinder*, 160–3.

110. "auf diejenige, so die kinder zu der Statt schleichen und hinsetzen gut Achtung zu geben." RV 1936: 3r (23 April 1617); "vielerley frembdte soldaten weiber, hin und wider." RV 2574: 45v–46r (10 July 1665).

111. FB 2: 95 (25 January 1645).

112. "die Nachbarn, die solch gesehen zuvernemen, wie sie gestaltet gewest, zuvernennen und auff sie nitt allein in der Statt alhie zu straifen, sonder auch gen Schweinau kuntshafft zu machen." RV 1943: 15r–v (11 November 1617).

113. The entire city of Nuremberg had only fifty archers (*Schützen*) in 1450, a number that declined to twenty-three by 1569. In 1614, thirteen archers were responsible for eight city gates and four begging police covered the entire city. The number of begging police was raised to six in 1615 and eight in 1638 (Bedencken on Bettelordnung [30 March 1615 and 6 June 1625]; StadtAN D1/545 and 546), but according to Andrea Bendlage and Peter Schuster ("Hüter der Ordnung. Bürger, Rat, und Polizei in Nürnberg in 15. und 16. Jahrhundert," *MVGN* 82 [1995], 38–53): "According to the surviving sources, the archers of every era were unreliable and for the most part unfit." There were also frequent complaints about excessive beating and the Bettelstreifer making themselves "despised" (RV 17 May 1564 and 25 February 1568) as well as accusations of incompetence and bribery (1665); StadtAN D1/560. Cf. Spierenburg, *Prison Experience* (77–81), on similar complaints about the begging police of Amsterdam and Hamburg.

114. RV 1897: 43r, 46r (11 and 14 June 1614).

115. RV 1942: 46v (22 October 1617); RV 1969: 67r (6 September 1620); RV 1980: 107v–108r (6 September 1620). Cf. a fourth case where two archers were reprimanded for not bringing in a suspicious maid. RV 1972: 33v (18 January 1620).

116. "gantz falsh unrecht und wider wertig aufgeshriben worden . . . bei etlichen Jaren hero der böse und unleidliche gebrauch." RV 1594: 27v (19 May 1591).

117. "eine verzeichnus solches hingesezten kinder machen und alle quartal verzulegen, damit man den Eltern nachfragen lassen könne." RV 1941: 41v (25 September 1617). See also RV 1557: 58r (30 June 1588); RV 1841: 41v (12 April 1610).

118. "es sein gleich reich od. Arme." RV 1469: 55r (26 November 1581). For an example of this method in practice, see RV 2121: 40r–v (21 April 1631) and RV 2535: 3v (26 July 1662).

119. RV 2092: 89r–v, 100r–v; RV 2093: 85v (13, 17 February and 11 March 1629).

120. RV 2615: 86r–v (10 August 1668).

121. "noch auch die schrift des beygelegten Zedulleins känne." RV 2535: 3r, 3v–4r, 58v–59r (26 July and 11 August 1662); see the similar case of RV 2545: 55v–56r (5 May 1663).

122. See below, chapter 5.

123. As specified in Nuremberg's 1564 civil code. Roetzer, "Die Delikte der Abtreibung," 116. In a sample of 261 criminal arrests between 1562–1696 in Frankfurt, 47 percent were the result of general gossip and 27 percent were caught in the act. Maria Boes,

"Public Appearance and Criminal Judicial Practices in Early Modern Germany," *Social Science History* 20, no. 2 (1996): 262.

124. Hans Durer, a baker who had also previously housed the child's mother, Maria Steudtlin from Gunzbachhausen, was initially imprisoned for perjury and after release fined 50 fl. and told to marry the young woman outside the city. RV 2044: 82v (9 July 1625).

125. Both the mother, a tailor's daughter, and the beggar woman were to be arrested if they returned to Schwerzelohe. RV 1975: 37v (11 April 1620). Mars Lumago endured an ordeal of the same nature, with the same result. RV 2036: 25r (20 November 1624); RV 2037: 65v (1 December 1624).

126. See Roetzer, "Die Delikte der Abtreibung," 125.

127. RV 1925: 25r (5 July 1616).

128. "soll man mit Zacharias Kriegs gennandt handeln solch kind anzunemen, wo nit in die findel thun." RV 1357: 8r (26 May 1573). The usual phrase was "wann anderst nitt freund verhanden die sich derselben annemen." RV 1881: 6r–v (20 March 1613).

129. Saloman Zorn was paid 20 kreuzer weekly "out of the municipal alms bureau" for care of his grandson. RV 2522: 39r (22 August 1661); see also RV 2568: 33v–34r (30 January 1665). For a case in which the Findel's budget was specified, see RV 1878: 13v (30 December 1612). When confronted with an overwhelming number of Findel petitions in December 1632, the inner council repeatedly implored petitioners to locate relatives "bey gegenwertigen schweren Zeiten" and promised to pay stipends out of the alms bureau." RV 2142: 68v (3 December 1632).

130. RV 1298: 16r (15 January 1569); RV 1959: 1r (14 January 1619). Another guardian a little more than a week later was granted 33 fl. annually for three children. RV 1959: 12r (23 January 1619). For other examples, see RV 1878: 13v (30 December 1612); RV 1896: 10r (29 April 1614); RV 1925: 25r (5 July 1616); RV 1977: 13v (28 August 1616); RV 1928: 33r (2 October 1616); RV 1928: 37r (4 October 1616; RV 2011: 33r (28 November 1622); and RV 2142: 8v–9r (16 November 1632).

131. Wiesner, *Working Women*, 54.

132. RV 1936: 33v, 66v–67r (3 and 14 May 1617).

133. RV 1863: 47r (27 November 1611).

134. RV 1391: 20v–21r (27 December 1575); RV 1947: 30v (6 March 1618); RV 1587: 43r, 50v (22 and 26 October 1590) .

135. StadtAN D1/430 (1668).

136. "darbey gleichfalls zu bedencken wie es mitt solchen Findelkinder auff dem land zu halten, damit die Findel mitt denselben nit beshwert werde." RV 1882: 60r (30 April 1613).

137. RV 2522: 39r (22 August 1661). See also the request for assistance from foster mother Margareta Selnerin from Wöhrd. RV 1107: 19v (27 October 1553).

138. Wiesner, *Working Women*, 48.

139. See an example two months before Albrecht Pömer took office, with his predecessor typically offering to accept the sickly and youngest of three orphans if the petitioning godfather would agree to care of other two. RV 2145: 48v–49r (19 February 1633).

140. "das Jungere kindt in die Findel enzunemmen, dem Pfleger aber befehlen, das eltere umb ein gering ziehgelt unterbringen, biss es sein Brod verdienen könne." RV 1857: 49r (11 June 1611). See also RV 1860: 67v (11 September 1611).

141. RV 1853: 11v (18 February 1611); also RV 2251: 53v (26 October 1663). Cf. three children whose mother lay sick in the hospital and the council's directions to the Fin-

del administrator to "make further inquiries whether one or two of them might be housed at different places." RV 1868: 27v and 1869: 1v–2r (4 and 14 April 1612).

142. FKD. Of 1541 petitions in which siblings were mentioned, 1049 (68.1 percent) had one or two siblings admitted simultaneously, 199 (12.9 percent) had three or more siblings admitted with the petitioner, and 172 (11.2 percent) had some admitted and some declined—a total of 92.2 percent. Further, 96 (6.2 percent) saw one or two siblings turned down, and 25 (1.6 percent) had three or more siblings turned down.

143. RV 1439: 1r (16 July 1579).

144. Vassberg, "Orphans and Adoption," 445; Gager, *Blood Ties and Fictive Ties,* 142

145. "weg entlof. und drei kind. siz. lassen." FB 2: 34 (2 June 1627; 4 May 1628); FB 1: 165 (8 June 1598).

146. FB 2: 124 (20 April 1666); RV 1939: 37r, 73v (29 July and 9 August 1617). See a similar case of an anonymously abandoned baby later returned to its mother and banished with her: FB 2: 2 (1 November 1615; 2 May 1616). Safley finds the same pattern in Augsburg (*Charity and Economy,* 5).

147. Emphasis added. "welchs aber bisshero nitt gethan, sonder das kind herumb und lam geshlagen, dann wann sie dem nitt nachkummen solte, werde man sie mitt sampt dem kind zur statt hinauss weisen." RV 1860: 27v (27 August 1611).

148. "und Ime sagen man könne frembde kinder nitt herein in die findel nemen." RV 1905: 34v (18 January 1615).

149. "soll man dieselben auff einen karren hinausfahren und daselbe niedersetzen lassen." RV 1853: 24r–v, 30r (25 February 1611). In 1614 a woman from Eger who abandoned her two children at the Heilig-Geist Spital was briefly imprisoned and then given 1 gulder and banished with her children. RV 1901: 36v. (11 September 1614). See also the 1614 case of two abandoned children, one of them "already seven years old," who were ordered interrogated on the identity and location of their parents and then "sent back home." RV 1901: 7v (16 September 1614).

150. "von Wasserzell ein halbe meil wegs von widerumb daselbst hinführen und sizen lassen." RV 2071: 28r (27 June 1627).

151. FB 2: 1 (25 May 1615; 10 June 1615).

152. RV 2166: 29v (3 October 1634).

153. Bologna's San Giussepe began taking paying customers, usually the daughters of well-to-do citizens, around 1629, and when the governors of the London Foundling Home announced in June of 1756 that they would accept any child aged two months to two years for the exorbitant fee of £100, they still found seventeen willing takers over the next fifteen years. Nicholas Terpstra, "Making a Living, Making a Life: Work in the Orphanages of Florence and Bologna," *Sixteenth Century Journal* 31, no. 4 (2000): 1077; McClure, *Coram's Children,* 86.

154. "biss sie zu handwerkch tuglich und Ihr Brod selbs erwerben mögen." I have found only one reference of the practice before 1618 (FB 1: 150 [20 December 1595]) and only two after 1649 (FB 2: 125 [22 October 1666]; and RV 2625: 26v–27r, RV 2627: 23v [21 April, 18 June 1669]). The remainder appeared during the intervening years: RV 1947: 30v (6 March 1618); RV 1959: 12r (25 January 1619); RV 2060: 3r–v (31 August 1626); RV 2142: 68r (3 December 1632); RV 2142: 69r (3 December 1632); FB 2: 50 (29 December 1633); RV 2158: 47v (20 March 1634); FB 2: 47 (8 April 1634; originally admitted 24 November 1632); RV 2170: 1r (15 January 1635); RV 2227: 26r–v (20 June 1639); and FB 2: 103 (13 December 1649).

155. RV 27 1892: 36v (January 1614). FKD: 60 of 1449 cases in which property is mentioned; 47 were above 10 fl.

156. RV 2169: 19r, RV 2171: 2v (21 January and 13 February 1635). See the acceptance of Jeronimus Erhardt's blind orphan in November 1634 with 25fl. property and some clothing, and another child's accepted admission the following year, once he was found to have 50 fl. property. RV 2168: 1r (20 November 1634); RV 2182: 62r–v (29 December 1635).

157. In 1634–35, inheritance and fees brought in 177 fl.; in 1635–36, 72 fl.; 1636–37, 55 fl.; 1637–38, 38 fl; 1638–39 191 fl. (one inheritance of the three Metz children was worth over 188 fl.); and 1639–40, 158 fl. The following year, that income dropped to 22 fl, and the two years after that was only 43 and 42 fl., respectively. StadtAN D10 2/ix: 16r–19v, 137r.

158. "grosser armuth . . . auff wass weis und weg derselbe in so grosse armuth kammen, was er an Losung schuldig, wie alt die drey kinder ob es knäblein oder mägdlein, wer dero befreundte und tauftdote, und ob sie nicht bey denselben unterzubringen." RV 2534: 42r–v, 65r (10 and 17 July 1662).

159. "ein armen dienstmagd . . . bey der Nachbarschafft und sunsten nachzufragen, ob die Armut so gross, als sie by der Supplicantin angeben worden." RV 2141: 80r–v (9 November 1632).

160. RV 1722: 4r (26 February 1601).

161. "welche bede [Eltern] gestorben und grosse shulden verlassen." FB 2: 32 (21 February 1627); RV 2213: 23v (4 May 1638). In Augsburg, most orphans brought little or no property with them and those who did had the capital invested as soon as possible for them. Safley, *Charity and Economy*, 122.

162. "in gdenck sein, ohne erhebliche ursach keine frembde zu Burgern anzunemen." RV 1924: 38r (12 June 1616).

163. RV 23 March 1634, StadtAN D1/561.

164. RV 2169: 13v–14r, 49v, 66v–67r (20 December 1634; 5 and 10 January 1635).

165. FKD: 92 of 936 (9.8 percent) fathers where citizenship status was known.

166. For instance, "dieweil in hohe notturfft, daran zusein das die arme nachdem befelch Gottes gepürlich versorget, und die heufig herumb straifende arme unmündige waysen." RV 2178 (16 September 1635).

167. RV 1924: 71r–v, RV 1925: 31v (26 June and 8 July 1616).

168. Natalie Zemon Davis, *Fiction in the Archives: Pardon Tales and Their Tellers in Sixteenth-century France* (Stanford: Stanford University Press, 1987).

169. For instance, the widow of the executioner's late assistant had her petition denied (albeit with a small annual stipend of 12 fl.), while the six-year-old orphan of a former begging beadle was accepted right away. RV 2011: 33r (28 November and 16 December 1622); RV 2093: 76r–v, 95v; RV 2094: 5r (7, 11, and 20 March 1629).

170. "gantz keine befreundte . . . zur Reformirten Religion würde gebrachte warden." RV 2523: 37r–v (16 September 1661). "damit es nit in Pabstumb kome." FB 2: 24 (23 July 1624). The council also urged craft masters to take on all evangelical local children as apprentices before any Catholics (RV 9 May 1659; StadtAN D1/430). On the role of denominational factors in admission decisions, see Meumann, *Findelkinder*, 282.

171. "sie soll das kind nitt verworlosen oder wider hinsezen, man werde sie sonsten darum zu finden wissen." RV 1896: 10r, 38v (29 April and 11 May 1614).

172. "Auff Hanns Maisenbuchs zum Weickershof bey idem Jungern Herrn Burgermeister beshehens anpringen, was massen Ime ein neugeporn Jung kindlein, welches ungeverlich bei 14 tagen alt in seinen stadel eigeshoben worden, soll man mit Ime handeln dasselbig zuerziehen und jerlich ein hulf von dem landalmesnamten darzu

geben oder do solches bei Ime nit zuerhalten, sonsten weg suchen wie das kindlein undergebracht und erzogen warden mog damit es nicht verder." RV 1409: 16r–v, 42r (16 and 25 April 1577).

173. "jämmerlich . . . wegen grosser kälte . . . ein gar kleiner seher übelgekleidter knab . . . ganz und verlassen uff der gassen ligen." RV 2141: 106v (15 September 1632); RV 2142: 58v (29 November 1632). Two months later magistrates felt similarly compelled to take in a three-year-old girl left in front of the Findel "on account of the great cold" and the next day accepted "a very small, poorly clothed boy . . . left to lie on the streets." Cf. similar complaints by Dresden magistrates during the Thirty Years' War about children who "auf den Gassen bei grosser Kälte nicht vor den Türen bleiben und sonderlich bei der Nacht mit jämmerlichem Geschrei u. Winseln, wie bisher u. vorige Jahre leider oftmals geschehen, den Leutern beschwerlich sein oder gar umkommen und erfrieren möchten." Mummenhoff, "Das Findel- und Waisenhaus," 1: 78.

174. "damit andern noth leidenden armen kindern und waissn auch umb so viel mehr geholffen warden können." RV 2139: 107r (14 September 1632); RV 2145: 97r (2 March 1633); RV 2148: 48v–49r (4 June 1633).

175. FKD. Thirty of sixty-four orphan petitions in 1633 were denied. Six boys and two girls were placed into service.

176. "bis anhero auss der Statt führen und weisen, noch dieselb, so wohl bey tags als nachts, uff der gassen lign und verderbe . . . bey der burgerschaffte ein stücklein brot beten und heishen . . . und dannach sich viel arme weisen und kinder, so wol man meine herrn unterthene uff dem land, alss hiesigen burgershafft, sich alhier befind., die uff abgang Ihre Eltern sich das Pettels behelten, uber nacht aber uff der gass. Ligen, und Iemmerlich verderben und erfruren mussen . . . alss soll man hinfuro die spitalstuben oder dess Streunerloch in der Findel tuglich, uff den Abent, einheizen und werm machen, auch den Schuzen befohlen lassen, wo sie dergleichen areme weisen, die sonsten keinen untershlaif heben, uff der gassen bey nacht entroffen worden, dass sie solche mit guten glimpf und bescheid enhelt an ermelt. Ort fuhren sollen, damit sie also dem leben erhalten warden und folgenden tags etwan ein stucklein brot wenig mögen. Nachdem aber das Petteln von andern starcken streuners gesind gar zu sehr widerumb uberhand nimmet." RV 2154: 17r–v (12 November 1633); also RV 2154: 60v–61r (28 November 1633). The policy was reaffirmed on 15 May 1634 and on 16 September 1635 (StadtAN D1/547).

177. RV 2154: 60v–61r (28 November 1633).

178. Cf. three lists of 12 and 28 November 1633, and 23 March 1634, the last containing the names of seventy-one children, more than ninety percent of them foreigners. StadtAN DA/561. Another large transfer of sixty beggar children, most of them ill, took place on 23 March 1636 (RV 2185: 73v–74r).

179. "sehr gebrechliches . . . damit es nicht gar verderb und vershmachten, dasselbig auss der Findel ziehen, und darbei gut ufsicht machen lassen, damit ds. Kind nicht wie bissher, im Pettel herumb geshlappent und dz sein gesundheit ferner verwehert sonder mit behörigen notwendig werdt versorget wurde." RV 2157: 48v (12 February 1634).

180. FKD. Seventy-six deaths from June 1632 to May 1633, fifteen deaths for the following twelve months.

181. "welche anders nichts dann ein Stuckh brod zuerhaltung Ihres lbens bitten und suchen müssen, auch andwerths keine mittel haben, ein untershiedt zumachen und zuhalten." StadtAN 547: Kriegsamt Bedencken (18 April 1634).

182. "der Waisen seindt auch Zweyerley, frembde und aigen, da sich dann mit den ersten
     also zuerhalten, dass zwar selbiger hershafften nach müglichkeit zukundig, und auf-
     sehen fall, woran sie auf einen sondbar hie zu bestellten weg an behörige ort andern
     gantze zu verführen, welche aber Ihr haimath nicht zunemen wissen, wer aber man
     mit solchen ein werkh d. barmherzigkeit für zunehmen, und selbige in die Findel an
     aein besond. Ort und mit gewiese mass gleich od. Feindligen so lang zu unterhalten
     biss sie entwed. Verdingt od. Zuhandwerkhen könten gebracht warden." Vorshläg des
     Findelpflegers (15 May 1634); StadtAN 547.
183. RV 2165: 57r (13 September 1634); Mummenhoff, "Das Findel- und Waisenhaus,"
     1: 145. See also RV 2170: 14v–15r (20 January 1635).
184. "auf einen absonderlichen Ort zu denken, darin solche Kinder enthalten, bis man se-
     hen möge, ob sie gesund und alsdann in die Findel genommen warden." This clearly
     implies that the children's house in Wöhrd, discussed later in chapter 5, was for some
     reason no longer in use. RV 2166: 27r (2 October 1634); RV 2168: 48r (9 December
     1634). The city construction engineer was told to use stone and old iron in construct-
     ing the annex so as to cut costs. RV 2167: 64v (14 November 1634).
185. "dergleich begern täglich und häuffig einkommen, soll man die herrn depurtirte
     ersuch., mit fleiss zubedencken, wohin, doch solche Elterlose kinder transportirtiert
     und welcher gestalt sie unterhalt. Ihr d. können." RV 2168: 50v, 61v (9 and 12 De-
     cember 1634).
186. RV 2172: 7r (13 March 1635); RV 2185: 73v–74r (23 March 1636); RV 2170: 28v
     (24 January and 9 February 1635).
187. RV 2173: 30v (9 April 1635). This policy was reiterated in March 1636, with the
     many "damaged and sick" ones put in the new chamber under the care of a nurse.
     Those who were "grown and big" were sent to the hospital where they were cured
     and, if not citizen children, were to be banished from the city. Between 1 June 1634
     and 31 May 1635, 294 children, including only 8 abandoned babies, were admitted
     to the Findel; 147 (50 percent) of those died within the year.
188. "eine anzahl armer kinder." RV 2170: 15r, 28v (20 and 24 January 1635); RV 2172:
     1v (12 March 1635); RV 2173: 4r–v, 28r, 47r–v (1, 8, 14 April 1635).
189. According to the new ordinance, for every 42 pounds of grain delivered to them,
     millers would donate 4 pounds to the Findel and 2 pounds to the hospital. RV 2173:
     28v, 55r–v, 58r–v, 86r (8, 16, 17, and 26 April 1635); RV 2174: 31r–v (12 May 1635).
     On 7 February 1639, there was further negotiation between the inner council and
     local millers on supplies of grain to the Findel and Spital.
190. RV 2173: 58r (17 April 1635).
191. "obwohl meine Herren nichts Lieberes wünschen wollten, denn daß die Bürgerschaft
     mit dergleichen Oneribus unbeschwert verbleiben könnte . . . dafern anderst die Ob-
     rigkeit und Untertanen ferners ein corpus reipublicae [sic] machen und noch länger
     beisammen wohnen sollen, unumgänglich mit dergleichen Mitteln unter die Arme
     gegriffen warden muß." RV 2182: 122v (18 January 1636); StaatsAN Älternverlässe
     41: 294. "jeder, den dieser Aufschlag treffen möchte, denselben als ein Almosen mit
     getreuem Herzen entrichten werde." RV 2173: 58v (17 April 1635).
192. The wedding and new officeholder taxes together brought in 99 fl. during the first
     five months of implementation and more than twice that amount during fiscal year
     1636–37. The occupational tax, on the other hand, spurred two contributions by
     the beer brewers of 75 fl. each but otherwise generated no new funds. The most suc-
     cessful new Findel tax was also the most inconsistent and shortest lived. During its
     first year of implementation in 1633–34, the *Straffen* tax generated over 504 fl. but

the following year no income whatsoever, followed by 298 fl. in 1635–36 and then no more income until 1644, with the tax eventually sputtering out in 1657. StadtAN D 10 2/ix: 20r–v, 88r–191r; RV 1829: 17v–18r (25 April 1609); Mummenhoff, "Das Findel- und Waisenhaus," 1: 321.

193. StadtAN D10 Sch. 2/ix: 62r–68v. The two exceptional years for the coffin pillows were mainly a function of high mortality, and the tax subsequently settled in at a steady level of 200–300 fl. annually. Extreme fluctuations in wine sales often spelled some very lean years right on the heels of bountiful ones. At the beginning of the Thirty Years' War, for instance, the annual income provided to the Findel plummeted to 30 fl.; six years later it soared to a high of 743 fl. and then sank to 27 fl. during 1628–29. Income from the wine tax rebounded to 173 fl. during Pömer's first year as Findel administrator in 1633–34, but by the time of his 1635 reforms, it was only bringing in 19 fl. a year.

194. StadtAN D10 Sch. 2/ix: 5r–v. See Mummenhoff, "Das Findel- und Waisenhaus," 1: 280–281, on the origin of this practice.

195. StadtAN D10 Sch. 2/ix: 29r–30r; StadtAN D 10 Sch. 3/vii.

196. Apparently no voluntary contributions were taken in during 1629–32, then 97 fl. in 1633, then no entries whatsoever for the following year, and a total of only 100 fl. over the next five years. StadtAN D 10 3/vii: StadtAN D10 2/ix: 9r. StadtAN F1–2/ VII, 742–743. See Mummenhoff, "Das Findel- und Waisenhaus," 1: 289ff., and cf. Meumann, *Findelkinder*, 380ff., on private foundations for orphans and foundlings in Hannover and Hildesheim.

197. Rüger, *Mittelalterliches Almosenwesen*, 49; StadtAN D10/Schubl. 2, Bde 1, 2, 3, 7, 9, 10; Mummenhoff, "Das Findel- und Waisenhaus," 1: 294.

198. "weilln dieser Zeit die Findel kinder ganz nichts zu arbeiten haben, soll man dem Rugshreiber befohlen, bey den geshwornen uff etlich handwerken nach zu fragen, was diesen armen waisen fur eine arbeit zushaffen, damit sie etwas verdienen, und nicht ganz müßig sizen mög." RV 2145: 24r–v (12 February 1633).

199. StadtAN D10/2/ix: 54r–59v.

200. StadtAN D10/2/ix: 72r–73r.

201. The Findel's new butter enterprise got big results immediately: from 90 to 144 fl. in the first year and over 239 fl. the following year. It continued to rise until its peak of 330 fl. in 1690–91; it dropped precipitously during the next fifty years, then re-bounded to 772 fl. in 1750–51, by which point the Findel owned seventeen cows. Income from selling animals for slaughter also remained low. StadtAN D 10 Sch. 2/ ix: 3r–4r; Mummenhoff, "Das Findel- und Waisenhaus," 1: 258–59, 261–62.

202. "die heufig gerumb straifende arme unmündige waysen . . . und wegen der einbre-chenden kalten nächt, darbey keine zeit versaumen." StadtAN 547: RV 16 September 1635.

203. FKD. Of 116 children admitted during 1635–36, 53 (45.7 percent) died before release.

204. The first transfer from the municipal alms bureau was 100 fl. on 2 July 1634. On 24 December 1634 the Findel borrowed 2,275 fl. five months later and a little more than a week later (2 January 1635) 2,025 fl. There were subsequent transfers in the amount of 195 fl. on 20 May 1635, 200 fl. total for 1635–36 and fourteen payments totaling 2,930 fl. in 1636–37. During 1637–38 the Findel borrowed 3,500 fl.; in 1638–39, 2,525 fl.; and then finally in 1639–40, 275 fl. The total amount borrowed between July 1634 and June 1640 was 14,025 fl. StadtAN D 10 2/ix: 69r–70r. Augs-burg's orphanage also borrowed heavily during this period, about 10,000 fl. Safley, *Charity and Economy*, 179.

205. Mummenhoff, "Das Findel- und Waisenhaus," pt. 2, 11, 31 ff.
206. Nuremberg figures are based on a 1586–87 alms bureau expenditure of 16,091 fl. when the city's population was about 35,000. The city maintained several other social welfare programs that might be added to this total. Augsburg spent perhaps 900 fl. per thousand inhabitants during the same period. Total English poor relief went from about £35,000 in 1614 to £350,000 by 1695 and £690,000, 1 percent of the national income, by 1750. Endres, "Einwohnerzahl," 266; Jütte, *Poverty and Social Deviance*, 141; Beier, *Masterless Men*, 174; Slack, *From Reformation*, 163.
207. Roughly 1,600 fl. annually in Regensburg versus about 3,200 fl. each in Augsburg in 1572. The latter cost had almost doubled by the eighteenth century. Mummenhoff, "Das Findel- und Waisenhaus," pt. 1, 86; Safley, *Charity and Economy*, 181, 183. By 1456, only a few years after its opening, the Florentine Innocenti Hospital was already 75,000 fl. in debt and continued to be a drain on city coffers throughout subsequent centuries. Food expenditures took up more than two-thirds of the Augsburg orphanages' budgets. Apprenticeship fees and staff salaries went up everywhere over the course of the seventeenth century. Gavitt, *Charity and Children*, 81–90; Safley, *Charity and Economy*, 182–85.
208. In 1627–28, the Findel spent 5,496 fl. with 156 children; during the 1640s, the Findel's average expenditures were 5,543 fl., while the number of children in residence dropped from 149 in 1640–41 to 61 in 1649–50. The cost per child thus fluctuated from 35.2 fl. annually in 1627–28, to 18.5 fl. during 1633–35, to 60.4 fl. in 1640–51. StaatsAN 53.
209. See 1653 Stadtalmosenamt Bericht; StadtAN D1/564. The value of the endowment in 1653–54 was estimated at 6,796 fl., and the Keyper Foundation paid only a total of 560 fl. to sixteen households. StadtAN B35, B455.
210. The Augsburg alms bureau generated 31.6 percent of its income from donations in 1600; by 1670 that share was 17.7 percent. Meanwhile, public funds increased to 46.3 percent of alms office's revenue in 1670. Safley, *Charity and Economy*, 36–40, 80–83.
211. This total included 2,719 children among alms recipients, sixty children in the Findel, and twenty youths among the *Springbuben*. 1668. Almosspfleger Gutachten (22 April 1668); StadtAN D1/564.
212. Georg Schrötter, *Geschichte der Stadt Nürnberg* (Nuremberg: C. Koch, 1909), 113, 130–32; Bernhard Stier and Wolfgang von Hippel, "War, Economy, and Society," in Olgivie, *Germany*, 241. On the wide-ranging impact of the Thirty Years' War on municipal budgets, see Wallace, *Communities and Conflict*, 146–78. Some Hanseatic towns, such as Hamburg, Lübeck, and Bremen, actually prospered during the war.
213. Rüger, *Mittelalterliches Almosenwesen*, 65.
214. See RV 2170: 28v, 30v (24 January 1635), RV 2171: 75r (10 March 1635), RV 2172: 2r (12 March 1635), RV 2173: 28r (8 April 1635), RV 2173: 55r–v, 58r–v (16 and 17 April 1635), RV 2174: 22r–v (6 May 1635), RV 2174: 31r–v (12 May 1635).
215. From fiscal year 1633–37, 235 children died, 27.3 percent of the 862 children resident or at wet nurses during the same period. Fiscal year 1634–35 accounted for almost two-thirds of the total deaths (147). See below, chapter 5, on institutional death rates among children.
216. StaatsAN 53, years 1633–37. From 1637–41, the Findel would place another 97 children.
217. The three children were Martin Seyfried (12 November 1627–6 March 1632), Georg Albrecht (2 June 1630–10 January 1634), and Maria Barbara (3–22 December 1634).

Biedermann, *Geschlechtsregister,* 578; Christoph Friedrich Wilhelm von Volckhamer, *Johann Gottfried Biedermann's Geschlechtsregister des Patriciats der vormaligen Reichsstadt Nürnberg (von 1749) bis zum Jahre 1796 fortgesetzt* (Nuremberg, 1797), 143–45.

218. "um allerhand ungehorsamer Buben willen." These new institutions included the Zurich Waisen- und Zuchthaus (1639), Basel Zucht- und Waisenhaus (1659), Frankfurt am Main Armen-, Waisen-, und Arbeits- (Korrektions-) Haus (1679), Dresden Zuchtanstalt (1685), Grosses Friedrichs-Waisenhaus of Berlin (1702), Stuttgart Waisen-, Zucht- und Arbeithaus (1710), Pforzheim Zucht- und Tollhaus (1718), Manheim Zuchthaus (1730), and similar institutions in Worms, Lübeck, Würzburg, and Bruchsal. Fumasoli, *Ursprünge und Anfänge der Schellenwerke,* 170–71, 180–84; Eduard Lempp, *Geschichte des Stuttgarter Waisenhauses, 1710–1910* (Stuttgart: Verlag des Evangelischen Gesellschaft, 1910); Mummenhoff, "Das Findel- und Waisenhaus," 1: 79, 86, 87, 90.

219. Rüger, *Die Kinderfürsorge,* 122, 124.

220. The most notable of these were in Nördlingen (1715), Wiesbaden (1725), and Ansbach (1709). Mummenhoff, "Das Findel- und Waisenhaus," 1: 86–89.

221. von Volckhamer, *Biedermanns Geschlechtsregister,* 41.

CHAPTER FOUR

1. The full interrogation transcripts are found in ASB 215: 272v–304v.

2. ASB 215: 303r–304v. The offer to go to Hungary came at the end of his third interrogation. Mayr's last recorded statement was "darumb bitt meine herrn er ganz diemütig und umb Gottes willen, Ihne bey angezaigter warheit gnedig bleiben zulassen, und Ime seine Junge tag lenger zuvergonnen, die sache der Jugent und dem unverstandt zuerrechnen, und deme schuld zugeben, das er als ein Jung unverstendig blut, von andern sey verührt worden, er wolle sich bessern, und gar ein Neuer Mensh werden."

3. ASB 215: 274r.

4. There has been much research done on early modern poverty (see above, chap. 2, n. 2, and the overview in Fritz, *Eine Rotte,* 219ff.), but only relatively recently have a few microhistorical studies of individual beggars appeared and of those only one, an article by Norbert Schindler, deals in detail with youthful beggars (albeit as a collective): Norbert Schindler, "Die Entstehung der Unbarmherzigkeit. Zur Kultur und Lebensweise der Salzburger Bettler am Ende des 17. Jahrhunderts," in *Widerspenstige Leute. Studien zur Volkskultur in der frühen Neuzeit* (Frankfurt am Main: Fischer Taschenbuch Verlag, 1992), 258–314. For an English translation, see "The Origins of Heartlessness: The Culture and Way of Life of Beggars in Late Seventeenth-century Salzburg," in, *Rebellion, Community and Custom,* 236–92. See also the excellent study of Ulbricht, "World of a Beggar," as well as Sabine Kienitz's study of a twenty-five-year-old vagrant woman accused of killing an older widow, *Unterwegs—Frauen zwischen Not und Normen. Lebensweise und Mentalität vagierender Frauen um 1800* (Tübingen: Tübinger Vereinigung für Volkskunde, 1989); and Norbert Schindler, "Die Ramingsteiner Bettlerhochzeit von 1688/89. Armut, Sexualität und Hexenpolitik in einem Salzburger Bergwerkort des 17. Jahrhunderts," *Historische Anthropologie* 2, no. 2 (1994): 165–92.

With the exception of witchcraft cases, the *Alltagsgeschichte* of early modern crime is similarly sparse, despite the abundance of sources, and I know of no microhistory of juvenile criminals in Germany during the early modern period. See Gerd Schwerhoff, *Aktenkundig und Gerichtsnotorisch: Einführung in die historische Kriminalitätsfor-*

schung (Tübingen: Edition Diskord, 1999). Maria Boes, "The Treatment of Juvenile Delinquents in Early Modern Germany: A Case Study," *Continuity and Change* 11, no. 1 (1996): 145–67, is an excellent analysis of criminal statistics but in no sense a microhistory.

5. *Straßenjunge* ("street youths") was already current by the seventeenth century in Germany. Grimm, *Deutsches Wörterbuch*, 19: 916. "Urchin," which was applied to London's street children as early as the sixteenth century, originally meant a hedgehog. *OED*, 19: 322–23. See also the long usage in English of "beggar children" (*OED*, 2: 67) and "street arab" (*OED*, 16: 876); as well as Angela Veale, Max Taylor, and Carol Linehan, "Psychological Perspectives of 'Abandoned' and 'Abandoning' Street Children," in *Abandoned Children*, ed. Painter-Brick and Smith, 132ff, on the difficulties of both defining "street children" and determining an accurate count. In modern Brazil, the terms for such children vary, depending on the context: *meninos carentes* ("needy children"), *crianças abandonandas* ("abandoned children"), or the more pejorative *pivetes* ("knaves"), *trombadinhas* ("scroundrels"), or *cheira-cola* ("glue sniffers"), in the same volume, Tobias Hecht, "In Search of Brazil's Street Children," 147–48.

6. A pathbreaking study by J. K. Felsman ("Street Urchins of Columbia," *Natural Histories* [April 1981]: 41–49) found that only 7 percent of 300 children on the streets of Cali, Columbia, had been abandoned by their parents. Another Latin American study found that 80–90 percent lived most of the time with their parents. Studies based in Sudan and Ethiopia found similar proportions. Baker and Painter-Brick, "Comparative Perspective on" in Painter-Brick, ed., *Abandoned Children*, 161–62; and in the same volume, see a summary of results by Veale et al., "Psychological Perspectives," 137, table 8.1.

7. A certain Ule took stolen goods to his mother's house "in ein klein gesslein am Vischbach nit weit von ein Ochsenhandler." ASB 210: 97r; also GNM Hs 3857: 39v; ASB 210: 87r; ASB 212: 109v, 116v.

8. Four years previously Mayr visited (and stole from) "ein karrenman zu Peckhofen und ein wenig sein vetter sey." There are also references to seinen vattern zu Wessstatt" and his travelling "gen Gozaw zu seiner Bruder Paulussen Mayrn." These relatives were in fact the source of the nickname the Little Castle Seventh (*der Schloß Sieptlein*), based on his grandfather's status as a sharecropper (*Halbpenner*) at the Driessdorf castle. ASB 215: 273v, 282r–v, 284v–285r. See also Schindler, *Widerspenstige Leute*, 285–89, on youths clinging to such fragments of family ties in their own unstable lives.

9. Hans Jakob Christoph von Grimmelshausen, *Simplicissimus*, trans. Mike Mitchell (Sawtry: Dedalus, 1999), 33–34, 110. "ein kleins baurn mägdlein . . . wisse doch nicht anzuzeigen, wo her sie sey, oder wer Ihre eltern sein." RV 2073: 39v (27 August 1627).

10. RV 2181: 21r (21 November 1635); RV 2185: 73v–74r (23 March 1636).

11. See, for instance the recommendation of 15 May 1634 on the council's "werckh d. barmherzigkeit" as well as the RV of 16 September 1635, describing "die heufig herumb straifende arme unmündige waysen." StadtAN D1/547. See also chapter 3.

12. RV 1272: 2r, 3v (24 and 25 January 1567).

13. In Beier's sample, which covers the period from 1570 to 1622, 67.1 percent were under 21, and 42.7 percent were under 16; in the sample for1623–39, these percentages had dropped to 46.8 percent and 28.7 percent, respectively. *Masterless Men*, 25, table 4. Schindler's sample from the Zauberjackl trials found one-half of the vagrants in question to be under the age of sixteen. *Widerspenstige Leute*, 279.

14. "umstreuenden Landtschüpfeln," referring to Creuzmayr (ASB 212: 115v). Cf. complaints about "starken Stirnenstüßeln" in 1580 Zurich (Boes, "Treatment," 45). Over two-thirds of vagrants in contemporary England were under the age of twenty-one and the great majority of those (93 percent in Cologne) were male. Jütte, *Poverty and Deviance*, 150. This issue is examined thoroughly in Griffiths, *Youth and Authority;* and Beier, *Masterless Men.*

15. Only 15 percent of the vagrants in Ammerer's study came from over 200 kilometers away from the site of their arrest (*Heimat Straße*, 473). Beier's study of vagrants in contemporary England found that at least half of all vagrant apprentices and journeymen stayed within fifty miles of their home and those who went further, went much further. Beier, *Masterless Men*, 70–71. See also Rolf Wolfensberger, "'Heimathlose und Vaganten': Die Kultur der Fahrenden im 19. Jahrhundert in der Schweiz" (Ph.D. diss., University of Bern, 1996), 118 ff.

16. ASB 215: 285r–286r.

17. See complaints about sturdy beggars in the suburbs in the *Ordnung der Pettelrichter* (19 August 1636), StadtAN D1/563: 28r; also Stadtalmosenamt memo of 20 October 1649, StadtAN D1/563.

18. Cf. estimates of one-third under fifteen for fifteenth-century German lands and one-third under twelve in late seventeenth-century Münster (Kurt Wesoly, *Lehrlinge und Handwerksgesellen am Mittelrhein: Ihre soziale Lage und ihre Organisation vom 14. bis ins 17. Jahrhundert* [Frankfurt am Main: W. Kramer, 1985], 23), one-half under twenty in seventeenth-century Lautern and Nürtingen (Wunder, *He Is the Sun*, 17), one-half under twenty-five and one-third under eighteen in eighteenth-century Flanders (Lis, *Disordered Lives*, 47–48).

19. I base these estimates of vagrant and begging children on a Nuremberg population of 40,000, of which 8–10 percent are vagrants and on Beier's findings that 42.79 percent of all arrested vagrants in England were under the age of sixteen between 1570 and 1620, and 28.7 percent during 1623–39 (*Masterless Men*, 25). Taking an average of 35.74 percent for minors and applying it to an estimated vagrant population of 3,200–4,000 yields 1,600–2,000 vagrant minors. To this I added the 2,700 children receiving some form of poor relief from the *Almosenamt* at the city's peak in the early seventeenth century for a total of 4,300–4,700 (Rüger, *Die Kinderfürsorge*, 52). Once again, these are very rough estimates, intended mainly to convey the relatively high number of children and youths under discussion.

20. In June 1634, the Findel admitted a group of 68 boys and 64 girls; on 17 January 1635, 5 boys and 8 girls; on 21 March 1636, 66 boys and 39 girls; on 14 June 1637, 13 boys and 8 girls; on 17 June 1637, 19 boys and 10 girls; on 21 June 1637, 8 boys and 4 girls; on 26 June 1637, 3 boys and 4 girls; on 28 September 1637, 11 boys and 2 girls; and on 23 December 1637, 9 boys and 7 girls. StadtAN D10/3–6: 53–66, 73–78, 80–87. One late seventeenth-century sample from Salzburg found that boys comprised two-thirds of arrested beggars, with half of those under the age of sixteen, while only one-quarter of female beggars were under twenty. Schindler, *Widerspenstige Leute*, 279; also Garrioch, *Neighborhood and Community*, 58–59.

21. "mit gots lestern / jauchzen/ shreyen / Weerzucken und andern mer unschicklichkeyten erscheyne . . . Mandate of 30 December 1537, repeated in the *Bettelmandat* of 15 October 1567 (StaatsAN 63Ia, vol. A: 117–118, volume C: 158).

22. Mandate of 18 December 1669; StaatsAN 63Ia/Volume M: 17. Cf. similar disruptions associated with New Year: mandates of 2 July 1557 and 28 December 1675;

StaatsAN 63Ia, volume B: 151, Volume M: 58; Stadtalmosenamt report of 1 March 1653; StadtAN D1/564. See also RV 7, August 1662 in StadtAN D1/560.

23. "wann andere leuth, gesundte unnd krancke personen, in ihre Ruhe ligen." Mandate of 11 September 1563; StaatsAN 63Ia, vol. C: 59. On youthful nocturnal activities, see Norbert Schindler, "Nocturnal Disturbances: On the Social History of the Night in the Early Modern Period," in Rebellion, Community and Custom, 132–33, 203–10.

24. Mandate of 24 March 1553 (StaatsAN 63Ia, vol. B: 105); Strauss, Nuremberg, 214. Cf. similar patterns among English youths, described in Griffiths, Youth and Authority, 132–14, and Beier, Masterless Men, 75, as well as Mitterauer, History of Youth, 157ff.

25. See Rüger, Die Kinderfürsorge, 59–60; Leder, Kirche und Jugend, 204; and Griffiths, Youth and Authority, 128.

26. They were also accused of harassing pedestrians. StadtAN D1/560; Stadtalmosenamt Actum of 7 and 26 July 1662; RV 7 and 8 August 1662.

27. 53 percent, based on a random survey of some 85,000 young people in various early modern central European populations, conducted by the Insitut für Wirtschafts- und Sozialgeschichte at the University of Vienna. Mitterauer, History of Youth, 67ff.

28. Wunder, He Is the Sun, 72; Griffiths, Youth and Authority, 360.

29. "ein Schritt ohne Wiederkehr." One-fifth of the children arrested for begging in late seventeenth-century Salzburg claimed that their parents raised them as beggars. Schindler, Widerspenstige Leute, 282–83. See also Rublack, Crimes of Women, 117–18, on parents who taught their children to steal.

30. In eighteenth-century Flanders, two out of three juvenile offenders were brought up in single-parent households, usually headed by women. Lis, Disordered Lives, 49–50; also Jütte, Poverty and Deviance, 37.

31. GNM Hs 3857: 103v.

32. "der kleine Dick" and "Pufferla." ASB 210: 100v; StaatsAN 51, 43: 156v (1583).

33. In Nuremberg, see the release of juvenile vandal Martin Steiner from Salzburg "wegen seines shadhaften kopf." StadtAN D1/560 (RV of 7 August 1662). Cf. Ulbricht, "World of a Beggar," 155, on number of Gesellen who have some sort of injury; as well as Franz Irsigler and Arnold Lassotta (Bettler und Gaukler, Dirnen und Henker. Außenseiter in einer mittelalterlichen Stadt Köln, 1300–1600 [Munich: Deutscher Taschenbuch Verlag, 1989], 87–96), on treatment of the physically and mentally ill during this period. Fritze (Eine Rotte, 244–45) estimates that 10 percent of all vagrants had serious illnesses or disabilities, while Ammerer (Heimat Straße, 142) postulates a slightly higher rate of disability among males.

34. "die Baurn Ketterla" and "die Schutzen Maria," "zwei verückte leichfertige schloppen und Diebin." ASB 210: 86v (1584).

35. "ein schoenes junges Leid." Keller, Maister Franntzn Schmidts, 86.

36. The youth received "55 rutenstreiche [!] auf die hinterbacken erhalten hatte, nachdem ihm zuvor hände und Fuße mit stricken gebunden und große stein daran gehängt." Soden, Kriegs- und Sittengeschichte, 1: 425; cited in Rüger, Die Kinderfürsorge, 61–62.

37. StaatsAN 51, 45: 358v–360r.

38. Apprentices had to provide birth certificates or up to three witnesses affirming their legitimacy (Wesoly, Lehrlinge und Handwerksgesellen, 56ff.). The topic of illegitimacy is treated in the 1484 Gewohnheitsrecht und Wandelbücher in Ref. Tit. 30, Ges 1.1, and in the 1564 Reformatio at Ref. Tit. 30, 3, Ges. 9.1. The Reformatio of 1564, divided all illegitimate births into three categories: naturales (simply born out of wedlock, where the father is acknowledged), spurii ("whore children," where the father is unknown)

and *incestuosi* (the products of incest or adultery). Illegitimate children of the first two categories were without honor (*ehrlos*) but not "infamous," a much more severe stigmatization. They could therefore be witnesses at trials, inherit from their fathers (if there were no legitimate heirs) and most importantly for our concerns, be admitted to the crafts (though not the professions of law, medicine, and government). Rüger, *Die Kinderfürsorge*, 62–65, 71; Walter Riedl, "Die rechtliche Stellung der Lehrjungen und Gesellen des Nürnberger Handwerks" (J.D. diss., Friedrich-Alexander Universität Erlangen, 1948), 24–25.

39. Based on applying the average official illegitimacy rate in Nuremberg before 1650 of 2 percent (see above, chap. 1) to the city's annual birth rate of 1,200–1,500 (Wiesner, *Working Women*, 59), yielding 24–30 officially illegitimate children, and then multiplying this by eleven (i.e., children aged 7–17), yielding 264–330 illegitimate resident children, with at least 200 more (a conservative estimate) illegitimate vagrant children, totaling 464–530. Schindler ("Origins of Heartlessness," 255) found that 15 percent of the beggar youths in the Zauberjackl trials were illegitimate—twice the ratio of the general population.

40. Stadtalmosenamt Acta of 7 and 36 July 1662; StadtAN D1/560. Runaway apprentices Balthasar Reuth and Hans Pühlman were also illegitimate (Stadtalmosenamt Acta of 4 and 13 March, 5 and 11 April 1661).

41. "So Im stehlen aufferwachsen," ASB 223: 117r.; RV 1636: 44v (20 August 1594). See also the Ratschlag (StaatsAN 51, 43), especially the opinion of Dr. Bussenreuter on 359v–360r; also StadtAN F1, 109: 65 on his execution.

42. "bereit bey einen Cardetshenmacher gewesen, hab auch demselben mit dem drotbeigen und stöcken, so guth alss ein gesell, helffen arbeiten können, also, das der meister mit ihme wohl zu frieden gewesen, und ihn so lang bey sich behalten hette, biss er etlicher massen erstarckt were und einen hausknecht hette abgeben können weilen er weder sein noch ander handwerck lernen dürffte. Er were aber bereit vor einen viertel Jahr davon geloffen und wolte also nicht gueth thun." Stadtalmosenamt Actum 5 and 11 April 1661; StadtAN D1/560.

43. ASB 215: 171v–172v.

44. ASB 212: 126v–132r (1 and 17 August 1594). Cf. Schwerhoff, *Köln im Kreuzverhör*, 178ff., who finds that 80 percent of his samples of convicted males from 1568 to 1612 had been journeymen or apprentices at some point; also Shore, *Artful Dodgers*, 40, where 81 percent of a Middlesex sample of early nineteenth-century juvenile delinquents acknowledged training in a trade.

45. GNM Hs 3857, 48r; ASB, 212: 115v–126v; StaatsAN 52a, 475: 135r.

46. "so sey er doch, wann er wider zu der Gesellschaft gerathen, ferner verführt worden." ASB 213: 290v. Those few street children in modern Nepal who had left home permanently or at least for a lengthy period did so because of a fight with a parent. Baker and Painter-Brick, "Comparative Perspective," 164. See also Ammerer, *Heimat Straße*, 131–48, on early modern child and youth vagrants.

47. "aber weiln ihrer Herrshafft den dienst zimlich sauer gemacht ohne einigen bedacht und hahrung, auch offters wieder willens der Eltern oder Vormunder." Stadtalmosenamt Bericht of 1 March 1653; StadtAN D1/564.

48. Beier (*Masterless Men*, 24–25), for instance, estimates that one-quarter to two-thirds of all farm servants switched masters yearly and also notes that "it was almost customary to lift something from masters when quitting their service." Griffiths (*Youth and Authority*, 327–34) found that most runaway servants remained in the vicinity of their employers and only a small number remained missing after two weeks.

49. The origins of the seventy-one beggar children are reported in a Stadtalmosenamt Actum of 23 March 1634; StadtAN D1/561. Only two members of a group of seven young burglars—Hans Schober and Catharina Schwartzin—came from the Nuremberg area, in this instance both from suburban Wöhrd. ASB 210.

50. Cf. Baker and Painter-Brick, "Comparative Perspective," 174, on a survey of 130 boys in 1993, with only half still around two years later.

51. These included *Winkelwirtshäuser*, which catered especially to vagrants. A group of seven juvenile thieves regularly stayed at an inn in suburban Wöhrd (ASB 210: 96v–97r, 102v; RV 1499: 30v–31r [23 January 1584]); seventeen-year-old Hans Creuzmeyer often spoke of staying in inns (ASB 210: 118r, 120v); eighteen-year-old Hensa Baur similarly mentioned staying at inns on occasion and even once paid the exorbitant price of half a gulden for one night in an inn the night before his arrest (ASB 212: 118r, 120v). See also Ammerer, *Heimat Straße*, 476–88.

52. Cf. account of squatters on the Schütt in *Bettelstreiferordnung* of 4 September 1638; StadtAN D1/99; also the arrest of Maria Kürshnerin in a public garden in suburban Wöhrd (ASB 210: 86v), and the arrest of Hans von Geiselwindt "in der Schüpfer bei der Weidenmühl" (52b, 210: 96r). See also Beier, *Masterless Men*, 77, 82–85; and Schubert, *Arme Leute*, 104–5, on the harshness of winter for vagrants.

53. "sträffliche Red." RV 1484: 38r (19 December 1582); RV 1498: 29r (27 December 1583); RV 1499: 30v–31r (23 January 1584).

54. Wunder, *He Is the Sun*, 22.

55. ASB 212: 117r.

56. Tlusty, *Bacchus and Civil Order*, passim.

57. On the use of conscription as an alternative to prison or a workhouse, see Burschel, *Söldner im Nordwestdeutschland*, 90–95, 100–3. The average ages of soldiers is based on the combined totals of two late seventeenth-century samples (118–19), with 6.5 percent of one company of 443 soldiers under 20, and another 65 man company with half 19 or younger, including six under 15 and 3 under 10 (!).

58. Report of the Comité de Mendicité in the 1770s. Hufton, *Poor in Eighteenth-century France*, 108–9. For the late Middle Ages through the seventeenth century, see Irsigler and Lassotta, *Bettler und Gaukler*, 62–67, on youth begging.

59. Hufton, *Poor of Eighteenth-Century France*, 204, 213, 228; and see Joel F. Harrington, "'Singing for his supper': The Reinvention of Juvenile Streetsinging in Early Modern Nuremberg," *Social History* 22, no. 1 (1997): 167ff.

60. "wie auch umb den letzigen drey konig tag an der altmühl gesehen hab, das er selb dritt gesungen." ASB 215: 288r; see also 281r on working.

61. Adult protection of young beggars from the *Bettelrichter* and *Almosendiener* was frequently cited in the city's begging ordinances. Rüger, *Mittelalterliches Almosenwesen*, 45.

62. Albrecht Bohn complained of the begging police "dass sie in zu weilen von armen leuth geldt nehmen, und dieselben betteln lassen sollen." StadtAN D1 560: Stadtalmosenamt Actum 28 April 1665. See also similar concerns a century earlier in the *Pettelrichter ordnung* of 29 November 1566; StadtAN D1/2 on daily rounds and commissions of 5–10 d; later 8d.

63. *Almosenordnung* of 1588, text in Rüger, *Mittelalterliches Almosenwesen*, 48. See also Knapp, *Nürnberger Kriminalrecht*, 10; and instructions of the *Bettelrichter Ordnung* of 19 August 1636 (StadtAN D1/2: 29r).

64. On 1 November 1578, *Bettelrichter* Joseph Pernmüler was flogged for raping a minor girl in the *Bettelstock*; three years later (9 January 1581), another *Bettelrichter*, Lien-

hardt Hertl (later beheaded as a robber) was flogged for the same offense. Keller, *Maister Franntzn Schmidts*, 16, 81, 83; StaatsAN 52a, 447: 1013.

65. See the example of sixteen-year-old Balthasar Reuth, "so ehedessen shon einmahl mit andern Jungen in loch gelegen, und ietzo wider gebettelt hette." StadtAN D1/560 (Stadtalmosenamt Actum 5 and 11 April 1661); also 1588 *Almosenordnung*; Rüger, *Mittelalterliches Almosenwesen*, 48ff., 53–54.

66. Rüger, *Die Kinderfürsorge*, 187.

67. Not until 1584 was there a register of arrested begging youths kept in the city's begging stockade and even after that it was poorly maintained and unreliable. RV 1499: 28r (28 January 1584).

68. Adam Heinrich Neumann (17) served one month, Simon Stengel (under 18) served at least three months, Hans Pühlhofman (13) served two months, and Jacob Kreuth (under 18) served four and one-half months. At least half of the twenty-two youths named in this collection of *Ratsverlässe* were later placed with craftsmen. In view of the records' incompleteness, we must rely on an *Almosenamt* report of 19 June 1666 that estimates about 20 youths per year for the previous five years. StadtAN D1/560. *See also* Rüger, *Die Kinderfürsorge*, 158–59.

69. Lazarillo, for instance, writes of his time on the street that "I almost died of hunger more than once," and he often goes two to three days with no food at all (*Two Spanish Picaresque Novels: Lazarillo de Tormes [Anon.] and The Swindler [El Buscón]*, trans. and ed. Michael Alpert [Baltimore: Penguin, 1969], 29, 59). See also *Simplicissimus*, 114, 145.

70. ASB 210: 90r, 102r.

71. "do er doch kein brodt noch nicht gehabt, vielwenniger sonsten etwas geloeht, oder gestolen habe . . . seithero habe er soviel nicht gestolen, was er aber gethan sey armut halben geschehen, dann er nichts erbetteln noch zu driessen. kommen können, sintmal er gar zerrissen gewesen, dannenhero er nothalben stelen müssen, hülff Ime aber Gott noch einmal davon, so wollte ers sein Lebenlang nicht mehr thun." ASB 215: 274r, 285r–v.

72. Here I disagree with those anthropologists who apply rational choice theory to modern street children. See especially Veale et al., "Psychological Perspectives," in Painter-Brick, *Abandoned Children*, 139.

73. "how he also regularly gorged, guzzled, and gambled with the common sluts in the sandpits."ASB 210: 120r. Beggar youth Andreas Wild was similarly tainted by the perception that he "would not stay with any master but instead hung out with other loose fellows, roaming around the city and begging with the same." Stadtalmosenamt Actum of 7 July 1665; StadtAN D1/560.

74. "seinen Eltern seyen Ihme zufrüe gestorben, also das er In die frembde gemüst, habe demnach das umbziehen gewohnet, und nicht mehr guet gethan, ob er gleich einmahl davon kommen, und hinten sich gedacht, so sey er doch, wann er wider zu der Gesellshafft gerathen, ferner verführt worden." ASB 215: 290v.

75. ASB 215: 282v, 285r.

76. "Wie er vor vier jahren, mit dem Steffan und seinem weib stettigs herumbgezogen und dazumal der Erndt der Steffan zu Windtsheim geschnitten" ASB 215: 297v–298r). There are also references to all three working in the fields (280v, 302r–v) as well as a mention of "the Shepherd" actually tending sheep for one year (280r).

77. ASB 215: 285r.

78. Griffiths, *Youth and Authority*, 339ff; and for a later period see Shore, *Artful Dodgers*, 35.

79. "gar zu arm und unausehenlich darzu gewest." ASB 212: 121r, 122v.

80. Based on his own testimony Mayr's thefts over the previous two years netted him at least 109 fl. and possibly as much as 194 fl. over the course of four years. The higher figure is based on unresolved accusations in the interrogation. Assuming that Mayr left out or undervalued some crimes during his testimony means that the actual figure was probably much higher. Endres, "Zur wirtschaftlichen und sozialen Lage," 21–25.

81. Cf. complaints that he "mit dem Steffan theilen müssen" (ASB 215, 295v) usually "dieweil er dem Steffan etwas schuldig" (ASB 215, 296v–297r, 298r); also reference to Hensa Baur to gambling with an innkeeper (ASB 212, 127v). See also Ammerer, *Heimat Straße*, 324–30, on the consumption of alcohol and luxury items in general among vagrants.

82. "Ein Dieb stiehlt sich selten reich." Karl Simrock, *Die deutschen Sprichwörter* (Frankfurt am Main: Winter, 1881), 99, no. 1598.

83. "nackent und bloss." Keller, *Maister Franntzn Schmidts*, 15.

84. Alpert, *Two Spanish Picaresque Novels*, 65, 76.

85. "das er ein Spizbueb sey oder das er ein falsch uff dem spilen gebrauchen könne, noch das er uff den kugelpläzen so starck gespillet haben sollt, sonder gibt für er seye gar zu arm, und unausehenlich darzu gewest, dann sich die andern Spizbueben mit Ihme zu spilen geshembt haben würden, weil dieselben alle stattlich geklaidet, und alss kauffmansdiener im Land umzherziehen theten . . . wie er sich dann damals von fuess auf neu gekleidet." ASB 212: 121r, 123v–124r. Cruezmayr claimed that the wool pants were a gift from a sick Frenchmen he served, who also gave him 12 Bazen. The leather vest was similarly supposed to have been given to him by a baker.

86. ASB 212: 127v; RV 1636: 31v–32r (12 August 1594).

87. RV 1478: 5r (15 June 1582); ASB 210: 92r.

88. The two also kept two wool shirts, a shawl, a bonnet, and a green plait. ASB 210: 87v, 90v, 91r–v, 92v, 94v.

89. ASB 209: 92r; also 116r. On *kocheme Gesellschaft* and *wittiche Gesellschaft*, see Richard J. Evans, *The German Underworld: Deviants and Outcasts in German History* (London and New York: Routledge, 1988), 2ff; also Küther, *Menschen auf der Straße*, 60–73.

90. See Florike Egmond, *Underworlds: Organized Crime in the Netherlands, 1650–1800* (Cambridge: Polity Press, 1993), 37ff., on the difficulties in speaking of an early modern "criminal subculture" and her conclusion that "there existed no dangerous or subversive criminal counter-society or counter-culture, then, in the Dutch Republic [from 1650–1800]" (181). Similar observations are made by Mitterauer, *History of Youth*, 195–96; Beier, *Masterless Men*, 14, 57; Lis, *Disordered Lives*, 62–67; Burschel, *Söldner in Nordwestdeutschland*, 291ff.; and Ulbricht, "World of a Beggar," 181–84.

91. "deren keiner über zwölff Jahr alt war." StadtAN F1-2/VII: 529 (August 1575). Georg Müllner was executed on 21 June 1593 (ASB 211: 231r). See also Keller, *Maister Franntzn Schmidts*, 33–34.

92. ASB 210: 87r, 110r, 103v, 108r; ASB 215: 288r.

93. Tlusty, *Bacchus and Civil Order*, 115ff. See also Hartinger, "Bayerisches Dienstboten auf dem Lande," 629, on *Bierbrüder* and *Weinschäche* among early modern male vagrants.

94. Cf. Robert Muchembled, *Popular Culture and Elite Culture in France, 1400–1750* (Baton Rouge: Louisiana State University Press, 1985), 119, on the popular perception of taverns as schools for crime. See also Hennslein Creuzmayr's comments on drinking and friendship in ASB 212: 117r.

95. The drinking bout was known among patricians as a *Zutrinken* and popularly as a *Zech*. Tlusty, *Bacchus and Civil Order*, 104, 125ff.
96. ASB 210: 105r; ASB 212: 125r. Cf. nineteenth-century parallels in Shore, *Artful Dodgers*, 70; and modern parallels in Martin S. Fleisher, *Beggars and Thieves: Lives of Urban Street Criminals* (Madison: University of Wisconsin Press, 1991), 118–20.
97. Rotwelsch was a combination of the Latin jargon of wandering monks and students and Hebrew, Yiddish, and Romany (gypsy). Like English cockney, the majority of words were created by a change in meaning (through metaphor or "formal techniques such as substitution, affixing, or reversal of consonants, vowels, and syllables"). Jütte, *Poverty and Deviance*, 182–83; and see his *Abbild und soziale Wirklichkeit des Bettler- und Gaunertums zu Beginn der Neuzeit: Sozial-, mentalitäts- und sprachgeschichtliche Studien zum Liber vagatorum* (1510) (Cologne and Vienna: Bohlau Verlag, 1988), esp. 26–106.
98. der Frösh Hennsle, der Kleine Dick, der Schwartzpeck, der Rote Lienl, der Rabenröder, der Stopfer, der Haugk, der Packele. ASB 210: 74vff., 112 r. Irsigler and Lassotta, *Bettler und Gaukler*, 65. Cf. modern street children in Brazil who call themselves *maloqueiros* ("bad boys") and the street children of Mumbai who refer to themselves as *sadak chap* ("those who carry the stamp of the street"). Hecht, "In Search of Brazil's Street Children," 156–58.
99. Spitzkopf and Pufferla. ASB 210: 106r–v; Schindler, "The World of Nicknames: On the Logic of Popular Nomenclature," in *Rebellion, Community, and Custom*, esp. 57–62; also F. Bock, "Nürnberger Spitzname von 1200 bis 1800," *MVGN* 45 (1954): 1–147, and idem, "Nürnberger Spitzname von 1200 bis 1800—Nachlese," *MVGN* 49 (1959): 1–33.
100. GNM Hs 3857: 39v.
101. Keller, *Maister Franntzn Schmidts*, 34.
102. ASB 212: 115v–132v.
103. See especially John Bowlby, *Attachment and Loss*, 3 vols. (New York: Basic Books, 1969–81); as well as the criticisms of James P. Comer, *Black Child Care: How to Bring Up a Healthy Black Child in America; A Guide to Emotional and Psychological Development* (New York: Simon and Schuster, 1975).
104. "Uf sein vernainen ist Ime der hennsle von Geiselwundt unnd hennsle schober unter augen gefurt worden, die haben bede ausstrucklich gesagt, das sie Ine wol kennen, und das er In irer gesellshafft sey, unnd dann das man Ine nur dem packele haisse." ASB 210: 101r, 106r.
105. ASB 212: 119v.
106. "haben sie doch sehr geweint und oft nach ihrem Gesellen und Bruder umbgesehen . . . wenn sie nur ein Karten hetten, wolten sie spielen, welcher unter inen am ersten gehenkt werden solte." Cited in Hampe, *Malefizbücher*, 84.
107. "dass shier keiner sein eigen wort hören können. . . . Mein junges Leben hat ein End." GNM Hs 3857: 104r.
108. On the frequent appearance of this kind of temporary *Zeitfamilie* among vagrants, see Claus Kappl and Franz Bittner, *Die Not der kleinen Leute: der Alltag der Armen im 18. Jahrhundert im Spiegel der Bamberger Malefizamtsakten* (Bamberg: Selbstverlag des Historischen Vereins Bamberg, 1984), 100ff.
109. "sey ein lange person röthliche bart, trage schwarze Parchete Pumphosen rot lindische strumpff, ein Lidern wannes mit zwilchen Ermeln und ein shwarzen filzhuet." ASB 215: 275v, for the references to Adam, 292r, 295r.
110. On the ubiquity of the *Hausvater* image in early modern Germany, see Julius Hoff-

mann, *Die "Hausväterliteratur" und die "Predigten über den christlichen Hausstand": Lehre vom Hause und Bildung für das häusliche Leben im 16., 17., und 18. Jahrhundert* (Weinheim, 1959); as well as the more recent Harrington, *"Hausvater* and *Landesvater,"* 52–75. On sexual relations and informal partnerships among vagrants, see Fritze, *Eine Rotte,* 319–23.

111. ASB 215: 275v–276r.

112. ASB 215: 276v–277r, 284v–285r, 298r.

113. "Ernannt Maussmaidtlein habe in der nechsten zweyen Jahren er, nicht mehr gesehen, weisse also nicht, ob sie mehr Im Leben sey, oder nit." In addition to the imminent execution of Steffan and his wife in Cadoltzburg, Jörg mentions the deaths of König, "der Shopfenbub," and Adam, a suicide in prison. ASB 215: 277r, 278r, 293r, 293r. Cf. Beier, *Masterless Men,* 68ff. on the effect of disease, jail, and execution on personal relationships and groups among vagrants.

114. Green Cap was the one major exception, but given his known involvement in accused crimes of arson and assault, Mayr has no choice but to put all the blame on him.

115. ASB 210: 87r–v.

116. The art of scamming was *burlar* in Castilian. Alpert, *Two Spanish Picaresque Novels,* 28.

117. For instance, on one job with Adam and "the Cobbler," Jörg's two accomplices take off with all of the loot; at later points he continues to associate and steal with them. ASB 215: 298v.

118. A sociological study of modern urban street youths finds that most such individuals have low self-esteem, no hope for the future, and assume that life is both exploitive and mostly monotonous. Fleisher, *Beggars and Thieves,* esp. 3–14.

119. ASB 215: 284r, 299r. Mayr was also caught and forced to return property on three other occasions: in Hinterloch (282v–283r), Gözendorff (297r–v), and Burckoberbach (302r). Cf. Ulbricht, "World of a Beggar," 159, on beggars often "geschimpfet by others;" also Jütte, *Poverty and Deviance,* 158–77, on patterns of stigmatization of the poor.

120. ASB 215: 280v–281r, 283v.

121. ASB 215: 282r, 282v–283r.

122. ASB 215: 283r.

123. "gedingte Jungen" ASB 211: 213r (21 June 1593); ASB 212: 128r. Cf. magisterial references to "Diebshandwerk" and "journeymen in crime" in Hampe, *Malefizbücher,* 13, and Rublack, *Crimes of Women,* 124. Cf. similar professionalization among street children in Nepal (Baker and Painter-Brick, "Comparative Perspective," 163) and juvenile delinquents in nineteenth-century London (Shore, *Artful Dodgers,* 56ff.).

124. Bader Jackel and Schifferlein. ASB 212: 118r–v, 120v. Shoplifting appears to have been especially common among women and girls, who were better able to hide items in their clothing (Ammerer, *Heimat Straße,* 431, also on purse-cutting, pickpocketing [443–44], and on confidence schemes [446–57]).

125. "Und als ser einsmals uff derselben Strassen einen fuhrman dergleichen auch machen wöllen, hab Ihme derselbe die handt im Peutel erdapt, Ihne darbey gehalten, und darüber mit feüsten, wie auch seiner Gaissel waidtlich abgeleuet." ASB 212: 1220v–121r.

126. The *Neuwalderinnen* ("New Forest women") competed with the *Sandgrüberinnen* ("sandpit women"). Wiesner, *Working Women,* 106.

127. Based on a study of young prostitutes in modern Thailand: Heather Montgomery,

"Abandonment and Child Prostitution in a Thai Slum Community," in Painter-Brick, *Abandoned Children*, 184.

128. See especially Schuster, *Die Freien Frauen*, 194–204; and Fritze, *Eine Rotte*, 299–305. Here again a comparison with modern prostitution in a developing country is instructive. "Far from abdicating responsibility for kin, the women and girls in [this Thai study] remained in close contact with their families, sending them money regularly." Thai parents in the study all denied forcing their children into prostitution, and the girls tended to confirm that they just wished to contribute to the household income. The reporting anthropologist thus concluded that "prostitution enables these children to keep their families and communities together." Montgomery, "Abandonment and Child prostitution," 184, 192–96.

129. Catharina Schwartzin testified that she and other girls usually received 20 d. per break-in. ASB 210: 93r. The rates for tricks come from Irsigler and Lasotta, *Bettler und Gaukler*, 209–10, 217.

130. Between 1432 and 1502, the "Office of the Night" made arrests involving as many as 16,000 people, leading to about 60 convictions per year. Younger males were passive in 90 percent of cases involving anal sex, though roles were usually reversed in instances of fellatio. Rocke found that at least 30 percent of boys admitted to 7–20 partners during the year previous to their arrests and a significant minority of those to many more. Michael Rocke, *Forbidden Friendships: Homosexuality and Male Culture in Renaissance Florence* (New York: Oxford University Press, 1996), 4, 88, 92, 106ff.

131. Cf. Mary Elizabeth Perry, *Gender and Disorder in Early Modern Seville* (Princeton: Princeton University Press, 1990), 198–99. In Germany the most common terms were *pasquille* and *Knabenschande*. See the fascinating discussion of related words, actions, and concepts in Helmut Puff, *Sodomy in Reformation Germany and Switzerland, 1400–1600* (Chicago: University of Chicago Press, 2003), esp. 12–14; and Maria R. Boes, "On Trial for Sodomy in Early Modern Germany," in *Sodomy in Early Modern Europe*, ed. Tom Betteridge (Manchester: Manchester University Press, 2002), 27–45.

132. Keller, *Maister Franntzn Schmidts*, 88 (2 December 1584).

133. Maria Kürshnerin confessed to seventeen burglaries within the previous month, Catharina Schwartzin to sixteen during the same period, Hans Baldauf to sixteen during the previous five weeks, Kilian Wurmb to twenty-four in the last two months, and Hans Klopfer to fourteen during an unspecified recent period. ASB 210.

134. Anna Steinfelderin, for example, provided the group with "bekunntschaft" for the burglary of one shop, and Hans Kopfer similarly identified at least one "gute gelegenheit." ASB 210: 90v, 97r, 109v.

135. Beier, *Masterless Men*, 130ff.

136. Thirteen-year-old Hans von Geiselwindt, Catharina Schwartzin, and the mentally retarded Hans Schober were the usual lookouts for the Seven. Catharina's usual cut was 20 d., Geiselwindt's and Schober's 8–15d. ASB 210: 89v, 90v, 93r, 96r, 101r.

137. ASB 210: 89r, 90r–v.

138. See Groebner, *Ökonomie ohne Haus*, 235–43 on the thriving secondhand clothing market in Nuremberg.

139. "hab vil maidle und ein grosse Nasen." ASB 210: 89v. See Schwerhoff, *Köln im Kreuzverhör*, 355–56, on Jewish fences; and Shore, *Artful Dodgers*, 76–80, on juveniles' fences in general.

140. See, for instance, a group of boys pulling all of the feathers out of a mattress and pillows they had just stolen. ASB 210: 109r–v.

141. Cf. same pattern among nineteenth-century delinquents in Shore, *Artful Dodgers*, 45.

142. ASB 212: 118r–119v. See Ulbricht, "World of a Beggar," 181, on the role of *Altgesellen* and the importance of the guild model in training young beggars and thieves; also Rublack, *Crimes of Women*, 117–19, 130–31, for examples of older women teaching younger girls.

143. "mit einer Ahln dann er überall die Schlosser damit aufmachen khönen." ASB 210: 110v. Cf. Hensa Baur using "ein Schissele in vernen spizzig gefeylet" to open several chests. ASB 212: 130r. See also Fritze, *Eine Rotte*, 369–75 and 403–6, on burglary techniques among early modern vagrants.

144. ASB 210: 107v. Cf. the similar importance of age in the pecking order in rural fraternities and journeymen's associations, as described in Mitterauer, *History of Youth*, 174ff.

145. "du Schelm, du dieb, Ich will dir noch ein Bein abhauen . . . gehe her du Sackramendts dieb, gehe her und damit seinen waidt herauss gerissen, und gesaget, es sollt Ihme nicht so gut warden." ASB 212: 123r.

146. "Women never committed violent robbery, used weapons, and stole only small animals, such as hens or ducks." Rublack, *Crimes of Women*, 120.

147. Tlusty, for instance, found that of her sample of 114 cases of male violence in Augsburg, 111 involved social drinking. *Bacchus and Civil Order*, 127ff.

148. ASB 210: 108r–v, 109v, 111r. See also the admission of consorting with the later executed robber Heinrich Heut (115r).

149. "ein feuerschlagende püchsen." ASB 212: 127v. Hennslein Creuzmayr had similarly bought "Püpen und Wöhr" shortly before his arrest (123v).

150. "der Haugk" claimed that his brother Bastl and "der Frosh" committed the murder itself. ASB 210: 78r–v, 111r, 114r.

151. "aus Zorn ein Sacrament schwur gethane habe." Magistrates accused Creuzmayr of "viel hundert tausend Sackwertfluchen." ASB 212: 121r–122v, 125v–126r.

152. ASB 223: 172r.

153. ASB 215: 131r–132r.

154. StaatsAN 51, 45: 357v; GNM Hs 3857: 48; ASB 212: 121v, 123v–126r.

155. ASB 210: 109r, 112v. See also thefts of five and eight gulden respectively (78r–v).

156. Cf. refusal of innkeeper in Stainbach based on this suspicion. ASB 215: 282r. Among other fences, there are references to "einen Juden verkaufft" (ASB 215: 278v, 281v), "einer dienstmagt" (281r), "die Wirtin zu Haundorf" (281r), "einer Peurin" (281r), "ein Weib" (284r), "ein Taglöhner" (296r), and "ein Wirth" (300r).

157. "dass hausses gelegenheit erlernet" ASB 215: 302r–v and also 280r, 280v, 293v. See Jütte, *Poverty and Deviance*, 180ff., on the specialized vocabulary of marginalized beggars and criminals.

158. ASB 215: 287r–v. Regarding the assumption of gambling, we must remember that despite his relatively high income, Mayr maintained no permanent residence and spent long periods begging or even working as a day laborer.

159. See Ammerer, *Heimat Straße*, 348–78, on sickness and death among early modern vagrants in general. Skin diseases, especially smallpox, were especially common. Some studies of modern street children have found that young runaways and quasi-independent youths are often in better health than their counterparts who spend most of their time in residential slums. Veale et al., "Psychological Perspectives," 136.

160. See, for example, various accounts of dead beggar boys: RV 1701: 3v–4r (3 August

1599); RV 1968: 14v (22 September 1619); RV 2048: 75r, 82v (26 and 29 October 1625). See also the group admission of seventy-one beggar children in March 1634, "diese ligen fast alle kranck." StadtAN D1/561 (23 March 1634).

161. "Sonsten habe er den Winter uber nichts mehr gestolen, dann er so elendt und erforen gewessen, das er den frörer Zehen woch lang gehabt, davon er gar ausgefallen, also das er kaumm von ainen dorff zum andern gehen können . . . sonder sey auch am ganzen leib mit den bösen dingen des franzosen behafftet." ASB 215: 275r, 287r.

162. Alpert, *Two Spanish Picaresque Novels*, 77–79; Thomas Platter, *Lebenbeschreibung*, ed. Alfred Hartmann, 2nd expanded ed., ed. Ueli Dill (Basel: Schwab & Co., 1999).

163. Precisely eight weeks and five days. StaatsAN 54a, 468.

164. "Sagt, ernannter Schafer, oder könig, sey zu Eschenbach Jezo balden ein Jahr mit dem streng gericht worden, weil nun derselbe bekennt haben möge, wie er mit Ihme gestolen, so woll ers auch bekennen, und annzaigen, man soll Ihn nur besinnen lassen, damit er eines nach den andern sagen könne." ASB 215: 277v.

165. One theft, for instance, involved six pieces of clothing, "von hosen und wöllenhembt, nicht wisse er was es mehr gewesen," which he sold for 18 Batzen. Another consisted of a small fur and a set of bed sheets. ASB 215: 278r–280r.

166. "Sagt, er sey an keinem ort noch so hartt gehalten worden, wie alhie, sondern zu Wintspach habe man Ihn nur in einer futterwamen gestrichen und widerlauffen lassen, seithero habe er soviel nicht gestolen, was er aber gethan sey armut halben geschehen, dann er nichts erbetteln noch zu driessen kommen können, sintmal er gar zerrissen gewessen, dannenhero er nothalben stelen müssen, hülff Ime aber Gott noch einmal davon, so wollte ers sein Lebenlang nicht mehr thun . . . Seiner verübten diebstell haben sey er nicht unshuldig zu verhafft kommen, dann er darzumal damit den Galgen verdient." ASB 215: 285r–v.

167. See Bob Scribner, "The Mordbrenner Panic in Sixteenth Century Germany," in Evans, *German Underworld*, 29–56.

168. "Sagt, hiebey hab er bey seiner Armen Seelseeligkeit, anders nicht gethan, dann das er uff das Grünhütleins anraizen an beede ortt mit gangen, sey aber heraussen vor den Höfen geblieben, was nun der Grünhütlein zu einem, oder dem andern gesagt, oder was er von Ihnen empfangen, das könne er nicht wissen." ASB 215: 285v–286r. Hennslein Creuzmayr similarly refuses under torture to admit to a charge of arson. ASB 212: 121r–v.

169. "darbey er dann gesehen, wie der Grünhütlein beim Endressen die Wöhr herauss gerissen, und sich darbey vernemen lassen, Er sollt Ime Im hauss nicht sicher sein, so wey er auch beim Bastlein mit einer stangen zum hoff herauss gesprengt worden." ASB 215: 286r.

170. "Sagt, dergleichen habe man Ihne auch zu Lichtenaw gefragt, er bitte aber umb Jessu Christi willen, Ihme nicht unrecht geshehen zulassen, er habe es bey seinem Theuern Aidt nicht gethan, wisse auch nichts davon, das soll Gott in seinem Reich wissen . . . wiss auch nicht aigentlich, ob sie auch stehlen, oder sonsten andere Unthaten begehen." ASB 215: 287v–288r.

171. "Sagt, wieviel dieses gestolnen geldts eigentlich gewesen, wisse er bey seiner Seelseeligkeit nicht mehr, dann es albereit lang angestanden es möge aber wol sein, das es 17 fl. Gewesen, das er nicht wider streitten wolle. Er habe aber dessen mehr nit genossen, dann das er davon wie zuvor angezaigt drey krz. für ein Weck ausgeben, habe alsdann, we er sich bessinne, zu Orberg drey Panzen, für ein Par schuch, und

zu Gunzenhaussen umb ein weisse Perlem huetschnur, drey kreuzer ausgeben, dass ander geldt sey vor dem dorff Ah, nicht weit von Gunzenhaussen eingegraben worden, diweil aber ein Schneider dessen Im nachgehen gewahr worden, habe derselbe solch geldt mit hillff anderer wider ausgegraben und ist Badthauss zu Ah begraben, Und soll bey solchem abholn, ermellter Volgelhenslein Personlich gewessen sein, und wie er berichtet, sein Geldt wider bekommen haben." ASB 215: 288v–289r.

172. "Sagt er habe sich erst recht besonnen, und wisse das dess geldts gar viel in zweyen Peuteln, und das sein Gesell der Grünhütlein, mit und darbey gewesen, wie sie es auss der Cammern und einer Truhen gestolen, haben solch geldt auch miteinander getheilt, und er von seiner theil, dem Pecken Enderlein zu Riet zehn gulden, auf zubehallten geben, weiln er aber hernacher vorstanden, wie es bey Ihnen von dem Pauern zu Niderndombach verbotten worden, sey er nicht mehr darnach gangen, habe es also ermellter Pecken Enderlein noch beyhanden. Vom übrigen geldt, hatt er und Grünhütlein zugleich dem Schmidt zu Hirschlaw 21 fl. In einem Peutel gelihen, und aufzubehalten geben, zum wahrzaichen, wohren unter solchem geldt drey ducaten gewesen, dass andern tags hette ermellter Schmidt Ime sagern alssbalden 15 fl. Wider zugestellt, welches In beysein seines weibs In der kirchen geschehen, darbey gesagt, er dörffe dess geldte nicht, möchte darzu vielleicht zu gefahr kommen. Und alss er nach den goldtstucken gefragt, dann er sie beim geldt nicht gefunden, wer Ihme zur anttwortt worden, er hette an den 15 fl. ein weil genug, ein andermal wolt er Ime das ubrige auch geben welches aber bisshero herblieben ware, und das sey bey seiner seelseligkeit die lautter warhait, ander werde sich die sache nicht finden, und habe er solch geldt allenthalben wider anwohrden." ASB 215: 289v–290r.

173. "weil es nit viel berathschlagen bedarff, was er verdiene." RV 1764: 11v, 35v (14 and 23 May 1604).

174. "Sagt, mit der warheit, wisse er nicht mehr anzuzaigen, es sey dessen, was er bekannt habe zuviel und sollt es nicht getan habe." ASB 215: 303v.

175. Cf. directions to the *Pfleger* of Lichtenau and the Vogt of Waisenbach, especially to compare the testimonies of Mayr and Steffan the Grocer to see if they agreed. RV 1763: 49v, 52v (27 and 28 April 1604).

176. "mit vielfältigen diebereyen, einstiegen, und einbrechen, uberal hin und wider Im Land offenmals und ein mit vielen unterschiedliche orthen, vergriffen, dass also kain einige hoffnung seiner besserung nicht zu schöpffen." ASB 215: 272v. Other reference to his "numerous" thefts are found on 275r, 280r, and 286v.

177. Van Dülmen, *Theatre of Horror*, 84. The figures were 33 percent from 1541–60, 68.5 percent from 1561 to 1640, and 17 percent from 1641–50. Nuremberg was not unique in this respect; thieves and robbers constituted over three-quarters of Cologne's 193 executions between 1568 and 1617. Schwerhoff, *Köln im Kreuzverhör*, 324–25.

178. Between 1540 and 1675, at least three minors were executed for murder in Nuremberg and two for incest (Keller, *Maister Franntzn Schmidts*, 21, 70; StaatsAN 226a: 61; ASB 21: 248v–251v; Knapp, *Das alte Nürnberger Kriminalrecht*, 9). Outside of Nuremberg, witchcraft remains the one major exception to the rule in executions of minors, at least in terms of significant numbers. For example, one-third of those executed for witchcraft during the *Zauberjackl* trials of the late seventeenth century were under the age of fifteen. Schindler, "Origins of Heartlessness," 238. See also the late accusations examined in Lyndal Roper, "'Evil Imaginings and Fantasies': Child Witches and the End of the Witch Craze," *Past and Present* 167 (May 2000): 107–39.

179. Based on the calculations for a later period in Shore, *Artful Dodgers*, 63. Overall, Boes ("Treatment of Juvenile Delinquents," 50) found that property offenses accounted for 90 percent of juvenile crime in Frankfurt between 1562 and 1696.

180. The actual number in Nuremberg is perhaps a bit higher, but this is the number substantiated by at least one reliable source. ASB: 209–217. It is difficult to be precise on this issue given both the vagueness of records on age and the occasional tendency to define minority as under age 25 or 21. The statement that Zurich executed over one hundred "young people" for various crimes between 1500 and 1750 offers no help on the question of thieves under the age of 18 (Kathleen Alaimo, "Juvenile Delinquency and Hooliganism," *Encyclopedia of Social History*, 3: 387). The same is true of Frankfurt's execution between 1562 and 1623 of fourteen minors (defined as under age 25) for theft and in one case for arson (Boes, "Treatment of Juvenile Delinquents," 46, 51–52). Schwerhoff (*Köln im Kreuzverhör*, 350) tells us that at least 60 of the 292 condemned convicts in one sample were under 20 and some were as young as 10, though he also notes the frustration in interpreting vague phrases such as "youth" or "girl." We also don't know how many of the thirty-eight thieves executed (113–14) fall into that category. Overall I have found no explicit reference to a minor under the age of 18 executed for theft in a German land outside this window of 1560–1620.

181. In her sample from early modern Frankfurt, Maria Boes found that half of all sentenced juvenile offenders had been tortured before 1602, before the practice was abandoned entirely for minors. Boes, "Treatment of Juvenile Delinquents" 46, 52.

182. "welches biss auf diese zeit, zu Nürnberg unverhört gewest." This comment refers to the hanging of women, who were usually drowned or beheaded in executions. StadtAN F1-2/VII: 660. See Rublack, *Crimes of Women*, 124, on the similarly exceptional 1599 execution of a sixteen-year-old female thief in Esslingen, as well as Boes, "Treatment of Juvenile Delinquents," 52–55, on the equally uncommon executions of one girl thief and one girl arsonist during the same period. In Frankfurt, boys constituted 93.4 percent of all juvenile criminals, and women under twenty-five made up only 1.6 percent of all female convictions (Boes, "Treatment of Juvenile Delinquents," 49). Schwerhoff concurs that the typical thief was young, foreign-born, and male (*Köln im Kreuzverhör*, 350).

183. "weil sie aber zum Galgen noch zu jung gewesen." (StadtAN F1-2/VII: 525); "zu jung zum henken" (Hampe, *Malefizbücher*, 84). The five boys in the first group were forced to watch the execution of their eighteen-year-old leader, Heinrich Lind, before public they were publicly flogged and banished. A group of thirteen boys the same year, "deren keiner über zwölff Jahr alt gewest," were also banished after flogging (StadtAN F1-2/VII: 529).

184. Boes, "Treatment of Juvenile Delinquents," 52–53. Again it must be stressed that the age of majority in this sample is 25. There is no way to determine how many of the 69 were aged 18 or younger.

185. "aber von herrn Siegmundt Pfintzing und den ganzen Metzger handwerck erbetten." Imhoff'sche Chronik, vol. 4 (StadtAN F1-14/IV: 1634). See a similar case of the pardoning of Hans Mayr, a thief of "about twenty," in response to the pleas of his mother and her other five children (15 March 1610), cited in Hampe, *Malefizbücher*,

186. "ungeacht Irer Jugendt." RV 1500: 9v (10 February 1584).

187. GNM Hs 3857: 39v. We must approach with great caution, however, Hagendorn's hearsay report of the number of detentions, including 35 imprisonments in the Hole for Hans Schober, 30 times in the begging stockade and five in the Hole for Hennsle

Baldauf, and 110 times (!) in the begging stockade and three times in the Hole for says Hennsle von Geiselwindt. See also the flogging accounts of Meister Frantz in Keller, *Maister Franntzn Schmidts*, 85–87.

188. ASB 212: 115v; GNM Hs 3857: 48r.

189. "Welches sie Inen kein warnung sein lassen sond. Daruber nichts weniges frefenlich widerumb herein gangen, sich an andere leichtfertige diebspursh gehenckt." ASB 210: 86v.

190. "Sie wisse das nhun zum oftermal Irer dieberei halben alhie gefangen gelegen, mit knechten wid. hinaus gefurt, Ir meiner herrn gipiet. verpotten, auch mit ruten alhie ausgehauen worden . . . warumb sie sich nhun widerumb hab betretten lassen. Sagt, sie hab nit gewusst, wo sie hin sollen ziehen, hab sie auch niemands wollen anne-men, wolt sunst nit hie pleiben sein." ASB 210: 95r. Hans Baldauf, asked the same question by Holzshuher, responded in a strikingly similar manner: "Sagt, er hab niergends konnen unterkommen und hab Ir nit gewust, wor er hin sollen ziehen" (105v).

191. "gleich gar zu todt gemarttert warden soll . . . alle die furta die er bekannt hab, funf Ungarische ducaten nich austragen." StaatsAN 51, 45: 358v–360r. In 1584, before ex-ecuting the Seven, magistrates asked the *Konsulenten* (357r) to reexamine their advice on juvenile executions from a few years earlier (RV 1499: 38r [28 January 1584]). Neither document, unfortunately, has been preserved. Nuremberg's preservation of the medieval custom of oath finger amputation was unusual among early modern German jurisdictions. Schwerhoff, *Köln im Kreuzverhör*, 146.

192. "dz er durch meiner herren diener so heftig geshedigt, und zur einen armselligen menshen gemacht wordten sey, dahero nich wenig zue zweiffeln, ob nicht der sa-chen zue vill geshehen, unnd man befugt were, ihne allein umb diss willen mit dem strang hinrichten zulassen, dz er den leutten nicht weitters shaden zuefugen sollte." StaatsAN 51, 45: 358r.

193. ASB 212: 116r.

194. "ungeacht dessen alles, sonderlich sovielfältiger empfangener gnediger Straff und Warnungen zut ettlich mahlen widerumb heren gangen, mainaydig worden." StaatsAN 51, 45: 359v–360r; ASB 212: 116r; also RV 1637: 19r–20r (3 September 1594).

195. "Man kenne den Schloss Sipten im ganzen Landt und wisse, das er ein arder dieb sey, für deme man nichts behalten kan." ASB 215: 274r.

196. "uff garner begangene diebstall, dern er ungehlig uber de bekannte, nach verüebt zu verdencken." ASB 215: 303v. The characterization of "frevenlich" recurs often in the magistrates' question, for instance, "meine herren werden sich am stein freven-lich falsh schweren weniger als nichts keeren, viel wenig damit abweissen lassen" (286v).

197. Of all the condemned juveniles, only Henslein Creuzmayr was tortured more than Mayr, twice with the strappado, three times with the "crown," and once with fire. ASB 212: 116v, 120r, 121r, 124r, 125v. Five of the Seven were also tortured one time each, including the two girls. ASB 210.

198. "Ihme unrecht geshehe und das er das leben mit verwurckt, und das man seine gesellen so eben soviel, alz er gestolen mit dem leben davon kommen lassen." RV 1637: 19r–v (3 September 1594).

199. Convicted of a stabbing death, Wild spent six weeks in the Hole before being released on 11 May 1604. "zwey Jar lang Inn hungar wider den Türggen zustreitten." StadtAN F1/47: 830v. Boes ("Treatment of Juvenile Delinquents," 53) cites two similar cases

in Frankfurt (1590 and 1607), where youths convicted of manslaughter had their sentence commuted to military service against the Turks in Hungary.

200. "... er wolle sich bessern, und gar ein Neuer Mensh werden." ASB 215: 304v (2 June 1604).

201. Despite this caveat, I am not sure that Schindler doesn't minimize the importance of the connection: "Trotzdem bleibt zu betonen, dass die Übergänge zu kriminellen Verhaltensweisen keineswegs so gleitend waren, wie die Obrigkeit ständig argwöhnte." "Die Entstehung der Unbarmherzigkeit," in *Widerspenstige Leute*, 291.

202. "dieweil keine besserung zu hofen." RV 1764: 66v 69v; RV 1765, 5r–v, 33r (4, 5, 7, and 18 June 1604).

CHAPTER FIVE

1. The twins were baptized on 21 November 1637 in Nuremberg's Saint Lorenz church. Their father Stephan Schier (also spelled Schür), described as a "Brillenmacher an Tafferlberlein gegen Muckhofflein," was buried on 22 August 1638 in Saint Johannis Cemetery. The date of Sibylla's death is not recorded. LKAN L-23 Taufen, 1627–45, Saint Lorenz: 787; L-81 Beerdigungen, 1637–67, Saint Lorenz: 16.

2. I will also draw on the valuable comparative research for Augsburg (Safley, *Children of the Laboring Poor*), Florence (Gavitt, *Charity and Children*; Terpstra, *Abandoned Children*), London (McClure, *Coram's Children*), Amsterdam (McCants, *Civic Charity*); and Saxony (Meumann, *Findelkinder*).

3. Minimum age for residence in foundling homes elsewhere ranged from four to eight. In Amsterdam and Florence a foundling left its foster mother for the home at age four; in Paris, Rennes, and London at age five; and in Lisbon, like Nuremberg, at age seven. Gavitt, *Charity and Children*, 188; McClure, *Coram's Children*, 46; Hufton, *Poor of Eighteenth-century France*, 338.

4. RV 2248: 18r (12 October 1647); FB 2: 99.

5. FKD: 663 of 913 abandoned children (72.6 percent) where the age is known were under the age of seven; 391 of the 663 (59 percent) were under the age of two. Only 4 percent (18 of 449) were eight or older.

6. FKD: Among Findel children under two, the abandonment proportion is 85.9 percent (336 of 391); for those under six months the figure rises to 92.1 percent (210 of 227). In most Italian and French cities, anonymously abandoned children were overwhelmingly young, with nine in ten under a year old and the great majority of those less than a week old. During the fifteenth century, 89 percent of babies whose age was provided in Florence were between three hours and three weeks old; by the nineteenth century, virtually all were less than a year old, with 84 percent of those only a few days old. Gavitt, "'Perche non avea chi la ghovernasse,'" in Henderson and Wall, *Poor Women and Children*, 72; Pier Paolo Viazzo, Maria Bortolotto, and Andrea Zanotta, "Five Centuries of Foundling History in Florence: Changing Patterns of Abandonment, Care and Mortality," in Painter-Brick, *Abandoned Children*, 78.

7. By the seventeenth century, these *Ziehmütter* earned 6–8 fl. annually, in addition to supplies, such as diapers, straw sacks, shirts, and blankets. Mummenhoff, "Das Findel- und Waisenhaus," 1:153.

8. Gavitt, *Children and Charity*, 180ff..

9. FB 2: 118 (5 April 1662).

10. "ad 12 July 1649 ist das kindt in der findel gestorben." FB 2: 99 (9 October 1649). See also the case of Kunigunda and Magdalena Schneiderin, admitted to the Findel at the ages of two years and one month, respectively (FB 2: 118; 30 April 1662); Anna

Maria Mayin, who returned to the Findel at the age of two and remained there until she was placed as a maid, fourteen years later (FB 2: 115; 26 May 1658; 11 May 1660; 1 November 1674); and Margaretha Sturmin, who lived in the Findel from eighteen months old onward (FB 2: 133; 18 July 1670).

In Florence, infants were first fed by in-house nurses and then after a week or two sent to a nurse in the country. Once babies were weaned (between eighteen and twenty-four months) they were briefly returned to the hospital before being assigned foster parents who would keep them until the age of four. Gavitt, *Charity and Children*, 188–89.

11. See Gavitt, "'Perche non avea chi la ghovernasse,'" 81.
12. "wie lang sie burger weren und warumb sie das kindt also verderben lassen." RV 1270: 11r, 12r (7 and 9 December 1566). The foundling homes of Florence displayed similar reluctance to prosecute wet nurses for questionable deaths, even refusing to prosecute two cases of open infanticide. Gavitt, *Children and Charity*, 219, 234–35.
13. FB 1: 271 (10 January 1612; ran away on 11 July 1614); "sehr ubel gehalten werde." RV 1932: 41v (23 January 1617).
14. "so übel geshlag. das es wenig stund daran todtes verfahren, und es den laut habe, das dies Wernerin in Kurzer zeit, funff solcher armen waisen begraben lassen." RV 2158: 55r (11 March 1634); also RV 2158: 88v, 106v, RV 2159: 8r, 8v–9r (18, 22, 29 March), and RV 2160: 7v (9 April 1634).
15. Schubert, *Arme Leute*, 132. Schubert notes that in the eighteenth century, "Eva Keller was no isolated case; there were other such women in Würzburg"—though unlikely as prolific!
16. Foster families were so often the destination for runaways from the London Foundling Home they were always the first places authorities checked. McClure, *Coram's Children*, 130.
17. FB 2: 92 (1 and 2 June 1642). In at least three instances, foster parents returned for children after almost two years: StadtAN D 10 3–5, 19 (2 November 1590 and 22 September 1592); FB 1: 173 (5 July 1599 and 1 May 1601); FB 2: 91 (3 October 1641 and 28 April 12 1643). Another mother returned after less than four months: FB 2: 121 (27 August 1663 and 19 December 1663). Usually the annotation simply reads "[the child's name] ist wieder zu Ihrer Ziehmutter komen," without a date (e.g., FB 2: 63 [5 June 1634]). See similar cases in Gavitt, *Charity and Children*, 236; McClure, *Coram's Children*, 129–30.
18. Directors of the Parisian Hôpital général and other French foundling homes intentionally left children with wet nurses beyond the usual pick-up age of five or six, so that emotional bonds might grow. Gager, *Blood Ties and Fictive Ties*, 154.
19. In the Lisbon Porto, one-third of wet nurses whose children had died "adopted" a foundling, as did one-quarter of those who still had children alive. Sá, "Circulation of Children," 36. As David Vassberg ("Orphans and Adoption," 445), observes, "From a strictly economic sense, if a family was looking only for labor, it would probably have been better off hiring a servant than adopting a child."
20. Kunigunda Ammenin dropped Diener off at the Findel on 2 November 1590; he was reclaimed on 22 September 1592 by "Hans Ammen, wirdt zu Potenglocken in Gostenhof, der will Im aufziehen und ein Jar oder Zwey lassen Inn die Schuel gehn und war zu er darnach dauglich sein wird zu lernen zu dem selben will er Im behulflich sein." Diener entered his apprenticeship on 2 February 1601 (StadtAN D 10 3–5: 19).
21. Schlumbohm (*Familien, Höfe*, 152, 156) found a mortality rate of 29.9 percent by

age fifteen in Belm, while Zschunke (*Oppenheim*, 162) found that 49 percent of all children died by age ten. Estimates of first-year mortality range from 15.2 percent in Belm (northern Germany) to 16 percent for England, 23.2 percent in Oppenheim (Germany), 33 percent for Muscovy, 40 percent for parts of seventeenth-century France, and 50 percent in parts of Bavaria and Württemberg (Kertzer, *Family Life in Early Modern Times, 1500–1789*, xiii). Katherine Lynch (*Individuals, Families, and Communities*, 43) reckons a general early modern infant mortality rate of 250–300 per 1,000. See also André Burgière, *Histoire de la famille* (Paris: A. Colin, 1986), 2: 18ff.; Pier Paolo Viazzo, "Mortality, Fertility, and Family," 165 (table 6.1) for early modern infant mortality rates; and Imhof, *Lost Worlds*, 80–87.

22. FKD: In a sample of 85 cases of children six months or younger where nature of departure was indicated, 51.8 percent (44) died within a month of admission; 87 percent (74) were dead at the end of two years.

23. FKD: 103 of a sample of 107 anonymous abandonments where age of six months or newborn was indicated. The London Foundling Hospital, which at one point experienced an annual mortality of 95 percent for infants under one, averaged 86 percent for the years 1741–60. Eighteenth-century Castile as a whole had a 90 percent fatality rate for foundling babies by age ten. The Lisbon Porto average of 63 percent dead by age seven appears good by comparison, as does the 52.2 percent rate of Saint-Yves in Rennes by the same age. McClure, *Coram's Children*, 102; Vassberg, "Orphans and Adoption," 448; Sá, "Circulation of Children," 36; Hufton, *Poor of Eighteenth-Century France*, 338.

24. FB 2: 99 (9 October 1647).

25. Gavitt, "'Perche non avea chi la ghovernasse,'" 73. This represents a revision of Gavitt's earlier estimates of 52.2 percent for girls and 44.3 percent for boys (*Charity and Children*, 211).

26. Richard C. Trexler, "The Foundlings of Florence, 1395–1455," *History of Childhood Quarterly* 1 (1973–74): 279–97. See also the even more provocative and less substantiated interpretations of Edward Shorter, *The Making of the Modern Family* (London: Collins, 1976).

27. Gavitt, *Charity and Children*, 213–14; Gavitt, "'Perche non avea chi la ghovernasse,'" 73.

28. See an intriguing recent discussion of this question in Katherine A. Lynch, "Infant Mortality, Child Neglect, and Child Abandonment in European History: A Comparative Analysis," in *Population and Economy: From Hunger to Modern Economic Growth*, ed. Tommy Bengtsson and Osamu Saito (Oxford: Oxford University Press, 2000), 133–64.

29. FKD: 531 (47.5 percent) of a sample of Nuremberg's 1,118 abandonments where gender was indicated were girls. Of these total abandonments, the anonymous component comprised 530 abandonments, of which 266 (50.2 percent) were boys and 264 (49.8 percent) were girls. The component of known abandonments comprised 588 cases, of which 312 (53.3 percent) were boys and 273 (46.7 percent) were girls. The total number of abandonment cases in the database was 1,347, including 622 (46.2 percent) anonymous and 725 (53.8 percent) known abandonments.

Based on a sample of 133 anonymous abandonment deaths, 74 (55.7 percent) were girls and 59 (44.3 percent) were boys. Overall, in anonymous abandonment cases where gender was indicated, 266 were boys and 264 were girls. In a sample of 181 anonymous abandonment cases where age, gender, and nature of departure were indicated, 73 of 76 girl foundlings under the age of two (96.1 percent) died, while 58 of 64 boys (90.6 percent) died. The death rates among foundlings under six months were virtually identical, with 98.1 percent (54 of 55) for girls and 94.2 percent (49 of 52) for boys. The mortality rates for anonymously abandoned children between the ages of two and seven were 73.1 percent (19 of 26) for boys and 66.6 percent (10 of 15) for girls.

There was also apparently no gender discrepancy whatsoever in the death rates among Nuremberg foundlings until the mid-seventeenth century, by which time the Findel's admissions numbers had plummeted to a handful a year. Based on a sample of 233 anonymous abandonment cases where both gender and nature of departure are known, the years 1610–34 recorded 143 deaths, an annual average of 5.72, compared to 90 deaths between 1560–1609 and 1635–69, an annual average of 1.06. Within the same sample, the total recorded deaths for foundling girls from 1645 to 1669 was 19, compared to 11 for boys. Based on a sample of 70 newborn anonymous abandonment cases where nature of departure was known, the years 1615–29 recorded 32 deaths, an average of 2.13 per year, as contrasted with a total of 38 for the years 1560–1614, an average of 0.4 deaths per year.

30. Infant mortality rate in nineteenth-century children's hospitals was still 50–90 percent and as late as 1900, the premier foundling home in Germany had an infant mortality rate of 71.5 percent—still better than a contemporary Baltimore facility with a 90 percent rate. In 1945, René Spitz argued that the problem was not hygiene, since the precautions of such hospitals were "impeccable." Institutional care just made children much more susceptible. Evelyn McRitchie, "Krankenbehandlung im Hamburger Waisenhaus in der Zeit von 1604 bis 1921. Die Krankenstation des Hamburger Waisenhauses als Vorläufer einer Kinderklinik" (M.D. diss., Universität Hamburg, 1983), 10; Gavitt, *Charity and Children*, 224; Pier Paolo Viazzo, "Mortality, Fertility, and Family," in Kertzer, *Family Life in Early Modern Times*, 178.

31. Records of both the London Foundling Hospital and Florence's Innocenti Hospital show an improvement of at least 10–20 percent when rural nurses become involved and the virtual 100 percent fatality rate of English parish workhouses plunged to about 40 percent among country nurses. Pier Paolo Viazzo has stressed that the key element in improving survivability was less the involvement of a wet nurse than the promptness with which an infant was dispatched to the countryside. In 1629, when two of three foundlings were sent out from the Innocenti within four days and 95 percent within a week, the mortality rate was 29.7 percent; in 1777, when the median waiting period before departure was 21.8 days, the mortality rate rose to 80 percent. McClure, *Coram's Children*, 87, 261 (app. 3); Viazzo, "Five Centuries," 81–84. Meumann (*Findelkinder*, 298) attributed the much lower fatality rates among his nursing foundlings with a strict enforcement of 1:1 nursing, as opposed to multiple nursing as in contemporary France.

32. Women whose own children had died of infectious diseases were supposedly banned from taking on foster children in Nuremberg (RV 2166: 27r; 2 October 1634). Based on a very small sample of the twenty-three cases from 1445 to 1450 where the cause of death was listed, Gavitt found that the most common causes for the deaths of children with foster mothers were convulsions or plague; others were overlaying, smallpox, worms, and accidents. Gavitt, *Charity and Children*, 219.

33. This differs markedly from some Italian institutions. In the Florentine conservatory Pietá's first two years of operation (1555–56), 39.8 percent of orphaned girls admitted were age fourteen or older. Over three-quarters of the girls admitted to nearby S. Caterina during the same period were older than ten, despite a policy of admitting

only girls between the ages of six and ten. The Oespedale degli Innocenti, by contrast, housed exclusively children under the age of ten, while its partner institution of San Gallo handled older children (Gavitt, *Charity and Children*, 169). Other European cities similarly divided wards of the state by age, as in Aix-en-Provence, where younger children went to the Hôtel-Dieu and older children were housed and eventually placed by the city's Charité. Nicholas Terpstra, "Making a Living,"1070.

34. FKD: In a sample of 360 cases where the age of admitted orphans was known, 1.1 percent (4) were newborns, 0.8 percent (3) were one to six months old, 7.5 percent (27) were six months to two years old, 31.1 percent (112) were aged two to seven years old, 42.2 percent (152) were eight to twelve years old, and 17.2 percent (62) were over twelve years old.

35. FKD: 6 (3.6 percent) of 167 cases where age and date of departure known.

36. "ein alten Beltz, ein schwarze Beltzheub, zwey Küslein, ein Plabe mitz, ein Baurngesesla, ein schw. Leinshurtz, ein klein tüchlein, unnd alt tuch darin die gemelt studck gebund. sein." Loose note between pp. 159 and 160 of FB *I* (19 July 1597).

37. Final authorization of renovations came on 23 December 1563 (RV 1231: 2v). The water wheel was constructed in 1565 (RV 1248: 16v; 18 April 1565). See Mummenhoff, "Das Findel- und Waisenhaus," 1: 188f., on all structural changes from 1560 to 1650.

38. The semblance to a monastic routine continued to apply to many Catholic and Protestant orphanages and hospitals throughout Europe into the nineteenth century. Harrington, "Genealogy of a German Workhouse," 324–26; Safely, *Charity and Economy*, 248; Safley, *Children of the Laboring Poor*, 207ff.; McClure, *Coram's Children*, 74; Meumann, *Findelkinder*, 284–92. See also Rüger, *Die Kinderfürsorge*, 121ff., on the similar routine followed in Nuremberg's Zucht- und Arbeitshaus.

39. Around 1600, the Findel had forty-five beds, each shared by two children. During the 1630s each bed slept three or more children, depending on their size. Mummenhoff, "Das Findel- und Waisenhaus," 1: 73.

40. "saubere Liegerstat . . . es ward ihnen täglich gebüstet und gestrählt." ASB 101: 76r.

41. RV 1292: 24v (4 August 1568). Children received clean sheets every Sunday (Mummenhoff, "Das Findel- und Waisenhaus," 1: 163).

42. Based on various expenditures with explicit references to haircutting and bathing. Mummenhoff, "Das Findel- und Waisenhaus," 1: 111, 243. In the Hamburg orphanage, haircuts occurred every Christmas, Easter, Saint John's Day, and Saint Michael's. McRitchie, "Krankenbehandlung im Hamburger Waisenhaus," 80.

43. Mummenhoff, "Das Findel- und Waisenhaus," 1: 163.

44. Blue and red were apparently the most common colors of uniforms among early modern orphans. The orphans of Christ's Hospital in London were know as bluecoats, while those of Amsterdam's Weehuijs were known for their black garments with a small red, white, and black shield on the upper sleeve. Orphans in Venice and the bishopric of Hildesheim wore red uniforms, those in Paris brown, and the boys of Augsburg's orphanage were recognizable by their cloaks of blue Meixner. Children of Florence's Abandonati wore distinctive brown robes while collecting in public; orphans of Bologna's S. Bartolomeo di Reno orphanage wore red. Hogarth designed the uniforms of London's Coram Hospital, brown drugget outfits trimmed in scarlet. McClure, *Coram's Children*, 74, 193–94; Safley, *Charity and Economy*, 18, idem, *Children of the Laboring Poor*, 209–10; Meumann, *Findelkinder*, 292–92; Terpstra, "Making a Living," 1067, 1069.

45. For example: "Was auf die hailung der findelkinder dis Jahr sol man aus dem Almusen zalen, und dem fundelpfleger sagen die kinder so hoch nit zuverlassen und etwas sperlich zu sein." RV 1303: 8r (20 May 1569). See also Mummenhoff, "Das Findel- und Waisenhaus," 1: 181–83, for an extensive list of herbs and other medications appearing in the Findel's expenditure books.
46. There is an early reference to Jörg Geiger who acted as bathmaster (RV 1404: 16r; 15 December 1576), and see Mummenhoff, "Das Findel- und Waisenhaus," 1: 243–244, on various other payments to barbers and bathmasters.
47. Mummenhoff, "Das Findel- und Waisenhaus," 1: 176, 242.
48. Dr. Johann Kuhn was paid 6 fl. in 1592, as well as a lamb shank and liter of wine at Easter. By the middle of the seventeenth century the honorarium had risen to 8 fl., still a modest amount, where it would remain until the early nineteenth century. A Findel decree from 7 September 1599 mentions the appointment of the widow Walburg Friedrichin for the care of poor children. Mumenhoff, "Die öffentliche Gesundheits- und Krankenpflege," 60.
49. "mit den schadhafften kinden sehr schlecht umbgehe und sie ziemlich verwarlosse." The bathmaster, Hans Striegel, had previously directed the city's Rosenbad and worked on children of the Findel since at least 1638. Johann Daunestock was paid 24 fl. a year "fur pflaster und seine mühe"; Dr. Gärtner was paid 30 fl. per year. RV 2208: 62r (4 January 1638); RV 2237: 1r–v (19 March 1640); RV 2237: 47v (1 April 1640); RV 2292: 63r (13 June 1644).
50. By 1645 all of the staff received meat daily and by the end of the seventeenth century, the children were to receive it at least three times a week. See Mummenhoff, "Das Findel- und Waisenhaus," 1: 332–33, on this and eighteenth-century revisions to the Findel's official menu. Children in Augsburg's Lutheran orphanage did not receive meat until 1780 (Safley, Children of the Laboring Poor, 211–12).
51. Ruth McClure (Coram's Children, 201) comes to a similar conclusion for the Coram Hospital in eighteenth-century London: "[Children of the orphanage] enjoyed a more ample diet, one of better quality and with more variety, than poor children who lived with their parents." Children in Florence's Innocenti averaged a little over five ounces of bread for breakfast, four times that for children out at work, five times that for wet nurses in residence, and each chaplain got a half loaf of bread and received meat twice a week. Overall, Gavitt considers this a "varied and adequate diet" for children over two, with average of twenty-two ounces of bread per day. Gavitt, Charity and Children, 170–72; see also Safley, Charity and Economy, 195. For a useful overview on this subject, see Robert Jütte, "Diets in Welfare Institutions and in Outdoor Relief in Early Modern Western Europe," Ethnologia Europaea 16 (1987): 117–35.
52. Mummenhoff, "Das Findel- und Waisenhaus," 1: 164, on Findel ordinance of 1530.
53. FB 1: 122 (22 July 1588).
54. The expenses report for 1550–51 mentions paying two "grosse Schüler" four florins for weekly catechism lessons. From 1635–44, the Findel father taught writing and math, for which he received the tutor's annual fee of 10 fl. In 1644 the Findel appointed Magister Johann Sauer, chaplain of Saint Lorenz, to a continuing position at the home. Peter Hoffman, appointed in 1647, was a former Findel child himself (FB 2: 41). The Findel did not employ a full-time scribe or teacher until 1710. Mummenhoff, "Das Findel- und Waisenhaus," 1: 164, 217, 236.
55. "Erlernung, Kleidung, Lohn, und anderer Notdurft." The endowment, dating back

to 1514, yielded 100 fl. annually, or 12.5 fl. each, for four boys and four girls. Testament des Bürgers und Genannten des grossen Raths Konrad Horn (22 December 1514), cited in Mummenhoff, "Das Findel- und Waisenhaus," 1: 165. The tuition for the Latin schools came out of the budget of the city alms bureau. See payment instructions for 12 May 1564 and 17 May 1570 (StadtAN D1/2: 81r). In Augsburg's orphanages, only 20 of 5734 children received special schooling and only a few of those went on to university. Safley, *Children of the Laboring Poor*, 402.

56. Augsburg' Lutheran orphanage, by contrast, saw nine boys go into the ministry, just within the samples' sixty years. Safley, *Charity and Economy*, 235; also *Children of the Laboring Poor*, 229–32. On the failure of many Protestant school reforms, see Strauss, *Luther's House of Learning*.

57. On this oft-iterated goal, see especially Safley, *Children of the Laboring Poor*, 13–29, 261–62.

58. The seamstress also trained boys who had no craft and was charged with the general moral conduct of all girls in the Findel. Mummenhoff, "Das Findel- und Waisenhaus," 1: 117, 122, 257, 264.

59. Ibid., 1: 305. Even at its peak in 1640, the Findel's spinning only brought in a bit more than 68 fl. annually.

60. RV 1233: 20r (3 March 1564).

61. Cf. description of children's work in the Nuremberg workhouse during the eighteenth century (Rüger, *Die Kinderfürsorge*, 121–22) and S. Caterina and S. Maria of Florence, which "were most like factories, with dedicated work-rooms and specialized superintendents who trained and supervised piecework of various types," as well as the heavy industrial labor of Stuttgart's Waisen-, Zucht-, und Arbeithaus, established in 1710. Terpstra, "Making a Living," 1071; Eduard Lempp, *Geschichte des Stuttgarter Waisenhauses, 1710–1910* (Stuttgart: Verlag der Evangelischen Gesellschaft, 1910). See also Cunningham, *Children and Childhood*, 75–76, 129–30; and Meumann, *Findelkinder*, 235–40, on the "Schools of Industry" and *Spinnschulen* of the seventeenth and eighteenth centuries. The Augsburg orphanages, on the other hand, also resisted industrial production at least until the nineteenth century (Safley, *Charity and Economy*, 209).

62. Mummenhoff, "Das Findel- und Waisenhaus," 1: 173.

63. Cf. Safley's speculation that "it seems unlikely that free time was spent in undirected play" and instead was spent in some "useful" activities. Safley, *Charity and Economy*, 250.

64. By the middle of the eighteenth century, with under eighty children resident, the Findel's staff and children were consuming over 8,000 Mass of beer (about 8,000 liters) and 7,000 lb. of meat per year. Mummenhoff, "Das Findel- und Waisenhaus," 1: 167.

65. See, for example, FB 2: 116 (14 March 1659), 125 (9 June and 7 August 1665), 126 (3 March 1668), and 129 (4 March 1669).

66. Mummenhoff, "Das Findel- und Waisenhaus," 1: 170–73.

67. On December 5, 1599, the Muscovite envoy to the Teutonic Knights visited Nuremberg with a large retinue. Since the next day was the feast of Saint Nicholas, the inner council arranged a small performance by the city's Findel children. StadtAN F1-2/VII: 900–902.

68. Mummenhoff ("Das Findel- und Waisenhaus," 1: 297) speculates that the practice dates back to the late fourteenth-century origins of the Findel itself but the earliest

explicit documentation is a 1512 indulgence for related alms and a council decree of 27 December 1522, recording a performance before the town council (RV 684: 16v). The longevity of the practice is also explicitly mentioned in a begging ordinance of 20 August 1580 (StaatsAN 63Ia/ Bd. E).

69. Begging ordinance of 20 August 1588 (StaatsAN 63Ia/ Bd. E).

70. RV 24 December 1636, cited in Mummenhoff, "Das Findel- und Waisenhaus," 1: 294.

71. Expenses for each of the homes for 1550 included 1 fl. 1 lb. 18 d. for 100 Mass of beer—approximately 1.23 liters per boy and girl every night. Mummenhoff, "Das Findel- und Waisenhaus," 1: 295. Subsequent expenses also listed large amounts of veal, fish, cheese, and onions.

72. Though evident by the late eighteenth century, it is not clear when either practice started. Ibid., 1: 293.

73. Ibid., 1: 290.

74. Some institutions also made money by having funerals in the orphanage's chapel. S. Onofrio in Bologna derived 17.7–27.3 percent of its annual income this way during the first three years of operation. Terpstra, "Making a Living," 1064, 1073. In seventeenth-century Stockholm, orphans were singing at up to three hundred funerals every year. Eventually the custom was suppressed because of the cost to the family of the deceased. Cunningham, *Children and Childhood*, 117.

75. Cf. 1575 *Schulbericht* of Paul Praetorius, rector of Saint Sebaldus in Leder, *Kirche und Jugend*, 91; also RV 1143: 9r (24 May 1557).

76. RV 2019: 34r (18 July 1623). See Mummenhoff, "Die öffentliche Gesundheits- und Krankenpflege," 25, on the renting of Findel pillows.

77. Cf. the Florentine Innocenti foundling home's frequent references to the institution as a *famiglia, brigata*, and *casa*. Gavitt, *Charity and Children*, 143–44, 189–90. Meumann (*Findelkinder*, 292 ff., 312) also debates the question in a section entitled "Anstalts- oder Familienerziehung?"

78. High staff turnover was also a problem at Florence's Oespedale dell'Innocenti, Saxon orphanages and foundling homes, and the London Foundling Hospital. Gavitt, *Charity and Children*, 155–58; McClure, *Coram's Children*, 177; Meumann, *Findelkinder*, 256–58.

79. StaatsAN 62, 146–173 (1627–54).

80. "Nutz und From." Mummenhoff, "Das Findel- und Waisenhaus," 1: 215, 229. According to Safley (*Charity and Economy*, 248), "the [Augsburg] orphanages strove . . . to inculcate habits of mind and body."

81. From the Findel father's oath of office in a 1562 municipal collection. ASB 101: 76r–77r.

82. The size of the staff tended to vary with the number of children resident, though this was not always true. In 1550, for instance, the Findel employed a cook and three maids; ten years later during the epidemic of the early 1560s two more women were hired. After that, the number of servants fluctuated until the mid-seventeenth century, when the female staff was reduced to one cook, one milkmaid, and one nurse. Based on study of expenses in Mummenhoff, "Das Findel- und Waisenhaus," 1: 214–41.

83. This is quite a good ratio compared to the Amsterdam orphanage, which had only four pairs of house parents for four times as many children. At the end of the sixteenth century, the Augsburg orphanage maintained staff of twenty-six full- and part-

time workers for about three hundred children, a comparable ratio of about 1:12. Safley, *Charity and Economy,* 185; Mummenhoff, "Das Findel- und Waisenhaus," 1: 81, 217

84. Mummenhoff, "Das Findel- und Waisenhaus," 1: 211.

85. RV 1966: 78v; RV 1967: 24v–25r, 33v (16, 26, 29 August 1619). See also RV 1973: 4v, 24v, 36r, 52r, 84r (3, 9, 12, 17, and 29 March 1620); RV 2034: 26v (26 August 1624).

86. See, for instance, FB 2: 118 (10 February 1662).

87. FB 1: 136 (25 November 1591); "den 17. Dezember 1685 nach 6 der grossen Uhr ist dieser Michael Saloman an einer Leibsschwacheit und geschwuhr auf der brust seelig vershieden." FB 2: 127 (admitted 29 June 1668).

88. RV 1277: 13r (9 June 1567); RV 2578: 85v–86r (8 November 1665); RV 1801: 2r–v (27 March 1607). See also FB 1: 19 (18 December 1570); RV 2578: 85v–86r (8 November 1665).

89. FB 2: 97 (4 April 1646), 102 (10 February 1648).

90. "ein recht traueriges, einförmiges, und gedrüktes Leben." Mummenhoff, "Das Findel- und Waisenhaus," 1: 169.

91. FKD: 1541 of 2849 cases (54.1 percent) where type known. 1420 of these 1541 (92.1 percent) known to have siblings were admitted with at least one.

92. After a two-month investigation, two men, Peter Fisher and Paulus Bedner, were imprisoned for the offense and Bedner, the self-acknowledged father, was later banished, despite his offer to provide for the child. RV 2025: 57v (20 January 1624); also RV 2029: 6r, 14r, 22v (31 March, 2, 6, and 9 April 1624).

93. Hans Christoff Korner "auss der findel entloffen ursach hat er dem Gabriel Ritter der Blind Baberla genannt 10 Batz gestollen" FB 1: 99 (10 October 1583). In 1600, the culprits were Walter Beckh, Jorgla Mezenhoffer, Veitla Leiherer, and Hennsa Schnela. FB 1: loose note between pp. 49 and 50, 136 (6 April 1592; 1600), 151 (22 December 1591); StadtAN D10 3–5: 4, 17, 19.

94. Cf. Safley, *Charity and Economy,* 250ff.

95. Augsburg's orphanages recorded several cases of incontinence (*unsauberkeit*), leading to at least four expulsions and one suicide. Safley, *Children of the Laboring Poor,* 206.

96. Augsburg's Lutheran orphanage had its own lockup for children but only twenty-six recorded cases of discipline. Safley, *Children of the Laboring Poor,* 186.

97. RV 1170: 18r, 19r (8 and 9 June 1559).

98. RV 1723: 19v (1 April 1601).

99. RV 2171: 70r (9 February 1635).

100. After an extensive investigation, the council released Anna N. "wie gebrauchlich" but ordered that the prison guards should be consulted "ob sie dasselbst nicht etwa zum seubern von der gefangen gerauchen können, damit es undergerbracht werde." RV 2240: 41r, 63r–v; 2244: 14r (15 June, 20 July, 28 September 1640). FB 2: 110 (28 March 1653).

101. FB 2: 26 (20 September 1625). For more on the development of the chain gang in Nuremberg, see pp. 145–46 above.

102. "ihrere ungestümm wegen aus den Findel verlassen worden." FB 2: 112 (admitted 11 November 1656, expelled 1667, died at foster mother's on 12 December 1681).

103. Thirty-seven runaways are recorded from 1560 to 1670 in FB 1 and FB 2, an average of one every 3.0 years. There were undoubtedly more than this. At least 165 of the 5,734 orphans in Safley's Augsburg sample ran away. *Children of the Laboring Poor,* 363.

104. According to the Findel registry, Bischoff ran off to a weaver. FB 2: 79 (2 April 1652).
105. "auss anraizung seiner schwester." FB 1: 107 (7 June 1585; 2 April 1599).
106. For instance, Elisabeth Erhartin, Anna Margreta Pöppin, and Georg Leypel all ran away during the same week in June 1637. FB 2: 81, 84 (14, 21 June 1637).
107. Hensla Stutz, "one alle ursache." FB 1, loose note between 148 and 149, also 117 (20 February 1594).
108. RV 1289: 24v (11 May 1568); FB 1: 45 (10 July 1572); FB 2: 64 (5 June 1634); FB: 81 (14 June 1637—two girls). All of the runaways in Meumann's small sample for Hildesheim (1694–1726) were boys. Findelkinder, 348.
109. RV 1162: 5v, 15v (31 October and 10 November 1558); FB 2: 64 (5 June 1634).
110. RV 1289: 24v (11 May 1568).
111. "zum virten mal hat in d. herr Pfleger inss Sighauss furen lassen, hab. in seine freund auss dem Sighauss wieder zu einen gelonnen." FB 1: 158 (4 June 1597).
112. FKD: In a sample of 996 cases where length of time in the Findel's care was indicated, 60.7 percent (605) spent less than a year and only 21.3 percent (212) remained after five years. The sample might be skewed by a surge of 67 boys staying more than five years from 1570–85, with only 14 girls in the same category.
113. FKD: In a sample of 363 cases where age and length of time in the Findel were indicated, 68 of 74 (91.9 percent) children aged eight or older stayed at least one year and 26 of 74 (35.1 percent) stayed five years or more.
114. FKD: Based on a sample of 956 cases where gender and length of stay were indicated, 306 of 567 boys (53.9 percent) stayed longer than a year while only 174 of 389 girls (44.7 percent) stayed more than one year. Both of the Schier twins were admitted on 7 March 1647; Eberhardt was released on 3 May 1653 and Susanna on 10 August 1654.
115. FKD: In 2,045 cases where nature of departure was indicated, 58.3 percent (1,193) of children died. This breaks down to 70.1 percent (350 of 499) abandoned children, 56.7 percent (327 of 577) orphans, and 35.3 percent (83 of 235) fostered children. The annual mortality rates Florence's Oespedale degli Innocenti ranged between 37.8 percent in 1763 to 73.8 percent in 1792. Almost half (74 of 156; 47.4 percent) of the Florentine Pietá's 1555 cohort died within five years of admission. At least 41.9 percent of these children died within the first year after admission. The mortality rate in Toledo foundling home during the sixteenth century fluctuated between 44 percent (1518) and 77 percent (1574, 1599); Murcia declined during the seventeenth century from 67.5 percent (ca. 1620) to 52.6 percent (by 1700). The Göttingen orphanage death rate in 1750 was 58.3 percent; by 1820 down to 38.7 percent. Hannover's death rate was 37.3 percent and Mainz 43 percent by age 11 (both seventeenth and eighteenth century). Safley's Augsburg sample from 1572 to 1806 saw an overall fatality rate of 52.9 percent. The lowest mortality rates recorded were those of the Coburg orphanage from 1702 to 1727 (11.3 percent) and the Stuttgart orphanage from 1710 to 1760 (26 percent). Terpstra, "Making a Living, 1071; Vassberg, "Orphans and Adoption," 448; Meumann, Findelkinder, 349–350; Safley, Children of the Laboring Poor, 308.
116. FKD: 69 or 184 (37.5 percent). Findel children over seven whose nature of departure is known.
117. FKD: 1632–39: 424 total deaths. Other years with high numbers of fatalities were 1570–77 (384 total), 1586–87 (30), 1601–3 (63), and 1615–16 (43).
118. FKD: In a sample of 198 cases of anonymous abandonments where the month of

death is known, 40.4 percent (80) died in July through October, July being the dead-liest month with 13.1 percent (26) and June the least deadly with 5.6 percent (11). The Spanish even had a proverb: "The month of August made them ill and Septem-ber carried them off." Pier Paolo Viazzo, "Mortality, Fertility, and Family," 165; also Pfister, "Population of Late Medieval and Early Modern Germany," 51.

119. Hans Peck's daughter was so examined and allowed to enter the Findel (RV 1270: 11r; 7 December 1566), as was the child of leper Katharina Donissin (RV 1499: 39v; 29 January 1584), the two children of Hans Bern (RV 1503: 32r; 8 May 1584), Stef-fan Schmid's son (RV 1525: 9v; 28 December 1585), Benedict Maur (RV 1560: 12r; 4 September 1588), Marx Vogelgesang's daughter (RV 1597: 50r; 16 August 1591), two "frembdte" children (RV 1686: 42v; 8 July 1598), Durla Geislerin (FB 1: 179; 2 July 1600), and Margaretha Engelbrechtin (RV 2058: 89r; 26 July 1626). For the leprous child quarantined for six months in the *Franzosenhaus*, see RV 1856: 29r, and FB 1: 263 (7 May 1611). See also rejections of contagious children on 6 November 1562 (RV 1215: 28r), 14 January 1634 (RV 2156: 42r) and 23 October 1654 (RV 2431: 36v).

120. RV 1583: 39v (9 July 1590); RV 1600: 11v (26 October 1591); RV 1643: 14v (12 Feb-ruary 1595); RV 1697: 22r (21 April 1599); FB 1: 255 (16 February 1610); FB 2: 8 (23 July 1617).

121. Initially, children were not to spend more than six months to a year in the house; if healthy for four weeks, they could move to the Findel, otherwise at the end of their stay they were transferred to the Lazareth hospice. Over time, the Wöhrd house began to fill up with contagious children transferred out of the Findel as well, particularly during the epidemics of 1585, 1599, and 1601. There are no surviving records of admissions to the Wöhrd children's house but linen and bed supplies expenditures for the plague year of 1585 alone—431 fl.—give some idea of the great numbers of sick and dying children who passed through it. Mummenhoff, "Das Findel- und Waisenhaus," 1: 180. The Wöhrder house's *Hofmeister* was to be given 2 fl. a week "fur sein muhe." The house was administered by the hospital, not the Findel. RV 1213: 3v (21 August 1562); RV 1218: 29v (25 January 1563). RV 1807: 1v (27 August 1607); RV 1866: 50v (19 February 1612); RV 1889: 28v (30 October 1613); RV 1881: 6r–v (20 March 1613); RV 1893: 7v (12 February 1614); FB 2: 31 (22 November 1626).

122. The last mention in official records is a 1633 order from the head of the hospi-tal "denen in Kinderhaus Rotbier, so lang das alte Bier währt, zu geben." Spitalp-flegerverlass of 6 December 1633, cited in Mummenhoff, "Das Findel- und Waisen-haus," 1:181.

123. StaatsAN 51, 63: 321; RV 1779: 104r (27 July 1605); StaatsAN Ratsbuch 64, fol. 221/224; RV 1785: 87r–v (15 January 1606); RV 2194: 18v (5 December 1636); also RV 2058: 25v (12 July 1626). For examples of hospital orphans, see RV 2072: 77v (10 August 1627); FB 2: 36 (1 January 1628), 38 (8 May 1628), 42 (7 July 1630), 70 (10 April 1635).

124. RV 1580: 64r (8 April 1590); RV 1605: 14r–v (14 March 1592); RV 1853: 73r.

125. "ob dise kranckheit al seine seuch von einen zum andern kumenn, und ob disem Junge nitt zu helffen sein möchte." RV 1961: 6v (12 March 1619). "das die kinder in der findel, durch Shrecken, wegen hannsen jörg Paumans hinfallender kranckheit, dieselb wol auch bekummen können, soll man den findelpfleger befehlen, den Pau-man umb ein Costgelt ander orten unterzubringen." RV 1961: 11r (13 March 1619). Cf. case of epileptic girl (FB 1: 91; 2 September 1581), reference to Balthasar Neu-man's epileptic son (RV 1957: 4r; 20 November 1618) as well as a 1625 reference to

transferring children afflicted with "der schweren hinfallenden Krankheit" from the hospital to the children's house at Wöhrd. RV 2044: 33r (14 June 1625).

126. "mit der shwehrn kranckheit behafft, mehrmaln überfallen würde und unter den findel kindern grossen shrecken verursach, und durch forch ander auch anstecken dürffte." RV 2569: 17r (22 February 1665).

127. I have found five explicit references to lame Findel children (RV 1643: 12v [11 February 1595]; FB 1: 220 [16 January 1606]; FB 2: 15 [19 October 1620]; RV 2052: 32v [3 February 1626], FB 2: 110–111 [14 April 1654]); six references to blind children (FB 1: 99, 214 [10 October 1592; 29 August 1604]; FB 1: 118 [2 August 1587], FB 2: 72 [10 February 1635], 89 [22 April 1639], 110–111 [21 January 1654]); and five mentions of deaf and dumb boys (RV 1535: 4v [22 September 1586]; RV 1643: 13v [12 February 1595]; RV 1947: 30v [6 March 1618]; RV 1980: 36r–v [19 August 1620]; FB 2: 108 [3 February 1653]).

128. gebrechlich, prechenhafft, schadhafft, so gar elend, krankh. In addition to a mass admission of seventy-one street children in 1635, "most of whom were sickly," see RV 1297: 5v (7 December 1568); RV 1688: 9r (16 August 1598); RV 2149: 53v–54r (3 July 1633); RV 2194: 18v (5 December 1636); RV 2583: 60r–v (21 March 1666); FB 1: 175 (13 December 1599), 210 (11 February 1604), 211 (22 April 1604), 217 (18 April 1605), 220 (20 July 1605), 252 (7 September 1609); FB 2: 15 (26 October 1620), 19 (16 February 1622), 27 (10 December 1625), 30 (7 August 1626), 38 (9 May 1629), 44 (2 September 1630), 74 (21 March 1636), 111 (14 April 1654).

129. In the institutions of Augsburg and Florence, such individuals accounted for a remarkable 20 percent of residents at any given time. 20.4 percent (11) of the 1579 cohort of Florence's S. Niccolo's Conservatory for girls remained at the institution until death at old age.); the fate of seven members of the cohort (13 percent) is unknown (Terpstra, "Making a Living," 1071). In a sample from 1723, Safley found that disabled orphans from age 11 to 71 constituted 20–25 percent of the population of the Lutheran and Catholic houses combined. Safley, Charity and Economy, 264. The governors of the London Foundling Hospital accepted total responsibility for the handicapped foundlings, even for life." McClure, Coram's Children, 218, 236ff.

130. "so Alber und seiner fünff sinn sich nicht gebrauchen kan." FB 2: 111 (1 July 1654); "wegen seines blöden verstands 2 jar verblieben," FB 2: 94 (24 September 1644); "welches drey od. Vier Jarn alt, aber weder redden noch stehen könne." RV 2083: 54r (27 May 1628). See also reference to "Christianishen Eheleuth blüder sohn hanss, seines alters in 15 Jahr." FB 2: 110 (21 January 1654).

131. "one henden und fuessen . . . auch ein klein persone, wie ein Zwerich." FB 1: 219 (3 June 1605). FB 1: 176 (25 January 1600).

132. RV 1980: 36r–v (19 August 1620); FB 2: 89 (22 April 1639).

133. "bis es etwas erstarkt, und zu drauss undergebracht w. können . . . mehr eine melancholy, als etwas and. es sey." The initial petition by Anna Schäferin (RV 2225: 68r; 3 May 1639) was granted conditionally, pending further investigation. Less than two weeks later (RV 2225: 109v; 14 May 1639) came the report from the Saint Egidien chaplain, prompting the council to order the Findel administrator reimbursed for his expenses up to that point and the girl "etwa uff einen thurm zu transferieren."

134. "auch in haupt der gestalt verruckt . . . und sich anfangs im Gebeth und die arbeit fein angelassen, aber weil. sie gantz kein shlaff hat, uf neu sehr verruckt in haupt und also erwiesen, dass hat gefahr bey den findelweisen sie länger nicht zu verbleiben, doch auch nicht allein zu lassen, und einzusperren, ist erthailt, zu trachten, wie sie in dei weiber eissen transfirt, und alda beobachtet, vorderst durch den Medicum

besucht, und Ihr nothwendige arzney, wegen dess Schlaffs, und in andere weg, damit sie wider zu recht und gesundheit gelange, verordnet warden möge." RV 2550: 58v–59r, 68r–v (23 September and 1 October 1663).

135. FKD: 27.7 percent (567) of the 1311 children whose nature of departure from the Findel is known were reclaimed by parents or other adults. Of those, 74.8 percent (424) were picked up by parents, 4.4 percent (25) by other relatives, 3.7 percent (20) by godparents or guardians, and 17.3 percent (98) by adults whose relationship to the child was not specified. The reclaim rates by case type were 57 percent (134 of 235) for fostered children, 20.5 percent (120 of 499) for abandoned children, and 11.9 percent (69 of 577) for orphans.

136. FB 2: 84 (admitted 4 March 1647; picked up on 19 September 1654), 90 (admitted 10 December; picked up in 1650), 90 (admitted 12 December 1640; picked up in 1650), 94 (admitted 13 September 1643; picked up in 1650), 94 (admitted 28 September 1644; picked up on 2 May 1654), 97 (picked up 8 March 1652). FKD: Of the 1426 cases where gender and nature of departure was indicated, 142 of 608 girls (23.7 percent) were reclaimed and 169 of 818 boys (20.7 percent) were picked up. Cf. the reclaim rate in contemporary Spain, where 53.2 percent of males were picked up while only 46.4 percent of females (Sherwood, *Poverty*, 139) and in Lisbon only 8.8 percent were reclaimed by relatives (Sá, "Circulation of Children," 34).

137. FKD: In a sample of 193 cases where the length of time until reclaim was indicated, forty children (20.7 percent) left within one month, 100 (51.8 percent) within three months, 144 (74.6 percent) within a year, and thirteen (6.7 percent) after five years. 78.5 percent (139 of 177) parents and 87.5 percent (7 of 8) guardians or godparents picked up a child within one year. Only 35.7 percent (5 of 14) other relatives picked up children by one year. The long-term reclaim rate for orphans was slightly higher: in a sample of 184 cases, where type and length of time before pick-up was indicated, 65 percent (13 of 20) orphans were picked up in three months or less, 20 percent (4 of 20) after five years.

138. Kurt Wesoly, *Lehrlinge und Handwerksgesellen am Mittelrhein: ihre soziale Lage und ihre Organisation vom 14. bis ins 17. Jahrhundert* (Frankfurt am Main: W. Kramer, 1985), 61–62; Walter Riedl, "Die rechtliche Stellung der Lehrjungen und Gesellen des Nürnberger Handwerks" (J.D. Diss., Friedrich-Alexander Universität Erlangen, 1948), 27. Safley mentions first communion as marking a life-cycle transition for the orphanage's Catholic wards and as especially significant in the commencement of apprenticeships (*Charity and Economy*, 215). I have not found any such corollary in Lutheran Nuremberg.

139. *Mägdezubringerin*. Rüger, *Die Kinderfürsorge*, 123.

140. McClure, *Coram's Children*, 132.

141. Cf. RV 2201: 90r (1 July 1637): "dass der Almoss shreiber und findelvatter sich unterstehen, von den Jenien handwercks leuthen, welche lehriungen aus dem Allmosen oder der findel annehmen." See also Riedl, "Die rechtliche Stellung," 30–31.

142. "Zaiger diss Hans Ritscher is ad 27 July der lengst abgewichenen 1583 Jars von einem Erb. Rath nach dem sein vatter Wendel Rütsch ein Zimmerman gesel in krieg gezogen, und die muter alhie gestorben, neben seinen Bruder Leonhard Rütscher in die Findel vershafft worden, zu erfund hab ich in diessen shein auf sein begeren unter meinen gewöhnlich Pottshafft mit gehandt. Actum Nurmberg Mittwochs den 27 April A[nn]o 97. .[P.S.] mag darzu die zeit ho sovil mir bewust, ehrlich unnd wol verhalten." Loose note between 128 and 129 of FB 1.

143. Rüger, *Die Kinderfürsorge*, 48.

144. FB 1: 66 (admitted on 17 June 1574 and apprenticed on 26 January 1591). See also the examples of a godfather (FB 1: 123, 4 October 1588); FB 1: 143, 27 May 1594), brother (FB 2: 55, 5 June 1634), brother-in-law (FB 2: 70, 10 April 1635), and unspecified male relative (FB 1: 140, 2 November 1593). By contrast, very few Augsburg orphans learned the craft of their fathers. Safley, *Children of the Laboring Poor*, 320.

145. RV 1963: 17r–v (5 May 1619). Gavitt, *Children and Charity*, 249; Safley, *Charity and Economy*, 222.

146. Masons, bookbinders, smiths, potters, wire pullers, spectacle makers. gold and silver smiths (several times), and thimble makers, In eighteenth-century Saxony and seventeenth-century Augsburg, orphans were most often placed with shoemakers, tailors, and table makers. Meumann, *Findelkinder*, 353; Safley, *Charity and Economy*, 226–28; *Children of the Laboring Poor*, 314.

147. The average length of service appears to have shortened during the late sixteenth and early seventeenth centuries. Hanns Planck contracted for five years (FB 1: 119; 11 November 1587), Hans Kopp for six years (FB 1: 108; 15 September 1585), Christoph Resch for three years (StadtAN 10 3/5: 1; 1 May 1601), Bastlein Mey for four years (FB 1: 199; 12 May 1602), and Lienhart Bertholt for four years (StadtAN D 10 3/5: 14).

148. "weil er klein ist" FB 1: 108 (24 August 1592). Durr's contract with a wheelmaker also specified that "gibt Im alletag neben seiner zimlichen speiss und cost ein mass pier und diss jar zu lon 4 fl." FB 1: 0 (Durr was admitted on 4 September 1572 (age not indicated) and apprenticed to a wheelmaker on 19 August 1594). Other Findel youths who were older when placed include twenty-two-year-old Hans Heraldt (1642), and twenty-year-old Anna Luzin (1644). FB 2: 76 (admitted on 21 March 1636, placed on 20 November 1644), 92 (admitted on 5 December 1642, placed on 17 April 1654).

149. FB 1: 98 (13 October 1595). Sometimes apprentices received weekly wages of 5–15 d. per week, totaling about 1 fl. annually. StadtAN 10 3/5: cases of Jörgla Rösner (9; 30 April 1593), Wölfflein Schein (15; 27 May 1594), and Wastla Schwarz (18; 26 October 1600). See also Riedl, "Die rechtliche Stellung," 30–44; Safley, *Charity and Economy*, 221ff.

150. The 1602 Speyer *Schneiderordnung* says that in cases of "poor orphans," two years should be added on to the contract in lieu of *Lehrgeld*. Wesoly, *Lehrlinge und Handwerksgesellen*, 66. For examples, see the 1601 case of *Lehrgeld* of 12 fl. for three years (FB 1: 107; Christoff Pesh); 1601 case of 24 fl. for three years (StadtAN D10/3–4: 112; Steffan Dehn); 1599 case of 28 fl. for an unspecified number of years (FB 1: 108; Michel Schuster) Wesoly (*Lehrlinge und Handwerksgesellen*, 64) found fees ranging from 12 fl. to 28 fl. with an average of 20 fl. in Rhine valley by late sixteenth century. Safley found a range of 3–60 fl. in fees among Augsburg's apprenticed orphans, most between 15 and 30 fl. *Children of the Laboring Poor*, 328–30 (table 15).

151. In 1480, the council offered to pay for a second apprentice for every master who took one from the Findel. Variations on this scheme were offered in 1493 and 1526. In 1633, children of thirty-three families on poor relief given *Lehrgeld*, a practice that appears sporadically in the records of the alms bureau and Findel. Rüger, *Die Kinderfürsorge*, 49. See also Mummenhoff, "Das Findel- und Waisenhaus," 1: 183 on foundations such as the Konrad Hornscher Stiftung and its stipends for selected children entering an apprenticeship or domestic service.

152. See example of Christoff Pesh (FB 1: 107; 1 May 1601) and cf. Safley, *Economy and Charity*, 131, 223.

153. An imperial ordinance of 1548 barred all "dishonorable people" from serving as apprentices, a sweeping proscription that included the children of shepherds, musicians, executioners, gravediggers, night watchmen, and many others. Wesoly, *Lehrlinge und Handwerksgesellen*, 56–60; Riedl," Die rechtliche Stellung," 26–27.

154. StadtAN D10 3/5, 16. Mandates of 4 May 1630, 9 March 1659, and 14 January 1676, cited in Rüger, *Die Kinderfürsorge*, 47. Ekkehard Wiest (*Die Entwicklung des Nürnberger Gewerbes zwischen 1648 und 1806* [Stuttgart, 1968], 77) characterizes post-1648 Nuremberg crafts as governed by "ein kompliziertes System von Restriktionen und Diskriminierungen." See also Riedl, "Die rechtliche Stellung," 24–25; Ernst Mummenhoff, *Handwerker in der deutschen Vergangenheit* (Leipzig: E. Diederichs, 1901), 2ff.; and Walker, *German Home Towns*, 102–7, on the moralism of German guilds.

155. "ob die ienige findelkinder, von denen man nicht gewiss weiss, ob sie ehelichen od. unehelichen geborn worden, auff den handwercken nicht passirt, od. wie es damit gehalten worde." RV 2349: 50v (7 September 1648).

156. FB 2: 122 (23 September 1664).

157. Twenty-one illegitimate Findel boys were placed during 1711 to 1772. Roetzer, "Die Delikte der Abtreibung," 176–77; Schubert, *Arme Leute*, 133.

158. "Auff der voerordneten herren zue handwerckhs Rug bericht, dass die handwercken keine hiesige burgerskinder zu LehrJung bekommen können, und dahero getrungen worden, nach frembden Jungen zu trachte." RV 2126: 106r–v (26 September 1631). See also Riedl, "Die rechtliche Stellung," 23.

159. See the example of citizen child Matthes Bauman, who was placed immediately with a goldsmith in 1633. FB 2: 49 (13 May 1633).

160. Wesoly, *Lehrlinge und Handwerksgesellen*, 69.

161. FKD: 238 of 1311 (18.2 percent) cases where child's nature of departure was indicated. Among older orphans such as Susanna and Eberhardt, the placement rate rises to one in three, though this figure is skewed by the exceptional number of placements amidst the Findel overcrowding of 1635–36; 191 of 577 (33.5 percent) cases where orphans' nature of departure was indicated. This rate is slightly lower than Augsburg's 40.1 percent rate, based on six decade samples during 1580–1770 in Augsburg: 439 of 1094 orphans. Safley, *Charity and Economy*, 235. In *Children of the Laboring Poor* (299), this figure is revised to 47.4 percent of all orphans.

162. FKD: Based on 187 cases of known placement, of which 35 were for girls and 152 for boys. Twenty-seven Findel youths were placed between 1647 and 1654, the period of the Schiers' residency. During only one fiscal year between 1557 and 1670, were significantly more Findel girls placed than boys: twelve girls and two boys were placed in 1572–73. There is no apparent explanation for the anomaly. FB 1: loose note between pages 49 and 50.

Based on Safley's six decade-long samples from 1580–1770, the Augsburg orphanage placed 174 girls (19.1 percent of total girls admitted, with peak of 35 percent during the 1680s) and 265 boys (44.1 percent). This amounts to an average annual placement of 2.9 girls and 4.3 boys (*Charity and Economy*, 235). Meumann, on the other hand, found that boys fared only slightly better than girls in placement (52 percent versus 45 percent) in his eighteenth-century sample of 108 placed orphans (*Findelkinder*, 353–55).

163. FKD: 63.2 percent (74 of 117) cases in the sample occurred between 1635 and 1640. See the exceptions of Maria Schmidtin, placed with a goldspinner in 1636, and Gertraut Sauberin, placed with a silver and gold worker in 1643. FB 2: 82 (17 June 1636), 93 (17 April 1643). The Augsburg orphanages saw a decline in placement

numbers by at least half in all crafts but food and decorative arts, from 1610 to 1720. Safley, *Charity and Economy*, 224.

164. Griffiths, *Youth and Authority*, 327–29, 334.
165. Riedl, "Die rechtliche Stellung," 33–34. Some of the orphanages and hospitals examined by Terpstra had two-month probationary periods ("Making a Living,," 1069).
166. *Rugamtordnung*: "Wie es mit Leerjungen uff den Hanndtwercken gehalten warden soll," (early seventeenth century), cited in Rüger, *Die Kinderfürsorge*, 18. See also Riedl, "Die rechtliche Stellung," 35–36.
167. RV 1319: 3r, 1320: 26v, 29v (20 July, 6 and 7 September 1570). Cf. similar case of beaten apprentice and council's decision "eine empfindliche straff zuffzulegen, damit andere maister ursach haben, ihre lehrjungen, etwas gellinde zu practirn." RV 2510; 84r–v (3 October 1660). McClure (*Coram's Children*, 150) found the same quick action among authorities of the London Foundling Hospital.
168. Thirty-four Findel children were known to have run away from an apprenticeship or domestic service position between 1557 and 1670, almost half (14) during the crisis year of 1634–35 alone, with twelve from one large group admitted on 5 June 1534. Only six runaways were noted before that date, though there were probably more that simply weren't known to Findel authorities. FB 1: 108 (Michl Schuster); FB 2: 48 (Hans Schmidt), 53 (Hanns Rost), 53 (Mattheus Hoffensummer), 54 (Jörg Kreuselman), 54 (Hanns Cunzman), 55 (Leonhart Seushal), 56 (Lorenz Mülfriz), 56 (Hanns Segenstein), 57 (Thomas N.), 58 (Hanns Rüppel), 58 (Paulus Weisshamer), 64 (Catharina Mollebreünin), 65 (Hieronymuss Giesswein), 73 (Jörg Denerla), 74 (Adam Wild). 75 (Ballus Fisher), 75 (Lorenz Albrecht), 82 (Margreta Geissbärtin), 82 (Maria N.).
169. Jochum was accepted into the Findel on 6 March 1583 with his sister, Saloma (who died on 22 November 1595), and apprenticed on 29 June 1595. FB 1: 96.
170. FB 1: 134 (23 September 1592, placed 13 August 1592, replaced 20 February 1592).
171. Cf. similar complaints by Hannover pastor Philipp Gerhard Scholvia in 1729 testament that despite all of his efforts at placing boys during the previous forty years, many don't finish and run away, often as soldiers. Meumann, *Findelkinder*, 355–56.
172. "ist ohne Weg gelauffen." FB 2: 64 (5 June 1634).
173. Very few deaths during apprenticeships were officially noted in the Findel register: FB 1: 79 (admitted 6 October 1575, apprenticed 11 June 1595, died in 1597). FB 2: 9 (9 December 1615), 57 (5 June 1634), 82 (17 June 1637), 121 (admitted 4 April 1664). My overall failure rate is based on the estimate of Griffiths (*Youth and Authority*, 330) that as many as one in ten apprentices and maids died during service, and also on the 34 known instances of runaways among at least 409 placements (not including multiple placements of the same children). There were both more placements and more runaways that were not recorded. Successful placement rates could also fluctuate considerably from year to year. In 1798 the schoolmaster of the London Foundling Hospital reported that only one in seven placements "turned out ill," yet less than a decade later a new report found that 40 percent of the boys that year had either run away or been sent off to sea. McClure, *Coram's Children*, 150–51.
174. Fifteen of thirty-four. FB 1: 82 (Lienhart Hawenstein; admitted 15 November 1576, placed 10 May 1591, ran away 1 November 1591, placed again 6 December 1591), 91 (Wolff Baumhawer; admitted 21 August 1581, placed 28 November 1587, runs back to Findel, re-placed 10 September 1589), 111 (Henssla Kumpass; admitted 5 January 1583, placed 5 June 1592, ran away, placed again 2 April 1593), 134 (Enderla Pilman; admitted 23 September 1571, placed 13 August 1592, placed again

20 February 1593); FB 2: 55 (Michel Müllner; admitted 5 June 1634, placed 7 July 1635, runs away and re-placed), 58 (Hanns Sipt, admitted 5 June 1634, placed, runs away, re-placed), 69 (Nicolaus Beuerlein; admitted 17 June 1637, placed 25 February 1650, runs away, replaced on 10 February 1651), 92 (Jacob Altreiss; admitted 24 May 1642, placed 26 May 1642, runs away, replaced 18 January 1644), 99 (Valentin Kostner; admitted 8 May 1644, placed, returns and stays at Findel); StadtAN D 10 3–5: 1 (Christoph Reich; placed 29 August 1600, replaced on 1 May 1601), 3 (Hennsa Schleiffer; placed on 19 April 1596; replaced on 4 June 1599), 7 (Wolffla Barmhauer; placed, returns to Findel on 28 November 1587, replaced 10 September 1589), 7 (Hensa Plannckh; placed 3 October 1596, replaced). Cf. a similar pattern in Safley's Augsburg sample, where 407 orphans required a second placement and 68 a third. *Children of the Laboring Poor*, 317.

175. FB 2: 69 (admitted 17 June 1637, placed with goldsmith 27 February 1650, replaced with dyer 10 February 1651). FB 1: 111 (5 June 1592 and 2 April 1593).
176. For example, Lienhart Hawenstein ran back to the Findel from his apprenticeship but after a month returned to the same position. FB 1: 82 (admitted 15 November 1576, placed 10 May 1591, runs back to Findel on 1 November 1591, returns to position 6 December 1591).
177. FB 1: 156 (17 February 1597); FB 2: 82 (17 June 1636) 93 (8 May 1644). See the similar case of Oswald Rau (FB 2: 58; admitted 5 June 1634).
178. Barbara Huberin spent 36 years in Findel, Elisabeth Engelmayerin 30 years, Anna Wickin 27 years, Michael Salomon 17 years and, Christof Brabi 32 years, in each instance punctuated by death as a young adult. FB 2: 1 (admitted 13 July 1615, dies 6 March 1651), 76 (admitted 14 April 1654; dies 1 October 1684), 92 (admitted 4 August 1642, dies 22 January 1670), 127 (admitted 29 June 1668, dies 17 December 1685), 112 (admitted 5 December 1654, dies 19 January 1686).
179. FB 2: 110. Admitted on 23 February 1653 at the age of four; "ad. 27 Marti 1699 in der Nacht nach 5 der grössen Uhr ist diese Maria Magdalena Liesserin seel vershieden und darauf christlich zur Erden bestattet worden."
180. The same is true at Augsburg, where Safley says "Indeed the orphanages of Augsburg stood behind their orphans throughout their adult lives" (*Charity and Economy*, 259). See several examples in Augsburg of orphanages officials helping young journeymen get started, not just with the necessary paperwork attesting to legitimate birth and the apprentice contract, but with cash as well (137–38, 260–61, table 8.1, 270–72 (table 8.2); also idem, *Children of the Laboring Poor*, 214.
181. StadtAN D 10/3–5: 7. FB 2: 126: admitted at age seven on 21 February 1668, placed with a silversmith in 1687 and a bellmaker on 23 November 1690, returned to the Findel on 19 June 1692.
182. Safley, *Charity and Economy*, 268; also *Children of the Laboring Poor*, 1–4.
183. "ist denselben aber zu den S[to]y beckin kommen unnd gebettelt, da hat sie im ein brot geben, das hat er nicht nemen, sondern ein semmel haben wollen, seithenn haben wir uber alle auff gestelte kundschafften das wenigste nicht mehr von Ime erfahren können." FB 1: 144 (20 July 1594).
184. "Ist nichts mehr von ihm gehört word." FB 2: 53 (5 June 1634).
185. "mütwilliger weiss, ohn ainige Ursach auss der fundel entloffe, man hat in fleissig zum schreiben gehalten, weil er Brechenhafftig ist, hat man nit d. Zeit, an Ei[m]ess Schriebers statt Bräuchen wöllen, also wie der Jacob Seliger." FB 1: loose note between 141 and 142.

186. FB 2: 65 (30 December 1634). "drotzieher . . . büchsenmacher . . . aber kein gutt gethan darvon gelauffen." FB 2: 53 (5 June 1634).

187. FB 2: 112 (1667).

188. FB 1: 66 (Hans Jacob Halle; admitted 17 June 1574; apprenticed on 26 January 1591), 118 (Hennsa Hess; admitted on 5 September 1587 and apprenticed on 11 June 1595); FB 2: 108 (Hans Paulus Pittelmayr; admitted on 25 May 1652 and apprenticed on 1 August 1663), 112 (Adam Diez; admitted 28 March 1655 and apprenticed 22 August 1659), 112 (Benedict Deckhert; admitted 18 March 1656 and apprenticed on 13 July 1665), 113 (Georg Mauer; admitted 27 August 1657 and apprenticed on 4 February 1667), 118 (Georg Hopff; admitted on 22 March 1662 and apprenticed on 6 May 1667), 129 (Martin Mauer; admitted on 8 October 1668 and apprenticed in 1672). On relative successes, see also McClure, *Coram's Children*, 240; and Safley, *Children of the Laboring Poor*, 397–436.

189. FB 2: 41, 75.

190. For a brief period at the beginning of the seventeenth century, we find occasional mention of Findel boys who were registered as Nuremberg citizens with the usual fee of 2–4 fl waived. Hans Jacob Halle not only became a master but also a citizen. FB 1: 66 (admitted 17 June 1574; apprenticed on 26 January 1591; citizen in 1601). See also ASB: 308: 142v (Michael Wolf and Bastian Moy; 23 January 1604), 143r (Jacob Nürmberger and Jobst Klein; 18 February 1604), 151v (Jacob Dorsch; 4 February 1610), 158r (Niclas Prückner and Stoffel Höltzlein; 12 March 1617). By the 1640s, the annual number of successful applicants for citizenship had dropped off by more than 80 percent, with each claiming at least 100–200 fl. property. The number of new citizens began to rise again during the 1650s, but there is no mention of any Findel boy achieving this status in Nuremberg. Georg Mauer later became a compassmaker master and citizen in Augsburg. FB 2: 129 (admitted 8 October 1668).

191. Strauss, *Nuremberg*, 150.

192. The Innocenti of Florence permitted the creation of such funds but unlike the municipal Monte della Doti, did not return the money to a girl's family upon her premature death. Gavitt, *Charity and Children*, 79.

193. This was already referred to as "an old custom" in 1493. Roetzer, "Die Delikte der Abtreibung," 8; Rüger, *Die Kinderfürsorge*, 84.

194. By contrast, in institutions for older girls, such as S. Niccolo's Conservatory in Florence, at least 13.2 percent of the 1570 cohort and 24 percent of the 1579 cohort left the conservatory to marry. That figure might be higher still, since the immediate fate of 32.1 percent of the 1570 cohort and 13 percent of the 1579 cohort is unknown. The Pietá of Florence, an institution more comparable to Nuremberg's Findel, did not have any members of its 1555 cohort go directly into marriage. Poor conservatories in Italy had very small dowry funds. Terpstra, "Making a Living," 1070–71.

195. McClure, *Coram's Children*, 237; Gavitt, *Charity and Children*, 259ff.

196. Cf. a rare early mention of an alumnus's marriage: FB 2: 119 (Hans Schnitzer; admitted 13 November 1587).

197. Safley argues, however, that Augsburg's city fathers would have viewed their placement of 75.7 percent of surviving orphans as a successful fulfillment of their responsibility to provide children with *Nahrung* ("living"). *Children of the Laboring Poor*, 409.

198. Conradt Krafft "ist zu Wehrd an die kus werber verquartirt und wider seinen willen gleich des andern tags fruh ehe man vor der kriegstuben hült haben könen, fortgeführt worden." FB 2: 116 (Conradt Kabes; admitted 14 March 1659 and appren-

ticed in 1666), 117 (Andreas Krafft; admitted on 11 April 1661 and apprenticed on 28 October 1668), 120 (Georg Schiller; admitted on 27 March 1663 and apprenticed on 1 September 1667), 121 (Basilius Seyer; admitted on 23 August 1663 and apprenticed on 1 May 1678), 121 (Sebalt Maister; admitted on 2 November 1663 and apprenticed on 8 September 1667), 127 (Gustavius Phillippus Dombach; admitted on 11 September 1668 at the age of ten and date of apprenticeship not indicated).

199. Safley, *Children of the Laboring Poor,* 387.

200. "eine unnüze dirrn, welche die straiffer gehendet und geshmehet." StadtAN D1 563: Stadalmosenamt Ansag of 11 April 1668, no. 1. Wahlman entered the Findel on 16 March 1648 at the unprecedented age of eighteen and was released to a linen weaver (*Schwabenweber*) on 14 January 1656. FB 2: 99

201. Bock, "Nürnberger Spitznamen von 1200 bis 1800—Nachlese," 18.

202. FB 1: 96 (admitted 6 March 1583 and apprenticed on 29 June 1595). Only 28 in Safley's Augsburg sample of 5734 orphans (0.4 percent) were known to have been convicted of a crime. *Children of the Laboring Poor,* 363. Cf. the failures described in McClure, *Coram's Children,* 238–40.

203. FB 2: 120 (admitted 9 June 1663).

204. FB 2: 93 (both admitted on 17 April 1643; Christof Wilhem was placed in 1655 and Gerdtraut in 1656), 99 (both admitted 23 March 1648, Christoph was placed in 1654 and Anna on 10 August 1656).

205. FB 2: 92 (both Wiechin girls were admitted on 4 August 1642; Regina died on 15 March 1643 and Anna on 22 January 1670); 100 (both Hirshmänin girls were admitted 18 June 1648, Ursula Susanna died on 11 April 1651 and Anna Maria on 24 February 1652).

206. FB 2: 97 (both Lorenz and Helena Sabina Schmitt were admitted 4 March 1647, Lorenz's date of death unknown, and Helena Sabina picked up on 19 September 1654); 106 (both Elisabeth and Hans Melchior Holstein were admitted on 1 October 1651; they were both picked up by their father on 8 March 1652).

207. FKD: Based on a sample of 1311 cases where the nature of departure was indicated, 760 (58 percent) died, 299 (22.8 percent) were reclaimed, 238 (18 percent) were placed, and fourteen (1.1 percent) ran away or were released on their own recognizance. Augsburg has significant cohort, about one in five, who were simply released on their own recognizance. Safley, *Charity and Economy,* 235.

208. FKD: death for 70.1 percent (350 of 499) abandonment cases where the nature of departure was indicated, reclaim for 57.1 percent (134 of 235) foster children, and placement of 33.1 percent (191 of 577) orphans.

209. More than one-third of the girls at a Florentine conservatory died while still in state care during the seventeenth and eighteenth centuries. There was a marked difference in the fate of girls whether orphaned. Sonnino, "Between the Home and the Hospice," in Henderson and Wall, *Poor Women and Children,* 104, 114. By the late sixteenth century, a boy of fifteen could expect to live to at least fifty-seven and a girl of the same age to at least thirty-eight. Pfister, "Population of Late Medieval and Early Modern Germany," 54.

210. Pick-up rates for boys and girls, virtually identical before the 1630s, also shifted to the disadvantage of girls from this time on. FKD: Between 1570 and 1629, 82 boys were recorded as reclaimed, compared to 75 girls. By the time of Eberhardt and Susanna, when reclaims had become much less common, boys were picked up at three times the rate of girls. In 1630–69, 24 boys were picked up while only 8 girls

were—much too small of a sample to be considered significant. Cf. similar conclusions about the gender disparity in Safley, *Children of the Laboring Poor*, 445.

211. Magdalena Erhardin was born on 2 February 1634 to Nicolaus Erhard, ringmaker, and his wife Magdalena. Hans Schwartz and Magdalena Erhardin were married on 11 September 1654. Maria Magdalena Schwartzin was born on 30 May 1655, and her sister Anna Catherina on 7 November 1656. Hans Schwartz was buried on 5 May 1657 Eberhardt Schier and Magadalena Schwartzin were married on 12 October 1658. LKAN L-56 Proclamationen, 1646–68, Saint Lorenz und Saint Sebaldus: 375; LKAN S-8 Taufen, 1632–54, Saint Sebald: 93; LKAN L-41: Trauungen, 1609–63, Saint Lorenz: 607; LKAN L-24 Taufen, 1646–67, Saint Lorenz, 459, 473; LKAN L-81 Beerdigungen, 1637–67, Saint Lorenz, 221.

212. Hans Schörbel's first marriage, to Anna Wagnerin, was on 29 May 1654. Susanna's stepchildren Johannes and Georgius were born on 28 February 1657 and 8 October 1663, respectively; twins Andreas and Anna were born on 8 October 1663 and died on 19 October and 1 November. Anna Schörblin was buried on 28 October 1665. Susanna Schierin married Hans Schörbel on 19 November 1666 in the Nuremberg suburb of Mögeldorf. Nicolaus Schörbel was born on 18 January 1668, Jacob on 16 July 1672, and Nicolaus on 3 May 1675. The only child whose death is recorded in Johannes, who was buried on 28 July 1674. LKAN M-5 Taufen/Trauungen, 1654–84, St. Leonhard (Mögeldorf): 2, 35, 53, 100, 110, 166, 230, 277; LKAN M-9 Beerdingungen, 1653–1713 Nbg Mögeldorf: 102v, 103v, 106v; LKAN L-56 Proclamationen, 1646–68, Saint Lorenz and Saint Sebaldus: 657.

213. Admitted on 11 May 1660 (RV 2479: 45r; FB 2: 115). Only two other older children known to have been anonymously abandoned survived to job placement as a teenager: Hensla Schenck, admitted on 23 June 1582 (FB 1: 82); and Anna Margreta Rumradin, admitted 3 November 1655 (FB 2: 106).

CHAPTER SIX

1. In the words of Nicholas Terpstra, "And while we look at the variety of shelters that stood in for family and that became models in one way or another for institutional orphanages, we should never forget that the great majority of these children were simply absorbed without a trace into households of grandparents, uncles, aunts, and siblings." *Abandoned Children*, 9–10.

2. I am paraphrasing Grassby, *Kinship and Capitalism*, 388.

3. Cf. criticisms of the microhistorical approach leveled at Robert Darnton and Natalie Zemon Davis in Giovanni Levi, "On Microhistory," in *New Perspectives*, ed. Peter Burke (University Park: Pennsylvania State University Press, 1992), 93–113. See also Sabean, *Property, Production, and Family*, 7–12, on the question of typicality for this type of approach.

4. See especially Crawford, *Blood, Bodies and Families*, passim; Capp, *When Gossips Meet*, esp. 365–73; and Ulrich, *Midwife's Tale*, chap. 7.

5. *Power Elites and State Building*, ed. Reinhard, 9.

6. Cf. the conclusion of Mitterauer (*Ledige Mütter*, 50ff.): "Die Höhe des Heiratalters erscheint als der beste generelle Indikator" of high illegitimacy.

7. See especially Claude Delasselle, "Les enfants abandonnés à Paris au XIIIe siècle," *Annales* (1975): 208; Jean-Claude Peyronnet, "Les enfants abandonnés et leurs nourrices à Limoges au XVIIIe siècle," *Revue d'Histoire moderne et contemporaine* (1976): 425–27; Sherwood, *Poverty in Eighteenth-Century Spain*, 113–14; and Katherine A.

Lynch, *Family, Class, and Ideology in Early Industrial France, 1830–1848* (Madison: University of Wisconsin, 1988), 125–26. David Ransel and Rachel Fuchs even refer to abandoned babies as "commodities," that are balanced with a household's other needs and assets. Fuchs, "Child Abandonment in European History," 11.

8. The numbers are admittedly small (particularly for known infanticides) and there is not a proportionate increase or decrease in the two phenomena, for example, between 1575 and 1590, when anonymous abandonments drop from 10 to 3.6 per year and known infanticides increase from 0.6 to 1.8 per year.

9. In the Basque parishes of Asteasu and Villafranca, the combined illegitimacy rate for 1560–89 was 17.6 percent (compared to less than 1 percent of all baptisms in nearby La Bañesa [Léon] from 1650 to 1700), with no reported foundlings (compared to an annual average of almost 500 foundling admissions, sometimes near 1,000, to La Inclusa in Madrid). Lola Valverde, "Illegitimacy and the Abandonment of Children in the Basque Country," in Henderson and Wall, *Poor Women and Children*, 51–53. See also Hunecke, *Findelkinder*, 27; Kertzer, *Sacrificed for Honor*, 25–28; and Jean Meyer, "Illegitimates and Foundlings in Pre-industrial France," in Laslett, *Bastardy*, 251–53, as well as Laslett's introduction to the volume (3ff.) on the structural patterns of illegitimacy over the course of the past five centuries.

10. See above, figure 6.4.

11. Kertzer, *Family Life*, 177. In Spain this was fuelled in part by a much greater number of legitimate children being abandoned to the foundling home. Sherwood, *Poverty in Eighteenth-century Spain*, 111.

12. By the end of the seventeenth century, the illegitimacy rate had risen back up to 5 percent of all births in Nuremberg and as much as 10 percent in other German lands; by the end of the eighteenth century the rate soared to 20–30 percent in some areas. Nearby Würzburg, with an illegitimacy rate similar to that of Nuremberg at the beginning of the eighteenth century, witnessed a tripling of its proportion of births outside of wedlock, from one in 37 births during 1701–25 to one in 13.5 births in the city and one in seven births in the countryside. Mitterauer, *Ledige Mütter*, 29–35; Schubert, *Arme Leute*, 111, 131.

13. This was noted by the two nineteenth-century pioneers of historical child abandonment: S. Hügel, *Die Findelhäuser und das Findelwesen Europas, ihre Geschichte, Gesetzgebung, Verwaltung, Statistik und Reform* (Vienna, 1863), 337ff.; Léon Lallemand, *Histoire des Enfants Abandonnés et Délaissés* (Paris: A. Picard, 1885), 643 ff.

14. Viazzo, "Family Structures," 34–35. Gavitt proposes "that where patrilineal inheritance was the most rigid, the south of Europe, both abandonment and institutions modeled on the Innocenti thrived," but there were many parts of northern Europe where patrilineal inheritance prevailed where this pattern was not found. Gavitt, "'Perche non avea chi la ghovernasse,'" 85.

15. David Kertzer, for instance, notes that by the early nineteenth century, one in five babies was abandoned in the Catholic cities of Madrid, Dublin, and Warsaw, one in three in Milan, and as many as one in two in Vienna, while during the same time period, hardly any were abandoned in the Protestant nations of Prussia, England, Switzerland, and the United States. Kertzer's religious argument is twofold, stressing both the tradition of individual (as opposed to communal) responsibility for illegitimate children in Protestant areas, as well as the "new" emphasis on "family values" starting with the Council of Trent in the mid-sixteenth century and intensifying during the nineteenth century in Italian states, with the introduction of various "pro-family" laws. Kertzer, *Sacrificed for Honor*, 9–18. Eugenio Sonnino similarly

connects rise of closed almshouses in seventeenth-century Italy with the spread of the Counter-Reformation. Eugenio Sonnino, "Between the Home and the Hospice: The Plight of Girl Orphans in Seventeenth- and Eighteenth-century Rome," in *Poor Women and Children*, ed. Henderson and Wall, 96. On German anonymous abandonment and infanticide practices, see especially Schulte, *Village in Court*; also Hunecke, *Findelkinder*, 19.

16. *La ruota* (Italian)—also known as *la tour* (French), *il torno* (Spanish), *la roda* (Portuguese)—first appeared in Bologna during the late sixteenth century and spread over the next two centuries throughout Italy, France, Spain, and Portugal, with the universal effect of higher foundling admissions. By 1800 almost 1200 cities and villages in Italy alone had wheels. The admissions trend began to reverse in French cities during the 1830s to 1860s, and in Italian cities from the 1860s on, declining to one half of the 1800 peak by 1888 and none by 1923. The last to close in Europe were Greek and Spanish localities during the 1930s. Kertzer, *Sacrificed for Honor*, 85, 105, 154–69; Hunecke, *Findelkinder*, 36, 91; Pier Paolo Viazzo, Mario Borolotto, and Andrea Zanotto, "Five Centuries of Foundling History in Florence: Changing Patterns of Abandonment, Care and Mortality," in Painter-Brick, *Abandoned Children*, 70; David L. Ransel, *Mothers of Misery: Child Abandonment in Russia* (Princeton: Princeton University Press, 1988), 62–83.

17. Even Brian Pullan, who presents an otherwise nuanced and circumspect argument, proceeds from this common assumption (*Orphans and Foundlings in Early Modern Europe* [Reading: University of Reading Press, 1989], 6ff.). The largely demographically driven expansion of European foundling homes during the nineteenth century is likewise often viewed through the prism of rationalist reform ambitions and governmental concerns about the unruly lower classes. See especially the discussion in David I. Kerzer, "The Lives of Foundlings in Nineteenth-century Italy," in Painter-Brick, *Abandoned Children*, 41–69; also Louise Tilly, Joan W. Scott, and Miriam Cohen, "Women's Work and European Fertility Patterns," *Journal of Interdisciplinary History* 6, no. 3 (1976): 447–76; and W. R. Lee, "Bastardy and the Socioeconomic Structure of South Germany," *Journal of Interdisciplinary History* 7 (1976–77): 403ff. Historians of the nineteenth century also look to the population surge in Europe from 1750 to 1850 that coincided with growth in the number and size of foundling homes and similar institutions as well as the effects of industrialization on migration patterns. Volker Hunecke, the historian of the Milan Foundling home, actually writes of two stages of differing levels of expansion: one from the Renaissance to Enlightenment, the other from 1750 to 1900 (*Findelkinder*, 156).

18. In Milan, the Ospedal Maggiore was admitting about 100 foundlings per year in 1471, over 1,000 by 1508, dipping down to some 400 in 1660, then 800 in 1780 over 2,600 per year in the 1830s, peaking at 4,700 per year in 1860; ten years later down to 2,000. Hunecke, *Findelkinder*, 56.

19. Gavitt, "Perche non avea chi la ghovenasse,'" 84; Gager, *Blood Ties*, 120, 145; Boswell, *Kindness of Strangers*, 15; Kertzer, *Sacrificed for Honor*, 10; Hunecke, *Findelkinder*, 34.

20. Ransel, *Mothers of Misery*, 294; Kertzer, *Sacrificed for Honor*, 7.

21. These are especially the arguments of Richard Trexler, John Boswell, and Rachel Fuchs. Sá even argues that the entire foundling apparatus was predicated on high infant mortality, since no state had the financial or other resources to care for all of the infants admitted to foundling homes. Sá, "Circulation of Children," 27ff.

22. I make a similar argument about Nuremberg's discipline- and workhouse in "Escape from the Great Confinement," 308–45.

23. See a similar correlation between city and foundling home population in Rome (Eugenio Sonnino, "Between the Home and the Hospice," in Henderson and Wall, *Poor Women and Children*, 97–100).

24. There were 7,924 baptisms in 1610–14; 5,433 in 1665–69 (Rüger, *Die Kinderfürsorge*, 126–29, table 1; FKD: 223 Findel admission 1610–14; 49 for 1665–69).

25. Cf. RV 1897: 43r (11 June 1614) and RV 1897: 46r (14 June 1614). Cf. acceptance of a female day laborer's ten-year-old daughter into the Findel but clear directions to guards in Steinbühl on tracking down and arresting the child's father. RV 1868: 24v (3 April 1612).

26. FKD: 9 of 61 abandonment cases (15 percent) where the abandoner was identified were turned down between 1610 and 1614 and 11 of 102 (10.8 percent) from 1615–34. Fourteen of forty-nine foster petitions (28. percent) between 1610 and 1635, compared to seven of ninety petitions (7.7 percent) between 1560 and 1614. In both types of cases, it must be noted, the numbers involved are relatively small.

27. FKD: 3650 of 3935 (93 percent) overall acceptance rate, 576 of 605 (95 percent) for fosters, 1262 of 1340 (94 percent) for abandonments, and 1361 of 1500 (91 percent) for orphans. Orphans were overrepresented in rejections (57 percent of total vs. 42 percent of admissions) while both foster (25 percent vs. 10 percent) and anonymous abandonments (10 percent vs. 19 percent) were underrepresented. Orphans had the lowest acceptance rate because of 1632–36 refusals, which represented over one-third of all rejections from 1557 to 1670. If these years are removed from the sample, the overall acceptance rate for the Findel rises to 94.1 percent. 98 of all applications for admission were turned down from 1632–38, 34.4 percent of a total of 285 rejections from 1557–1670. If the years of 1632–36 are excluded from the sample, 2968 of 3155 petitions (94.1 percent) were granted.

28. FKD: Beginning in 1633, the annual rates of admission were 55 percent (30 of 67) in 1633, 86 percent in 1634 (200 of 233), 85 percent (83 of 98) in 1635, 97 percent (95 of 98) in 1636, 100 percent (95 of 95) in 1637, 88 percent (15 of 17) in 1638, and 100 percent (12 of 12) in 1639. 1632 saw 6 of 11 foster petitions rejected, but all 22 foster petitions for the next six years granted. During the period of 1633–35, the inner council turned away seventy-eight applicants, all but two of them orphans. This three-year period witnessed more than one-quarter of all rejections for 1557–1669. Only 1633 was really low (55 percent) the rest of the 1630s hovered at 85–100 percent.

29. For a fuller description of early modern bureaucratic momentum, see my "Escape from the Great Confinement," 317–19 and 341–45.

30. Even David Ransel, who describes the irony of Russian governmental intervention "intended to save the lives of young children end[ing up] as a conduit of disease and death," concedes that the new programs did contribute to the growth of pediatric medicine in Russia as well as greater training of midwives and an overall increased awareness of hygiene among the general populace. *Mothers of Misery*, 290–93.

31. Beier believes that Tudor and Stuart officials—unlike their French counterparts—did make effective responses to serious problems with their poor-relief programs. Beier, *Masterless Men*, 175.

32. Nuremberg's Findel rarely accepted more than five foundlings per year after 1640 and none after 1831. Meanwhile, the smaller German cities of Hildesheim and Kassel each saw on average forty anonymous abandonments per year during the eighteenth century. Meumann, *Findelkinder*, 143–44. On the question of overall German exceptionalism on the foundling question, see Mummenhoff, "Das Findel- und Waisen-

haus," 2: 96–97; also Hunecke, *Findelkinder*, 133; Mummenhoff, "Das Findel- und Waisenhaus," 1: 243; Kertzer, "Lives of Foundlings," 41–42.

33. Boswell, *Kindness of Strangers*, 26.
34. See, for instance, the variety of institutional responses to child abandonment within Renaissance Florence alone: Terpstra, *Abandoned Children*, 187–244.
35. Thomas Safley has reached a similar conclusion: "Contrary to the emphasis of most modern scholarship, state intervention immediately altered neither the structure nor the foundation of charity, because charity drew its inspiration from social and economic realities rather than political or ideological impulses" (*Charity and Economy*, 50).

BIBLIOGRAPHY

MANUSCRIPT SOURCES

Bayerisches Staatsarchiv Nürnberg (StaatsAN)

10a	Heilig-Geist Spital, Akten
15a	A-Laden, Akten (pre-1558)
16a	B-Laden, Akten (1550–1648)
17a	C-Laden, Akten (1648–1806)
18a	D-Laden, Akten (fifteenth–eighteenth century)
25	Kirchen und Vormundamt, Akten (1776–1808)
25a	Nürnberg Lateinschulen, Akten (1620–1808)
44a	Losungsamt, Akten, 5 volumes
51	Ratschlagbücher (1442–1730)
52a	Handschriften
52b	Amts- und Standbücher (including Achtbücher), 350 volumes
53	Finanzbücher: Findelamt
58	Karten und Pläne
60a	Verlässe des inneren Rates (1449, 1452, 1458–61, 1471, 1474–1808), 4,456 volumes
60b	Ratsbücher (1400–15, 1441–1619), 74 volumes
60c	Verlässe des inneren Rates zum Losungsamt (1528–1647), 11 volumes
60d	Verlässe der Herrn Älteren (1543–1807), 75 volumes
61a	Briefbücher des inneren Rates (1404–1738), 350 volumes
61b	Briefbücher der Herrn Älteren (1576–89; 1603–21), 4 volumes
62	Ämterbüchlein (1396–1476, 1476–1806), 325 volumes
63Ia	Mandate in Bänden gesammelt (1491–1806), 20 volumes
63II	Mandate (Lose) (1497–1807)
65	Nürnberg Totengeläuterbücher u. Ratstotenbücher (1461–1522, 1564–71, 1573–1674, 1686–1743, 1775–91), 54 volumes
72	Landalmosenamt
77	Stadtgericht, Prozessakten (16th–18th century)
78a	Geburts u. Lehrbriefe (1598–1768)
88	Justiz u. Polizei

90   Stiftungen
94b   Losungsamt: Strafbücher (1597–1806)

Landeskirchliches Archiv Nürnberg (LKAN)

L-23   Taufen, 1627–45, Saint Lorenz
L-24   Taufen, 1646–67, Saint Lorenz
L-41   Trauungen, 1609–1663, Saint Lorenz
L-52   Proclamatinen, 1602–10, Saint Sebaldus and Saint Lorenz
L-56   Proclamationen, 1646–1668, Saint Lorenz und Saint Sebaldus
L-81   Beerdigungen, 1637–1667, Saint Lorenz
L-82   Beerdigungen, 1668–1702, Saint Lorenz
LH-56   Beerdigungen, 1703–1810, Saint Leonhard (register only; burial book lost)
M-5   Taufen/Trauungen, 1654–84, Saint Leonhard (Mögeldorf)
M-9   Beerdigungen, 1653–1713 Nürnberg Mögeldorf
S-8   Taufen, 1632–54, Saint Sebaldus
S23   Trauungen, 1587–1616 Saint Sebaldus

Stadtarchiv Nürnberg (StadtAN)

A4   Karten und Pläne (ca. sixteenth–twentieth century)
A6   Mandate und Ordnungen
A7   Stiche und Drucke
A7/I   Porträts
B1   Bauamt (fifteenth–nineteenth century)
B1/I   Bauamt, Amstbücher (fifteenth –19th century)
B 1/II   Bauamt, Akten (sixteenth–nineteenth century)
B 1/III   Bauamt, Rechnungen (sixteenth–nineteenth century)
B2   Bürger und Unbürgeramt
B5   Kirchen-, Grabstätten-, und Vormundamt
B11   Ratskanzlei (sixteenth–eighteenth century)
B12   Rugamt (sixteenth–nineteenth century)
B13   Schöffenamt (eighteenth and nineteenth century)
B14   Stadtgericht, Gerichte (fifteenth–eighteenth century)
B14/I   LL Libri litteratum, Grundverbriefungsbücher (1475–1770)
B14/III   Sonstige Gerichtsbücher (fifteenth–eighteenth century)
B14/IV   Stadtgericht, Akten (sixteenth–eighteenth century)
B16   Pflegamt Wöhrd (fifteenth–nineteenth century)
B32   Land- und Bauerngericht; 1529–40 (Händelbücher); sixteenth–eighteenth century (misc. Manuale)
B33   Kriminalgericht
B35   Losungsamt
D1   Stadtalmosenamt (sixteenth–eighteenthth century)
D2   Heilig-Geist-Spital II Bände III Rechnungen IV Akten
D10   Findelamt
D15   Wohltätigkeitsstiftungen ältere Spezialregistratur
D17   Landalmosenamt
D23   Elisabeth Kraus'sche Stiftung (1447, 1545–1990)
E5   Handwerksarchive
F1   Nürnberger Chroniken

PRINTED SOURCES

Alpert, Michael, trans. and ed. *Two Spanish Picaresque Novels: Lazarillo de Tormes (Anonymous) and The Swindler (El Buscón)*. Baltimore: Penguin, 1969.

Biedermann, Johann Gottfried. *Geschlechtsregister des Hochadelichen Patriciats zu Nürnberg*. Nuremberg, 1750.

Boesch, Hans. *Kinderleben in der deutschen Vergangenheit mit Abbildungen nach den Originalen aus 15.–18. Jahrhundert*. Monographien zur Deutschen Kulturgeschichte, 5. Leipzig and Cologne, 1900.

Dilherr, Johann Michael. *Christliche Gedächtnis-Münze, d. i. etliche Lehren, Trost u. Vermahnungen für Eltern u. Kindern*. Nuremberg, 1655.

Grimmelshausen, Hans Jakob Christoph von. *Simplicissimus*. Translated and with an introduction by Mike Mitchell. Sawtry: Dedalus, 1999.

Luther, Martin. *D. Martin Luthers Werke: Kritische Gesamtausgabe*. Weimar, 1883– ; reprint, 1964–68.

Menagius, Philemon, *Die Sieben Teuffel / welche fast in der gantzen Welt die heutige Dienst-Mägde beherrschen und verführen . . .* Frankfurt, 1693.

Müllner Johannes. *Die Annalen der Reichsstadt Nürnberg von 1623*. Ed. Gerhard Hirschmann. Teil 2, 1351–1469. Nuremberg, 1984.

Peters, Jan, ed. *Ein Söldnerleben im Dreißigjährigen Krieg. Eine Quelle zur Sozialgeschichte*. Berlin: Akademie Verlag, 1993.

Siebenkees, Johann Christian, ed. *Kleine Chronik der Reichsstadt Nürnberg*. Altdorf: Meyer, 1790.

——, ed. *Materialien zur Nürnbergischen Geschichte*. 4 volumes. Nuremberg, 1792–95.

——, ed. *Nachrichten von Armenstiftungen in Nürnberg*. 2 volumes. Nuremberg, 1792 and 1794.

Volckhamer, Christoph Friedrich Wilhelm von. *Johann Gottfried Biedermanns Geschlechtsregister des Patriciats der vormalige Reichsstadt Nürnberg (von 1749) bis zum Jahre 1796 fortgesetzt*. Nuremberg, 1797.

SELECT SECONDARY LITERATURE

Amussen, Susan. *An Ordered Society: Gender and Class in Early Modern England*. New York: Blackwell, 1988.

Ariès, Philippe. *Centuries of Childhood: A Social History of Family Life*. Translated by Robert Baldwick. New York: Knopf, 1962.

Bardet, Jean-Pierre. "Enfants abandonés et assistés à Rouen dans la seconde motié du XVIIe. Siècle." In *Sur la population française au XVIIe et au XVIIe siècles: Homages à Marcel Reinhard*. Edited by Marcel Reinhard, 19–47. Paris: Société de Demographie Historique, 1973.

Baruch, Friedrich. "Das Hebammenwesen im Reichsstädtischen Nürnberg," Ph.D. dissertation, Friedrich-Alexander Universität Erlangen, 1955.

Beck, Rainer. "Illegitimität und voreheliche Sexualität auf dem Land. Unterfinning 1671–770." In *Die Kultur der einfachen Leute*. Edited by Richard van Dülmen, 112–50. Munich: Beck, 1983.

Beer, Mathias. *Eltern und Kinder des späten Mittelalters in ihren Briefen: Familienleben in der Stadt des Spätmittelaters und der frühen Neuzeit mit besonderer Berücksichtigung Nürnberg (1400–1550)*. Nürnberger Werkstücke zur Stadt- und Landesgeschichte, 44. Nuremberg: 1990.

Beier, A. L. *Masterless Men: The Vagrancy Problem in England, 1560–1640*. London and New York: Methuen, 1985.

Bendlage, Andrea, and Peter Schuster. "Hüter der Ordnung. Bürger, Rat, und Polizei in Nürnberg im 15. und 16. Jahrhundert." *MVGN* 82 (1995): 37–56.

Bode, Gustav. "Die Kindestötung und ihre Bestrafung im Nürnberg des Mittelalters." *Archiv für Strafrecht und Strafprozess* 61 (1914): 430–81.

Boes, Maria. "Public Appearance and Criminal Judicial Practices in Early Modern Germany." *Social Science History* 20, no. 2 (1996): 259–79.

———. "The Treatment of Juvenile Delinquents in Early Modern Germany: A Case Study." *Continuity and Change* 11, no. 1 (1996): 43–60.

Bog, Ingomar. "Über Arme und Armenfürsorge in Oberdeutschland und in der Eidgenossenschaft im 15. und 16. Jahrhundert." *Jahrbuch für fränkische Landesforschung* 34–35 (1974–75): 244–87.

Boswell, John. *The Kindness of Strangers: The Abandonment of Children in Western Europe from Late Antiquity to the Renaissance*. New York: Pantheon, 1988.

Boulton, Jeremy. *Neighbourhood and Society in a London Suburb in the Seventeenth Century*. Cambridge: Cambridge University Press, 1987.

Brady, Thomas A., Heiko Oberman, and James D. Tracy, eds. *Handbook of European History, 1400–1600, Late Middle Ages, Renaissance and Reformation*. Two volumes. Leiden: Brill, 1994.

Brady, Thomas A. *Ruling Class, Regime and Reformation in Strasbourg, 1520–1555*. Leiden: Brill, 1978.

Briggs, Robin. *Witches and Neighbors. The Social and Cultural Contexts of European Witchcraft*. New York: Viking, 1996.

Burghartz, Susanna. *Zeiten der Reinheiten, Orte der Unzucht. Ehe und Sexualität in Basel während der Frühen Neuzeit*. Paderborn: Schöningh, 1999.

Burschel, Peter. *Söldner im Nordwestdeutschland des 16. und 17. Jahrhunderts. Sozialgeschichtliche Studien*. Göttingen: Vandenhoeck & Ruprecht, 1994.

Capp, Bernard. *When Gossips Meet: Women, Family, and Neighbourhood in Early Modern England*. Oxford: Oxford University Press, 2003.

Chvojka, Erhard. *Geschichte der Großelternrollen vom 16. bis zum 20 Jahrhundert*. Vienna: Böhlau Verlag, 2003.

Coing, Helmut. *Handbuch der Quellen und Literatur der neueren europäischen Privatrechtsgeschichte*. 3 volumes. Munich: Beck, 1976–77.

Corbier, Mireille, ed. *Adoption et fosterage*. Paris: DeBoccard, 1999.

Crawford, Patricia. *Blood, Bodies and Families in Early Modern England*. Harlow: Longman, 2004.

Cunningham, Hugh. *Children and Childhood in Western Society since 1500*. London: Longman, 1995.

DeLacy, Margaret. *Prison Reform in Lancashire, 1700–1850: A Study in Local Administration*. Palo Alto: Stanford University Press, 1986.

DesBrisay, Gordon. "Wet Nurses and Unwed Mothers in Seventeenth-Century Aberdeen." In *Women in Scotland, c. 100–1750*. Edited by Elizabeth Ewan and Maureen Meikle, 210–21. East Linton: Tuckwell Press, 1999.

Dinges, Martin. "Frühneuzeitliche Armenfürsorge als Sozialdisziplinierung? Probleme mit einem Konzept." *Geschichte und Gesellschaft* 17 (1991): 5–29.

———. "Self-Help and Reciprocity in Parish Assistance: Bordeaux in the Sixteenth and Seventeenth Centuries." In *The Locus of Care: Families, Institutions, and the Provision of Welfare since Antiquity*. Edited by Peregrine Horden and Richard Smith. London and New York: Routledge, 1998.

——. *Stadtarmut in Bordeaux, 1525–1675: Alltag, Politik, Mentalitäten.* Bonn: Edition Röhrscheid, 1988.

Dülmen, Richard van. *Frauen vor Gericht. Kindsmord in der frühen Neuzeit.* Frankfurt am Main: Fischer, 1991.

——. *Historische Anthropologie. Entwicklung, Probleme, Aufgaben.* Cologne: Böhlau, 2000.

——. *Theatre of Horror: Crime and Punishment in Early Modern Germany.* Translated by Elisabeth Neu. Cambridge: Polity Press, 1990.

Dürr, Renate. *Mägde in der Stadt. Das Beispiel Schwäbisch Hall in der Frühen Neuzeit.* Frankfurt: Campus, 1995.

Eberle, Ernst. *Probleme zur Rechtsstellung der Frau nach der kursächsischen Konstitution von 1572.* Stuttgart: Photo-Offsetdrucke P. Illg, 1964.

Egmond, Florike. *Underworlds: Organized Crime in the Netherlands, 1650–1800.* Cambridge: Cambridge University Press, 1993.

Eichler, Helga. "Zucht- und Arbeitshäuser in den mittleren und östlichen Provinzen Brandenburg-Preußens; Ihr Anteil an der Vorbereitung des Kapitalismus. Eine Untersuchung für die Zeit vom Ende des 17. bis zum Ausgang des 18. Jahrhunderts." *Jahrbuch für Wirtschaftsgeschichte* 1, no. 1 (1970): 127–147.

Eisenbichler, Konrad, ed. *The Premodern Teenager: Youth in Society, 1150–1650.* Toronto: Centre for Reformation and Renaissance Studies, 2002.

Endres, Rudolf. "Armenstiftungen und Armenschulen in Nürnberg in der Frühneuzeit." *Jahrbuch für fränkische Landesforschung* 53 (1992): 156–89.

——. "Zur Einwohnerzahl und Bevölkerungsstruktur Nürnbergs im 15./16. Jahrhundert." *MVGN* 57 (1970): 242–71.

——. "Das Schulwesen in Franken in ausgehenden Mittelalter." In *Studien zum städtischen Bildungswesen des späten Mittelalters und der frühen Neuzeit.* Edited by Bernd Moeller et al., 173–215. Göttingen, 1983.

——. "Zur wirtschaftlichen und sozialen Lage in Franken vor den Dreißigjährigen Krieg." *Jahrbuch fü fränkische Landesforschung* 28 (1968): 5–52.

Engelsing, R. "Der Arbeitsmarkt der Dienstboten im 17., 18., und 19. Jahrhundert." In *Wirtschaftspolitik und Arbeitsmarkt. Bericht über die 4. Arbeitstagung der Gesellschaft für Sozial- und Wirtschaftsgeschichte in Wien am 14. und 15. April 1971.* Edited by H. Kellenbenz, 159–237. Munich, 1974.

——. "Einkommen der Dienstboten in Deutschland zwischen dem 16. und 20. Jahrhunderte." *Jahrbuch des Instituts für Deutsche Geschichte der Universität Tel Aviv* 2 (1973): 11–65.

Erler, A., and E. Kaufmann, eds. *Handwörterbuch zur deutschen Rechtsgeschichte.* Berlin: E. Schmidt, 1964ff.

Evans, Richard J. *Rituals of Retribution: Capital Punishment in Germany, 1600–1987.* Oxford: Oxford University Press, 1996.

Evans, Richard J., ed. *The German Underworld: Deviants and Outcasts in German History.* London and New York: Routledge, 1988.

Fagerlund, Solveig. "Women and Men as Godparents in an Early Modern Swedish Town." *History of the Family* 5, no. 3 (2000): 347–57.

Farge, Arlette. *Fragile Lives: Violence, Power and Solidarity in Eighteenth-century Paris.* Translated by Carol Shelton. Cambridge: Harvard University Press, 1993.

——. *Vivre dans la rue à Paris au XVIIIe siècle.* Paris: Gallimard, 1979.

Fauve-Chamoux, Antoinette. "Beyond Adoption: Orphans and Family Strategies in Pre-Industrial France." *History of the Family* 1, no. 1 (1996): 1–13.

———. "Introduction: Adoption, Affiliation, in Family Recomposition—Inventing Family Continuity." *History of the Family* 3, no. 4 (1998): 385–92.

Felber, Alfons. "Unzucht und Kindsmord in der Rechtsprechung der freien Reichsstadt Nördlingen vom 15.–19." Jahrhundert. Ph.D. dissertation: Universität Bonn, 1961.

Feldbauer, Peter. *Kinderelend in Wien. Von der Armenpflege zur Jugendfürsorge, 17.–19. Jahrhundert.* Vienna: Verlag für Gesellschaftkritik, 1980.

Fine, Agnès, ed. *Adoptions. Ethnologie des parentés choisies.* Paris: Éditions de la Maison des sciences de l'homme, 1998.

———. *Parrains, Marraines. La parenté spirituelle en Europe.* Paris: Fayard, 1994.

Fontaine, Laurence and Jürgen Schlumbohm, eds. *Household Strategies for Survival 1600–2000: Fission, Faction and Cooperation. International Review of Social History Supplement,* 45 (2000).

Foucault, Michel. *Discipline and Punish: The Birth of the Prison.* Translated by Alan Sheridan. New York: Pantheon, 1977.

Friedrichs, Christopher R. *The Early Modern City, 1450–1750.* London and New York: Longman, 1995.

Fuchs, Rachel G. *Abandoned Children: Foundlings and Child Welfare in Nineteenth-Century France.* Albany: State University of New York Press, 1984.

———. *Poor and Pregnant in Paris: Strategies for Survival in the Nineteenth Century.* New Brunswick: Rutgers University Press, 1992.

Fumasoli, Georg. *Ursprünge und Anfänge der Schellenwerke. Ein Beitrag zur Frühgeschichte des Zuchthauswesens.* Zurich: Schultheiss Polygraphischer Verlag, 1981.

Gager, Kristin Elizabeth. *Blood Ties and Fictive Ties: Adoption and Family Life in Early Modern France.* Princeton: Princeton University Press, 1996.

Garrioch, David. *Neighborhood and Community in Paris, 1740–1790.* Cambridge: Cambridge University Press, 1986.

Gavitt, Philip. *Charity and Children in Renaissance Florence: The Ospedale degli Innocenti, 1410–1536.* Ann Arbor: University of Michigan Press, 1990.

Geremek, Bronislaw. *Poverty: A History.* Translated by Agnieska Kolokowska. Cambridge: Blackwell, 1994.

Goody, Jack. "Adoption in Cross-cultural Perspective." In *Production and Reproduction: A Comparative Study of the Domestic Domain,* 66–85. Cambridge: Cambridge University Press, 1976.

Gowing, Laura. "Secret Births and Infanticide in Seventeenth-century England." *Past and Present* 156 (1997): 87–115.

Grassby, Richard. *Kinship and Capitalism: Marriage, Family, and Business in the English-speaking world, 1580–1740.* New York: Cambridge University Press, 2001.

Griffiths, Paul. *Youth and Authority: Formative Experiences in England, 1560–1640.* Oxford: Clarendon Press, 1996.

Groebner, Valentin. *Ökonomie ohne Haus. Zum Wirtschaften armer Leute in Nürnberg am Endes des 15. Jahrhunderts.* Göttingen: Max-Plank Institut für Geschichte, 1993.

Haas, Louis. *The Renaissance Man and His Children: Childbirth and Early Childhood in Florence, 1300–1600.* New York: St. Martin's, 1997.

Hagemann, Karen and Rolf Pröve, eds. *Landsknechte, Soldatenfrauen, und Nationalkrieger. Militär, Krieg, und Geschlechterordnung im historischen Wandel.* Frankfurt: Campus Verlag, 1998.

Hampe, Theodor. *Die Nürnberger Malefizbücher als Quellen der reichsstädtischen Sittengeschichte von 14. bis zum 18. Jahrhundert.* Nuremberg: Gesellschaft für frankische Geschichte, 1927.

Harrington, Joel F. "Bad Parents, the State, and the Early Modern Civilising Process." *German History* 16, no. 1 (1998): 16–28.

———. "Escape from the Great Confinement: The Genealogy of a German Workhouse." *Journal of Modern History* 71 (1999): 308–45.

———. "Historians without Borders? *L'histoire croisée* and Early Modern Social History." In *Politics and Reformation; Histories and Reformations: Essays in Honor of Thomas A. Brady, Jr.* Edited by Christopher Ocker, Michael Printy, Peter Starenko, and Peter Wallace, 79–90. Leiden: E. J. Brill, 2007.

———. *Reordering Marriage and Society in Reformation Germany.* Cambridge: Cambridge University Press, 1995.

———. "'Singing for his supper': The Reinvention of Juvenile Streetsinging in Early Modern Nuremberg." *Social History* 22, no. 1 (1997): 27–45.

Hartinger, Walter. "Bayerisches Dienstboten auf dem Lande vom 16. bis zum 18. Jahrhundert." *Zeitschrift für Bayerische Landesgeschichte* 38 (1975): 598–638.

Henderson, John, Richard Wall, eds. *Poor Women and Children in the European Past.* New York: Routledge, 1994.

Hindle, Steve. *The State and Social Change in Early Modern England, c. 1550–1640.* New York: St. Martin's, 2000.

Hippel, Robert von. "Beiträge zur Geschichte der Freiheitsstrafe." Teil 2, *Zeitschrift für die gesamte Strafrechtswissenschaft* 18 (1898): 608–66.

Hoffer, Peter C., and N. E. H. Hull. *Murdering Mothers: Infanticide in England and New England, 1558–1803.* New York: New York University Press, 1981.

Hufton, Olwen H. *The Poor of Eighteenth-Century France, 1750–1789.* Oxford: Clarendon Press, 1974.

Hunecke, Volker. *Die Findelkinder von Mailand. Kindesaussetzung und aussetzende Eltern vom 17. bis zum 19. Jahrhundert.* Stuttgart: Klett-Cotta, 1987.

Imhof, Arthur E. *Lost Worlds: How Our European Ancestors Coped with Everyday Life and Why Life Is So Hard Today.* Translated by Thomas Robisheaux. Charlottesville: University Press of Virginia, 1996.

Imhoff, Christoph. *Berühmte Nürnberger aus neun Jahrhunderten.* Nuremberg: A. Hofmann, 1984.

Irsigler, Franz, and Arnold Lassotta. *Bettler und Gaukler, Dirnen und Henker. Außenseiter in einer mittelalterlichen Stadt Köln, 1300–1600.* Munich: Deutsches Taschenbuch Verlag, 1989.

Jütte, Robert, ed. *Geschichte der Abtreibung. Von der Antike bis zur Gegenwart.* Munich: Beck, 1993.

———. *Lust ohne Last. Geschichte der Empfängnisverhütung.* Munich: Beck, 2003.

———. *Poverty and Deviance in Early Modern Europe.* Cambridge: Cambridge University Press, 1994.

Kallert, Heide. "Waisenhaus und Arbeitserziehung im 17. und 18. Jahrhundert." Ph.D. dissertation, Johann Wolfgang Goethe Universität, 1964.

Kertzer, David I., ed. *Family Life in Early Modern Times, 1500–1789.* New Haven: Yale University Press, 2001.

———. *Sacrificed for Honor: Italian Infant Abandonment and the Politics of Reproductive Control.* Boston: Beacon, 1993.

Kipfmüller, Bertha. "Die Frau im Recht der freien Reichsstadt Nürnberg. Eine rechtsgeschichtliche Darlegung auf grund der verneuerten Reformation des Jahres 1564." Ph.D. dissertation, Universität-Erlangen, 1929.

Knapp, Hermann. *Das alte Nürnberger Kriminalrecht.* Berlin: J. Guttentag, 1896.

———. *Das Lochgefängnis, Tortur, und Richtung im alten Nürnberg*. Nuremberg: Heerdegen-Barbeck, 1907.

Küther, Carsten. *Menschen auf der Straße. Vagierende Unterschichten in Bayern, Franken und Schwaben in der zweiten Hälfte des 18. Jahrhunderts*. Göttingen: Vandenhoeck & Ruprecht, 1983.

Lallemand, Léon. *Histoire des enfants abandonnés et délaissés*. Paris: A. Picard, 1885.

Lallemand, Suzanne. *La circulation des enfants en société traditionelle. Prêt, don, échange*. Paris: Éditions L'Harmattan, 1993.

Langer, William. "Infanticide: A Historical Survey." *History of Childhood Quarterly* 1 (1973–74): 353–74.

Laslett, Peter. *Family Life and Illicit Love in Earlier Generations*. Cambridge: Cambridge University Press, 1977.

Laurence, A. *Women in England, 1500–1760: A Social History*. New York: St. Martin's Press, 1994.

Leder, Klaus. *Kirche und Jugend in Nürnberg und seinem Landgebiet: 1400–1800*. Neustadt an der Aisch: Degener, 1973.

Leibrock-Plehn, Larissa. "Frühe Neuzeit. Hebammen, Kräutermedizin und weltliche Justiz." In *Geschichte der Abtreibung. Von der Antike bis zur Gegenwart*. Edited by Robert Jütte, 68–90. Munich: C. H. Beck, 1993.

Levi, Giovanni, and Jean-Claude Schmitt, eds. *A History of Young People in the West*. Volume 2, *Stormy Evolution to Modern Times*. Translated by Carol Volk. Cambridge: Belknap Press, 1997.

Lind, Vera. *Selbstmord in der frühen Neuzeit. Diskurs, Lebenswelt und kultureller Wandel am Beispiel der Herzogtümer Schleswig und Holstein*. Göttingen: Vandenhoeck und Ruprecht, 1999.

Lindemann, Mary. *Patriots and Paupers: Hamburg, 1712–1830*. Oxford: Oxford University Press, 1990.

Lis, Catherine, and Hugo Soly. *Disordered Lives: Eighteenth-Century Families and Their Unruly Relatives*. Cambridge: Polity Press, 1996.

Lynch, Katherine A. *Individuals, Families, and Communities in Europe, 1200–1800: The Urban Foundations of Western Society*. Cambridge: Cambridge University Press, 2003.

———. "Infant Mortality, Child Neglect, and Child Abandonment in European History: A Comparative Analysis." In *Population and Economy: From Hunger to Modern Economic Growth*. Edited by Tommy Bengtsson and Osamu Saito, 133–64. Oxford: Oxford University Press, 2000.

McCants, Anne E. C. *Civic Charity in a Golden Age: Orphan Care in Early Modern Amsterdam*. Urbana and Chicago: University of Illinois Press, 1997.

McClure. Ruth. *Coram's Children: The London Foundling Hospital in the Eighteenth Century*. New Haven: Yale University Press, 1981.

McCracken, G. "The Exchange of Children in Tudor England: An Anthropological Phenomenon in Historical Context." *Journal of Family History* 8 (1983): 303–13.

McGinn, Thomas A. *Widows and Patriarchy: Ancient and Modern*. London: Duckworth, 2008.

McRitchie, Evelyn. "Krankenbehandlung im Hamburger Waisenhaus in der Zeit von 1604 bis 1921. Die Krankenstation des Hamburger Waisenhauses als Vorläufer einer Kinderklinik." M.D. dissertation, Universität Hamburg, 1983.

Martz, Linda. *Poverty and Welfare in Habsburg Spain: The Example of Toledo*. New York: Cambridge University Press, 1983.

Meumann, Markus. *Findelkinder, Waisenhäuser, Kindsmord und unversorgte Kinder in der Frühen Neuzeit.* Munich: Oldenburg, 1995.

Mitterauer, Michael. "Gesindedienst und Jugendphase im europäischen Vergleich." *Geschichte und Gesellschaft* 11 (1985): 177–204.

———. *A History of Youth.* Translated by R. Graeme Dunphy. Oxford: Blackwell, 1992.

———. *Ledige Mütter: Zur Geschichte unehelicher Geburten in Europa.* Munich: C. H. Beck, 1983.

Mitterauer, Michael, and Reinhard Seider. *The European Family: Patriarchy to Partnership from the Middle Ages to the Present.* Translated by Karla Oosterveen and Manfred Horzinger. Oxford: Basil Blackwell, 1982.

Mummenhoff, Ernst. "Das Findel- und Waisenhaus zu Nürnbergs, orts-, kultur-, und wirtschaftsgeschichtlich." *MVGN* 21 (1915): 57–336; 22 (1918): 1–146.

———. *Der Handwerker in der deutschen Vergangenheit.* Leipzig: E. Diederichs, 1901.

———. "Die öffentliche Gesundheits- und Krankenpflege im alten Nürnberg. Das Spital zum heilige Geist." In *Festschrift zur Eröffnung des Neuen Krankenhauses der Stadt Nürnberg,* 1–122. Nuremberg, 1898, reprint, Neustadt/Aisch: C. Schmitt, 1986.

Obermeier, Anita. "Findel- und Waisenkinder: Zur Geschichte des Sozialfürsorge in der Reichsstadt Augsburg." *Zeitschrift des historischen Vereins für Schwaben* 83 (1990): 129–62.

Ogilvie, Sheilaugh, and Robert Scribner, eds. *Germany: A Social and Economic History.* 2 vols. London: Edward Arnold, 1996.

Ozment, Steven. *Ancestors: The Loving Family in Old Europe.* Cambridge: Harvard University Press, 2001.

———. *When Fathers Ruled: Family Life in Reformation Europe.* Cambridge: Harvard University Press, 1983.

Painter-Brick, Catherine, and Malcolm T. Smiths, eds. *Abandoned Children.* Cambridge: Cambridge University Press, 2000.

Parker, Charles H. *The Reformation of Community: Social Welfare and Calvinist Charity in Holland, 1572–1620.* Cambridge: Cambridge University Press, 1998.

Pollock, Linda A. *Forgotten Children: Parent-child relations from 1500 to 1900.* New York: Cambridge University Press, 1983.

Pullan, Brian. *Orphans and Foundlings in Early Modern Europe.* Reading: University of Reading Press, 1989.

Quanter, Rudolf. *Deutsches Zuchthaus- und Gefängniswesen von den ältesten Zeiten bis in die Gegenwart.* Aalen: Scientia Verlag, 1905.

Ransel, David. *Mothers of Misery: Child Abandonment in Russia.* Princeton: Princeton University Press, 1988.

Reicke, Emil. *Geschichte der Reichsstadt Nürnberg.* Nuremberg: Schmidt, 1896; reprint, Neustadt an der Aisch: C. Schmitt, 1983.

Reif, Heinz, ed. *Räuber, Volk und Obrigkeit. Studien zur Geschichte der Kriminalität in Deutschland seit dem 18. Jahrhundert.* Frankfurt am Main: Suhrkamp, 1984.

Riddle, John M. *Contraception and Abortion from the Ancient World to the Renaissance.* Cambridge: Harvard University Press, 1992.

Riedl, Walter. "Die rechtliche Stellung der Lehrjungen und Gesellen des Nürnberger Handwerks." J.D. dissertation, Friedrich-Alexander Universität Erlangen, 1948.

Roche, Daniel. *The People of Paris: An Essay in Popular Culture in the Eighteenth Century.* Translated by Marie Evans, in association with Gwynne Lewis. Berkeley: University of California Press, 1987.

Roetzer, Karl. "Die Delikte der Abtreibung, Kindstötung sowie Kindaussetzung und ihre Bestrafung in der Reichsstadt Nürnberg." Ph.D. dissertation, Friedrich-Alexander Universität Erlangen, 1957.

Rogg, Matthias. "'Wol auff mit mir, du schoenes weyb.' Anmerkungen zu Konstruktion von Mänlichkeit im Soldatenbild des 16. Jahrhunderts." In *Landsknechte, Soldatenfrauen und Nationalkrieger. Militär, Krieg und Geschlechterordnung im historischen Wandel*. Edited by Karen Hagemann. Frankfurt: Campus, 1998.

Romano, Dennis. *Housecraft and Statecraft: Domestic Service in Renaissance Venice, 1400–1600*. Baltimore: Johns Hopkins University Press, 1996.

Roper, Lyndal. *The Holy Household: Women and Morals in Reformation Augsburg*. Oxford: Clarendon Press, 1989.

———. *Oedipus and the Devil: Witchcraft, Sexuality, and Religion in Early Modern Europe*. London: Routledge, 1994.

———. *Witch Craze: Terror and Fantasy in Baroque Germany*. New Haven: Yale University Press, 2004.

Rowlands, Alison. "In Great Secrecy: The Crime of Infanticide in Rothenburg ob der Tauber, 1501–1618." *German History* 15, no. 2 (1997): 179–200.

———. *Witchcraft Narratives in Germany: Rothenburg, 1561–1562*. Manchester: Manchester University Press, 2003.

Rublack, Ulinka. *The Crimes of Women in Early Modern Germany*. Oxford: Oxford University Press, 1999.

———. "The Public Body: Policing Abortion in Early Modern Germany." In *Gender Relations in Germany History: Power, Agency and Experience from the Sixteenth to the Twentieth Century*. Ed. Lynn Abrams and Elizabeth Harvey, 57–79. Durham: Duke University Press, 1997.

Rüger, Willi. *Die Kinderfürsorge im Almosenwesen des XVII Jahrhunderts*. Nürnberger Beiträge zu den Wirtschafts- und Sozialwissenschaften, 47–48. Nuremberg: Krische, 1934.

———. *Mittelalterliches Almosenwesen. Die Almosenordnungen der Reichsstadt Nürnberg*. Nürnberger Beiträge zu den Wirtschafts- und Sozialwissenschaften, 31. Nuremberg: Krische, 1932.

Sabean, David. *Kinship in Neckarshausen, 1700–1870*. Cambridge: Cambridge University Press, 1998.

———. *Power in the Blood: Popular Culture and Village Discourse in Early Modern Germany*. Cambridge: Cambridge University Press, 1984.

———. *Property, Production, and Family in Neckarshausen, 1700–1870*. Cambridge: Cambridge University Press, 1990.

Sachße, Christoph, and Florian Tennstedt. *Geschichte der Armenfürsorge in Deutschland*. Volume 1, *Vom Spätmittelalter bis zum 1. Weltkrieg*. Second revised edition. Stuttgart: Kohlhammer, 1998.

Safley, Thomas Max. *Charity and Economy in the Orphanages of Early Modern Augsburg*. Atlantic Highlands: Humanities Press, 1997.

———. *Children of the Laboring Poor: Expectation and Experience among the Orphans of Early Modern Augsburg*. Leiden: Brill, 2005.

———. *Let No Man Put Asunder: The Control of Marriage in the German Southwest; A Comparative Study, 1550–1600*. Kirksville: Sixteenth-Century Publications, 1984.

Schlumbohm, Jürgen. *Lebensläufe, Familien, Höfe. Die Bauern und Heuerleute des Osnabrückischen Kirchspiels Belm in proto-industrieller Zeit, 1650–1860*. Göttingen: Vandenhoeck & Ruprecht, 1994.

Schindler, Norbert. *Rebellion, Community and Custom in Early Modern Germany.* Translated by Pamela E. Selwyn. Past and Present Publications. Cambridge: Cambridge University Press, 2003.

Schmelzeisen, Gustav K. *Die Rechtsstellung der Frau in der deutschen Stadtwirtschaft.* Arbeiten zur deutschen Rechts- und Verfassungsgeschichte, 10. Stuttgart, 1935.

Schubert, Ernst. *Arme Leute. Bettler und Gauner im Franken des 18. Jahrhunderts.* Neustadt an der Aisch: Kommissionsverlage Degener & Col, 1983.

Schulze, Winfried, ed. *Ego-Dokumente. Annäherung an den Menschen in der Geschichte.* Berlin: Akademie Verlag, 1996.

Schwerhoff, Gerd. *Köln im Kreuzverhör. Kriminalität, Herrschaft, und Gesellschaft in einer frühneuzeitlichen Stadt.* Bonn: Bouvieu, 1991.

Scribner, Bob, ed. *Germany: A New Social and Economic History, Volume 1, 1450–1630.* London: Arnold, 1996.

———. *Religion and Culture in Germany (1400–1800).* Ed. Lyndal Roper. Leiden: Brill, 2001.

Sherwood, Joan. *Poverty in Eighteenth-Century Spain: The Women and Children of the Inclusa.* Toronto: University of Toronto Press, 1988.

Shore, Heather. *Artful Dodgers: Youth and Crime in Early Nineteenth-century London.* Bury St. Edmunds: Royal Historical Society, 1999.

Slack, Paul. *From Reformation to Improvement: Public Welfare in Early Modern England; The Ford Lectures Delivered in the University of Oxford, 1995–95.* Oxford: Clarendon Press, 1999.

Sothmann, Marlene. *Das Armen-, Arbeits-, Zucht- und Werkhaus in Nürnberg bis 1806.* Nürnberger Werkstücke zur Stadt- und Landesgeschichte, 2. Nuremberg, 1970.

Spierenburg, Pieter. *The Emergence of Carceral Institutions: Prisons, Galleys, and Lunatic Asylums, 1550–1900.* Rotterdam: Erasmus Universiteit, 1984.

———. *The Prison Experience: Disciplinary Institutions and Their Inmates in Early Modern Europe.* New Brunswick: Rutgers University Press, 1991.

Strauss, Gerald. *Luther's House of Learning: Indoctrination of the Young in the German Reformation.* Baltimore: Johns Hopkins University Press, 1978.

———. *Nuremberg in the Sixteenth Century.* New York: John Wiley & Sons, 1966.

Stuart, Kathy. *Defiled Trades and Social Outcasts; Honor and Ritual Pollution in Early Modern Germany.* Cambridge: Cambridge University Press, 1999.

Symonds, Deborah A. *Weep Not for Me. Women, Ballads and Infanticide in Early Modern Scotland.* University Park: Penn State University, 1997.

Tadmor, Naomi. *Family and Friends in Eighteenth-Century England: Household, Kinship, and Patronage.* Cambridge: Cambridge University Press, 2001.

Terpstra, Nicholas. *Abandoned Children of the Italian Renaissance: Orphan care in Florence and Bologna.* Baltimore: Johns Hopkins University Press, 2005.

———. "Making a Living, Making a Life: Work in the Orphanages of Florence and Bologna." *Sixteenth Century Journal* 31, no. 4 (2000): 1063–79.

———. "*In loco parentis*: Confraternities and Abandoned Children in Florence and Bologna." In *The Politics of Ritual Kinship: Confraternities and Social Order in Early Modern Italy.* Edited by Nicholas Terpstra, 115–20. Cambridge: Cambridge University Press, 2000.

Tilly, Charles. "Family History, Social History, and Social Change." *Journal of Family History* 12, nos. 1–3 (1987): 319–30.

Tilly, Louise A., et al. "Child Abandonment in European History: A Symposium." *Journal of Family History* 17, no. 1 (1992): 1–23.

Tlusty, B. Ann. *Bacchus and Civil Order: The Culture of Drink in Early Modern Germany*. Charlottesville: University of Virginia Press, 2001.

Trexler, Richard. "The Foundlings of Florence, 1395–1455." *History of Childhood Quarterly* 1 (1973): 259–84.

———. "Infanticide in Florence: New Sources and First Results." *Journal of Psychohistory* 1, no. 1 (1973): 98–117.

Ulbricht, Otto. *Kindsmord und Aufklärung in Deutschland*. Munich: Oldenburg, 1990.

———. "The World of a Beggar around 1775." *Central European History* 27 (1994): 153–84.

Ulbricht, Otto, ed. *Von Huren und Rabenmüttern. Weibliche Kriminalität in der Frühen Neuzeit*. Cologne: Böhlau, 1995.

Valverde, Lola. "Illegitimacy and the Abandonment of Children in the Basque Country, 1550–1800." In *Poor Women and Children in the European Past*. Edited by John Henderson and Richard Wall, 51–65. London: Routledge, 1994.

Vassberg, David E. "Orphans and Adoption in Early Modern Castilian Villages." *History of the Family* 3, no. 4 (1998): 441–58.

Walker, Mack. *German Home Towns: Community, State and General Estate, 1648–1971*. Ithaca: Cornell University Press, 1971.

Watt, Jeffrey. *The Making of Modern Marriage: Matrimonial Control and the Rise of Sentiment in Neuchâtel, 1550–1800*. Ithaca: Cornell University Press, 1992.

Weber, Hellmuth von. "Die Entwicklung des Zuchthauswesens in Deutschland im 17. und 18. Jahrhundert." In *Abhandlungen zur Rechts- und Wirtschaftsgeschichte. Festschrift für Adolf Zycha zum 70. Geburtstag*. Edited by Adolf Zycha, 427–68. Weimar: Böhlhaus, 1941.

Werner, Michael, and Bénédicte Zimmerman. "Penser l'histoire croisée: Entre empirie et réflexivité." *Annales Histoire, Sciences sociales* 58, no. 1 (Jan.–Feb. 2003): 7–36.

Wesoly, Kurt. *Lehrlinge und Handwerksgesellen am Mittelrhein: Ihre soziale Lage und ihre Organisation vom 14. bis ins 17. Jahrhundert*. Frankfurt am Main: W. Kramer, 1985.

Wiesner, Merry E. "Paternalism in Practice: The Control of Servants and Prostitutes in Early Modern Germany Cities." In *The Process of Change in Early Modern Europe. Essays in Honor of Miriam Usher Chrisman*. Edited by Phillip N. Bebb and Sherrin Marshall. Athens: Ohio University Press, 1988.

———. *Working Women in Renaissance Germany*. New Brunswick: Rutgers University Press, 1986.

Wiesner-Hanks, Merry. *Women and Gender in Early Modern Europe*. Second edition. Cambridge: Cambridge University Press, 2000.

Wiest, Ekkehard. *Die Entwicklung des Nürnberger Gewerbes zwischen 1648 und 1806*. Forschungen zur Sozial und Wirtschaftsgeschichte, 12. Stuttgart: G. Fischer, 1968.

Wiltenburg, Joy. *Disorderly Women and Female Power in the Street Literature of Early Modern England and Germany*. Charlottesville: University Press of Virginia, 1992.

Wunder, Heide. *He Is the Sun, She Is the Moon: Women in Early Modern Germany*. Translated by Thomas Dunlap. Cambridge: Harvard University Press, 1998.

Zimmerman, Clemens. "'Behörigs Orthen angezeigt.' Kindsmörderinnen in der ländlichen Gesellschaft Württembergs, 1581–1792." *Medizin, Gesellschaft und Geschichte* 10 (1991): 67–102.

Zschunke, Peter. *Konfession und Alltag in Oppenheim*. Wiesbaden: F. Steiner, 1984.

INDEX

www.ingramcontent.com/pod-product-compliance
Lightning Source LLC
Chambersburg PA
CBHW022129020426
42334CB00015B/829